MFC Programming
from the Ground Up

About the Author ...

Herbert Schildt is the world's leading programming author. He is an authority on the C and C++ languages, a master Windows programmer, and an expert on Java. His programming books have sold more than two million copies worldwide and have been translated into all major foreign languages. He is the author of numerous best-sellers including, *Windows NT 4 Programming from the Ground Up*, *Windows 98 Programming from the Ground Up*, *C: The Complete Reference*, *C++ the Complete Reference*, *C++ from the Ground Up*, and co-author of *Java: The Complete Reference*. Schildt is president of Universal Computing Laboratories, Inc., a software consulting firm in Mahomet, Illinois. He is a member of both the ANSI C and C++ standardization committees. He holds a master's degree in computer science from the University of Illinois.

MFC Programming
from the Ground Up

Herbert Schildt

Osborne/**McGraw-Hill**

Berkeley New York St. Louis San Francisco
Auckland Bogotá Hamburg London Madrid
Mexico City Milan Montreal New Delhi Panama City
Paris São Paulo Singapore Sydney
Tokyo Toronto

Osborne/**McGraw-Hill**
2600 Tenth Street
Berkeley, California 94710
U.S.A.

For information on translations or book distributors outside the U.S.A., or to arrange bulk purchase discounts for sales promotions, premiums, or fund-raisers, please contact Osborne/**McGraw-Hill** at the above address.

MFC Programming from the Ground Up

1234567890 AGM AGM 901987654321098

ISBN 0-07-882573-3

Publisher
Brandon A. Nordin

Editor-in-Chief
Scott Rogers

Acquisitions Editor
Wendy Rinaldi

Project Editor
Heidi Poulin

Editorial Assistant
Marlene Vasilieff

Technical Editor
Paul Garland

Copy Editor
Salome Hancock

Proofreader
Laurie Stewart

Indexer
Sheryl Schildt

Computer Designer
Ann Sellers

Illustrator
Brian Wells

Series Design
Peter Hancik

Cover Design
John Nedwidek

Contents at a Glance

Contents

Introduction

The Microsoft Foundation Classes (MFC) were created to make programming for the Windows environment easier and the code that you produce more portable. As you may know, writing Windows programs using the traditional, API-based approach is both a challenging and, at times, frustrating job. The sheer size and complexity of the Windows environment can make the creation of even a small utility program daunting. Furthermore, in a traditional-style API-based Windows program you, the programmer, must manage all of the details explicitly. The Microsoft Foundation Classes were invented for the express purpose of alleviating much of the drudgery associated with Windows programming. As you will see as you work your way through this book, to a very great extent they have succeeded in their purpose.

If you are like most programmers, then you are, or soon will be, actively engaged in the process of creating new programs. There are schedules to meet, bugs to kill, and design changes to incorporate. Sometimes it is useful to step back and put things in perspective. Although programmers have been working nearly non-stop for years, the vast majority of Windows applications have yet to be written! Demand for quality software far outstrips its supply.

This is the main reason the impact of the Microsoft Foundation Classes is so significant. MFC provides a faster and easier way to produce solid code. Put simply, Windows is the most important operating system for which programs are being written—and MFC is the fastest way that you can write programs for it. Be assured, there will be a large demand for programmers able to put MFC to good use.

By reading this book, you will learn the foundation of MFC programming. You will also learn many of the tricks and techniques that you will need to become a first-rate MFC programmer.

What's New in the Second Edition

This is the second edition of *MFC Programming from the Ground Up*. In the years that have passed since the first edition, a new version of Windows has appeared (Windows 98, with NT 5 just around the corner), technologies such as ActiveX are entering the mainstream, and the Web has reshaped the computing universe. Through all of these changes, one thing has remained constant: MFC. Because MFC was designed with portability in mind, the same programs written years ago can be compiled using today's compilers and run using today's operating systems. This is the beauty and power of MFC.

Since MFC was designed to produce long-lasting, portable code, no major changes have been made to the first part of the book. However, each chapter has been updated to reflect the inclusion of new options. For example, MFC now allows smooth and vertical progress bars and the options that support these features has been included in this book. In a few places, coverage of entirely new Windows' innovations has been added, such as the new Month Calendar common control. The one new feature found throughout the book is the In Depth box. These boxes contain supplemental material that expands upon some topic, illustrates a programming technique, or points you in a direction for further exploration.

The major change to the book is the addition of two new chapters, 18 and 19, which cover ActiveX controls, and Visual C++'s AppWizard and ClassWizard. ActiveX is an emerging technology that will grow in importance. No professional programmer can afford to be without a minimal understanding of this pivotal subsystem. Visual C++ is the most widely used compiler for generating MFC code and its wizards can streamline development.

Which Version of Windows?

There are four flavors of Windows in widespread use: Windows 3.1, Window 95, Window 98, and the various versions of Windows NT. Since MFC-based code is largely platform-independent, much of the information and examples in this book will apply to all four environments. However, the future belongs to the 32-bit world. As you will see, there are several aspects of MFC that cannot be applied to the older, 16-bit Windows 3.1 environment. Since all modern software is being built upon the 32-bit versions of Windows, the 16-bit material is included mostly for those programmers charged with maintaining 16-bit legacy code.

Who Is this Book For?

This book is designed specifically for programmers who have already mastered the fundamentals of programming. For example, you must be an accomplished C++ programmer. Specifically, you must be fluent with such concepts as virtual functions, constructors, function overloading, and inheritance. If your C++ skills are not what you would like them to be, take a little time to improve them before attempting to learn the Microsoft Foundation Classes.

It is not necessary for you to have written a traditional, non-MFC Windows program before. However, familiarity with a few of the rudimentary Windows programming concepts will be helpful and allow you to progress faster. But even if you have no previous experience with Windows programming, as long as you know C++, then you can learn to program Windows using this book.

What Programming Tools You Will Need

The code in this book was written, compiled, and tested using Microsoft's Visual C++ version 6. You will need either this compiler or another C/C++ compiler that is designed to produce Windows-compatible object code. The compiler must also be able to compile MFC-based programs.

The examples in this book must be compiled as C++ programs. This is to be expected since MFC is a C++-based class hierarchy. This means that your source files must use the .CPP extension. Furthermore, you must set the proper options (in your compiler) that relate to MFC-based compilation. For example, when using Visual C++, you must tell it to use the MFC static library or shared DLL.

Don't Forget: Code on the Web

Remember, the source code for all of the programs in this book is available free-of-charge on the Web at **www.osborne.com**. Downloading this code prevents you from having to type in the examples.

—HS
Mahomet, Illinois

Special Thanks

Special thanks go to Frank Crockett for his help in preparing the second edition of this book. He checked and updated all of the existing chapters, helped with the In Depth boxes, and provided the chapters on ActiveX and the Visual C++ wizards (Chapters 18 and 19). His expertise, ideas, and suggestions were appreciated.

For Further Study

MFC Programming From the Ground Up is just one of the many programming books written by Herbert Schildt. Here are some others that you will find of interest.

To learn more about programming Windows, we recommend the following:

Windows 98 Programming from the Ground Up

Windows NT 4 Programming from the Ground Up

Schildt's Windows 95 Programming in C and C++

Schildt's Advanced Windows 95 Programming in C and C++

If you want to learn more about the C language, then the following titles will be of interest:

C: The Complete Reference, Third Edition

The Annotated ANSI C Standard

Teach Yourself C, Third Edition

To learn more about C++, you will find these books especially helpful:

C++: The Complete Reference, Third Edition

Teach Yourself C++, Third Edition

C++ from the Ground Up, Second Edition

If you are interested in Web programming, we recommend:

Java: The Complete Reference

Co-authored by Herbert Schildt and Patrick Naughton

When you need solid answers, fast, turn to Herbert Schildt, the recognized authority on programming.

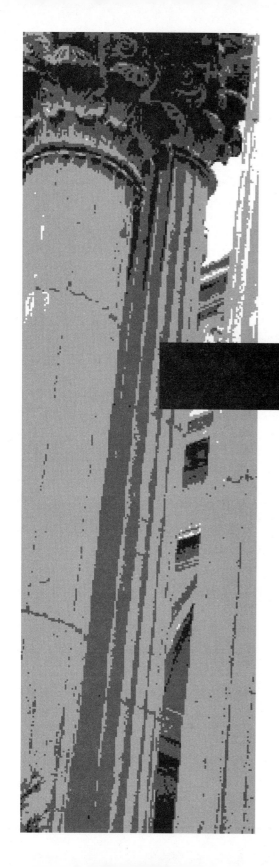

CHAPTER 1

MFC and Windows

This book teaches you to program for Windows using the Microsoft Foundation Classes (MFC). It is first and foremost a practical guide that provides a hands-on approach that will have you writing MFC-based Windows programs in the shortest possible time. As such, this book does not delve deeply into theoretical aspects of either Windows or MFC. However, before you can begin using the Foundation Classes to program for Windows you must understand, in a general way, what MFC is and why it was created. Further, you must know how Windows operates, how it interacts with your programs, what constitutes the basic elements of any Windows application, and what rules your programs must follow. Toward these ends, this chapter begins with a brief description of the philosophy and design criteria behind MFC. It concludes with an overview of Windows from the programmer's perspective.

Before beginning, it is important to remember that both Windows and MFC are very large, complex software systems. Neither can be fully described in one book. (Indeed, a full description would require several volumes!) This book covers those elements of MFC-based Windows programming that are common to all programs, that are frequently used, or that are important innovations. After you have completed this book, you will have sufficient understanding of the Microsoft Foundation Classes to begin writing your own Windows programs and to easily explore any of its various subsystems in detail.

What Is MFC?

In the simplest terms, MFC is a system of C++ classes designed to make Windows programming easier and quicker. MFC consists of a multi-layered class hierarchy that defines approximately 200 classes. These classes allow you to construct a Windows application using object-oriented principles. As you will see, MFC provides you, the programmer, with a framework upon which you can build Windows applications.

MFC was developed as a means of simplifying Windows programming. As you may know, the traditional method of programming for Windows requires rather long, complex programs that have many idiosyncrasies. For example, even a minimal, skeletal program written the traditional way requires about 75 lines of code. As a program becomes more complex, the amount of Windows-related code can become unwieldy. By contrast, the same program written using MFC is about one third as long. This is because MFC handles many of the clerical details for you.

MFC offers the convenience of reusable code. Because many of the tasks common to all Windows programs are provided by MFC, you don't need to re-create these each time you write a new program. Instead, your programs can simply inherit this functionality from MFC as needed. Also, MFC programs are highly portable, because the interface provided by the Foundation Class library is largely independent from the details of its underlying implementation. Your MFC-based programs will be able to be ported to new versions of Windows more easily than will traditional-style Windows programs.

Another way that MFC simplifies Windows programming is by organizing the Windows Application Programming Interface (API). An application program interfaces with Windows through the API, which contains several hundred functions. The sheer size of the API makes it difficult to grasp and understand in its entirety. For example, it is often hard to know what part of the API relates to what other parts! Because the Microsoft Foundation Classes encapsulate much of the API in a set of logically organized classes, the API is easier to manage. (We will return to the topic of the API shortly.)

One last point: A small number of classes defined by MFC do not directly relate to Windows programming. For example, MFC defines classes that create strings, manage files, and implement exception handling. Sometimes referred to as *general purpose classes*, these elements of MFC can be used by both Windows and non-Windows programs. Since this book is about programming for Windows using MFC, its focus is on the Windows-related classes. However, by the time you finish this book, you will be able to easily explore any of the general purpose classes on your own.

MFC Requires C++

Since MFC is a tool kit constructed from a hierarchy of C++ classes, you must use a C++ compiler when compiling MFC programs. Fortunately, any compiler that supports the MFC library also supports C++, so this is not generally a problem. It is important to understand that the programs you write that use the Microsoft Foundation Classes must also be C++ programs. Thus, in order to utilize MFC you must be a proficient C++ programmer. For example, you must be able to create your own classes, understand the principles of inheritance, and override virtual functions. Frankly, if your C++ skills are not as strong as you would like, you might want to build them up a bit before continuing. Although MFC programs *do not* use the most advanced or esoteric features of C++, they still require a solid knowledge of its fundamentals. If you are not well grounded in C++, you will quickly be lost when trying to understand the MFC programs shown in this book.

NOTE: If you need to bolster your C++ skills, we recommend Herb Schildt's book *C++: The Complete Reference, 3rd edition* (Osborne/McGraw-Hill, 1998). If you don't know C++ at all, try Herb's book *C++ from the Ground Up, 2nd edition* (Osborne/McGraw-Hill, 1998).

16 Bits or 32 Bits?

There are currently several versions of Windows in general use. The most common are Windows 3.1, Windows 95, Windows 98, and Windows NT. Windows 3.1 is a 16-bit system that runs on top of DOS. Although still in use at the time of this writing, it is, for all practical purposes, a dead system. Few new applications are being written for it because the 16-bit environment has been superseded by the 32-bit environment. (Windows 3.1 does, however, support a limited subset of 32-bit code.)

Windows 95, Windows 98, and Windows NT are 32-bit, stand-alone operating systems. They support all of the functionality originally provided by Windows 3.1. They also contain many additional features. For example, they support 32-bit, flat addressing, thread-based multitasking, sophisticated control elements, and the console-based interface. When Windows moved to a 32-bit implementation it left behind many of the quirks and problems associated with the older, 16-bit system.

Just as Windows has migrated from 16 to 32 bits, so has MFC. Beginning with MFC version 3.0, the 32-bit environment preempted the 16-bit world. The differences between the two environments are caused not so much because modern versions of MFC are specifically designed for 32 bits—although they are—but because so many new features of Windows are supported only by 32-bit environments. Since MFC provides full support for those 32-bit platforms, you will be unable to use many of its 32-bit-only features if you use MFC to create 16-bit code.

Since the 32-bit Windows environment is the target of virtually all new software development, this book teaches MFC programming from the 32-bit perspective. However, much of the information and examples can also be used for Windows 3.1. So if you need to create programs that are backward compatible with Windows 3.1, don't worry. The general techniques taught in this book will still apply. However, the future is a 32-bit world!

For the rest of this book, a 32-bit environment is assumed. For the purposes of illustration and discussion, Windows 98 will be used because it is the most popular and readily available 32-bit Windows platform. However, the information is applicable to any 32-bit environment.

What Version of MFC?

There have been several versions of MFC since version 1 was introduced in 1992. This book describes the latest version of MFC: version 6. This is the version supplied with Visual C++ 6. MFC 6 fully supports the modern, 32-bit Windows application environment and interface elements, including those features added by Windows 98. However, much of the information in this book is applicable to all versions of MFC. The reason for this is easy to understand: MFC was designed with portability in mind.

The Windows Programming Environment

If you have never programmed for Windows before, then you may be in for a shock. Windows programs are not like other types of programs that you have been writing. While MFC helps soften some of the blow, writing a Windows program is just plain harder than writing a console-based program for an operating system such as DOS or Unix. Before you can understand why a Windows program is structured the way it is, you need to know something about the way Windows works and how your programs interact with it. Let's begin by looking at some of Windows' key features.

The Windows Call-Based Interface

Windows uses a *call-based interface* to access the operating system. The Windows call-based interface is a rich set of system-defined functions that perform all necessary operating system–related activities, such as memory allocation, outputting to the screen, creating windows, and the like. As mentioned earlier, these functions are called the Application Programming Interface, or API. An application program calls the API functions to communicate with Windows.

MFC encapsulates the API. While it is still permissible for an MFC program to directly call an API function, most often your MFC program will interact with the API through MFC member functions. For the most part, these member functions parallel the API functions and often simply map directly onto their corresponding API counterparts.

Dynamic Link Libraries (DLLs)

Because the API consists of a large number of functions, you might be thinking that a large amount of code is linked into every program compiled for Windows, causing each program to contain much duplicate code. However, this is not the case. Instead, the Windows API functions are contained in *Dynamic Link Libraries*, or DLLs, which each program has access to when it is executed. Here is how dynamic linking works.

The Windows API functions are stored in a relocatable format within a DLL. During the compilation phase, when your program calls an API function, the linker does not add the code for that function to the executable version of your program. Instead, it adds loading instructions for that function, such as what DLL it resides in and its name. When your program is executed, the necessary API routines are also loaded by the Windows loader. In this way, each application program does not need to contain the actual API code. The API functions are added only when the application is loaded into memory for execution.

Dynamic linking has some very important benefits. First, since virtually all programs will use the API functions, DLLs prevent disk space from being wasted by the significant amount of duplicated object code that would be created if the API functions were actually added to each program's executable file on disk. Second, updates and enhancements to Windows can be accomplished by changing the dynamic link library routines. Existing application programs do not need to be recompiled.

Win16 vs. Win32

There are two versions of the Windows API. The first is called Win16, which is the 16-bit version of the API utilized by Windows 3.1 The other is called Win32. This is the 32-bit version used by all 32-bit versions of Windows, such as Windows 95/98/NT. For the most part, Win32 is a superset of the older Win16. Indeed, most functions are called by the same name and are used in the same way. However, while similar in spirit and purpose, the two APIs differ. Win32 supports 32-bit, flat addressing, while Win16 supports only the 16-bit, segmented memory model. This difference has caused several API functions to be widened to accept 32-bit arguments and return 32-bit values. Also, a few API functions were altered to accommodate the 32-bit architecture. API functions have also been added to support thread-based multitasking, new interface elements, and other enhanced Windows features. If you are new to Windows programming in general, these changes will not affect you significantly because you will probably be writing 32-bit code from the start. However, if you will be porting older code from Windows 3.1 to a 32-bit platform, you may need to deal with these differences.

As mentioned earlier, modern versions of MFC require the Win32 API. However, if you restrict your programs a bit, you can use MFC to create Windows 3.1 applications as long as they use a restricted set of the Win32 API, called Win32s.

Because Win32 supports full 32-bit addressing, it makes sense that integers are also 32 bits long. This means that types **int** and **unsigned** will be 32 bits long, not 16 bits long, as is the case for Windows 3.1. If you want to use a 16-bit integer, it must be declared as **short**. (Portable **typedef** names are provided for these types, as you will see shortly.) Therefore, if you will be porting code from the 16-bit environment, you will need to check your use of integers because they will automatically be expanded from 16 to 32 bits and side effects may result.

Another result of 32-bit addressing is that pointers no longer need to be declared as **near** or **far**. Any pointer can access any part of memory. In a Win32 environment, both **far** and **near** are defined (using **#define**) as nothing.

The GDI

There is a subset to the API called the GDI (Graphics Device Interface), which is the part of Windows that provides device-independent graphics support. The GDI functions are what make it possible for a Windows application to run on a variety of different hardware.

Windows Is Multitasking

As you almost certainly know, all versions of Windows support multitasking. Windows 3.1 supports only process-based multitasking. All 32-bit versions of Windows support both process-based and thread-based multitasking. Let's look more closely at these two types of multitasking.

A *process* is a program that is executing. In process-based multitasking, two or more programs may be run concurrently. Of course, the programs share the CPU and do not technically run simultaneously, but appear to because of the speed of the computer.

A *thread* is a dispatchable unit of executable code. The name comes from the concept of a "thread of execution." In thread-based multitasking, individual threads within a single process are multitasked. All processes have at least one thread. However, a Win32-process may have several.

Since a Win32 environment multitasks threads and since each process can have more than one thread, this implies that it is possible for one process to have two or more pieces of itself executing simultaneously. As it turns out, this implication is correct. Therefore, when working with Windows 95/98/NT, it is possible to multitask both programs and pieces of a single program. As you will see later in this book, this capability makes it possible to write very efficient programs.

There is another very important difference between Windows 3.1 multitasking and the multitasking provided by Windows 95/98/NT. Windows 3.1 uses *nonpreemptive* multitasking. This means that the currently executing process retains control of the CPU until it (the process) relinquishes it. Thus, it is possible for a misbehaving program to dominate the CPU, preventing other processes from executing. By contrast, Windows 95/98/NT use *preemptive* multitasking. In this approach, each active thread of execution is granted a slice of CPU time. When that time slice ends, execution automatically moves on to the next thread. This prevents a program from dominating the CPU. Most programmers feel that preemptive multitasking is an important improvement.

How Windows and Your Program Interact

When you write a program for many operating systems, it is your program that initiates interaction with the operating system. For example, in a DOS program, it is the program that requests such things as input and output. Put differently, non-Windows programs call the operating system. The operating system does not call your program. However, in a large measure, Windows works in the opposite way. It is Windows that calls your program. The process works like this: A program waits until it is sent a *message* by Windows. When it receives a message, the program takes appropriate action. After completing that action, the program once again waits for the next message.

There are many different types of messages that Windows may send your program. For example, each time the mouse is clicked on a window belonging to your program, a mouse-clicked message will be sent. Another type of message is sent each time a window belonging to your program must be redrawn. Still another message is sent each time the user presses a key when your program is the focus of input. Keep one fact firmly in mind: as far as your program is concerned, messages arrive randomly. This is why Windows programs resemble interrupt-driven programs. You can't know what message will be next.

Some Windows Programming Fundamentals

Because of its message-based architecture, all Windows programs contain
certain common components. In a traditional Windows program, you must
provide all of these elements explicitly in your program's source code.
Fortunately, when using MFC, these components are provided automatically;
you don't have to waste time and effort on them. However, to fully grasp
what your MFC-based Windows program is actually doing—and why it is
doing it—you need to understand in a general way the operation and
purpose of these essential items. Also, because they are referred to by most
literature on Windows programming, you should know what they are. For
these reasons, each is briefly described in the following sections.

1

NOTE: If you have never seen a traditional-style Windows program and
are interested in how one is written, refer to Appendix A. For comparison
purposes, it provides a brief overview of traditional Windows programming
and develops a traditional skeletal Windows program.

WinMain( )

All Windows programs begin execution with a call to the **WinMain( )**
function. In a traditional program, you must explicitly provide the
WinMain( ) function. When using MFC, it is provided for you. However, it ·
still does exist.

The Window Procedure

All Windows programs must contain a special function that is *not* called by
your program but is called by Windows. This function is generally called the
window function or the *window procedure*. The window procedure is called by
Windows when it needs to pass a message to your program. It is through this
function that Windows communicates with your program. The window
procedure receives the message in its parameters. In Windows terminology,
any function called by Windows is referred to as a *callback function*. Thus, the
window procedure is a callback function.

In addition to receiving the messages sent by Windows, the window
procedure must initiate any actions indicated by a message. Of course, your
program need not respond to every message that Windows sends. For
messages that your program doesn't care about, you can let Windows provide
default processing of them. Since there are hundreds of different messages

that Windows can generate, it is common for most messages to simply be processed by Windows and not your program.

In a traditional Windows program, the window procedure is a function provided by you. In an MFC-based program, the window procedure is provided by MFC. This is one of the benefits of using MFC for Windows programming. In either case, once a message is received, your program is expected to take an appropriate action. While your program may call one or more API functions when responding to a message, it is still Windows that initiates the activity. More than anything else, it is the message-based interaction with Windows that dictates the general form of all Windows programs—MFC-based or traditional.

The Message Loop

As explained earlier, Windows communicates with your program by sending it messages. All Windows applications must establish a *message loop* (usually inside the **WinMain( )** function). This loop reads any pending message from the application's message queue and then dispatches that message back to Windows, which then calls your program's window procedure with that message as a parameter. In a traditional Windows program, you must create and activate the message loop. When using MFC, the message loop is provided for you. Remember, however, that the message loop still exists. It is an integral part of a Windows application.

The process of receiving and dispatching messages may seem to be an overly complex way of doing things; but it is, nevertheless, the way that all Windows programs must function. When using the Microsoft Foundation Classes, these clerical details are taken care of for you. However, they do still exist in your program.

Window Classes

As you will learn, each window in a Windows application is defined by certain attributes, called its *class*. (Here, the word *class* is not being used in its C++ sense. Rather, it means *style* or *type*.) In a traditional-style program, a window class must be defined and registered before a window can be created. When you register a window class, you are telling Windows about the form and function of the window. However, registering the window class does not cause a window to come into existence. To actually create a window requires additional steps. In an MFC program, you can define your own window class, but you don't have to. Instead, you can use the default class provided by MFC. This is another benefit of writing Windows programs using the Microsoft Foundation Classes.

Windows Programs Are Unique

1

As you have seen, Windows programs are structured differently from other types of programs. The unique structure of a Windows-style program is dictated by two constraints. The first is determined by the way your program interacts with Windows, as just described. The second is governed by the rules that must be followed to create a standard, Windows-style application interface (that is, to make a program that "looks like" a Windows program).

The goal of Windows is to enable a person who has basic familiarity with the system to sit down and run virtually any application without prior training. Toward this end, Windows provides a consistent interface to the user. In theory, if you can run one Windows-based program, you can run them all. In actuality, most useful programs will still require some sort of training in order to be used effectively; but at least this instruction can be restricted to *what* the program *does*, not *how* the user must *interact* with it. In fact, much of the code in a Windows application is there just to support the user interface.

Although creating a consistent, Windows-style interface is a crucial part of writing any Windows program, it does not happen automatically. That is, it is possible to write Windows programs that do not take advantage of the Windows interface elements. To create a Windows-style program, you must purposely do so using the techniques described in this book. Only those programs written to take advantage of Windows will look and feel like Windows programs. While you can override the basic Windows design philosophy, you had better have a good reason to do so; otherwise, the users of your programs will be disappointed. In general, if you are writing application programs for Windows, they should utilize the normal Windows interface and conform to the standard Windows design practices.

Windows Data Types

As you will soon see, Windows programs in general, and MFC programs in particular, do not make extensive use of standard C/C++ data types, such as **int** or **char ***. Instead, all data types have been defined within the various header files. Some of the most common types are **HANDLE**, **HWND**, **BYTE**, **WORD**, **DWORD**, **UINT**, **LONG**, **BOOL**, **LPSTR**, and **LPCSTR**. **HANDLE** is a 32-bit integer that is used as a handle. There are a number of handle types, but they all are the same size as **HANDLE**. A *handle* is simply a value that identifies some resource. For example, **HWND** is a 32-bit integer that is used as a window handle. All handle types begin with an "H." Handles are not used as extensively in an MFC-based program as they are in a traditional-style program. **BYTE** is an 8-bit unsigned character. **WORD** is a 16-bit unsigned short integer. **DWORD** is an unsigned long integer. **UINT** is an unsigned

32-bit integer. **LONG** is another name for **long**. **BOOL** is an integer; it is used to indicate values that are either true or false. **LPSTR** is a pointer to a string and **LPCSTR** is a **const** pointer to a string.

Naming Conventions

If you are new to Windows programming, several of the variable and parameter names in the programs shown in this book will probably seem rather unusual. This is because they follow a set of naming conventions invented by Microsoft for Windows programming. For functions, the name consists of a verb followed by a noun. The first character of the verb and the first character of the noun are capitalized. For the most part, this book will use this convention for function names.

For variable names, Microsoft chose to use a rather complex system of embedding the data type into a variable's name. To accomplish this, a lowercase type prefix is added to the start of the variable's name. The name itself is begun with a capital letter. The type prefixes are shown in Table 1-1. Frankly, the use of type prefixes is controversial and is not universally supported. Many Windows programmers use this method, many do not. It will be used by the programs in this book when it seems reasonable to do so. However, you are free to use any naming convention you like.

Prefix	Data Type
b	Boolean (one byte)
c	Character (one byte)
C	Class type
dw	Long unsigned integer
f	16-bit bitfield (flags)
fn	Function
h	Handle
l	Long integer
lp	Long pointer
n	Short integer
p	Pointer

Variable Type
Prefix
Characters
Table 1-1.

Prefix	Data Type
pt	Long integer holding screen coordinates
w	Short unsigned integer
sz	Pointer to null-terminated string
lpsz	Long pointer to null-terminated string
rgb	Long integer holding RGB color values

Variable Type
Prefix
Characters
(*continued*)
Table 1-2.

1

The Components of a Window

Before moving on, a few important terms need to be defined. Figure 1-1 shows a standard window with each of its elements pointed out.

All windows have a border that defines the limits of the window and is used to resize the window. At the top of the window are several items. On the far left is the System menu icon (also called the Title Bar icon). Clicking on this box displays the System menu. To the right of the System menu icon is the window's title. At the far right are the Minimize, Maximize, and Close icons. The client area is the part of the window in which your program activity takes place. Most windows also have horizontal and vertical scroll bars that are used to move text through the window.

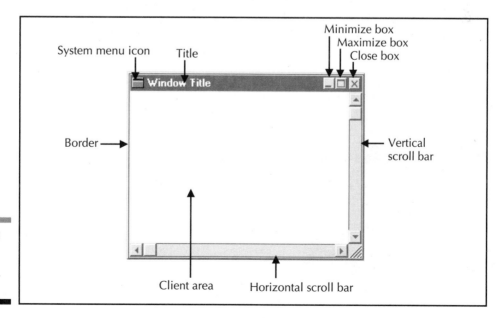

The elements
of a standard
window
Figure 1-1.

CHAPTER 2

MFC
Fundamentals

This chapter discusses the fundamental elements of an MFC program. It also develops a minimal MFC program that will be used as the basis for all other programs in this book. As such, this chapter lays the foundation for MFC programming. In it you will learn about the Microsoft Foundation Classes class hierarchy, how MFC programs are structured, how to create a window, and how to instantiate an application. Since the class hierarchy is at the core of MFC, we will begin there.

NOTE: If you know how to write traditional-style Windows programs, you might be tempted to skip ahead. However, this is not a good idea because MFC programs have several important differences from their traditional counterparts. Also, MFC programs have several unique attributes with which you will not be familiar. So, even if you are already an accomplished Windows programmer, a careful reading of this chapter is advised.

The MFC Class Hierarchy

As mentioned in Chapter 1, the Microsoft Foundation Classes are a C++-based class hierarchy. The MFC class hierarchy is shown in Figure 2-1. At the top is a class called **CObject**. **CObject** provides various run-time support features, including run-time type information, serialization, and diagnostics. As it applies to **CObject**, serialization is the feature that allows an object to store itself on disk (or some other type of storage device) and be restored later—usually by a subsequent invocation of your program. We won't be making direct use of any of the features defined by **CObject**. Of course, programs that you write might. However, since **CObject** is the top-level base class of most of the MFC library, its functionality is contained in all of its derived classes.

Looking at Figure 2-1 you can see that several classes are derived directly from **CObject**. Some of the most commonly used derived classes are **CCmdTarget**, **CFile**, **CDC**, **CGdiObject**, **CException**, and **CMenu**. **CCmdTarget** provides support for message processing. As you may recall from Chapter 1, Windows communicates with your program by passing it messages. It is **CCmdTarget** that encapsulates this process. **CFile** provides support for file operations, including disk files. **CDC** encapsulates device-context support. You will learn about device contexts later, but briefly, a device context defines a display environment (such as a window on the screen). In addition, it provides functions that allow your application to draw various objects (such as lines and circles) in a window. **CGdiObject** is the base class for various GDI objects. You will be using GDI objects frequently in your Windows programs because they consist of such things as bitmaps, brushes, and pens. **CException** provides exception handling. **CMenu** helps you manage menus. In addition to these classes, several other classes are directly derived from **CObject**, supporting such things as thread synchronization, databases, arrays, lists, and maps.

From **CCmdTarget** is derived one very important class: **CWnd**. **CWnd** is the base class from which all windows are derived, including frame windows ("normal" windows), dialog boxes, and the various control windows. One of the most commonly used classes derived from **CWnd** is **CFrameWnd** because it creates a frame window. This class provides support for SDI (Single Document Interface) windows and in the past, nearly all MFC applications used the SDI model. Over the years, Windows applications have become more complex and more diverse, and some have outgrown the abilities of the SDI window type. In response, additional types, such as MDI (Multiple Document Interface), dialog-based, or form-based windows, were created and are now also commonly used. No matter what type of application you are creating, it is within classes implementing these various window types that you will typically declare your application's main message map. (You will learn about message maps shortly.) For the simple sample applications used by this book the SDI type of Windows application is more than adequate, and is used exclusively. However, the same general techniques apply to all types of applications.

Another class derived directly from **CCmdTarget** is **CWinThread**. **CWinThread** defines a thread of execution for your application and provides support for thread-based multitasking. You will learn how to manage multithreaded programs later in this book.

From **CWinThread** is derived what is probably the single most important class that you will deal with directly in your MFC programs: **CWinApp**. Even though **CWinApp** is four levels deep in the MFC hierarchy, it is one of its most fundamental classes because it encapsulates your MFC-based application. Specifically, **CWinApp** is the class that controls the startup, initialization, execution, and shutdown of your program. Each MFC program that you write will have one (and only one) object of type **CWinApp**. When this object is instantiated, your application begins running.

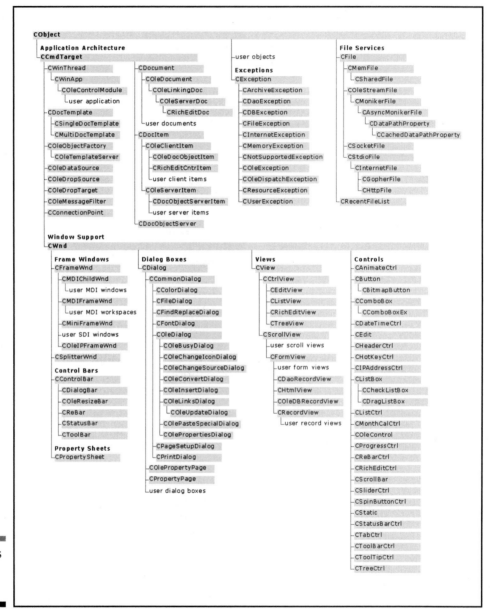

The MFC class heirarchy

Figure 2-1.

Classes Not Derived
from CObject

Graphical Drawing
CDC
└CClientDC
└CMetaFileDC
└CPaintDC
└CWindowDC

Control Support
CDockState
CImageList

**Graphical
Drawing Objects**
CGdiObject
└CBitmap
└CBrush
└CFont
└CPalette
└CPen
└CRgn

Menus
CMenu

Command Line
CCommandLineInfo

**ODBC Database
Support**
CDatabase
CRecordset
└user recordsets
CLongBinary

**DAO Database
Support**
CDaoDatabase
CDaoQueryDef
CDaoRecordset
CDaoTableDef
CDaoWorkspace

Synchronization
CSyncObject
└CCriticalSection
└CEvent
└CMutex
└CSemaphore

Windows Sockets
CAsyncSocket
└CSocket

Arrays
CArray (template)
CByteArray
CDWordArray
CObArray
CPtrArray
CStringArray
CUIntArray
CWordArray
arrays of user types

Lists
CList (template)
CPtrList
CObList
CStringList
lists of user types

Maps
CMap (template)
CMapWordToPtr
CMapPtrToWord
CMapPtrToPtr
CMapWordToOb
CMapStringToPtr
CMapStringToOb
CMapStringToString
maps of user types

Internet Services
CInternetSession
CInternetConnection
└CFtpConnection
└CGopherConnection
└CHttpConnection
CFileFind
└CFtpFileFind
└CGopherFileFind
CGopherLocator

**Internet
Server API**
CHtmlStream
CHttpFilter
CHttpFilterContext
CHttpServer
CHttpServerContext

**Run-time Object
Model Support**
CArchive
CDumpContext
CRuntimeClass

**Simple
Value Types**
CPoint
CRect
CSize
CString
CTime
CTimeSpan

Structures
CCreateContext
CMemoryState
COleSafeArray
CPrintInfo

Support Classes
CCmdUI
└COleCmdUI
CDaoFieldExchange
CDataExchange
CDBVariant
CFieldExchange
COleDataObject
COleDispatchDriver
CPropExchange
CRectTracker
CWaitCursor

**Typed Template
Collections**
CTypedPtrArray
CTypedPtrList
CTypedPtrMap

**OLE Type
Wrappers**
CFontHolder
CPictureHolder

**OLE Automation
Types**
COleCurrency
COleDateTime
COleDateTimeSpan
COleVariant

Synchronization
CMultiLock
CSingleLock

The MFC class
heirarchy
(*continued*)
Figure 2-1.

As you will see, the MFC skeleton application developed in this chapter directly uses only two classes in the MFC hierarchy. However, later examples will make extensive use of many others. In fact, part of learning to write Windows applications using MFC is understanding the class hierarchy.

Although the MFC hierarchy is quite large, don't be intimidated by it. You will see as you progress through this book that each class addresses a specific Windows-related operation or subsystem. By the time you finish this book, you will have no trouble navigating the MFC classes.

MFC Member Functions

When you write an MFC program you will find that many of the functions you call will be members of a class defined by MFC. Here are some examples:

◆ The function that displays a window is called **ShowWindow( )**, and it is a member of the **CWnd** class.

◆ To output a string in a window, you will use the **CDC** member function **TextOut( )**.

◆ To load a bitmap, you will use **CBitmap::LoadBitmap( )**.

As mentioned in Chapter 1, most of the API functions provided by Win32 (and Win16) are available through MFC member functions. In fact, for the most part, MFC encapsulates the API. This is one reason why you will be making such extensive use of MFC member functions. However, it is important to remember that your MFC program can always call an API function directly. It's just more convenient to use the MFC member functions for most operations.

MFC Global Functions

Most of the time you will be using member functions of the MFC classes to interface with Windows. However, this will not always be the case. MFC also defines several global functions that your MFC-based programs are free to use. These functions all begin with the **Afx** prefix. For example, one commonly used **Afx** function is called **AfxMessageBox( )**. As you will see in Chapter 4, it displays a message box on the screen. Since message boxes are predefined windows, it is possible to activate one independently from the rest of your application. (It is also possible to activate a message box relative to your application. In this case, you *will* use an MFC member function.) In a general sense, the **Afx** functions are either independent of or span the class hierarchy.

AFXWIN.H

All MFC Windows programs must include AFXWIN.H. This file (and its various support files) define the MFC classes. The AFXWIN.H header file automatically includes most of the header files related to MFC, and also includes WINDOWS.H. As you may know, WINDOWS.H is the header file used by traditional-style Windows programs. WINDOWS.H includes the prototypes for the API functions and defines numerous constants used by Windows programs. By including AFXWIN.H, you are including all necessary support for your Windows application.

2

An MFC Application Skeleton

Now that the necessary background information has been covered, it is time to develop a minimal MFC application skeleton. As stated, all Foundation Classes programs have certain things in common. In this section a short MFC program containing these necessary features is developed. This simple application will be used as a starting point for the rest of the programs in this book.

In its simplest form, an MFC program consists of two classes that you must derive from the MFC hierarchy: an application class and a window class. Put differently, to create a minimal MFC program you must derive one class that defines your application and another class that defines your application's main window. For the programs in this book, the main window class is derived from **CFrameWnd**. The application is derived from **CWinApp**. While your program is free to derive additional classes as needed, these are the only two that every program must have.

In addition to creating the application and window classes, an MFC program must also respond to all relevant messages passed to it by Windows. Since the skeleton program shown in this section does nothing but display its window, it does not respond explicitly to any messages. However, the message-handling mechanism must still be present in its skeletal form.

To create an MFC program, follow these steps:

1. Derive a window class from **CFrameWnd**.
2. Derive an application class from **CWinApp**.
3. Define a message map.
4. Override **CWinApp**'s **InitInstance( )** function.
5. Create an instance of your application class.

Before discussing the details, examine the following minimal MFC program. It creates a standard window that includes a title, a system menu, and the standard minimize, maximize, and close boxes. It is, therefore, capable of being minimized, maximized, moved, resized, and closed.

```cpp
// A minimal MFC program.
#include <afxwin.h>

// Derive essential classes.

// This is the main window class.
class CMainWin : public CFrameWnd
{
public:
  CMainWin();
  DECLARE_MESSAGE_MAP()
};

// Construct a window.
CMainWin::CMainWin()
{
  Create(NULL, "An MFC Application Skeleton");
}

// This is the application class.
class CApp : public CWinApp
{
public:
  BOOL InitInstance();
};

// Initialize the application.
BOOL CApp::InitInstance()
{
  m_pMainWnd = new CMainWin;
  m_pMainWnd->ShowWindow(m_nCmdShow);
  m_pMainWnd->UpdateWindow();

  return TRUE;
}

// This is the application's message map.
BEGIN_MESSAGE_MAP(CMainWin, CFrameWnd)
END_MESSAGE_MAP()

CApp App; // instantiate the application
```

2

When you run this program, you will see a window similar to that shown in Figure 2-2. Let's go through this program step by step.

As you can see, nearly all the code in this example exists to derive two classes from MFC base classes. As mentioned, almost all Windows applications (including the applications in this book) must derive at least two classes. The first creates a frame window class, which serves as the main window for the application. The second creates the application class. Your application begins running when an object of the application class is instantiated.

To create a frame window, your application must derive one from the **CFrameWnd** class. In the program, this derived class is called **CMainWin**. Inside **CMainWin** two members are declared: the **CMainWin( )** constructor and the **DECLARE_MESSAGE_MAP( )** macro. As you will see, **DECLARE_-MESSAGE_MAP( )** declares a message map for the **CMainWin** class, which allows it to respond to messages. Any window that will process messages must include **DECLARE_MESSAGE_MAP( )**. Also, **DECLARE_MESSAGE_-MAP( )** should be the last member declared within the class. (If it isn't, then you must precede the next member with an access specifier.)

The frame window itself is created inside **CMainWin**'s constructor using a call to the **Create( )** member function. As described earlier, **CFrameWnd** is derived from **CWnd**, which is derived from **CCmdTarget**, which is derived from **CObject**. This means that any class derived from **CFrameWnd** has access to all of the member functions and variables declared anywhere in this hierarchy. While only a few of these members will be needed by the programs in this book, you will want to explore them fully when writing

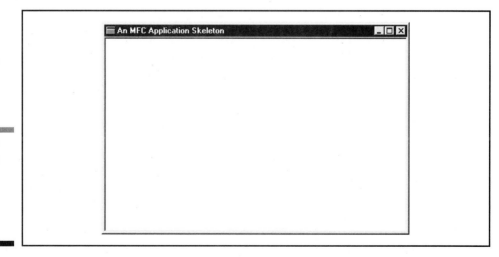

The window produced by the MFC skeleton program

Figure 2-2.

your own programs. However, the one function that nearly every Windows application will use is called **Create( )**. This function is used to create a window and is a member of **CFrameWnd**. In our program, it is used in its most simple form. Although you will learn about **Create( )** in detail shortly, it is apparent that its second parameter specifies the title of the window.

The application class, **CApp**, is derived from **CWinApp**. As mentioned, this is the class that encapsulates your program. It is derived from **CWinThread**, which is derived from **CCmdTarget**. **CWinApp** contains a number of member functions and variables. Only one member function, **InitInstance( )**, is used by the skeletal program. Its prototype is shown here:

    virtual BOOL CWinApp::InitInstance( );

InitInstance( ) is a virtual function that must be overridden by your application class. It is called each time a new instance of your program is started. Inside **InitInstance( )** you will perform any initializations related to this instance of your program. This function must return nonzero if successful and zero upon failure.

Inside **InitInstance( )** three statements execute. An object of type **CMainWin** is created and a pointer to this object stored in **m_pMainWnd**. **m_pMainWnd** is a member variable of the **CWinThread** class, which is indirectly inherited by **CApp**. It is a pointer of type **CWnd ***. This variable is used by nearly all MFC-based programs because it is a pointer to your program's main window object. It will be used to call various member functions related to your main window, as the next two lines of code in **InitInstance( )** show.

Once the main window has been created, two member functions of **CWnd** are called using **m_pMainWnd**. The first is **ShowWindow( )**. Its prototype is shown here:

    BOOL CWnd::ShowWindow(int *How*);

ShowWindow( ) determines how the main window will be displayed. The display mode is specified in *How*. The first time the window is displayed, you will want to pass **m_nCmdShow** as the *How* parameter. This member variable of **CWinApp** determines how the window will be displayed when the program begins execution. Subsequent calls can display (or remove) the window as necessary. Some common values for *How* are shown next.

Display Macro	Effect
SW_HIDE	Removes the window.
SW_MAXIMIZE	Maximizes the window.
SW_MINIMIZE	Minimizes the window into an icon.
SW_SHOW	Displays the window.
SW_RESTORE	Returns the window to normal size.

The **ShowWindow( )** function returns the previous display status of the window. If the window was displayed, then nonzero is returned. If the window was not displayed, zero is returned.

The next function called by **InitInstance( )** is **UpdateWindow( )**, which is also a member of the **CWnd** class. Although not technically necessary for this simple program, a call to **UpdateWindow( )** is included because it is needed by virtually every Windows application that you will create. It essentially tells Windows to send a message to your application that the main window needs to be updated. (This message will be discussed in the next chapter.)

Near the end of the program you can see the rather odd-looking bit of code shown here:

```
// This is the application's message map.
BEGIN_MESSAGE_MAP(CMainWin, CFrameWnd)
END_MESSAGE_MAP()
```

This is your main window's *message map*. Every Windows application receives and processes messages. It is inside this message map that you will declare those functions that will process the messages related to your application. Since our skeletal application does not process any messages, none are included in its map. However, message processing is an important—indeed, fundamental—part of any actual Windows application.

Up to this point, the nature and form of a simple window and application have been defined, but neither exist until an application object derived from **CWinApp** is instantiated. This happens when the following statement executes:

```
CApp App;
```

As mentioned, there can only be one object of type **CWinApp** in your program. Once it is created, your application begins execution.

Before moving on, you should enter this simple program, compile it, and run it. Doing so will confirm that you have set all of your compiler's options correctly so that it will compile MFC-based Windows programs.

Using a Definition File

As mentioned in Chapter 1, the focus of this book is the creation of MFC programs for a modern, 32-bit environment. However, much of the information does apply to the older, 16-bit world. There is, however, one important additional step that you must take if you want to compile an MFC program for a 16-bit version of Windows, such as Windows 3.1: you must define a *definition file* for each program that you create. Remember, a definition file is *not needed* when compiling most types of programs for Windows 95, Windows 98, or Windows NT (or any other modern, 32-bit environment). It *is* needed for 16-bit Windows programs. A definition file defines certain attributes required by your program, such as the amount of memory required for the stack and heap. Some compilers will automatically generate this information if no definition file is present. Since definition files are largely vestiges of an earlier time and are becoming obsolete, this book does not spend much time on them. However, if you find that you need one, the following definition file should be sufficient for the programs in this book; but be sure to consult your compiler's user manual for details concerning this file.

```
DESCRIPTION 'Skeleton Program'
EXETYPE WINDOWS
CODE PRELOAD MOVEABLE DISCARDABLE
DATA PRELOAD MOVEABLE MULTIPLE
HEAPSIZE 8192
STACKSIZE 8192
```

All definition files use the extension .DEF. For example, the definition file for the skeleton program could be called SKEL.DEF.

A Closer Look at Creating Frame Windows

The preceding program creates a default-style frame window. For simple applications, this may be sufficient, but usually you will need more control over the form and nature of your application's main window. Fortunately, this control is easy to obtain using the **Create( )** function. The prototype for **CFrameWnd::Create( )** is shown here:

```
BOOL CFrameWnd::Create(LPCSTR ClassName, // window class name
              LPCSTR Title, // title of window
              DWORD Style = WS_OVERLAPPEDWINDOW, // style
              const RECT &XYsize = rectDefault, // position and size
              CWnd *Parent = NULL, // parent window
              LPCSTR MenuName = NULL, // name of main menu
              DWORD ExStyle = 0, // extended style specifier
              CCreateContext *Context = NULL // optional context structure
);
```

As you can see, all but the first two parameters specify default arguments. This is why the skeletal program was able to use a very simple form of **Create( )**.

The first parameter, *ClassName*, specifies a pointer to the name of the window class. In this context, the term *class* does not refer to a C++ class, but rather to a style of Window. When this parameter is **NULL** (as it typically is) the default window class (created by MFC) associated with a frame window is used. However, you may register your own window class name, using **AfxRegisterWndClass( )**. This function constructs the window class according to your own specification and returns a pointer to its name. You can then use this name as the first parameter to **Create( )**. Of course, it is usually easier to simply use the default window class defined by **CFrameWnd**, which is what the examples in this book do.

The title of the window is a string pointed to by *Title*. This can be a null string, but usually a window will be given a title. The style (or type) of window actually created is determined by the value of *Style*. The macro **WS_OVERLAPPEDWINDOW** specifies a standard window that has a system menu; a border; and minimize, maximize, and close boxes. This is the default style if no *Style* parameter is specified. While this style of window is the most common, you can construct one to your own specifications. To accomplish this, simply OR together the various style macros that you want. Some other common styles are shown here:

Style Macro	Window Feature
WS_OVERLAPPED	Overlapped window with border
WS_MAXIMIZEBOX	Maximize box
WS_MINIMIZEBOX	Minimize box

Style Macro	Window Feature
WS_SYSMENU	System menu
WS_HSCROLL	Horizontal scroll bar
WS_VSCROLL	Vertical scroll bar

The initial location and size of the window is specified by *XYsize*. If this parameter is allowed to default (as is most typical), then the window is displayed at a location and size chosen by Windows. However, you can specify these items explicitly by passing a reference to a **RECT** structure. **RECT** is defined like this:

```
typedef struct tagRECT {
 LONG left;
 LONG top;
 LONG right;
 LONG bottom;
} RECT;
```

Specify the coordinates of the upper-left corner of the window in **left** and **top**, and the coordinates of the lower-right corner in **right** and **bottom**. When determining the location and dimensions of a window, keep in mind that these are specified in *device units,* which are the physical units used by the device (in this case, pixels). This means that the coordinates are relative to the screen. Output to a window is generally specified in terms of *logical units*, which are mapped to a window according to the current mapping mode. However, since the position of a window is relative to the entire screen, it makes sense that **Create( )** would require physical units rather than logical ones.

The *Parent* parameter must be a pointer to the window that is the parent of the one being created. However, for top-level windows, such as the main window of your application, this parameter must be **NULL**.

Although the skeletal application does not use a top-level menu, most real applications do. When used, the name of this menu must be specified by the *MenuName* parameter. (You will learn about menus later in this book.)

Any extended style attributes are specified by the *ExStyle* parameter. Use **NULL** if no extended styles are needed. (Extended styles are also discussed later in this book.)

The last parameter, *Context,* is normally **NULL**. It is a pointer to a **CCreateContext** structure. Customizing context structures is a specialized programming task and is seldom required.

Create( ) returns nonzero if it creates the window or zero if the window cannot be created.

To see how some of the additional parameters to **Create( )** can be used, try substituting the following version of the **CMainWin( )** constructor in the skeletal program.

```
CMainWin::CMainWin()
{
  RECT r;

  r.top = 10; r.left = 10;
  r.bottom = r.right = 200;

  Create(NULL, "A Small Window",
         WS_OVERLAPPEDWINDOW, r);
}
```

This version creates a standard, overlapped window that has its upper-left corner at location 10,10 and its lower-right corner at location 200,200. This window is shown here:

A Closer Look at CWinApp

In addition to **InitInstance( )** and **m_nCmdShow**, **CWinApp** has several other members that you will find useful. Here are a few:

IN DEPTH

ANSI vs. Unicode?

In the **CFrameWnd::Create( )** function, notice the data type **LPCSTR** for several of the parameters, such as *ClassName*. If you look up **CFrameWnd::Create( )** in the Visual C++ online documentation, you will find this type shown as **LPCTSTR**, instead of **LPCSTR**. **LPCTSTR** is a placeholder type that is automatically replaced by either **LPCSTR** or **LPCWSTR** when your program is compiled. The type **LPCSTR** specifies a pointer to a **const** string that uses 8-bit ANSI characters and **LPCWSTR** specifies a pointer to a **const** wide-character string represented in Unicode. A discussion of the reason for the **LPCTSTR** placeholder type and its replacement follows.

In the past, **CFrameWnd::Create( )** used a pointer to a constant ANSI string, **LPCSTR**, as the data type for strings passed into the **Create( )** function because it could be assumed that the target platform expected ANSI strings. Therefore, an ANSI string worked perfectly. However, due to the internationalization of the software market, you can no longer assume that the platform you are targeting expects an ANSI string. As you probably know, the ANSI character set is restricted to no more than 256 characters. However, some human languages require far more; for these languages a wide-character string is required. Wide-character strings use 16-bit Unicode characters, which can accommodate the large character sets of some languages. To accommodate both ANSI and Unicode, the header files associated with MFC (and Windows in general) use the placeholder type **LPCTSTR** for functions that receive pointers to **const** strings. If you build an ANSI version of your program, **LPCSTR** is automatically substituted. If you build a Unicode version, the type **LPCWSTR** is used. Aside from the strings, themselves, no other changes are required in your program. Thus, one source file can be used to target both types of character environments.

The preceding discussion also applies to non-**const** strings. In this case, **LPTSTR** is the placeholder type that is automatically substituted for by using either **LPSTR** or **LPWSTR**. For the sake of simplicity, this book will assume that the target platform expects ANSI strings and all prototypes will be shown using the **LPCSTR** and **LPSTR** types.

◆ Any command-line parameters associated with your application are found in a string pointed to by **m_lpCmdLine**.

◆ The name of the application is contained in the string pointed to by **m_pszAppName**.

◆ When your application is idle, it calls the **OnIdle( )** function. Your application can override this function to perform background processing.

2

In the course of this book, we will be making use of several of the members of **CWinApp**.

Organizing Your Program's Source Code

Although the skeleton program is quite short, most Windows programs that you write will be quite long. As you will soon see, even the examples in this book will frequently extend over several pages. To aid in the organization of MFC-based Windows programs, a style of file management has evolved that has become common among MFC programmers. When writing MFC programs, put all of your class derivations in one file and the code that implements those classes in another. Call the first file something like CLASSES.H and include it in the other file. Since most real-world projects consist of multiple source files, this approach is useful because it allows you to easily include your class hierarchy in all of the files used by your program.

To see an example, let's reorganize the skeleton program shown earlier so that it uses this approach. First, the class hierarchy is contained in the following file. Call this file SKEL.H.

```
//  This file derives the necessary classes.

// This is the main window class.
class CMainWin : public CFrameWnd
{
public:
  CMainWin();
  DECLARE_MESSAGE_MAP()
};

// This is the application class.
class CApp : public CWinApp
{
public:
  BOOL InitInstance();
};
```

Next, the code that implements these classes is put into the following file:

```
// A minimal MFC program.
#include <afxwin.h>
#include "skel.h"

// Construct a window.
CMainWin::CMainWin()
{
  Create(NULL, "An MFC Application Skeleton");
}

// Initialize the application.
BOOL CApp::InitInstance()
{
  m_pMainWnd = new CMainWin;
  m_pMainWnd->ShowWindow(m_nCmdShow);
  m_pMainWnd->UpdateWindow();

  return TRUE;
}

// This is the application's message map.
BEGIN_MESSAGE_MAP(CMainWin, CFrameWnd)
END_MESSAGE_MAP()

CApp App; // instantiate the application
```

As you can see, this file first includes AFXWIN.H and then includes SKEL.H. The order of these inclusions is important because SKEL.H requires the information in AFXWIN.H but does not include it itself.

Since this style of program organization is very common when writing MFC-based Windows programs, it is the style used in this book. It is also an effective way to organize your programs. Of course, you need not use this approach. You are free to organize your programs however you choose.

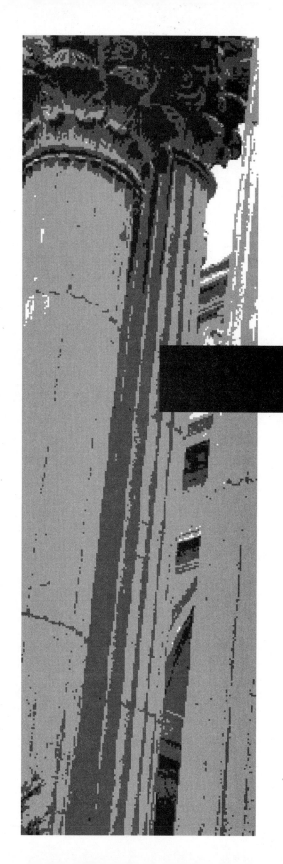

CHAPTER 3

Processing Messages

Windows communicates with your application by sending it messages. For this reason, the processing of messages is at the core of all Windows applications. In the preceding chapter you learned how to create a skeletal MFC Windows application. In this chapter, that skeleton will be expanded to receive and process several common messages.

What Are Messages?

There are a large number of Windows messages. Each message is represented by a unique integer value. In the header file WINDOWS.H there are standard names for these messages. For example, here are some common Windows messages:

WM_CHAR	WM_PAINT	WM_MOVE	WM_CLOSE
WM_LBUTTONUP	WM_LBUTTONDOWN	WM_COMMAND	WM_SIZE

Often, a message will be accompanied by other values that contain additional, related information. This related information includes things such as cursor or mouse coordinates; the value of a keypress; or a system-related value.

Windows interacts with your program using messages. Specifically, each time an event occurs to which your program may need to respond, it is sent a message that identifies that event. It is important to understand that your program doesn't need to respond explicitly to all messages that it is sent. In fact, since Windows can generate a large number of messages, your program probably won't respond to most. It need only process those messages that relate to it. For messages that your program doesn't explicitly handle, MFC supplies a default message handler.

In a traditional-style Windows program, your program's window procedure receives each message, plus any additional information associated with that message, in its parameters. Inside the window procedure, a large **switch** statement determines what type of message has been received and then processes it accordingly. Frankly, this approach is both clumsy and prone to trouble. Fortunately, when using the Microsoft Foundation Classes, responding to messages is much easier.

Responding to Messages—MFC Style

MFC encapsulates the message-handling mechanism. By doing so, it greatly simplifies the way your program must respond to messages. MFC provides a set of predefined message handler functions that your program may implement. If your program implements one of these handlers, then that function will be called whenever its associated message is received. When a message has additional information associated with it, this information will be passed to the handler as an argument.

3

To respond to a message, your program must perform these three steps:

1. The message macro corresponding to the message must be added to your program's message map.
2. The prototype for the message handler must be added to the window class that will process the message.
3. You must implement the message handler associated with the message.

Let's take a closer look at these now.

Adding Message Macros to Your Message Map

In order for your program to respond to a message, the message macro corresponding to that message must be included in your program's message map. MFC message macros have the same name as standard Windows messages, except that they all begin with **ON_** and end with a set of parentheses. There is one exception to this rule: the **WM_COMMAND** message uses **ON_COMMAND** for its message macro. This is because **WM_COMMAND** is a rather special Windows message, and it requires unique treatment by MFC. (You will learn about **WM_COMMAND** messages in Chapter 4.) Here are the MFC message macros that correspond to the messages shown in the previous section:

ON_WM_CHAR( )	ON_WM_PAINT( )	ON_WM_MOVE( )
ON_WM_CLOSE( )	ON_WM_LBUTTONUP( )	ON_WM_LBUTTONDOWN( )
ON_COMMAND( )	ON_WM_SIZE( )	

To add a message macro to your message map, simply include it between **BEGIN_MESSAGE_MAP** and **END_MESSAGE_MAP**. For example, if you want your program to handle **WM_CHAR** messages, then you will use the following message map:

```
BEGIN_MESSAGE_MAP(CMainWin, CFrameWnd)
  ON_WM_CHAR()
END_MESSAGE_MAP()
```

Of course, you may have more than one message macro declared in your message map. For example, the following map allows your program to process **WM_CHAR** and **WM_LBUTTONDOWN** messages:

```
BEGIN_MESSAGE_MAP(CMainWin, CFrameWnd)
  ON_WM_CHAR()
  ON_WM_LBUTTONDOWN()
END_MESSAGE_MAP()
```

As you will soon see, **WM_CHAR** is the message that your program receives when the user presses a key, and the **WM_LBUTTONDOWN** message is sent each time the left mouse button is pressed.

Adding Message Handlers to Your Window Class

Each message that your program responds to must be associated with a message handler. All message handlers are members of the **CWnd** class, and may be overidden by your program. As a general rule, the name of a message handler function is constructed using the name of the message preceded by **On**. For example, the handler for **WM_CHAR** is **OnChar( )**, the handler for **WM_LBUTTONDOWN** is **OnLButtonDown( )**, and the handler for **WM_PAINT** is **OnPaint( )**.

To respond to a message, you must add the message handler to the window class that your program defines. This is done by including its prototype in the class declaration. The following example adds the **OnPaint( )** handler to the **CMainWin** class:

```
class CMainWin : public CFrameWnd
{
public:
  CMainWin();
  afx_msg void OnPaint();
  DECLARE_MESSAGE_MAP()
};
```

As you can see, **OnPaint( )** uses the **afx_msg** type specifier. All message handlers are prototyped using **afx_msg**. Now that **OnPaint( )** is part of **CMainWin**, this class will receive—and must respond to—**WM_PAINT** messages.

As a technical note, although message handlers "feel like" virtual functions, they are not. Instead, message handlers are defined within a message table by MFC for reasons of efficiency. As stated, all message handler functions are prototyped as type **afx_msg**. At this time, this is simply a placeholder type specification. However, this may change in the future.

Implementing Message Handlers

Once the message macro has been added to your program's message map and the handler's prototype has been added to your program's window class, you may define the message handler itself. Exactly how you implement each message handler depends upon two things: one, the nature of the message being handled; and two, the meaning this message has for your program. Therefore, it is not possible to describe a generic message handler. However, in this chapter, several message handlers are examined. Throughout the remainder of this book, additional message handlers are discussed as needed.

A Closer Look at the BEGIN_MESSAGE_MAP( ) Macro

Although we have been speaking of message maps in the singular, it is possible for your program to have more than one. In fact, any window can receive messages. You specify which window a message map is for in the parameters of **BEGIN_MESSAGE_MAP( )**. The general form of **BEGIN_MESSAGE_MAP( )** is shown here:

```
BEGIN_MESSAGE_MAP(Owner, Base)
  // add message macros here
END_MESSAGE_MAP( )
```

Here, the name of the class that the map is for is specified by *Owner*. *Base* specifies the name of the base class used to derive the owner of the map. For example, the map

```
BEGIN_MESSAGE_MAP(CMainWin, CFrameWnd)
  ON_WM_CHAR()
  ON_WM_LBUTTONDOWN()
END_MESSAGE_MAP()
```

specifies an owner class called **CMainWin**, which is derived from the standard MFC frame window class **CFrameWnd**.

Now that you know the theory behind messages, message maps, and message macros, the rest of this chapter shows how they can be applied.

Responding to a Keypress

One of the most common Windows messages is generated when a key is pressed. This message is called **WM_CHAR** and uses the **ON_WM_CHAR** message macro. It is important to understand that your application never receives keystrokes directly from the keyboard. Instead, each time a key is pressed, a **WM_CHAR** message is sent to the active window. To illustrate how this process works, this section extends the skeletal application developed in Chapter 2 so that it processes keystroke messages.

The message handler that processes **WM_CHAR** messages is called **OnChar( )**. Its prototype is shown here:

afx_msg void OnChar(UINT *Ch*, UINT *Count*, UINT *Flags*);

Each time **WM_CHAR** is received, **OnChar( )** is called. The ASCII value of the key pressed is passed in *Ch*. The number of times the key has been repeated as a result of the key being held down is passed in *Count*. The *Flags* parameter is encoded as shown here:

Bit	Meaning
0–15	Contains the number of times the key has been repeated as a result of the key being held down.
16–23	Manufacturer-dependent key code (i.e., the scan code).
24	Set if the key pressed is a function key or an extended key; cleared otherwise.
25–28	Used by Windows.
29	Set if the ALT key is also being pressed; cleared if ALT is not pressed.
30	Set if the key was pressed before the message was sent; cleared if it was not pressed.
31	Set if the key is being released; cleared if the key is being pressed.

For our purposes, the only parameter important at this time is *Ch*, since it holds the key that was pressed. However, notice how detailed the information is that Windows supplies about the state of the system. Of course, you are free to use as much or as little of this information as you like.

To process a **WM_CHAR** message, you must add its message macro to your message map, add the prototype for its handler to your main window's class, and then implement the **OnChar( )** function. For example, here is a version of **OnChar( )** that processes a keystroke by displaying it on the screen:

3

```
char str[80]; // holds output string

// Process a WM_CHAR message.
afx_msg void CMainWin::OnChar(UINT ch,
                              UINT count, UINT flags)
{
  CClientDC dc(this);

  dc.TextOut(1, 1, "   ", 3); // erase previous char

  wsprintf(str, "%c", ch);
  dc.TextOut(1, 1, str, strlen(str));
}
```

The purpose of the code inside **OnChar( )** is very simple: it echoes the key to the screen! You are probably surprised that it takes so many lines of code to accomplish this seemingly trivial feat. The reason for this is that Windows must establish a link between your program and the screen. This is called a *device context*, or *DC*, and it is acquired by declaring an object of type **CClientDC**, which is derived from **CDC**. **CClientDC** obtains a device context for the client area of the window. Don't worry about the precise definition of a device context at this time. It will be discussed in the next section. For now, it is sufficient to know that once you obtain a device context, you may write to the screen.

The function that actually outputs the character is the function **TextOut( )**, which is a member of the **CDC** class. It has two versions. The prototypes for both are shown here:

virtual BOOL CDC::TextOut(int *X*, int *Y*, LPCSTR *lpszStr*, int *Length*);

BOOL CDC::TextOut(int *X*, int *Y*, const CString &*StrOb*);

The first version of **TextOut( )** outputs the string pointed to by *lpszStr* at the window coordinates specified by *X,Y*. (By default, these coordinates are in terms of pixels.) The length of the string is specified in *Length*. The second version outputs the string contained in *StrOb*. **CString** is one of MFC's stand-alone classes. It implements a string class. For the purposes of this chapter, we will be using the first form of **TextOut( )**. (However, you are free to experiment with **CString** on your own.) In both cases, the **TextOut( )** function returns nonzero if successful, zero otherwise.

In the function, each time **OnChar( )** is called, the character that is typed by the user is converted, using **wsprintf( )**, into a string that is one character long and then displayed using **TextOut( )** at location 1,1. (**wsprintf( )** is the Windows-specific version of the standard **sprintf( )** function.) The string **str** is global because it will need to keep its value between function calls in later examples. In a window, the upper-left corner of the client area is location 0,0. Window coordinates are always relative to the window, not the screen. Therefore, as characters are entered, they are displayed in the upper-left corner no matter where the window is physically located on the screen.

The reason for the first call to **TextOut( )** is to erase whatever character had been previously displayed. Because Windows is a graphics-based system, characters are of different sizes and the overwriting of one character by another does not necessarily cause all of the previous character to be erased. For example, if you typed a "w" followed by an "i," part of the "w" would still be displayed if it weren't manually erased. (Try commenting out the first call to **TextOut( )** and observe what happens.)

At first you might think that using **TextOut( )** to output a single character is not an efficient application of the function. The fact is that MFC (and Windows, in general) does not contain a function that simply outputs a character. As you will see, Windows performs much of its user interaction through dialog boxes, menus, toolbars, etc. For this reason, it contains only a few functions that output text to the client area.

Here is the entire program that processes keystrokes, beginning with the class derivation header file called MESSAGE1.H:

```
// MESSAGE1.H

// This is the main window class.
```

```cpp
class CMainWin : public CFrameWnd
{
public:
  CMainWin();
  afx_msg void OnChar(UINT ch, UINT count, UINT flags);
  DECLARE_MESSAGE_MAP()
};

// This is the application class.
class CApp : public CWinApp
{
public:
  BOOL InitInstance();
};
```

Here is the program file:

```cpp
// An MFC program that processes WM_CHAR messages.

#include <afxwin.h>
#include <string.h>
#include "message1.h"

char str[80]; // holds output string

CMainWin::CMainWin()
{
  Create(NULL, "Processing WM_CHAR Messages");
}

// Initialize the application.
BOOL CApp::InitInstance()
{
  m_pMainWnd = new CMainWin;
  m_pMainWnd->ShowWindow(m_nCmdShow);
  m_pMainWnd->UpdateWindow();

  return TRUE;
}

// This is the application's message map.
```

```
BEGIN_MESSAGE_MAP(CMainWin, CFrameWnd)
  ON_WM_CHAR()
END_MESSAGE_MAP()

// Process a WM_CHAR message.
afx_msg void CMainWin::OnChar(UINT ch,
                              UINT count, UINT flags)
{
  CClientDC dc(this);

  dc.TextOut(1, 1, "   ", 3); // erase previous char

  wsprintf(str, "%c", ch);
  dc.TextOut(1, 1, str, strlen(str));
}

CApp App; // instantiate the application
```

Figure 3-1 shows the window produced by this program.

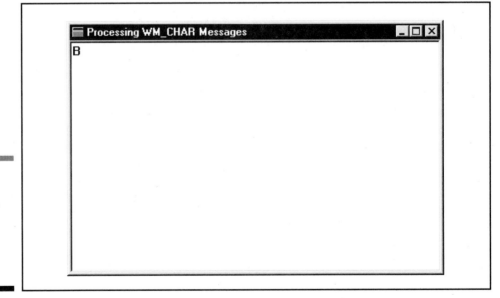

Sample
window
produced by
the
WM_CHAR
program
Figure 3-1.

Device Contexts

The program in the previous section had to obtain a device context prior to outputting to the window. It is now time to understand what a device context is. A device context is a structure that describes the display environment of a window, including its device driver and various display parameters, such as the current type font. Before your application can output information to the client area of the window, a device context must be obtained. Until this is done, there is no linkage between your program and the window relative to output. Since **TextOut( )** and other output functions require a device context for their operation, this is a self-enforcing rule.

3

If you have written traditional-style Windows programs, then you know that a device context is obtained using a call to **GetDC( )**, and must be released using a call to **ReleaseDC( )**. Because Windows provides a finite number of device contexts, it is important that your program release a device context when it is done with it. Fortunately, the MFC device context classes encapsulate this process. Specifically, when you instantiate an object of type **CClientDC**, a device context is obtained. When that object goes out of scope, **ReleaseDC( )** is called. Thus, in an MFC program, the device context is automatically released when the **CClientDC** object is destroyed. This is another advantage of using the Microsoft Foundation Classes.

The device context obtained by creating an object of type **CClientDC** is the device context of the client area of the window. The constructor function for **CClientDC** is shown here:

```
CClientDC(CWnd *Window);
```

Here, *Window* is a pointer to the window for which the device context is being obtained. To obtain a DC for the invoking window, specify **this**. If the device context cannot be granted, **CClientDC( )** throws a **CResourceException**.

In general, you will use **CClientDC** to obtain a device context of the client area of a window whenever your program needs to perform output. However, there is one special case in which you will obtain a device context in a different way. This is when a **WM_PAINT** message is being processed, which is the subject of the next section.

Processing the WM_PAINT Message

Before continuing, run the program from the previous section and enter a
few characters. Next, minimize and then restore the window. As you will see,
the last character typed is not displayed after the window is restored. Also, if
the window is overwritten by another window and then redisplayed, the
character is not redisplayed. The reason for this is simple: in general,
Windows does not keep a record of what a window contains. Instead, it is
your program's job to maintain the contents of a window. To help your
program accomplish this, each time the contents of a window must be
redisplayed, your program will be sent a **WM_PAINT** message. (This message
will also be sent when your window is first displayed.) Each time your
program receives this message, it must redisplay the contents of the window.
In this section, you will add a message handler that processes the
WM_PAINT message.

NOTE: When the window is moved or resized, its contents are
redisplayed. However, this will not occur when the window is minimized or
overwritten and then redisplayed.

Before explaining how to respond to a **WM_PAINT** message, it might be
useful to explain why Windows does not automatically rewrite your window.
The answer is short and to the point: in many situations, it is easier for your
program, which has intimate knowledge of the contents of the window, to
rewrite it than it would be for Windows to do so. While the merits of this
approach have been much debated by programmers, you should simply
accept it, because it is unlikely to change.

The message handler associated with **WM_PAINT** is called **OnPaint( )**. Its
prototype is shown here:

    afx_msg void OnPaint( );

The message macro associated with **WM_PAINT** is **ON_WM_PAINT**.

To process a **WM_PAINT** message, you must add the prototype for its
message handler to **CMainWin**, add its macro to your message map, and
then define its handler. For example, the handler shown here will output
the current contents of **str**, which will be the last character typed.

```
// Process a WM_PAINT message.
afx_msg void CMainWin::OnPaint()
{
  CPaintDC dc(this);

  // this line redisplays the last character
  dc.TextOut(1, 1, str, strlen(str));
}
```

3

Let's look at this closely. First, notice that a device context is obtained by creating an object of type **CPaintDC** instead of **CClientDC**. For various reasons, when you process a **WM_PAINT** message, you must obtain a device context using **CPaintDC**. Its constructor has this prototype:

CPaintDC(CWnd *Window);

Here, *Window* is a pointer to the window for which the device context is being obtained. To obtain a DC for the invoking window, specify **this**. If the device context cannot be granted, **CPaintDC( )** throws a **CResource-Exception**. Remember, this DC must only be used in reponse to a **WM_PAINT** message.

CPaintDC includes an important member, called **m_ps**, which contains a structure of type **PAINTSTRUCT**. When a **CPaintDC** object is created, this structure contains information relating to the current state of the device context. **PAINTSTRUCT** is defined as follows:

```
typedef struct tagPAINTSTRUCT {
  HDC hdc; // handle to device context
  BOOL fErase; // true if background must be erased
  RECT rcPaint; // coordinates of region to redraw
  BOOL fRestore; // reserved
  BOOL fIncUpdate; // reserved
  BYTE rgbReserved[32]; // reserved
} PAINTSTRUCT;
```

Here, **hdc** is a *handle* to the device context. In a traditional-style Windows program, device contexts are operated upon through handles. However, when using MFC, you operate on a device context through an object, so the handle is seldom needed. If the background needs to be erased, then **fErase** will be nonzero. (For now, you don't need to worry about this.) The **rcPaint** member contains the coordinates of the region of the window that needs to be repainted. The type **RECT** is a structure that specifies the upper-left and lower-right coordinates of a rectangular region. This structure is shown here:

```
typedef tagRECT {
  LONG left, top; /* upper left */
  LONG right, bottom; /* lower right */
} RECT;
```

For now, you will not need to use the contents of **rcPaint** because you can assume that the entire window must be redisplayed.

Here is a program that processes **WM_PAINT** messages, with the class derivation header file, MESSAGE2.H, shown first:

```
// MESSAGE2.H

// This is the main window class.
class CMainWin : public CFrameWnd
{
public:
  CMainWin();
  afx_msg void OnChar(UINT ch, UINT count, UINT flags);
  afx_msg void OnPaint();
  DECLARE_MESSAGE_MAP()
};

// This is the application class.
class CApp : public CWinApp
{
public:
  BOOL InitInstance();
};
```

The program file is shown here:

```
/*
   An MFC program that processes WM_CHAR and
   WM_PAINT messages.
*/
#include <afxwin.h>
#include <string.h>
#include "message2.h"
```

```
char str[80] = "Sample Output"; // holds output string

CMainWin::CMainWin()
{
  Create(NULL, "Processing WM_PAINT Messages");
}

// Initialize the application.
BOOL CApp::InitInstance()
{
  m_pMainWnd = new CMainWin;
  m_pMainWnd->ShowWindow(m_nCmdShow);
  m_pMainWnd->UpdateWindow();

  return TRUE;
}

// This is the application's message map.
BEGIN_MESSAGE_MAP(CMainWin, CFrameWnd)
  ON_WM_CHAR()
  ON_WM_PAINT()
END_MESSAGE_MAP()

// Process a WM_CHAR message.
afx_msg void CMainWin::OnChar(UINT ch,
                                UINT count, UINT flags)
{
  CClientDC dc(this);

  dc.TextOut(1, 1, "    ", 3); // erase previous char

  wsprintf(str, "%c", ch);
  dc.TextOut(1, 1, str, strlen(str));
}

// Process a WM_PAINT message.
afx_msg void CMainWin::OnPaint()
{
  CPaintDC dc(this);

  // this line redisplays the last character
  dc.TextOut(1, 1, str, strlen(str));
}

CApp App; // instantiate the application
```

Before continuing, enter, compile, and run this program. Try typing a few characters and then minimizing and restoring the window. As you will see, each time the window is redisplayed, the last character you typed is automatically redrawn. Notice that the global array **str** is initialized to **Sample Output** and that this is displayed when the program begins execution. The reason for this is that when a window is created, a **WM_PAINT** message is automatically generated.

While the handling of the **WM_PAINT** message in this example is quite simple, it must be emphasized that most real-world versions of this will be more complex because most windows contain considerably more output.

Since it is your program's responsibility to restore the window if it is overwritten, you must always provide some mechanism to accomplish this. This is usually handled in one of three ways. First, your program can simply regenerate the output by computational means. This is most feasible when no user input is used. Second, in some instances, you can keep a record of display events and replay the events when the window needs to be redrawn. Finally, your program can maintain a virtual window that you simply copy to the physical window each time it must be redrawn. This is the most general method. (The implementation of this approach is described later in this book.) Which approach is best depends completely upon the application. Most of the examples in this book won't bother to redraw the window because doing so typically involves substantial additional code, which often just muddies the point of an example. However, your programs will need to restore their windows in order to be conforming Windows applications.

Responding to Mouse Messages

Since Windows is, to a great extent, a mouse-based operating system, all Windows programs should respond to mouse input. Because the mouse is so important, there are several different types of mouse messages. This section examines the two most common: **WM_LBUTTONDOWN** and **WM_RBUTTONDOWN**, which are generated when the left button and right buttons are pressed, respectively. The message handlers for these two messages are **OnLButtonDown( )** and **OnRButtonDown( )**. Their prototypes are shown here:

afx_msg void OnLButtonDown(UINT *Flags*, CPoint *Loc*);

afx_msg void OnRButtonDown(UINT *Flags*, CPoint *Loc*);

The value contained in the *Flags* parameter tells you if the control key, SHIFT key, or any other mouse button was pressed when the message was generated. It may contain any combination of the following values:

    MK_CONTROL
    MK_SHIFT
    MK_MBUTTON
    MK_RBUTTON
    MK_LBUTTON

3

If the control key is pressed when a mouse button is pressed, then *Flags* will contain **MK_CONTROL**. If the SHIFT key is pressed when a mouse button is pressed, then *Flags* will contain **MK_SHIFT**. If the right button is down when the left button is pressed, then *Flags* will contain **MK_RBUTTON**. If the left button is down when the right button is pressed, then *Flags* will contain **MK_LBUTTON**. If the middle button (if it exists) is down when one of the other buttons is pressed, then *Flags* will contain **MK_MBUTTON**. More than one of these values may be present. Although we won't make use of the *Flags* parameter at this time, you might want to try experimenting with it on your own.

The **CPoint** object pointed to by *Loc* specifies the location of the mouse when the button was pressed. The **CPoint** class is derived from and encapsulates the **POINT** structure, which is defined as follows:

```
typedef struct tagPOINT {
  LONG x;
  LONG y;
} POINT;
```

The **POINT** structure contains the X,Y coordinates of the location of the mouse when its button was pressed. Thus, its X location is found at *Loc.x* and its Y location is found at *Loc.y*.

The following example adds the necessary elements to the preceding program so that it can respond to the mouse messages. Each time a left or right mouse button is pressed, it displays a message at the current location of the mouse pointer. Here is the class derivation header file:

```
// MESSAGE3.H

// This is the main window class.
class CMainWin : public CFrameWnd
```

```
{
public:
  CMainWin();
  afx_msg void OnChar(UINT ch, UINT count, UINT flags);
  afx_msg void OnPaint();
  afx_msg void OnLButtonDown(UINT flags, CPoint loc);
  afx_msg void OnRButtonDown(UINT flags, CPoint loc);
  DECLARE_MESSAGE_MAP()
};

// This is the application class.
class CApp : public CWinApp
{
public:
  BOOL InitInstance();
};
```

The program code is shown here:

```
// An MFC program that processes mouse messages.

#include <afxwin.h>
#include <string.h>
#include "message3.h"

char str[80] = "Sample Output"; // holds output string

CMainWin::CMainWin()
{
  Create(NULL, "Processing Mouse Messages");
}

// Initialize the application.
BOOL CApp::InitInstance()
{
  m_pMainWnd = new CMainWin;
  m_pMainWnd->ShowWindow(m_nCmdShow);
  m_pMainWnd->UpdateWindow();

  return TRUE;
}

// This is the application's message map.
BEGIN_MESSAGE_MAP(CMainWin, CFrameWnd)
  ON_WM_CHAR()
  ON_WM_PAINT()
```

```
      ON_WM_LBUTTONDOWN()
      ON_WM_RBUTTONDOWN()
END_MESSAGE_MAP()

// Process a WM_CHAR message.
afx_msg void CMainWin::OnChar(UINT ch,
                              UINT count, UINT flags)
{
  CClientDC dc(this);

  dc.TextOut(1, 1, "    ", 3); // erase previous char

  wsprintf(str, "%c", ch);
  dc.TextOut(1, 1, str, strlen(str));
}

// Process a WM_PAINT message.
afx_msg void CMainWin::OnPaint()
{
  CPaintDC dc(this);

  // this line redisplays the last character
  dc.TextOut(1, 1, str, strlen(str));
}

// Process left mouse button.
afx_msg void CMainWin::OnLButtonDown(UINT flags, CPoint loc)
{
  CClientDC dc(this);

  wsprintf(str, "Left button is down.");
  dc.TextOut(loc.x, loc.y, str, strlen(str));
}

// Process right mouse button.
afx_msg void CMainWin::OnRButtonDown(UINT flags, CPoint loc)
{
  CClientDC dc(this);

  wsprintf(str, "Right button is down.");
  dc.TextOut(loc.x, loc.y, str, strlen(str));
}

CApp App; // instantiate the application
```

Figure 3-2 shows sample output from this program.

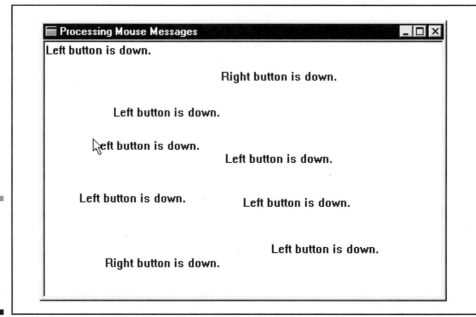

Sample output
from the
mouse
messages
program
Figure 3-2.

Generating a WM_PAINT Message

It is possible for your program to cause a **WM_PAINT** message to be
generated. At first, you might wonder why your program would need to
generate a **WM_PAINT** message since it seems that it can repaint its window
whenever it wants. However, this is a false assumption. Remember, updating
a window is a costly process in terms of time. Because Windows is a
multitasking system that might be running other programs that are also
demanding CPU time, your program should simply tell Windows that it
wants to output information, but let Windows decide when it is best to
actually perform that output. This allows Windows to better manage the
system and efficiently allocate CPU time to all the tasks in the system. Using
this approach, your program simply holds all output until a **WM_PAINT**
message is received.

In the previous examples, the **WM_PAINT** message was received only
when the window was uncovered. However, if all output is held until a
WM_PAINT message is received, then to achieve interactive I/O, there must
be some way to tell Windows that it needs to send a **WM_PAINT** message to
your window whenever output is pending. As expected, Windows includes

such a feature. Thus, when your program has information to output, it simply requests that a **WM_PAINT** message be sent when Windows is ready to do so.

To cause Windows to send a **WM_PAINT** message, your program will call the **InvalidateRect( )** function, which is a member of **CWnd**. Its prototype is shown here:

```
void CWnd::InvalidateRect(LPCRECT lpRegion, BOOL Erase = TRUE);
```

3

Here, *lpRegion* points to an object of type **CRect**, which specifies the region within the window that must be redrawn. The **CRect** class is derived from and encapsulates the **RECT** structure described earlier. The region to be repainted is specified in the members of the **RECT** structure. However, if this value is **NULL**, then the entire window will be specified. If *Erase* is nonzero, then the background will be erased. (This is its default value.) If it is zero, then the background is left unchanged.

When **InvalidateRect( )** is called, it tells Windows that the window is invalid and must be redrawn. This, in turn, causes Windows to send a **WM_PAINT** message to your program.

Here is a reworked version of the previous program that routes all output through the **WM_PAINT** handler. It does this by generating a **WM_PAINT** message whenever output needs to be performed. The other message handlers simply prepare the information to be displayed and then call **InvalidateRect( )**. Here is the class derivation header file:

```
// MESSAGE4.H

// This is the main window class.
class CMainWin : public CFrameWnd
{
public:
  CMainWin();
  afx_msg void OnChar(UINT ch, UINT count, UINT flags);
  afx_msg void OnPaint();
  afx_msg void OnLButtonDown(UINT flags, CPoint loc);
  afx_msg void OnRButtonDown(UINT flags, CPoint loc);
  DECLARE_MESSAGE_MAP()
};

// This is the application class.
class CApp : public CWinApp
```

```
{
public:
  BOOL InitInstance();
};
```

Here is the program file:

```
/*
   An MFC program that routes all output
   through the WM_PAINT message.
*/
#include <afxwin.h>
#include <string.h>
#include "message4.h"

char str[80] = "Sample Output"; // holds output string
int X = 1, Y = 1; // current window location

CMainWin::CMainWin()
{
  Create(NULL, "Routing Output Through WM_PAINT");
}

// Initialize the application.
BOOL CApp::InitInstance()
{
  m_pMainWnd = new CMainWin;
  m_pMainWnd->ShowWindow(m_nCmdShow);
  m_pMainWnd->UpdateWindow();

  return TRUE;
}

// This is the application's message map.
BEGIN_MESSAGE_MAP(CMainWin, CFrameWnd)
  ON_WM_CHAR()
  ON_WM_PAINT()
  ON_WM_LBUTTONDOWN()
  ON_WM_RBUTTONDOWN()
END_MESSAGE_MAP()

// Process a WM_CHAR message.
afx_msg void CMainWin::OnChar(UINT ch,
```

```
                                      UINT count, UINT flags)
{
  X = Y = 1;
  wsprintf(str, "%c", ch);
  InvalidateRect(NULL);
}

// Process a WM_PAINT message.
afx_msg void CMainWin::OnPaint()
{
  CPaintDC dc(this);

  // this line redisplays the last character
  dc.TextOut(X, Y, str, strlen(str));
}

// Process left mouse button.
afx_msg void CMainWin::OnLButtonDown(UINT flags, CPoint loc)
{
  wsprintf(str, "Left button is down.");
  X = loc.x;
  Y = loc.y;
  InvalidateRect(NULL);
}

// Process right mouse button.
afx_msg void CMainWin::OnRButtonDown(UINT flags, CPoint loc)
{
  wsprintf(str, "Right button is down.");
  X = loc.x;
  Y = loc.y;
  InvalidateRect(NULL);
}

CApp App; // instantiate the application
```

3

Notice that the program adds two new global variables called **X** and **Y** that hold the location at which the text will be displayed when a **WM_PAINT** message is received.

As you can see, by channeling all output through **WM_PAINT**, the program has actually become smaller and, in some ways, easier to understand. Also, as stated at the beginning of this section, the program allows Windows to decide when it is most appropriate to update the window.

NOTE: Many Windows applications route all (or most) output through **WM_PAINT**, for the reasons already stated. However, the previous programs are not technically wrong in outputting text when they respond to a message. It is just that this approach may not be best for all purposes.

Responding to WM_DESTROY Messages

There is one special message to which your program may need to respond: **WM_DESTROY**. This message is sent to a window when it is being destroyed. When the main window of your application receives this message, it means that the entire application is being terminated. When it is received, your application can perform any shutdown operations that it may require. The message handler for **WM_DESTROY** is called **OnDestroy( )** and its prototype is shown here:

    afx_msg void OnDestroy( );

Up to this point, there has been no need to explicitly handle **WM_DESTROY** messages because none of the programs have required that any special actions be taken when they are terminated. However, often the opposite will be the case. In situations in which your program has to perform actions when it is being destroyed, you may perform those actions inside **OnDestroy( )**. The example program in the next section makes use of this fact.

IN DEPTH

Exploring Windows Messages

This chapter describes a few of the most commonly used Windows messages. In later chapters of the book, more will be introduced. However, Windows defines hundreds of other messages—many more than can be described in this book. Part of being an accomplished Windows programmer is a thorough understanding of these messages. The best way to gain this knowledge is to explore the various Windows messages on your own. (Most compilers supply an online reference to the Windows messages.) To help you get started, here is a sampling of some of the more common messages that are not discussed elsewhere in this book.

Message	Description
WM_ACTIVATE	Sent when a window is being activated or deactivated.
WM_CREATE	Sent when a window is first created.
WM_ERASEBKGND	Sent when the background of a window needs erasing.
WM_INITMENU	Sent when a menu is activated.
WM_LBUTTONUP	Sent when the left mouse button is released.
WM_MDIACTIVATE	Sent when one child window is deactivated and another is activated. Both windows receive this message. This message applies to MDI (multiple document interface) applications.
WM_MOUSEWHEEL	Sent when the user rotates the mouse wheel and encounters the wheel's next notch.
WM_MOVE	Sent after a window has been moved.
WM_PALETTECHANGED	Sent when there is a change in the system color palette.
WM_POWERBROADCAST	Notifies your program about a power-related event. For example, this message is sent just before the computer enters power-down mode.
WM_RBUTTONUP	Sent when the right mouse button is released.
WM_SETFOCUS	Sent when a window gains the input focus.
WM_SYSCHAR	Sent when the user presses a system key (such as, ALT-X or F10).
WM_SYSCOLORCHANGE	Sent when the system color settings change.

3

One last point: Remember that the names of the MFC message handlers are created by adding **On** to the name of the message and using mixed case. Thus, the handler for **WM_SYSCHAR** is **OnSysChar( )**.

Generating Timer Messages

The last message that will be discussed here is **WM_TIMER**. Using Windows, it is possible to establish a timer that will interrupt your program at periodic intervals. Each time the timer goes off, it sends a **WM_TIMER** message to your program. Using a timer is a good way to "wake up your program" every so often. This is particularly useful when your program is running as a background task.

To start a timer, use the **SetTimer( )** function, which is a member of **CWnd**. Its prototype is shown here:

UINT CWnd::SetTimer(UINT *ID*, UINT *Length*,
        void (CALLBACK EXPORT **TFunc*)(HWND, UINT, UINT,
            DWORD));

Here, *ID* specifies a value that will be associated with this timer. (More than one timer can be active.) The value of *Length* specifies the length of the period, in milliseconds. That is, *Length* specifies how much time there is between interrupts. The function pointed to by *TFunc* is the timer function that will be called when the timer goes off. This must be a callback function that returns **VOID CALLBACK** and takes the same type of parameters as a traditional-style window procedure. However, if the value of *TFunc* is **NULL**, as it commonly is, then timer messages are sent to your program's main window. In this case, each time the timer goes off, a **WM_TIMER** message is put into the message queue for your program, and your program processes it like any other message. This is the approach used by the example that follows. The function returns *ID* if successful. If the timer cannot be allocated, zero is returned.

Once a timer has been started, it continues to interrupt your program until your program executes a call to the **CWnd::KillTimer( )** function, whose prototype is shown here:

BOOL CWnd::KillTimer(int *ID*);

Here, *ID* is the value that identifies that particular timer. **KillTimer( )** returns nonzero if successful and zero otherwise.

Timer messages are handled by **OnTimer( )**, which has the following prototype:

afx_msg void OnTimer(UINT *ID*);

Each time **OnTimer( )** is called, the value of *ID* contains the ID of the timer that went off. If your program uses more than one timer, then you must check the value of *ID* to determine which timer sent the message.

To demonstrate the use of a timer, the following program uses one to create a clock. It uses the MFC class **CTime** to obtain and display the current system time and date. (**CTime** encapsulates the standard C/C++ time and date library functions.) Each time the timer goes off, which is approximately once each second, the time is updated. Thus, the time displayed is accurate to within one second. Since timers should be canceled when they are no longer in use, the timer is killed when the program receives a **WM_DESTROY** message. The program's class derivation header file is shown here:

3

```
// MESSAGE5.H

// This is the main window class.
class CMainWin : public CFrameWnd
{
public:
  CMainWin();
  afx_msg void OnPaint();
  afx_msg void OnTimer(UINT ID);
  afx_msg void OnDestroy();
  DECLARE_MESSAGE_MAP()
};

// This is the application class.
class CApp : public CWinApp
{
public:
  BOOL InitInstance();
};
```

The program file is shown here:

```
// A clock program

#include <afxwin.h>
#include <string.h>
#include <time.h>
#include "message5.h"
```

```
char str[80] = ""; // holds output string

CMainWin::CMainWin()
{
  RECT r;

  r.left = r.top = 10;
  r.right = 200;
  r.bottom = 60;

  Create(NULL, "A Clock Program", WS_OVERLAPPEDWINDOW, r);
}

// Initialize the application.
BOOL CApp::InitInstance()
{
  m_pMainWnd = new CMainWin;

  // start the timer
  if(m_pMainWnd->SetTimer(1, 1000, NULL) != 1) return FALSE;

  m_pMainWnd->ShowWindow(m_nCmdShow);
  m_pMainWnd->UpdateWindow();

  return TRUE;
}

// This is the application's message map.
BEGIN_MESSAGE_MAP(CMainWin, CFrameWnd)
  ON_WM_PAINT()
  ON_WM_TIMER()
  ON_WM_DESTROY()
END_MESSAGE_MAP()

// Process a WM_PAINT message.
afx_msg void CMainWin::OnPaint()
{
  CPaintDC dc(this);

  // this line redisplays the last character
  dc.TextOut(1, 1, str, strlen(str));
}

// Process WM_TIMER messages
```

```
afx_msg void CMainWin::OnTimer(UINT ID)
{
  CTime curtime = CTime::GetCurrentTime();
  struct tm *newtime;

  newtime = curtime.GetLocalTm();
  wsprintf(str, asctime(newtime));
  str[strlen(str)-1] = '\0'; // remove /r/n
  InvalidateRect(NULL, 0);
}

// Exit the application
afx_msg void CMainWin::OnDestroy()
{
  KillTimer(1);
}

CApp App; // instantiate the application
```

Sample output from this program is shown here in the Clock window:

As mentioned, this program uses the **CTime** class to obtain the current time. The static function **GetCurrentTime( )** obtains the current system time. The **GetLocalTm( )** function returns a pointer to the standard **TM** structure defined by the C/C++ library. This pointer is then used by the standard library function **asctime( )** to return a pointer to a string that contains the current time. If you will be working with times and dates, you might want to examine the **CTime** class on your own.

Now that you have learned how a Windows program processes messages, you can move on to creating message boxes and menus, which is the subject of the next chapter.

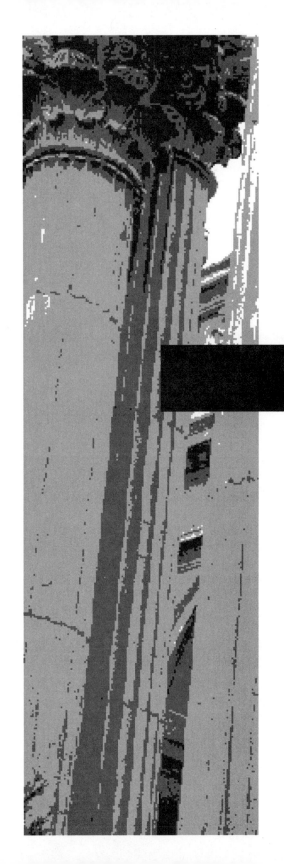

CHAPTER 4

Message Boxes
and Menus

Now that you know how to construct a basic MFC application and receive and process messages, it is time to begin exploring Windows' user interface components. If you are learning to program Windows for the first time, it is important to understand that your application will most often communicate with the user through one or more predefined interface components. There are several different types of interface elements supported by Windows. This chapter discusses two: message boxes and menus. These are the most fundamental. Virtually any program you write will use both of them. As you will see, the basic style of the message box and the menu is predefined. You need only supply the specific information that relates to your application.

This chapter also introduces the *resource*. A resource is, essentially, an object defined outside your program but used by your program. Icons, cursors, menus, and bitmaps are common resources. Resources are a crucial part of nearly all Windows applications.

Message Boxes

By far, the simplest interface window is the message box. A message box displays a message to the user and waits for an acknowledgment. It is possible to construct message boxes that allow the user to select between a few basic alternatives, but in general, the purpose of a message box is to inform the user that some event has taken place.

To create a message box, use the **MessageBox( )** function, which is a member of **CWnd**. Its prototype is shown here:

    int CWnd::MessageBox(LPCSTR *lpszText*,
                         LPCSTR *lpszTitle* = NULL,
                         UINT *MBType* = MB_OK);

Here, the *lpszText* parameter is a pointer to a string that will appear inside the message box. The string pointed to by *lpszTitle* is used as the caption for the box. The value of *MBType* determines the exact nature of the message box, including what type of buttons and icons will be present. Some of its most common values are shown in Table 4-1. These macros are defined by including AFXWIN.H, and you can OR together two or more as long as they are not mutually exclusive. **MessageBox( )** returns the user's response to the

box or zero if the box could not be created. The possible return values are
shown here:

Button Pressed	Return Value
Abort	IDABORT
Retry	IDRETRY
Ignore	IDIGNORE
Cancel	IDCANCEL
No	IDNO
Yes	IDYES
OK	IDOK

Remember, depending upon the value of *MBType*, only certain buttons will
be present. Thus, only certain return values will be possible for any given
message box.

Value	Effect
MB_ABORTRETRYIGNORE	Displays Abort, Retry, and Ignore push buttons.
MB_ICONEXCLAMATION	Displays exclamation-point icon.
MB_ICONINFORMATION	Displays an information icon.
MB_ICONQUESTION	Displays a question mark icon.
MB_ICONSTOP	Displays a stop sign icon.
MB_OK	Displays OK push button.
MB_OKCANCEL	Displays OK and Cancel push buttons.
MB_RETRYCANCEL	Displays Retry and Cancel push buttons.
MB_YESNO	Displays Yes and No push buttons.
MB_YESNOCANCEL	Displays Yes, No, and Cancel push buttons.

Some
Common
Values for
MBType
Table 4-1.

To display a message box, just call the **MessageBox( )** function. Windows will display it at its first opportunity. You do not need to obtain a device context or generate a **WM_PAINT** message. **MessageBox( )** handles all of these details for you. Because message boxes are so easy to use, they make excellent debugging tools when you need a simple way to output something to the screen.

The following short example displays a message box when you press a mouse button. Here is the class derivation file:

```
// MESSBOX.H

// This is the main window class.
class CMainWin : public CFrameWnd
{
public:
  CMainWin();
  afx_msg void OnLButtonDown(UINT flags, CPoint loc);
  afx_msg void OnRButtonDown(UINT flags, CPoint loc);
  DECLARE_MESSAGE_MAP()
};

// This is the application class.
class CApp : public CWinApp
{
public:
  BOOL InitInstance();
};
```

Here is the message box program file:

```
// Demonstrate a Message Box

#include <afxwin.h>
#include "messbox.h"

CMainWin::CMainWin()
{
  Create(NULL, "Using Message Boxes");
}

// Initialize the application.
BOOL CApp::InitInstance()
{
```

```
    m_pMainWnd = new CMainWin;
    m_pMainWnd->ShowWindow(m_nCmdShow);
    m_pMainWnd->UpdateWindow();

    return TRUE;
}

// This is the application's message map.
BEGIN_MESSAGE_MAP(CMainWin, CFrameWnd)
  ON_WM_LBUTTONDOWN()
  ON_WM_RBUTTONDOWN()
END_MESSAGE_MAP()

// Process left mouse button.
afx_msg void CMainWin::OnLButtonDown(UINT flags, CPoint loc)
{
  int i;

  i = MessageBox("Press One", "Left Button",
                 MB_ABORTRETRYIGNORE);

  switch(i) {
    case IDABORT:
      MessageBox("", "Abort");
      break;
    case IDRETRY:
      MessageBox("", "Retry");
      break;
    case IDIGNORE:
      MessageBox("", "Ignore");
      break;
  }
}

// Process right mouse button.
afx_msg void CMainWin::OnRButtonDown(UINT flags, CPoint loc)
{
  int i;

  i = MessageBox("Press One", "Right Button",
                 MB_ICONSTOP | MB_YESNO);

  switch(i) {
    case IDYES:
      MessageBox("", "Yes");
```

4

```
      break;
    case IDNO:
      MessageBox("", "No");
      break;
  }
}

CApp App; // instantiate the application
```

Each time a button is pressed, a message box is displayed. For example, pressing the left button displays the message box shown in the following illustration.

As you can see, when you press the left button a message box displays the buttons Abort, Retry, and Ignore. Depending upon your response, a second message box will be displayed that indicates which button you pressed. Pressing the right mouse button causes a message box displaying a stop sign to be displayed. This box allows a Yes or a No response.

Using AfxMessageBox( )

Occasionally you will want to display a message box before the main window of your application has been created. For example, an error may occur prior to the creation of your program's main window. In this case, you will still want to inform the user that a problem occurred. In order to display a message box prior to (or independently of) your program's main window, you can use the MFC global function **AfxMessageBox( )**. It has the following prototype:

int AfxMessageBox(LPCSTR *lpszText*, UINT *MBType* = MB_OK,
                  UINT *HelpID* = 0);

Here, *lpszText* is the message displayed within the message box. The title of the message box is automatically the name of your application and cannot be specified otherwise. *MBType* is the same as for the standard **MessageBox( )** function. *HelpID* specifies the help context identifier related to the message box. If there is no context-sensitive help, let this parameter default to zero.

(The Windows help system is examined later in the book.) **AfxMessageBox( )** returns zero if the box cannot be displayed. Otherwise, it returns the value selected by the user.

Here is a modified version of **InitInstance( )** that displays a message box prior to the creation of the main window. Substitute this function into the preceding program and observe the results. As you will see, the message box is displayed before the main window is shown.

```
// Initialize the application.
BOOL CApp::InitInstance()
{
  // display a message box before creating main window
  AfxMessageBox("This is displayed first.");

  m_pMainWnd = new CMainWin;
  m_pMainWnd->ShowWindow(m_nCmdShow);
  m_pMainWnd->UpdateWindow();

  return TRUE;
}
```

Before continuing, experiment with message boxes by trying different types.

Introducing Menus

In Windows, the most common element of control is the menu. Virtually all main windows have some type of menu associated with them. Because menus are so common and important in Windows applications, Windows provides substantial built-in support for them. As you will see, adding a menu to a window involves these relatively few steps:

1. Define the form of the menu in a resource file.
2. Load the menu when your program creates its main window.
3. Process menu selections.

In Windows, the top level of a menu is displayed across the top of the window as a menu bar. Submenus are displayed as pop-up menus. (You should be accustomed to this approach because it is used by virtually all Windows programs.)

Before beginning an in-depth discussion of menus, it is necessary to explain resources and resource files.

4

Using Resources

Windows defines several common types of objects as *resources*. As mentioned at the beginning of this chapter, resources are essentially objects that are used by your program, but are defined outside of your program. They include items such as menus, icons, dialog boxes, and bitmapped graphics. Since a menu is a resource, you need to understand resources before you can add a menu to your program.

A resource is created separately from your program, but is added to the .EXE file when your program is linked. Resources are contained in *resource files*, which have the extension .RC. In general, the resource filename should be related to the name of your program's .EXE file. For example, if your program is called PROG.EXE, then its resource file should be called PROG.RC. Of course, you are free to use any name you like. You may also have more than one resource file associated with your program.

Depending upon the resource, some may be described using text descriptions. For example, a standard menu is a text-based resource. Text-based resources are typically defined within the resource file itself. Others, such as icons, are graphics-based and are most easily generated using an image editor. However, they still must be referred to in the .RC file that is associated with your application. Also, it is possible to automate the construction of your resource file using a resource editor, which is supplied by most integrated development environments. This will be helpful for real-world applications in which the number of resources is quite large.

Sometimes you will need access to the various macros defined by Windows. To gain this access, your resource files should include AFXRES.H.

Compiling .RC Files

Resource files are not C or C++ files. Instead, they contain a special resource language, or *script*, that must be compiled using a *resource compiler*. Often, the resource compiler is called RC.EXE, but this varies. Exactly how you compile a resource file will depend upon what compiler you are using. Also, most integrated development environments automatically handle this phase for you. For example, both Microsoft's Visual C++ and Borland's C++ automatically compile resource files as long as they are part of your project. In any event, the output of the resource compiler will be a .RES file and it is this file that you will link with your program to build the final Windows application.

NOTE: Remember that you must consult your compiler's user manual for instructions on including resource files with your programs.

Creating a Simple Menu

Before a menu can be included in your program, you must define its content in a resource file. All menu definitions have this general form:

MenuName MENU [*options*]
{
  menu items
}

4

Here, *MenuName* is the name of the menu. (It may also be an integer value identifying the menu, but all examples in this book will use the name when referring to the menu.) The keyword **MENU** tells the resource compiler that a menu is being created. Several options can be specified when creating the menu. The most common are shown in Table 4-2. The examples in this book simply use the default settings and specify no options.

Option	Meaning
DISCARDABLE	Menu may be removed from memory when no longer needed.
CHARACTERISTICS *info*	Application-specific information, which is specified as a LONG value in *info*.
FIXED	Menu is fixed in memory. Ignored for 32-bit applications.
LANGUAGE *lang, sub-lang*	The language used by the resource is specified by *lang* and *sub-lang*. This is used by internationalized menus.
LOADONCALL	Menu is loaded when used. Ignored for 32-bit applications.

The **MENU** Options
Table 4-2.

The **MENU**
Options
(*continued*)
Table 4-2.

Option	Meaning
MOVEABLE	Menu may be moved in memory. Ignored for 32-bit applications.
PRELOAD	Menu is loaded when your program begins execution. Ignored for 32-bit applications.
VERSION *ver*	Application-defined version number is specified in *ver*.

Two types of items can be used to define the menu: **MENUITEM**s and **POPUP**s. A **MENUITEM** specifies a final selection. A **POPUP** specifies a pop-up submenu, which may, in itself, contain other **MENUITEM**s or **POPUP**s. The general forms of these two statements are shown here:

MENUITEM "*ItemName*", *MenuID* [,*Options*]

POPUP "*PopupName*" [,*Options*]

Here, *ItemName* is the name of the menu selection, such as "Help" or "File." *MenuID* is a unique integer associated with a menu item that will be sent to your application when a selection is made. Typically, these values are defined as macros inside a header file that is included in both your application code and in the .RC resource file. *PopupName* is the name of the pop-up menu. For both cases, the values for *Options* are shown in Table 4-3.

The
MENUITEM
and **POPUP**
Options

Table 4-3.

Option	Meaning
CHECKED	A check mark is displayed next to the name. Not applicable to top-level menus.
GRAYED	The name is shown in gray and may not be selected.
HELP	May be associated with a help selection. This applies to MENUITEMs only.
INACTIVE	The option may not be selected.

Option	Meaning
MENUBARBREAK	For menu bar, causes the item to be put on a new line. For pop-up menus, causes the item to be put in a different column. In this case, the item is separated using a bar.
MENUBREAK	Same as MENUBARBREAK except that no separator bar is used.
SEPARATOR	Creates an empty menu item that acts as a separator. Applies to MENUITEMs only.

The **MENUITEM** and **POPUP** Options (*continued*)
Table 4-3.

Here is an example of a simple menu that you should enter at this time. Call the file MENU1.RC.

```
// MENU1.RC

// Sample menu resource file.
#include "ids.h"

MYMENU MENU
{
  POPUP "&One"
  {
    MENUITEM "&Alpha", IDM_ALPHA
    MENUITEM "&Beta", IDM_BETA
  }
  POPUP "&Two"
  {
    MENUITEM "&Gamma", IDM_GAMMA
    POPUP "&Delta"
    {
      MENUITEM "&Epsilon", IDM_EPSILON
      MENUITEM "&Zeta", IDM_ZETA
    }
    MENUITEM "&Eta", IDM_ETA
    MENUITEM "&Theta", IDM_THETA
  }
  MENUITEM "&Help", IDM_HELP
}
```

This menu, called **MYMENU**, contains three top-level, menu bar options: One, Two, and Help. The One and Two options contain pop-up submenus.

The Delta option activates a pop-up submenu of its own. Notice that options that activate submenus do not have menu ID values associated with them. Only actual menu items have ID numbers. In this menu, all menu ID values are specified as macros beginning with **IDM**. (These macros are defined in the header file IDS.H.) What names you give these values is arbitrary.

An **&** in an item's name causes the key that it precedes to become the shortcut key associated with that option. That is, once that menu is active, pressing that key causes that menu item to be selected. It doesn't have to be the first key in the name, but it should be unless a conflict with another name exists.

NOTE: As the resource file shows, you can embed remarks into a resource file using C- and C++-style comments.

The IDS.H header file, which is included in MENU1.RC, contains the macro definitions of the menu ID values. It is shown here. Enter it at this time.

```
// IDS.H

#define IDM_ALPHA    100
#define IDM_BETA     101
#define IDM_GAMMA    102
#define IDM_DELTA    103
#define IDM_EPSILON  104
#define IDM_ZETA     105
#define IDM_ETA      106
#define IDM_THETA    107
#define IDM_HELP     108
```

This file defines the menu ID values that will be returned when the various menu items are selected. This file will also be included in the program that uses the menu. Remember, the actual names and values you give the menu items are arbitrary. But each value must be unique. Also, the valid range for ID values is 0 through 65,565.

Including a Menu in Your Program

Once you have defined a menu, you include that menu in a program by specifying its name when you create the window. Specifically, you pass a pointer to its name in the last parameter of **Create( )**. For example, to load the menu **MYMENU**, you could use this call to **Create( )**:

```
Create(NULL, "Using Menus", WS_OVERLAPPEDWINDOW,
        rectDefault, NULL, "MYMENU");
```

After this statement executes, the menu named **MYMENU** will be displayed. However, simply including the menu does not enable your program to respond to it. That is, the menu will be displayed, but otherwise inactive. To enable your program to process menu selections, you must provide **WM_COMMAND** message handlers, as described in the next section.

4

Handling WM_COMMAND Messages

Each time the user makes a menu selection, your program is sent a **WM_COMMAND** command message. Associated with this message is the ID value of the item selected. Thus, when a **WM_COMMAND** message is received, it is the ID value linked with that message that determines which item has been chosen. As mentioned in the preceding chapter, **WM_COMMAND** messages are managed differently by MFC than are the other messages. This is because the specific meaning of each **WM_COMMAND** message depends upon the ID value. Therefore, it is the ID value that determines which handler must be called. In a traditional-style Windows program, ID values are usually decoded using a large **switch** statement, which is both awkward and error-prone. Fortunately, MFC provides a mechanism that automates this process. It does so by linking each ID value with its own handler inside the message map. After this is done, each time a **WM_COMMAND** message is received, the handler associated with the current ID value is executed.

To add **WM_COMMAND** messages to your message map, use the **ON_COMMAND** message macro, shown here:

ON_COMMAND(*ID*, *HandlerName*)

Here, *ID* is the ID value being handled and *HandlerName* is the name of the function that processes that ID.

Each **WM_COMMAND** handler must include the **afx_msg** type specifier and return **void**. Command handlers do not have parameters. The name of each command handler is up to you. However, most programmers use the **On** prefix and the same naming style as the built-in handlers.

Responding to Menu Selections

To allow your program to respond to a menu selection, follow these steps:

1. Add an **ON_COMMAND** message macro to your program's message map for each menu ID value.

2. Add the prototype for each command handler to your main window class.

3. Implement each command handler.

Remember that you must provide a handler for each item in the menu.

A Sample Menu Program

The following program demonstrates a menu by adding one to the previous program. For the sake of illustration, the response to each selection simply displays an acknowledgment of that selection on the screen. However, in real applications, the response to menu selections will generally be more complex.

The menu program uses the IDS.H and MENU1.RC files shown earlier. The class derivation file, MENU.H, is shown here:

```
// MENU.H

// This is the main window class.
class CMainWin : public CFrameWnd
{
public:
  CMainWin();
  afx_msg void OnLButtonDown(UINT flags, CPoint loc);
  afx_msg void OnRButtonDown(UINT flags, CPoint loc);

  // define menu handlers
  afx_msg void OnAlpha();
  afx_msg void OnBeta();
  afx_msg void OnGamma();
  afx_msg void OnEpsilon();
  afx_msg void OnZeta();
  afx_msg void OnEta();
  afx_msg void OnTheta();
  afx_msg void OnHelp();

  DECLARE_MESSAGE_MAP()
```

```
};

// This is the application class.
class CApp : public CWinApp
{
public:
  BOOL InitInstance();
};
```

The menu program file is shown here:

```
// Demonstrate a Menu

#include <afxwin.h>
#include "menu.h"
#include "ids.h"

CMainWin::CMainWin()
{
  Create(NULL, "Using Menus", WS_OVERLAPPEDWINDOW,
         rectDefault, NULL, "MYMENU");
}

// Initialize the application.
BOOL CApp::InitInstance()
{
  m_pMainWnd = new CMainWin;
  m_pMainWnd->ShowWindow(m_nCmdShow);
  m_pMainWnd->UpdateWindow();

  return TRUE;
}

// This is the application's message map.
BEGIN_MESSAGE_MAP(CMainWin, CFrameWnd)
  ON_WM_LBUTTONDOWN()
  ON_WM_RBUTTONDOWN()
  ON_COMMAND(IDM_ALPHA, OnAlpha)
  ON_COMMAND(IDM_BETA, OnBeta)
  ON_COMMAND(IDM_GAMMA, OnGamma)
  ON_COMMAND(IDM_EPSILON, OnEpsilon)
  ON_COMMAND(IDM_ZETA, OnZeta)
  ON_COMMAND(IDM_ETA, OnEta)
  ON_COMMAND(IDM_THETA, OnTheta)
  ON_COMMAND(IDM_HELP, OnHelp)
```

4

```
END_MESSAGE_MAP()

// Process left mouse button.
afx_msg void CMainWin::OnLButtonDown(UINT flags, CPoint loc)
{
  int i;

  i = MessageBox("Press One", "Left Button",
                 MB_ABORTRETRYIGNORE);

  switch(i) {
    case IDABORT:
      MessageBox("", "Abort");
      break;
    case IDRETRY:
      MessageBox("", "Retry");
      break;
    case IDIGNORE:
      MessageBox("", "Ignore");
      break;
  }
}

// Process right mouse button.
afx_msg void CMainWin::OnRButtonDown(UINT flags, CPoint loc)
{
  int i;

  i = MessageBox("Press One", "Right Button",
                 MB_ICONHAND | MB_YESNO);

  switch(i) {
    case IDYES:
      MessageBox("", "Yes");
      break;
    case IDNO:
      MessageBox("", "No");
      break;
  }
}

// Process IDM_ALPHA
afx_msg void CMainWin::OnAlpha()
{
   MessageBox("Alpha", "Alpha");
}
```

```
// Process IDM_BETA
afx_msg void CMainWin::OnBeta()
{
    MessageBox("Beta", "Beta");
}

// Process IDM_GAMMA
afx_msg void CMainWin::OnGamma()
{
    MessageBox("Gamma", "Gamma");
}

// Process IDM_EPSILON
afx_msg void CMainWin::OnEpsilon()
{
    MessageBox("Epsilon", "Epsilon");
}

// Process IDM_ZETA
afx_msg void CMainWin::OnZeta()
{
    MessageBox("Zeta", "Zeta");
}

// Process IDM_ETA
afx_msg void CMainWin::OnEta()
{
    MessageBox("Eta", "Eta");
}

// Process IDM_THETA
afx_msg void CMainWin::OnTheta()
{
    MessageBox("Theta", "Theta");
}

// Process IDM_HELP
afx_msg void CMainWin::OnHelp()
{
    MessageBox("Menu Demo", "Help");
}

CApp App; // instantiate the application
```

Sample output from the program is shown in Figure 4-1.

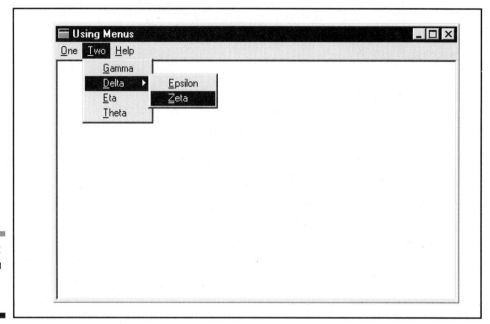

Sample output
from the menu
example

Figure 4-1.

Adding Menu Accelerator Keys

Another feature provided by Windows often used in conjunction with a menu is the *accelerator key*. Accelerator keys are special keystrokes you define that, when pressed, automatically select a menu option even though the menu in which that option resides is not displayed. Put differently, you can select an item directly by pressing an accelerator key, bypassing the menu entirely. *Accelerator key* is an accurate name because pressing one is generally a faster way to select a menu item than is first activating its menu and then selecting the item.

To define accelerator keys relative to a menu you must add an accelerator key table to your resource file. All accelerator table definitions have this general form:

```
TableName ACCELERATORS
{
  Key1, MenuID1 [,type] [option]
  Key2, MenuID2 [,type] [option]
  Key3, MenuID3 [,type] [option]
     .
     .
     .
}
```

Here, *TableName* is the name of the accelerator table. *Key* is the keystroke that selects the item, and *MenuID* is the ID value associated with the desired item. The *type* specifies whether the key is a standard key (the default) or a virtual key (discussed shortly). The options may be one of the following macros: **NOINVERT**, **ALT**, **SHIFT**, and **CONTROL**. **NOINVERT** prevents the selected menu item from being highlighted when its accelerator key is pressed. **ALT** specifies an ALT key. **SHIFT** specifies a SHIFT key. **CONTROL** specifies a control key.

The value of *Key* will be either a quoted character, an ASCII integer value corresponding to a key, or a virtual key code. If a quoted character is used, then it is assumed to be an ASCII character. If it is an integer value, then you must tell the resource compiler explicitly that this is an ASCII character by specifying *type* as **ASCII**. If it is a virtual key, then *type* must be **VIRTKEY**.

4

If the key is an uppercase quoted character, then its corresponding menu item will be selected if it is pressed while holding down SHIFT. If it is a lowercase character, then its menu item will be selected if the key is pressed by itself. If the key is specified as a lowercase character and **ALT** is specified as an option, then pressing ALT and the character will select the item. (If the key is uppercase and **ALT** is specified, then you must press SHIFT and ALT to select the item.) Finally, if you want the user to press CTRL and the character to select an item, precede the key with a ^.

A virtual key is a system-independent code for a variety of keys. Virtual keys include the function keys F1 through F12, the arrow keys, and various non-ASCII keys. They are defined by including AFXRES.H. All virtual key macros begin with **VK_**. The function keys are **VK_F1** through **VK_F12**, for example. To use a virtual key as an accelerator, simply specify its macro for the *Key* and specify **VIRTKEY** for its *type*. You may also specify **ALT**, **SHIFT**, or **CONTROL** to achieve the desired key combination. Here are some examples:

```
"A", IDM_x ; select by pressing Shift-A
"a", IDM_x ; select by pressing a
"^A", IDM_x ; select by pressing Ctrl-A
"a", IDM_x, ALT ; select by pressing Alt-a
VK_F2, IDM_x ; select by pressing F2
VK_F2, IDM_x, SHIFT ; select by pressing Shift-F2
```

The following menu resource file also contains accelerator key definitions for the menu specified in the previous section. Call this file MENU2.RC.

```
// MENU2.RC

// Sample menu resource file.
#include <afxres.h>
#include <ids.h>

MYMENU MENU
{
  POPUP "&One"
  {
    MENUITEM "&Alpha\tF2", IDM_ALPHA
    MENUITEM "&Beta\tF3", IDM_BETA
  }
  POPUP "&Two"
  {
    MENUITEM "&Gamma\tShift-G", IDM_GAMMA
    POPUP "&Delta"
    {
      MENUITEM "&Epsilon\tCntl-E", IDM_EPSILON
      MENUITEM "&Zeta\tCntl-Z", IDM_ZETA
    }
    MENUITEM "&Eta\tCntl-F4", IDM_ETA
    MENUITEM "&Theta\tF5", IDM_THETA
  }
  MENUITEM "&Help", IDM_HELP
}

// Define menu accelerators.
MYMENU ACCELERATORS
{
  VK_F2, IDM_ALPHA, VIRTKEY
  VK_F3, IDM_BETA, VIRTKEY
  "G", IDM_GAMMA
  "^E", IDM_EPSILON
  "^Z", IDM_ZETA
  VK_F4, IDM_ETA, VIRTKEY, CONTROL
  VK_F5, IDM_THETA, VIRTKEY
  VK_F1, IDM_HELP, VIRTKEY
}
```

Notice that the menu definition has been enhanced to display which accelerator key selects which option. Each item is separated from its accelerator key using a tab. The header file AFXRES.H is included because it defines the virtual key macros.

Loading the Accelerator Table

Even though the accelerators are contained in the same resource file as the menu, they must be loaded separately using **LoadAccelTable( )**, a member function of **CFrameWnd**. Its prototype is shown here:

    BOOL CFrameWnd::LoadAccelTable(LPCSTR *lpszName*);

Here, *lpszName* is the name of the accelerator table. The function returns nonzero if successful or zero if the table cannot be loaded.

You must call **LoadAccelTable( )** soon after the window is created. Typically, you will load the accelerators inside your main window's constructor function. The following example shows how to load the **MYMENU** accelerator table for **CMainWin**:

```
CMainWin::CMainWin()
{
  Create(NULL, "Demonstrate Accelerators",
         WS_OVERLAPPEDWINDOW, rectDefault,
         NULL, "MYMENU");

  // Load accelerator table
  if(!LoadAccelTable("MYMENU"))
     MessageBox("Cannot Load Accelerators", "Error");
}
```

To see the effect of the accelerator keys, substitute this function into the preceding menu program and use MENU2.RC as its resource file.

Creating a Hot Key

Although keyboard accelerators are most commonly used to provide a fast means of selecting menu items, they are not limited to this role. For example, you can define an accelerator key for which there is no corresponding menu item. This type of accelerator is sometimes called a *hot key*. A hot key is used to directly activate a specific feature. For example, you might use a hot key to activate a keyboard macro, to initiate some frequently used option, or as an

4

"emergency stop" signal. To define a non-menu accelerator key, simply add it to the accelerator table, assigning it a unique ID value.

As an example, let's add a hot key to the sample menu program. The hot key will be CTRL-T and each time it is pressed, the current time and date will be displayed in a message box. To begin, add CTRL-T to the accelerator table of MENU2.RC. That is, MENU2.RC should now look like this:

```
// MENU2.RC

// Sample menu resource file.
#include <afxres.h>
#include <ids.h>

MYMENU MENU
{
  POPUP "&One"
  {
    MENUITEM "&Alpha\tF2", IDM_ALPHA
    MENUITEM "&Beta\tF3", IDM_BETA
  }
  POPUP "&Two"
  {
    MENUITEM "&Gamma\tShift-G", IDM_GAMMA
    POPUP "&Delta"
    {
      MENUITEM "&Epsilon\tCntl-E", IDM_EPSILON
      MENUITEM "&Zeta\tCntl-Z", IDM_ZETA
    }
    MENUITEM "&Eta\tCntl-F4", IDM_ETA
    MENUITEM "&Theta\tF5", IDM_THETA
  }
  MENUITEM "&Help", IDM_HELP
}

// Define menu accelerators.
MYMENU ACCELERATORS
{
  VK_F2, IDM_ALPHA, VIRTKEY
  VK_F3, IDM_BETA, VIRTKEY
  "G", IDM_GAMMA
  "^E", IDM_EPSILON
  "^Z", IDM_ZETA
  VK_F4, IDM_ETA, VIRTKEY, CONTROL
```

```
        VK_F5, IDM_THETA, VIRTKEY
        VK_F1, IDM_HELP, VIRTKEY
         "^T", IDM_TIME
}
```

Next, add this line to IDS.H:

```
#define IDM_TIME  500
```

This is the ID value associated with CTRL-T.

Next, add the prototype for the command handler **OnTime( )** to **CMainWin** within the class derivation file MENU.H. It should look like this:

4

```
// MENU.H

// This is the main window class.
class CMainWin : public CFrameWnd
{
public:
  CMainWin();
  afx_msg void OnLButtonDown(UINT flags, CPoint loc);
  afx_msg void OnRButtonDown(UINT flags, CPoint loc);

  // define menu handlers
  afx_msg void OnAlpha();
  afx_msg void OnBeta();
  afx_msg void OnGamma();
  afx_msg void OnEpsilon();
  afx_msg void OnZeta();
  afx_msg void OnEta();
  afx_msg void OnTheta();
  afx_msg void OnHelp();

  afx_msg void OnTime(); // process the hot key

  DECLARE_MESSAGE_MAP()
};

// This is the application class.
class CApp : public CWinApp
{
public:
  BOOL InitInstance();
};
```

Finally, implement **OnTime( )** in your main program file. Your program file should now look like this:

```
// Add a Hot Key

#include <afxwin.h>
#include <string.h>
#include "menu.h"
#include "ids.h"

CMainWin::CMainWin()
{
  Create(NULL, "Adding a Hot Key",
         WS_OVERLAPPEDWINDOW, rectDefault,
         NULL, "MYMENU");

  // Load accelerator table
  if(!LoadAccelTable("MYMENU"))
     MessageBox("Cannot Load Accelerators", "Error");
}

// Initialize the application
BOOL CApp::InitInstance()
{
  m_pMainWnd = new CMainWin;
  m_pMainWnd->ShowWindow(m_nCmdShow);
  m_pMainWnd->UpdateWindow();

  return TRUE;
}

// This is the application's message map.
BEGIN_MESSAGE_MAP(CMainWin, CFrameWnd)
  ON_WM_LBUTTONDOWN()
  ON_WM_RBUTTONDOWN()
  ON_COMMAND(IDM_ALPHA, OnAlpha)
  ON_COMMAND(IDM_BETA, OnBeta)
  ON_COMMAND(IDM_GAMMA, OnGamma)
  ON_COMMAND(IDM_EPSILON, OnEpsilon)
  ON_COMMAND(IDM_ZETA, OnZeta)
  ON_COMMAND(IDM_ETA, OnEta)
  ON_COMMAND(IDM_THETA, OnTheta)
  ON_COMMAND(IDM_HELP, OnHelp)
  ON_COMMAND(IDM_TIME, OnTime) // handle the hot key
END_MESSAGE_MAP()
```

```
// Process left mouse button.
afx_msg void CMainWin::OnLButtonDown(UINT flags, CPoint loc)
{
  int i;

  i = MessageBox("Press One", "Left Button",
                 MB_ABORTRETRYIGNORE);

  switch(i) {
    case IDABORT:
      MessageBox("", "Abort");
      break;
    case IDRETRY:
      MessageBox("", "Retry");
      break;
    case IDIGNORE:
      MessageBox("", "Ignore");
      break;
  }
}


// Process right mouse button.
afx_msg void CMainWin::OnRButtonDown(UINT flags, CPoint loc)
{
  int i;

  i = MessageBox("Press One", "Right Button",
                 MB_ICONHAND | MB_YESNO);

  switch(i) {
    case IDYES:
      MessageBox("", "Yes");
      break;
    case IDNO:
      MessageBox("", "No");
      break;
  }
}


// Process IDM_ALPHA
afx_msg void CMainWin::OnAlpha()
{
  MessageBox("Alpha", "Alpha");
}
```

4

```
// Process IDM_BETA
afx_msg void CMainWin::OnBeta()
{
    MessageBox("Beta", "Beta");
}

// Process IDM_GAMMA
afx_msg void CMainWin::OnGamma()
{
    MessageBox("Gamma", "Gamma");
}

// Process IDM_EPSILON
afx_msg void CMainWin::OnEpsilon()
{
    MessageBox("Epsilon", "Epsilon");
}

// Process IDM_ZETA
afx_msg void CMainWin::OnZeta()
{
    MessageBox("Zeta", "Zeta");
}

// Process IDM_ETA
afx_msg void CMainWin::OnEta()
{
    MessageBox("Eta", "Eta");
}

// Process IDM_THETA
afx_msg void CMainWin::OnTheta()
{
    MessageBox("Theta", "Theta");
}

// Process IDM_HELP
afx_msg void CMainWin::OnHelp()
{
    MessageBox("Menu Demo", "Help");
}

// Process IDM_TIME
afx_msg void CMainWin::OnTime()
```

```
{
  char str[80];
  CTime curtime = CTime::GetCurrentTime();
  struct tm *newtime;

  newtime = curtime.GetLocalTm();
  wsprintf(str, asctime(newtime));
  str[strlen(str)-1] = '\0'; // remove /r/n
  MessageBox(str, "Time and Date");
}

CApp App; // instantiate the application
```

4

When you run this program, each time you press CTRL-T, you will see a
message box similar to the following:

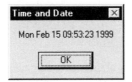

Before moving on to the next chapter, you should experiment on your own
using message boxes, menus, and accelerators. Try the various options and
see what they do. Menus and message boxes will be used by most of the other
programs in this book so a thorough understanding is important.

IN DEPTH

Some Menu Style Rules

While the precise structure and functionality of the menus associated
with your applications are under your control, there are some guidelines
that you should follow. By following these suggestions, your applications
will have the same look and feel as most other Windows programs. Here
are a few of the most important rules.

First, menu bar options should activate pop-up menus. They should not
directly activate program functionality. That is, a menu bar option

should act only as a gateway to another menu. The selection of menu items is best left to pop-up menus. This is the way most Windows applications function.

Second, if your application performs any type of file operation, such as opening, saving, or closing, then it should include a File menu bar item. This should be the first entry in the menu bar (that is, it should be on the far left). It should also include the Exit option. If your application does not have a File menu bar entry, then the far-left pop-up menu should include the Exit option.

Third, if your application supports editing, such as cut and paste, then the menu bar should include the Edit option.

Fourth, if your application supports different viewing options, the menu bar should support the View item.

Finally, all applications should provide the Help option on the far-right side of the menu bar.

While there are certainly going to be exceptions to these rules, they apply to the vast majority of Windows applications. Also, if you will be designing the menus for a sophisticated application, you will want to consult Microsoft's standard style guide for further suggestions.

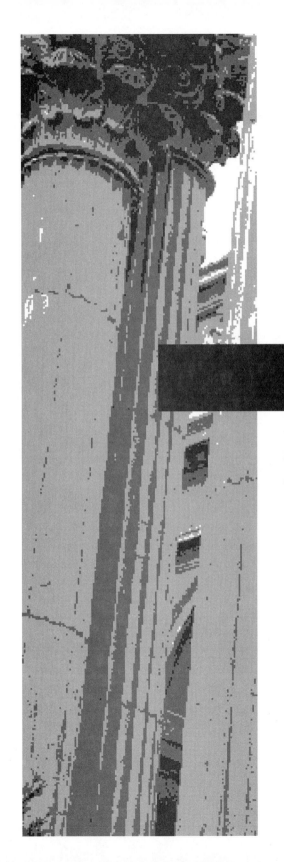

CHAPTER 5

Introducing Dialog Boxes

This chapter introduces the *dialog box*. After menus, there is no more important interface element. A dialog box is a type of window that provides a more flexible means by which the user can interact with your application. In general, dialog boxes allow the user to select or enter information that would be difficult or impossible to enter using a menu.

Dialog boxes (and the controls that occur within them) are a large topic. In this chapter you will learn the basics of dialog box management, including how to create a dialog box and process dialog box messages. In subsequent chapters, we will use a dialog box to explore several elements of the Windows interface.

How Dialog Boxes Interact with the User

A dialog box interacts with the user through one or more *controls*. A control is a specific type of input or output window. It is owned by its parent window, which, for the examples presented in this chapter, is the dialog box. All versions of Windows support several basic controls, including push buttons, check boxes, radio buttons, list boxes, edit boxes, combo boxes, scroll bars, and static controls. Each is briefly described here:

◆   A *push button* is a control that the user "pushes on" (by clicking the mouse or tabbing to, and then pressing ENTER) to activate some response. You have already been using push buttons in message boxes. For example, the OK button that we have been using in most message boxes is a push button.

◆   A *check box* can be either checked or not checked. If the box is checked, it means that the item associated with that box is selected. If there is more than one check box in a dialog box, more than one item may be selected.

◆   A *radio button* is essentially a check box. However, when there is more than one radio button, one and only one item may be selected. Thus, radio buttons are mutually exclusive check boxes.

◆   A *list box* displays a list of items from which the user selects. List boxes are commonly used to display things such as filenames.

◆   An *edit box* allows the user to enter a string. Edit boxes provide all necessary text-editing features required by the user. Therefore, to input a string, your program simply displays an edit box and waits until the user has finished typing in the string.

◆   A *combo box* is a combination of a list box and an edit box.

◆ A *scroll bar* is used to scroll the contents of a window.

◆ A *static control* is used to output text (or graphics) that provides information to the user, but accepts no input.

NOTE: All 32-bit versions of Windows, including Windows 95, Windows 98, and Windows NT, support several enhanced controls, such as toolbars, tree views, and tab controls. These controls are discussed later in this book.

In the course of explaining how to use dialog boxes with Windows, the examples in this chapter illustrate three of these controls: the push button, the list box, and the edit box. Later in this book, the other controls will be examined.

5

It is important to understand that controls both generate messages (when accessed by the user) and receive messages (from your application). A message generated by a control indicates what type of interaction the user has had with the control. A message sent to the control is essentially an instruction to which the control must respond. You will see examples of each type of message passing later in this chapter.

The Control Classes

MFC defines classes for the standard controls. These classes encapsulate the controls and the functions that manipulate them. The control classes are derived from **CWnd**. Thus, a control has access to the same general functionality that is available to any other type of window. The classes for the standard controls are shown here:

Class	Controls
CButton	Push buttons, radio buttons, and check boxes
CEdit	Edit boxes
CListBox	List boxes
CComboBox	Combo boxes
CScrollBar	Scroll bars
CStatic	Static controls

Although MFC allows you to access the various controls directly, without going through a control class object, you will seldom want to do so. Accessing and managing most controls through their control classes greatly simplifies their usage. As you will soon see, the only exceptions to this rule are very simple uses of the push button. But even the push button should be encapsulated when sophisticated control is required.

One last point: Although you will most frequently use controls within a dialog box, it is possible to create freestanding controls within your program's main window. Remember, controls are simply special types of windows.

Modal vs. Modeless Dialog Boxes

There are two types of dialog boxes: *modal* and *modeless*. The most common dialog boxes are modal. A modal dialog box demands a response before the parent program will continue. That is, a modal dialog box will not allow you to refocus input to another part of the parent application without first responding to the dialog box. A modeless dialog box does not prevent the parent program from running. That is, it does not demand a response before input can be refocused to another part of the program. We will examine modal dialog boxes first since they are the most common. A modeless dialog box example concludes this chapter.

The Dialog Box Resource

A dialog box is another resource that is contained in your program's resource file. Before developing a program that uses a dialog box, you will need a resource file that specifies one. Although it is possible to specify the contents of a dialog box using a text editor and enter its specifications as you do when creating a menu, this is seldom done. Instead, most programmers use a dialog editor. The main reason for this is that dialog box definitions involve the positioning of the various controls inside the dialog box, which is best done interactively. However, since the complete .RC files for the examples in this chapter are supplied in their text form, you should simply enter them using a text editor. Just remember that when creating your own dialog boxes, you will want to use a dialog editor.

NOTE: Since, in practice, most dialog boxes are created using a dialog editor, only a brief explanation of the dialog box definition in the resource file is given for the examples in this chapter.

Dialog boxes are defined within your program's resource file using the **DIALOG** statement. Its general form is shown here:

Dialog-name DIALOG [*options*] *X, Y, Width, Height*
Features
{
  Dialog-items
}

The *Dialog-name* is the name of the dialog box. The box's upper-left corner will be at *X,Y* and the box will have the dimensions specified by *Width* × *Height*. Dialog boxes allow various loading and memory options to be specified in *options*. However, for Win32, most of these options are ignored. (If you are using Windows 3.1, then you will want to examine the options that apply to that environment on your own.) One or more features of the dialog box may be specified. As you will see, two of these are the caption and the style of the box. The *Dialog-items* are the controls that comprise the dialog box. Each control resource statement will be explained when its corresponding control is described.

5

The CDialog Class

Dialog boxes are encapsulated by the **CDialog** class, which is derived from **CWnd**. In MFC, all dialog boxes are objects that are instances of either **CDialog** itself, or a class derived from **CDialog**. However, only the most trivial dialog boxes are objects of **CDialog**, and these are better implemented as message boxes. In general, when your program requires a dialog box, you will derive your own dialog box class. For this reason, all of the dialog box examples in this book use a derived dialog box class.

To create a dialog box object, the constructor of your derived class will execute a call to the **CDialog** constructor. Its prototypes are shown here:

CDialog(LPCSTR *lpszDialogName*, CWnd **Owner* = NULL);

CDialog(UINT *ID*, CWnd **Owner* = NULL);

CDialog( );

In the first form, *lpszDialogName* specifies the name of the dialog box template in the resource file. In the second form, *ID* is the ID of the dialog box template. (Most resources can be referred to either by name or by number. The examples in this book use names.) In both cases, *Owner* is a pointer to the parent window that owns the dialog box. If *Owner* is **NULL**, then the parent window is the application's main window. The third form of **CDialog( )** is used to create a modeless dialog box, and its use is described later in this chapter.

Processing Dialog Box Messages

Since **CDialog** is derived from **CWnd**, all dialog boxes are windows (albeit, a special kind of window). Events that occur within a dialog box are sent to your program using the same message-passing mechanism the main window uses. However, dialog box messages are not sent to your program's main window and do not use its message map. Instead, each dialog box that you define will need its own message map and handlers. (Remember, any window can define a message map and process messages.)

In general, each control within a dialog box will be given its own resource ID. Each time that control is accessed by the user, a **WM_COMMAND** message will be sent to your dialog box window. Associated with that message will be the ID of the control that was accessed. The dialog box message map can use the **ON_COMMAND** macro to decode and handle each message. This process parallels the way that menu messages are processed. Remember, however, that dialog box messages are sent to your dialog box's message map, not to your main window's message map.

Many controls also generate a *notification code* that describes precisely what type of action has taken place. In many cases, it is the notification code that will determine which message handler is called when a control is accessed. As you will see, MFC provides a mechanism similar to **ON_COMMAND** that allows you to link notification codes with their own specific handlers.

Activating a Dialog Box

After you have created a dialog box template in your resource file and derived a dialog class from **CDialog**, you can activate the dialog box using the member function **DoModal( )**. This causes the modal version of the dialog box to be displayed. The prototype for **DoModal( )** is shown here:

```
virtual int CDialog::DoModal( );
```

The function returns the termination code generated by the dialog box when it is closed, or –1 if the dialog box could not be displayed. It returns

IDABORT if an error occurs after the box is displayed. **DoModal( )** does not return until the dialog box has been closed.

Deactivating a Dialog Box

By default, a modal dialog box is closed whenever it receives either an **IDCANCEL** or an **IDOK** message. These messages are defined by Windows and are normally linked to the Cancel and OK push buttons. The **CDialog** class provides built-in handlers for these two messages, called **OnCancel( )** and **OnOK( )**. Since these handlers are built in, you do not need to include them in a dialog box message map. As you will see, it is possible to override these handlers and implement your own custom termination functions.

A Simple Dialog Box Example

5

As a first example, a simple dialog box will be created. This dialog box will contain three push buttons called Red, Green, and Cancel. When either the Red or Green button is pressed, it will activate a message box indicating the choice selected. The box will be removed from the screen when the Cancel button is pressed.

The program will have a top-level menu containing two options: Dialog and Help. While this and other examples in this chapter don't do much with the information provided by the dialog box, they illustrate the central features that you will use in your own applications.

The Dialog Box Resource File

The following resource file defines the dialog box that will be used by the first example program. It includes a menu that is used to activate the dialog box, the menu accelerator keys, and then the dialog box itself. You should enter it into your computer at this time, calling it DIALOG.RC.

```
// DIALOG.RC
// Sample dialog box and menu resource file.
#include <afxres.h>
#include "ids.h"

DialogMenu MENU
{
  POPUP "&Dialog"
```

```
  {
    MENUITEM "&Sample Dialog",   IDM_DIALOG
    MENUITEM "&Exit", IDM_EXIT
  }
  MENUITEM "&Help", IDM_HELP
}


DialogMenu ACCELERATORS
{
  VK_F1, IDM_HELP, VIRTKEY
  VK_F2, IDM_DIALOG, VIRTKEY
  VK_F3, IDM_EXIT, VIRTKEY
}


SampleDialog DIALOG 18, 18, 142, 92
CAPTION "Sample Dialog Box"
STYLE DS_MODALFRAME | WS_POPUP | WS_CAPTION | WS_SYSMENU
{
  DEFPUSHBUTTON "Red",  IDD_RED, 32, 40, 30, 14,
            WS_CHILD | WS_VISIBLE | WS_TABSTOP
  PUSHBUTTON "Green", IDD_GREEN, 74, 40, 30, 14,
            WS_CHILD | WS_VISIBLE | WS_TABSTOP
  PUSHBUTTON "Cancel", IDCANCEL, 52, 65, 37, 14,
            WS_CHILD | WS_VISIBLE | WS_TABSTOP
}
```

This defines a dialog box called **SampleDialog** that has its upper-left corner at location 18,18. Its width is 142 and its height is 92. The string after **CAPTION** becomes the title of the dialog box. The **STYLE** statement determines what type of dialog box is created. Some common style values, including those used later in this chapter, are shown in Table 5-1. You can OR together the values that are appropriate for the style of dialog box that you desire. These style values may also be used by other controls.

Within the **SampleDialog** definition are defined three push buttons. The first is the default push button. This button is automatically highlighted when the dialog box is first displayed. The general form of a push button declaration is shown here:

   PUSHBUTTON "*string*", *PBID, X, Y, Width, Height* [, *Style*]

Here, *string* is the text that will be shown inside the push button. *PBID* is the value associated with the push button. This is the value returned to your program when this button is pushed. The button's upper-left corner will be at *X,Y* and the button will have the dimensions specified by *Width* × *Height*.

Value	Meaning
DS_MODALFRAME	Dialog box has a modal frame; this style can be used with either modal or modeless dialog boxes.
WS_BORDER	Include a border.
WS_CAPTION	Include title bar.
WS_CHILD	Create as child window.
WS_HSCROLL	Include horizontal scroll bar.
WS_MAXIMIZEBOX	Include maximize box.
WS_MINIMIZEBOX	Include minimize box.
WS_SYSMENU	Include system menu.
WS_TABSTOP	Control may be tabbed to.
WS_VISIBLE	Box is visible when activated.
WS_VSCROLL	Include vertical scroll bar.

Some Common Dialog Box Style Options
Table 5-1.

5

Style determines the exact nature of the push button. To define a default push button, use the **DEFPUSHBUTTON** statement. It has the same parameters as the regular push buttons.

The IDS.H Header File

The header file IDS.H shown here defines the ID values needed by the program:

```
// IDS.H

#define IDM_DIALOG   100
#define IDM_EXIT     101
#define IDM_HELP     102

#define IDD_RED      200
#define IDD_GREEN    201
```

Enter this file now.

The Class Derivation File

Here is the file that contains the class derivations for the dialog box example:

```
// DIALOG.H

// This is the main window class.
class CMainWin : public CFrameWnd
{
public:
  CMainWin();

  // define menu handlers
  afx_msg void OnDialog();
  afx_msg void OnExit();
  afx_msg void OnHelp();

  DECLARE_MESSAGE_MAP()
};

// This is the application class.
class CApp : public CWinApp
{
public:
  BOOL InitInstance();
};

// This is a dialog class.
class CSampleDialog : public CDialog
{
public:
  CSampleDialog(char *DialogName, CWnd *Owner) :
    CDialog(DialogName, Owner) {}

  afx_msg void OnRed();
  afx_msg void OnGreen();

  DECLARE_MESSAGE_MAP()
};
```

Notice that the **CSampleDialog( )** constructor simply passes along its arguments to the **CDialog( )** constructor.

The Program File

Here is the dialog box program. When the program begins execution, only the top-level menu is displayed on the menu bar. Selecting **Dialog**, then selecting **Sample Dialog** in the popup menu, causes the dialog box to be displayed. Once the dialog box is displayed, selecting a push button causes the appropriate response. A sample screen is shown in Figure 5-1.

```
// Demonstrate a Dialog Box

#include <afxwin.h>
#include "dialog.h"
#include "ids.h"

CMainWin::CMainWin()
{
  Create(NULL, "Demonstrate Dialog Boxes",
         WS_OVERLAPPEDWINDOW, rectDefault,
         NULL, "DialogMenu");

  // Load accelerator table.
  if(!LoadAccelTable("DialogMenu"))
    MessageBox("Cannot Load Accelerators", "Error");
}

// Initialize the application.
BOOL CApp::InitInstance()
{
  m_pMainWnd = new CMainWin;
  m_pMainWnd->ShowWindow(m_nCmdShow);
  m_pMainWnd->UpdateWindow();

  return TRUE;
}

// This is the application's message map.
BEGIN_MESSAGE_MAP(CMainWin, CFrameWnd)
  ON_COMMAND(IDM_DIALOG, OnDialog)
  ON_COMMAND(IDM_EXIT, OnExit)
  ON_COMMAND(IDM_HELP, OnHelp)
END_MESSAGE_MAP()

// Process IDM_DIALOG
afx_msg void CMainWin::OnDialog()
{
```

5

```
  CSampleDialog diagOb("SampleDialog", this);

  diagOb.DoModal(); // activate modal dialog box
}

// Process IDM_EXIT
afx_msg void CMainWin::OnExit()
{
  int response;

  response = MessageBox("Quit the Program?",
                        "Exit", MB_YESNO);

  if(response == IDYES)
    SendMessage(WM_CLOSE); // terminate app
}

// Process IDM_HELP
afx_msg void CMainWin::OnHelp()
{
    MessageBox("Dialog Demo", "Help");
}

// This is SampleDialog's message map.
BEGIN_MESSAGE_MAP(CSampleDialog, CDialog)
  ON_COMMAND(IDD_RED, OnRed)
  ON_COMMAND(IDD_GREEN, OnGreen)
END_MESSAGE_MAP()

// Process IDD_RED
afx_msg void CSampleDialog::OnRed()
{
  MessageBox("Red", "Color Selected");
}

// Process IDD_GREEN
afx_msg void CSampleDialog::OnGreen()
{
  MessageBox("Green", "Color Selected");
}

CApp App; // instantiate the application
```

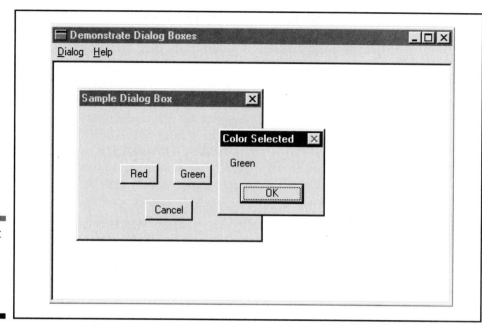

Sample output
from the first
dialog box
program

Figure 5-1.

A Closer Look at the First Dialog Box Example

Each time a control within the dialog box is accessed, a **WM_COMMAND** message is sent to your program. This message is handled by the message map associated with the dialog class **CSampleDialog**. This map processes two of the three messages that can be generated by the box. If the user presses the Red push button, then **IDD_RED** is generated and this is handled by the **OnRed( )** handler. If the user presses the Green push button, then **IDD_GREEN** is generated and this is handled by the **OnGreen( )** handler.

As you can see, the message map provides no handler for the Cancel button. As mentioned earlier, this is because **CDialog** provides default handlers for two IDs: **IDCANCEL** and **IDOK**. **IDCANCEL** is handled by the member function **OnCancel( )**. **IDOK** is handled by **OnOK( )**. Both of these built-in handlers close the dialog box. As you can see by looking at the DIALOG.RC resource file, the Cancel button is given the **IDCANCEL** ID. This means that when it is pressed, the built-in **OnCancel( )** function is automatically called. The prototypes for **OnCancel( )** and **OnOK( )** are shown here:

```
virtual void CDialog::OnCancel( );

virtual void CDialog::OnOK( );
```

Your application is free to override either handler. If it does, you will need to close the dialog box manually, as described in the next section. Remember that since these handlers are built in, they are not included in the dialog box message map.

As mentioned earlier in this chapter, MFC provides the standard class **CButton** that encapsulates buttons, including push buttons. This class is not used in this program because there is no interaction between the push button and the program except for the receipt of the button's ID when one is pressed—and this is sent as a **WM_COMMAND** message. Thus, there is no need to create a push button object inside the program. However, the **CButton** class will be used extensively when other types of buttons are implemented.

There is something interesting to notice about the main menu to this program. Look at the handler associated with the Exit option. This handler terminates the program by sending a **WM_CLOSE** message to the main window. This message tells your program to perform any necessary shutdown operations and then stop execution. To send the message, the handler calls the **SendMessage( )** function, which is a member of **CWnd**. Its prototype is shown here:

LRESULT CWnd::SendMessage(UINT *Message*, WPARAM *wParam* = 0,
LPARAM *lParam* = 0);

This function sends the specified message to the calling window. *Message* is the message that is being sent. Some messages require extra information to be associated with them. When this information is needed, it is passed in *wParam* and *lParam*. The standard types **WPARAM** and **LPARAM** are defined by Windows expressly for this purpose.

Manually Closing a Dialog Box

As mentioned, you may override the standard handlers **OnCancel( )** and **OnOK( )**. If you do, then your handler must close the dialog box manually. To close a modal dialog box, you must use the **EndDialog( )** function, which is a member of **CDialog**. Its prototype is shown here:

void CDialog::EndDialog(int *Status*);

Here, *Status* is a status code returned by the **DoModal( )** function.

For example, here is one way that you could implement **OnCancel( )** for the preceding program:

```
// Handle IDCANCEL explicitly.
afx_msg void CSampleDialog::OnCancel()
{
  int response;

  response = MessageBox("Are You Sure?", "Cancel", MB_YESNO);

  if(response==IDYES) EndDialog(0);
}
```

This function displays a message box that confirms the user's desire to cancel the dialog box. To try this function, add its prototype to the **CSampleDialog** class in DIALOG.H and then add the following message handler to the **CSampleDialog** message map:

```
ON_COMMAND(IDCANCEL, OnCancel)
```

After making these changes, the user will see the message box shown in the following illustration when the Cancel button is pressed:

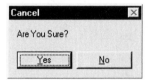

It is important to remember that **EndDialog( )** must only be used with modal dialog boxes. Modeless dialog boxes are closed using a different function.

Initializing a Dialog Box

Sometimes you will need to initialize various variables or controls associated with a dialog box before it is displayed. To allow a dialog box to perform these initializations, Windows automatically sends it a **WM_INITDIALOG** message when the dialog box is first created. When this message is received, MFC automatically calls **OnInitDialog( )**, which is a built-in message handler defined by **CDialog**. Your program may override **OnInitDialog( )**

and perform any required initializations. The prototype for **OnInitDialog( )** is shown here:

virtual BOOL CDialog::OnInitDialog( );

This function will be called before the dialog box is displayed. It must return **TRUE** to allow Windows to set input focus to the first control in the box. Since **OnInitDialog( )** is a built-in message handler, it does not need to be added to the message map.

There is one important constraint that you must adhere to if you override **OnInitDialog( )**: Your implementation of **OnInitDialog( )** must call **CDialog::OnInitDialog( )** as the first thing that it does. That is, your version of **OnInitDialog( )** must first call the version defined by **CDialog**.

While the preceding program did not make use of **OnInitDialog( )**, subsequent examples will.

Adding a List Box

To continue exploring dialog boxes, let's add another control to the dialog box defined in the previous program. One of the most common controls after the push button is the list box. List boxes are managed in an MFC program through the **CListBox** class.

Adding a List Box Resource

To add a list box to a dialog box, include a **LISTBOX** statement inside the dialog box definition of your program's resource file. The **LISTBOX** statement has this general form:

LISTBOX *LBID*, *X*, *Y*, *Width*, *Height* [,*Style*]

Here, *LBID* is the value that identifies the list box. The box's upper-left corner will be at *X,Y* and the box will have the dimensions specified by *Width* × *Height*. *Style* determines the exact nature of the list box.

To add a list box, you must change the dialog box definition in DIALOG.RC. First, add the following list box description to the dialog box definition:

```
LISTBOX IDD_LB1, 2, 10, 47, 32, LBS_NOTIFY | WS_CHILD |
        WS_VISIBLE | WS_BORDER | WS_VSCROLL | WS_TABSTOP
```

Second, add this push button to the dialog box definition:

```
PUSHBUTTON "Select Fruit", IDD_SELFRUIT, 5, 45, 42, 14,
         WS_CHILD | WS_VISIBLE | WS_TABSTOP
```

Finally, the positions of the Red and Green push buttons must be changed slightly, with the Red button located at 56,45 and the Green button located at 96,45. After these changes, your dialog box definition should now look like this:

```
SampleDialog DIALOG 18, 18, 142, 92
CAPTION "Sample Dialog Box"
STYLE DS_MODALFRAME | WS_POPUP | WS_CAPTION | WS_SYSMENU
{
  DEFPUSHBUTTON "Red", IDD_RED, 56, 45, 30, 14,
            WS_CHILD | WS_VISIBLE | WS_TABSTOP
  PUSHBUTTON "Green", IDD_GREEN, 96, 45, 30, 14,
            WS_CHILD | WS_VISIBLE | WS_TABSTOP
  PUSHBUTTON "Cancel", IDCANCEL, 52, 65, 37, 14,
            WS_CHILD | WS_VISIBLE | WS_TABSTOP
  LISTBOX IDD_LB1, 2, 10, 47, 32, LBS_NOTIFY | WS_CHILD |
            WS_VISIBLE | WS_BORDER | WS_VSCROLL | WS_TABSTOP
  PUSHBUTTON "Select Fruit", IDD_SELFRUIT, 5, 45, 42, 14,
            WS_CHILD | WS_VISIBLE | WS_TABSTOP
}
```

5

You will also need to add these macros to IDS.H:

```
#define IDD_SELFRUIT 202
#define IDD_LB1      203
```

IDD_LB1 identifies the list box specified in the dialog box definition in the resource file. **IDD_SELFRUIT** is the ID value of the Select Fruit push button.

List Box Basics

List boxes are controls that require bi-directional communication between themselves and your program. That is, a list box will both generate and receive messages. For example, you will send a list box messages when initializing it. This consists of sending the list box the list of strings that it will display. (By default, the list box will be empty.) Once the list box has been initialized, it will generate messages in response to user actions. Let's look closely at how list boxes send and receive messages.

Receiving List Box Notification Codes

A list box generates various types of messages. For example, it will generate a message when an item in the box has been double-clicked, when the box is losing input focus, and when the selection inside the box is being changed. These events are described by their corresponding *notification codes*. A notification code is part of a **WM_COMMAND** message and is, in essence, a secondary message that describes the event. As you will see, several controls make use of notification codes.

The only notification code that we will use at this time is **LBN_DBLCLK**. This code is sent when the user has double-clicked on an entry in the list. (The list box must have the **LBS_NOTIFY** style flag included in its definition in order to generate **LBN_DBLCLK** messages.) Once a selection has been made, you will need to query the list box to find out which item has been selected.

To process the **LBN_DBLCLK** notification message, you will need to add its message handler to your message map. However, you will not use **ON_COMMAND** to process it. Instead, you will use a special notification message macro to handle notification codes. For **LBN_DBLCLK**, the message macro is **ON_LBN_DBLCLK**. It has this general form:

ON_LBN_DBLCLK(*ID*, *HandlerName*)

Here, *ID* is the ID value being handled and *HandlerName* is the name of the function that processes that ID.

Although **LBN_DBLCLK** is the only list box notification message that the example program will process, other notification codes will be handled in the same way. All list box notification macros begin with **ON_LBN**. For example, here are a few more list box notification macros:

Macro	Meaning
ON_LBN_ERRSPACE	Out of memory
ON_LBN_KILLFOCUS	List box losing input focus
ON_LBN_SELCHANGE	Selection changing
ON_LBN_SETFOCUS	List box gaining input focus

As you will see, the notification codes associated with other controls use a similar message macro mechanism.

Sending List Box Messages

In a traditional-style Windows program, you will send messages to a control using an API function such as **SendDlgItemMessage( )**. However, in an MFC program, you will use member functions to communicate with a control. These member functions automatically send the correct message to the control. This is another advantage that MFC offers over the traditional approach to Windows programming.

There are several different messages that can be sent to a list box. Thus, the **CListBox** class contains several member functions that send these messages. However, the example in this chapter uses only the three shown here:

    int CListBox::AddString(LPCSTR *lpszStr*);

    int CListBox::GetCurSel( ) const;

    int CListBox::GetText(int *Index*, LPCSTR *lpszStr*) const;

Let's look at each of these.

5

◆ **AddString( )** inserts the specified string into the list box. By default, the string is inserted at the end of the current list. (However, if the list box specification includes the **LBS_SORT** style, then the string will be inserted in order.) It returns the index of the string in the list. List box indexes start at zero. If an error occurs, then either **LB_ERR** or **LB_ERRSPACE** (out of space) is returned.

◆ **GetCurSel( )** returns the index of the currently highlighted (i.e., selected) item in the list. If no item is currently selected, then **LB_ERR** is returned.

◆ **GetText( )** obtains the string associated with the specified index. It returns the number of characters in the string or **LB_ERR** if there is no string at the specified index. The string is copied into the character array pointed to by *lpszStr*.

Other commonly used list box functions include **DeleteString( )** (removes a string from the list box), **FindString( )** (finds a string), **SetCurSel( )** (sets the current selection), **InsertString( )** (inserts a string at a specific index), and **GetCount( )** (returns the number of items in the list box). You will want to explore these and other **CListBox** member functions on your own.

Obtaining a Pointer to a List Box

Since the **CListBox** member functions must operate on a **CListBox** object, you might be wondering how they are used to operate on a list box that is defined as a resource within a resource file. Fortunately, the answer to this question is quite easy. You will simply obtain a pointer to the list box using **GetDlgItem( )**, which is a member of the **CWnd** class.

  CWnd *CWnd::GetDlgItem(int *ID*) const;

GetDlgItem( ) returns a pointer to the object whose ID is specified by *ID*. If the object does not exist, **NULL** is returned. It is important to understand that the pointer returned by **GetDlgItem( )** is temporary. This means that you must obtain it each time that your program needs it. You can't store it in a global variable for later use, for example.

When obtaining a pointer to a control object, the pointer returned by **GetDlgItem( )** must be cast into a pointer to the type of object that is being obtained. For list box objects, this means that the return value will be cast into a **CListBox *** pointer.

Initializing the List Box

Since a list box is empty by default, you will need to initialize it each time the dialog box that contains it is displayed. To do this, you will need to implement your own version of the **OnInitDialog( )** handler so that it adds strings to the list box. For example, here is the version of **OnInitDialog( )** that will be used to initialize the list box:

```
// Initialize the dialog box.
BOOL CSampleDialog::OnInitDialog()
{
  CDialog::OnInitDialog(); // Call base class version

  CListBox *lbptr = (CListBox *) GetDlgItem(IDD_LB1);

  // initialize the list box
  lbptr->AddString("Apple");
  lbptr->AddString("Orange");
  lbptr->AddString("Pear");
  lbptr->AddString("Grape");

  return TRUE;
}
```

This code loads the list box with the strings "Apple", "Orange", "Pear", and "Grape". Each string is added to the list box by calling **AddString( )**. Notice how a pointer to the list box is obtained using **GetDlgItem( )** and is then used to call **AddString( )**. This procedure can be generalized. The same mechanism will be used to call other **CListBox** member functions. Further, the same basic approach will be used whenever you need to communicate with other types of controls.

Each string is added to the list box in the order it is sent. (However, depending upon how you construct the list box, it is possible to have the items displayed in alphabetical order.) If the number of items you send to a list box exceeds what it can display in its window, vertical scroll bars will be added automatically.

The Entire List Box Example

5

Here is the entire dialog box program, which now includes a list box, beginning with the updated class derivation file, DIALOG.H.

```
// DIALOG.H

// This is the main window class.
class CMainWin : public CFrameWnd
{
public:
  CMainWin();

  // define menu handlers
  afx_msg void OnDialog();
  afx_msg void OnExit();
  afx_msg void OnHelp();

  DECLARE_MESSAGE_MAP()
};

// This is the application class.
class CApp : public CWinApp
{
public:
  BOOL InitInstance();
};

// This is a dialog class.
class CSampleDialog : public CDialog
{
```

```
public:
  CSampleDialog(char *DialogName, CWnd *Owner) :
    CDialog(DialogName, Owner) {}

  BOOL OnInitDialog();

  afx_msg void OnRed();
  afx_msg void OnGreen();
  afx_msg void OnSelect();

  DECLARE_MESSAGE_MAP()
};
```

The program file is shown here:

```
// Using a list box.

#include <afxwin.h>
#include <string.h>
#include "dialog.h"
#include "ids.h"

CMainWin::CMainWin()
{
  Create(NULL, "Demonstrate Dialog Boxes",
         WS_OVERLAPPEDWINDOW, rectDefault,
         NULL, "DialogMenu");

  // Load accelerator table.
  if(!LoadAccelTable("DialogMenu"))
    MessageBox("Cannot Load Accelerators", "Error");
}

// Initialize the application.
BOOL CApp::InitInstance()
{
  m_pMainWnd = new CMainWin;
  m_pMainWnd->ShowWindow(m_nCmdShow);
  m_pMainWnd->UpdateWindow();

  return TRUE;
}

// This is the application's message map.
BEGIN_MESSAGE_MAP(CMainWin, CFrameWnd)
  ON_COMMAND(IDM_DIALOG, OnDialog)
```

```
      ON_COMMAND(IDM_EXIT, OnExit)
      ON_COMMAND(IDM_HELP, OnHelp)
END_MESSAGE_MAP()

// Process IDM_DIALOG
afx_msg void CMainWin::OnDialog()
{
  CSampleDialog diagOb("SampleDialog", this);

  diagOb.DoModal(); // activate modal dialog box
}

// Process IDM_EXIT
afx_msg void CMainWin::OnExit()
{
  int response;

  response = MessageBox("Quit the Program?",
                        "Exit", MB_YESNO);

  if(response == IDYES)
    SendMessage(WM_CLOSE); // terminate app
}

// Process IDM_HELP
afx_msg void CMainWin::OnHelp()
{
    MessageBox("Dialog Demo", "Help");
}

// This is SampleDialog's message map.
BEGIN_MESSAGE_MAP(CSampleDialog, CDialog)
  ON_COMMAND(IDD_RED, OnRed)
  ON_COMMAND(IDD_GREEN, OnGreen)
  ON_COMMAND(IDD_SELFRUIT, OnSelect)
  ON_LBN_DBLCLK(IDD_LB1, OnSelect)
END_MESSAGE_MAP()

// Initialize the dialog box.
BOOL CSampleDialog::OnInitDialog()
{
  CDialog::OnInitDialog(); // Call base class version

  CListBox *lbptr = (CListBox *) GetDlgItem(IDD_LB1);

  // initialize the list box
  lbptr->AddString("Apple");
```

5

```
  lbptr->AddString("Orange");
  lbptr->AddString("Pear");
  lbptr->AddString("Grape");

  return TRUE;
}

// Process IDD_RED
afx_msg void CSampleDialog::OnRed()
{
  MessageBox("Red", "Color Selected");
}

// Process IDD_GREEN
afx_msg void CSampleDialog::OnGreen()
{
  MessageBox("Green", "Color Selected");
}

// Process IDD_SELFRUIT and LBN_DBLCLK
afx_msg void CSampleDialog::OnSelect()
{
  CListBox *lbptr = (CListBox *) GetDlgItem(IDD_LB1);
  char str1[80], str2[80];
  int i;

  i = lbptr->GetCurSel(); // get index of selection

  if(i==LB_ERR) wsprintf(str1, "No Selection");
  else {
    lbptr->GetText(i, str1); // get string
    wsprintf(str2, " at index %d.", i);
    strcat(str1, str2);
  }

  MessageBox(str1, "Selection Made");
}

CApp App; // instantiate the application
```

When compiling this program, be sure to use the updated versions of
DIALOG.RC and IDS.H, shown earlier. Sample output from this program is
shown in Figure 5-2.

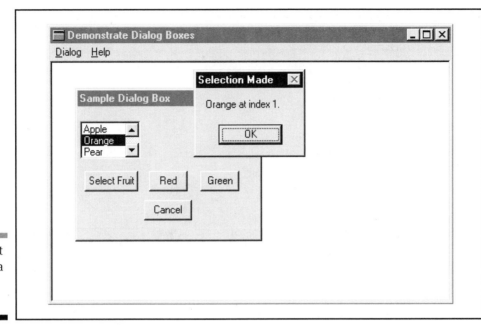

Sample output
that includes a
list box
Figure 5-2.

There are essentially two ways a user makes a selection from a list box. First, the user may double-click on an item in the list box. This causes an **LBN_DBLCLK** notification message to be generated. Double-clicking causes your program to be immediately aware of the user's selection. The other way to use a list box is to simply highlight a selection (either by single-clicking or by using the arrow keys to move the highlight), and then press the Select Fruit push button to obtain the selection. Both methods are demonstrated in the example program. Also, both methods are processed by the same message handler: **OnSelect( )**.

Inside **OnSelect( )**, the member function **GetCurSel( )** is called to obtain the index of the current selection. If this function is called before an item has been selected, the list box returns **LB_ERR**. To obtain the text associated with the selection, **OnSelect( )** calls **GetText( )**. After obtaining the index and text associated with the current selection, this information is displayed in a message box.

Adding an Edit Box

The last control that we will add to the sample dialog box is the edit box. Edit boxes are particularly useful because they allow users to enter a string of their own choosing. Before you can use an edit box, you must define one in your resource file. For this example, change DIALOG.RC so that it looks like this:

```
SampleDialog DIALOG 18, 18, 142, 92
CAPTION "Sample Dialog Box"
STYLE DS_MODALFRAME | WS_POPUP | WS_CAPTION | WS_SYSMENU
{
  DEFPUSHBUTTON "Red", IDD_RED, 56, 45, 30, 14,
            WS_CHILD | WS_VISIBLE | WS_TABSTOP
  PUSHBUTTON "Green", IDD_GREEN, 96, 45, 30, 14,
            WS_CHILD | WS_VISIBLE | WS_TABSTOP
  PUSHBUTTON "Cancel", IDCANCEL, 52, 65, 37, 14,
            WS_CHILD | WS_VISIBLE | WS_TABSTOP
  LISTBOX IDD_LB1, 2, 10, 47, 32, LBS_NOTIFY | WS_CHILD |
            WS_VISIBLE | WS_BORDER | WS_VSCROLL | WS_TABSTOP
  PUSHBUTTON "Select Fruit", IDD_SELFRUIT, 5, 45, 42, 14,
            WS_CHILD | WS_VISIBLE | WS_TABSTOP
  PUSHBUTTON "Edit OK", IDD_EDITOK, 68, 22, 30, 14,
            WS_CHILD | WS_VISIBLE | WS_TABSTOP
  EDITTEXT IDD_EB1, 68, 8, 72, 12, ES_LEFT | ES_AUTOHSCROLL |
            WS_CHILD | WS_VISIBLE | WS_BORDER | WS_TABSTOP
}
```

This version adds a push button called Edit OK, which will be used to tell the program that you are done editing text in the edit box. It also adds the edit box itself. The ID for the edit box is **IDD_EB1**. The ID for the Edit OK button is **IDD_EDITOK**.

The EDITTEXT statement has this general form:

EDITTEXT *EDID*, *X*, *Y*, *Width*, *Height* [,*Style*]

Here, *EDID* is the value that identifies the edit box. The box's upper-left corner will be at *X*,*Y* and its dimensions are specified by *Width* × *Height*. *Style* determines the exact nature of the edit box. Edit boxes come in two basic flavors: single-line and multi-line. A single-line edit box allows only one line of text. EDITTEXT creates a single-line edit box.

Next, add these macro definitions to IDS.H:

```
#define IDD_EB1     204
#define IDD_EDITOK  205
```

Edit boxes recognize many messages and generate several of their own. However, for the purposes of this example, there is no need for the program to respond to any messages. As you will see, edit boxes perform the editing function on their own. No program interaction is required. Your program simply decides when it wants to obtain the current contents of the edit box.

To obtain the current contents of a single-line edit box, use the function **GetWindowText( )**. This function is a member of **CWnd**, not **CEdit**. (Remember, **CEdit** is derived from **CWnd**.) It has this prototype:

> int CWnd::GetWindowText(LPSTR *lpszStr*, int *Max*) const;

This function causes the edit box to copy the current contents of the box to the string pointed to by *lpszStr*. The maximum number of characters to copy is specified by *Max*. The function returns the length of the string. **GetWindowText( )** will obtain the text associated with any window or control. When applied to a window, it obtains the window's title. When applied to a control, it obtains the text in that control. You will only use **GetWindowText( )** to obtain the text from a single-line edit control. (For multi-line controls, you will use other **CEdit** member functions.)

When first created, edit boxes are empty. If you want to initialize the contents of an edit box, use another **CWnd** member function called **SetWindowText( )**. This function sets the text within the control that calls it. Its prototype is shown here:

> void CWnd::SetWindowText(LPCSTR *lpszStr*);

Here, *lpszStr* is a pointer to the string that will be displayed within the edit box.

The following program adds the edit box and the Edit OK push button. Here is the updated DIALOG.H class derivation file:

```
// DIALOG.H

// This is the main window class.
class CMainWin : public CFrameWnd
{
public:
  CMainWin();

  // define menu handlers
```

5

```
  afx_msg void OnDialog();
  afx_msg void OnExit();
  afx_msg void OnHelp();

  DECLARE_MESSAGE_MAP()
};

// This is the application class.
class CApp : public CWinApp
{
public:
  BOOL InitInstance();
};

// This is a dialog class.
class CSampleDialog : public CDialog
{
public:
  CSampleDialog(char *DialogName, CWnd *Owner) :
    CDialog(DialogName, Owner) {}

  BOOL OnInitDialog();

  afx_msg void OnRed();
  afx_msg void OnGreen();
  afx_msg void OnSelect();
  afx_msg void OnEditOK();

  DECLARE_MESSAGE_MAP()
};
```

Here is the program file that includes support for the edit box:

```
// Add an edit box.

#include <afxwin.h>
#include <string.h>
#include "dialog.h"
#include "ids.h"

CMainWin::CMainWin()
{
```

```
    Create(NULL, "Demonstrate Dialog Boxes",
           WS_OVERLAPPEDWINDOW, rectDefault,
           NULL, "DialogMenu");

    // Load accelerator table.
    if(!LoadAccelTable("DialogMenu"))
      MessageBox("Cannot Load Accelerators", "Error");
}

// Initialize the application.
BOOL CApp::InitInstance()
{
    m_pMainWnd = new CMainWin;
    m_pMainWnd->ShowWindow(m_nCmdShow);
    m_pMainWnd->UpdateWindow();

    return TRUE;
}

// This is the application's message map.
BEGIN_MESSAGE_MAP(CMainWin, CFrameWnd)
    ON_COMMAND(IDM_DIALOG, OnDialog)
    ON_COMMAND(IDM_EXIT, OnExit)
    ON_COMMAND(IDM_HELP, OnHelp)
END_MESSAGE_MAP()

// Process IDM_DIALOG
afx_msg void CMainWin::OnDialog()
{
    CSampleDialog diagOb("SampleDialog", this);

    diagOb.DoModal(); // activate modal dialog box
}

// Process IDM_EXIT
afx_msg void CMainWin::OnExit()
{
    int response;

    response = MessageBox("Quit the Program?",
                          "Exit", MB_YESNO);

    if(response == IDYES)
      SendMessage(WM_CLOSE); // terminate app
```

5

```
}

// Process IDM_HELP
afx_msg void CMainWin::OnHelp()
{
   MessageBox("Dialog Demo", "Help");
}

// This is SampleDialog's message map.
BEGIN_MESSAGE_MAP(CSampleDialog, CDialog)
  ON_COMMAND(IDD_RED, OnRed)
  ON_COMMAND(IDD_GREEN, OnGreen)
  ON_COMMAND(IDD_SELFRUIT, OnSelect)
  ON_COMMAND(IDD_EDITOK, OnEditOK)
  ON_LBN_DBLCLK(IDD_LB1, OnSelect)
END_MESSAGE_MAP()

// Initialize the dialog box.
BOOL CSampleDialog::OnInitDialog()
{
  CDialog::OnInitDialog(); // Call base class version

  CListBox *lbptr = (CListBox *) GetDlgItem(IDD_LB1);

  // initialize the list box
  lbptr->AddString("Apple");
  lbptr->AddString("Orange");
  lbptr->AddString("Pear");
  lbptr->AddString("Grape");

  // initialize edit box
  CEdit *ebptr = (CEdit *) GetDlgItem(IDD_EB1);
  ebptr->SetWindowText("Sample Text");

  return TRUE;
}

// Process IDD_RED
afx_msg void CSampleDialog::OnRed()
{
  MessageBox("Red", "Color Selected");
}
```

```
// Process IDD_GREEN
afx_msg void CSampleDialog::OnGreen()
{
  MessageBox("Green", "Color Selected");
}

// Process IDD_SELFRUIT and LBN_DBLCLK
afx_msg void CSampleDialog::OnSelect()
{
  CListBox *lbptr = (CListBox *) GetDlgItem(IDD_LB1);
  char str1[80], str2[80];
  int i;

  i = lbptr->GetCurSel(); // get index of selection

  if(i==LB_ERR) wsprintf(str1, "No Selection");
  else {
    lbptr->GetText(i, str1); // get string
    wsprintf(str2, " at index %d.", i);
    strcat(str1, str2);
  }

  MessageBox(str1, "Selection Made");
}

// Process IDD_EDITOK
afx_msg void CSampleDialog::OnEditOK()
{
  CEdit *ebptr = (CEdit *) GetDlgItem(IDD_EB1);
  char str[80];
  int i;

  i = ebptr->GetWindowText(str, sizeof str-1);

  MessageBox(str, "Edit Box Contains");
}

CApp App; // instantiate the application
```

As you can see, the contents of the edit box are initialized inside
OnInitDialog( ). Each time the push button Edit OK is pressed, the current
contents of the edit box are displayed. Figure 5-3 shows sample output
created by the edit box.

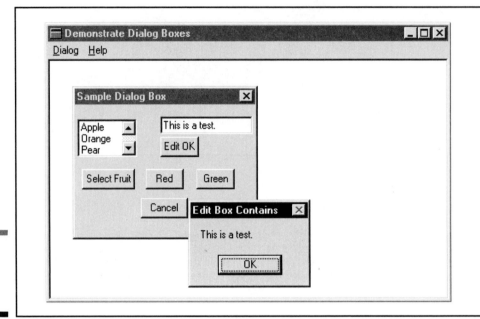

Sample
output using
the edit box
Figure 5-3.

Exploring Edit Boxes

Edit boxes are powerful controls that respond to a wide range of
messages. While none of the examples in this book make full use of their
capabilities, you will want to explore them on your own. To understand
why, here is a list of just a few of their messages, shown with their
corresponding **CEdit** member functions.

5

Message	CEdit Member Function	Description
EM_GETLIMITTEXT	GetLimitText( )	Gets the current text limit in an edit box.
EM_GETLINE	GetLine( )	Obtains a line of text from the edit box.
EM_GETLINECOUNT	GetLineCount( )	Obtains the number of lines of text currently in a multi-line edit control.
EM_GETMODIFY	GetModify( )	Determines if the text in an edit box has been modified.
EM_LIMITTEXT	LimitText( )	Limits the number of characters that the user can enter into an edit box.
EM_LINELENGTH	LineLength( )	Obtains the number of characters currently in the edit box.
EM_REPLACESEL	ReplaceSel( )	Replaces the currently selected text.
EM_SETLIMITTEXT	SetLimitText( )	Limits the number of characters that an edit box can hold.
EM_SETSEL	SetSel( )	Selects text.
EM_UNDO	Undo( )	Undoes the last edit operation.

Using a Modeless Dialog Box

To conclude this chapter, the modal dialog box used by the preceding program will be converted into a modeless dialog box. As you will see, using a modeless dialog box requires a little more work. The main reason for this is that a modeless dialog box is a more independent window. Specifically, the rest of your program is still active when a modeless dialog box is displayed. Also, both it and your application's main window continue to receive messages. Thus, as you will see, some additional overhead is required to accommodate the modeless dialog box.

To create a modeless dialog box, you must follow a two-step process. First, you must create an "empty" **CDialog** object. That is, you must create a **CDialog** object that is not associated with a dialog box resource template. Second, you must associate that object with a dialog box resource using the **CDialog** member function **Create( )**. Let's look at each of these steps.

To create a modeless dialog box object, use the following version of the **CDialog** constructor:

    CDialog( );

As you can see, this constructor does not take any parameters. Its sole purpose is to instantiate the mechanism necessary to manage a modeless dialog box. This constructor is declared as **protected** inside **CDialog**. This means that it can be executed only by members of a class derived from **CDialog**. (That is, you cannot use this form outside of a derived class.) Thus, you will typically call this version of **CDialog( )** from within the constructor of your derived dialog class.

Once you have instantiated a dialog box object, you can link it to a dialog box template using **Create( )**, which is shown here:

    BOOL CDialog::Create(LPCSTR *lpszDialogName*, CWnd *Owner* = NULL);

    BOOL CDialog::Create(UINT *ID*, CWnd *Owner* = NULL);

In the first form, *lpszDialogName* specifies the name of the dialog box template in the resource file. In the second form, *ID* is the ID of the dialog box template. In both cases, *Owner* is a pointer to the parent window object that owns the dialog box. If *Owner* is **NULL**, then the main application window is the parent. **Create( )** returns nonzero if successful and zero otherwise. After calling **Create( )**, the modeless dialog box will be active.

It is important to remember that the modeless dialog box object that you create must stay in existence the entire time that your dialog box is being used. This means that it will have to be declared as either a global object or as a static local object. If the object goes out of scope, then the dialog box will be destroyed by **CDialog**'s destructor. This wasn't an issue for modal dialog boxes because the **DoModal( )** function does not return until the dialog box is terminated by the user. However, **Create( )** returns immediately after it has activated the modeless dialog box.

Unlike a modal dialog box, a modeless dialog box is not automatically visible unless you include the **WS_VISIBLE** style in the dialog box template definition. Alternatively, you may call **ShowWindow( )** to cause it to be displayed after it has been created. However, using **WS_VISIBLE** is easier because the box will automatically be displayed.

To close a modeless dialog box, your program must call **DestroyWindow( )** rather than **EndDialog( )**, which is used only for modal dialog boxes. This means that your dialog box class must override **OnCancel( )** and/or **OnOK( )** if your program uses them because their default implementations call **EndDialog( )**. **DestroyWindow( )** is a member of **CWnd** and its prototype is shown here:

```
BOOL CWnd::DestroyWindow( );
```

It returns nonzero if successful and zero otherwise.

Creating a Modeless Dialog Box

To convert the modal dialog box shown in the preceding example into a modeless one, you will need to make a few changes. The first is to the dialog box definition in the DIALOG.RC resource file. Since a modeless dialog box is not automatically visible, add **WS_VISIBLE** to the dialog box definition. Because we have made many changes to DIALOG.RC since the start of this chapter, the entire file is shown here for your convenience:

```
// Sample dialog box and menu resource file.
#include <afxres.h>
#include "ids.h"

DialogMenu MENU
{
  POPUP "&Dialog"
  {
```

5

```
      MENUITEM "&Sample Dialog",   IDM_DIALOG
      MENUITEM "E&xit", IDM_EXIT
    }
    MENUITEM "&Help", IDM_HELP
}


DialogMenu ACCELERATORS
{
  VK_F1, IDM_HELP, VIRTKEY
  VK_F2, IDM_DIALOG, VIRTKEY
  VK_F3, IDM_EXIT, VIRTKEY
}


SampleDialog DIALOG 18, 18, 142, 92
CAPTION "Sample Dialog Box"
STYLE DS_MODALFRAME | WS_POPUP | WS_CAPTION |
      WS_SYSMENU | WS_VISIBLE
{
  DEFPUSHBUTTON "Red", IDD_RED, 56, 45, 30, 14,
            WS_CHILD | WS_VISIBLE | WS_TABSTOP
  PUSHBUTTON "Green", IDD_GREEN, 96, 45, 30, 14,
            WS_CHILD | WS_VISIBLE | WS_TABSTOP
  PUSHBUTTON "Cancel", IDCANCEL, 52, 65, 37, 14,
            WS_CHILD | WS_VISIBLE | WS_TABSTOP
  LISTBOX IDD_LB1, 2, 10, 47, 32, LBS_NOTIFY | WS_CHILD |
            WS_VISIBLE | WS_BORDER | WS_VSCROLL | WS_TABSTOP
  PUSHBUTTON "Select Fruit", IDD_SELFRUIT, 5, 45, 42, 14,
            WS_CHILD | WS_VISIBLE | WS_TABSTOP
  PUSHBUTTON "Edit OK", IDD_EDITOK, 68, 22, 30, 14,
            WS_CHILD | WS_VISIBLE | WS_TABSTOP
  EDITTEXT IDD_EB1, 68, 8, 72, 12, ES_LEFT | ES_AUTOHSCROLL |
            WS_CHILD | WS_VISIBLE | WS_BORDER | WS_TABSTOP
}
```

Since several changes have been made to IDS.H through the course of this chapter, its final form is also shown here:

```
// IDS.H

#define IDM_DIALOG   100
#define IDM_EXIT     101
#define IDM_HELP     102

#define IDD_RED      200
#define IDD_GREEN    201
#define IDD_SELFRUIT 202
```

```
#define IDD_LB1      203
#define IDD_EB1      204
#define IDD_EDITOK   205
```

Next, you must make the following changes to the program:

1. Create a global **CDialog** object.
2. Activate the dialog box using **Create( )** rather than **DoModal( )**.
3. Override **OnCancel( )** so that it closes the dialog box by calling **DestroyWindow( )**.

Here is the complete modeless dialog box program that implements these changes, beginning with the class derivation file:

```
// DIALOG.H -- modeless dialog box version

// This is the main window class.
class CMainWin : public CFrameWnd
{
public:
  CMainWin();

  // define menu handlers
  afx_msg void OnDialog();
  afx_msg void OnExit();
  afx_msg void OnHelp();

  DECLARE_MESSAGE_MAP()
};

// This is the application class.
class CApp : public CWinApp
{
public:
  BOOL InitInstance();
};

// This is a dialog class.
class CSampleDialog : public CDialog
{
public:
  CSampleDialog() : CDialog() {}

  BOOL OnInitDialog();
  void OnCancel();
```

5

```
    afx_msg void OnRed();
    afx_msg void OnGreen();
    afx_msg void OnSelect();
    afx_msg void OnEditOK();

    DECLARE_MESSAGE_MAP()
};
```

Here is the program file:

```
// Demonstrate a Modeless Dialog Box

#include <afxwin.h>
#include <string.h>
#include "dialog.h"
#include "ids.h"

 // create a modeless dialog box object
CSampleDialog diagOb;

int DlgActive = 0; // nonzero if dialog box is active

CMainWin::CMainWin()
{
  Create(NULL, "Demonstrate a Modeless Dialog Box",
         WS_OVERLAPPEDWINDOW, rectDefault,
         NULL, "DialogMenu");

  // Load accelerator table.
  if(!LoadAccelTable("DialogMenu"))
    MessageBox("Cannot Load Accelerators", "Error");
}

// Initialize the application.
BOOL CApp::InitInstance()
{
  m_pMainWnd = new CMainWin;
  m_pMainWnd->ShowWindow(m_nCmdShow);
  m_pMainWnd->UpdateWindow();

  return TRUE;
}

// This is the application's message map.
BEGIN_MESSAGE_MAP(CMainWin, CFrameWnd)
  ON_COMMAND(IDM_DIALOG, OnDialog)
  ON_COMMAND(IDM_EXIT, OnExit)
  ON_COMMAND(IDM_HELP, OnHelp)
```

```
END_MESSAGE_MAP()


// Process IDM_DIALOG
afx_msg void CMainWin::OnDialog()
{
  if(DlgActive) return; // dialog box already active
  DlgActive = 1;

  // link the modeless dialog box object with a resource
  diagOb.Create("SampleDialog", this);
}

// Process IDM_EXIT
afx_msg void CMainWin::OnExit()
{
  int response;

  response = MessageBox("Quit the Program?",
                        "Exit", MB_YESNO);

  if(response == IDYES)
    SendMessage(WM_CLOSE); // terminate app
}

// Process IDM_HELP
afx_msg void CMainWin::OnHelp()
{
    MessageBox("Dialog Demo", "Help");
}

// This is SampleDialog's message map.
BEGIN_MESSAGE_MAP(CSampleDialog, CDialog)
  ON_COMMAND(IDD_RED, OnRed)
  ON_COMMAND(IDD_GREEN, OnGreen)
  ON_COMMAND(IDD_SELFRUIT, OnSelect)
  ON_COMMAND(IDD_EDITOK, OnEditOK)
  ON_LBN_DBLCLK(IDD_LB1, OnSelect)
END_MESSAGE_MAP()

// Initialize the dialog box.
BOOL CSampleDialog::OnInitDialog()
{
  CDialog::OnInitDialog(); // Call base class version

  CListBox *lbptr = (CListBox *) GetDlgItem(IDD_LB1);
```

5

```
  // initialize the list box
  lbptr->AddString("Apple");
  lbptr->AddString("Orange");
  lbptr->AddString("Pear");
  lbptr->AddString("Grape");

  CEdit *ebptr = (CEdit *) GetDlgItem(IDD_EB1);
  ebptr->SetWindowText("Sample Text");

  return TRUE;
}

// Destroy the modeless dialog box.
void CSampleDialog::OnCancel()
{
  DlgActive = 0; // dialog box is deactivated
  DestroyWindow();
}

// Process IDD_RED
afx_msg void CSampleDialog::OnRed()
{
  MessageBox("Red", "Color Selected");
}

// Process IDD_GREEN
afx_msg void CSampleDialog::OnGreen()
{
  MessageBox("Green", "Color Selected");
}

// Process IDD_SELFRUIT and LBN_DBLCLK
afx_msg void CSampleDialog::OnSelect()
{
  CListBox *lbptr = (CListBox *) GetDlgItem(IDD_LB1);
  char str1[80], str2[80];
  int i;

  i = lbptr->GetCurSel(); // get index of selection

  if(i==LB_ERR) wsprintf(str1, "No Selection");
  else {
    lbptr->GetText(i, str1); // get string
    wsprintf(str2, " at index %d.", i);
    strcat(str1, str2);
```

```
    }

    MessageBox(str1, "Selection Made");
}

// Process IDD_EDITOK
afx_msg void CSampleDialog::OnEditOK()
{
    CEdit *ebptr = (CEdit *) GetDlgItem(IDD_EB1);
    char str[80];
    int i;

    i = ebptr->GetWindowText(str, sizeof str-1);

    MessageBox(str, "Edit Box Contains");
}

CApp App; // instantiate the application
```

5

Sample output from the modeless dialog box program is shown in Figure 5-4. Notice how both the dialog box and the application itself (as evidenced by the activation of the Exit message box) are active at the same time.

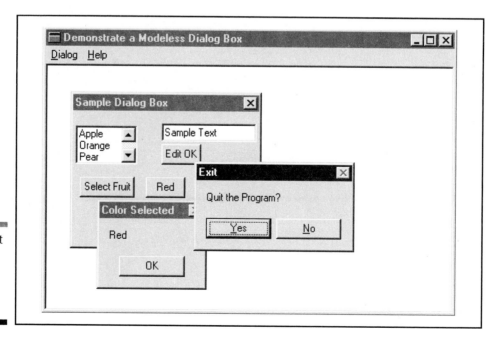

Sample output using the modeless dialog box

Figure 5-4.

If you look at the program file, you will see that a global variable called **DlgActive** is declared and initialized to zero. This variable is used to prevent multiple activations of the dialog box. While it is not always improper to allow multiple activations, it often is. Further, since this program uses a global variable to hold the **CDialog** object, a second activation while the first is still present would overwrite the first, causing a run-time error.

This chapter only scratches the surface of what you can do using dialog boxes and the various controls. Additional controls are covered throughout this book. Also, you will want to experiment on your own, exploring how the various controls function and interact with your program.

CHAPTER 6

More Controls

Controls were introduced in the preceding chapter when dialog boxes were first discussed. This chapter continues the topic of controls by examining several more, including check boxes, radio buttons, group boxes, static text controls, and scroll bars. As you will see, many of the techniques that you learned when using the controls in Chapter 5 will apply to the controls discussed here.

Using Check Boxes

A *check box* is a control that is used to turn an option on or off. It consists of a small rectangle that either does or does not contain a check mark. A check box has associated with it a label that describes what option the box represents. If the box contains a check mark, the box is said to be *checked* and the option is selected. If the box is empty, the option is deselected. Check boxes are encapsulated in MFC by the **CButton** class.

A check box is a control that is typically part of a dialog box and is generally defined within the dialog box's definition in your program's resource file. To add a check box to a dialog box definition, use the **CHECKBOX** command, which has this general form:

CHECKBOX "*string*", *CBID, X, Y, Width, Height* [, *Style* [, *Extended-style*]]

Here, *string* is the text that will be shown alongside the check box. *CBID* is the value associated with the check box. The box's upper-left corner will be at *X,Y* and the box plus its associated text will have the dimensions specified by *Width* × *Height*. *Style* determines the exact nature of the check box. If no explicit style is specified, then the check box defaults to displaying the *string* on the right and allowing the box to be tabbed to. *Extended-style* determines which extended styles the check box implements. By default, the check box does not implement any extended styles.

As you know from using Windows, check boxes are toggles. Each time you select a check box, its state changes from checked to unchecked, and vice versa. However, this is not necessarily automatically accomplished. When you use the **CHECKBOX** resource command, you are creating a *manual check box*, which your program must manage by checking and unchecking the box each time it is selected. (You will see how, shortly.) However, you can have Windows perform this housekeeping function for you if you create an *automatic check box*. An automatic check box is created using the **AUTOCHECKBOX** resource command. It has exactly the same form as the **CHECKBOX** command. When you use an automatic check box, Windows automatically toggles its state (between checked and unchecked) each time it is selected.

NOTE: If you are programming for Windows 3.1, then your development environment may not support the **AUTOCHECKBOX** resource command. If it does not, then you can either manage your check boxes manually or create an automatic check box using the **CONTROL** resource command, specifying the **BUTTON** class and the **BS_AUTOCHECKBOX** style.

Before continuing, you need to create the following resource file, which defines a dialog box that contains both a manual and an automatic check box. The file also defines a top-level menu. Enter this file into your computer now:

```
// DIALOG.RC
#include <afxres.h>
#include "ids.h"

DialogMenu MENU
{
  POPUP "&Dialog"
  {
    MENUITEM "&Dialog", IDM_DIALOG
    MENUITEM "&Status", IDM_STATUS
    MENUITEM "E&xit", IDM_EXIT
  }
    MENUITEM "&Help", IDM_HELP
}


DialogMenu ACCELERATORS
{
  VK_F1, IDM_HELP, VIRTKEY
  VK_F2, IDM_DIALOG, VIRTKEY
  VK_F3, IDM_STATUS, VIRTKEY
  VK_F4, IDM_EXIT, VIRTKEY
}


SampleDialog DIALOG 18, 18, 142, 92
CAPTION "Test Dialog Box"
STYLE DS_MODALFRAME | WS_POPUP | WS_CAPTION | WS_SYSMENU
{
  PUSHBUTTON "OK", IDOK, 77, 44, 30, 13,
             WS_CHILD | WS_VISIBLE | WS_TABSTOP
  PUSHBUTTON "Cancel", IDCANCEL, 74, 65, 37, 14,
             WS_CHILD | WS_VISIBLE | WS_TABSTOP
```

6

```
   CHECKBOX "Checkbox 1" , IDD_CB1, 4, 10, 52, 12
   AUTOCHECKBOX "Checkbox 2" , IDD_CB2, 4, 22, 52, 12
}
```

You will also need to create the header file IDS.H, which is shown below. This file also defines values that will be needed by other examples later in this chapter.

```
// IDS.H

#define IDM_DIALOG    100
#define IDM_EXIT      101
#define IDM_HELP      102
#define IDM_STATUS    103

#define IDD_CB1       200
#define IDD_CB2       201

#define IDD_CT1       300

#define IDD_RB1       400
#define IDD_RB2       401

#define IDD_GB1       500
#define IDD_GB2       501
```

Check Box Messages

Each time that the user clicks on a check box or selects the check box and then presses the SPACEBAR, a **WM_COMMAND** message is sent to the dialog box window along with the notification code **BN_CLICKED**. You can process this message using the **ON_BN_CLICKED** message macro. For automatic check boxes, your program will not need to respond when the button is clicked—Windows does the work for you. However, if you are using a manual check box, then you will want to respond to this command by changing the state of the box. To do this, add an **ON_BN_CLICKED** message macro to the dialog box's message map and then implement a message handler that checks the box as described in the next section.

Setting and Retrieving the State of a Check Box

To set the state of a check box, you will use the **CButton** member function **SetCheck( )**. Its prototype is shown here:

void CButton::SetCheck(int *How*);

When **SetCheck( )** is called, the value of *How* determines whether the box will be checked or cleared. If *How* is 1, then the box will be checked. If it is 0, the box will be cleared. By default, when a dialog box is first displayed, all check boxes will be unchecked.

Remember, if you use an automatic check box, then the state of the box will be changed automatically each time it is selected. You do not need to call **SetCheck( )** to perform this function. However, you will still use **SetCheck( )** to set the state of an automatic check box when initializing it.

You can determine the status of a check box by calling the **GetCheck( )** function. It has the following prototype:

    int CButton::GetCheck( ) const;

This function returns 1 if the box is checked, and zero otherwise.

IN DEPTH

6

The 3-State Check Box

There is an interesting variation of the check box called the *3-state* box. This check box has three possible states: checked, cleared, or grayed. (When the control is grayed, it is disabled.) Like its relative, the 3-state check box can be implemented as either an automatic or manually managed control using the **AUTO3STATE** and **STATE3** resource commands, respectively. Their general forms are shown here:

    STATE3 "*string*", *ID, X, Y, Width, Height* [, *Style* [, *Extended-style*]]

    AUTO3STATE "*string*", *ID, X, Y, Width, Height* [, *Style* [,
                Extended-style]]

Here, *string* is the text that will be shown alongside the check box. *ID* is the value associated with the check box. The box's upper-left corner will be at *X,Y* and the box plus its associated text will have the dimensions specified by *Width* × *Height*. *Style* determines the exact nature of the check box. If no explicit style is specified, then the check box defaults to displaying the *string* on the right and allowing the box to be tabbed to. *Extended-style* determines which extended styles the check box implements. By default, the check box does not implement any extended styles. When a 3-state check box is first created, it is unchecked.

> In response to a call to **GetCheck( )**, 3-state check boxes return 0 if unchecked, 1 if checked, and 2 if grayed. Correspondingly, when setting a 3-state check box using **SetCheck( )**, use 0 to clear it, 1 to check it, and 2 to gray it.

Here is a program that demonstrates both an automatic and a manual check box. For the sake of illustrating the difference between the two, when the manual check box is selected it is always checked. It is not possible to uncheck the box. You will see how to manage a manual check box in the next example.

The class derivation file called DIALOG.H is shown below. Notice that the **CDialog** function **OnOK( )** is overridden by **CSampleDialog**.

```
// DIALOG.H

// This is the main window class.
class CMainWin : public CFrameWnd
{
public:
  CMainWin();

  // define menu handlers
  afx_msg void OnDialog();
  afx_msg void OnStatus();
  afx_msg void OnExit();
  afx_msg void OnHelp();

  DECLARE_MESSAGE_MAP()
};

// This is the application class.
class CApp : public CWinApp
{
public:
  BOOL InitInstance();
};

// This is a dialog class
class CSampleDialog : public CDialog
{
public:
  CSampleDialog(char *DialogName, CWnd *Owner) :
```

```
      CDialog(DialogName, Owner) {}

  afx_msg void OnOK();

  afx_msg void OnCB1();

  DECLARE_MESSAGE_MAP()
};
```

The program file is shown here:

```
// Demonstrate a Check Box

#include <afxwin.h>
#include <string.h>
#include "dialog.h"
#include "ids.h"

int cbstatus1=0, cbstatus2=0; // status of check boxes

CMainWin::CMainWin()
{
  Create(NULL, "Using Check Boxes",
         WS_OVERLAPPEDWINDOW, rectDefault,
         NULL, "DialogMenu");

  // Load accelerator table
  if(!LoadAccelTable("DialogMenu"))
    MessageBox("Cannot Load Accelerators", "Error");
}

// Initialize the application.
BOOL CApp::InitInstance()
{
  m_pMainWnd = new CMainWin;
  m_pMainWnd->ShowWindow(m_nCmdShow);
  m_pMainWnd->UpdateWindow();

  return TRUE;
}

// This is the application's message map.
BEGIN_MESSAGE_MAP(CMainWin, CFrameWnd)
  ON_COMMAND(IDM_DIALOG, OnDialog)
  ON_COMMAND(IDM_STATUS, OnStatus)
```

6

```
  ON_COMMAND(IDM_EXIT, OnExit)
  ON_COMMAND(IDM_HELP, OnHelp)
END_MESSAGE_MAP()

// Process IDM_DIALOG
afx_msg void CMainWin::OnDialog()
{
  CSampleDialog diagOb("SampleDialog", this);

  diagOb.DoModal(); // activate modal dialog box
}

// Process IDM_STATUS
afx_msg void CMainWin::OnStatus()
{
  char str[255];

  if(cbstatus1)
    wsprintf(str, "Checkbox 1 is checked.\n");
  else
    wsprintf(str, "Checkbox 1 is cleared.\n");

  if(cbstatus2)
    strcat(str, "Checkbox 2 is checked.");
  else
    strcat(str, "Checkbox 2 is cleared.");

  MessageBox(str, "Status");
}

// Process IDM_EXIT
afx_msg void CMainWin::OnExit()
{
  int response;

  response = MessageBox("Quit the Program?",
                        "Exit", MB_YESNO);

  if(response == IDYES)
    SendMessage(WM_CLOSE); // terminate app
}

// Process IDM_HELP
```

```
afx_msg void CMainWin::OnHelp()
{
   MessageBox("More Controls", "Help");
}

// This is SampleDialog's message map.
BEGIN_MESSAGE_MAP(CSampleDialog, CDialog)
  ON_BN_CLICKED(IDD_CB1, OnCB1)
END_MESSAGE_MAP()

// Handle IDOK explicitly.
afx_msg void CSampleDialog::OnOK()
{
  // update check box status
  CButton *cb1ptr = (CButton *) GetDlgItem(IDD_CB1);
  CButton *cb2ptr = (CButton *) GetDlgItem(IDD_CB2);
  cbstatus1 = cb1ptr->GetCheck();
  cbstatus2 = cb2ptr->GetCheck();

  EndDialog(0);
}

// Process ON_BN_CLICKED on CB1
afx_msg void CSampleDialog::OnCB1()
{
  CButton *cb1ptr = (CButton *) GetDlgItem(IDD_CB1);

  cb1ptr->SetCheck(1);
}

CApp App; // instantiate the application
```

6

To try the check boxes, select the Dialog option. To see the status of the check boxes, select the Status option. Sample output is shown in Figure 6-1.

Let's take a closer look at parts of this program. First, notice that it contains two global variables, called **cbstatus1** and **cbstatus2**, which hold the state of the two check boxes. These variables are updated by the overridden **OnOK( )** function when the OK button is selected inside the dialog box. The variables are not updated when the dialog box is closed by pressing Cancel. This reflects a fundamental rule of Windows programming: user interaction with a control takes effect only if the user closes the dialog box by selecting OK, not if the box is canceled.

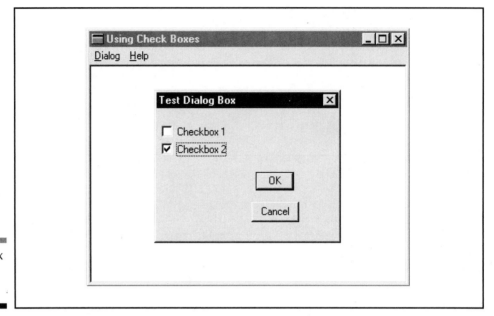

The check box
dialog box
Figure 6-1.

Next, notice that the program uses **GetDlgItem( )** to obtain a **CButton** pointer to a check box object. This allows the **CButton** member functions to manipulate the check box. This process was described in Chapter 5, along with the **GetDlgItem( )** function.

Finally, notice that the message handler **OnCB1( )** handles the **BN_CLICKED** message that is generated when the user clicks on the first check box (which is the manual check box). This function manually places a check mark inside the box.

Managing Check Boxes

The check box program, as it stands, has two serious flaws. First, the state of each check box is reset each time the dialog box is displayed. That is, the previous setting of each box is lost. Second, while the manual check box can be set, it cannot be cleared. That is, the manual check box is not fully implemented as a toggle, the way check boxes are expected to function. In this section, you will see how to manage check boxes more effectively.

Toggling a Check Box

While it is far easier to simply use automatic check boxes, it is possible to implement a toggled check box by managing a manual check box. To do this means that your program will have to perform all the necessary overhead itself, instead of letting Windows handle it. To accomplish this, the program first finds out the current state of the check box and then sets it to the opposite state. The following change to the **OnCB1( )** function accomplishes this:

```
// Process ON_BN_CLICKED on CB1
afx_msg void CSampleDialog::OnCB1()
{
  CButton *cb1ptr = (CButton *) GetDlgItem(IDD_CB1);

  // toggle check box
  if(cb1ptr->GetCheck()) cb1ptr->SetCheck(0);
  else cb1ptr->SetCheck(1);
}
```

6

Initializing a Check Box

As mentioned, both the manual and the automatic check boxes are cleared (that is, unchecked) each time the dialog box that contains them is activated. While this might be desirable in some situations, it is not what is normally expected. Generally, check boxes are set to their previous state each time the dialog box is displayed. If you want the check boxes to reflect their previous state, then you must initialize them each time the dialog box is activated. Remember, each time a dialog box is activated, the **OnInitDialog( )** member function is called. If you override this function, then you can perform any initializations required by the controls within your dialog box. In this example, **OnInitDialog( )** is used to set the initial state of the check boxes.

The **OnInitDialog( )** function that initializes the check boxes is shown here:

```
// Initialize the dialog box.
BOOL CSampleDialog::OnInitDialog()
{
  CDialog::OnInitDialog(); // Call base class version
```

```
  // initialize check boxes
  CButton *cb1ptr = (CButton *) GetDlgItem(IDD_CB1);
  CButton *cb2ptr = (CButton *) GetDlgItem(IDD_CB2);
  cb1ptr->SetCheck(cbstatus1);
  cb2ptr->SetCheck(cbstatus2);

  return TRUE;
}
```

The entire program that incorporates the check box initialization and manages the manual check box is shown below. You should compare its operation to the preceding example. As you might expect, it now behaves in a way that is common to most all other Windows applications. Here is the updated DIALOG.H class derivation file that adds **OnInitDialog( )** to the **CSampleDialog** class:

```
// DIALOG.H
// Updated version that includes OnInitDialog().

// This is the main window class.
class CMainWin : public CFrameWnd
{
public:
  CMainWin();

  // define menu handlers
  afx_msg void OnDialog();
  afx_msg void OnStatus();
  afx_msg void OnExit();
  afx_msg void OnHelp();

  DECLARE_MESSAGE_MAP()
};

// This is the application class.
class CApp : public CWinApp
{
public:
  BOOL InitInstance();
};

// This is a dialog class.
class CSampleDialog : public CDialog
```

```
{
public:
  CSampleDialog(char *DialogName, CWnd *Owner) :
    CDialog(DialogName, Owner) {}

  afx_msg void OnOK();
  BOOL OnInitDialog();

  afx_msg void OnCB1();

  DECLARE_MESSAGE_MAP()
};
```

The updated program file is shown here:

```
// Demonstrate a Check Box -- Improved Version

#include <afxwin.h>
#include <string.h>
#include "dialog.h"
#include "ids.h"

int cbstatus1=0, cbstatus2=0; // status of check boxes

CMainWin::CMainWin()
{
  Create(NULL, "Using Check Boxes",
         WS_OVERLAPPEDWINDOW, rectDefault,
         NULL, "DialogMenu");

  // Load accelerator table.
  if(!LoadAccelTable("DialogMenu"))
    MessageBox("Cannot Load Accelerators", "Error");
}

// Initialize the application.
BOOL CApp::InitInstance()
{
  m_pMainWnd = new CMainWin;
  m_pMainWnd->ShowWindow(m_nCmdShow);
  m_pMainWnd->UpdateWindow();

  return TRUE;
```

6

```
}

// This is the application's message map.
BEGIN_MESSAGE_MAP(CMainWin, CFrameWnd)
  ON_COMMAND(IDM_DIALOG, OnDialog)
  ON_COMMAND(IDM_STATUS, OnStatus)
  ON_COMMAND(IDM_EXIT, OnExit)
  ON_COMMAND(IDM_HELP, OnHelp)
END_MESSAGE_MAP()

// Process IDM_DIALOG
afx_msg void CMainWin::OnDialog()
{
  CSampleDialog diagOb("SampleDialog", this);

  diagOb.DoModal(); // activate modal dialog box
}

// Process IDM_STATUS
afx_msg void CMainWin::OnStatus()
{
  char str[255];

  if(cbstatus1)
    wsprintf(str, "Checkbox 1 is checked.\n");
  else
    wsprintf(str, "Checkbox 1 is cleared.\n");

  if(cbstatus2)
    strcat(str, "Checkbox 2 is checked.");
  else
    strcat(str, "Checkbox 2 is cleared.");

  MessageBox(str, "Status");
}

// Process IDM_EXIT
afx_msg void CMainWin::OnExit()
{
  int response;

  response = MessageBox("Quit the Program?",
                        "Exit", MB_YESNO);
```

```
    if(response == IDYES)
      SendMessage(WM_CLOSE); // terminate app
  }

// Process IDM_HELP
afx_msg void CMainWin::OnHelp()
{
    MessageBox("More Controls", "Help");
}

// This is SampleDialog's message map.
BEGIN_MESSAGE_MAP(CSampleDialog, CDialog)
  ON_BN_CLICKED(IDD_CB1, OnCB1)
END_MESSAGE_MAP()

// Initialize the dialog box.
BOOL CSampleDialog::OnInitDialog()
{
  CDialog::OnInitDialog(); // Call base class version

  // initialize check boxes
  CButton *cb1ptr = (CButton *) GetDlgItem(IDD_CB1);
  CButton *cb2ptr = (CButton *) GetDlgItem(IDD_CB2);
  cb1ptr->SetCheck(cbstatus1);
  cb2ptr->SetCheck(cbstatus2);

  return TRUE;
}

// Handle IDOK explicitly.
afx_msg void CSampleDialog::OnOK()
{
  // update check box status
  CButton *cb1ptr = (CButton *) GetDlgItem(IDD_CB1);
  CButton *cb2ptr = (CButton *) GetDlgItem(IDD_CB2);

  cbstatus1 = cb1ptr->GetCheck();
  cbstatus2 = cb2ptr->GetCheck();

  EndDialog(0);
}

// Process ON_BN_CLICKED on CB1
afx_msg void CSampleDialog::OnCB1()
```

6

```
{
  CButton *cb1ptr = (CButton *) GetDlgItem(IDD_CB1);

  // toggle check box
  if(cb1ptr->GetCheck()) cb1ptr->SetCheck(0);
  else cb1ptr->SetCheck(1);
}

CApp App; // instantiate the application
```

Adding Static Controls

A *static control* is one that neither receives nor generates any messages. The term "static control" is a formal way of describing something that is simply displayed in a dialog box, such as a text message or a simple box used to group other controls. The two static controls that we will look at here are the *centered text box* and the *group box*. Both of these controls are included in the dialog definition in your program's resource file using the commands **CTEXT** and **GROUPBOX**, respectively.

The **CTEXT** control outputs a string that is centered within a predefined area. The general form for **CTEXT** is shown here:

CTEXT "*string*", *CTID*, *X, Y, Width, Height* [, *Style* [, *Extended-style*]]

Here, *string* is the text that will be displayed. *CTID* is the value associated with the text. The text will be shown in a box whose upper-left corner will be at *X,Y* and whose dimensions are specified by *Width* × *Height*. The *Style* determines the exact nature of the text box. If no explicit style is specified, then **CTEXT** defaults to displaying the *text* centered within the box. *Extended-style* determines which extended styles the text box implements. By default, the text box does not implement any extended styles. Understand that the box itself is *not* displayed. The box simply defines the space that the text is allowed to occupy.

The **GROUPBOX** control draws a box. This box is generally used to visually group other controls. The box may contain a title. The general form for **GROUPBOX** is shown here:

GROUPBOX "*title*", *GBID*, *X, Y, Width, Height* [, *Style* [, *Extended-style*]]

Here, *title* is the title to the box. *GBID* is the value associated with the box. The upper-left corner will be at *X,Y* and its dimensions are specified by *Width* × *Height*. The *Style* determines the exact nature of the group box. *Extended-style* determines which extended styles the group box implements. By default, the group box does not implement any extended styles. Generally, the default setting is sufficient.

To see the effects of using these two static controls, add the following statements to the dialog box definition in the resource file you created for the preceding examples:

```
GROUPBOX "Checkboxes", IDD_GB1, 1, 1, 56, 34
CTEXT "This is text", IDD_CT1, 1, 44, 50, 24
```

After you have added these lines, recompile the preceding example, execute the program, and select the Dialog option. The dialog box will now look like that shown in Figure 6-2. Remember that although the static controls make the dialog box look different, its function has not been changed.

6

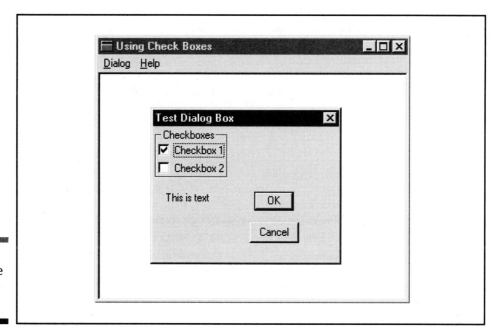

Adding static controls to the dialog box

Figure 6-2.

Adding Radio Buttons

The next control that we will examine is the *radio button*. Radio buttons are used to present mutually exclusive options. A radio button consists of a label and a small circular button. If the button is empty, then the option is not selected. If the button is filled, then the option is selected. Windows supports two types of radio buttons: manual and automatic. The manual radio button (like the manual check box) requires that you perform all management functions. The automatic radio button performs the management functions for you. Because managing radio buttons is more complex than managing check boxes and because automatic radio buttons are the type generally used by applications, they are the only ones examined here. Radio buttons are also encapsulated by the **CButton** class.

Like other controls, automatic radio buttons are defined in your program's resource file within a dialog definition. To create an automatic radio button, use **AUTORADIOBUTTON**, which has this general form:

AUTORADIOBUTTON "*string*", *RBID*, *X*, *Y*, *Width*, *Height* [, *Style* [, *Extended-style*]]

Here, *string* is the text that will be shown alongside the button. *RBID* is the value associated with the radio button. The button's upper-left corner will be at *X,Y* and the button plus its associated text will have the dimensions specified by *Width* × *Height*. The *Style* determines the exact nature of the radio button. If no explicit style is specified, then the button defaults to displaying the *string* on the right and allowing the button to be tabbed to. *Extended-style* determines which extended styles the radio button implements. By default, the radio button does not implement any extended styles.

NOTE: If you are programming for Windows 3.1, then your development environment may not support the **AUTORADIOBUTTON** resource command. If it does not, then you can either manage your radio buttons manually or use the **CONTROL** resource command, specifying the **BUTTON** class and the **BS_AUTORADIOBUTTON** style.

As stated, radio buttons are generally used to create groups of mutually exclusive options. When you use automatic radio buttons to create such a group, then Windows automatically manages the buttons in a mutually exclusive manner. That is, each time you select one button, the previously selected button is turned off. Also, it is not possible to select more than one button at any one time.

A radio button (even an automatic one) may be set to a known state by your program by calling **CButton::SetCheck( )**. You can obtain the status of a radio button by calling **CButton::GetCheck( )**. Both of these functions operate on radio buttons in the same way as they do on check boxes.

NOTE: Even using automatic radio buttons, it is possible to manually check more than one button or to uncheck all buttons using **SetCheck( )**. However, normal Windows style dictates that radio buttons be used in a mutually exclusive fashion, with one (and only one) option selected. It is strongly suggested that you do not violate this rule.

To add radio buttons to the example program, first add the following lines to the dialog box definition in the resource file. Notice that another group box is added to surround the radio buttons. This is not necessary, of course, but such groupings are common in dialog boxes.

6

```
AUTORADIOBUTTON "Radio 1", IDD_RB1, 66, 10, 48, 12
AUTORADIOBUTTON "Radio 2", IDD_RB2, 66, 22, 48, 12
GROUPBOX "Radio Group", IDD_GB2, 64, 1, 51, 34
```

Since we have made several changes to the resource file since the start of this chapter, the entire resource file is shown here for your convenience:

```
// DIALOG.RC -- Includes Radio buttons

#include <afxres.h>
#include "ids.h"

DialogMenu MENU
{
  POPUP "&Dialog"
  {
    MENUITEM "&Dialog", IDM_DIALOG
    MENUITEM "&Status", IDM_STATUS
    MENUITEM "E&xit", IDM_EXIT
  }
    MENUITEM "&Help", IDM_HELP
}


DialogMenu ACCELERATORS
```

```
{
  VK_F1, IDM_HELP, VIRTKEY
  VK_F2, IDM_DIALOG, VIRTKEY
  VK_F3, IDM_STATUS, VIRTKEY
  VK_F4, IDM_EXIT, VIRTKEY
}

SampleDialog DIALOG 18, 18, 142, 92
CAPTION "Test Dialog Box"
STYLE DS_MODALFRAME | WS_POPUP | WS_CAPTION | WS_SYSMENU
{
  PUSHBUTTON "OK", IDOK, 77, 44, 30, 13,
             WS_CHILD | WS_VISIBLE | WS_TABSTOP
  PUSHBUTTON "Cancel", IDCANCEL, 74, 65, 37, 14,
             WS_CHILD | WS_VISIBLE | WS_TABSTOP
  CHECKBOX "Checkbox 1" , IDD_CB1, 4, 10, 52, 12
  AUTOCHECKBOX "Checkbox 2" , IDD_CB2, 4, 22, 52, 12

  GROUPBOX "Checkboxes", IDD_GB1, 1, 1, 56, 34
  CTEXT "This is text", IDD_CT1, 1, 44, 50, 24

  AUTORADIOBUTTON "Radio 1", IDD_RB1, 66, 10, 48, 12
  AUTORADIOBUTTON "Radio 2", IDD_RB2, 66, 22, 48, 12
  GROUPBOX "Radio Group", IDD_GB2, 64, 1, 51, 34
}
```

Below is the preceding sample program, expanded to accommodate the two radio buttons. (It uses the same DIALOG.H class derivation file as the preceding program.) Notice that since the radio buttons are automatic, there are only a few additions to the program. The state of the radio buttons is stored in two global variables: **rbstatus1** and **rbstatus2**. They are updated by **OnOK( )** when the user closes the dialog box. The values of these variables are used to set the initial button states and to display the status of the buttons when the Status option is selected.

```
// Add Radio Buttons

#include <afxwin.h>
#include <string.h>
#include "dialog.h"
#include "ids.h"

int cbstatus1=0, cbstatus2=0; // status of check boxes
int rbstatus1=1, rbstatus2=0; // status of radio buttons

CMainWin::CMainWin()
```

```
{
  Create(NULL, "Try Radio Buttons",
         WS_OVERLAPPEDWINDOW, rectDefault,
         NULL, "DialogMenu");

  // Load accelerator table
  if(!LoadAccelTable("DialogMenu"))
    MessageBox("Cannot Load Accelerators", "Error");
}

// Initialize the application.
BOOL CApp::InitInstance()
{
  m_pMainWnd = new CMainWin;
  m_pMainWnd->ShowWindow(m_nCmdShow);
  m_pMainWnd->UpdateWindow();

  return TRUE;
}

// This is the application's message map.
BEGIN_MESSAGE_MAP(CMainWin, CFrameWnd)
  ON_COMMAND(IDM_DIALOG, OnDialog)
  ON_COMMAND(IDM_STATUS, OnStatus)
  ON_COMMAND(IDM_EXIT, OnExit)
  ON_COMMAND(IDM_HELP, OnHelp)
END_MESSAGE_MAP()

// Process IDM_DIALOG
afx_msg void CMainWin::OnDialog()
{
  CSampleDialog diagOb("SampleDialog", this);

  diagOb.DoModal(); // activate modal dialog box
}

// Process IDM_STATUS
afx_msg void CMainWin::OnStatus()
{
  char str[255];

  if(cbstatus1)
    wsprintf(str, "Checkbox 1 is checked.\n");
  else
    wsprintf(str, "Checkbox 1 is cleared.\n");

  if(cbstatus2)
```

6

```
      strcat(str, "Checkbox 2 is checked.\n");
    else
      strcat(str, "Checkbox 2 is cleared.\n");

    if(rbstatus1)
      strcat(str, "Radio 1 is checked.\n");
    else
      strcat(str, "Radio 1 is cleared.\n");

    if(rbstatus2)
      strcat(str, "Radio 2 is checked.");
    else
      strcat(str, "Radio 2 is cleared.");

    MessageBox(str, "Status");
}

// Process IDM_EXIT
afx_msg void CMainWin::OnExit()
{
  int response;

  response = MessageBox("Quit the Program?",
                        "Exit", MB_YESNO);

  if(response == IDYES)
    SendMessage(WM_CLOSE); // terminate app
}

// Process IDM_HELP
afx_msg void CMainWin::OnHelp()
{
   MessageBox("More Controls", "Help");
}

// This is SampleDialog's message map.
BEGIN_MESSAGE_MAP(CSampleDialog, CDialog)
  ON_BN_CLICKED(IDD_CB1, OnCB1)
END_MESSAGE_MAP()

// Initialize the dialog box.
BOOL CSampleDialog::OnInitDialog()
{
  CDialog::OnInitDialog(); // Call base class version

  // initialize check boxes
  CButton *cb1ptr = (CButton *) GetDlgItem(IDD_CB1);
```

```
  CButton *cb2ptr = (CButton *) GetDlgItem(IDD_CB2);
  cb1ptr->SetCheck(cbstatus1);
  cb2ptr->SetCheck(cbstatus2);

  // initialize radio buttons
  CButton *rb1ptr = (CButton *) GetDlgItem(IDD_RB1);
  CButton *rb2ptr = (CButton *) GetDlgItem(IDD_RB2);
  rb1ptr->SetCheck(rbstatus1);
  rb2ptr->SetCheck(rbstatus2);

  return TRUE;
}

// Handle IDOK explicitly.
afx_msg void CSampleDialog::OnOK()
{
  // update check box status
  CButton *cb1ptr = (CButton *) GetDlgItem(IDD_CB1);
  CButton *cb2ptr = (CButton *) GetDlgItem(IDD_CB2);
  cbstatus1 = cb1ptr->GetCheck();
  cbstatus2 = cb2ptr->GetCheck();

  // update radio button status
  CButton *rb1ptr = (CButton *) GetDlgItem(IDD_RB1);
  CButton *rb2ptr = (CButton *) GetDlgItem(IDD_RB2);
  rbstatus1 = rb1ptr->GetCheck();
  rbstatus2 = rb2ptr->GetCheck();

  EndDialog(0);
}

// Process ON_BN_CLICKED on CB1
afx_msg void CSampleDialog::OnCB1()
{
  CButton *cb1ptr = (CButton *) GetDlgItem(IDD_CB1);

  // toggle check box
  if(cb1ptr->GetCheck()) cb1ptr->SetCheck(0);
  else cb1ptr->SetCheck(1);
}
CApp App; // instantiate the application
```

When you run this program, the dialog box will now look like that shown in Figure 6-3.

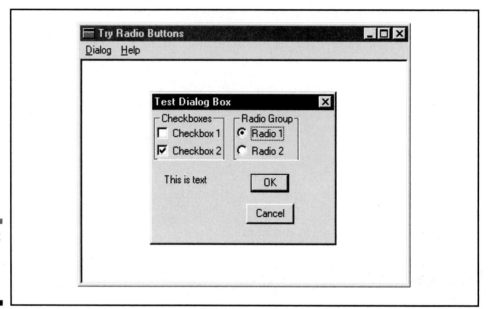

The dialog box
with radio
buttons
Figure 6-3.

Using a Scroll Bar Control

The last control examined in this chapter is the scroll bar. Scroll bars exist in
two forms in Windows. The first type of scroll bar is an integral part of a
window (including dialog box windows). This type of scroll bar is called a
window scroll bar (or, sometimes a *standard scroll bar*). The other type of scroll
bar exists separately as a control and is called a *scroll bar control*. Window
scroll bars are encapsulated by **CWnd**. Control scroll bars are encapsulated
by the **CScrollBar** class. While both types of scroll bars are managed in
essentially the same way, the scroll bar control requires a little additional
work. For this reason, both are discussed here. Many beginning Windows
programmers have the impression that using scroll bars is difficult. As you
will see, scroll bars are one of Windows' easiest controls.

Generating Window Scroll Bars

For a window to include standard scroll bars, you must explicitly request
them. In the case of the main window, this means including the
WS_VSCROLL and/or **WS_HSCROLL** styles as part of the style parameter

when **Create( )** is called. To add standard scroll bars to a dialog box, include the **WS_VSCROLL** and/or **WS_HSCROLL** to the box's definition in its resource file. As you might expect, the **WS_VSCROLL** causes a standard vertical scroll bar to be included and **WS_HSCROLL** activates a horizontal scroll bar. After you have added these styles, the window will automatically display the standard vertical and horizontal scroll bars.

Creating Scroll Bar Controls

To create a scroll bar control, you will generally use the **SCROLLBAR** resource statement, which has this general form:

SCROLLBAR *SBID, X, Y, Width, Height* [, *Style* [, *Extended-style*]]

Here, *SBID* is the value associated with the scroll bar. The scroll bar's upper-left corner will be at *X,Y* and the scroll bar will have the dimensions specified by *Width* × *Height*. *Style* determines the exact nature of the scroll bar. Its default style is **SBS_HORZ**, which creates a horizontal scroll bar. For a vertical scroll bar, specify the **SBS_VERT** style. If you want the scroll bar to be able to receive keyboard focus, include the **WS_TABSTOP** style. For example, the following creates a vertical scroll bar:

```
SCROLLBAR ID_SB1, 130, 10, 10, 70, SBS_VERT | WS_TABSTOP
```

Finally, *Extended-style* determines the extended styles implemented by the scroll bar. By default, the scroll bar does not implement any extended styles. We won't be using any extended styles.

Receiving Scroll Bar Messages

Unlike other controls, a scroll bar does not generate a **WM_COMMAND** message. Instead, scroll bars, whether control scroll bars or window scroll bars, send either a **WM_VSCROLL** or a **WM_HSCROLL** message when either a vertical or horizontal scroll bar is accessed, respectively. These messages are handled by the **OnVScroll( )** and **OnHScroll( )** message handlers, shown here:

afx_msg void CWnd::OnVScroll(UINT *SBCode*, INT *Pos*, CScrollBar **SB*);

afx_msg void CWnd::OnHScroll(UINT *SBCode*, INT *Pos*, CScrollBar **SB*);

6

SBCode contains a value that describes what type of scroll bar activity has occurred. Here are the most commonly used values:

SB_LINEUP	SB_LINEDOWN	SB_PAGEUP
SB_PAGEDOWN	SB_LINELEFT	SB_LINERIGHT
SB_PAGELEFT	SB_PAGERIGHT	SB_THUMBPOSITION
SB_THUMBTRACK	SB_TOP	SB_BOTTOM

For vertical scroll bars, each time the user moves the scroll bar up one position, **SB_LINEUP** is sent. Each time the scroll bar is moved down one position, **SB_LINEDOWN** is sent. **SB_PAGEUP** and **SB_PAGEDOWN** are sent when the scroll bar is moved up or down one page.

For horizontal scroll bars, each time the user moves the scroll bar left one position, **SB_LINELEFT** is sent. Each time the scroll bar is moved right one position, **SB_LINERIGHT** is sent. **SB_PAGELEFT** and **SB_PAGERIGHT** are sent when the scroll bar is moved left or right one page.

For both types of scroll bars, the **SB_THUMBPOSITION** value is sent each time the slider box (thumb) of the scroll bar is dragged to a new position. The **SB_THUMBTRACK** message is also sent when the thumb is dragged to a new position. However, it is sent each time the thumb passes over a new position. This allows you to "track" the movement of the thumb before it is released.

The **SB_TOP** value is sent when the thumb is dragged to the top of the scroll bar. The **SB_BOTTOM** value is sent when the user drags the thumb to the bottom of the scroll bar.

The value of *Pos* indicates the current position of the scroll bar slider box, or *thumb*, as it is sometimes called.

If a standard window scroll bar generates the message, then *SB* will be **NULL**. However, if the message is generated by a scroll bar control, then *SB* will point to the scroll bar object that generated the message.

Setting and Obtaining the Scroll Bar Range

Before you can use a scroll bar control, you must define its range. The range of the scroll bar determines how many positions there are between one end and the other. By default, window scroll bars have a range of 0 to 100.

However, control scroll bars have a default range of 0 to 0, which means that the range needs to be set before the scroll bar control can be used. To set the range of a scroll bar, use the **SetScrollRange( )** function. This function has two forms: one for standard window scroll bars and the other for scroll bar controls. The one for window scroll bars is a member function of **CWnd**. Its prototype is shown here:

> void CWnd::SetScrollRange(int *Which*, int *Min*, int *Max*,
> BOOL *Redraw* = TRUE);

The value of *Which* determines which scroll bar is having its range set. If you are setting the range of the vertical window scroll bar, then this parameter must be **SB_VERT**. If you are setting the range of the horizontal window scroll bar, this value must be **SB_HORZ**. The values of *Min* and *Max* determine the range. If *Redraw* is true, then the scroll bar is redrawn after the range is set. If false, the bar is not redisplayed.

To set the range of a scroll bar control, use the version of **SetScrollRange( )** that is a member function of **CScrollBar**. It is shown here:

6

> void CScrollBar::SetScrollRange(int *Min*, int *Max*, BOOL *Redraw* = TRUE);

Here, *Min*, *Max*, and *Redraw* have the same meaning as before.

Although seldom required in practice, your program can obtain the current scroll bar range by calling **GetScrollRange( )**, which is a member function of both **CWnd** and **CScrollBar**. Its prototypes are shown here:

> void CWnd::GetScrollRange(int *Which*, LPINT *lpMin*, LPINT *lpMax*) const;

> void CScrollBar::GetScrollRange(LPINT *lpMin*, LPINT *lpMax*) const;

For **CWnd::GetScrollRange( )**, *Which* must be either **SB_VERT** or **SB_HORZ**. For both, the minimum and maximum ranges are returned in the variables pointed to by *lpMin* and *lpMax*, respectively.

Setting and Retrieving the Scroll Bar Slider Box Position

Scroll bars are manually managed controls. Thus, it is necessary for your program to move the slider box (thumb) as needed. To do this, use the

SetScrollPos( ) function. For window scroll bars, you will use the version of **SetScrollPos( )** defined by **CWnd**, whose prototype is shown here:

int CWnd::SetScrollPos(int *Which*, int *Pos*, BOOL *Redraw* = TRUE);

Here, the value of *Which* determines which scroll bar is having its slider box set. If you are setting the position of the box of the vertical window scroll bar, then this parameter must be **SB_VERT**. If you are setting the position of the box in the horizontal window scroll bar, this value must be **SB_HORZ**. The value of *Pos* determines where the slider box will be positioned. It must contain a value that is within the range of the scroll bar. If *Redraw* is true, then the scroll bar is redrawn after the box is set so that the slider box reflects its new position. If false, the bar is not redisplayed. The function returns the previous position.

To set the position of the slider box in a scroll bar control, use the version of **SetScrollPos( )** defined by **CScrollBar**. Its prototype is

int CScrollBar::SetScrollPos(int *Pos*, BOOL *Redraw* = TRUE);

Here, *Pos* and *Redraw* have the same meaning as before. The function returns the previous position of the slider box.

Your program can obtain the current position of the slider box by calling **GetScrollPos( )**. This function is a member of both **CWnd** and **CScrollBar**. Its prototypes are shown here:

int CWnd::GetScrollPos(int *Which*) const;

int CScrollBar::GetScrollPos( ) const;

For **CWnd::GetScrollPos( )**, *Which* must be either **SB_VERT** or **SB_HORZ**. For both functions, the current position of the slider box is returned.

A Sample Scroll Bar Program

In this section, a simple program is shown that demonstrates the standard window scroll bars and a vertical scroll bar control. The program requires the following resource file:

```
// SCROLL.RC
// Demonstrate Scroll Bars
#include <afxres.h>
```

```
#include "scrlids.h"

DialogMenu MENU
{
  POPUP "&Dialog"
  {
    MENUITEM "&Scroll Bar Dialog", IDM_DIALOG
    MENUITEM "E&xit", IDM_EXIT
  }
    MENUITEM "&Help", IDM_HELP
}

DialogMenu ACCELERATORS
{
  VK_F1, IDM_HELP, VIRTKEY
  VK_F2, IDM_DIALOG, VIRTKEY
  VK_F3, IDM_EXIT, VIRTKEY
}

SampleDialog DIALOG 18, 18, 142, 92
CAPTION "Using a Scroll Bar Control"
STYLE DS_MODALFRAME | WS_POPUP | WS_CAPTION | WS_SYSMENU
{
  GROUPBOX "Slider Position", IDD_GB1, 15, 5, 60, 30
  SCROLLBAR  IDD_SB1, 130, 10, 10, 70, SBS_VERT | WS_TABSTOP
}
```

The header file SCRLIDS.H is shown here:

```
// SCRLIDS.H

#define IDM_DIALOG    100
#define IDM_EXIT      101
#define IDM_HELP      102

#define IDD_SB1       200

#define IDD_GB1       300
```

The class derivation file for the scroll bar demonstration program is shown below. Call this file SCROLL.H.

```
// SCROLL.H
```

```
// This is the main window class.
class CMainWin : public CFrameWnd
{
public:
  CMainWin();

  // define menu handlers
  afx_msg void OnDialog();
  afx_msg void OnExit();
  afx_msg void OnHelp();

  afx_msg void OnVScroll(UINT SBCode, UINT Pos,
                         CScrollBar *SB);
  afx_msg void OnHScroll(UINT SBCode, UINT Pos,
                         CScrollBar *SB);

  DECLARE_MESSAGE_MAP()
};

// This is the application class.
class CApp : public CWinApp
{
public:
  BOOL InitInstance();
};

// This is a dialog class
class CSampleDialog : public CDialog
{
public:
  CSampleDialog(char *DialogName, CWnd *Owner) :
    CDialog(DialogName, Owner) {}

  BOOL OnInitDialog();

  afx_msg void OnVScroll(UINT SBCode, UINT Pos,
                         CScrollBar *SB);

  DECLARE_MESSAGE_MAP()
};
```

The scroll bar demonstration program is shown here:

```
// Demonstrate Scroll Bars

#include <afxwin.h>
```

```
#include "scroll.h"
#include "scrlids.h"

#define RANGEMAX 50

int ctlsbpos = 0;
int vsbpos = 0;
int hsbpos = 0;


CMainWin::CMainWin()
{
  Create(NULL, "Using Scroll Bars",
         WS_OVERLAPPEDWINDOW | WS_VSCROLL | WS_HSCROLL,
         rectDefault, NULL, "DialogMenu");

  // Load accelerator table.
  if(!LoadAccelTable("DialogMenu"))
    MessageBox("Cannot Load Accelerators", "Error");

  SetScrollRange(SB_VERT, 0, RANGEMAX);
  SetScrollRange(SB_HORZ, 0, RANGEMAX);
}

// Initialize the application.
BOOL CApp::InitInstance()
{
  m_pMainWnd = new CMainWin;
  m_pMainWnd->ShowWindow(m_nCmdShow);
  m_pMainWnd->UpdateWindow();

  return TRUE;
}

// This is the application's message map.
BEGIN_MESSAGE_MAP(CMainWin, CFrameWnd)
  ON_COMMAND(IDM_DIALOG, OnDialog)
  ON_COMMAND(IDM_EXIT, OnExit)
  ON_COMMAND(IDM_HELP, OnHelp)
  ON_WM_VSCROLL()
  ON_WM_HSCROLL()
END_MESSAGE_MAP()

// Process IDM_DIALOG
```

6

```
afx_msg void CMainWin::OnDialog()
{
  CSampleDialog diagOb("SampleDialog", this);

  diagOb.DoModal(); // activate modal dialog box
}

// Process IDM_EXIT
afx_msg void CMainWin::OnExit()
{
  int response;

  response = MessageBox("Quit the Program?",
                        "Exit", MB_YESNO);

  if(response == IDYES)
    SendMessage(WM_CLOSE); // terminate app
}

// Process IDM_HELP
afx_msg void CMainWin::OnHelp()
{
    MessageBox("Scroll Bars", "Help");
}

// Process WM_VSCROLL
afx_msg void CMainWin::OnVScroll(UINT SBCode, UINT Pos,
                                 CScrollBar *SB)
{
  char str[255];

  if(SB) return; // Error, SB should be NULL

  CClientDC dc(this);

  switch(SBCode) {
    case SB_LINEDOWN:
      vsbpos++;
      if(vsbpos>RANGEMAX) vsbpos = RANGEMAX;
      break;
    case SB_LINEUP:
      vsbpos--;
      if(vsbpos<0) vsbpos = 0;
      break;
    case SB_THUMBPOSITION:
```

```
        vsbpos = Pos; // get current position
        break;
      case SB_THUMBTRACK:
        vsbpos = Pos; // get current position
        break;
      case SB_PAGEDOWN:
        vsbpos += 5;
        if(vsbpos>RANGEMAX) vsbpos = RANGEMAX;
        break;
      case SB_PAGEUP:
        vsbpos -= 5;
        if(vsbpos<0) vsbpos = 0;
        break;
    }
    SetScrollPos(SB_VERT, vsbpos);
    wsprintf(str, "Vertical Scroll Bar: %d    ", vsbpos);
    dc.TextOut(2, 2, str, strlen(str));

}

// Process WM_HSCROLL
afx_msg void CMainWin::OnHScroll(UINT SBCode, UINT Pos,
                                  CScrollBar *SB)
{
  char str[255];

  if(SB) return; // Error, SB should be NULL

  CClientDC dc(this);

  switch(SBCode) {
    case SB_LINERIGHT:
      hsbpos++;
      if(hsbpos>RANGEMAX) hsbpos = RANGEMAX;
      break;
    case SB_LINELEFT:
      hsbpos--;
      if(hsbpos<0) hsbpos = 0;
      break;
    case SB_THUMBPOSITION:
      hsbpos = Pos; // get current position
      break;
    case SB_THUMBTRACK:
      hsbpos = Pos; // get current position
      break;
```

6

```
      case SB_PAGERIGHT:
        hsbpos += 5;
        if(hsbpos>RANGEMAX) hsbpos = RANGEMAX;
        break;
      case SB_PAGELEFT:
        hsbpos -= 5;
        if(hsbpos<0) hsbpos = 0;
        break;
  }
  SetScrollPos(SB_HORZ, hsbpos);
  wsprintf(str, "Horizontal Scroll Bar: %d     ", hsbpos);
  dc.TextOut(200, 2, str, strlen(str));
}

// This is SampleDialog's message map.
BEGIN_MESSAGE_MAP(CSampleDialog, CDialog)
  ON_WM_VSCROLL()
END_MESSAGE_MAP()

// Initialize the dialog box.
BOOL CSampleDialog::OnInitDialog()
{
  CDialog::OnInitDialog(); // Call base class version

  CScrollBar *SB = (CScrollBar *) GetDlgItem(IDD_SB1);
  SB->SetScrollRange(0, RANGEMAX);
  ctlsbpos = 0; // reset scroll bar position

  return TRUE;
}

// Process WM_VSCROLL Messages
afx_msg void CSampleDialog::OnVScroll(UINT SBCode, UINT Pos,
                             CScrollBar *SB)
{
  char str[255];

  if(!SB) return; // Error, SB must point to scroll bar control

  CClientDC dc(this);

  switch(SBCode) {
    case SB_LINEDOWN:
      ctlsbpos++;
      if(ctlsbpos>RANGEMAX) ctlsbpos = RANGEMAX;
```

```
      break;
    case SB_LINEUP:
      ctlsbpos--;
      if(ctlsbpos<0) ctlsbpos = 0;
      break;
    case SB_THUMBPOSITION:
      ctlsbpos = Pos; // get current position
      break;
    case SB_THUMBTRACK:
      ctlsbpos = Pos; // get current position
      break;
    case SB_PAGEDOWN:
      ctlsbpos += 5;
      if(ctlsbpos>RANGEMAX) ctlsbpos = RANGEMAX;
      break;
    case SB_PAGEUP:
      ctlsbpos -= 5;
      if(ctlsbpos<0) ctlsbpos = 0;
      break;
  }
  SB->SetScrollPos(ctlsbpos);
  wsprintf(str, "%d", ctlsbpos);
  dc.TextOut(55, 30, "        ", 5);
  dc.TextOut(55, 30, str, strlen(str));
}

CApp App; // instantiate the application
```

6

The main window has both a horizontal and a vertical standard scroll bar. The dialog box contains a vertical scroll bar control. The range of each scroll bar is set to 0 through 50. The scroll bars respond to the various scroll bar messages by moving the slider box appropriately. When you move one of the main window scroll bars, the current position of the slider box is displayed in the client area of the main window. The current position of the "thumb" in the control scroll bar is shown in the "Slider Position" group box inside the dialog box. Of course, you must activate the dialog box to try the control scroll bar. Sample output from the program is shown in Figure 6-4.

One other thing to notice about this program is that the thumb position of the scroll bar control is displayed by outputting text to the client area of the dialog box using **TextOut( )**. Although a dialog box performs a special purpose, it is still a window with the same basic characteristics as the main window. Thus, text can be output to its client area using the same mechanism that is used for the main window.

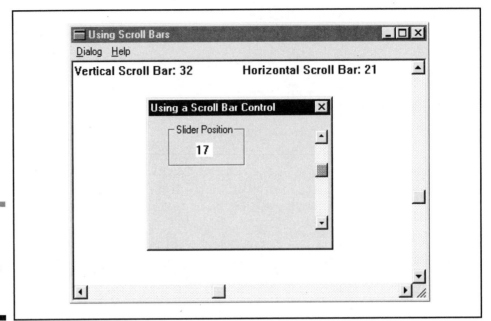

Sample
output from
the scroll bar
demonstration
program

Figure 6-4.

Using SetScrollInfo( ) and GetScrollInfo( )

The scroll bar management functions described in the preceding section can
be used to write MFC programs that will run under any version of Windows,
including Windows 3.1. However, if you will be using MFC to write programs
for modern, 32-bit versions of Windows, such as Windows 95, Windows 98,
or Windows NT, then you will want to use two newer scroll bar functions to
manage scroll bars. These functions are called **GetScrollInfo( )**, which is
used to read various attributes associated with a scroll bar, and
SetScrollInfo( ), which sets the various scroll bar attributes. There are
versions of these functions for both window scroll bars and scroll bar
controls.

In a 32-bit Windows environment, **GetScrollInfo( )** and **SetScrollInfo( )**
replace functions such as **GetScrollPos( )** and **SetScrollRange( )**. The
reason for this change is that **GetScrollInfo( )** and **SetScrollInfo( )** utilize
32-bit position data. The other scroll bar functions use only 16-bit data.
Although you can still use the older, 16-bit functions, **GetScrollInfo( )** and
SetScrollInfo( ) are the recommended way for Windows 95/98/NT
programs to interact with scroll bars because of their 32-bit capabilities. (Of
course, if your program doesn't require 32-bit scroll bar data, then it doesn't

matter which scroll bar functions you use.) In this section we will take a look at **GetScrollInfo( )** and **SetScrollInfo( )**.

For window scroll bars, use the version of **SetScrollInfo( )** defined by **CWnd**. It has the following prototype:

```
BOOL CWnd::SetScrollInfo(int Which, LPSCROLLINFO lpSI,
                         BOOL Redraw = TRUE);
```

The value of *Which* determines which scroll bar is affected. If you are setting the attributes of the vertical window scroll bar, then this parameter must be **SB_VERT**. If you are setting the attributes of the horizontal window scroll bar, this value must be **SB_HORZ**. The attributes are set according to the information pointed to by *lpSI* (discussed shortly). If *Redraw* is true, then the scroll bar is redrawn. If false, the bar is not redisplayed. The function returns nonzero if successful and zero otherwise.

The version of **SetScrollInfo( )** used for scroll bar controls is shown here:

```
BOOL CScrollBar::SetScrollInfo(LPSCROLLINFO lpSI,
                               BOOL Redraw = TRUE);
```

6

Its two parameters are the same as just described. It returns nonzero if successful and zero otherwise.

To obtain the attributes associated with a scroll bar, use **GetScrollInfo( )**. The version defined with **CWnd** is used for the standard scroll bars. Its prototype is shown here:

```
BOOL CWnd::GetScrollInfo(int Which,  LPSCROLLINFO lpSI,
                         UINT Mask = SIF_ALL);
```

The *Which* parameter is either **SB_VERT** or **SB_HORZ**. The information obtained by **GetScrollInfo( )** is put into the structure pointed to by *lpSI*. The function returns nonzero if successful and zero on failure. The value of *Mask* determines which information will be obtained. The mask values are described shortly.

The **CScrollBar** version of **GetScrollInfo( )** is shown here:

```
BOOL CScrollBar::GetScrollInfo(LPSCROLLINFO lpSI,
                               UINT Mask = SIF_ALL);
```

The parameters are the same as just described.

The *lpSI* parameter of both functions points to a structure of type **SCROLLINFO**, which is defined as follows:

```
typedef struct tagSCROLLINFO
{
  UINT cbSize; // size of SCROLLINFO
  UINT fMask; // Operation performed
  int nMin; // minimum range
  int nMax; // maximum range
  UINT nPage; // Page value
  int nPos; // slider box position
  int nTrackPos; // current tracking position
} SCROLLINFO;
```

Here, **cbSize** must contain the size of the **SCROLLINFO** structure. The value or values contained in **fMask** determine which of the remaining members contain valid information. **fMask** must be one or more of these values. (To combine values, simply OR them together.)

SIF_ALL	Same as SIF_PAGE	SIF_POS	SIF_RANGE	SIF_TRACKPOS.
SIF_DISABLENOSCROLL	Scroll bar is disabled rather than removed if its range is set to zero.
SIF_PAGE	**nPage** contains valid information.
SIF_POS	**nPos** contains valid information.
SIF_RANGE	**nMin** and **nMax** contain valid information.
SIF_TRACKPOS	**nTrackPos** contains valid information.

These are the same values that may be used in the *Mask* parameter of **GetScrollInfo( )**.

nPage contains the current page setting for proportional scroll bars. **nPos** contains the position of the slider box. **nMin** and **nMax** contain the minimum and maximum range of the scroll bar. **nTrackPos** contains the current tracking position. The tracking position is the current position of the slider box while it is being dragged by the user. This value cannot be set.

Using SetScrollInfo( )

To see how the new scroll bar functions can be applied, the preceding scroll bar demonstration program is re-coded to use **SetScrollInfo( )** instead of **SetScrollRange( )** and **SetScrollPos( )**. Remember, this program will only work for 32-bit versions of Windows. The program uses the same SCROLL.H class derivation file as the preceding program. The program file is shown here:

```
// Using ScrollInfo()

#include <afxwin.h>
#include <string.h>
#include "scroll.h"
#include "scrlids.h"

#define RANGEMAX 50

int ctlsbpos = 0;
int vsbpos = 0;
int hsbpos = 0;


CMainWin::CMainWin()
{
  SCROLLINFO si; // scroll bar info

  Create(NULL, "Using Scroll Bars",
         WS_OVERLAPPEDWINDOW | WS_VSCROLL | WS_HSCROLL,
         rectDefault, NULL, "DialogMenu");

  // Load accelerator table.
  if(!LoadAccelTable("DialogMenu"))
    MessageBox("Cannot Load Accelerators", "Error");

  si.cbSize = sizeof(SCROLLINFO);
  si.fMask = SIF_RANGE;
  si.nMin = 0;
  si.nMax = RANGEMAX;
  SetScrollInfo(SB_VERT, &si);
  SetScrollInfo(SB_HORZ, &si);
}

// Initialize the application.
BOOL CApp::InitInstance()
{
```

6

```
  m_pMainWnd = new CMainWin;
  m_pMainWnd->ShowWindow(m_nCmdShow);
  m_pMainWnd->UpdateWindow();

  return TRUE;
}

// This is the application's message map.
BEGIN_MESSAGE_MAP(CMainWin, CFrameWnd)
  ON_COMMAND(IDM_DIALOG, OnDialog)
  ON_COMMAND(IDM_EXIT, OnExit)
  ON_COMMAND(IDM_HELP, OnHelp)
  ON_WM_VSCROLL()
  ON_WM_HSCROLL()
END_MESSAGE_MAP()

// Process IDM_DIALOG
afx_msg void CMainWin::OnDialog()
{
  CSampleDialog diagOb("SampleDialog", this);

  diagOb.DoModal(); // activate modal dialog box
}

// Process IDM_EXIT
afx_msg void CMainWin::OnExit()
{
  int response;

  response = MessageBox("Quit the Program?",
                        "Exit", MB_YESNO);

  if(response == IDYES)
    SendMessage(WM_CLOSE); // terminate app
}

// Process IDM_HELP
afx_msg void CMainWin::OnHelp()
{
  MessageBox("Scroll Bars", "Help");
}

// Process WM_VSCROLL
afx_msg void CMainWin::OnVScroll(UINT SBCode, UINT Pos,
                                        CScrollBar *SB)
```

```
  {
    char str[255];
    SCROLLINFO si; // scroll bar info

    if(SB) return; // Error, SB should be NULL

    CClientDC dc(this);

    switch(SBCode) {
      case SB_LINEDOWN:
        vsbpos++;
        if(vsbpos>RANGEMAX) vsbpos = RANGEMAX;
        break;
      case SB_LINEUP:
        vsbpos--;
        if(vsbpos<0) vsbpos = 0;
        break;
      case SB_THUMBPOSITION:
        vsbpos = Pos; // get current position
        break;
      case SB_THUMBTRACK:
        vsbpos = Pos; // get current position
        break;
      case SB_PAGEDOWN:
        vsbpos += 5;
        if(vsbpos>RANGEMAX) vsbpos = RANGEMAX;
        break;
      case SB_PAGEUP:
        vsbpos -= 5;
        if(vsbpos<0) vsbpos = 0;
        break;
    }
    si.cbSize = sizeof(SCROLLINFO);
    si.fMask = SIF_POS;
    si.nPos = vsbpos;
    SetScrollInfo(SB_VERT, &si);
    wsprintf(str, "Vertical Scroll Bar: %d     ", vsbpos);
    dc.TextOut(2, 2, str, strlen(str));

  }

// Process WM_HSCROLL
afx_msg void CMainWin::OnHScroll(UINT SBCode, UINT Pos,
                                 CScrollBar *SB)
  {
```

```
    SCROLLINFO si; // scroll bar info
    char str[255];

    if(SB) return; // Error, SB should be NULL

    CClientDC dc(this);

    switch(SBCode) {
      case SB_LINERIGHT:
        hsbpos++;
        if(hsbpos>RANGEMAX) hsbpos = RANGEMAX;
        break;
      case SB_LINELEFT:
        hsbpos--;
        if(hsbpos<0) hsbpos = 0;
        break;
      case SB_THUMBPOSITION:
        hsbpos = Pos; // get current position
        break;
      case SB_THUMBTRACK:
        hsbpos = Pos; // get current position
        break;
      case SB_PAGERIGHT:
        hsbpos += 5;
        if(hsbpos>RANGEMAX) hsbpos = RANGEMAX;
        break;
      case SB_PAGELEFT:
        hsbpos -= 5;
        if(hsbpos<0) hsbpos = 0;
        break;
    }
    si.cbSize = sizeof(SCROLLINFO);
    si.fMask = SIF_POS;

    si.nPos = hsbpos;
    SetScrollInfo(SB_HORZ, &si);
    wsprintf(str, "Horizontal Scroll Bar: %d    ", hsbpos);
    dc.TextOut(200, 2, str, strlen(str));
  }

// This is SampleDialog's message map.
BEGIN_MESSAGE_MAP(CSampleDialog, CDialog)
  ON_WM_VSCROLL()
END_MESSAGE_MAP()
```

```
// Initialize the dialog box.
BOOL CSampleDialog::OnInitDialog()
{
  SCROLLINFO si; // scroll bar info

  CDialog::OnInitDialog(); // Call base class version

  CScrollBar *SB = (CScrollBar *) GetDlgItem(IDD_SB1);

  si.cbSize = sizeof(SCROLLINFO);
  si.fMask = SIF_RANGE;
  si.nMin = 0;
  si.nMax = RANGEMAX;
  SB->SetScrollInfo(&si);

  ctlsbpos = 0; // reset scroll bar position

  return TRUE;
}

// Process WM_VSCROLL Messages
afx_msg void CSampleDialog::OnVScroll(UINT SBCode, UINT Pos,
                          CScrollBar *SB)
{
  SCROLLINFO si; // scroll bar info
  char str[255];

  if(!SB) return; // Error, SB must point to scroll bar control

  CClientDC dc(this);

  switch(SBCode) {
    case SB_LINEDOWN:
      ctlsbpos++;
      if(ctlsbpos>RANGEMAX) ctlsbpos = RANGEMAX;
      break;
    case SB_LINEUP:
      ctlsbpos--;
      if(ctlsbpos<0) ctlsbpos = 0;
      break;
    case SB_THUMBPOSITION:
      ctlsbpos = Pos; // get current position
      break;
    case SB_THUMBTRACK:
      ctlsbpos = Pos; // get current position
```

6

```
      break;
    case SB_PAGEDOWN:
      ctlsbpos += 5;
      if(ctlsbpos>RANGEMAX) ctlsbpos = RANGEMAX;
      break;
    case SB_PAGEUP:
      ctlsbpos -= 5;
      if(ctlsbpos<0) ctlsbpos = 0;
      break;
  }
  si.cbSize = sizeof(SCROLLINFO);
  si.fMask = SIF_POS;
  si.nPos = ctlsbpos;
  SB->SetScrollInfo(&si);
  wsprintf(str, "%d", ctlsbpos);
  dc.TextOut(55, 30, "     ", 5);
  dc.TextOut(55, 30, str, strlen(str));
}

CApp App; // instantiate the application
```

Using DDX and DDV Functions

Before leaving the topic of controls, it is necessary to discuss two categories of functions that can be used to simplify the management of controls in certain circumstances. To understand the purpose of these functions, consider the following. Often a program variable is linked to a control. For example, in the check box example at the beginning of this chapter the variables **cbstatus1** and **cbstatus2** are used to hold the check status of the boxes. As you saw, some code is required to update these variables when a check box changes state. In the example, the **OnOK( )** function is overloaded so that **cbstatus1** and **cbstatus2** are updated when the user selects OK to close the dialog box. They are not updated (i.e., changed) if the user exits via the Cancel button. This same general process occurs frequently when working with other types of controls and dialog boxes. Data must be moved into a dialog box control when it is initialized and out of the control when the control is closed. Also, sometimes the data entered by the user (such as a string in an edit control) must be validated.

While the situation just described is easy to handle, it can occur quite often in the real world. For this reason, MFC provides a mechanism by which you can automate this process. This mechanism uses two categories of functions: DDX and DDV. DDX stands for *dialog data exchange*, and the DDX functions handle the exchange of data between a control and a variable. DDV stands for *dialog data validation* and DDV functions validate that data. Since not all controls provide data that must be validated, the DDX functions are used more extensively. (For example, you will not validate check boxes, push buttons, radio buttons, or, in most cases, scroll bars.) The DDX/DDV functions operate on member variables defined within your dialog box class. That is, you must define a member variable for each control that you want to use.

Here are some common DDX functions:

Function	Purpose
DDX_Check	Manages a check box variable
DDX_Text	Manages an edit box string variable
DDX_Radio	Manages a variable for a set of radio buttons
DDX_Scroll	Manages a scroll bar variable

Here are some common DDV functions:

Function	Purpose
DDV_MaxChars	Validates the length of a string
DDV_MinMaxDouble	Validates a double
DDV_MinMaxDWord	Validates a DWORD
DDV_MinMaxInt	Validates an integer
DDV_MinMaxLong	Validates a long integer
DDV_MinMaxUnsigned	Validates an unsigned integer

To use the DDX and DDV functions, you must override the **DoDataExchange( )** function in your dialog box class. It is a virtual member of **CWnd** and its prototype is shown here:

    void CWnd::DoDataExchange(CDataExchange *Data);

Here, *Data* is a pointer to a **CDataExchange** object that is used by the DDX and DDV functions. (You will not use this object directly.) Inside your overridden version of **DoDataExchange( )**, you will call the necessary DDX and DDV functions. You should immediately follow each call to a DDX function with its associated DDV function (if applicable).

Inside **DoDataExchange( )**, each DDX/DDV function links a member variable of your dialog class with a control and then provides the necessary data exchange or validation. For example, the **DDX_Check( )** function has this prototype:

   void AFXAPI DDX_Check(CDataExchange *Data*, int *ID*, int &*var*);

Here, *Data* is a pointer to the **CDataExchange** object passed to **DoDataExchange( )**, *ID* is the ID of the control, and *var* is the member variable that will be updated. When this function is called within **DoDataExchange( )**, the information in the specified control is automatically moved into or out of its corresponding variable.

A DDX Demonstration

To fully appreciate the power of DDX, you need to see it in action. As a demonstration, we will modify the second check box program shown at the beginning of this chapter so that it transfers data to and from the check box controls using DDX. This will allow you to compare the manual transfer code in the original version with the automated DDX approach.

In general, here are the changes we will need to make. Two new member variables will be added to the **CSampleDialog** class. These member variables are used by the DDX mechanism to initialize the two check box controls before the dialog box is displayed and to store the current value when the dialog box is dismissed. As before, the current status of the check boxes is stored in the global variables **cbstatus1** and **cbstatus2**. It's just that now they will be maintained automatically through DDX. The **CDialog::DoDataExchange( )** function will be overridden, and it is here that the actual data exchange will occur. In addition, the **OnDialog( )** and **OnOk( )** functions will be modified to use the DDX method. The remainder of this section describes the changes in detail.

The IDS.H and DIALOG.RC files used in this example are the same as those used in the original program.

Modifying the CSampleDialog Class Declaration
The first step in switching to DDX involves modifications to the **CSampleDialog** class inside DIALOG.H. You must add two new member variables (**m_check1Val** and **m_check2Val**) and override the

CDialog::DoDataExchange( ) function. Also, remove the override of
OnInitDialog( ); it is no longer needed. The modified file is shown here:

```
// DIALOG.H -- DDX version

// This is the main window class.
class CMainWin : public CFrameWnd
{
public:
  CMainWin();

  // define menu handlers
  afx_msg void OnDialog();
  afx_msg void OnStatus();
  afx_msg void OnExit();
  afx_msg void OnHelp();

  DECLARE_MESSAGE_MAP()
};

// This is the application class.
class CApp : public CWinApp
{
public:
  BOOL InitInstance();
};

// This is a dialog class.
class CSampleDialog : public CDialog
{
public:
  CSampleDialog(char *DialogName, CWnd *Owner) :
    CDialog(DialogName, Owner) {}

  afx_msg void OnOK();
  afx_msg void OnCB1();

  virtual void DoDataExchange(CDataExchange* pDX);
  int m_check1Val, m_check2Val;

  DECLARE_MESSAGE_MAP()
};
```

Implementing the DoDataExchange Function

The remaining modifications occur in the program file. Briefly, they are as follows:

◆ Initialize the new member variables.

◆ Implement **CSampleDialog::DoDataExchange( )**.

◆ Modify the **OnOK( )** function.

◆ Remove the previous data exchange code.

The first step is to initialize **m_check1Val** and **m_check2Val** using the values stored in **cbstatus1** and **cbstatus2**. Because they are members of **CSampleDialog**, the best place would be after the dialog box is created, in the **CMainWin::OnDialog( )** function. Add the following lines before the call to **DoModal( )**:

```
diagOb.m_check1Val = cbstatus1;
diagOb.m_check2Val = cbstatus2;
```

Next, you must implement the **DoDataExchange( )** function. It must first call **CDialog::DoDataExchange( )** and then make calls to **DDX_Check( )**, as shown here:

```
// Transfer the new check box data.
void CSampleDialog::DoDataExchange(CDataExchange* pDX)
{
  CDialog::DoDataExchange(pDX);

  DDX_Check(pDX, IDD_CB1, m_check1Val);
  DDX_Check(pDX, IDD_CB2, m_check2Val);
}
```

Next, the existing **OnOK( )** function needs to be changed to use DDX. Remove the existing transfer code. Then add code that first makes a call to **CDialog::OnOK( )** and then stores the new check box values in the proper global variables. The following **OnOK( )** function is the result of these changes. Notice that the new function is smaller and more efficient.

```
afx_msg void CSampleDialog::OnOK()
{
  CDialog::OnOK(); // transfer the new check box control data
```

```
cbstatus1 = m_check1Val;
cbstatus2 = m_check2Val

EndDialog(IDOK);
}
```

Finally, you must remove the remaining data-exchange code from the original program. This code is contained in the **CDialog::OnInitDialog( )** function. Since the only purpose for this function was to initialize the check boxes, it can be removed in its entirety.

NOTE: Even though we don't override the **CDialog::OnInitDialog( )** function, a critical step in the DDX process is taken by the MFC library. In **CDialog::OnInitDialog( )**, a call is made to the **CWnd::UpdateData( )** function. This call initializes the controls in the dialog box with the values stored in **m_check1Val** and **m_check2Val**.

6

We have made a lot of changes to the program file. It is shown here for your convenience:

```
// Demonstrate DDX Transfer

#include <afxwin.h>
#include <string.h>
#include "dialog.h"
#include "ids.h"

int cbstatus1=0, cbstatus2=0; // status of check boxes

CMainWin::CMainWin()
{
  Create(NULL, "Using Check Boxes",
         WS_OVERLAPPEDWINDOW, rectDefault,
         NULL, "DialogMenu");

  // Load accelerator table.
  if(!LoadAccelTable("DialogMenu"))
     MessageBox("Cannot Load Accelerators", "Error");
}

// Initialize the application.
BOOL CApp::InitInstance()
```

```
{
  m_pMainWnd = new CMainWin;
  m_pMainWnd->ShowWindow(m_nCmdShow);
  m_pMainWnd->UpdateWindow();

  return TRUE;
}

// This is the application's message map.
BEGIN_MESSAGE_MAP(CMainWin, CFrameWnd)
  ON_COMMAND(IDM_DIALOG, OnDialog)
  ON_COMMAND(IDM_STATUS, OnStatus)
  ON_COMMAND(IDM_EXIT, OnExit)
  ON_COMMAND(IDM_HELP, OnHelp)
END_MESSAGE_MAP()

// Process IDM_DIALOG
afx_msg void CMainWin::OnDialog()
{
  CSampleDialog diagOb("SampleDialog", this);

  diagOb.m_check1Val = cbstatus1;
  diagOb.m_check2Val = cbstatus2;
  diagOb.DoModal(); // activate modal dialog box
}

// Process IDM_STATUS
afx_msg void CMainWin::OnStatus()
{
  char str[255];

  if(cbstatus1)
    wsprintf(str, "Checkbox 1 is checked.\n");
  else
    wsprintf(str, "Checkbox 1 is cleared.\n");

  if(cbstatus2)
    strcat(str, "Checkbox 2 is checked.");
  else
    strcat(str, "Checkbox 2 is cleared.");

  MessageBox(str, "Status");
}

// Process IDM_EXIT
```

```
afx_msg void CMainWin::OnExit()
{
  int response;

  response = MessageBox("Quit the Program?",
                        "Exit", MB_YESNO);

  if(response == IDYES)
    SendMessage(WM_CLOSE); // terminate app
}

// Process IDM_HELP
afx_msg void CMainWin::OnHelp()
{
    MessageBox("More Controls", "Help");
}

// This is SampleDialog's message map.
BEGIN_MESSAGE_MAP(CSampleDialog, CDialog)
  ON_BN_CLICKED(IDD_CB1, OnCB1)
END_MESSAGE_MAP()

// Transfer the new check box data.
void CSampleDialog::DoDataExchange(CDataExchange* pDX)
{
  CDialog::DoDataExchange(pDX);

  DDX_Check(pDX, IDD_CB1, m_check1Val);
  DDX_Check(pDX, IDD_CB2, m_check2Val);
}

// Handle IDOK explicitly.
afx_msg void CSampleDialog::OnOK()
{
  CDialog::OnOK(); // transfer the new check box control data

  cbstatus1 = m_check1Val;
  cbstatus2 = m_check2Val;

  EndDialog(IDOK);
}

// Process ON_BN_CLICKED on CB1
afx_msg void CSampleDialog::OnCB1()
{
```

6

```
CButton *cb1ptr = (CButton *) GetDlgItem(IDD_CB1);

// toggle check box
if(cb1ptr->GetCheck()) cb1ptr->SetCheck(0);
else cb1ptr->SetCheck(1);
}

CApp App; // instantiate the application
```

After following these steps, data is automatically transferred to your new check box control when the dialog box is created, and transferred to the global variable if the user selects OK. Data is not moved out if the user cancels the box.

Frankly, it is often easier to handle controls directly, rather than using the DDX/DDV functions. This is especially true for the simple controls, such as push buttons, check boxes, and the like. However, you will find the DDX/DDV functions useful if you use Microsoft's application and class wizards to generate the framework for your programs. Since the purpose of this book is to show the details and fundamentals of MFC programming, the examples will continue to manage controls manually, without using the DDX/DDV functions. However, if automating the exchange and validation of data affected by controls within a dialog box is important to you, then you will want to explore the DDX/DDV subsystem of functions.

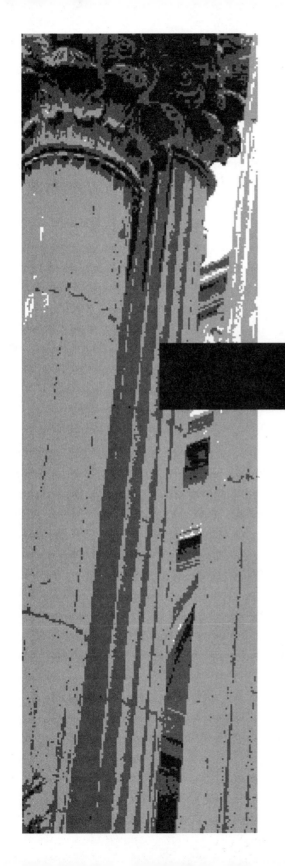

CHAPTER 7

Working with Icons, Cursors, and Bitmaps

This chapter explains how to control the appearance of two important items linked with all Windows applications: the icon and the mouse cursor. Up to this point, the programs in this book have used the icon and cursor defaults supplied by Windows. Here you will learn how to create your own custom versions of these items. In addition, you will see how to use other built-in icons and cursors defined by Windows. This chapter also shows how to display a bitmapped graphics image.

Icons, cursors, and bitmaps are resources that consist of graphical information. These resources are created using an *image editor*. (An image editor is generally supplied with a compiler that is capable of compiling Windows programs.) Once you have defined the nature of the icon, cursor, or bitmap, the image must be incorporated into the resource file associated with your program. Finally, before the image is used, it must be loaded by your program. This chapter discusses the necessary details required to accomplish this.

Defining an Icon and a Cursor

For the examples that will follow, you will need to create your own custom icon and cursor. As stated, when you create your own icons or cursors, you will need to use an image editor. An image editor displays an enlarged view of your icon or cursor. This allows you to easily construct or alter the image. For example, the custom icon and cursor shown in the examples is displayed inside the Microsoft image editor in Figure 7-1.

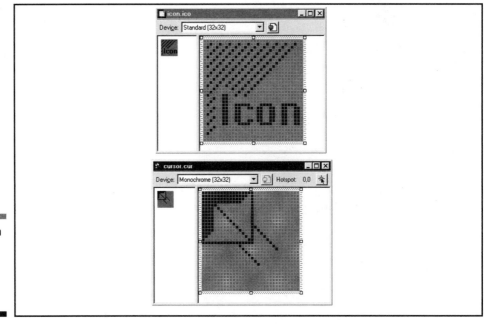

A custom icon and cursor within an image editor

Figure 7-1.

All cursors have the same size: 32 pixels by 32 pixels. For Windows 3.1, the standard icon associated with an application is also 32×32. However, if you are programming for 32-bit versions of Windows, such as Windows 95, Windows 98, or modern versions of Windows NT, then you will want to define two icons. The first is the standard icon, which is a 32×32 pixel bitmap. The second is the small icon, which is a 16×16 pixel bitmap. The small icon is not supported by older versions of Windows. The standard icon (also called the large icon) is used whenever a large icon is needed. For example, the standard icon is used when you select Large Icons in the Explorer. It is also used when an icon is moved to the desktop. The small icon is used for small icon display lists and is shown in the system menu box and the task bar. If you are using the Microsoft image editor provided with Visual C++, then you will be able to define both icons within the same icon file. If you fail to define a small icon, then the large icon is simply "shrunk" when a small icon is needed. Once you have defined both icons, MFC will automatically use the correct one. One final point: for modern versions of Windows you can also define 48×48 icons, but they are currently seldom used.

After you have defined the icon and cursor images, you will need to add an **ICON** and a **CURSOR** statement to your program's resource file. These statements have the following general forms:

7

> *IconName* ICON *filename*

> *CursorName* CURSOR *filename*

Here, *IconName* is the name that identifies the icon and *CursorName* is the name that identifies the cursor. These names are used by your program to refer to the icon and cursor. The *filename* specifies the file that holds the custom icon or cursor.

For the examples that follow, you should call your icon **MYICON** and your cursor **MYCURSOR**. Store your icon in a file called ICON.ICO and your cursor in a file CURSOR.CUR. Next, create the following resource file, called IC.RC:

```
MYCURSOR CURSOR CURSOR.CUR
MYICON ICON ICON.ICO
```

Changing the Icon and the Cursor

The window class of an application defines the attributes of the window, including the shape of the application's icon and mouse cursor. Up to this point, we have just been using the default class that is generated automatically by MFC when a frame window is created. However, to specify a custom icon and/or cursor requires that you define your own class. As mentioned in Chapter 2, to create your own window class, use the **AfxRegisterWndClass( )** function. Its prototype is shown here:

LPCSTR AFXAPI AfxRegisterWndClass(UINT *Style*,
                    HCURSOR *hCur* = 0, // cursor handle
                    HBRUSH *hBrush* = 0, // background color
                    HICON *hIcon* = 0); // icon handle

AfxRegisterWndClass( ) returns the name of the newly created class if successful. This name can then be passed to the **Create( )** function when a window is created.

The *Style* parameter specifies any additional style parameters that your window may require. Most of the time you can use the default style. In this case, specify *Style* as zero. The next three parameters specify the handles of three items that are defined by the window class: the shape of its cursor, the brush used to paint the background of the window, and its icon. That is, *hCur* specifies the handle of the cursor, *hBrush* specifies the handle of the brush used to paint the background of the client area of the window, and *hIcon* specifies the icon used by the window. It is important to understand that handles are not objects. Handles are used extensively in traditional-style Windows programs to identify various items. This is not the case in MFC because most items are encapsulated by objects—handles are not usually needed. However, handles *are* needed by the **AfxRegisterWndClass( )** function. Fortunately, MFC provides an easy means by which we can obtain these three handles. The next two sections explain how.

Loading the Icon and Cursor

To use a custom icon and mouse cursor, you must load the new icon and the new cursor and obtain their handles. To accomplish this you must use the functions **LoadIcon( )** and **LoadCursor( )**, which are members of the **CWinApp** class. The prototypes for the versions of these functions used in this chapter are shown here:

HICON CWinApp::LoadIcon(LPCSTR *lpszIconName*) const;

HCURSOR CWinApp::LoadCursor(LPCSTR *lpszCurName*) const;

lpszIconName specifies the name of an icon resource. *lpszCurName* specifies the name of a cursor. **LoadIcon( )** loads the specified icon and returns its handle. **LoadCursor( )** loads the specified cursor and returns its handle. The functions return **NULL** if the resource cannot be loaded.

Since both **LoadIcon( )** and **LoadCursor( )** return handles to their respective items, these handles can be used as parameters to **AfxRegisterWndClass( )**.

Obtaining a Background Brush

A detailed examination of brushes is deferred until Chapter 9 when various GDI objects are examined. However, in order to register a window class, you must pass the handle of the brush that will be used to paint the background color of the client area of the window. A *brush* is a resource that paints the screen using a predetermined size, color, and pattern. Your application can either define its own brush or use one of the predefined brushes. For the purposes of this chapter, we will use one of the built-in brushes to paint the background. (Later in this book you will see how to create your own brushes.) Brushes are encapsulated by the **CBrush** class, which is derived from **CGdiObject**.

7

To obtain a predefined brush, use the **CreateStockObject( )** function, which is a member of **CGdiObject**. It has this prototype:

BOOL CGdiObject::CreateStockObject(int *Item*);

Here, *Item* is the stock GDI item being obtained (which can be one of the stock brushes). Here are some of the built-in brushes available to your program:

Brush Macro	Background Type
BLACK_BRUSH	Black
DKGRAY_BRUSH	Dark gray
HOLLOW_BRUSH	See-through window
LTGRAY_BRUSH	Light gray
WHITE_BRUSH	White

The function returns nonzero if it can obtain the built-in item and zero otherwise.

To create a background brush for use with **AfxRegisterWndClass( )**, you will use the following sequence:

```
CBrush bkbrush;

// standard background
bkbrush.CreateStockObject(WHITE_BRUSH);
```

This creates a brush object and then links it with the stock white brush. After this sequence executes, you can use **bkbrush** as the **HBRUSH** parameter in **AfxRegisterWndClass( )**. This is because the **CBrush** class defines a conversion from **CBrush** to **HBRUSH**.

When you create a window using MFC's default window class, the background brush is white. That is, it uses the stock brush **WHITE_BRUSH**. This is the brush that the subsequent examples in this chapter will use, too. You might want to try using other brushes on your own, as an experiment.

A Sample Program That Demonstrates a Custom Icon and Cursor

The following program uses a custom icon and cursor. The icon will be shown whenever the program is represented in its iconic form. If you are running Windows 95/98/NT, then the small icon is displayed in the main window's system menu box and in the program's entry in the task bar. The standard icon will be used when you move your program to the desktop or view it using a large icon list. The cursor will be used when the mouse pointer is over the window. That is, the shape of the mouse cursor will automatically change to the one defined by your program when the mouse moves over the program's window. It will automatically revert to its default shape when it moves off the program's window.

Remember, before you try to compile this program, you must define the custom icons and cursor using an image editor and then add these resources to the resource file associated with the program. The custom icon and cursor program uses the following class derivation file, called IC.H:

```
// IC.H

// This is the main window class.
class CMainWin : public CFrameWnd
```

```
{
public:
  CMainWin(LPCSTR ClassName); // now includes class name parameter
  DECLARE_MESSAGE_MAP()
};

// This is the application class.
class CApp : public CWinApp
{
public:
  BOOL InitInstance();
};
```

Notice that the **CMainWin( )** constructor now includes a parameter that receives the class name when the main window is created. This parameter will be used when the frame window is created.

The program file, called IC.CPP, is shown here:

```
// A program that uses a custom cursor and icon.

#include <afxwin.h>
#include "ic.h"

// Construct window using custom class.
CMainWin::CMainWin(LPCSTR ClassName)
{
  Create(ClassName, "Custom Icon and Cursor");
}

// Initialize the application.
BOOL CApp::InitInstance()
{
  CBrush bkbrush;

  // standard background
  bkbrush.CreateStockObject(WHITE_BRUSH);

  LPCSTR cname = AfxRegisterWndClass(0,
                   LoadCursor("MYCURSOR"),
                   bkbrush,
                   LoadIcon("MYICON"));

  m_pMainWnd = new CMainWin(cname);
```

```
    m_pMainWnd->ShowWindow(m_nCmdShow);
    m_pMainWnd->UpdateWindow();

    return TRUE;
}

// This is the application's message map.
BEGIN_MESSAGE_MAP(CMainWin, CFrameWnd)
END_MESSAGE_MAP()

CApp App; // instantiate the application
```

Look carefully at the code inside **CApp::InitInstance( )**. First it creates a brush object and then initializes it to the stock, white brush. Next, a window class is registered using the custom icon and cursor and a stock brush. The class name returned by **AfxRegisterWndClass( )** is then passed as a parameter to **CMainWin( )**, which uses this class to construct the main window of the application. By specifying the name of a class in **Create( )**, a frame window with the attributes linked to that name will be created.

The custom icon is shown in the following illustration. (Of course, your custom icon may look different.) You will also see the small icon. The custom mouse cursor will appear when you move the mouse over the window. Try this before continuing.

Using the Built-in Cursors and Icons

Windows defines several of its own icons and cursors, which your program is free to use. However, you will not use **LoadIcon( )** or **LoadCursor( )** to load built-in icons or cursors. Instead, you will use **LoadStandardIcon( )** to load a predefined icon and **LoadStandardCursor( )** to load a predefined cursor. Their prototypes are shown here:

HICON CWinApp::LoadStandardIcon(LPCSTR *lpszIcon*) const;

HCURSOR CWinApp::LoadStandardCursor(LPCSTR *lpszCursor*) const;

Here, *lpszIcon* specifies the predefined icon and it must be one of these values:

Icon Macro	Shape
IDI_APPLICATION	Default icon
IDI_ASTERISK	Information icon
IDI_EXCLAMATION	Exclamation point icon
IDI_HAND	Stop sign
IDI_QUESTION	Question mark icon
IDI_WINLOGO	Windows Logo

lpszCursor specifies the name of a predefined cursor. Some of its common values are shown here:

Cursor Macro	Shape
IDC_ARROW	Default arrow pointer
IDC_CROSS	Cross hairs
IDC_IBEAM	Vertical I-beam
IDC_WAIT	Hourglass

7

Both functions return nonzero if successful and **NULL** on failure.

Here is a program that uses a predefined cursor and icon, beginning with its class derivation file, called SYSIC.H:

```
// SYSIC.H

// This is the main window class.
class CMainWin : public CFrameWnd
{
public:
  CMainWin(LPCSTR ClassName);
  DECLARE_MESSAGE_MAP()
};

// This is the application class.
class CApp : public CWinApp
{
public:
```

```
  BOOL InitInstance();
};
```

Here is the program file, called SYSIC.CPP:

```
// A program that uses a predefined cursor and icon.

#include <afxwin.h>
#include "sysic.h"

// Construct window using custom class.
CMainWin::CMainWin(LPCSTR ClassName)
{
  Create(ClassName, "Using a Predefined Icon and Cursor");
}

// Initialize the application.
BOOL CApp::InitInstance()
{
  CBrush bkbrush;

  // standard background
  bkbrush.CreateStockObject(WHITE_BRUSH);

  LPCSTR cname = AfxRegisterWndClass(0,
                 LoadStandardCursor(IDC_CROSS),
                 bkbrush,
                 LoadStandardIcon(IDI_QUESTION));

  m_pMainWnd = new CMainWin(cname);

  m_pMainWnd->ShowWindow(m_nCmdShow);
  m_pMainWnd->UpdateWindow();

  return TRUE;
}

// This is the application's message map.
BEGIN_MESSAGE_MAP(CMainWin, CFrameWnd)
END_MESSAGE_MAP()

CApp App; // instantiate the application
```

When you run this program, its icon will be the standard question mark icon, and the mouse cursor will change into a set of cross hairs when it is moved over the client area.

Using a Bitmap

A bitmap is a graphics image. Since Windows is a graphics-based operating system, it makes sense that you can include graphics images in your applications. It is important to understand that you can draw graphics images such as lines, circles, and boxes, inside the client area of a window using the rich set of graphics functions contained in the Windows API and encapsulated by MFC. However, a bitmap, and the mechanism used to display one, is separate from those types of graphics. A bitmap is a self-contained graphical resource that your program utilizes as a single entity. A bitmap contains a bit-by-bit representation of the image that ultimately will be displayed on the screen. Put differently, a bitmap contains a complete image that your program generally displays in its totality. Bitmaps are encapsulated by the **CBitmap** class.

Creating a Bitmap

Before continuing, you must create a bitmap resource if you wish to try the sample program that displays a bitmap. As with other graphical resources, you must use an image editor to create your bitmap. Unlike icons and cursors that have a fixed size, the size of a custom bitmap is under your control. To use the example that follows, your bitmap must be 64 × 64 pixels. Call your bitmap file BP.BMP. Next, create a resource file, called BMP.RC, that contains the following line:

7

```
MYBP1 BITMAP BP.BMP
```

As you can guess, the **BITMAP** resource command defines a bitmap resource. Its general form is shown here:

BitmapName BITMAP *filename*

Here, *BitmapName* is the name that identifies the bitmap. This name is used by your program to refer to the bitmap. The *filename* specifies the file that holds the bitmap.

Displaying a Bitmap

Once you have created a bitmap and included it in your application's resource file, you may display it as many times as you want. However, displaying a bitmap requires a little more work than using a custom cursor or icon. The following discussion explains the proper procedure.

To use a bitmap, you must create a **CBitmap** object and then load the bitmap specified in your program's resource file into this object. To load the bitmap, use the member function **LoadBitmap( )**. The prototype for the form used in this chapter is shown here:

BOOL CBitmap::LoadBitmap(LPCSTR *lpszBitmapName*);

Here, *lpszBitmapName* specifies the name of the bitmap. The function returns nonzero if successful or zero on failure.

The following fragment declares a bitmap object and loads a bitmap called **MYBIT**:

```
CBitmap bit;

bit.LoadBitmap("MYBIT");
```

Loading a bitmap is only half the story. When it comes time to display the bitmap, your program must follow these four steps:

1. Obtain the device context so that your program can output to the window.
2. Obtain an equivalent memory device context that will hold the bitmap until it is displayed. (A bitmap is held in memory until it is copied to your window.)
3. Select the bitmap into the memory device context.
4. Finally, copy the bitmap from the memory device context to the window device context. This causes the bitmap to actually be displayed.

To see how the preceding four steps can be implemented, consider the following fragment. It causes a bitmap to be displayed each time the left mouse button is pressed. (It assumes that the bitmap has already been loaded and is stored in a **CBitmap** object called **m_bmp1**.)

```
// Display the bitmap.
afx_msg void CMainWin::OnLButtonDown(UINT flags, CPoint loc)
{
  CClientDC DC(this);
  CDC memDC;

  // create a compatible DC
  memDC.CreateCompatibleDC(&DC);
```

```
    // Select bitmap into memory DC
    memDC.SelectObject(&m_bmp1);

    // copy bitmap to window DC
    DC.BitBlt(loc.x, loc.y, 64, 64, &memDC, 0, 0, SRCCOPY);
}
```

Let's examine this code, step by step. First, two device contexts are declared. **DC** will hold the current window device context. The other, called **memDC**, is an uninitialized device context that will be used to hold the device context of the memory that stores the bitmap. Next, a memory device context is created that will hold the bitmap. This DC will be compatible with the window device context. The compatible memory device context is created using the **CDC** member function **CreateCompatibleDC( )**. Its prototype is shown here:

   virtual BOOL CDC::CreateCompatibleDC(CDC *pDC);

This function creates a memory DC that is compatible with the device context pointed to by *pDC*. This memory will be used to construct an image before it is actually displayed. The function returns nonzero if successful and zero if an error occurs.

Before a bitmap can be displayed, it must be selected into the memory device context using the **SelectObject( )** member function. Since there can be several bitmaps associated with an application, you must select the one you want to display before it can actually be output to the window. The **SelectObject( )** function has several forms since it can be used to select several different types of objects. The prototype for the one used to select a bitmap is shown here:

   CBitmap *CDC:: SelectObject(CBitmap *pBitmap);

Here, *pBitmap* is a pointer to the bitmap object being selected into the device context. The function returns a pointer to the previously selected object, allowing it to be reselected later, if desired. **NULL** is returned on error. It is important to understand that a bitmap can be selected only into a memory device context—it cannot be selected into a window DC, for example.

To actually display the object once it has been selected, use the **BitBlt( )** function. This function copies a bitmap from the source device context to that of the invoking object. Its prototype is shown here:

   BOOL CDC::BitBlt(int *X*, int *Y*, int *Width*, int *Height*, CDC *pSourceDC*,
          int *SourceX*, int *SourceY*, DWORD *dwRasterOp*);

7

Here, *X* and *Y* are the upper-left coordinates at which point the bitmap will be drawn. The width and height of the bitmap are specified in *Width* and *Height*. The *pSourceDC* parameter is a pointer to the source device context, which in this case will be the memory context obtained using **CreateCompatibleDC( )**. *SourceX* and *SourceY* specify the upper-left coordinates in the bitmap. These values are usually 0. The value of *dwRasterOp* determines how the bit-by-bit contents of the bitmap will actually be drawn on the screen. Some of its most common values are shown here:

dwRasterOp Macro	Effect
SRCAND	ANDs bitmap with current destination.
SRCCOPY	Copies bitmap as is, overwriting existing information.
SRCINVERT	XORs bitmap with current destination.
SRCPAINT	ORs bitmap with current destination.

The function returns nonzero if successful and zero otherwise.

In the example, the call to **BitBlt( )** displays the entire bitmap at the destination location at which the left mouse button was pressed, copying the bitmap to the window.

A bitmap is a resource that must be removed before your application ends. Generally, this is done automatically when a **CBitmap** object is destroyed. However, you can delete a bitmap manually by calling the function **CGdiObject::DeleteObject( )**, which has the following prototype:

    BOOL CGdiObject::DeleteObject( );

The function returns nonzero if successful and zero on failure.

The Complete Bitmap Example Program

Here is a program that displays a custom bitmap each time you press the left mouse button. The bitmap is displayed at the location pointed to by the mouse. Sample output is shown in Figure 7-2. The class derivation file, BMP.H, is shown here:

```
// BMP.H

// This is the main window class.
```

```
class CMainWin : public CFrameWnd
{
public:
  CBitmap m_bmp1; // member bitmap object

  CMainWin();

  afx_msg void OnLButtonDown(UINT flags, CPoint loc);

  DECLARE_MESSAGE_MAP()
};

// This is the application class.
class CApp : public CWinApp
{
public:
  BOOL InitInstance();
};
```

Notice that the member variable **m_bmp1** has been added to **CMainWin**. This **CBitmap** object will be used to hold the bitmap. It is not technically necessary that the bitmap be a member of **CMainWin** (or any other class). It is just that it makes sense for this to be the case here.

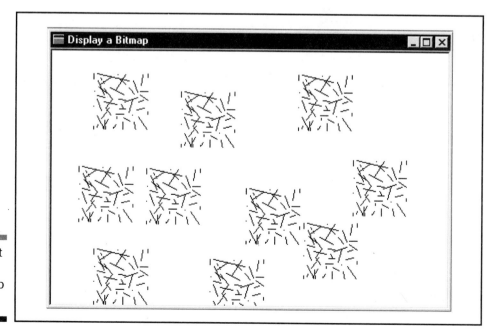

Sample output using the custom bitmap

Figure 7-2.

The bitmap program file, called BMP.CPP, is shown here:

```cpp
// A program that displays a bitmap.

#include <afxwin.h>
#include "bmp.h"


// Construct window.
CMainWin::CMainWin()
{
  Create(NULL, "Display a Bitmap");

  // load the bitmap
  m_bmp1.LoadBitmap("MYBP1");
}

// Initialize the application.
BOOL CApp::InitInstance()
{
  m_pMainWnd = new CMainWin();

  m_pMainWnd->ShowWindow(m_nCmdShow);
  m_pMainWnd->UpdateWindow();

  return TRUE;
}

// This is the application's message map.
BEGIN_MESSAGE_MAP(CMainWin, CFrameWnd)
  ON_WM_LBUTTONDOWN()
END_MESSAGE_MAP()

// Display the bitmap.
afx_msg void CMainWin::OnLButtonDown(UINT flags, CPoint loc)
{
  CClientDC DC(this);
  CDC memDC;

  // create a compatible DC
  memDC.CreateCompatibleDC(&DC);

  // Select bitmap into memory DC
  memDC.SelectObject(&m_bmp1);
```

```
  // copy bitmap to window DC
  DC.BitBlt(loc.x, loc.y, 64, 64, &memDC, 0, 0, SRCCOPY);
}

CApp App; // instantiate the application
```

As you can see, the bitmap is loaded inside the **CMainWin( )** constructor.
Since the bitmap will be displayed each time the left mouse button is pressed,
it makes sense to load the bitmap once, at the start of the program, so that it
is on hand when needed. This is not technically necessary—you could load
the bitmap each time the left mouse button is pressed, for example. However,
when you know in advance that you will be repeatedly using a resource, such
as a bitmap, it is better to load it once.

IN DEPTH

XORing an Image to a Window

7

As explained, **BitBlt( )** can copy the bitmap contained in one device
context into another device context a number of different ways. For
example, if you specify **SRCPAINT**, the image is ORed with the
destination. Using **SRCAND** causes the bitmap to be ANDed with the
destination. Perhaps the most interesting way to copy the contents of
one DC to another uses **SRCINVERT**. This method XORs the source
with the destination. There are two reasons this is particularly valuable.

First, XORing an image onto a window guarantees that the image will be
visible. It doesn't matter what color or colors the source image or the
destination uses, a XORed image is always visible. Second, XORing an
image to the same destination twice removes the image and restores the
destination to its original condition. As you might guess, XORing is an
efficient way to temporarily display and then remove an image from a
window without disturbing its original contents.

To see the effects of XORing an image to a window, you can modify the
preceding sample by handling the **WM_RBUTTONUP** and
WM_RBUTTONDOWN messages. First, declare these two handler
functions in your main window class in the file BMP.H.

```
afx_msg void OnRButtonUp(UINT nFlags, CPoint point);
afx_msg void OnRButtonDown(UINT nFlags, CPoint point);
```

Next, add the **WM_RBUTTONUP** and **WM_RBUTTONDOWN** messages to your message map, located in the program file.

```
ON_WM_RBUTTONUP()
ON_WM_RBUTTONDOWN()
```

Finally, add the following code to your program file.

```
// XOR the bitmap.
afx_msg void CMainWin::OnRButtonDown(UINT flags, CPoint loc)
{
  CClientDC DC(this);
  CDC memDC;

  // create a compatible DC
  memDC.CreateCompatibleDC(&DC);

  // Select bitmap into memory DC
  memDC.SelectObject(&m_bmp1);

  // XOR image onto the window
  DC.BitBlt(loc.x, loc.y, 64, 64, &memDC, 0, 0, SRCINVERT);
}

afx_msg void CMainWin::OnRButtonUp(UINT flags, CPoint loc)
{
  CClientDC DC(this);
  CDC memDC;

  // create a compatible DC
  memDC.CreateCompatibleDC(&DC);

  // Select bitmap into memory DC
  memDC.SelectObject(&m_bmp1);
```

```
   // XOR image onto the window
   DC.BitBlt(loc.x, loc.y, 64, 64, &memDC, 0, 0, SRCINVERT);
}
```

Notice that both the button-down and button-up handlers do exactly the same thing.

The code works like this: Each time the right mouse button is pressed, the bitmap is XORed to the window starting at the location of the mouse pointer. This causes an inverted image of the bitmap to be displayed. When the button is released, the image is XORed a second time, causing the bitmap to be removed and the previous contents to be restored.

Using Multiple Bitmaps

Before concluding the topic of bitmaps, one last point must be emphasized: It is possible (indeed, easy) to use more than one bitmap within your program. Your application can include as many bitmaps as necessary. Whenever you need to display one, simply select the desired bitmap and display it using the method described in the previous section.

7

To illustrate how easy it is to use multiple bitmaps, let's add another one to the preceding program. The second bitmap will be displayed when you press the right mouse button. To begin, add this line to your resource file, BMP.RC:

```
MYBP2 BITMAP BP2.BMP
```

Then, using an image editor, create a second 64 × 64 pixel bitmap. When you are done, save the second bitmap in a file called BP2.BMP.

Next, enter this class derivation file, calling it BMP2.H. It is an updated version of the previous class derivation file.

```
// BMP2.H

// This is the main window class.
class CMainWin : public CFrameWnd
{
public:
```

```
CBitmap m_bmp1, m_bmp2; // bitmap members

CMainWin();

afx_msg void OnLButtonDown(UINT flags, CPoint loc);
afx_msg void OnRButtonDown(UINT flags, CPoint loc);

DECLARE_MESSAGE_MAP()
};

// This is the application class.
class CApp : public CWinApp
{
public:
  BOOL InitInstance();
};
```

This version adds the **m_bmp2** bitmap object and the **OnRButtonDown( )** message handler to **CMainWin**.

Below is the updated program file—call it BMP2.CPP. It loads the second bitmap, adds **ON_WM_RBUTTONDOWN** to the message map, and implements the **OnRButtonDown( )** message handler.

```
// A program that displays two bitmaps.

#include <afxwin.h>
#include "bmp2.h"


// Construct window.
CMainWin::CMainWin()
{
  Create(NULL, "Display Two Bitmaps");

  m_bmp1.LoadBitmap("MYBP1");
  m_bmp2.LoadBitmap("MYBP2");
}

// Initialize the application.
BOOL CApp::InitInstance()
{
  m_pMainWnd = new CMainWin();

  m_pMainWnd->ShowWindow(m_nCmdShow);
```

```
   m_pMainWnd->UpdateWindow();

   return TRUE;
}

// This is the application's message map.
BEGIN_MESSAGE_MAP(CMainWin, CFrameWnd)
  ON_WM_LBUTTONDOWN()
  ON_WM_RBUTTONDOWN()
END_MESSAGE_MAP()

// Display first bitmap.
afx_msg void CMainWin::OnLButtonDown(UINT flags, CPoint loc)
{
  CClientDC DC(this);
  CDC memDC;

  // create a compatible DC
  memDC.CreateCompatibleDC(&DC);

  // Select bitmap into memory DC
  memDC.SelectObject(&m_bmp1);

  // copy bitmap to window DC
  DC.BitBlt(loc.x, loc.y, 64, 64, &memDC, 0, 0, SRCCOPY);
}

// Display second bitmap.
afx_msg void CMainWin::OnRButtonDown(UINT flags, CPoint loc)
{
  CClientDC DC(this);
  CDC memDC;

  // create a compatible DC
  memDC.CreateCompatibleDC(&DC);

  // Select bitmap into memory DC
  memDC.SelectObject(&m_bmp2);

  // copy bitmap to window DC
  DC.BitBlt(loc.x, loc.y, 64, 64, &memDC, 0, 0, SRCCOPY);
}

CApp App; // instantiate the application
```

7

After making these changes, the program will display the first bitmap when you press the left mouse button. It will display the second bitmap when you press the right mouse button. Sample output from the dual-bitmap program is shown in Figure 7-3.

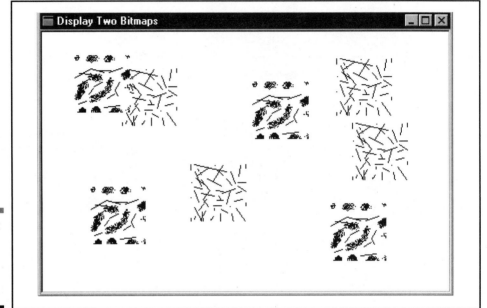

Sample output
from the
dual-bitmap
program
Figure 7-3.

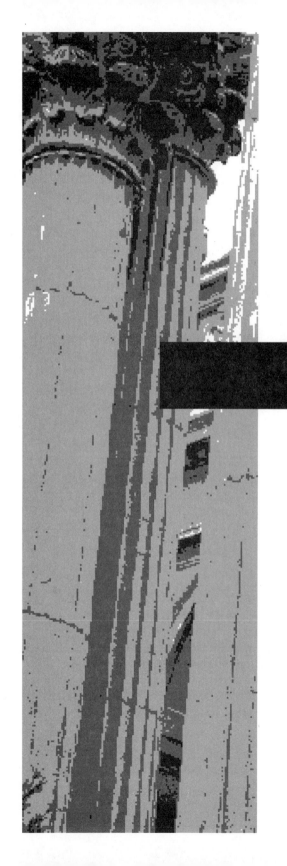

CHAPTER 8

Managing Text and Solving the Repaint Problem

For the past several chapters, output has been handled using message and dialog boxes—the client area of the window has been ignored. However, this chapter returns to the client area and explores various ways that you can manage text output to using MFC. Also, some important techniques are developed that make it easier for you to repaint the window when it has been overwritten. The chapter concludes with a discussion of how additional text fonts can be used by your application.

As with most other aspects of the Windows environment, you, the programmer, have virtually unlimited control over the way that text is displayed and managed within the client area of a window. As such, it is far beyond the scope of this chapter to cover all features relating to text manipulation in Windows. However, you will be able to easily explore other related topics after understanding the basics introduced here.

This chapter begins with a discussion of the window coordinate system and how text is mapped to it. Then several MFC member functions are described. These functions help you control and manage text output to the client area of a window.

Window Coordinates

As you know, **CDC::TextOut( )** is MFC's text output function. It displays a string at the specified coordinates, which are always relative to the window. Therefore, where a window is positioned on the screen has no effect upon the coordinates passed to **TextOut( )**. By default, the upper-left corner of the client area of the window is location 0,0. The X value increases to the right and the Y value increases downward.

So far, we have been using window coordinates for **TextOut( )** and for positioning various elements within a dialog box without any specific mention of to what those coordinates actually refer. Now is the time to clarify a few details. First, the coordinates that are specified in **TextOut( )** are *logical coordinates*. That is, the units used by **TextOut( )** (and other window display functions, including the graphics functions described in Chapter 9) are *logical units*. Windows maps these logical units onto pixels when output is actually displayed. The reason that we haven't had to worry about this distinction is that, by default, logical units are the same as pixels. In other words, by default, logical units are pixels. It is important to understand, however, that different mapping modes can be selected in which this convenient default will not be the case.

Setting the Text and Background Color

By default, when you output text to the window using **TextOut( )**, it is shown as black text against the current background. However, you can determine both the color of the text and the background color using the **CDC** member functions **SetTextColor( )** and **SetBkColor( )**. Their prototypes are shown here:

virtual COLORREF CDC::SetTextColor(COLORREF *Color*);

virtual COLORREF CDC::SetBkColor(COLORREF *Color*);

The **SetTextColor( )** function sets the current text color of the invoking device context to that specified by *Color* (or closest color that the display device is capable of displaying). The **SetBkColor( )** function sets the current text background color to that specified by *Color* (or nearest possible). For both functions, the previous color setting is returned.

The color is specified as a value of type **COLORREF**, which is a 32-bit integer. Windows allows colors to be specified in three different ways. The first, and by far most common, way is as an RGB (red, green, blue) value. In an RGB value, the relative intensities of the three colors are combined to produce the actual color. The second way a color can be specified is as an index into a logical palette. The third is as an RGB value relative to a palette. In this chapter, only the first way will be discussed.

8

A **COLORREF** value that holds an RGB color is passed to either **SetTextColor( )** or **SetBkColor( )** using the following encoding:

Byte	Color
Byte 0 (low-order byte)	Red
Byte 1	Green
Byte 2	Blue
Byte 3 (high-order byte)	Must be zero

Each color in an RGB value is in the range 0 through 255, with 0 being the lowest intensity and 255 being the brightest intensity.

Although you are free to manually construct a **COLORREF** value, Windows defines the macro **RGB( )** that does this for you. It has this general form:

COLORREF RGB(BYTE *red*, BYTE *green*, BYTE *blue*);

Here, *red*, *green*, and *blue* must be values in the range 0 through 255. Therefore, to create bright magenta, use **RGB(255, 0, 255)**. To create white, use **RGB(255, 255, 255)**. To create black, use **RGB(0, 0, 0)**. To create other colors, combine the three basic colors in varying intensities. For example, **RGB(0, 100, 100)** creates a light aqua. You can experiment to determine which colors are best for your application.

Setting the Background Display Mode

You can control the way that the background is affected when text is displayed on the screen by using the **SetBkMode( )** function, whose prototype is shown here:

int CDC::SetBkMode(int *mode*);

This function determines what happens to the current background color when text (and some other types of output) is displayed. The background mode of the invoking device context is set as specified by *mode*, which must be one of these two macros: **OPAQUE** or **TRANSPARENT**. The function returns the previous setting.

If *mode* is **OPAQUE**, then each time text is output, the background is changed to that of the current background color. If *mode* is **TRANSPARENT**, then the background is not altered. In this case, any effects of a call to **SetBkColor( )** are ignored. By default, the background mode is **OPAQUE**.

Obtaining the Text Metrics

As you know from Chapter 3, characters are not all the same dimension. That is, in Windows, most text fonts are proportional. Therefore, the character "i" is not as wide as the character "w." Also, the height of each character and of descenders varies between fonts. In addition, the amount of space between horizontal lines is also changeable. That these (and other) attributes are variable would not be of too much consequence except for the fact that Windows demands that you, the programmer, manually manage virtually all text output.

Windows provides only the minimal support for text output to the client area of a window. The main output function is **TextOut( )**. This function will only display a string of text beginning at a specified location. It will not format output or even automatically perform a carriage return/linefeed sequence, for example. Instead, managing output to the client window is completely your job.

Given that the size of each font may be different (and that fonts may be changed while your program is executing), there must be some way to determine the dimensions and various other attributes of the currently selected font. For example, writing one line of text after another implies that you have some way of knowing how tall the font is and how many pixels are between lines. The **CDC** member function that obtains information about the current font is called **GetTextMetrics( )**, and it has this prototype:

BOOL CDC::GetTextMetrics(LPTEXTMETRIC *lpTextAttrib*) const;

Here, *lpTextAttrib* is a pointer to a structure of type **TEXTMETRIC**, which upon return, will contain the text metrics for the currently selected font in the invoking device context. The function returns nonzero if successful and zero on failure. The **TEXTMETRIC** structure is defined as shown here:

8

```
typedef struct tagTEXTMETRIC
{
  LONG tmHeight; // total height of font
  LONG tmAscent; // height above base line
  LONG tmDescent; // length of descenders
  LONG tmInternalLeading; // space above characters
  LONG tmExternalLeading; // space between rows
  LONG tmAveCharWidth; // average width
  LONG tmMaxCharWidth; // maximum width
  LONG tmWeight;    // weight
  LONG tmOverhang; // extra width added to special fonts
  LONG tmDigitizedAspectX; // horizontal aspect
  LONG tmDigitizedAspectY; // vertical aspect
  BYTE tmFirstChar; // first character in font
  BYTE tmLastChar; // last character in font
  BYTE tmDefaultChar; // default character
  BYTE tmBreakChar; // character used to break words
  BYTE tmItalic; // non-zero if italic
  BYTE tmUnderlined; // non-zero if underlined
  BYTE tmStruckOut; // non-zero if struckout
  BYTE tmPitchAndFamily; // pitch and family of font
  BYTE tmCharSet; // character set identifier
} TEXTMETRIC;
```

While most of the values obtained by this function will not be used in this chapter, two are very important because they are used to compute the vertical distance between lines of text. This value is needed if you want to output more than one line of text to a window. Unlike a console-based application in which there is only one font of fixed size, there may be several Windows fonts and they may vary in size. Specifically, each font defines the height of its characters and the amount of space required between lines. This means that it is not possible to know in advance the vertical (Y) coordinate of the next line of text. To determine where the next line of text will begin you must call **GetTextMetrics( )** to acquire two values: the character height and the amount of space between lines. These values are given in the **tmHeight** and **tmExternalLeading** fields, respectively. By adding together these two values, you obtain the number of vertical units between lines.

NOTE: Remember that the value **tmExternalLeading** contains, in essence, the number of vertical units that should be left blank between lines of text. This value is separate from the height of the font. Thus, both values are needed to compute where the next line of text will begin. You will see this applied shortly.

NEWTEXTMETRIC and NEWTEXTMETRICEX

While the **TEXTMETRIC** structure has served and continues to serve well, there are two enhanced versions of **TEXTMETRIC** that have been recently created. The first is called **NEWTEXTMETRIC**. It is exactly the same as **TEXTMETRIC** except for four additional fields. These fields provide support for TrueType fonts. (TrueType fonts provide superior scalability features.) The new fields for **NEWTEXTMETRIC** are shown here:

```
DWORD ntmFlags; /* indicates style of font */
UINT ntmSizeEM; /* size of an em */
UINT ntmCellHeight; /* font height */
UINT ntmAvgWidth; /* average character width */
```

An extension to **NEWTEXTMETRIC**, called **NEWTEXTMETRICEX**, is the second enhanced version of **TEXTMETRIC**. It has the following definition:

```
typedef struct tagNEWTEXTMETRICEX
{
  NEWTEXTMETRIC ntmentm;
  FONTSIGNATURE ntmeFontSignature; /* font signature */
} NEWTEXTMETRICEX;
```

As you can see, it includes all of **NEWTEXTMETRIC** and adds the structure **FONTSIGNATURE**, which contains information relating to Unicode and code pages.

While **GetTextMetrics( )** does not currently make use of either **NEWTEXTMETRIC** or **NEWTEXTMETRICEX**, it might in the future. These structures are used by a few API functions, however, and they may be of value to applications that you create. As Windows continues to evolve, you can expect the use of these two structures to expand.

8

Computing the Length of a String

Because characters in the current font are not the same size, it is not possible to know the length of a string, in logical units, by simply knowing how many characters are in it. That is, the result returned by **strlen( )** is not meaningful to managing output to a window because characters are of differing widths. To solve this problem, the **CDC** class includes the function **GetTextExtent( )**, whose prototype is shown here:

CSize CDC::GetTextExtent(LPCSTR *lpszString*, int *Len*) const;

Here, the string whose length you want is pointed to by *lpszString*. The number of characters in the string is specified in *Len*. The width and height of the string, in logical units, are returned in a **CSize** object. **CSize** encapsulates the standard Windows **SIZE** structure, which is defined as follows:

```
typedef struct tagSIZE {
  LONG cx; // width
  LONG cy; // height
} SIZE;
```

Upon return from a call to **GetTextExtent( )**, the **cx** field will contain the length of the string. Therefore, this value can be used to determine the starting point for the next string to be displayed if you want to continue on from where the previous output left off.

Obtaining the System Metrics

Although Windows maintains and automatically translates logical coordinates into pixels, sometimes you will want to know the actual display size of the computer being used to run your application. To obtain this and other information, use the **GetSystemMetrics( )** API function, whose prototype is shown here:

int GetSystemMetrics(int *what*);

Notice that this function is not a member of an MFC class. Since system-wide information is independent of any application, we will simply use the standard API function to obtain system metrics. Here, *what* is a value that specifies the metric that you want to obtain. **GetSystemMetrics( )** can obtain many different values. The values for screen coordinates are returned in pixel units. Following are the macros for some common values:

Value	Metric Obtained
SM_CXFULLSCREEN	Width of maximized client area
SM_CYFULLSCREEN	Height of maximized client area
SM_CXICON	Width of large icon
SM_CYICON	Height of large icon
SM_CXSMICON	Width of small icon
SM_CYSMICON	Height of small icon
SM_CXSCREEN	Width of entire screen
SM_CYSCREEN	Height of entire screen

A Short Text Demonstration

Now that you have learned about some of Windows' text functions, a short demonstration of these features will be useful. Here is the program's resource file:

```
// TEXT.RC

#include <afxres.h>
#include "ids.h"

TextMenu MENU
{
  POPUP "Demonstrate Text"
  {
    MENUITEM "&Show\tF2", IDM_SHOW
    MENUITEM "&Reset\tF3", IDM_RESET
    MENUITEM "E&xit\tF4", IDM_EXIT
  }

  MENUITEM "&Help", IDM_HELP
}

TextMenu ACCELERATORS
{
  VK_F2, IDM_SHOW, VIRTKEY
  VK_F3, IDM_RESET, VIRTKEY
  VK_F4, IDM_EXIT, VIRTKEY
  VK_F1, IDM_HELP, VIRTKEY
}
```

The header file IDS.H is shown here. The value **IDM_FONT** is not used until later in this chapter.

```
// IDS.H

#define IDM_SHOW    100
#define IDM_RESET   101
#define IDM_FONT    102
#define IDM_EXIT    103
#define IDM_HELP    104
```

The class derivation file for the program is shown here. Call it TEXT.H.

```
// TEXT.H

// This is the main window class.
```

```
class CMainWin : public CFrameWnd
{
public:
  int m_X, m_Y; // current output location
  char m_str[255]; // holds output string

  CMainWin();

  afx_msg void OnShow();
  afx_msg void OnReset();
  afx_msg void OnExit();
  afx_msg void OnHelp();

  DECLARE_MESSAGE_MAP()
};

// This is the application class.
class CApp : public CWinApp
{
public:
  BOOL InitInstance();
};
```

The program file is shown here:

```
// Demonstrate text output.
#include <afxwin.h>
#include <string.h>
#include "text.h"
#include "ids.h"

int maxX, maxY; // screen dimensions

CMainWin::CMainWin()
{
  Create(NULL, "Demonstrate Text Output",
         WS_OVERLAPPEDWINDOW, rectDefault,
         NULL, "TextMenu");

  // Load accelerator table
  if(!LoadAccelTable("TextMenu"))
    MessageBox("Cannot Load Accelerators", "Error");

  m_X = m_Y = 0;
```

```
    maxX = GetSystemMetrics(SM_CXSCREEN);
    maxY = GetSystemMetrics(SM_CYSCREEN);
}

// Initialize the application.
BOOL CApp::InitInstance()
{
  m_pMainWnd = new CMainWin;
  m_pMainWnd->ShowWindow(m_nCmdShow);
  m_pMainWnd->UpdateWindow();

  return TRUE;
}

// This is the application's message map.
BEGIN_MESSAGE_MAP(CMainWin, CFrameWnd)
  ON_COMMAND(IDM_SHOW, OnShow)
  ON_COMMAND(IDM_RESET, OnReset)
  ON_COMMAND(IDM_EXIT, OnExit)
  ON_COMMAND(IDM_HELP, OnHelp)
END_MESSAGE_MAP()

// Process IDM_EXIT.
afx_msg void CMainWin::OnExit()
{
  int response;

  response = MessageBox("Quit the Program?",
                        "Exit", MB_YESNO);

  if(response == IDYES)
    SendMessage(WM_CLOSE); // terminate app
}

// Process IDM_HELP.
afx_msg void CMainWin::OnHelp()
{
   MessageBox("Text Demo", "Help");
}

// Display text.
afx_msg void CMainWin::OnShow()
{
  CClientDC DC(this);
  TEXTMETRIC tm;
```

8

```
  CSize size;

  // set text color to black
  DC.SetTextColor(RGB(0, 0, 0));

  // set background color to turquoise
  DC.SetBkColor(RGB(0, 255, 255));

  // get text metrics
  DC.GetTextMetrics(&tm);

  wsprintf(m_str, "The font is %ld pixels high.", tm.tmHeight);
  DC.TextOut(m_X, m_Y, m_str, strlen(m_str)); // output string
  m_Y = m_Y + tm.tmHeight + tm.tmExternalLeading; // next line

  strcpy(m_str, "This is on the next line. ");
  DC.TextOut(m_X, m_Y, m_str, strlen(m_str)); // output string

  // compute length of a string
  size = DC.GetTextExtent(m_str, strlen(m_str));

  wsprintf(m_str, "Previous string is %ld units long", size.cx);
  m_X = size.cx; // advance to end of previous string
  DC.TextOut(m_X, m_Y, m_str, strlen(m_str));
  m_Y = m_Y + tm.tmHeight + tm.tmExternalLeading; // next line
  m_X = 0; // reset X coordinate

  wsprintf(m_str, "Screen dimensions: %d %d", maxX, maxY);
  DC.TextOut(m_X, m_Y, m_str, strlen(m_str));
  m_Y = m_Y + tm.tmHeight + tm.tmExternalLeading; // next line
}

// Reset screen coordinates and erase window.
afx_msg void CMainWin::OnReset()
{
  m_X = m_Y = 0;
}

CApp App; // instantiate the application
```

Enter these files and compile and run the program. Each time you select Show from the Demonstrate Text menu, you will cause a few lines of text to be displayed. The text will be black and the background turquoise. Sample output is shown in Figure 8-1.

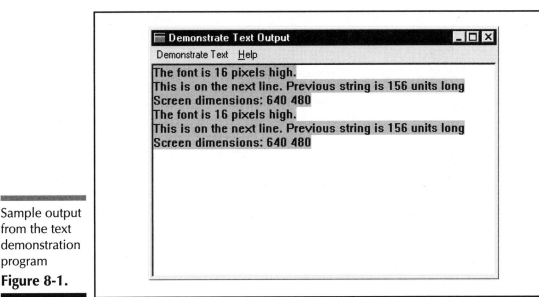

Sample output
from the text
demonstration
program

Figure 8-1.

When the window is created, the global integers **maxX** and **maxY** are initialized to the coordinates of the screen using the **GetSystemMetrics( )** function. While these values serve no special purpose in this program, they will in later examples.

Notice that **CMainWin** declares two member variables called **m_X** and **m_Y** and initializes both of these to 0 when a window is constructed. These variables will contain the current window location at which text will be displayed. They will be continually updated by the program after each output sequence.

The interesting part of this program is mostly contained within the **OnShow( )** message handler. Let's examine it closely. Each time **OnShow( )** is called, a device context is obtained. Then, the text color is set to black and the background color is set to turquoise. Since the device context is obtained each time an **IDM_SHOW** message is received, the colors must be set each time. That is, they cannot be set once, at the start of the program for example.

After the colors have been set, the text metrics are obtained. Next, the first line of text is output. Notice that it is constructed using **wsprintf( )** and then actually output using **TextOut( )**. As you know from earlier in this book, neither **TextOut( )** nor any other output function performs text formatting,

8

so it is up to you, the programmer, to construct your output first and then display it using **TextOut( )**. After the string is displayed, the **m_Y** coordinate is advanced to the next line by applying the formula developed earlier.

The program then continues by outputting the line "This is on the next line." Then, before that string is overwritten by the next call to **wsprintf( )**, its length is computed using a call to **GetTextExtent( )**. This value is then used to advance the **m_X** coordinate to the end of the previous line before the next line is printed. Notice that here the **m_Y** coordinate is unchanged. This causes the next string to be displayed immediately following the previous one on the same line. Before continuing, the program advances **m_Y** to the next line and resets **m_X** to 0, which is the leftmost coordinate. This causes subsequent output to once again be started at the beginning of the next line. Finally, the screen dimensions are displayed and the **m_Y** coordinate is advanced to the next line.

Each time you select Show, the text is displayed lower down in the window and does not overwrite the preceding text. Instead each set of lines is displayed beneath the previous set.

To start over, select Reset from the Demonstrate Text menu. This causes the coordinates to be reset to 0,0.

Solving the Repaint Problem

While the preceding program demonstrates some text handling functions, it reintroduces a fundamental problem that was first discussed in Chapter 3. The problem is this: When you run the program, display some text, and then overlay the window with another, the text is lost. When the window is then redisplayed, the part of the text that was covered will be missing. Of course, the reason for this is that each program must repaint its window when it receives a **WM_PAINT** message and the preceding program does not do this. However, this raises the larger question: What mechanism should one use to restore the contents of a window that has been overwritten? As mentioned in Chapter 3, there are three basic methods. First, you can regenerate the output if that output is created by some computational method. Second, you can store a record of display events and "replay" those events. Third, you can maintain a virtual window and simply copy the contents of the virtual window each time a **WM_PAINT** message is received. The most general of these is, of course, the third mechanism, and this is the method that will be developed here. As you will see, Windows and MFC provide substantial support for this method.

Virtual Window Theory

Here is how output will be accomplished using a virtual window. First, a memory device context is created that is compatible with the window DC. Then, all output is written to the memory device context. Each time a **WM_PAINT** message is received, the contents of the memory device context are copied into the physical DC, causing output to be displayed on the screen. Because all output has been written to the memory DC, there is always a record of the current contents of the physical window. Whenever the physical window is covered and then uncovered, a **WM_PAINT** message will be sent to your program, causing the contents of the virtual window to be copied to the physical window, restoring it. As you will see, this scheme is surprisingly easy to implement and convenient to use.

Some Additional API Functions

Implementing a virtual window requires the use of several MFC member functions. Four have been discussed already. These are **CreateCompatibleDC( )**, **SelectObject( )**, **CreateStockObject( )**, and **BitBlt( )**. We will also be using **CreateCompatibleBitmap( )** and **PatBlt( )**, which are described here.

CreateCompatibleBitmap( ) creates a bitmap that is compatible with a specified device context. Further, this bitmap can be used by any memory device context that is compatible with the specified DC. **CreateCompatibleBitmap( )** is a member of **CBitmap** and its prototype is shown here:

BOOL CBitmap::CreateCompatibleBitmap(CDC *pDC, int *Width*,
                                            int *Height*);

Here, the dimensions of the bitmap are specified in *Width* and *Height*. These values are in pixels. The function returns nonzero if successful or zero on failure.

PatBlt( ) fills a rectangle with the color and pattern of the currently selected brush. It is a member of **CDC**. Filling an area using a brush is also commonly referred to as *painting* the region. **PatBlt( )** has this prototype:

BOOL CDC::PatBlt(int *X*, int *Y*, int *Width*, int *Height*,
                    DWORD *dwRasterOp*);

8

Here, the coordinates *X* and *Y* specify the upper-left corner of the region to be filled. The width and height of the region are specified in *Width* and *Height*. The value passed in *dwRasterOp* determines how the brush will be applied. It must be one of the following macros:

dwRasterOp	Meaning
BLACKNESS	Region is black (brush is ignored)
WHITENESS	Region is white (brush is ignored)
PATCOPY	Brush is copied to region
PATINVERT	Brush is ORed to region
DSTINVERT	Region is inverted (brush is ignored)

Therefore, if you wish to apply the current brush unaltered, you would select **PATCOPY** for the value of *dwRasterOp*. The function returns nonzero if successful, zero otherwise.

Now that you know about the functions that will be used, it is time to see how to implement a virtual window.

Creating and Using a Virtual Window

Let's begin by restating the procedure that will be implemented. To create an easy and convenient means of restoring a window after a **WM_PAINT** message has been received, a virtual window will be maintained and all output will be written to that virtual window. Each time a repaint request is received, the contents of the virtual window are copied into the window that is physically on the screen. Now, let's implement this approach.

Creating the Virtual Window

First, a memory device context must be created that is compatible with the device context of the main window (i.e., the physical window). This will be done only once, when the main window is being created, inside the **CMainWin( )** constructor. This compatible device context will stay in existence the entire time the program is executing. Since the virtual window will be tightly linked to the main window of the program, the variables that support the virtual window will be members of the **CMainWin** class. These member variables are shown here:

```
CDC m_memDC; // virtual window device context
CBitmap m_bmp; // virtual window bitmap
CBrush m_bkbrush; // brush for virtual window
```

Here is the portion of code from **CMainWin( )** that constructs the virtual window:

```
maxX = GetSystemMetrics(SM_CXSCREEN);
maxY = GetSystemMetrics(SM_CYSCREEN);

CClientDC DC(this);

// Create bitmap for virtual window
m_memDC.CreateCompatibleDC(&DC);
m_bmp.CreateCompatibleBitmap(&DC, maxX, maxY);
m_memDC.SelectObject(&m_bmp);

// use standard background
m_bkbrush.CreateStockObject(WHITE_BRUSH);
m_memDC.SelectObject(&m_bkbrush);
// paint background of virtual window
m_memDC.PatBlt(0, 0, maxX, maxY, PATCOPY);
```

Let's examine this code carefully. First, the dimensions of the screen are obtained. They will be used to create a compatible bitmap. Next, the current device context is obtained. This DC is then used to create a compatible memory device context. Then, a compatible bitmap is created. This establishes a one-to-one mapping between the virtual window and the physical window. The dimensions of the bitmap are those of the maximum screen size. This ensures that the bitmap will always be large enough to fully restore the window regardless of the window's size. (Actually, slightly smaller values could be used, since the borders aren't repainted, but this minor improvement is left to you, as an exercise.) The bitmap is then selected into the memory DC. Next, a stock white brush is obtained. This brush is selected into the memory device context and then **PatBlt( )** paints the entire virtual window using the brush. Thus, the virtual window will have a white

8

background, which matches the background of the physical window in the example program that follows. (Remember, these colors are under your control. The colors used here are arbitrary.) Finally, the physical device context is released when **DC** goes out-of-scope. However, the memory device context stays in existence until the program ends.

Using the Virtual Window

Once the virtual window has been created, all output is directed to it. (The only time output is actually directed to the physical window is when a **WM_PAINT** message is received.) For example, here is a reworked version of the **OnShow( )** message handler from the previous program, which uses the virtual window.

```
// Display text using virtual window.
afx_msg void CMainWin::OnShow()
{
  TEXTMETRIC tm;
  CSize size;

  // set text color to black
  m_memDC.SetTextColor(RGB(0, 0, 0));

  // set background color to turquoise
  m_memDC.SetBkColor(RGB(0, 255, 255));

  // get text metrics
  m_memDC.GetTextMetrics(&tm);

  wsprintf(m_str, "The font is %ld pixels high.", tm.tmHeight);
  m_memDC.TextOut(m_X, m_Y, m_str,
                  strlen(m_str)); // output string
  m_Y = m_Y + tm.tmHeight + tm.tmExternalLeading; // next line

  strcpy(m_str, "This is on the next line. ");
  m_memDC.TextOut(m_X, m_Y, m_str,
                  strlen(m_str)); // output string

  // compute length of a string
  size = m_memDC.GetTextExtent(m_str, strlen(m_str));
```

```
wsprintf(m_str, "Previous string is %ld units long", size.cx);
m_X = size.cx; // advance to end of previous string
m_memDC.TextOut(m_X, m_Y, m_str, strlen(m_str));
m_Y = m_Y + tm.tmHeight + tm.tmExternalLeading; // next line
m_X = 0; // reset X coordinate

wsprintf(m_str, "Screen dimensions: %d %d", maxX, maxY);
m_memDC.TextOut(m_X, m_Y, m_str, strlen(m_str));
m_Y = m_Y + tm.tmHeight + tm.tmExternalLeading; // next line
InvalidateRect(NULL);
}
```

As you can see, this version directs all output to **m_memDC**. It calls **InvalidateRect( )** to cause the physical window to be updated.

Each time a **WM_PAINT** message is received, the contents of the virtual device are copied into the physical device. This is accomplished by the following **OnPaint( )** handler:

```
// Update screen using contents of virtual window.
afx_msg void CMainWin::OnPaint()
{
  CPaintDC DC(this);

  DC.BitBlt(0, 0, maxX, maxY, &m_memDC, 0, 0, SRCCOPY);
}
```

8

The **BitBlt( )** function is used to copy the image from **m_memDC** to the physical window. Remember, the parameter **SRCCOPY** simply means to copy the image as is without alteration directly from the source to the target. Because all output has been stored in **m_memDC**, this statement causes that output to actually be displayed. More important, if the window is covered and then uncovered, **WM_PAINT** will be received and this code causes the contents of that window to be restored automatically.

As stated earlier, there are many ways to approach the restoring of a window, but the method just developed is applicable to a wide range of situations and is, generally, quite efficient. Also, since your program is passed the coordinates of the region that must be repainted, you can actually make the preceding routine more efficient by simply restoring only that part of the window that has been destroyed. (You might want to try implementing this enhancement on your own.)

The Entire Virtual Window Demonstration Program

Here is the complete program that demonstrates using a virtual window. It uses the same resource file and IDS.H header file as the previous program. Its class derivation file, called VIRTWIN.H, is shown here:

```
// VIRTWIN.H

// This is the main window class.
class CMainWin : public CFrameWnd
{
public:
  int m_X, m_Y; // current output location
  char m_str[255]; // holds output string
  CDC m_memDC; // virtual window device context
  CBitmap m_bmp; // virtual window bitmap
  CBrush m_bkbrush; // brush for virtual window

  CMainWin();

  afx_msg void OnPaint();

  afx_msg void OnShow();
  afx_msg void OnReset();
  afx_msg void OnExit();
  afx_msg void OnHelp();

  DECLARE_MESSAGE_MAP()
};

// This is the application class.
class CApp : public CWinApp
{
public:
  BOOL InitInstance();
};
```

The program file is shown here:

```
// Demonstrate text output.
#include <afxwin.h>
#include <string.h>
#include "virtwin.h"
#include "ids.h"
```

```
int maxX, maxY; // screen dimensions

CMainWin::CMainWin()
{
  Create(NULL, "Demonstrate Text Output",
         WS_OVERLAPPEDWINDOW, rectDefault,
         NULL, "TextMenu");

  // Load accelerator table
  if(!LoadAccelTable("TextMenu"))
    MessageBox("Cannot Load Accelerators", "Error");

  m_X = m_Y = 0;

  maxX = GetSystemMetrics(SM_CXSCREEN);
  maxY = GetSystemMetrics(SM_CYSCREEN);

  CClientDC DC(this);

  // Create bitmap for virtual window
  m_memDC.CreateCompatibleDC(&DC);
  m_bmp.CreateCompatibleBitmap(&DC, maxX, maxY);
  m_memDC.SelectObject(&m_bmp);

  // use standard background
  m_bkbrush.CreateStockObject(WHITE_BRUSH);
  m_memDC.SelectObject(&m_bkbrush);
  // paint background of virtual window
  m_memDC.PatBlt(0, 0, maxX, maxY, PATCOPY);
}

// Initialize the application.
BOOL CApp::InitInstance()
{
  m_pMainWnd = new CMainWin;
  m_pMainWnd->ShowWindow(m_nCmdShow);
  m_pMainWnd->UpdateWindow();

  return TRUE;
}

// This is the application's message map.
BEGIN_MESSAGE_MAP(CMainWin, CFrameWnd)
  ON_WM_PAINT()
```

```
  ON_COMMAND(IDM_SHOW, OnShow)
  ON_COMMAND(IDM_RESET, OnReset)
  ON_COMMAND(IDM_EXIT, OnExit)
  ON_COMMAND(IDM_HELP, OnHelp)
END_MESSAGE_MAP()

// Update screen using contents of virtual window.
afx_msg void CMainWin::OnPaint()
{
  CPaintDC DC(this);

  DC.BitBlt(0, 0, maxX, maxY, &m_memDC, 0, 0, SRCCOPY);
}


// Process IDM_EXIT.
afx_msg void CMainWin::OnExit()
{
  int response;

  response = MessageBox("Quit the Program?",
                        "Exit", MB_YESNO);

  if(response == IDYES)
    SendMessage(WM_CLOSE); // terminate app
}

// Process IDM_HELP.
afx_msg void CMainWin::OnHelp()
{
    MessageBox("Text Demo", "Help");
}

// Display text using a virtual window.
afx_msg void CMainWin::OnShow()
{
  TEXTMETRIC tm;
  CSize size;

  // set text color to black
  m_memDC.SetTextColor(RGB(0, 0, 0));

  // set background color to turquoise
```

```
m_memDC.SetBkColor(RGB(0, 255, 255));

// get text metrics
m_memDC.GetTextMetrics(&tm);

wsprintf(m_str, "The font is %1d pixels high.", tm.tmHeight);
m_memDC.TextOut(m_X, m_Y, m_str,
                strlen(m_str)); // output string
m_Y = m_Y + tm.tmHeight + tm.tmExternalLeading; // next line

strcpy(m_str, "This is on the next line. ");
m_memDC.TextOut(m_X, m_Y, m_str,
                strlen(m_str)); // output string

// compute length of a string
size = m_memDC.GetTextExtent(m_str, strlen(m_str));

wsprintf(m_str, "Previous string is %1d units long", size.cx);
m_X = size.cx; // advance to end of previous string
m_memDC.TextOut(m_X, m_Y, m_str, strlen(m_str));
m_Y = m_Y + tm.tmHeight + tm.tmExternalLeading; // next line
m_X = 0; // reset X coordinate

wsprintf(m_str, "Screen dimensions: %d %d", maxX, maxY);
m_memDC.TextOut(m_X, m_Y, m_str, strlen(m_str));
m_Y = m_Y + tm.tmHeight + tm.tmExternalLeading; // next line
InvalidateRect(NULL);
}

// Reset screen coordinates and erase window.
afx_msg void CMainWin::OnReset()
{
  m_X = m_Y = 0;
  m_memDC.PatBlt(0, 0, maxX, maxY, PATCOPY);
  InvalidateRect(NULL);
}

CApp App; // instantiate the application
```

8

When you run this program you will see two immediate improvements. First, each time you cover and then uncover the window, the contents are restored. Second, choosing Reset also causes the window to be cleared. This is accomplished by calling **PatBlt( )**, which repaints the background.

Changing Fonts

As you probably know, one of the main purposes of Windows is to provide complete control over the user interface. As such, it has a rich and varied set of text-based features you can use. One of its strongest text-based features is its collection of various type fonts. Using Windows you have several built-in type fonts from which to choose. You can also create custom fonts. Both of these topics are discussed here.

Using Built-in Fonts

The built-in fonts are stock objects that are selected using the MFC function **CreateStockObject( )**, which was described in Chapter 7. At the time of this writing, MFC supports seven built-in fonts. The macros associated with these fonts are shown here:

Font Macro	Description
ANSI_FIXED_FONT	Fixed-pitch font
ANSI_VAR_FONT	Variable-pitch font
DEVICE_DEFAULT_FONT	Default device font
DEFAULT_GUI_FONT	Font used by dialog boxes, etc.
OEM_FIXED_FONT	OEM defined font
SYSTEM_FONT	Font used by Windows
SYSTEM_FIXED_FONT	Font used by older versions of Windows

The system fonts are those character fonts used by Windows for things such as menus and dialog boxes. Older versions of Windows used a fixed-pitch system font, but beginning with Windows 3.0 a variable font was used. Of course, all 32-bit versions of Windows, including Windows 95, Windows 98, and Windows NT use the variable font.

Selecting and using a built-in font is very easy. To do so, your program must first create a font object of type **CFont**. Next, it must load the desired font, using **CreateStockObject( )**. To switch to the font, select the font using **SelectObject( )** with the new font as a parameter. **SelectObject( )** will return a pointer to the old font, which you may want to save so that you can switch back to it after you have finished using the other font. Keep in mind that the object pointed to by the return value of **SelectObject( )** may be temporary, however.

The following program demonstrates changing fonts. It adds another menu selection to the previous resource file called Change Font. Each time it is selected, the font is toggled between the default system font and the ANSI variable font. The program uses the same IDS.H header file described earlier. Here is the system-font program's resource file:

```
// SYSFONT.RC

#include <afxres.h>
#include "ids.h"

TextMenu MENU
{
  POPUP "Demonstrate Text"
  {
    MENUITEM "&Show\tF2", IDM_SHOW
    MENUITEM "&Reset\tF3", IDM_RESET
    MENUITEM "&Change Font\tF4", IDM_FONT
    MENUITEM "E&xit\tF5", IDM_EXIT
  }

  MENUITEM "&Help", IDM_HELP
}

TextMenu ACCELERATORS
{
  VK_F2, IDM_SHOW, VIRTKEY
  VK_F3, IDM_RESET, VIRTKEY
  VK_F4, IDM_FONT, VIRTKEY
  VK_F5, IDM_EXIT, VIRTKEY
  VK_F1, IDM_HELP, VIRTKEY
}
```

The class derivation file, called SYSFONT.H, is shown here:

```
// SYSFONT.H

// This is the main window class.
class CMainWin : public CFrameWnd
{
public:
```

8

```
  int m_X, m_Y; // current output location
  char m_str[255]; // holds output string
  CDC m_memDC; // virtual window device context
  CBitmap m_bmp; // virtual window bitmap
  CBrush m_bkbrush; // brush for virtual window
  CFont m_SystemFont, m_AnsiVarFont; // font objects

  CMainWin();

  afx_msg void OnPaint();

  afx_msg void OnShow();
  afx_msg void OnFont();
  afx_msg void OnReset();
  afx_msg void OnExit();
  afx_msg void OnHelp();

  DECLARE_MESSAGE_MAP()
};

// This is the application class.
class CApp : public CWinApp
{
public:
  BOOL InitInstance();
};
```

The system-font program file is shown here:

```
// Demonstrate built-in fonts.
#include <afxwin.h>
#include <string.h>
#include "sysfont.h"
#include "ids.h"

int maxX, maxY; // screen dimensions

CMainWin::CMainWin()
{
  Create(NULL, "Demonstrate Built-in Fonts",
         WS_OVERLAPPEDWINDOW, rectDefault,
         NULL, "TextMenu");

  // Load accelerator table
  if(!LoadAccelTable("TextMenu"))
```

```
        MessageBox("Cannot Load Accelerators", "Error");

    m_X = m_Y = 0;

    maxX = GetSystemMetrics(SM_CXSCREEN);
    maxY = GetSystemMetrics(SM_CYSCREEN);

    CClientDC DC(this);

    // Create bitmap for virtual window
    m_memDC.CreateCompatibleDC(&DC);
    m_bmp.CreateCompatibleBitmap(&DC, maxX, maxY);
    m_memDC.SelectObject(&m_bmp);

    // use standard background
    m_bkbrush.CreateStockObject(WHITE_BRUSH);
    m_memDC.SelectObject(&m_bkbrush);
    // paint background of virtual window
    m_memDC.PatBlt(0, 0, maxX, maxY, PATCOPY);

    // initialize built-in font objects
    m_AnsiVarFont.CreateStockObject(ANSI_VAR_FONT);
    m_SystemFont.CreateStockObject(SYSTEM_FONT);
}

// Initialize the application.
BOOL CApp::InitInstance()
{
    m_pMainWnd = new CMainWin;
    m_pMainWnd->ShowWindow(m_nCmdShow);
    m_pMainWnd->UpdateWindow();

    return TRUE;
}

// This is the application's message map.
BEGIN_MESSAGE_MAP(CMainWin, CFrameWnd)
    ON_WM_PAINT()
    ON_COMMAND(IDM_SHOW, OnShow)
    ON_COMMAND(IDM_FONT, OnFont)
    ON_COMMAND(IDM_RESET, OnReset)
    ON_COMMAND(IDM_EXIT, OnExit)
    ON_COMMAND(IDM_HELP, OnHelp)
END_MESSAGE_MAP()
```

8

```
// Update screen using contents of virtual window.
afx_msg void CMainWin::OnPaint()
{
  CPaintDC DC(this);

  DC.BitBlt(0, 0, maxX, maxY, &m_memDC, 0, 0, SRCCOPY);
}

// Process IDM_EXIT.
afx_msg void CMainWin::OnExit()
{
  int response;

  response = MessageBox("Quit the Program?",
                        "Exit", MB_YESNO);

  if(response == IDYES)
    SendMessage(WM_CLOSE); // terminate app
}

// Process IDM_HELP.
afx_msg void CMainWin::OnHelp()
{
    MessageBox("Text Demo", "Help");
}

// Display text.
afx_msg void CMainWin::OnShow()
{
  TEXTMETRIC tm;
  CSize size;

  // set text color to black
  m_memDC.SetTextColor(RGB(0, 0, 0));

  // get text metrics
  m_memDC.GetTextMetrics(&tm);

  wsprintf(m_str, "The font is %1d pixels high.", tm.tmHeight);
  m_memDC.TextOut(m_X, m_Y, m_str,
                  strlen(m_str)); // output string
  m_Y = m_Y + tm.tmHeight + tm.tmExternalLeading; // next line

  strcpy(m_str, "This is on the next line. ");
  m_memDC.TextOut(m_X, m_Y, m_str,
```

```
                            strlen(m_str)); // output string

   // compute length of a string
   size = m_memDC.GetTextExtent(m_str, strlen(m_str));

   wsprintf(m_str, "Previous string is %1d units long", size.cx);
   m_X = size.cx; // advance to end of previous string
   m_memDC.TextOut(m_X, m_Y, m_str, strlen(m_str));
   m_Y = m_Y + tm.tmHeight + tm.tmExternalLeading; // next line
   m_X = 0; // reset X coordinate

   wsprintf(m_str, "Screen dimensions: %d %d", maxX, maxY);
   m_memDC.TextOut(m_X, m_Y, m_str, strlen(m_str));
   m_Y = m_Y + tm.tmHeight + tm.tmExternalLeading; // next line
   InvalidateRect(NULL);
}

// Reset screen coordinates.
afx_msg void CMainWin::OnReset()
{
  m_X = m_Y = 0;
  m_memDC.PatBlt(0, 0, maxX, maxY, PATCOPY);
  InvalidateRect(NULL);
}

// Change fonts.
afx_msg void CMainWin::OnFont()
{
  static whichfont = 0;

  if(!whichfont) {
    m_memDC.SelectObject(&m_AnsiVarFont);
    whichfont = 1;
  }
  else {
    m_memDC.SelectObject(&m_SystemFont);
    whichfont = 0;
  }
}

CApp App; // instantiate the application
```

Sample output produced by this program is shown in Figure 8-2.

8

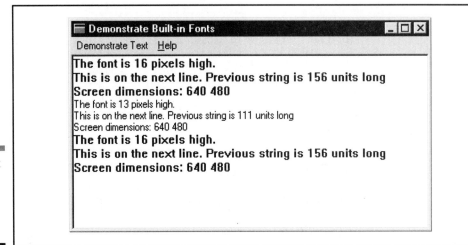

Sample output
from the
built-in font
program

Figur 8-2.

Creating Custom Fonts

Although it may sound complex, it is actually very easy to create a custom type font. There are two major advantages to doing this. First, a custom font gives your application a unique look that will set it apart. Second, creating your own font lets you control precisely what occurs when text is output. Before beginning, it is important to understand that you will not be defining a new font. Instead, you will be tailoring an existing font so that it meets the specifications you desire. (That is, you don't need to define the shape of each character in the font that you create.)

To create your own font, use the **CFont** member function **CreateFont( )**, whose prototype is shown here:

```
BOOL CFont::CreateFont(int Height, int Width, int Escapement,
                       int Orientation, int Weight,
                       BYTE Ital, BYTE Underline,
                       BYTE StrikeThru, BYTE Charset,
                       BYTE Precision, BYTE ClipPrecision,
                       BYTE Quality, BYTE Pitch,
                       LPCSTR FontName);
```

The height of the font is passed in *Height*. If *Height* is zero, then a default size is used. The width of the font is specified in *Width*. If *Width* is zero, then

Windows chooses an appropriate value based upon the current aspect ratio. Both *Height* and *Width* are in terms of logical units.

Text can be output at any angle within the window. The angle at which it is displayed is determined by the *Escapement* parameter. For normal, horizontal text, this value should be zero. Otherwise, it specifies the number of 1/10 degree increments through which the text should be rotated. For example, a value of 900 causes the text to be rotated 90 degrees, causing output to be vertical.

The angle of each individual character can also be specified using the *Orientation* parameter. It, too, uses 1/10 degree increments to specify the angle of each character relative to horizontal.

Weight specifies the preferred weight of the font in the range of zero to 1000. A value of zero specifies the default weight. To specify a normal weight, use 400; for bold, use 700. You can also use any of the following macros to specify the font weight.

```
FW_DONTCARE
FW_THIN
FW_EXTRALIGHT
FW_ULTRALIGHT
FW_LIGHT
FW_NORMAL
FW_REGULAR
FW_MEDIUM
FW_SEMIBOLD
FW_DEMIBOLD
FW_BOLD
FW_EXTRABOLD
FW_ULTRABOLD
FW_BLACK
FW_HEAVY
```

8

To create an italic font, specify *Ital* as nonzero. Otherwise, this parameter should be zero.

To create an underlined font, specify *Underline* as nonzero. Otherwise, this parameter should be zero.

To create a strike-through font, specify *StrikeThru* as nonzero. Otherwise, this parameter should be zero.

Charset indicates which character set is desired. The example that follows uses **ANSI_CHARSET**. *Precision* specifies the preferred output precision. This determines just how closely the output must match the requested font's characteristics. The example in this chapter uses **OUT_DEFAULT_PRECIS**. *ClipPrecision* specifies the preferred clipping precision. Clipping precision references just how each character that extends beyond the clipping region is to be "clipped." The value used by the example in this chapter is **CLIP_DEFAULT_PRECIS**.

Quality determines how closely the logical font will be matched with the actual physical fonts provided for the requested output device. It can be one of these three values:

    DEFAULT_QUALITY
    DRAFT_QUALITY
    PROOF_QUALITY

Pitch specifies the pitch and family of the font. There are three pitch choices:

    DEFAULT_PITCH
    FIXED_PITCH
    VARIABLE_PITCH

There are six possible font families:

    FF_DECORATIVE
    FF_DONTCARE
    FF_MODERN
    FF_ROMAN
    FF_SCRIPT
    FF_SWISS

To create the value for *Pitch*, OR together one pitch value and one font family value.

A pointer to the name of the font is passed in *FontName*. This name cannot be longer than 32 characters. The font you specify must be installed in your system.

If successful, **CreateFont( )** returns nonzero. On failure, zero is returned. It is important to understand that the **CreateFont( )** function does *not* technically create a new font. It simply tailors as closely as possible, based on the information that you specify, the actual physical fonts available in the system.

Fonts created using **CreateFont( )** must be deleted before your program ends. This will normally be done automatically by the **CFont** destructor. However, to delete a font manually, call **DeleteObject( )**.

Here is a program that demonstrates two custom fonts. The first is based upon Courier New, the second upon Century Gothic. Each time you choose the Change Font menu item, a new font is selected and displayed. This program uses the same resource file and IDS.H header file as the program in the preceding section. Its class derivation file, called USERFONT.H, is shown here:

```
// USERFONT.H

// This is the main window class.
class CMainWin : public CFrameWnd
{
public:
  int m_X, m_Y; // current output location
  char m_str[255]; // holds output string
  CDC m_memDC; // virtual window device context
  CBitmap m_bmp; // virtual window bitmap
  CBrush m_bkbrush; // brush for virtual window
  CFont m_SystemFont; // built-in font
  CFont m_CourierNew, m_CenturyGothic; // custom fonts
  char m_fontname[80]; // holds name of font

  CMainWin();

  afx_msg void OnPaint();

  afx_msg void OnShow();
  afx_msg void OnFont();
  afx_msg void OnReset();
  afx_msg void OnExit();
  afx_msg void OnHelp();

  DECLARE_MESSAGE_MAP()
};

// This is the application class.
class CApp : public CWinApp
{
public:
  BOOL InitInstance();
};
```

8

The custom font program file is shown here:

```
// Demonstrate custom fonts.
#include <afxwin.h>
#include <string.h>
#include "userfont.h"
#include "ids.h"

int maxX, maxY; // screen dimensions

CMainWin::CMainWin()
{
  Create(NULL, "Demonstrate Custom Fonts",
         WS_OVERLAPPEDWINDOW, rectDefault,
         NULL, "TextMenu");

  // Load accelerator table
  if(!LoadAccelTable("TextMenu"))
    MessageBox("Cannot Load Accelerators", "Error");

  m_X = m_Y = 0;

  maxX = GetSystemMetrics(SM_CXSCREEN);
  maxY = GetSystemMetrics(SM_CYSCREEN);

  CClientDC DC(this);

  // Create bitmap for virtual window
  m_memDC.CreateCompatibleDC(&DC);
  m_bmp.CreateCompatibleBitmap(&DC, maxX, maxY);
  m_memDC.SelectObject(&m_bmp);

  // use standard background
  m_bkbrush.CreateStockObject(WHITE_BRUSH);
  m_memDC.SelectObject(&m_bkbrush);
  // paint background of virtual window
  m_memDC.PatBlt(0, 0, maxX, maxY, PATCOPY);

  // initialize system font object
  m_SystemFont.CreateStockObject(SYSTEM_FONT);

  // initialize custom fonts
  m_CourierNew.CreateFont(14, 0, 0, 0, FW_NORMAL,
                          0, 0, 0, ANSI_CHARSET,
                          OUT_DEFAULT_PRECIS,
```

```
                                  CLIP_DEFAULT_PRECIS,
                                  DEFAULT_QUALITY,
                                  DEFAULT_PITCH | FF_DONTCARE,
                                  "Courier New");

  m_CenturyGothic.CreateFont(20, 0, 0, 0, FW_SEMIBOLD,
                                  0, 0, 0, ANSI_CHARSET,
                                  OUT_DEFAULT_PRECIS,
                                  CLIP_DEFAULT_PRECIS,
                                  DEFAULT_QUALITY,
                                  DEFAULT_PITCH | FF_DONTCARE,
                                  "Century Gothic");

  strcpy(m_fontname, "Default");
}

// Initialize the application.
BOOL CApp::InitInstance()
{
  m_pMainWnd = new CMainWin;
  m_pMainWnd->ShowWindow(m_nCmdShow);
  m_pMainWnd->UpdateWindow();

  return TRUE;
}

// This is the application's message map.
BEGIN_MESSAGE_MAP(CMainWin, CFrameWnd)
  ON_WM_PAINT()
  ON_COMMAND(IDM_SHOW, OnShow)
  ON_COMMAND(IDM_FONT, OnFont)
  ON_COMMAND(IDM_RESET, OnReset)
  ON_COMMAND(IDM_EXIT, OnExit)
  ON_COMMAND(IDM_HELP, OnHelp)
END_MESSAGE_MAP()

// Update screen using contents of virtual window.
afx_msg void CMainWin::OnPaint()
{
  CPaintDC DC(this);

  DC.BitBlt(0, 0, maxX, maxY, &m_memDC, 0, 0, SRCCOPY);
}

// Process IDM_EXIT.
```

8

```
afx_msg void CMainWin::OnExit()
{
  int response;

  response = MessageBox("Quit the Program?",
                        "Exit", MB_YESNO);

  if(response == IDYES)
    SendMessage(WM_CLOSE); // terminate app
}

// Process IDM_HELP.
afx_msg void CMainWin::OnHelp()
{
    MessageBox("Text Demo", "Help");
}

// Display text.
afx_msg void CMainWin::OnShow()
{
  TEXTMETRIC tm;
  CSize size;

  // set text color to black
  m_memDC.SetTextColor(RGB(0, 0, 0));

  // get text metrics
  m_memDC.GetTextMetrics(&tm);

  wsprintf(m_str, "%s is %ld pixels high.",
           m_fontname, tm.tmHeight);
  m_memDC.TextOut(m_X, m_Y, m_str,
                  strlen(m_str)); // output string
  m_Y = m_Y + tm.tmHeight + tm.tmExternalLeading; // next line

  strcpy(m_str, "This is on the next line. ");
  m_memDC.TextOut(m_X, m_Y, m_str,
                  strlen(m_str)); // output string

  // compute length of a string
  size = m_memDC.GetTextExtent(m_str, strlen(m_str));

  wsprintf(m_str, "Previous string is %ld units long", size.cx);
  m_X = size.cx; // advance to end of previous string
  m_memDC.TextOut(m_X, m_Y, m_str, strlen(m_str));
```

```
    m_Y = m_Y + tm.tmHeight + tm.tmExternalLeading; // next line
    m_X = 0; // reset X coordinate

    wsprintf(m_str, "Screen dimensions: %d %d", maxX, maxY);
    m_memDC.TextOut(m_X, m_Y, m_str, strlen(m_str));
    m_Y = m_Y + tm.tmHeight + tm.tmExternalLeading; // next line
    InvalidateRect(NULL);
}

// Reset screen coordinates.
afx_msg void CMainWin::OnReset()
{
    m_X = m_Y = 0;
    m_memDC.PatBlt(0, 0, maxX, maxY, PATCOPY);
    InvalidateRect(NULL);
}

// Change fonts.
afx_msg void CMainWin::OnFont()
{
    static whichfont = 0;

    switch(whichfont) {
        case 0:
            m_memDC.SelectObject(&m_CourierNew);
            whichfont = 1;
            strcpy(m_fontname, "Courier New");
            break;
        case 1:
            m_memDC.SelectObject(&m_CenturyGothic);
            whichfont = 2;
            strcpy(m_fontname, "Century Gothic");
            break;
        case 2:
            m_memDC.SelectObject(&m_SystemFont);
            whichfont = 0;
            strcpy(m_fontname, "Default");
            break;
    }
}

CApp App; // instantiate the application
```

8

Sample output is shown in Figure 8-3. Remember, Windows' support for fonts and text is quite rich. You will want to explore this area on your own. As you have seen, using MFC makes this process quite easy.

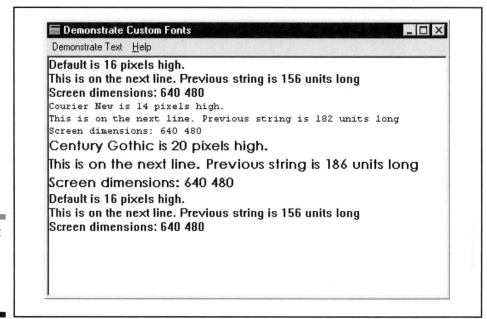

Sample output from the custom font program

Figure 8-3.

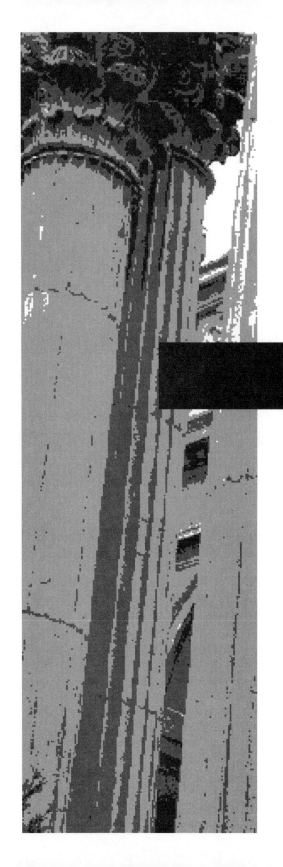

CHAPTER 9

Working with Graphics

Windows has a rich and flexible set of graphics functions available to the programmer. This is not surprising since it is a graphical operating system. However, what you might find surprising is how tightly integrated graphics are into the Windows display system. In fact, much of what you learned in the preceding chapter about text is applicable to graphics. For example, the same brush that is used to paint the window is used to fill an object. This chapter discusses and demonstrates several graphics functions.

This chapter also examines several features that control precisely how output is mapped to a window. Specifically, it discusses how to set the current mapping mode, how to change the logical coordinates associated with a window, and how to define a viewport. These factors have a profound effect on how both graphics and text are displayed.

Keep in mind that the discussion of graphics and related topics in this chapter only scratches the surface. The Windows graphics system is quite powerful, and you will want to explore it further on your own.

The Graphics Coordinate System

The graphics coordinate system is the same as that used by the text-based functions (discussed in Chapter 8). This means that, by default, the upper-left corner is location 0,0 and that logical units are equivalent to pixels. Remember that the coordinate system and the mapping of logical units to pixels is under your control and may be changed. You will see how, later in this chapter.

Windows maintains a *current position* that is used and updated by certain graphics functions. When your program begins, the current location is set to 0,0. Keep in mind that the location of the current position is completely invisible. That is, no graphics "cursor" is displayed. Instead, the current position is simply the next place in the window at which certain graphics functions will begin.

Pens and Brushes

The Windows graphics system is based upon two important objects: pens and brushes. You learned about stock brushes in Chapter 7. All of that information applies to the graphics functions described here as well. By default, closed graphics shapes, such as rectangles and ellipses, are filled using the currently selected brush. Pens are resources that draw the lines and curves specified by the various graphics functions. The default pen is black and one pixel thick. However, you can alter these attributes.

Until now, we have only been working with stock objects. In this chapter you will learn how to create custom brushes and pens.

Graphics Functions

Windows defines several graphics API functions. MFC encapsulates these functions within the **CDC** class. This section describes the most fundamental ones. There are a large number of additional graphics functions, including overloaded versions of the ones presented here, that you will want to explore on your own.

Setting a Pixel

You can set the color of any specific pixel using the **SetPixel( )** function. The form we will be using is shown here:

COLORREF CDC::SetPixel(int *X*, int *Y*, COLORREF *Color*);

Here, the point specified by *X,Y* is set to the color specified by *Color*. The function returns the actual color that the pixel is set to, which may differ slightly from that specified by *Color* because of device limitations. –1 is returned if an error occurs or if the location specified is outside the window.

NOTE: For many of the graphics functions, including **SetPixel( )**, MFC provides an overloaded form in which coordinates are specified using **POINT** structures. Therefore, if you would rather treat coordinate pairs as a single object, you will want to use these overloaded versions of the graphics functions.

9

Drawing a Line

To draw a line, use the **LineTo( )** function. This function draws a line using the currently selected pen. Its prototype is shown here:

BOOL CDC::LineTo(int *X*, int *Y*);

The line is drawn from the current graphics position to the coordinates specified by *X,Y*. The current position is then changed to *X,Y*. The function returns nonzero if successful (i.e., the line is drawn) and zero on failure.

Some programmers are surprised by the fact that **LineTo( )** uses the current position as its starting location and then sets the current position to the end point of the line that is drawn (instead of leaving it unchanged). However, there is a good reason for this. Many times, when displaying lines, one line will begin where the previous line ends. When this is the case, **LineTo( )** operates extremely efficiently because it avoids the additional overhead caused by an extra set of coordinate parameters. When this is not the case, you can set the current location to any position you like using the **MoveTo( )** function, described next, prior to calling **LineTo( )**.

Setting the Current Location

To set the current position, use the **MoveTo( )** function, whose prototype is shown here:

CPoint CDC::MoveTo(int *X*, int *Y*);

The coordinates of the new current position are specified by *X,Y*. The previous current position is returned as a **CPoint** object that encapsulates the standard **POINT** structure. **POINT** is defined as follows:

```
typedef struct tagPOINT {
  LONG x;
  LONG y;
} POINT;
```

Drawing an Arc

You can draw an elliptical arc (a portion of an ellipse) in the current pen color using the **Arc( )** function. The prototype for the version we will be using is shown here:

BOOL CDC::Arc(int *upX*, int *upY*, int *lowX*, int *lowY*,
              int *startX*, int *startY*, int *endX*, int *endY*);

The arc is defined by two objects. First, the arc is a portion of an ellipse that is bounded by the rectangle whose upper-left corner is at *upX,upY* and whose lower-right corner is at *lowX,lowY*. The portion of the ellipse that is actually drawn (i.e., the arc) starts at the intersection of a line from the center of the rectangle through the point specified by *startX,startY* and ends at the intersection of a line from the center of the rectangle through the point *endX,endY*. The arc is drawn counterclockwise starting from *startX,startY*. Figure 9-1 illustrates how **Arc( )** works. **Arc( )** returns nonzero if successful and zero on failure.

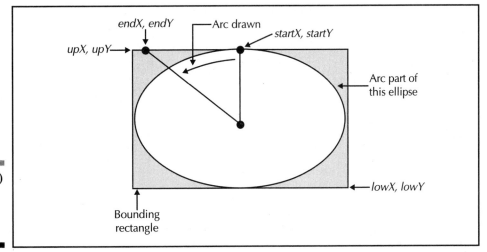

How the **Arc( )**
function
operates
Figure 9-1.

Displaying Rectangles

You can display a rectangle in the current pen using the **Rectangle( )**
function. The prototype for the version used in this chapter is shown here:

BOOL CDC::Rectangle(int *upX*, int *upY*, int *lowX*, int *lowY*);

The upper-left corner of the rectangle is specified by *upX,upY* and the
lower-right corner is specified by *lowX,lowY*. The function returns nonzero if
successful and zero if an error occurs. The rectangle is automatically filled
using the current brush.

You can display a rounded rectangle using the **RoundRect( )** function. A
rounded rectangle has its corners rounded slightly. The prototype for
RoundRect( ) is shown here:

BOOL CDC::RoundRect(int *upX*, int *upY*, int *lowX*, int *lowY*,
                    int *curveX*, int *curveY*);

The first four parameters are the same as for **Rectangle( )**. How the corners
are curved is determined by the values of *curveX* and *curveY*, which define the
width and the height of the ellipse that describes the curve. The function
returns nonzero if successful and zero if a failure occurs. The rounded
rectangle is automatically filled using the current brush.

9

Drawing Ellipses and Pie Slices

To draw an ellipse or a circle in the current pen, use the **Ellipse( )** function. The prototype for the version used in this chapter is shown here:

BOOL CDC::Ellipse(int *upX*, int *upY*, int *lowX*, int *lowY*);

The ellipse is defined by specifying its bounding rectangle. The upper-left corner of the rectangle is specified by *upX,upY* and the lower-right corner is specified by *lowX,lowY*. To draw a circle, specify a square.

Ellipse( ) returns nonzero if successful and zero if a failure occurs. The ellipse is filled using the current brush.

Related to the ellipse is the pie slice. A pie slice is an object that includes an arc and lines from each end point of the arc to the center. To draw a pie slice, use the **Pie( )** function. Its prototype is shown here:

BOOL CDC::Pie(int *upX*, int *upY*, int *lowX*, int *lowY*, int *startX*, int *startY*, int *endX*, int *endY*);

The arc of the slice is defined by two objects. First, the arc is a portion of an ellipse that is bounded by the rectangle whose upper-left corner is at *upX,upY* and whose lower-right corner is at *lowX,lowY*. The portion of the ellipse that is actually drawn (i.e., the arc of the slice) starts at the intersection of a line from the center of the rectangle through the point specified by *startX,startY* and ends at the intersection of a line from the center of the rectangle through the point *endX,endY*.

The slice is drawn in the current pen and filled using the current brush. The **Pie( )** function returns nonzero if successful and zero if an error occurs.

Working with Pens

Graphics objects are drawn using the current pen. In MFC, pens are encapsulated by the **CPen** class. The default pen is a black pen that is 1 pixel wide. There are three stock pens: black, white, and null. These can be obtained using **CreateStockObject( )**, discussed earlier in this book. The macros for these stock pens are **BLACK_PEN**, **WHITE_PEN**, and **NULL_PEN**, respectively.

Frankly, the stock pens are quite limited, and you will usually want to define your own pens for your application. This is accomplished by declaring a

CPen object and then calling **CreatePen( )**. There are several versions of this function. The one we will use is shown here:

BOOL CPen::CreatePen(int *Style*, int *Width*, COLORREF *Color*);

The *Style* parameter determines what type of pen is created. It must be one of the following values:

Style	Pen Style
PS_DASH	Dashed
PS_DASHDOT	Dash-dot
PS_DASHDOTDOT	Dash-dot-dot
PS_DOT	Dotted
PS_INSIDEFRAME	Solid pen that is within a bounded region
PS_NULL	None
PS_SOLID	Solid line

The dotted and/or dashed styles may be applied only to pens that are 1 unit thick. The **PS_INSIDEFRAME** pen is a solid pen that will be completely within the dimensions of any object that is drawn, even when that pen is more than 1 unit thick. For example, if a pen with **PS_INSIDEFRAME** style and width greater than 1 is used to draw a rectangle, then the outside of the line will be within the coordinates of the rectangle. (When a wide pen of a different style is used, the line may be partially outside the dimensions of the object.)

9

The thickness of a pen is specified by *Width*, which is in logical units. The color of the pen is specified by *Color*, which is a **COLORREF** value (discussed in Chapter 8). For the examples in this chapter, all colors are specified as RGB values.

CreatePen( ) returns nonzero if successful and zero on failure.

In some cases, it will be easier to create a pen when a **CPen** object is declared. To do this, you can use this form of the **CPen** constructor:

CPen(int *Style*, int *Width*, COLORREF *Color*);

Here, the parameters have the same meaning as they do for the **CreatePen( )** function. The **CPen** constructor throws a **CResourceException** on failure.

Once a pen has been created, it is selected into a device context using **SelectObject( )**.

Creating Custom Brushes

Custom brushes are created in a way similar to custom pens. Remember, a brush is encapsulated by the **CBrush** class.

There are various styles of brushes. The most common custom brush is a *solid brush*. A solid brush is created using the **CreateSolidBrush( )** function, whose prototype is shown here:

BOOL CBrush::CreateSolidBrush(COLORREF *Color*);

The color of the brush is specified in *Color*. The function returns nonzero if successful and zero on failure.

CBrush also has a constructor that can be used to create a solid brush when a brush object is created. This version of **CBrush( )** is shown here:

CBrush(COLORREF *Color*);

Using this constructor, you can create and initialize a brush object in one step. On failure, **CBrush( )** throws a **CResourceException**.

Once a custom brush has been created, it is selected into a device context using **SelectObject( )**.

Other types of brushes you might want to explore on your own are hatch and pattern brushes, which are created using **CBrush::CreateHatchBrush( )** and **CBrush::CreatePatternBrush( )**, respectively.

Deleting Custom Pens and Brushes

Before it terminates, your program must delete any custom pens or brushes that it creates. Most of the time, you will not need to worry about this because these objects remove themselves when their destructors are called. However, if you wish to delete a pen or brush manually, you do this using the **DeleteObject( )** function. Remember, you cannot (and must not) delete stock objects. Also, the object being deleted must not be currently selected into any device context.

A Graphics Demonstration

The following program demonstrates the various graphics functions just discussed. The program uses the virtual window technique developed in Chapter 8. It directs output to a memory device context, which is then copied to the physical window when a **WM_PAINT** message is received. (Remember, this approach to output allows a window's contents to be automatically updated each time a **WM_PAINT** message is received.)

The resource file for the program is shown here:

```
// GRAPH.RC

#include <afxres.h>
#include "ids.h"

GraphicsMenu MENU
{
  POPUP "Graphics Demo"
  {
    MENUITEM "&Lines\tF2", IDM_LINES
    MENUITEM "&Rectangles\tF3", IDM_RECTANGLES
    MENUITEM "&Ellipses\tF4", IDM_ELLIPSES
    MENUITEM "&Reset\tF5", IDM_RESET
    MENUITEM "E&xit\tF6", IDM_EXIT
  }
  MENUITEM "&Help", IDM_HELP
}


GraphicsMenu ACCELERATORS
{
  VK_F2, IDM_LINES, VIRTKEY
  VK_F3, IDM_RECTANGLES, VIRTKEY
  VK_F4, IDM_ELLIPSES, VIRTKEY
  VK_F5, IDM_RESET, VIRTKEY
  VK_F6, IDM_EXIT, VIRTKEY
  VK_F1, IDM_HELP, VIRTKEY
}
```

9

The header file, IDS.H, is shown here. It includes some values that will be used by a later example.

```
// IDS.H

#define IDM_LINES       100
#define IDM_RECTANGLES  101
#define IDM_ELLIPSES    102
#define IDM_ENLARGE     103
#define IDM_ORG         104
#define IDM_RESET       105
#define IDM_EXIT        106
#define IDM_HELP        107
```

The class derivation file, GRAPH.H, is shown here:

```
// GRAPH.H

// This is the main window class.
class CMainWin : public CFrameWnd
{
  CDC m_memDC; // virtual window device context
  CBitmap m_bmp; // virtual window bitmap
  CBrush m_bkbrush; // brush for virtual window

  // create pens
  CPen m_RedPen, m_YellowPen, m_GreenPen, m_BluePen;
  CPen m_OldPen;
public:
  CMainWin();

  afx_msg void OnPaint();

  afx_msg void OnLines();
  afx_msg void OnRectangles();
  afx_msg void OnEllipses();
  afx_msg void OnReset();
  afx_msg void OnExit();
  afx_msg void OnHelp();

  DECLARE_MESSAGE_MAP()
};
```

```
// This is the application class.
class CApp : public CWinApp
{
public:
  BOOL InitInstance();
};
```

The program file is shown here:

```
// Demonstrate Graphics
#include <afxwin.h>
#include "graph.h"
#include "ids.h"

int maxX, maxY; // screen dimensions

CMainWin::CMainWin()
{
  Create(NULL, "Demonstrate Graphics",
         WS_OVERLAPPEDWINDOW, rectDefault,
         NULL, "GraphicsMenu");

  // Load accelerator table
  if(!LoadAccelTable("GraphicsMenu"))
    MessageBox("Cannot Load Accelerators", "Error");

  maxX = GetSystemMetrics(SM_CXSCREEN);
  maxY = GetSystemMetrics(SM_CYSCREEN);

  CClientDC DC(this);

  // create a virtual output window
  m_memDC.CreateCompatibleDC(&DC);
  m_bmp.CreateCompatibleBitmap(&DC, maxX, maxY);
  m_memDC.SelectObject(&m_bmp);
  // use standard background
  m_bkbrush.CreateStockObject(WHITE_BRUSH);
  m_memDC.SelectObject(&m_bkbrush);
  // paint background of virtual window
  m_memDC.PatBlt(0, 0, maxX, maxY, PATCOPY);
```

9

```
  // create pens
  m_RedPen.CreatePen(PS_SOLID, 1, RGB(255,0,0));
  m_GreenPen.CreatePen(PS_SOLID, 2, RGB(0,255,0));
  m_BluePen.CreatePen(PS_SOLID, 3, RGB(0,0,255));
  m_YellowPen.CreatePen(PS_SOLID, 4, RGB(255, 255, 0));

  m_OldPen.CreateStockObject(BLACK_PEN);
}

// Initialize the application.
BOOL CApp::InitInstance()
{
  m_pMainWnd = new CMainWin;
  m_pMainWnd->ShowWindow(m_nCmdShow);
  m_pMainWnd->UpdateWindow();

  return TRUE;
}

// This is the application's message map.
BEGIN_MESSAGE_MAP(CMainWin, CFrameWnd)
  ON_WM_PAINT()
  ON_COMMAND(IDM_LINES, OnLines)
  ON_COMMAND(IDM_RECTANGLES, OnRectangles)
  ON_COMMAND(IDM_ELLIPSES, OnEllipses)
  ON_COMMAND(IDM_RESET, OnReset)
  ON_COMMAND(IDM_EXIT, OnExit)
  ON_COMMAND(IDM_HELP, OnHelp)
END_MESSAGE_MAP()

// Update screen using contents of virtual window.
afx_msg void CMainWin::OnPaint()
{
  CPaintDC DC(this);

  DC.BitBlt(0, 0, maxX, maxY, &m_memDC, 0, 0, SRCCOPY);
}

// Process IDM_EXIT.
afx_msg void CMainWin::OnExit()
{
  int response;
```

```
      response = MessageBox("Quit the Program?",
                            "Exit", MB_YESNO);

    if(response == IDYES)
      SendMessage(WM_CLOSE); // terminate app
}

// Process IDM_HELP.
afx_msg void CMainWin::OnHelp()
{
    MessageBox("Graphics Demo", "Help");
}

// Display lines and points.
afx_msg void CMainWin::OnLines()
{
  // draw 4 pixels
  m_memDC.SetPixel(40, 14, RGB(255, 0, 0));
  m_memDC.SetPixel(41, 14, RGB(0, 255, 0));
  m_memDC.SetPixel(42, 14, RGB(0, 0, 255));
  m_memDC.SetPixel(43, 14, RGB(0, 0, 0));

  m_memDC.LineTo(100, 50);
  m_memDC.MoveTo(100, 50);

  // change to green pen
  m_memDC.SelectObject(&m_GreenPen);
  m_memDC.LineTo(200, 100);

  // change to yellow pen
  m_memDC.SelectObject(&m_YellowPen);
  m_memDC.LineTo(0, 200);

  // change to blue pen
  m_memDC.SelectObject(&m_BluePen);
  m_memDC.LineTo(200, 200);

  // change to red pen
  m_memDC.SelectObject(&m_RedPen);
  m_memDC.LineTo(0, 0);

  m_memDC.LineTo(100, 150);
  m_memDC.MoveTo(0, 0);
```

9

```
  m_memDC.LineTo(100, 250);
  m_memDC.MoveTo(0, 0);
  m_memDC.LineTo(100, 350);

  // return to default pen
  m_memDC.SelectObject(&m_OldPen);

  m_memDC.Arc(0, 0, 300, 300, 0, 50, 200, 0);
  // show intersecting lines that define arc
  m_memDC.MoveTo(150, 150);
  m_memDC.LineTo(0, 50);
  m_memDC.MoveTo(150, 150);
  m_memDC.LineTo(200, 0);

  InvalidateRect(NULL);
}

// Display rectangles.
afx_msg void CMainWin::OnRectangles()
{
  CBrush HollowBrush;

  // display, but don't fill, rectangles
  HollowBrush.CreateStockObject(HOLLOW_BRUSH);
  m_memDC.SelectObject(&HollowBrush);

  // draw some rectangles
  m_memDC.Rectangle(50, 50, 300, 300);
  m_memDC.RoundRect(125, 125, 220, 240, 15, 13);

  // use a red pen
  m_memDC.SelectObject(&m_RedPen);
  m_memDC.Rectangle(100, 100, 200, 200);
  m_memDC.SelectObject(&m_OldPen); // return to default pen

  // restore default brush
  m_memDC.SelectObject(&m_bkbrush);

  InvalidateRect(NULL);
}

// Display ellipses.
afx_msg void CMainWin::OnEllipses()
{
```

```
    CBrush Brush;

    // make blue brush
    Brush.CreateSolidBrush(RGB(0, 0, 255));
    m_memDC.SelectObject(&Brush);

    // fill these ellipses with blue
    m_memDC.Ellipse(50, 200, 100, 280);
    m_memDC.Ellipse(75, 25, 280, 100);

    // use a red pen
    m_memDC.SelectObject(&m_RedPen);

    // create green brush
    Brush.DeleteObject(); // delete blue brush
    Brush.CreateSolidBrush(RGB(0, 255, 0));
    m_memDC.SelectObject(&Brush); // select green brush
    m_memDC.Ellipse(100, 100, 200, 200);

    // draw a pie slice
    m_memDC.Pie(200, 200, 340, 340, 225, 200, 200, 250);

    m_memDC.SelectObject(&m_OldPen); // return to default pen
    m_memDC.SelectObject(&m_bkbrush); // select default brush

    InvalidateRect(NULL);
}

// Reset screen coordinates and erase window.
afx_msg void CMainWin::OnReset()
{
  m_memDC.PatBlt(0, 0, maxX, maxY, PATCOPY);
  InvalidateRect(NULL);
}

CApp App; // instantiate the application
```

9

The program displays a menu that lets you display lines (plus four pixels), rectangles, and ellipses. It also lets you reset the window, which erases its contents and resets the current position, and start over. Sample output is shown in Figure 9-2.

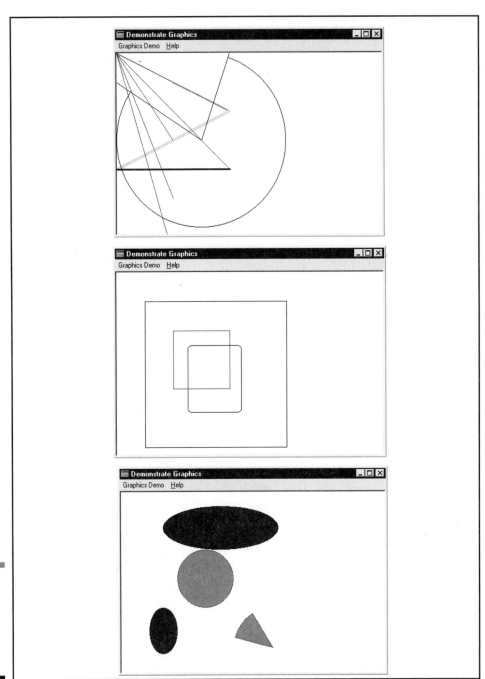

Sample output
from the
graphics
demonstration
program

Figure 9-2.

Understanding Mapping Modes and Viewports

As you know, the Windows text and graphics functions operate on logical units. These logical units are then translated by Windows into physical units defined by the device (i.e., pixels) when an object is displayed. How the translation from logical units to physical units is made is determined by the current *mapping mode*. By default, logical units are the same as pixels. However, you can change the ratio of logical units to physical units by changing the mapping mode.

In addition to changing the way Windows maps output to a window, for certain mapping modes you can also set two other attributes that affect the translation of logical to physical units. First, you can define the length and width of a window in terms of logical units that you select. Second, you can set the physical extents of a viewport. A *viewport* is a region that exists within a window. Once a viewport has been selected, all output is confined within its boundaries. In this section, the functions that allow you to set the mapping mode, the window extents, and viewport extents are examined.

The mapping mode and viewport functions are encapsulated by the **CDC** class.

Setting the Mapping Mode

To set the current mapping mode use **SetMapMode( )**. It has this prototype:

    virtual int CDC::SetMapMode(int *Mode*);

Mode specifies the new mapping mode, and it can be any one of the following constants:

Mapping Mode	Meaning
MM_ANISOTROPIC	Maps logical units to programmer-defined units with arbitrarily scaled axes.
MM_HIENGLISH	Maps each logical unit to 0.001 inch.
MM_HIMETRIC	Maps each logical unit to 0.01 millimeter.

9

Mapping Mode	Meaning
MM_ISOTROPIC	Maps logical units to programmer-defined units with equally scaled axes. (This establishes a one-to-one aspect ratio.)
MM_LOMETRIC	Maps each logical unit to 0.1 millimeter.
MM_LOENGLISH	Maps each logical unit to 0.01 inch.
MM_TEXT	Maps each logical unit to one device pixel.
MM_TWIPS	Maps each logical unit to one twentieth of a printer's point, or approximately 1/1440 inch.

SetMapMode( ) returns the previous mapping mode or zero if an error occurs.

The default mapping mode is **MM_TEXT**. There are several reasons why you might want to change the current mapping mode. First, if you want your program's output to be displayed in physical units, then you can select one of the real-world modes, such as **MM_LOMETRIC**. Second, you might want to define units for your program that best fit the nature of what you are displaying. Third, you might want to change the scale of what is displayed. (That is, you might want to enlarge or shrink the size of what is output.) Finally, you may want to establish a one-to-one aspect ratio between the X and Y axis. When this is done, each X unit represents the same physical distance as each Y unit.

NOTE: Remember that changing the mapping mode changes the way logical units are translated into physical units (pixels).

Defining the Window Extents

Selecting either the **MM_ISOTROPIC** or **MM_ANISOTROPIC** mapping mode allows you to define the size of the window in terms of logical units. In fact, if you select either of these mapping modes, you must define the dimensions of the window. (Since **MM_ISOTROPIC** and **MM_ANISOTROPIC** operate on programmer-defined units, the limits are technically undefined until you define them.) To define the X and Y extents of a window, use the **SetWindowExt( )** function. The version of this function used in this chapter is shown here:

virtual CSize CDC::SetWindowExt(int *Xextent,* int *Yextent*);

Xextent and *Yextent* specify the new horizontal and vertical extents measured in logical units. The previous window extents are returned in a **CSize** object (which encapsulates the standard **SIZE** structure). **SetWindowExt( )** only has effect when the mapping mode is **MM_ANISOTROPIC** or **MM_ISOTROPIC**.

Keep in mind that when you change the logical dimensions of a window you are not changing the physical size of the window on the screen. You are simply defining the size of the window in terms of logical units that you choose. (Or, more precisely, you are defining the relationship between the logical units used by the window and the physical units (pixels) used by the device.) For example, the same window could be given logical dimensions of 100×100 or 50×75. The only difference is the ratio of logical units to pixels when an image is displayed.

Defining a Viewport

As mentioned, a viewport is a region within a window that receives output. A viewport is defined using the **SetViewportExt( )** function. The prototype for the form used in this chapter is shown here:

virtual CSize CDC::SetViewportExt(int *Xextent,* int *Yextent*);

Xextent and *Yextent* specify the new horizontal and vertical viewport extents, in pixels. The previous viewport extents are returned. **SetViewportExt( )** has effect only when the mapping mode is **MM_ANISOTROPIC** or **MM_ISOTROPIC**.

A viewport may be any size you desire. That is, it may encompass the entire window or simply a part thereof. For the default mapping mode of **MM_TEXT**, the viewport and the window are the same.

Output is automatically mapped from the window device context (logical units) to the viewport (pixels) and scaled accordingly. Therefore, by changing

9

the X and Y extents of the viewport, you are in effect changing the size of anything displayed within it. Thus, if you make the viewport extents larger, the contents of the viewport will get larger. Conversely, if you make the extents smaller, the contents of the viewport will shrink. This fact is used in the following demonstration program.

Setting the Viewport Origin

By default, the origin of the viewport is at 0,0 within the window. However, you can change this using **SetViewportOrg( )**, shown here:

virtual CPoint CDC::SetViewportOrg(int *X*, int *Y*);

The new origin, specified in pixels, for the viewport is passed in *X,Y*. The previous origin is returned in a **CPoint** structure, which encapsulates the standard **POINT** structure.

Changing the origin of the viewport changes where images are drawn in the window. You will see the effect of this in the sample program that follows.

IN DEPTH

Converting Between Logical and Device Coordinates

As explained, Windows supports two coordinate systems: the logical coordinates used by your program and the physical coordinates used by the device. For the most part, Windows automatically converts between the two. Also, by default, logical units are the same as pixels (the physical device units) and the two coordinate systems are essentially equivalent. So the difference between the two isn't always an issue. However, if you change the mapping mode, viewport or window extents, or origin, this will not be the case. Since logical and device coordinates may differ, MFC provides two member functions of the **CDC** class to translate between the two. They are shown here.

Conversion Function	Description
DPtoLP( )	Converts a point, in the current device coordinates, to logical coordinates.
LPtoDP( )	Converts a point, in logical coordinates, to the current device coordinates.

Using these functions, you can easily convert between logical and device coordinates. This might be useful for several reasons. For example, when a mouse button is pressed, the coordinates of its location are passed in device units. To translate these into logical units you would use **DPtoLP( )**. For the purposes of this chapter, neither of these functions will be used. However, they may be of value to applications that you create. You might want to experiment with them on your own.

A Sample Viewport and Mapping Mode Program

The following program is an expanded version of the preceding graphics program, which sets the mapping mode, the window extents, and the viewport extents. Sample output from this program is shown in Figure 9-3. The program sets the mapping mode to **MM_ANISOTROPIC**, the window extents to 200 × 200, and the initial viewport extents to 10 × 10. When you run this program, each time you select the Magnify menu option, the viewport extents will be increased by ten units in each dimension, causing the image to become larger within the window. Selecting the Origin menu option causes the viewport origin to be moved 50 pixels in both the X and Y directions.

The program uses the same IDS.H header file that was shown earlier. The resource file for the viewport program is shown here:

```
// VIEWPORT.RC

#include <afxres.h>
```

9

```
#include "ids.h"

GraphicsMenu MENU
{
  POPUP "Graphics Demo"
  {
    MENUITEM "&Lines\tF2", IDM_LINES
    MENUITEM "&Rectangles\tF3", IDM_RECTANGLES
    MENUITEM "&Ellipses\tF4", IDM_ELLIPSES
    MENUITEM "&Magnify\tF5", IDM_ENLARGE
    MENUITEM "&Change Origin\tF6", IDM_ORG
    MENUITEM "&Reset\tF7", IDM_RESET
    MENUITEM "E&xit\tF8", IDM_EXIT
  }
  MENUITEM "&Help", IDM_HELP
}

GraphicsMenu ACCELERATORS
{
  VK_F2, IDM_LINES, VIRTKEY
  VK_F3, IDM_RECTANGLES, VIRTKEY
  VK_F4, IDM_ELLIPSES, VIRTKEY
  VK_F5, IDM_ENLARGE, VIRTKEY
  VK_F6, IDM_ORG, VIRTKEY
  VK_F7, IDM_RESET, VIRTKEY
  VK_F8, IDM_EXIT, VIRTKEY
  VK_F1, IDM_HELP, VIRTKEY
}
```

The class derivation file, VIEWPORT.H, is shown here:

```
// VIEWPORT.H

// This is the main window class.
class CMainWin : public CFrameWnd
{
  CDC m_memDC; // virtual window device context
  CBitmap m_bmp; // virtual window bitmap
  CBrush m_bkbrush; // brush for virtual window

  // create pens
  CPen m_RedPen, m_YellowPen, m_GreenPen, m_BluePen;
  CPen m_OldPen;
```

```
    int m_vpX, m_vpY; // viewport extents
    int m_orgX, m_orgY; // viewport origin
public:
  CMainWin();

  afx_msg void OnPaint();

  afx_msg void OnLines();
  afx_msg void OnRectangles();
  afx_msg void OnEllipses();
  afx_msg void OnEnlarge();
  afx_msg void OnOrg();
  afx_msg void OnReset();
  afx_msg void OnExit();
  afx_msg void OnHelp();

  DECLARE_MESSAGE_MAP()
};

// This is the application class.
class CApp : public CWinApp
{
public:
  BOOL InitInstance();
};
```

9

The program file is shown here:

```
// Demonstrate viewports and mapping modes.
#include <afxwin.h>
#include "viewport.h"
#include "ids.h"

int maxX, maxY; // screen dimensions

CMainWin::CMainWin()
{
  Create(NULL, "Viewports and Mapping Modes",
         WS_OVERLAPPEDWINDOW, rectDefault,
         NULL, "GraphicsMenu");

  // Load accelerator table
```

```
  if(!LoadAccelTable("GraphicsMenu"))
    MessageBox("Cannot Load Accelerators", "Error");

  maxX = GetSystemMetrics(SM_CXSCREEN);
  maxY = GetSystemMetrics(SM_CYSCREEN);

  CClientDC DC(this);

  // create a virtual output window
  m_memDC.CreateCompatibleDC(&DC);
  m_bmp.CreateCompatibleBitmap(&DC, maxX, maxY);
  m_memDC.SelectObject(&m_bmp);
  // use standard background
  m_bkbrush.CreateStockObject(WHITE_BRUSH);
  m_memDC.SelectObject(&m_bkbrush);
  // paint background of virtual window
  m_memDC.PatBlt(0, 0, maxX, maxY, PATCOPY);

  // create pens
  m_RedPen.CreatePen(PS_SOLID, 1, RGB(255,0,0));
  m_GreenPen.CreatePen(PS_SOLID, 2, RGB(0,255,0));
  m_BluePen.CreatePen(PS_SOLID, 3, RGB(0,0,255));
  m_YellowPen.CreatePen(PS_SOLID, 4, RGB(255, 255, 0));

  m_OldPen.CreateStockObject(BLACK_PEN);

  // initialize viewport extents and origin
  m_vpX = m_vpY = 10;
  m_orgX = m_orgY = 0;
}

// Initialize the application.
BOOL CApp::InitInstance()
{
  m_pMainWnd = new CMainWin;
  m_pMainWnd->ShowWindow(m_nCmdShow);
  m_pMainWnd->UpdateWindow();

  return TRUE;
}

// This is the application's message map.
BEGIN_MESSAGE_MAP(CMainWin, CFrameWnd)
```

```
      ON_WM_PAINT()
      ON_COMMAND(IDM_LINES, OnLines)
      ON_COMMAND(IDM_RECTANGLES, OnRectangles)
      ON_COMMAND(IDM_ELLIPSES, OnEllipses)
      ON_COMMAND(IDM_ENLARGE, OnEnlarge)
      ON_COMMAND(IDM_ORG, OnOrg)
      ON_COMMAND(IDM_RESET, OnReset)
      ON_COMMAND(IDM_EXIT, OnExit)
      ON_COMMAND(IDM_HELP, OnHelp)
    END_MESSAGE_MAP()

    // Update screen using contents of virtual window.
    afx_msg void CMainWin::OnPaint()
    {
      CPaintDC DC(this);

      // set mapping mode, window and viewport extents
      DC.SetMapMode(MM_ANISOTROPIC);
      DC.SetWindowExt(200, 200);
      DC.SetViewportExt(m_vpX, m_vpY);
      DC.SetViewportOrg(m_orgX, m_orgY);

      DC.BitBlt(0, 0, maxX, maxY, &m_memDC, 0, 0, SRCCOPY);
    }

    // Process IDM_EXIT.
    afx_msg void CMainWin::OnExit()
    {
      int response;

      response = MessageBox("Quit the Program?",
                            "Exit", MB_YESNO);

      if(response == IDYES)
        SendMessage(WM_CLOSE); // terminate app
    }

    // Process IDM_HELP.
    afx_msg void CMainWin::OnHelp()
    {
      MessageBox("Graphics Demo", "Help");
    }
```

9

```
// Display lines and points.
afx_msg void CMainWin::OnLines()
{
  // draw 4 pixels
  m_memDC.SetPixel(40, 14, RGB(255, 0, 0));
  m_memDC.SetPixel(41, 14, RGB(0, 255, 0));
  m_memDC.SetPixel(42, 14, RGB(0, 0, 255));
  m_memDC.SetPixel(43, 14, RGB(0, 0, 0));

  m_memDC.LineTo(100, 50);
  m_memDC.MoveTo(100, 50);

  // change to green pen
  m_memDC.SelectObject(&m_GreenPen);
  m_memDC.LineTo(200, 100);

  // change to yellow pen
  m_memDC.SelectObject(&m_YellowPen);
  m_memDC.LineTo(0, 200);

  // change to blue pen
  m_memDC.SelectObject(&m_BluePen);
  m_memDC.LineTo(200, 200);

  // change to red pen
  m_memDC.SelectObject(&m_RedPen);
  m_memDC.LineTo(0, 0);

  m_memDC.LineTo(100, 150);
  m_memDC.MoveTo(0, 0);
  m_memDC.LineTo(100, 250);
  m_memDC.MoveTo(0, 0);
  m_memDC.LineTo(100, 350);

  // return to default pen
  m_memDC.SelectObject(&m_OldPen);

  m_memDC.Arc(0, 0, 300, 300, 0, 50, 200, 0);
  // show intersecting lines that define arc
  m_memDC.MoveTo(150, 150);
  m_memDC.LineTo(0, 50);
  m_memDC.MoveTo(150, 150);
  m_memDC.LineTo(200, 0);
```

```
      InvalidateRect(NULL);
}

// Display rectangles.
afx_msg void CMainWin::OnRectangles()
{
  CBrush HollowBrush;

  // display, but don't fill, rectangles
  HollowBrush.CreateStockObject(HOLLOW_BRUSH);
  m_memDC.SelectObject(&HollowBrush);

  // draw some rectangles
  m_memDC.Rectangle(50, 50, 300, 300);
  m_memDC.RoundRect(125, 125, 220, 240, 15, 13);

  // use a red pen
  m_memDC.SelectObject(&m_RedPen);
  m_memDC.Rectangle(100, 100, 200, 200);
  m_memDC.SelectObject(&m_OldPen); // return to default pen

  // restore default brush
  m_memDC.SelectObject(&m_bkbrush);

  InvalidateRect(NULL);
}

// Display ellipses.
afx_msg void CMainWin::OnEllipses()
{
  CBrush Brush;

  // make blue brush
  Brush.CreateSolidBrush(RGB(0, 0, 255));
  m_memDC.SelectObject(&Brush);

  // fill these ellipses with blue
  m_memDC.Ellipse(50, 200, 100, 280);
  m_memDC.Ellipse(75, 25, 280, 100);

  // use a red pen
  m_memDC.SelectObject(&m_RedPen);
```

9

```
    // create green brush
    Brush.DeleteObject(); // delete blue brush
    Brush.CreateSolidBrush(RGB(0, 255, 0));
    m_memDC.SelectObject(&Brush); // select green brush
    m_memDC.Ellipse(100, 100, 200, 200);

    // draw a pie slice
    m_memDC.Pie(200, 200, 340, 340, 225, 200, 200, 250);

    m_memDC.SelectObject(&m_OldPen); // return to default pen
    m_memDC.SelectObject(&m_bkbrush); // select default brush

    InvalidateRect(NULL);
}

// Enlarge image.
afx_msg void CMainWin::OnEnlarge()
{
    m_vpX += 10;
    m_vpY += 10;
    InvalidateRect(NULL);
}

// Change origin.
afx_msg void CMainWin::OnOrg()
{
    m_orgX += 50;
    m_orgY += 50;
    InvalidateRect(NULL);
}

// Reset screen coordinates and erase window.
afx_msg void CMainWin::OnReset()
{
    m_vpX = m_vpY = 10;
    m_orgX = m_orgY = 0;

    m_memDC.PatBlt(0, 0, maxX, maxY, PATCOPY);
    InvalidateRect(NULL);
}

CApp App; // instantiate the application
```

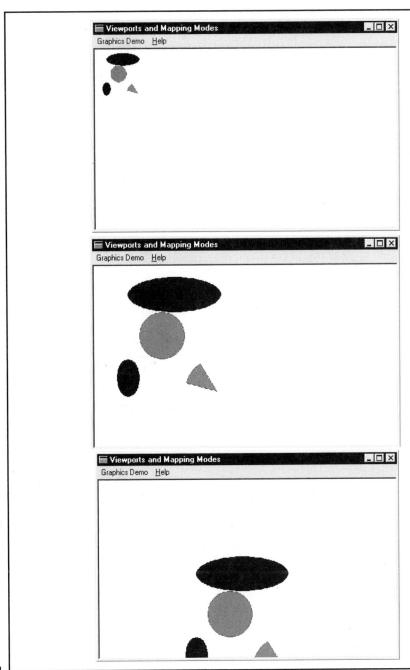

Sample output
from the
mapping mode
program at
various
modifications
and locations.

Figure 9-3.

9

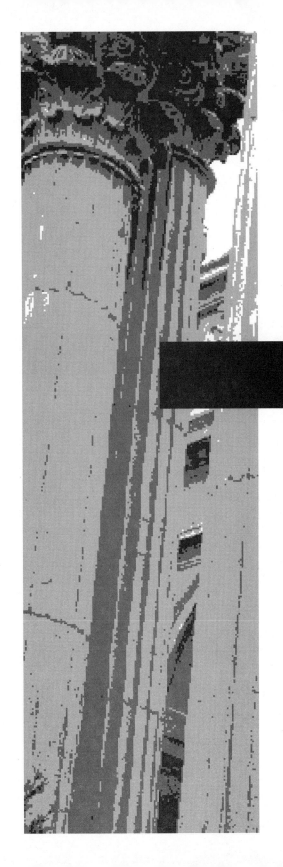

CHAPTER 10

Introducing Common Controls

This chapter introduces one of the most exciting dimensions in Windows programming: *common controls*. In the preceding chapters, you have learned about the standard controls supported by all versions of Windows. However, beginning with Windows 95, several new controls were defined that add excitement to your application and enhance the interface to any Windows application. The common controls are intended to supplement the standard controls and give you increased power and flexibility. They can also help give your application a polished look.

The original common controls have been support by MFC since version 4. Recently, several new controls and options were added by Windows 98 and Internet Explorer 4. These new features are fully supported by MFC version 6. (See the In Depth box.)

The common controls are listed here:

Control	Description
Animation control	Displays an AVI file.
ComboBoxEx control	Combo box with extended capabilities.
Date and Time Picker controls	Updates date and time.
Drag List box	A list box that allows items to be dragged.
Header control	A column heading.
Hot Key control	Supports user-created hot keys.
Image list	A list of graphical images.
IP control	Supports user-entered Internet Protocol (IP) addresses.
List View control	A list of icons and labels.
Month Calendar control	A calendar-based control used for dates.
Pager control	Scrollable control that contains other controls.
Progress bar	A visual gauge used to indicate the degree to which a task is completed.
Property sheet	A properties dialog box.
Rebar control	A bar that contains other controls.

Control	Description
Rich Edit control	A sophisticated edit box.
Status window	A bar that displays information related to an application.
Tab control	A tab-based menu. (This control looks like the tabs on file folders.)
Toolbar	A graphics-based menu.
Tooltip	Small pop-up text box. Typically used to describe toolbar buttons or other control elements.
Trackbar	A slider-based control. (Similar in concept to a scrollbar, but resembles a fader control on a stereo.)
Tree view control	A tree-structured display.
Up-down (spin) control	Up and down arrows. Called a spin control when linked with an edit box.

These controls are called common controls because they represent an extended set of controls that will be used by many applications. You have certainly encountered several (if not all) of these controls if you have been using a modern version of Windows for very long.

This chapter discusses the theory and general procedure for using a common control in your program. It then explores toolbars and tooltips. Additional common controls are examined in the following chapters.

Including and Initializing the Common Controls

Before you can use the common controls, you must include the standard header file AFXCMN.H in your program. You must also make sure that the common controls library (called COMCTL32.LIB) is linked into your program. Normally, this library is automatically included when you create an MFC program. But this may vary between compilers.

Applications that use one or more common controls must call the **InitCommonControlsEx( )** API function prior to using the first common control. **InitCommonControlsEx( )** ensures that the common controls

10

dynamic link library (DLL) is loaded and that the common controls subsystem is initialized. The prototype for **InitCommonControlsEx( )** is shown here:

BOOL InitCommonControlsEx(LPINITCOMMONCONTROLSEX *WhichControls*);

Here, *WhichControls* specifies which common controls you wish to initialize. The function returns nonzero if successful and zero on failure.

NOTE: Earlier versions of MFC used the **InitCommonControls ( )** API function. This function has been replaced by the more powerful **InitCommonControlsEx( )**, which should be used for new code.

The **INITCOMMONCONTROLSEX** structure is shown here:

```
typedef struct tagINITCOMMONCONTROLSEX {
  DWORD dwSize;
  DWORD dwICC;
} INITCOMMONCONTROLSEX;
```

The **dwSize** member must contain the size of the **INITCOMMONCON-TROLSEX** structure. The **dwICC** member specifies which control or set of controls is loaded and initialized. It must be one or more of the following values:

Macro	Loads and Initializes
ICC_ANIMATE_CLASS	Animation control
ICC_BAR_CLASSES	Status bar, toolbar, tooltip, and trackbar controls
ICC_COOL_CLASSES	Rebar control
ICC_DATE_CLASSES	Date and time picker control
ICC_HOTKEY_CLASS	Hot key control
ICC_INTERNET_CLASSES	Internet address control
ICC_LISTVIEW_CLASSES	List view and header controls
ICC_PAGESCROLLER_CLASS	Page scrolling control

Macro	Loads and Initializes
ICC_PROGRESS_CLASS	Progress bar
ICC_TAB_CLASSES	Tab and tooltip controls
ICC_TREEVIEW_CLASSES	Tree view and tooltip controls
ICC_UPDOWN_CLASSES	Up-down controls
ICC_USEREX_CLASSES	ComboBoxEx control
ICC_WIN95_CLASSES	Common controls supported by Windows 95

For example, the following code ensures that the toolbar control classes are loaded and initalized:

```
INITCOMMONCONTROLSEX initCtrls;

initCtrls.dwSize = sizeof(initCtrls);
initCtrls.dwICC= ICC_BAR_CLASSES;
InitCommonControlsEx(&initCtrls);
```

A good place to call **InitCommonControlsEx( )** is in the constructor for your application's main window.

IN DEPTH

10

Common Controls and Internet Explorer 4

The implementation of the common control set is contained in a system DLL called COMCTL32.DLL. With the introduction of Internet Explorer (IE) 4, and subsequently of Windows 98, this DLL was upgraded. The reason this is important is that the set of common controls available on any given machine depends upon the version of COMCTL32.DLL that is currently installed. The new DLL supports several new common controls, including the date and time picker, the extended combo box, the month calendar, and the IP address. Several new options to existing controls are also provided. For example, the transparent option was added to the toolbar.

While it is possible to determine what version of COMCTL32.DLL is installed on a machine and adjust accordingly, it is easiest to use only the original common controls and options when writing backwards-compatible code. However, if you are writing applications for Windows 98 or for systems that have IE 4 (or later) installed, then you can use all of the common controls and their features.

Common Controls Are Windows

Before continuing, it is important to understand that all of the common controls are child windows. They will be created using their corresponding class constructors. Because the common controls are windows, they can be managed in more or less the same way as you manage other windows used by your program.

Using a Toolbar

Perhaps the most sought-after common control is the *toolbar*. A toolbar is, essentially, a graphical menu. In the toolbar, menu items are represented by images, which form graphical buttons. Often, a toolbar is used in conjunction with a standard menu. As such, it provides an alternative means of making a menu selection. Toolbars are encapsulated by the **CToolBarCtrl** class.

 NOTE: Toolbars can also be created using the older **CToolBar** class. However, modern applications should use the **CToolBarCtrl** class, as described in this section.

To create a toolbar, you first declare an object of type **CToolBarCtrl** and then execute a call to **Create( )**. Its prototype is shown here:

BOOL CToolBarCtrl::Create(DWORD *dwStyle*, const RECT &*SizePos*,
                                        CWnd **Owner*, UINT *ID*);

The style of the toolbar is passed in *dwStyle*. The toolbar style must include
WS_CHILD. It can also include other standard styles, such as **WS_BORDER**
or **WS_VISIBLE**. Several toolbar style options are available. Here are some of
the most popular:

TBSTYLE_TOOLTIPS	Include tooltips.
TBSTYLE_WRAPABLE	Wrap a long toolbar to the next line.
TBSTYLE_FLAT	Toolbar is flat. Requires Windows 98 or IE 4 (or later).
TBSTYLE_TRANSPARENT	Toolbar is transparent. Requires Windows 98 or IE 4 (or later).

You can also include any of these common control styles:

Style	Effect
CCS_ADJUSTABLE	Toolbar can be adjusted by the user.
CCS_BOTTOM	Toolbar located at bottom of parent window.
CCS_LEFT	Toolbar located at left side of parent window. Requires Windows 98 or IE 4 (or later).
CCS_NODIVIDER	No dividing line between toolbar and parent.
CCS_NOMOVEX	Toolbar will not resize horizontally. Requires Windows 98 or IE 4 (or later).
CCS_NOMOVEY	Toolbar will not resize vertically.
CCS_NOPARENTALIGN	Toolbar does not automatically move between the top and bottom of the parent's window.
CCS_NORESIZE	Toolbar's size and position are fixed.
CCS_RIGHT	Toolbar located at right side of parent window. Requires Windows 98 or IE 4 (or later).
CCS_TOP	Toolbar located at top of parent window. (This is the default.)
CCS_VERT	Toolbar is aligned vertically. Requires Windows 98 or IE 4 (or later).

10

Generally, the *SizePos* parameter is ignored. However, if you include the **CCS_NORESIZE** style value, then the dimensions and position specified in *SizePos* will be used to position the control. By default, a toolbar is positioned at the top of the parent window and is automatically sized to fit the parent. Usually, you will not want to alter this default behavior.

A pointer to the parent window is passed in *Owner*. The identifier associated with the toolbar is passed in *ID*. **Create( )** returns nonzero if successful and zero on failure.

After calling **Create( )**, the toolbar has been created, but is neither initialized nor ready for use. Instead, your program must perform two more operations. First, it must add the buttons to the toolbar. Second, it must add the bitmap to each button. You can also add a label to each bitmap, but this is seldom done for two reasons. First, the labels take up space. Second, tooltips provide a better alternative.

Adding the Toolbar Buttons

Buttons are added to a toolbar using the **AddButtons( )** member function. Its prototype is shown here:

BOOL CToolBarCtrl::AddButtons(int *Num*, LPTBBUTTON *lpButtons*);

Here, *Num* specifies the number of buttons to add to the toolbar. *lpButtons* is a pointer to an array of **TBBUTTON** structures that describe the buttons. The function returns nonzero if successful and zero on failure.

Each **TBBUTTON** structure in the array pointed to by *lpButtons* defines one button in the toolbar. Thus, the array must contain as many elements as there are buttons in the toolbar. The **TBBUTTON** structure is shown here:

```
typedef struct _TBBUTTON {
  int iBitmap;
  int idCommand;
  BYTE fsState;
  BYTE fsStyle;
  DWORD dwData;
  int iString;
} TBBUTTON;
```

The index of the bitmap image associated with the button is contained in **iBitmap**. The buttons begin their indexing at zero and are displayed left to right.

The ID associated with the button is stored in **idCommand**. Each time the button is pressed, a **WM_COMMAND** message that contains the button's ID will be generated and sent to the parent window. Typically, you will handle the **WM_COMMAND** messages generated by a toolbar in the same way that you handle messages generated by a menu.

The initial state of the button is stored in **fsState**. It can be one (or more) of the following values:

State	Meaning
TBSTATE_CHECKED	Button is pressed.
TBSTATE_ELLIPSES	Ellipsis is shown when button text is truncated. Requires Windows 98 or IE 4 (or later).
TBSTATE_ENABLE	Button may be pressed.
TBSTATE_HIDDEN	Button is hidden and inactive.
TBSTATE_INDETERMINATE	Button is gray and inactive.
TBSTATE_MARKED	Button is marked. The appearance of the mark is determined by the application. Requires Windows 98 or IE 4 (or later).
TBSTATE_PRESSED	Button is pressed.
TBSTATE_WRAP	Following buttons are on new line.

The style of the button is contained in **fsStyle**. It can be any valid combination of the following values:

Style	Meaning
TBSTYLE_AUTOSIZE	The text in the button determines its size. Requires Windows 98 or IE 4 (or later).
TBSTYLE_BUTTON	Standard button.

10

Style	Meaning
TBSTYLE_CHECK	Button toggles between checked and unchecked each time it is pressed.
TBSTYLE_CHECKGROUP	A check button that is part of a mutually exclusive group.
TBSTYLE_DROPDOWN	Allows a drop-down list to be displayed from the button. Requires Windows 98 or IE 4 (or later).
TBSTYLE_GROUP	A standard button that is part of a mutually exclusive group.
TBSTYLE_NOPREFIX	No accelerator prefix is shown. Requires Windows 98 or IE 4 (or later).
TBSTYLE_SEP	Separates buttons. (**idCommand** must be zero when this style is used.)

Notice the **TBSTYLE_SEP** style. This style is used to provide a gap between buttons on the toolbar. This allows you to visually group buttons into clusters.

dwData contains user-defined data. The **iString** member is the index of an optional label associated with the button. These elements should be zero if they are unused.

Adding the Toolbar Bitmaps

After you have added the buttons to the toolbar, you will need to add the bitmapped images that will be shown inside each button. To do this, call **AddBitmap( )**, shown here:

    int CToolBarCtrl::AddBitmap(int *Num*, UINT *BitmapID*);

Here, *Num* specifies the number of images to add. The resource ID of the bitmap that contains the images is passed in *BitmapID*. An overloaded version of **AddBitmap( )** allows you to pass a pointer to a **CBitmap** object as the second parameter. This may be useful in some applications. The function returns the index of the first image or –1 on failure.

To create the bitmaps that form the graphics images inside each button, you will usually employ an image editor. The process is similar to creating an icon or bitmap (the way you did when working with custom icons in Chapter 7). The default image size for toolbars is 16 × 15 (that is, 16 pixels wide and 15 pixels tall). This dimension fits nicely inside the standard button size of 24 × 22.

There is one important point to remember when creating the bitmaps for a toolbar: Only one bitmap is associated with the toolbar and this bitmap must contain *all* of the button images. Thus, if your toolbar will have six buttons, then the bitmap associated with your toolbar must define six images. For example, if your toolbar images are each 16 × 15 and your toolbar has six buttons, then your toolbar bitmap will have to be 15 pixels high by 96 (6 times 16) pixels long.

For the toolbar examples presented in this chapter, you will need five images. Each image must be 16 × 15. This means that you will need to create a bitmap that is 80 × 15. Figure 10-1 shows how the toolbar bitmap used by the sample programs in this chapter looks inside the image editor. The toolbar will be used as an alternative menu for the graphics program developed in the preceding chapter. Store your bitmap in a file called TOOLBAR.BMP.

Resizing the Toolbar

When a toolbar is initialized, it is sized to fit the current dimensions of its parent window. However, if the parent window is resized, the toolbar is *not* automatically adjusted to fit the new dimensions. While this is not actually harmful, failure to resize the toolbar will cause it to be too short if the width of the window is enlarged. Fortunately, there is an easy way around this problem. Each time the parent window of the toolbar changes size, your program should call the **AutoSize( )** function, shown here:

10

```
void CToolBarCtrl::AutoSize( );
```

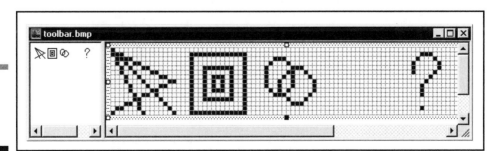

The toolbar bitmap while being edited

Figure 10-1.

This function automatically resizes the toolbar so that it fits the dimensions of the parent window.

Since you will want to readjust the size of a toolbar only when necessary, you will need some way to know when such an adjustment is required. Fortunately, this too is easy. Each time a window is resized, your program receives a **WM_SIZE** message. So far, we haven't needed to respond to this message because, for the most part, window resizing is handled automatically by Windows. However, any program that uses a toolbar will want to respond to this message by resizing the toolbar. The **WM_SIZE** message is processed by the standard **OnSize( )** message handler, whose prototype is shown here:

afx_msg void OnSize(UINT *What*, int *Width*, int *Height*);

If you are handling this message only to resize a toolbar, then all three parameters can be ignored. However, since you might want to handle this message for other reasons, here is a description of its parameters: The new dimensions of the window's client area are passed in *Width* and *Height*. *What* describes what type of resizing has occurred. The value of *What* will be one of the following values:

What	Meaning
SIZE_RESTORED	Window resized.
SIZE_MAXIMIZED	Window maximized.
SIZE_MINIMIZED	Window minimized.
SIZE_MAXHIDE	Another window has been maximized.
SIZE_MAXSHOW	Another window has been restored.

As stated, if your application is only processing **WM_SIZE** messages to resize a toolbar, then none of its parameters are needed. Your implementation of **OnSize( )** will consist solely of a call to **AutoSize( )**.

Some Additional CToolBarCtrl Member Functions

Toolbars are fully automated controls. However, they may also be manually managed. Here are a few of the many **CToolBarCtrl** member functions that help you do that.

You may change the "pressed state" of a button using the function **PressButton( )**. Its prototype is shown here:

BOOL CToolBarCtrl::PressButton(int *ID*, BOOL *Pressed* = TRUE);

Here, *ID* is the ID of the button being pressed. When *Pressed* is nonzero, the button will appear to be pressed. When *Pressed* is zero, the button will be returned to its normal state. The function returns nonzero if successful and zero on failure.

You may check a button using the function **CheckButton( )**. Its prototype is shown here:

BOOL CToolBarCtrl::CheckButton(int *ID*, BOOL *Checked* = TRUE);

Here, *ID* is the ID of the button being checked. When *Checked* is nonzero, the button will appear to be pressed and checked. When *Checked* is zero, the button will be returned to its normal state. The function returns nonzero if successful and zero on failure.

To hide a button, call **HideButton( )**. Its prototype is shown here:

BOOL CToolBarCtrl::HideButton(int *ID*, BOOL *Hidden* = TRUE);

Here, *ID* is the ID of the button being hidden. When *Hidden* is nonzero, the button will be hidden. When *Hidden* is zero, the button will be shown. The function returns nonzero if successful and zero on failure.

To enable/disable a button, call **EnableButton( )**. Its prototype is shown here:

BOOL CToolBarCtrl::EnableButton(int *ID*, BOOL *Enabled* = TRUE);

Here, *ID* is the ID of the button being affected. When *Enabled* is nonzero, the button will be enabled. This means that it can be pressed by the user. When *Enabled* is zero, the button will be disabled and may not be pressed. The function returns nonzero if successful and zero on failure.

There are many other **CToolBarCtrl** member functions that you will want to explore on your own.

10

A Toolbar Example Program

The following program adds a toolbar to the graphics program developed in
the preceding chapter. The toolbar duplicates the menu options. It allows
you to display lines, rectangles, and ellipses. You can also reset the window
and choose Help. The program handles **WM_SIZE** messages by resizing the
toolbar. The program also lets you hide or show the toolbar.

The resource file for the program is shown here:

```
// TOOLBAR.RC

#include <afxres.h>
#include "ids.h"

IDTB_BMP BITMAP "toolbar.bmp"

ToolbarMenu MENU
{
  POPUP "Draw"
  {
    MENUITEM "&Lines\tF2", IDM_LINES
    MENUITEM "&Rectangles\tF3", IDM_RECTANGLES
    MENUITEM "&Ellipses\tF4", IDM_ELLIPSES
    MENUITEM "&Reset\tF5", IDM_RESET
  }
  POPUP "Options"
  {
    MENUITEM "&Show Toolbar\tF6", IDM_SHOWTB
    MENUITEM "&Hide Toolbar\tF7", IDM_HIDETB
    MENUITEM "E&xit\tF8", IDM_EXIT
  }
  MENUITEM "&Help", IDM_HELP
}


ToolbarMenu ACCELERATORS
{
  VK_F2, IDM_LINES, VIRTKEY
  VK_F3, IDM_RECTANGLES, VIRTKEY
  VK_F4, IDM_ELLIPSES, VIRTKEY
  VK_F5, IDM_RESET, VIRTKEY
  VK_F6, IDM_SHOWTB, VIRTKEY
  VK_F7, IDM_HIDETB, VIRTKEY
  VK_F8, IDM_EXIT, VIRTKEY
```

```
    VK_F1, IDM_HELP, VIRTKEY
}
```

The IDS.H header file is shown here:

```
// IDS.H

#define IDM_LINES      100
#define IDM_RECTANGLES 101
#define IDM_ELLIPSES   102
#define IDM_ENLARGE    103
#define IDM_ORG        104
#define IDM_RESET      105
#define IDM_SHOWTB     106
#define IDM_HIDETB     107
#define IDM_EXIT       108
#define IDM_HELP       109

#define ID_TB          200

#define IDTB_BMP       300

#define NUMBUTTONS       6
```

The class derivation file, TOOLBAR.H, is shown here:

```
// TOOLBAR.H

#include "ids.h"

// This is the main window class.
class CMainWin : public CFrameWnd
{
  CDC m_memDC; // virtual window device context
  CBitmap m_bmp; // virtual window bitmap
  CBrush m_bkbrush; // brush for virtual window

  // create pens
  CPen m_RedPen, m_YellowPen, m_GreenPen, m_BluePen;
  CPen m_OldPen;

  CToolBarCtrl m_TB; // toolbar control
public:
```

```
    CMainWin();

    afx_msg void OnPaint();
    afx_msg void OnSize(UINT How, int Width, int Height);

    afx_msg void OnLines();
    afx_msg void OnRectangles();
    afx_msg void OnEllipses();
    afx_msg void OnReset();
    afx_msg void OnShowTB();
    afx_msg void OnHideTB();
    afx_msg void OnExit();
    afx_msg void OnHelp();

    void InitToolbar();

    DECLARE_MESSAGE_MAP()
};

// This is the application class.
class CApp : public CWinApp
{
public:
    BOOL InitInstance();
};
```

The program file is shown here:

```
// Demonstrate Toolbars
#include <afxwin.h>
#include <afxcmn.h>
#include "toolbar.h"
#include "ids.h"

int maxX, maxY; // screen dimensions

CMainWin::CMainWin()
{
    Create(NULL, "Using a Toolbar",
            WS_OVERLAPPEDWINDOW, rectDefault,
            NULL, "ToolbarMenu");

    // Load accelerator table
```

```
    if(!LoadAccelTable("ToolbarMenu"))
      MessageBox("Cannot Load Accelerators", "Error");

    maxX = GetSystemMetrics(SM_CXSCREEN);
    maxY = GetSystemMetrics(SM_CYSCREEN);

    CClientDC DC(this);

    // create a virtual output window
    m_memDC.CreateCompatibleDC(&DC);
    m_bmp.CreateCompatibleBitmap(&DC, maxX, maxY);
    m_memDC.SelectObject(&m_bmp);
    // use standard background
    m_bkbrush.CreateStockObject(WHITE_BRUSH);
    m_memDC.SelectObject(&m_bkbrush);
    // paint background of virtual window
    m_memDC.PatBlt(0, 0, maxX, maxY, PATCOPY);

    // create pens
    m_RedPen.CreatePen(PS_SOLID, 1, RGB(255,0,0));
    m_GreenPen.CreatePen(PS_SOLID, 2, RGB(0,255,0));
    m_BluePen.CreatePen(PS_SOLID, 3, RGB(0,0,255));
    m_YellowPen.CreatePen(PS_SOLID, 4, RGB(255, 255, 0));

    m_OldPen.CreateStockObject(BLACK_PEN);

    INITCOMMONCONTROLSEX initCtrls;

    initCtrls.dwSize = sizeof(initCtrls);
    initCtrls.dwICC= ICC_BAR_CLASSES;
    InitCommonControlsEx(&initCtrls);

    InitToolbar();
}

// Initialize the application.
BOOL CApp::InitInstance()
{
  m_pMainWnd = new CMainWin;
  m_pMainWnd->ShowWindow(m_nCmdShow);
  m_pMainWnd->UpdateWindow();

  return TRUE;
}
```

10

```
// This is the application's message map.
BEGIN_MESSAGE_MAP(CMainWin, CFrameWnd)
  ON_WM_PAINT()
  ON_WM_SIZE()
  ON_COMMAND(IDM_LINES, OnLines)
  ON_COMMAND(IDM_RECTANGLES, OnRectangles)
  ON_COMMAND(IDM_ELLIPSES, OnEllipses)
  ON_COMMAND(IDM_RESET, OnReset)
  ON_COMMAND(IDM_SHOWTB, OnShowTB)
  ON_COMMAND(IDM_HIDETB, OnHideTB)
  ON_COMMAND(IDM_EXIT, OnExit)
  ON_COMMAND(IDM_HELP, OnHelp)
END_MESSAGE_MAP()

// Update screen using contents of virtual window.
afx_msg void CMainWin::OnPaint()
{
  CPaintDC DC(this);

  DC.BitBlt(0, 0, maxX, maxY, &m_memDC, 0, 0, SRCCOPY);
}

// Resize toolbar when a WM_SIZE message is received.
afx_msg void CMainWin::OnSize(UINT How,
                              int Width, int Height)
{
  m_TB.AutoSize();
}

// Process IDM_EXIT.
afx_msg void CMainWin::OnExit()
{
  int response;

  response = MessageBox("Quit the Program?",
                  "Exit", MB_YESNO);

  if(response == IDYES)
    SendMessage(WM_CLOSE); // terminate app
}

// Process IDM_HELP.
afx_msg void CMainWin::OnHelp()
```

```
{
   m_TB.PressButton(IDM_HELP, TRUE);
   MessageBox("Toolbar Demo", "Help");
   m_TB.PressButton(IDM_HELP, FALSE);
}

// Display lines and points.
afx_msg void CMainWin::OnLines()
{
  // draw 4 pixels
  m_memDC.SetPixel(40, 14, RGB(255, 0, 0));
  m_memDC.SetPixel(41, 14, RGB(0, 255, 0));
  m_memDC.SetPixel(42, 14, RGB(0, 0, 255));
  m_memDC.SetPixel(43, 14, RGB(0, 0, 0));

  m_memDC.LineTo(100, 50);
  m_memDC.MoveTo(100, 50);

  // change to green pen
  m_memDC.SelectObject(&m_GreenPen);
  m_memDC.LineTo(200, 100);

  // change to yellow pen
  m_memDC.SelectObject(&m_YellowPen);
  m_memDC.LineTo(0, 200);

  // change to blue pen
  m_memDC.SelectObject(&m_BluePen);
  m_memDC.LineTo(200, 200);

  // change to red pen
  m_memDC.SelectObject(&m_RedPen);
  m_memDC.LineTo(0, 0);

  m_memDC.LineTo(100, 150);
  m_memDC.MoveTo(0, 0);
  m_memDC.LineTo(100, 250);
  m_memDC.MoveTo(0, 0);
  m_memDC.LineTo(100, 350);

  // return to default pen
  m_memDC.SelectObject(&m_OldPen);

  m_memDC.Arc(0, 0, 300, 300, 0, 50, 200, 0);
```

10

```
    // show intersecting lines that define arc
    m_memDC.MoveTo(150, 150);
    m_memDC.LineTo(0, 50);
    m_memDC.MoveTo(150, 150);
    m_memDC.LineTo(200, 0);

    InvalidateRect(NULL);
}

// Display rectangles.
afx_msg void CMainWin::OnRectangles()
{
    CBrush HollowBrush;

    // display, but don't fill, rectangles
    HollowBrush.CreateStockObject(HOLLOW_BRUSH);
    m_memDC.SelectObject(&HollowBrush);

    // draw some rectangles
    m_memDC.Rectangle(50, 50, 300, 300);
    m_memDC.RoundRect(125, 125, 220, 240, 15, 13);

    // use a red pen
    m_memDC.SelectObject(&m_RedPen);
    m_memDC.Rectangle(100, 100, 200, 200);
    m_memDC.SelectObject(&m_OldPen); // return to default pen

    // restore default brush
    m_memDC.SelectObject(&m_bkbrush);

    InvalidateRect(NULL);
}

// Display ellipses.
afx_msg void CMainWin::OnEllipses()
{
    CBrush Brush;

    // make blue brush
    Brush.CreateSolidBrush(RGB(0, 0, 255));
    m_memDC.SelectObject(&Brush);

    // fill these ellipses with blue
    m_memDC.Ellipse(50, 200, 100, 280);
    m_memDC.Ellipse(75, 25, 280, 100);
```

```
    // use a red pen
    m_memDC.SelectObject(&m_RedPen);

    // create green brush
    Brush.DeleteObject();
    Brush.CreateSolidBrush(RGB(0, 255, 0));
    m_memDC.SelectObject(&Brush); // select green brush
    m_memDC.Ellipse(100, 100, 200, 200);

    // draw a pie slice
    m_memDC.Pie(200, 200, 340, 340, 225, 200, 200, 250);

    m_memDC.SelectObject(&m_OldPen); // return to default pen
    m_memDC.SelectObject(&m_bkbrush); // select default brush

    InvalidateRect(NULL);
}

// Reset screen coordinates and erase window.
afx_msg void CMainWin::OnReset()
{
    m_memDC.PatBlt(0, 0, maxX, maxY, PATCOPY);
    InvalidateRect(NULL);
}

// Show toolbar.
afx_msg void CMainWin::OnShowTB()
{
    m_TB.ShowWindow(SW_RESTORE);
}

// Hide toolbar.
afx_msg void CMainWin::OnHideTB()
{
    m_TB.ShowWindow(SW_HIDE);
}

// Initialize the toolbar.
void CMainWin::InitToolbar()
{
    RECT r;
    TBBUTTON tbButtons[NUMBUTTONS];

    r.left = r.top = r.right = r.bottom = 0;
```

10

```
m_TB.Create(WS_VISIBLE | WS_CHILD | WS_BORDER,
            r, this, ID_TB);

tbButtons[0].iBitmap = 0;
tbButtons[0].idCommand = IDM_LINES;
tbButtons[0].fsState = TBSTATE_ENABLED;
tbButtons[0].fsStyle = TBSTYLE_BUTTON;
tbButtons[0].dwData = 0;
tbButtons[0].iBitmap = 0;
tbButtons[0].iString = 0;

tbButtons[1].iBitmap = 1;
tbButtons[1].idCommand = IDM_RECTANGLES;
tbButtons[1].fsState = TBSTATE_ENABLED;
tbButtons[1].fsStyle = TBSTYLE_BUTTON;
tbButtons[1].dwData = 0;
tbButtons[1].iString = 0;

tbButtons[2].iBitmap = 2;
tbButtons[2].idCommand = IDM_ELLIPSES;
tbButtons[2].fsState = TBSTATE_ENABLED;
tbButtons[2].fsStyle = TBSTYLE_BUTTON;
tbButtons[2].dwData = 0;
tbButtons[2].iString = 0;

tbButtons[3].iBitmap = 3;
tbButtons[3].idCommand = IDM_RESET;
tbButtons[3].fsState = TBSTATE_ENABLED;
tbButtons[3].fsStyle = TBSTYLE_BUTTON;
tbButtons[3].dwData = 0;
tbButtons[3].iString = 0;

/* button separator */
tbButtons[4].iBitmap = 0;
tbButtons[4].idCommand = 0;
tbButtons[4].fsState = TBSTATE_ENABLED;
tbButtons[4].fsStyle = TBSTYLE_SEP;
tbButtons[4].dwData = 0;
tbButtons[4].iString = 0;

tbButtons[5].iBitmap = 4;
tbButtons[5].idCommand = IDM_HELP;
tbButtons[5].fsState = TBSTATE_ENABLED;
tbButtons[5].fsStyle = TBSTYLE_BUTTON;
```

```
  tbButtons[5].dwData = 0;
  tbButtons[5].iString = 0;


  m_TB.AddButtons(NUMBUTTONS, tbButtons);
  m_TB.AddBitmap(NUMBUTTONS, IDTB_BMP);
}


CApp App; // instantiate the application
```

Most of the code in this program is straightforward. The following is a brief description. (Remember, the non-toolbar-related code was discussed in the preceding chapter.) The toolbar is supported by the **m_TB** object, which is a member of the **CMainWin** class. In **CMainWin( )**, the **InitCommonControlsEx( )** function is called, then the toolbar is initialized inside **InitToolbar( )**. The toolbar information is held in the **tbButtons** array. Notice that the fifth structure is simply a button separator. After **tbButtons** is initialized, the buttons are added to the toolbar by calling **AddButtons( )**. The bitmaps are added using **AddBitmap( )**.

Each button in the toolbar corresponds to a menu entry in the main menu. Specifically, each of the buttons (other than the separator) is associated with a menu ID. When a button is pressed, its associated ID will be sent to the program as part of a **WM_COMMAND** message in just the same way as if a menu item had been selected. In fact, the same message handler processes both toolbar button presses and menu selections.

Since a toolbar is a window, it may be displayed or hidden like any other window using the **ShowWindow( )** function. To hide the window, select Hide Toolbar in the Options menu. To redisplay the toolbar, select Show Toolbar. Since the toolbar overlays part of the client area of the main window, you should always allow the user to remove the toolbar if it is not needed. As the program illustrates, this is very easy to do.

There is one other point of interest in the program. Notice the code inside the **OnHelp( )** handler. When Help is selected (either through the main menu or by pressing the Help button), the Help toolbar button is manually pressed by calling **PressButton( )**. After the user closes the Help message box, the button is manually released—again, by calling **PressButton( )**. Thus, the Help button remains pressed while the Help message box is displayed. This is an example of how a toolbar can be manually managed by your program when necessary.

Sample output from the toolbar program is shown in Figure 10-2.

10

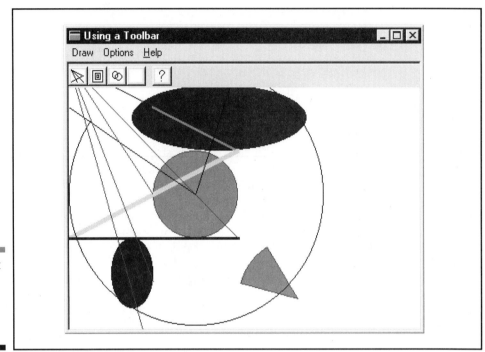

Sample output
from the
toolbar
program

Figure 10-2.

Adding Tooltips

As you have probably already seen when using Windows, some toolbars
automatically pop up small text windows when the mouse pointer pauses
over a toolbar button. These small text windows are called *tooltips*. Although
not technically required, tooltips should be included with most toolbars
because users will expect to see them. (They are also a better alternative than
including a label with each button.) In this section, we will add tooltips to
the toolbar developed in the preceding section.

To add tooltips to a toolbar, you must first include the
TBSTYLE_TOOLTIPS style when you create the toolbar. This allows
WM_NOTIFY messages to be sent when the mouse pointer lingers over a
button for more than about one half of a second. You can handle a
WM_NOTIFY message in various ways using MFC. When responding to
tooltip requests, Microsoft recommends the use of the **ON_NOTIFY_EX**
message macro.

As it applies to tooltips, the **ON_NOTIFY_EX** message macro takes this form:

ON_NOTIFY_EX(TTN_GETDISPINFO, *ID*, *TTipHandler*)

Here, **TTN_GETDISPINFO** is the notification code associated with the **WM_NOTIFY** message when a tooltip is needed. *ID* specifies the control ID and must be zero for tooltips. *TTipHandler* is the name of the message handler that processes the tooltip notification message. It must have this prototype:

afx_msg BOOL *TTipHandler*(UINT *IDnotUsed*, NMHDR **Hdr*,
                                                    LRESULT **ResultNotUsed*);

The function must return true if you have handled the notification and false otherwise. *IDnotUsed* is the control ID associated with the **WM_NOTIFY** message. Again, for tooltips, this ID is always zero and is not used. *ResultNotUsed* is also not used for tooltips. Instead, the information associated with a **WM_NOTIFY** message is found in the structure pointed to by *Hdr*. When processing tooltip requests, the type **NMHDR** is essentially a placeholder for the actual type of structure passed to the handler. You will normally need to cast this pointer into the proper structure type. For tooltips, this will be a **NMTTDISPINFO** structure, which is defined like this:

```
typedef struct tagNMTTDISPINFO {
  NMHDR hdr;
  LPSTR lpszText;
  char szText[80];
  HINSTANCE hinst;
  UINT uFlags;
  LPARAM lparam;
} NMTTDISPINFO;
```

The first member of **NMTTDISPINFO** is an **NMHDR** structure, which is defined like this:

```
typedef struct tagNMHDR
{
  HWND  hwndFrom; // handle of control
  UINT  idFrom; // control ID
  UINT  code; // notification code
} NMHDR;
```

10

If a tooltip is being requested, then **code** will contain **TTN_GETDISPINFO**, and **idFrom** will contain the ID of the button for which the tip is needed. Thus, you will use **idFrom** to identify which tooltip button is requesting a tooltip.

There are three ways to supply the required tooltip. You must either copy the tooltip text into the **szText** array of **NMTTDISPINFO**, point **lpszText** to the text, or supply the resource ID of a string resource. When using a string resource, the string ID is assigned to **lpszText** and **hinst** must be the handle of the string resource. By far the easiest way is to simply point **lpszText** to a string supplied by your program.

NOTE: The structure defined by **NMTTDISPINFO** was previously called **TOOLTIPTEXT**, and the **TTN_GETDISPINFO** message was previously called **TTN_NEEDTEXT**. The name changes have occurred to update these names with current Microsoft naming conventions. For the sake of portability, MFC programs may continue to use the old names. But, of course, new code should use the new names.

Putting into action the preceding discussion, the following function responds to tooltip requests for the graphics program:

```
// Respond to tooltip requests.
afx_msg BOOL CMainWin::OnTTip(UINT idNotUsed, NMHDR *hdr,
                              LRESULT *ResultNotUsed)
{
  switch(hdr->idFrom) {
    case IDM_LINES:
      ((NMTTDISPINFO *)hdr)->lpszText = "Lines";
      return TRUE;
    case IDM_RECTANGLES:
      ((NMTTDISPINFO *)hdr)->lpszText = "Rectangles";
      return TRUE;
    case IDM_ELLIPSES:
      ((NMTTDISPINFO *)hdr)->lpszText = "Ellipses";
      return TRUE;
    case IDM_RESET:
      ((NMTTDISPINFO *)hdr)->lpszText = "Reset";
      return TRUE;
    case IDM_HELP:
      ((NMTTDISPINFO *)hdr)->lpszText = "Help";
      return TRUE;
```

```
   }
   return FALSE;
}
```

Once the tooltip text has been set and control passes back to Windows, the tooltip will automatically be displayed. Your program need perform no further action. As you can see, tooltips are largely automated and easy to add to your toolbar.

NOTE: It is also possible to create stand-alone tooltips that can be used with types of controls other than toolbars. They are encapsulated by the **CToolTipCtrl** class. You may want to explore these on your own.

The Entire Toolbar Program Including Tooltips

The entire toolbar with tooltips program is shown here. Sample output from this program is shown in Figure 10-3. The program uses the same resource file and IDS.H header file as the previous program. The class derivation file, TOOLTIP.H, is shown here:

```
// TOOLTIP.H

#include "ids.h"

// This is the main window class.
class CMainWin : public CFrameWnd
{
  CDC m_memDC; // virtual window device context
  CBitmap m_bmp; // virtual window bitmap
  CBrush m_bkbrush; // brush for virtual window

  // create pens
  CPen m_RedPen, m_YellowPen, m_GreenPen, m_BluePen;
  CPen m_OldPen;

  CToolBarCtrl m_TB; // toolbar control
public:
  CMainWin();
```

10

```
afx_msg void OnPaint();
afx_msg void OnSize(UINT How, int Width, int Height);

afx_msg void OnLines();
afx_msg void OnRectangles();
afx_msg void OnEllipses();
afx_msg void OnReset();
afx_msg void OnShowTB();
afx_msg void OnHideTB();
afx_msg void OnExit();
afx_msg void OnHelp();

afx_msg BOOL OnTTip(UINT idNotUsed, NMHDR *hdr,
                    LRESULT *ResultNotUsed);

void InitToolbar();

DECLARE_MESSAGE_MAP()
};

// This is the application class.
class CApp : public CWinApp
{
public:
  BOOL InitInstance();
};
```

The tooltip program file is shown here:

```
// Demonstrate Tooltips
#include <afxwin.h>
#include <afxcmn.h>
#include "tooltip.h"
#include "ids.h"

int maxX, maxY; // screen dimensions

CMainWin::CMainWin()
{
  Create(NULL, "Adding Tooltips",
         WS_OVERLAPPEDWINDOW, rectDefault,
         NULL, "ToolbarMenu");
```

```
    // Load accelerator table
    if(!LoadAccelTable("ToolbarMenu"))
      MessageBox("Cannot Load Accelerators", "Error");

    maxX = GetSystemMetrics(SM_CXSCREEN);
    maxY = GetSystemMetrics(SM_CYSCREEN);

    CClientDC DC(this);

    // create a virtual output window
    m_memDC.CreateCompatibleDC(&DC);
    m_bmp.CreateCompatibleBitmap(&DC, maxX, maxY);
    m_memDC.SelectObject(&m_bmp);
    // use standard background
    m_bkbrush.CreateStockObject(WHITE_BRUSH);
    m_memDC.SelectObject(&m_bkbrush);
    // paint background of virtual window
    m_memDC.PatBlt(0, 0, maxX, maxY, PATCOPY);

    // create pens
    m_RedPen.CreatePen(PS_SOLID, 1, RGB(255,0,0));
    m_GreenPen.CreatePen(PS_SOLID, 2, RGB(0,255,0));
    m_BluePen.CreatePen(PS_SOLID, 3, RGB(0,0,255));
    m_YellowPen.CreatePen(PS_SOLID, 4, RGB(255, 255, 0));

    m_OldPen.CreateStockObject(BLACK_PEN);

    INITCOMMONCONTROLSEX initCtrls;

    initCtrls.dwSize = sizeof(initCtrls);
    initCtrls.dwICC= ICC_BAR_CLASSES;
    InitCommonControlsEx(&initCtrls);

    InitToolbar();
}

// Initialize the application.
BOOL CApp::InitInstance()
{
  m_pMainWnd = new CMainWin;
  m_pMainWnd->ShowWindow(m_nCmdShow);
  m_pMainWnd->UpdateWindow();
```

10

```
    return TRUE;
}

// This is the application's message map.
BEGIN_MESSAGE_MAP(CMainWin, CFrameWnd)
  ON_WM_PAINT()
  ON_WM_SIZE()
  ON_COMMAND(IDM_LINES, OnLines)
  ON_COMMAND(IDM_RECTANGLES, OnRectangles)
  ON_COMMAND(IDM_ELLIPSES, OnEllipses)
  ON_COMMAND(IDM_RESET, OnReset)
  ON_COMMAND(IDM_SHOWTB, OnShowTB)
  ON_COMMAND(IDM_HIDETB, OnHideTB)
  ON_COMMAND(IDM_EXIT, OnExit)
  ON_COMMAND(IDM_HELP, OnHelp)
  ON_NOTIFY_EX(TTN_GETDISPINFO, 0, OnTTip)
END_MESSAGE_MAP()

// Update screen using contents of virtual window.
afx_msg void CMainWin::OnPaint()
{
  CPaintDC DC(this);

  DC.BitBlt(0, 0, maxX, maxY, &m_memDC, 0, 0, SRCCOPY);
}

// Resize toolbar when a WM_SIZE message is received.
afx_msg void CMainWin::OnSize(UINT How,
                               int Width, int Height)
{
  m_TB.AutoSize();
}

// Process IDM_EXIT.
afx_msg void CMainWin::OnExit()
{
  int response;

  response = MessageBox("Quit the Program?",
                        "Exit", MB_YESNO);

  if(response == IDYES)
    SendMessage(WM_CLOSE); // terminate app
```

```
    }

    // Process IDM_HELP.
    afx_msg void CMainWin::OnHelp()
    {
        m_TB.PressButton(IDM_HELP);
        MessageBox("Toolbar Demo", "Help");
        m_TB.PressButton(IDM_HELP, FALSE);
    }

    // Display lines and points.
    afx_msg void CMainWin::OnLines()
    {
      // draw 4 pixels
      m_memDC.SetPixel(40, 14, RGB(255, 0, 0));
      m_memDC.SetPixel(41, 14, RGB(0, 255, 0));
      m_memDC.SetPixel(42, 14, RGB(0, 0, 255));
      m_memDC.SetPixel(43, 14, RGB(0, 0, 0));

      m_memDC.LineTo(100, 50);
      m_memDC.MoveTo(100, 50);

      // change to green pen
      m_memDC.SelectObject(&m_GreenPen);
      m_memDC.LineTo(200, 100);

      // change to yellow pen
      m_memDC.SelectObject(&m_YellowPen);
      m_memDC.LineTo(0, 200);

      // change to blue pen
      m_memDC.SelectObject(&m_BluePen);
      m_memDC.LineTo(200, 200);

      // change to red pen
      m_memDC.SelectObject(&m_RedPen);
      m_memDC.LineTo(0, 0);

      m_memDC.LineTo(100, 150);
      m_memDC.MoveTo(0, 0);
      m_memDC.LineTo(100, 250);
      m_memDC.MoveTo(0, 0);
      m_memDC.LineTo(100, 350);
```

10

```
   // return to default pen
   m_memDC.SelectObject(&m_OldPen);

   m_memDC.Arc(0, 0, 300, 300, 0, 50, 200, 0);
   // show intersecting lines that define arc
   m_memDC.MoveTo(150, 150);
   m_memDC.LineTo(0, 50);
   m_memDC.MoveTo(150, 150);
   m_memDC.LineTo(200, 0);

   InvalidateRect(NULL);
}

// Display rectangles.
afx_msg void CMainWin::OnRectangles()
{
   CBrush HollowBrush;

   // display, but don't fill, rectangles
   HollowBrush.CreateStockObject(HOLLOW_BRUSH);
   m_memDC.SelectObject(&HollowBrush);

   // draw some rectangles
   m_memDC.Rectangle(50, 50, 300, 300);
   m_memDC.RoundRect(125, 125, 220, 240, 15, 13);

   // use a red pen
   m_memDC.SelectObject(&m_RedPen);
   m_memDC.Rectangle(100, 100, 200, 200);
   m_memDC.SelectObject(&m_OldPen); // return to default pen

   // restore default brush
   m_memDC.SelectObject(&m_bkbrush);

   InvalidateRect(NULL);
}

// Display ellipses.
afx_msg void CMainWin::OnEllipses()
{
   CBrush Brush;
```

```
// make blue brush
Brush.CreateSolidBrush(RGB(0, 0, 255));
m_memDC.SelectObject(&Brush);

// fill these ellipses with blue
m_memDC.Ellipse(50, 200, 100, 280);
m_memDC.Ellipse(75, 25, 280, 100);

// use a red pen
m_memDC.SelectObject(&m_RedPen);

// create green brush
Brush.DeleteObject();
Brush.CreateSolidBrush(RGB(0, 255, 0));
m_memDC.SelectObject(&Brush); // select green brush
m_memDC.Ellipse(100, 100, 200, 200);

// draw a pie slice
m_memDC.Pie(200, 200, 340, 340, 225, 200, 200, 250);

m_memDC.SelectObject(&m_OldPen); // return to default pen
m_memDC.SelectObject(&m_bkbrush); // select default brush

InvalidateRect(NULL);
}

// Reset screen coordinates and erase window.
afx_msg void CMainWin::OnReset()
{
  m_memDC.PatBlt(0, 0, maxX, maxY, PATCOPY);
  InvalidateRect(NULL);
}

// Show toolbar.
afx_msg void CMainWin::OnShowTB()
{
  m_TB.ShowWindow(SW_RESTORE);
}

// Hide toolbar.
afx_msg void CMainWin::OnHideTB()
{
```

10

```
    m_TB.ShowWindow(SW_HIDE);
}

// Respond to tooltip requests.
afx_msg BOOL CMainWin::OnTTip(UINT idNotUsed, NMHDR *hdr,
                              LRESULT *ResultNotUsed)
{
  switch(hdr->idFrom) {
    case IDM_LINES:
      ((NMTTDISPINFO *)hdr)->lpszText = "Lines";
      return TRUE;
    case IDM_RECTANGLES:
      ((NMTTDISPINFO *)hdr)->lpszText = "Rectangles";
      return TRUE;
    case IDM_ELLIPSES:
      ((NMTTDISPINFO *)hdr)->lpszText = "Ellipses";
      return TRUE;
    case IDM_RESET:
      ((NMTTDISPINFO *)hdr)->lpszText = "Reset";
      return TRUE;
    case IDM_HELP:
      ((NMTTDISPINFO *)hdr)->lpszText = "Help";
      return TRUE;
  }
  return FALSE;
}

// Initialize the toolbar.
void CMainWin::InitToolbar()
{
  RECT r;
  TBBUTTON tbButtons[NUMBUTTONS];

  r.left = r.top = r.right = r.bottom = 0;

  m_TB.Create(WS_VISIBLE | WS_CHILD | WS_BORDER |
              TBSTYLE_TOOLTIPS, r, this, ID_TB);

  tbButtons[0].iBitmap = 0;
  tbButtons[0].idCommand = IDM_LINES;
  tbButtons[0].fsState = TBSTATE_ENABLED;
  tbButtons[0].fsStyle = TBSTYLE_BUTTON;
  tbButtons[0].dwData = 0;
```

```
            tbButtons[0].iBitmap = 0;
            tbButtons[0].iString = 0;

            tbButtons[1].iBitmap = 1;
            tbButtons[1].idCommand = IDM_RECTANGLES;
            tbButtons[1].fsState = TBSTATE_ENABLED;
            tbButtons[1].fsStyle = TBSTYLE_BUTTON;
            tbButtons[1].dwData = 0;
            tbButtons[1].iString = 0;

            tbButtons[2].iBitmap = 2;
            tbButtons[2].idCommand = IDM_ELLIPSES;
            tbButtons[2].fsState = TBSTATE_ENABLED;
            tbButtons[2].fsStyle = TBSTYLE_BUTTON;
            tbButtons[2].dwData = 0;
            tbButtons[2].iString = 0;

            tbButtons[3].iBitmap = 3;
            tbButtons[3].idCommand = IDM_RESET;
            tbButtons[3].fsState = TBSTATE_ENABLED;
            tbButtons[3].fsStyle = TBSTYLE_BUTTON;
            tbButtons[3].dwData = 0;
            tbButtons[3].iString = 0;

            /* button separator */
            tbButtons[4].iBitmap = 0;
            tbButtons[4].idCommand = 0;
            tbButtons[4].fsState = TBSTATE_ENABLED;
            tbButtons[4].fsStyle = TBSTYLE_SEP;
            tbButtons[4].dwData = 0;
            tbButtons[4].iString = 0;

            tbButtons[5].iBitmap = 4;
            tbButtons[5].idCommand = IDM_HELP;
            tbButtons[5].fsState = TBSTATE_ENABLED;
            tbButtons[5].fsStyle = TBSTYLE_BUTTON;
            tbButtons[5].dwData = 0;
            tbButtons[5].iString = 0;

            m_TB.AddButtons(NUMBUTTONS, tbButtons);
            m_TB.AddBitmap(NUMBUTTONS, IDTB_BMP);
        }

        CApp App; // instantiate the application
```

10

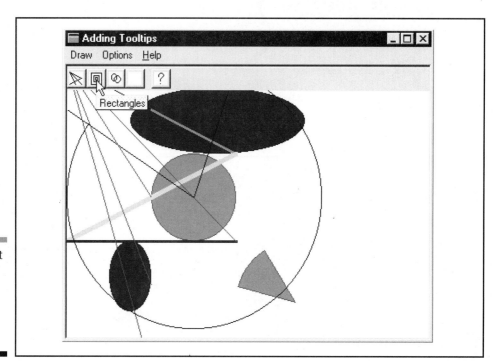

Sample output
from the
toolbar with
tooltips
program

Figure 10-3.

In the next chapter, we will continue to explore the common controls,
examining spin controls, track bars, and progress bars.

CHAPTER 11

More
Common Controls

This chapter continues our look at the common controls. In it we will examine the up-down, spin, and slider controls, and the progress bar.

 NOTE: Remember, the common controls are supported only by modern versions of Windows, such as Windows 95, Windows 98, and Windows NT 4. They are not supported by Windows 3.1.

Up-Down Controls

One control that you will find useful in a number of situations is the *up-down* control. An up-down control is essentially a scroll bar without the bar! That is, it consists only of the arrows found on the ends of a scroll bar, but there is no bar between them. As you may have seen while using various Windows applications, some scroll bars are so small that the bar is pointless. Also, some situations don't lend themselves to the concept of the bar, but benefit from the use of the up and down arrows. To accommodate these situations, the up-down control was invented. As you will see, using an up-down control is much like using a scroll bar.

An up-down control may be used two different ways. First, it may be used more or less like a stand-alone scroll bar. Second, it can be used in conjunction with another control, called its *buddy window*. The most common buddy window is an edit box. When this is the case, a *spin control* is created. When using a spin control, almost all of the overhead required to manage the control is provided automatically. This makes the spin control easy to add to your application. This chapter presents two up-down examples. The first creates a stand-alone up-down control. The second example uses a buddy window to create a spin control. Up-down controls are encapsulated in MFC by the **CSpinButtonCtrl** class. As you will see, this class is used to create both up-down and spin controls.

Creating an Up-Down Control

To create an up-down control, use the **Create( )** member function of the **CSpinButtonCtrl** class, shown here:

BOOL CSpinButtonCtrl::Create(DWORD *dwStyle*, const RECT &*SizePos*,
                             CWnd **Owner, UINT *ID*);

Here, *dwStyle* specifies the style of the up-down control. This parameter usually includes the standard styles **WS_CHILD**, **WS_VISIBLE**, and **WS_BORDER**.

It may also include one or more of the up-down styles shown in Table 11-1. The location and size of the up-down control is passed in the **RECT** structure specified by *SizePos*. A pointer to the parent window object is passed in *Owner*. The ID associated with the up-down control is specified in *ID*.

Create( ) returns nonzero if successful and zero on failure.

Up-Down Control Messages

When one of the arrows of an up-down control is pressed, it sends a **WM_VSCROLL** message to its parent window. You will handle this message by overriding the standard **OnVScroll( )** message handler, which was described in Chapter 6. As you should recall, **OnVScroll( )** has this prototype:

afx_msg void CWnd::OnVScroll(UINT *SBCode*, UINT *Pos*, CScrollBar **SB*);

SBCode contains a notification code that describes what type of activity has occurred. Since up-down controls are fully automated, this value is not

11

Style	Meaning
UDS_ALIGNLEFT	Aligns up-down control to the left of its buddy window.
UDS_ALIGNRIGHT	Aligns up-down control to the right of its buddy window.
UDS_ARROWKEYS	Enables arrow keys. (That is, the keyboard arrow keys may be used to move the control.) Applies to spin controls only.
UDS_AUTOBUDDY	Buddy window is previous window in Z order.
UDS_HORZ	Up-down control is horizontal. Up-down controls are vertical by default.
UDS_NOTHOUSANDS	Commas not used in large values. (Applies to spin controls only.)
UDS_SETBUDDYINT	Automatically sets the text within the buddy window when the control position is changed. This allows the buddy window to show the current position of the up-down control.
UDS_WRAP	Position of up-down control will "wrap around" when moved past an end.

The Up-Down (Spin) Control Styles

Table 11-1.

usually needed. *Pos* contains the position of the up-down control. When the **WM_VSCROLL** message is generated by an up-down control, then *SB* will point to the up-down control object that generated the message. Otherwise, *SB* will either be **NULL** if a standard window scroll bar generated the message or point to a scroll bar control if a stand-alone scroll bar generated the message. Since there may be more than one control that generates **WM_VSCROLL** messages, you will need to check the value of *SB* to determine if it is that of the up-down control.

Some CSpinButtonCtrl Member Functions

CSpinButtonCtrl contains several member functions that help you manage up-down controls. Some of the most commonly used are presented here.

An up-down control maintains its own current position (or count). Each time you press one of the arrow buttons, this position is incremented or decremented. To obtain the new position, call **GetPos( )**. Its prototype is shown here:

    int CSpinButtonCtrl::GetPos( ) const;

The current position of the control is returned in the low-order word. The high-order word is zero unless an error occurs or if there is no buddy window.

To set the position of the up-down control, call **SetPos( )**. Its prototype is shown here:

    int CSpinButtonCtrl::SetPos(int *NewPos*);

Here, *NewPos* specifies the new position. The previous position of the control is returned.

By default, the range of an up-down control is 0 through 100. You can set the range using **SetRange( )**, shown here:

    void CSpinButtonCtrl::SetRange(int *min*, int *max*);

Here, *min* must be greater than or equal to **UD_MINVAL** and *max* must be less than or equal to **UD_MAXVAL**. Also, *max* – *min* must not be greater than **UD_MAXVAL**. If *min* is greater than *max* then the control runs backward.

You can obtain the range of an up-down control by calling **GetRange( )**. Its prototype is shown here:

    void CSpinButtonCtrl::GetRange(int &*min*, int &*max*) const;

After the call, *min* will contain the minimum value and *max* will contain the maximum value. There is also an overloaded form of **GetRange( )** that returns the range encoded into a 32-bit value.

Using an Up-Down Control

The following program creates a stand-alone up-down control within a dialog box. In this example, the up-down control is not linked to a buddy window. The up-down control has a range of 0 to 99, with an initial position of 50. Each time the position of the control is changed (by pressing an arrow), the new position is displayed in the client area of the dialog box. Sample output from the program is shown in Figure 11-1.

The resource file for the program is shown here:

```
// UPDOWN.RC

#include <afxres.h>
#include "ids.h"

UpDownMenu MENU
{
  POPUP "Demo"
  {
    MENUITEM "&Up-Down Demo\tF2", IDM_DIALOG
    MENUITEM "E&xit\tF3", IDM_EXIT
  }
  MENUITEM "&Help", IDM_HELP
}

UpDownMenu ACCELERATORS
{
  VK_F1, IDM_HELP, VIRTKEY
  VK_F2, IDM_DIALOG, VIRTKEY
  VK_F3, IDM_EXIT, VIRTKEY
}
```

11

```
UpDownDialog DIALOG 18, 18, 142, 92
CAPTION "Demonstrate Up-Down Control"
STYLE DS_MODALFRAME | WS_POPUP | WS_CAPTION | WS_SYSMENU
{
  PUSHBUTTON "Cancel", IDCANCEL, 52, 65, 37, 14,
             WS_CHILD | WS_VISIBLE | WS_TABSTOP
}
```

The IDS.H header file is shown here. This file is used by all of the programs in this chapter and includes values used by later programs.

```
// IDS.H

#define IDM_DIALOG   100
#define IDM_HELP     101
#define IDM_EXIT     102

#define IDD_SPIN       200
#define IDD_EB1        201
#define IDD_TRACKBAR 202
#define IDD_PROGBAR    203
#define IDD_STATIC     204
```

The class derivation file for the up-down demo program is shown here. Call this file UPDOWN.H.

```
// UPDOWN.H

// This is the main window class.
class CMainWin : public CFrameWnd
{
public:
  CMainWin();

  // define menu handlers
  afx_msg void OnDialog();
  afx_msg void OnExit();
  afx_msg void OnHelp();

  DECLARE_MESSAGE_MAP()
};

// This is the application class.
class CApp : public CWinApp
```

```
{
public:
  BOOL InitInstance();
};

// This is a dialog class.
class CSampleDialog : public CDialog
{
  CSpinButtonCtrl m_UpDown; // up-down control

public:
  CSampleDialog(char *DialogName, CWnd *Owner) :
    CDialog(DialogName, Owner) {}

  BOOL OnInitDialog();

  afx_msg void OnVScroll(UINT SBCode, UINT Pos,
                         CScrollBar *SB);

  DECLARE_MESSAGE_MAP()
};
```

The up-down control program file is shown here:

```
// Demonstrate an up-down control.

#include <afxwin.h>
#include <afxcmn.h>
#include <string.h>
#include "updown.h"
#include "ids.h"

CMainWin::CMainWin()
{
  Create(NULL, "Demonstrate Up-Down Control",
         WS_OVERLAPPEDWINDOW, rectDefault,
         NULL, "UpDownMenu");

  INITCOMMONCONTROLSEX initCtrls;

  initCtrls.dwSize = sizeof(initCtrls);
  initCtrls.dwICC= ICC_UPDOWN_CLASS;
  InitCommonControlsEx(&initCtrls);

  // Load accelerator table.
  if(!LoadAccelTable("UpDownMenu"))
```

11

```
    MessageBox("Cannot Load Accelerators", "Error");
}

// Initialize the application.
BOOL CApp::InitInstance()
{
  m_pMainWnd = new CMainWin;
  m_pMainWnd->ShowWindow(m_nCmdShow);
  m_pMainWnd->UpdateWindow();

  return TRUE;
}

// This is the application's message map.
BEGIN_MESSAGE_MAP(CMainWin, CFrameWnd)
  ON_COMMAND(IDM_DIALOG, OnDialog)
  ON_COMMAND(IDM_EXIT, OnExit)
  ON_COMMAND(IDM_HELP, OnHelp)
END_MESSAGE_MAP()

// Process IDM_DIALOG.
afx_msg void CMainWin::OnDialog()
{
  CSampleDialog diagOb("UpDownDialog", this);

  diagOb.DoModal(); // activate modal dialog box
}

// Process IDM_EXIT.
afx_msg void CMainWin::OnExit()
{
  int response;

  response = MessageBox("Quit the Program?",
                        "Exit", MB_YESNO);

  if(response == IDYES)
    SendMessage(WM_CLOSE); // terminate app
}

// Process IDM_HELP.
afx_msg void CMainWin::OnHelp()
{
    MessageBox("Up-Down Control", "Help");
}
```

```
// This is SampleDialog's message map.
BEGIN_MESSAGE_MAP(CSampleDialog, CDialog)
  ON_WM_VSCROLL()
END_MESSAGE_MAP()

// Initialize the dialog box.
BOOL CSampleDialog::OnInitDialog()
{
  RECT r;

  CDialog::OnInitDialog(); // Call base class version

  // create up-down control
  r.left = r.top  = 10;
  r.right = r.bottom = 50;
  m_UpDown.Create(WS_VISIBLE | WS_CHILD | WS_BORDER,
                  r, this, IDD_SPIN);

  // set range and initial position of up-down control
  m_UpDown.SetRange(0, 99);
  m_UpDown.SetPos(50);

  return TRUE;
}

// Process WM_VSCROLL messages for up-down control.
afx_msg void CSampleDialog::OnVScroll(UINT SBCode, UINT Pos,
                             CScrollBar *SB)
{
  char str[255];

  // SB must point to up-down control
  if(SB != (CScrollBar *)&m_UpDown) return;

  CClientDC dc(this);

  dc.SetBkColor(RGB(200, 200, 200));

  wsprintf(str, "%d", LOWORD(m_UpDown.GetPos()));
  dc.TextOut(50, 22, "     ", 5);
  dc.TextOut(50, 22, str, strlen(str));
}

CApp App; // instantiate the application
```

11

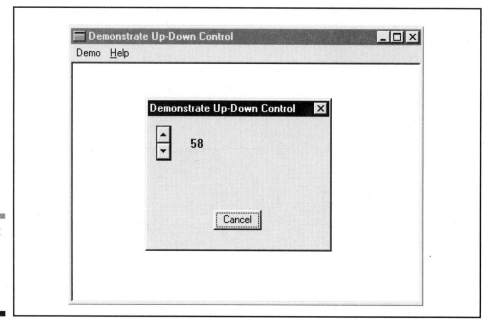

Sample output
from the first
up-down
example
Figure 11-1.

In the program, the up-down control is contained within the dialog box. The control is created when the dialog box is initialized by the **OnInitDialog( )** function, shown here:

```
// Initialize the dialog box.
BOOL CSampleDialog::OnInitDialog()
{
  RECT r;

  CDialog::OnInitDialog(); // Call base class version

  // create up-down control
  r.left = r.top  = 10;
  r.right = r.bottom = 50;
  m_UpDown.Create(WS_VISIBLE | WS_CHILD | WS_BORDER,
                  r, this, IDD_SPIN);

  // set range and initial position of up-down control
  m_UpDown.SetRange(0, 99);
  m_UpDown.SetPos(50);

  return TRUE;
}
```

The up-down control is encapsulated by the **CSampleDialog** member object **m_UpDown**. The call to **Create( )** creates an up-down control that is at location 10,10 within the dialog box. The control is 50 pixels wide and 50 pixels tall. Because the control is a child window of the dialog box, a pointer to the dialog box object (represented by **this**) is passed as the parent window. The ID of the up-down control is **IDD_SPIN**. The range of the up-down control is set at 0 through 99, and the initial position is 50.

Each time the up-down control is accessed, a **WM_VSCROLL** message is sent to the dialog box. This message is processed by **OnVScroll( )**, shown here:

```
// Process WM_VSCROLL messages for up-down control.
afx_msg void CSampleDialog::OnVScroll(UINT SBCode, UINT Pos,
                                CScrollBar *SB)
{
  char str[255];

  // SB must point to up-down control
  if(SB != (CScrollBar *)&m_UpDown) return;

  CClientDC dc(this);

  dc.SetBkColor(RGB(200, 200, 200));

  wsprintf(str, "%d", LOWORD(m_UpDown.GetPos()));
  dc.TextOut(50, 22, "       ", 5);
  dc.TextOut(50, 22, str, strlen(str));
}
```

Notice that **SB** is tested against the address of **m_UpDown** to confirm that it is the up-down control that generated the message. While there is only one control in this example, real-world applications may have several controls capable of generating a **WM_VSCROLL** message, so you should always confirm which control has been accessed.

11

To obtain the new up-down position, the **GetPos( )** function is called. As explained, the current position of the up-down control is contained in the low-order word of the value returned by **GetPos( )**. The low-order word is obtained through the use of the macro **LOWORD( )**. (See the In Depth box.) Since the up-down control's position is also contained in the **Pos** parameter to **OnVScroll( )**, **GetPos( )** is used only for the sake of demonstration. Once obtained, the position of the up-down control is then displayed in the client area of the dialog box.

IN DEPTH

LOWORD( ) and HIWORD( )

As illustrated by the return value of **CSpinButtonCtrl::GetPos( )**, in Windows programming two values are frequently encoded into the high- and low-order words of a single 32-bit integer. This means you often need access to either the high-order or low-order word of a given value. As a convenience, Windows provides the macros **LOWORD( )** and **HIWORD( )** that decode a 32-bit integer into its low-order and high-order words, respectively. These macros have the following general forms:

WORD LOWORD(DWORD *val*);

WORD HIWORD(DWORD *val*);

As you continue to program for Windows, you will find numerous opportunities to put these macros to good use.

Creating a Spin Control

While there is nothing whatsoever wrong with creating and using a stand-alone up-down control, the up-down control is most commonly linked with an edit box. As mentioned, this combination is called a *spin control*. Because the spin control is such a common use of an up-down control, Windows provides special support for it. In fact, a spin control is a completely automated control—your program incurs virtually no management overhead itself.

To create a spin control, you must specify an edit control as a buddy window to an up-down control. After you have done this, each time the up-down control is changed, its new position is automatically displayed in the edit box. Further, if you manually change the value in the edit box, the up-down control is automatically set to reflect that value.

Changing an up-down control into a spin control is an easy, two-step process. First, add an edit box to your program's resource file. Second, call the **SetBuddy( )** member function to link the edit box with the up-down control. The prototype for **SetBuddy( )** is shown here:

CWnd *CSpinButtonCtrl::SetBuddy(CWnd *BuddyWnd*);

Here, *BuddyWnd* is a pointer to the buddy window that will be linked to the up-down control to form the spin button. The function returns the previous buddy window (if there was one).

A Spin Control Sample Program

The following program demonstrates a spin control. Here is its resource file:

```
// SPIN.RC

#include <afxres.h>
#include "ids.h"

SpinMenu MENU
{
  POPUP "Demo"
  {
    MENUITEM "&Spin Control Demo\tF2", IDM_DIALOG
    MENUITEM "E&xit\tF3", IDM_EXIT
  }
  MENUITEM "&Help", IDM_HELP
}

SpinMenu ACCELERATORS
{
  VK_F1, IDM_HELP, VIRTKEY
  VK_F2, IDM_DIALOG, VIRTKEY
  VK_F3, IDM_EXIT, VIRTKEY
}

SpinDialog DIALOG 18, 18, 142, 92
CAPTION "Demonstrate Spin Control"
STYLE DS_MODALFRAME | WS_POPUP | WS_CAPTION | WS_SYSMENU
{
  PUSHBUTTON "Cancel", IDCANCEL, 52, 65, 37, 14,
             WS_CHILD | WS_VISIBLE | WS_TABSTOP
  EDITTEXT IDD_EB1, 10, 10, 26, 12, ES_LEFT | WS_CHILD |
             WS_VISIBLE | WS_BORDER
}
```

The SPIN.H class derivation file is shown here:

```
// SPIN.H
```

11

```
// This is the main window class.
class CMainWin : public CFrameWnd
{
public:
  CMainWin();

  // define menu handlers
  afx_msg void OnDialog();
  afx_msg void OnExit();
  afx_msg void OnHelp();

  DECLARE_MESSAGE_MAP()
};

// This is the application class.
class CApp : public CWinApp
{
public:
  BOOL InitInstance();
};

// This is a dialog class.
class CSampleDialog : public CDialog
{
  CSpinButtonCtrl m_Spin; // spin control

public:
  CSampleDialog(char *DialogName, CWnd *Owner) :
    CDialog(DialogName, Owner) {}

  BOOL OnInitDialog();

  DECLARE_MESSAGE_MAP()
};
```

The spin control program file is shown here:

```
// Demonstrate a Spin control.

#include <afxwin.h>
#include <afxcmn.h>
#include "spin.h"
#include "ids.h"

CMainWin::CMainWin()
```

```
  {
    Create(NULL, "Demonstrate Spin Control",
           WS_OVERLAPPEDWINDOW, rectDefault,
           NULL, "SpinMenu");

    INITCOMMONCONTROLSEX initCtrls;

    initCtrls.dwSize = sizeof(initCtrls);
    initCtrls.dwICC= ICC_UPDOWN_CLASS;
    InitCommonControlsEx(&initCtrls);

    // Load accelerator table
    if(!LoadAccelTable("SpinMenu"))
      MessageBox("Cannot Load Accelerators", "Error");
  }

// Initialize the application.
BOOL CApp::InitInstance()
{
  m_pMainWnd = new CMainWin;
  m_pMainWnd->ShowWindow(m_nCmdShow);
  m_pMainWnd->UpdateWindow();

  return TRUE;
}

// This is the application's message map.
BEGIN_MESSAGE_MAP(CMainWin, CFrameWnd)
  ON_COMMAND(IDM_DIALOG, OnDialog)
  ON_COMMAND(IDM_EXIT, OnExit)
  ON_COMMAND(IDM_HELP, OnHelp)
END_MESSAGE_MAP()

// Process IDM_DIALOG.
afx_msg void CMainWin::OnDialog()
{
  CSampleDialog diagOb("SpinDialog", this);

  diagOb.DoModal(); // activate modal dialog box
}

// Process IDM_EXIT.
afx_msg void CMainWin::OnExit()
{
  int response;
```

11

```
    response = MessageBox("Quit the Program?",
                          "Exit", MB_YESNO);

  if(response == IDYES)
    SendMessage(WM_CLOSE); // terminate app
}

// Process IDM_HELP.
afx_msg void CMainWin::OnHelp()
{
    MessageBox("Spin Control", "Help");
}

// This is SampleDialog's message map.
BEGIN_MESSAGE_MAP(CSampleDialog, CDialog)
END_MESSAGE_MAP()

// Initialize the dialog box.
BOOL CSampleDialog::OnInitDialog()
{
  RECT r;

  CDialog::OnInitDialog(); // Call base class version

  // create spin control
  r.left = r.top  = 10;
  r.right = r.bottom = 50;
  m_Spin.Create(WS_VISIBLE | WS_CHILD | WS_BORDER |
                UDS_SETBUDDYINT | UDS_ALIGNRIGHT,
                r, this, IDD_SPIN);

  // set range of spin control
  m_Spin.SetRange(0, 99);

  // Set buddy window
  m_Spin.SetBuddy(GetDlgItem(IDD_EB1));

  // set initial position
  m_Spin.SetPos(50);

  return TRUE;
}

CApp App; // instantiate the application
```

Sample output from the program is shown in Figure 11-2.

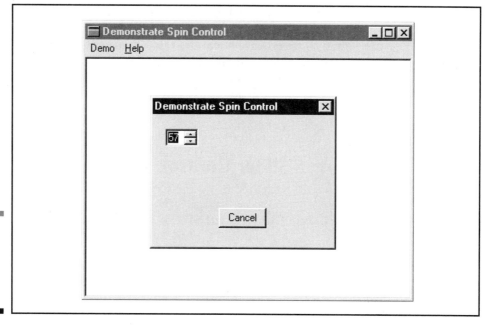

Sample output
from the spin
control
program
Figure 11-2.

As you can see by looking at the **OnInitDialog( )** function, the buddy
window is linked to the up-down control using the following call to
SetBuddy( ):

```
m_Spin.SetBuddy(GetDlgItem(IDD_EB1));
```

As you should recall from Chapter 5, **GetDlgItem( )** is a member function
of the **CWnd** class. It returns a pointer to the object whose ID is passed as a
parameter.

Once the up-down control has been created with an edit box as its buddy
window, the two controls are automatically linked together, forming the spin
control. Notice that the program does not handle **WM_VSCROLL** messages.
The reason for this is that a spin control automatically updates its buddy
window each time its position changes. Your program does not need to do
this manually.

Using a Slider Control

One of the most visually appealing of the common controls is the slider
control (also called a *trackbar*). A slider control is visually similar to the slide

11

control found on various types of electronic equipment, such as stereos. It consists of a pointer that moves within a track. Although it looks quite different, a slider control is handled in a manner similar to the way a scroll bar is handled by your program. Slider controls are particularly useful when your program is emulating a real device. For example, if your program is controlling a graphics equalizer, then sliders are an excellent choice for representing and setting the frequency curve. Slider controls are encapsulated by the **CSliderCtrl** class.

Creating a Slider Control

A slider control is created using the **Create( )** member function, shown here:

BOOL CSliderCtrl::Create(DWORD *dwStyle*, const RECT &*SizePos*,
CWnd **Owner*, UINT *ID*);

Here, *dwStyle* specifies the style of the slider control. This parameter usually includes the standard styles **WS_CHILD**, **WS_VISIBLE**, and **WS_BORDER**. It may also include one or more trackbar-specific styles. The most common styles are shown in Table 11-2. You will almost always want to include **TBS_AUTOTICKS** because this style causes small "tick" marks to be automatically shown on the bar. The tick marks provide a scale for the bar. The location and size of the slider control is passed in the **RECT** structure specified by *SizePos*. A pointer to the parent window object is passed in *Owner*. The ID associated with the slider control is specified in *ID*.

Create( ) returns nonzero if successful and zero on failure.

Slider Control Style	Effect
TBS_AUTOTICKS	Automatically adds tick marks to the trackbar.
TBS_TOOLTIPS	Trackbar includes a tooltip. By default, the tooltip displays the current position of the slider. Requires Windows 98 or IE 4 (or later).
TBS_NOTICKS	Trackbar does not have tick marks.
TBS_HORZ	Trackbar is horizontal. (This is the default.)
TBS_VERT	Trackbar is vertical.
TBS_BOTTOM	Tick marks on bottom of bar. (This is the default.)

Common Slider Control (Trackbar) Style Options

Table 11-2.

Common
Slider Control
(Trackbar)
Style Options
(*continued*)
Table 11-2.

Slider Control Style	Effect
TBS_TOP	Tick marks on top of bar.
TBS_LEFT	Tick marks on left of bar.
TBS_RIGHT	Tick marks on right of bar. (This is the default.)
TBS_BOTH	Tick marks on both sides of bar.

Processing Slider Control Messages

When a slider control is accessed, it generates a **WM_HSCROLL** message. Your program will handle this message by overriding the standard **OnHScroll( )** message handler. As you should recall, **OnHScroll( )** has this prototype:

afx_msg void CWnd::OnHScroll(UINT *SBCode*, UINT *Pos*, CScrollBar **SB*);

SBCode contains a notification code that describes what type of activity has occurred. Since slider controls are not scroll bars, they use a different set of notification codes. These notification codes are described in Table 11-3. *Pos* contains the position of the slider control. When the **WM_HSCROLL** message is generated by a slider control, then *SB* will point to the slider control object that generated the message. Otherwise, *SB* will either be **NULL** if a standard window scroll bar generated the message or point to a scroll bar control if a stand-alone scroll bar generated the message. Since there may be more than one control that generates **WM_HSCROLL** messages, you will need to check the value of *SB* to determine if it is that of the slider control.

11

Slider Control
Notification
Messages
Table 11-3.

Message	Meaning
TB_BOTTOM	END key is pressed. Slider is moved to minimum value.
TB_ENDTRACK	End of keyboard event. (Key is released.)
TB_LINEDOWN	Right or down arrow key pressed.
TB_LINEUP	Left or up arrow key pressed.

Message	Meaning
TB_PAGEDOWN	PAGE DOWN key pressed or mouse click before slider.
TB_PAGEUP	PAGE UP key pressed or mouse click after slider.
TB_THUMBPOSITION	Slider moved using the mouse.
TB_THUMBTRACK	Slider dragged using the mouse.
TB_TOP	HOME key pressed. Slider is moved to maximum value.

Slider Control Member Functions

Like the other common controls we have examined, you communicate with a slider control by calling member functions. Here are some frequently used members of **CSliderCtrl**.

A slider control maintains its own current position. Each time you move the slider, this position is incremented or decremented. To obtain the new position, call **GetPos( )**. Its prototype is shown here:

   int CSliderCtrl::GetPos( ) const;

The current position of the control is returned.

To set the position of the slider control, call **SetPos( )**. Its prototype is shown here:

   void CSliderCtrl::SetPos(int *NewPos*);

Here, *NewPos* specifies the new position of the slider control.

You set the range of a slider control using **SetRange( )**, shown here:

   void CSliderCtrl::SetRange(int *min*, int *max*, BOOL *Redraw* = FALSE);

If *Redraw* is nonzero, then the control is redrawn after the range is set.

You can obtain the range of a slider control by calling **GetRange( )**. Its prototype is shown here:

> void CSliderCtrl::GetRange(int &*min*, int &*max*) const;

After the call, *min* will contain the minimum value and *max* will contain the maximum value.

There are many other slider control functions that give you detailed control over the appearance and operation of the control. You will want to explore all of the slider control functions on your own.

A Slider Control Demonstration Program

The following program demonstrates the slider control by adding one to the previous spin control program. As you will see when you run the program, whenever you change the slider control, the spin control is updated. If you change the spin control, the slider control is changed. Sample output is shown in Figure 11-3.

The slider control program uses the following resource file:

```
// SLIDER.RC

#include <afxres.h>
#include "ids.h"

SliderMenu MENU
{
  POPUP "Demo"
  {
    MENUITEM "&Slider Demo\tF2", IDM_DIALOG
    MENUITEM "E&xit\tF3", IDM_EXIT
  }
  MENUITEM "&Help", IDM_HELP
}

SliderMenu ACCELERATORS
{
  VK_F1, IDM_HELP, VIRTKEY
  VK_F2, IDM_DIALOG, VIRTKEY
  VK_F3, IDM_EXIT, VIRTKEY
```

11

```
}

SliderDialog DIALOG 18, 18, 142, 92
CAPTION "Demonstrate Slider Control"
STYLE DS_MODALFRAME | WS_POPUP | WS_CAPTION | WS_SYSMENU
{
  PUSHBUTTON "Cancel", IDCANCEL, 52, 65, 37, 14,
             WS_CHILD | WS_VISIBLE | WS_TABSTOP
  EDITTEXT IDD_EB1, 10, 10, 26, 12, ES_LEFT | WS_CHILD |
           WS_VISIBLE | WS_BORDER
}
```

The class derivation file, SLIDER.H, is shown here:

```
// SLIDER.H

// This is the main window class.
class CMainWin : public CFrameWnd
{
public:
  CMainWin();

  // define menu handlers
  afx_msg void OnDialog();
  afx_msg void OnExit();
  afx_msg void OnHelp();

  DECLARE_MESSAGE_MAP()
};

// This is the application class.
class CApp : public CWinApp
{
public:
  BOOL InitInstance();
};

// This is a dialog class.
class CSampleDialog : public CDialog
{
  CSpinButtonCtrl m_Spin; // spin control
  CSliderCtrl m_Slider;   // slider control
```

```
public:
  CSampleDialog(char *DialogName, CWnd *Owner) :
    CDialog(DialogName, Owner) {}

  BOOL OnInitDialog();

  afx_msg void OnVScroll(UINT SBCode, UINT Pos,
                         CScrollBar *SB);
  afx_msg void OnHScroll(UINT SBCode, UINT Pos,
                         CScrollBar *SB);

  DECLARE_MESSAGE_MAP()
};
```

The slider control program file is shown here:

```
// Demonstrate a Slider (trackbar) control.

#include <afxwin.h>
#include <afxcmn.h>
#include "slider.h"
#include "ids.h"

CMainWin::CMainWin()
{
  Create(NULL, "Demonstrate Slider Control",
         WS_OVERLAPPEDWINDOW, rectDefault,
         NULL, "SliderMenu");

  INITCOMMONCONTROLSEX initCtrls;

  initCtrls.dwSize = sizeof(initCtrls);
  initCtrls.dwICC= ICC_BAR_CLASSES | ICC_UPDOWN_CLASS;
  InitCommonControlsEx(&initCtrls);

  // Load accelerator table.
  if(!LoadAccelTable("SliderMenu"))
     MessageBox("Cannot Load Accelerators", "Error");
}

// Initialize the application.
BOOL CApp::InitInstance()
{
```

11

```
  m_pMainWnd = new CMainWin;
  m_pMainWnd->ShowWindow(m_nCmdShow);
  m_pMainWnd->UpdateWindow();

  return TRUE;
}

// This is the application's message map.
BEGIN_MESSAGE_MAP(CMainWin, CFrameWnd)
  ON_COMMAND(IDM_DIALOG, OnDialog)
  ON_COMMAND(IDM_EXIT, OnExit)
  ON_COMMAND(IDM_HELP, OnHelp)
END_MESSAGE_MAP()

// Process IDM_DIALOG.
afx_msg void CMainWin::OnDialog()
{
  CSampleDialog diagOb("SliderDialog", this);

  diagOb.DoModal(); // activate modal dialog box
}

// Process IDM_EXIT.
afx_msg void CMainWin::OnExit()
{
  int response;

  response = MessageBox("Quit the Program?",
                        "Exit", MB_YESNO);

  if(response == IDYES)
    SendMessage(WM_CLOSE); // terminate app
}

// Process IDM_HELP.
afx_msg void CMainWin::OnHelp()
{
  MessageBox("Slider Control", "Help");
}

// This is SampleDialog's message map.
BEGIN_MESSAGE_MAP(CSampleDialog, CDialog)
  ON_WM_VSCROLL()
  ON_WM_HSCROLL()
```

```
END_MESSAGE_MAP()

// Initialize the dialog box.
BOOL CSampleDialog::OnInitDialog()
{
  RECT r;

  CDialog::OnInitDialog(); // Call base class version

  // create spin control
  r.left = r.top  = 10;
  r.right = r.bottom = 50;
  m_Spin.Create(WS_VISIBLE | WS_CHILD | WS_BORDER |
                UDS_SETBUDDYINT | UDS_ALIGNRIGHT,
                r, this, IDD_SPIN);

  // set range of spin control
  m_Spin.SetRange(0, 10);

  // Set buddy window
  m_Spin.SetBuddy(GetDlgItem(IDD_EB1));

  // set initial position
  m_Spin.SetPos(5);

  // Create slider control
  r.left = 10; r.top  = 50;
  r.right = 200; r.bottom = 80;
  m_Slider.Create(WS_VISIBLE | WS_CHILD | WS_BORDER |
                  TBS_AUTOTICKS | WS_TABSTOP,
                  r, this, IDD_TRACKBAR);

  // set range and position of slider
  m_Slider.SetRange(0, 10);
  m_Slider.SetPos(5);

  return TRUE;
}

// Process WM_HSCROLL messages for slider control.
afx_msg void CSampleDialog::OnHScroll(UINT SBCode, UINT Pos,
                              CScrollBar *SB)
{
  // SB must point to slider control
```

```
  if(SB != (CScrollBar *)&m_Slider) return;

  // update spin control
  m_Spin.SetPos(m_Slider.GetPos());
}

// Process WM_VSCROLL messages for spin control.
afx_msg void CSampleDialog::OnVScroll(UINT SBCode, UINT Pos,
                                      CScrollBar *SB)
{
  // SB must point to slider control
  if(SB != (CScrollBar *)&m_Spin) return;

  // update slider control
  m_Slider.SetPos(m_Spin.GetPos());
}

CApp App; // instantiate the application
```

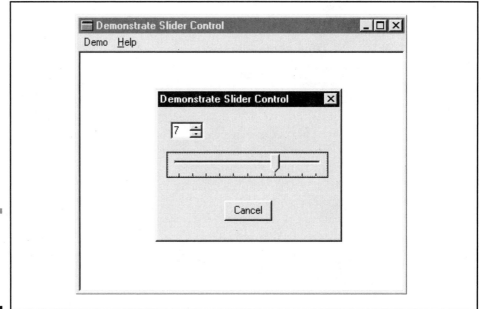

Sample output
from the slider
control
program

Figure 11-3.

Inside the program, both a slider control and a spin control are created when the dialog box is initialized. After the trackbar is created, its range is set to 0 through 10. Its initial position is set at 5. (The same range and initial value are also given to the spin control.) Whenever the spin control is changed, a **WM_VSCROLL** message is received. Whenever the trackbar is moved, a **WM_HSCROLL** message is received.

As the program is written, the spin control and slider control are synchronized. That is, each time you change one control, the other is automatically adjusted to reflect the change. Keep in mind, however, that the linkage of the slider control with the spin control within this program is purely arbitrary and for the sake of illustration. Slider controls can, obviously, be used entirely on their own.

Using a Progress Bar

One of the simpler common controls is the *progress bar*. You have probably seen progress bars in action. They are small windows in which the degree of completion of a long task is depicted. For example, progress bars are commonly used by installation programs, sorts, and file transfer programs. Progress bars are encapsulated by **CProgressCtrl**.

Creating a Progress Bar

To create a progress bar, use the **Create( )** member function, shown here:

```
BOOL CProgressCtrl::Create(DWORD dwStyle, const RECT &SizePos,
                           CWnd *Owner, UINT ID);
```

Here, *dwStyle* specifies the style of the progress bar. This parameter usually includes the standard styles **WS_CHILD**, **WS_VISIBLE**, and **WS_BORDER**. The location and size of the progress bar is passed in the **RECT** structure specified by *SizePos*. A pointer to the parent window object is passed in *Owner*. The ID associated with the progress bar is specified in *ID*.

Create( ) returns nonzero if successful and zero on failure.

Progress Bar Member Functions

You communicate with a progress bar through member functions. Here are some frequently used members of **CProgressCtrl**.

11

A progress bar maintains its own current position. To set the position of the progress bar, call **SetPos( )**. Its prototype is shown here:

   int CProgressCtrl::SetPos(int *NewPos*);

Here, *NewPos* specifies the new position of the progress bar. The previous position is returned.

You set the range of a progress bar using **SetRange( )**, shown here:

   void CProgressCtrl::SetRange(int *min*, int *max*);

By default, a progress bar has the range 0 through 100. However, you can set it to any value between 0 and 65,535.

After creating a progress bar, you will advance the bar by calling **StepIt( )**. This function causes the bar's current position to advance by a predetermined increment called a *step*. By default, the increment is 10, but it may be any value you like. As you increment the bar's position, more of the bar is filled. Since a progress bar is used to display the degree of completion of a long task, the task should end when the bar is fully filled. The **StepIt( )** function is shown here:

   int CProgressCtrl::StepIt( );

The function returns the previous position.

To set the step value, call **SetStep( )**, shown here:

   int CProgressCtrl::SetStep(int *Amount*);

Here, *Amount* specifies the size of the step value. The previous step value is returned.

A Simple Progress Bar Program

The following short program illustrates how to use a progress bar. It creates a dialog box that contains a progress bar and a push button named Progress. The progress bar has a range of 0 to 120 and an increment of 5. Each time you press the Progress push button, the progress bar is incremented another step. When the bar is filled, the dialog box automatically removes itself. Sample output is shown in Figure 11-4.

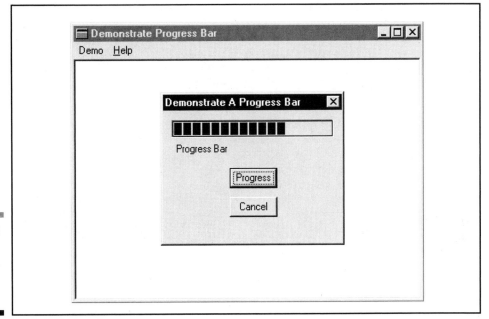

Sample output
from the
progress bar
program
Figure 11-4.

The progress bar program uses this resource file:

```
// PROGRESS.RC

#include <afxres.h>
#include "ids.h"

ProgMenu MENU
{
  POPUP "Demo"
  {
    MENUITEM "&Progress Bar Demo\tF2", IDM_DIALOG
    MENUITEM "E&xit\tF3", IDM_EXIT
  }
  MENUITEM "&Help", IDM_HELP
}

ProgMenu ACCELERATORS
{
  VK_F1, IDM_HELP, VIRTKEY
  VK_F2, IDM_DIALOG, VIRTKEY
```

11

```
    VK_F3, IDM_EXIT, VIRTKEY
}

ProgDialog DIALOG 18, 18, 140, 92
CAPTION "Demonstrate A Progress Bar"
STYLE DS_MODALFRAME | WS_POPUP | WS_CAPTION | WS_SYSMENU
{
  DEFPUSHBUTTON "Progress", IDD_PROGBAR, 52, 40, 37, 14,
            WS_CHILD | WS_VISIBLE | WS_TABSTOP
  PUSHBUTTON "Cancel", IDCANCEL, 52, 60, 37, 14,
            WS_CHILD | WS_VISIBLE | WS_TABSTOP
  LTEXT "Progress Bar",
        IDD_STATIC, 10, 22, 100, 10
}
```

The PROGRESS.H class derivation file is shown here:

```
// PROGRESS.H

// This is the main window class.
class CMainWin : public CFrameWnd
{
public:
  CMainWin();

  // define menu handlers
  afx_msg void OnDialog();
  afx_msg void OnExit();
  afx_msg void OnHelp();

  DECLARE_MESSAGE_MAP()
};

// This is the application class.
class CApp : public CWinApp
{
public:
  BOOL InitInstance();
};

// This is a dialog class
class CSampleDialog : public CDialog
{
```

```
  CProgressCtrl m_Prog; // progress bar
  int m_ProgPos; // progress bar position

public:
  CSampleDialog(char *DialogName, CWnd *Owner) :
    CDialog(DialogName, Owner) {}

  BOOL OnInitDialog();

  afx_msg void OnProgress();

  DECLARE_MESSAGE_MAP()
};
```

The progress bar program file is shown here:

```
// Demonstrate a progress bar.

#include <afxwin.h>
#include <afxcmn.h>
#include "progress.h"
#include "ids.h"

CMainWin::CMainWin()
{
  Create(NULL, "Demonstrate Progress Bar",
         WS_OVERLAPPEDWINDOW, rectDefault,
         NULL, "ProgMenu");

  INITCOMMONCONTROLSEX initCtrls;

  initCtrls.dwSize = sizeof(initCtrls);
  initCtrls.dwICC= ICC_PROGRESS_CLASS;
  InitCommonControlsEx(&initCtrls);

  // Load accelerator table
  if(!LoadAccelTable("ProgMenu"))
    MessageBox("Cannot Load Accelerators", "Error");
}

// Initialize the application.
BOOL CApp::InitInstance()
{
```

```
  m_pMainWnd = new CMainWin;
  m_pMainWnd->ShowWindow(m_nCmdShow);
  m_pMainWnd->UpdateWindow();

  return TRUE;
}

// This is the application's message map.
BEGIN_MESSAGE_MAP(CMainWin, CFrameWnd)
  ON_COMMAND(IDM_DIALOG, OnDialog)
  ON_COMMAND(IDM_EXIT, OnExit)
  ON_COMMAND(IDM_HELP, OnHelp)
END_MESSAGE_MAP()

// Process IDM_DIALOG.
afx_msg void CMainWin::OnDialog()
{
  CSampleDialog diagOb("ProgDialog", this);

  diagOb.DoModal(); // activate modal dialog box
}

// Process IDM_EXIT.
afx_msg void CMainWin::OnExit()
{
  int response;

  response = MessageBox("Quit the Program?",
                        "Exit", MB_YESNO);

  if(response == IDYES)
    SendMessage(WM_CLOSE); // terminate app
}

// Process IDM_HELP.
afx_msg void CMainWin::OnHelp()
{
  MessageBox("Progress Bar", "Help");
}

// This is SampleDialog's message map.
BEGIN_MESSAGE_MAP(CSampleDialog, CDialog)
  ON_COMMAND(IDD_PROGBAR, OnProgress)
END_MESSAGE_MAP()
```

```
// Initialize the dialog box.
BOOL CSampleDialog::OnInitDialog()
{
  RECT r;

  CDialog::OnInitDialog(); // Call base class version

  // create the progress bar
  r.left = 10; r.top  = 10;
  r.right = 200; r.bottom = 30;
  m_Prog.Create(WS_VISIBLE | WS_CHILD | WS_BORDER,
                r, this, IDD_PROGBAR);

  // Set range and step value
  m_Prog.SetRange(0, 120);
  m_Prog.SetStep(5);

  m_ProgPos = 0; // initialize counter
  return TRUE;
}

// Advance the bar.
afx_msg void CSampleDialog::OnProgress()
{
  m_Prog.StepIt(); // step the progress bar

  m_ProgPos += 5;
  if(m_ProgPos == 120) EndDialog(0);
}

CApp App; // instantiate the application
```

11

When using a progress bar, remember that one reason it exists is to reassure the user that the program is still proceeding normally. Therefore, you will want to increment the bar frequently. Remember, the user will be relying upon its progress as feedback that the program is still running. If you change it too slowly, a nervous user may reset the computer, thinking that the program has crashed!

In the next chapter we will continue to explore the common controls by examining the status bar, the tab control, the tree view, and the month calendar control.

Creating Smooth and Vertical Progress Bars

Originally, progress bars did not offer any style options, but two new styles have recently been added. The first is **PBS_SMOOTH**. By default, progress bars display their progress in steps. By specifying **PBS_SMOOTH**, the progress is shown in a smooth, continuous fashion. The second is **PBS_VERTICAL**. It creates a vertical progress bar. Normally, progress bars advance from left to right. A vertical progress bar advances from bottom to top.

Here is how the example progress bar appears with the **PBS_SMOOTH** style:

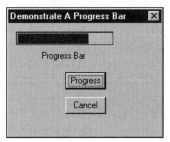

Here is the same bar with the **PBS_VERTICAL** style added:

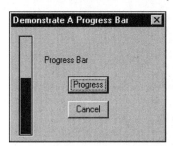

The addition of smooth and vertical progress styles gives you the ability to tailor a progress bar to the precise needs of your program. For example, using a small vertical progress bar saves a significant amount of screen space. A smooth progress bar is especially pleasing when the bar advances at a fairly rapid, fixed rate. Although the progress bar is one of the simplest common controls, its use is an important factor in inspiring confidence in your applications.

CHAPTER 12

Status Bars, Tab Controls, Tree Views, and the Month Calendar Control

This chapter takes a look at more of the common controls. In it we will examine the status bar, the tab control, the tree view control, and the month calendar control.

Status Bars

Frequently an application will need to keep the user apprised of the status of certain program variables, attributes, or parameters. In the early days of Windows programming, each application had to define its own way of accomplishing this. Fortunately, modern versions of Windows include a standard control for this purpose, called the *status bar* or *status window*. A status window is a bar that is typically displayed along the bottom of a window. It is used to display information related to the program. Status bars are encapsulated by the **CStatusBarCtrl** class.

NOTE: Status bars can also be implemented using the older **CStatusBar** class. However, for modern versions of windows, **CStatusBarCtrl** is recommended.

Creating a Status Bar

To create a status bar, you first declare an object of type **CStatusBarCtrl** and then call the **Create( )** member function, shown here:

BOOL CStatusBarCtrl::Create(DWORD *dwStyle*, const RECT &*SizePos*,
                            CWnd **Owner*, UINT *ID*);

Here, *dwStyle* specifies the style of the status bar. This parameter must include the standard style **WS_CHILD** and usually includes **WS_VISIBLE** and **WS_BORDER**. It may also include one or more of the status bar styles shown in Table 12-1. The position and dimensions of the status bar are specified by the **RECT** structure specified by *SizePos*. However, this parameter is ignored (unless the **CCS_NORESIZE** style is included). Instead, a status bar is automatically sized to fit its parent window. A pointer to the parent window object is passed in *Owner*. The ID associated with the status bar is specified in *ID*. **Create( )** returns nonzero if successful and zero on failure.

After a status bar has been created, it is generally divided into parts, with each part displaying one piece of status information. (However, a single-part status window is perfectly acceptable.) Once the parts have been established, you may write text to each part individually. Each part is referred to by its index.

Style	Description
CCS_BOTTOM	Status bar is located at bottom of parent window. (This is the default.)
CCS_NODIVIDER	There is no dividing line between status bar and parent.
CCS_NOHILITE	No highlight is shown on the top of the status bar.
CCS_NOMOVEY	Status bar will not resize vertically.
CCS_NOPARENTALIGN	Status bar does not automatically move between the top and bottom of the parent's window.
CCS_NORESIZE	Status bar's size and position are specified by **Create ( )**'s *SizePos* parameter and are fixed.
CCS_TOP	Status bar is located at top of parent window.

Status Bar
Styles
Table 12-1.

Setting the Status Bar's Parts

Almost all applications will divide a status bar into two or more parts. To do this, your program will call the **SetParts( )** member function, shown here:

BOOL CStatusBarCtrl::SetParts(int *NumParts*, int *WidthArray*);

Here, *NumParts* specifies the number of parts in the status bar, which must be less than 256. The integer array pointed to by *WidthArray* contains the Y coordinate of the right edge of each part. Thus, the number of elements in the array pointed to by *WidthArray* must be equal to the value passed in *NumParts*. The function returns nonzero if successful and zero on error.

Setting the Text in a Status Bar

12

After you have set the number of parts, you can write a string to each part of a status bar. To do so, use the **SetText( )** member function, shown here:

BOOL CStatusBarCtrl::SetText(LPCSTR *lpszString*, int *Part*, int *How*);

Here, *lpszString* is a pointer to the text that will be displayed in the partition specified by *Part*. *Part* is the index of the partition that receives the text. All status bar indexes begin at zero. How the text is drawn is determined by *How*.

For a normal status bar, *How* will be zero. This causes the text to appear below the status bar. To cause the text to appear above the status bar, specify **SBT_POPOUT**.

Using a Status Bar

Status bars are surprisingly easy to use. Here is the general procedure:

1. Create the status window.
2. Set the number of parts.
3. Set the text in each part.
4. Update the text in each part as program conditions change.

You can update each part of a status bar as needed by calling **SetText( )** whenever the status of your program changes.

The following program uses a status bar to report the settings within a dialog box. The dialog box contains a spin control and two check boxes. In the status bar, the status of each control is updated whenever the control is changed. Sample output from the program is shown in Figure 12-1.

The program uses this resource file:

```
// STATUS.RC

#include <afxres.h>
#include "statids.h"

StatusMenu MENU
{
  POPUP "&Demo"
  {
    MENUITEM "&Dialog\tF2", IDM_DIALOG
    MENUITEM "E&xit\tF3", IDM_EXIT
  }
  MENUITEM "&Help", IDM_HELP
}


StatusMenu ACCELERATORS
{
  VK_F2, IDM_DIALOG, VIRTKEY
  VK_F3, IDM_EXIT, VIRTKEY
  VK_F1, IDM_HELP, VIRTKEY
}
```

```
StatusDialog DIALOG 18, 18, 150, 92
CAPTION "Demonstrate a Status Bar"
STYLE DS_MODALFRAME | WS_POPUP | WS_CAPTION | WS_SYSMENU
{
  PUSHBUTTON "Reset", IDD_RESET, 92, 34, 37, 14,
            WS_CHILD | WS_VISIBLE | WS_TABSTOP
  PUSHBUTTON "OK", IDOK, 92, 53, 37, 14,
            WS_CHILD | WS_VISIBLE | WS_TABSTOP
  EDITTEXT IDD_EB1, 10, 10, 30, 12, ES_LEFT | WS_CHILD |
          WS_VISIBLE | WS_BORDER
  AUTOCHECKBOX "Option 1", IDD_CB1, 10, 40, 48, 12
  AUTOCHECKBOX "Option 2", IDD_CB2, 10, 60, 48, 12
}
```

The header file STATIDS.H is shown here:

```
// STATIDS.H

#define IDM_DIALOG    100
#define IDM_HELP      101
#define IDM_EXIT      103

#define IDD_EB1       200
#define IDD_CB1       201
#define IDD_CB2       202
#define IDD_RESET     203
#define IDD_SPIN      210

#define IDD_STATUS    300

#define NUMPARTS        3
```

The class derivation file STATUS.H is shown here:

```
// STATUS.H

// This is the main window class.
class CMainWin : public CFrameWnd
{
public:
  CMainWin();

  // define menu handlers
  afx_msg void OnDialog();
```

```
  afx_msg void OnExit();
  afx_msg void OnHelp();

  DECLARE_MESSAGE_MAP()
};

// This is the application class.
class CApp : public CWinApp
{
public:
  BOOL InitInstance();
};

// This is a dialog class.
class CSampleDialog : public CDialog
{
  CStatusBarCtrl m_Status; // status bar
  CSpinButtonCtrl m_Spin; // spin control

public:
  CSampleDialog(char *DialogName, CWnd *Owner) :
    CDialog(DialogName, Owner) {}

  BOOL OnInitDialog();

  afx_msg void OnVScroll(UINT SBCode, UINT Pos,
                         CScrollBar *SB);

  afx_msg void OnCB1();
  afx_msg void OnCB2();
  afx_msg void OnReset();

  DECLARE_MESSAGE_MAP()
};
```

The program file is shown here:

```
// Demonstrate a status bar control.

#include <afxwin.h>
#include <afxcmn.h>
#include <string.h>
#include "status.h"
#include "statids.h"

CMainWin::CMainWin()
{
```

```
    Create(NULL, "Using A Status Bar",
           WS_OVERLAPPEDWINDOW, rectDefault,
           NULL, "StatusMenu");
    INITCOMMONCONTROLSEX initCtrls;

    initCtrls.dwSize = sizeof(initCtrls);
    initCtrls.dwICC= ICC_BAR_CLASSES | ICC_UPDOWN_CLASS;
    InitCommonControlsEx(&initCtrls);

    // Load accelerator table.
    if(!LoadAccelTable("StatusMenu"))
      MessageBox("Cannot Load Accelerators", "Error");
}

// Initialize the application.
BOOL CApp::InitInstance()
{
  m_pMainWnd = new CMainWin;
  m_pMainWnd->ShowWindow(m_nCmdShow);
  m_pMainWnd->UpdateWindow();

  return TRUE;
}

// This is the application's message map.
BEGIN_MESSAGE_MAP(CMainWin, CFrameWnd)
  ON_COMMAND(IDM_DIALOG, OnDialog)
  ON_COMMAND(IDM_EXIT, OnExit)
  ON_COMMAND(IDM_HELP, OnHelp)
END_MESSAGE_MAP()

// Process IDM_DIALOG.
afx_msg void CMainWin::OnDialog()
{
  CSampleDialog diagOb("StatusDialog", this);

  diagOb.DoModal(); // activate modal dialog box
}

// Process IDM_EXIT.
afx_msg void CMainWin::OnExit()
{
  int response;

  response = MessageBox("Quit the Program?",
                        "Exit", MB_YESNO);
```

```
    if(response == IDYES)
      SendMessage(WM_CLOSE); // terminate app
}

// Process IDM_HELP.
afx_msg void CMainWin::OnHelp()
{
  MessageBox("Status Bar", "Help");
}

// This is CSampleDialog's message map.
BEGIN_MESSAGE_MAP(CSampleDialog, CDialog)
  ON_WM_VSCROLL()
  ON_COMMAND(IDD_CB1, OnCB1)
  ON_COMMAND(IDD_CB2, OnCB2)
  ON_COMMAND(IDD_RESET, OnReset)
END_MESSAGE_MAP()

// Initialize the dialog box.
BOOL CSampleDialog::OnInitDialog()
{
  RECT r;
  int i;
  int parts[NUMPARTS];

  CDialog::OnInitDialog(); // Call base class version

  // create spin control
  r.left = r.top  = 10;
  r.right = r.bottom = 50;
  m_Spin.Create(WS_VISIBLE | WS_CHILD | WS_BORDER |
                UDS_SETBUDDYINT | UDS_ALIGNRIGHT,
                r, this, IDD_SPIN);
  // set range of spin control
  m_Spin.SetRange(0, 20);
  // Set buddy window
  m_Spin.SetBuddy(GetDlgItem(IDD_EB1));
  // set initial position
  m_Spin.SetPos(10);

  // determine partitions for status bar
  GetClientRect(&r);
  for(i=1; i<=NUMPARTS; i++)
    parts[i-1] = r.right/NUMPARTS *i;
```

```
// create status control
r.left = r.top  = 0; // these coordinates are ignored
r.right = r.bottom = 0;
m_Status.Create(WS_VISIBLE | WS_CHILD,
                r, this, IDD_STATUS);

// set parts and text of status bar
m_Status.SetParts(NUMPARTS, parts);
m_Status.SetText("Spin Ctrl: 10", 0, 0);
m_Status.SetText("Option 1: OFF", 1, 0);
m_Status.SetText("Option 2: OFF", 2, 0);

return TRUE;
}

// Process WM_VSCROLL messages for spin control.
afx_msg void CSampleDialog::OnVScroll(UINT SBCode, UINT Pos,
                                CScrollBar *SB)
{
  char str[255];

  // SB must point to spin control
  if(SB != (CScrollBar *)&m_Spin) return;

  wsprintf(str, "Spin Ctrl: %d", Pos);

  m_Status.SetText(str, 0, 0);
}

// Handle IDD_CB1 commands.
afx_msg void CSampleDialog::OnCB1()
{
  CButton *cbptr = (CButton *) GetDlgItem(IDD_CB1);

  if(cbptr->GetCheck())
    m_Status.SetText("Option 1: ON", 1, 0);
  else
    m_Status.SetText("Option 1: OFF", 1, 0);
}

// Handle IDD_CB2 commands.
afx_msg void CSampleDialog::OnCB2()
{
  CButton *cbptr = (CButton *) GetDlgItem(IDD_CB2);
```

```
    if(cbptr->GetCheck())
      m_Status.SetText("Option 2: ON", 2, 0);
    else
      m_Status.SetText("Option 2: OFF", 2, 0);
}

// Handle IDD_RESET commands.
afx_msg void CSampleDialog::OnReset()
{
  CButton *cbptr = (CButton *) GetDlgItem(IDD_CB1);
  cbptr->SetCheck(0);
  cbptr = (CButton *) GetDlgItem(IDD_CB2);
  cbptr->SetCheck(0);

  m_Spin.SetPos(10);

  m_Status.SetText("Spin Ctrl: 10", 0, 0);
  m_Status.SetText("Option 1: OFF", 1, 0);
  m_Status.SetText("Option 2: OFF", 2, 0);
}


CApp App; // instantiate the application
```

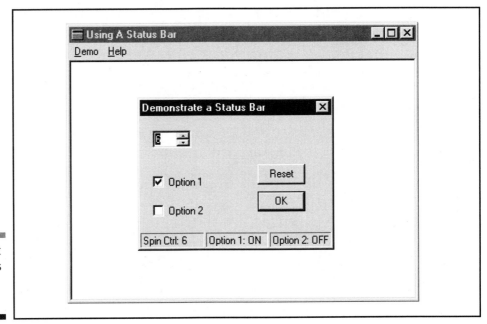

Sample output from the status bar program

Figure 12-1.

Inside the program, the function **OnInitDialog( )** creates and initializes the status bar. First, the status bar is divided into three equal parts. The division of the status bar is aided by the **GetClientRect( )** function. This function obtains the current size of the client area of the specified window. It has the following prototype:

    void CWnd::GetClientRect(RECT *Rect) const;

Here, *Rect* is a pointer to the **RECT** structure that receives the dimensions of the window's client area.

Since there are three parts to the status bar, the width of the dialog box (as obtained by **GetClientRect( )**) is divided into three parts. These become the end points for the status bar parts and are put into the **parts** array. Remember, the end point of each part must be passed to the status window—not the width of each part. Once the parts have been set, the initial text in each part is displayed. Each time a control within the dialog box is changed, the text within its part of the status bar is updated.

While this program illustrates the basic operation of a status bar, you will want to explore the **CStatusBarCtrl** class more fully on your own. It includes several member functions that allow fine-tuned control over a status bar.

Tab Controls

One of the more visually interesting common controls is the tab control. A tab control emulates the tabs on a set of file folders. Each time a tab is selected, its associated folder comes to the surface. Tab controls are encapsulated by the **CTabCtrl** class.

NOTE: A relative of the tab control is the property sheet control. As you will see in the next chapter, a property sheet is a better choice than a tab control in many situations.

12

Creating a Tab Control

To create a tab control, first declare an object of type **CTabCtrl** and then call the **Create( )** member function, shown here:

    BOOL CTabCtrl::Create(DWORD *dwStyle*, const RECT &*SizePos*,
                          CWnd *Owner, UINT *ID*);

Here, *dwStyle* specifies the style of the tab control. This parameter generally includes the standard styles **WS_CHILD** and **WS_VISIBLE**. It may also include one or more tab control styles. Several common ones are shown here:

Tab Style	Effect
TCS_BUTTONS	Use buttons, not tabs.
TCS_FIXEDWIDTH	All tabs are the same size.
TCS_MULTILINE	Tab control may use multiple lines of tabs.
TCS_TOOLTIPS	Tab control has tooltips.
TCS_SINGLELINE	Tab control uses a single line. Tabs can be scrolled into view.

The **RECT** structure specified by *SizePos* specifies the size and position of the tab control. A pointer to the parent window object is passed in *Owner*. The ID associated with the tab control is specified in *ID*. **Create( )** returns nonzero if successful and zero on failure.

Initializing a Tab Control

Once a tab control has been created, it must be initialized by adding tab headings to it. This is accomplished using the **InsertItem( )** member function, shown here:

BOOL CTabCtrl::InsertItem(int *Index*, TCITEM **Item*);

Here, *Index* is the index of the tab being added. Tab indexes begin at zero. *Item* is a pointer to a **TCITEM** structure that defines a tab. You will call **InsertItem( )** for each tab heading that you wish to add. **InsertItem( )** returns nonzero if successful and zero on failure.

The **TCITEM** structure is defined as follows:

```
typedef struct tagTCITEM
{
  UINT mask;
  DWORD dwState;
  DWORD dwStateMask;
```

```
    LPSTR pszText;
    int cchTextMax;
    int iImage;
    LPARAM lParam;
} TCITEM;
```

In this structure, the value contained in **mask** determines whether the **pszText**, **iImage**, or **lParam** members of the structure contain valid data. **mask** can contain one or more of the following values:

mask	Meaning
TCIF_IMAGE	**iImage** contains data.
TCIF_PARAM	**lParam** contains data.
TCIF_STATE	**dwState** contains data. (Requires a modern version of Windows.)
TCIF_TEXT	**pszText** contains data.

The value in **mask** may also include **TCIF_RTLREADING**, which means that the text should be displayed right to left.

When a tab is being created, the value of **dwState** is not used. When information is being obtained about an existing tab, **dwState** indicates its state. It will be either zero, **TCIS_BUTTONPRESSED** (the tab is selected), or **TCIS_HIGHLIGHTED** (the tab is highlighed). The value of **dwStateMask** determines which bits in **dwState** are valid. This field is not used when inserting items. The **dwState** and **dwStateMask** fields are available only for modern versions of Windows, such as Windows 98 or those that have IE 4 (or later) installed.

When a tab is being set, **pszText** points to the string that will be displayed within the tab. When information about a tab is being obtained, **pszText** must point to an array that will receive the text. In this case, the value of **cchTextMax** specifies the size of the array pointed to by **pszText**.

If there is an image list associated with the tab control, then **iImage** will contain the index of the image associated with the specified tab. If there is no image list associated with the tab control, **iImage** should be –1. (An image list defines a set of images that may be accessed via an index. Image lists are encapsulated by the **CImageList** class.) **lParam** contains application-defined data.

12

NOTE: The **TCITEM** structure replaces the older **TC_ITEM** structure. Also, in **TC_ITEM**, **dwState** and **dwStateMask** were reserved fields. For the sake of portability, MFC programs may continue to use the old structure. But, of course, new code should use the new one.

Some CTabCtrl Member Functions

CTabCtrl contains many member functions that give you detailed control over a tab control. Here are just a few of its most commonly used ones.

Frequently, your program will need to know which tab is currently selected. To obtain this information, use the **GetCurSel( )** member function, shown here:

    int CTabCtrl::GetCurSel( ) const;

The function returns the index of the currently selected tab or –1 if no tab has been chosen.

To select a tab, call **SetCurSel( )**, shown here:

    int CTabCtrl::SetCurSel(int *Index*);

Here, *Index* is the index of the tab to select. The index of the previously selected tab is returned. If no tab has been selected, –1 is returned.

To obtain the information associated with a tab, call **GetItem( )**, shown here:

    BOOL CTabCtrl::GetItem(int *Index*, TCITEM **Item*) const;

Here, *Index* is the index of the tab being obtained. *Item* points to the **TCITEM** structure that receives the information about the specified tab. You must initialize the **mask** member of this structure, specifying the information that you desire, prior to the call. On return, the structure will contain the information that you request. The function returns nonzero if successful and zero on failure.

To set the information associated with a tab, call **SetItem( )**, shown here:

    BOOL CTabCtrl::SetItem(int *Index*, TCITEM **Item*);

Here, *Index* is the index of the tab to set. *Item* points to the **TCITEM** structure that contains the information being set. You must initialize the

mask member of this structure, specifying the information that you desire to change. The function returns nonzero if successful and zero on failure.

Although the tab control example shown later does not require it, **AdjustRect( )**, shown here, is one function that your real-world applications will probably use.

        void CTabCtrl::AdjustRect(BOOL *How*, RECT **Rect*);

This function is used to obtain the dimensions of the display area of a tab control. Remember, when you create a tab control, its window contains the tabs themselves, as well as the area in which you will display information or pop up a dialog box. The display area is the part of a tab control window that excludes the tabs. That is, the display area is the part of the tab control window that you may use to display other items. Since it is the display area that will contain the information associated with the tab, you will usually need to know its dimensions. If *How* is nonzero, then *Rect* must point to a **RECT** structure that contains the dimensions of the desired display area. On return, this structure will contain the dimensions of the entire control. If *How* is zero, then *Rect* must point to the dimensions of the entire control, and the dimensions of the display area are returned.

Tab Notification Messages

When a tab control is accessed by the user, a **WM_NOTIFY** message is generated. Tab controls can generate two selection-change notification codes: **TCN_SELCHANGE** and **TCN_SELCHANGING**. **TCN_SELCHANGING** is sent when a tab selection is about to change. **TCN_SELCHANGE** is sent after a new tab is selected.

Tab control notification messages are handled using the standard **ON_NOTIFY** message macro, which has this general form:

        ON_NOTIFY(*notification-code, ID, handler*)

Here, *notification-code* is the notification code being handled. *ID* is the ID of the tab control. The name of the message handler is specified by *handler*. Notification message handlers for tab controls take this general form:

        afx_msg void handler(NMHDR **hdr*, LRESULT **Result*);

12

For **TCN_SELCHANGE**, *Result* is unused. For **TCN_SELCHANGING**, your message handler must set the value pointed to by *Result* to zero to allow the tab to change, or to nonzero to prevent it.

A Simple Tab Demonstration Program

The following short program demonstrates the tab control. It creates a tab control as a child window of the main window. The program then creates three tabs, labeled One, Two, and Three. Each time a new tab is selected, a message is displayed reporting this fact. Sample output is shown in Figure 12-2.

The tab control program does not require a resource file. The program uses the TABIDS.H header file shown here:

```
// TABIDS.H

#define ID_TAB 100
```

The tab program's class derivation file, TAB.H, is shown here:

```
// TAB.H

// This is the main window class.
class CMainWin : public CFrameWnd
{
  CTabCtrl m_Tab; // tab control
public:
  CMainWin();

  afx_msg void OnTabChange(NMHDR *hdr,
                           LRESULT *NotUsed);

  DECLARE_MESSAGE_MAP()
};

// This is the application class.
class CApp : public CWinApp
{
```

```
public:
  BOOL InitInstance();
};
```

The tab control program file is shown here:

```
// A simple tab control demonstration.

#include <afxwin.h>
#include <afxcmn.h>
#include <string.h>
#include "tabids.h"
#include "tab.h"

CMainWin::CMainWin()
{
  Create(NULL, "Using A Tab Control");

  INITCOMMONCONTROLSEX initCtrls;

  initCtrls.dwSize = sizeof(initCtrls);
  initCtrls.dwICC= ICC_TAB_CLASSES;
  InitCommonControlsEx(&initCtrls);

  RECT r;
  TCITEM tci;

  // get dimensions of client area
  GetClientRect(&r);

  // create tab control
  m_Tab.Create(WS_VISIBLE | WS_CHILD,
               r, this, ID_TAB);

  tci.mask = TCIF_TEXT;
  tci.iImage = -1;

  tci.pszText = "One";
  m_Tab.InsertItem(0, &tci);

  tci.pszText = "Two";
  m_Tab.InsertItem(1, &tci);
```

12

```
  tci.pszText = "Three";
  m_Tab.InsertItem(2, &tci);
}

// Initialize the application.
BOOL CApp::InitInstance()
{
  m_pMainWnd = new CMainWin;
  m_pMainWnd->ShowWindow(m_nCmdShow);
  m_pMainWnd->UpdateWindow();

  return TRUE;
}

// This is the application's message map.
BEGIN_MESSAGE_MAP(CMainWin, CFrameWnd)
  ON_NOTIFY(TCN_SELCHANGE, ID_TAB, OnTabChange)
END_MESSAGE_MAP()

// Process tab change.
afx_msg void CMainWin::OnTabChange(NMHDR *hdr,
                                   LRESULT *NotUsed)
{
  CClientDC DC(this);
  char str[255];

  wsprintf(str, "Changed to Tab %d  ",
           m_Tab.GetCurSel()+1);

  DC.SetBkColor(RGB(200, 200, 200));
  DC.TextOut(40, 100, str, strlen(str));
}

CApp App; // instantiate the application
```

In the **CMainWin( )** constructor, just before the tab control is created, a call is made to **GetClientRect( )** to obtain the size of the main window. When the tab control is created, it is sized to fill the entire client area of its parent window. While using this size is arbitrary, it is not uncommon. After the tab control has been created, three tabs are created. Each time a **WM_NOTIFY** message contains the **TCN_SELCHANGE** code, a message is displayed within the tab control display area, indicating that the selection has changed to the specified tab.

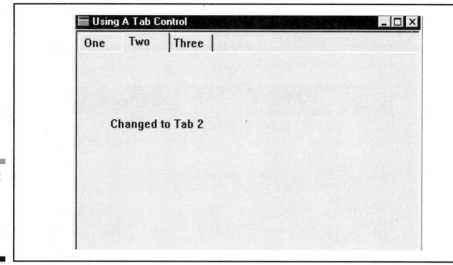

Tree View Controls

The next control that we will look at is the tree view control. Tree view controls are used to display information using a tree structure. For example, the file list used by Windows' Explorer is an example of a tree view control. Because trees imply a hierarchy, tree view controls should only be used to display hierarchical information. Tree view controls are very powerful and support a large number of options. In fact, one could easily write a book about tree view controls alone! For this reason, this section discusses tree view fundamentals only. However, once you understand the basics, you will be able to easily incorporate the other tree view features on your own. Tree view controls are encapsulated by the **CTreeCtrl** class.

NOTE: A tree view can also be created using the **CTreeView** class. However, in most situations you will want to use a **CTreeCtrl** object instead. **CTreeView** objects are most useful when you want a tree view to be the main view of your application.

12

Creating a Tree View Control

To create a tree view control, declare an object of type **CTreeCtrl** and then call the **Create( )** member function, shown here:

```
BOOL CTreeCtrl::Create(DWORD dwStyle, const RECT &SizePos,
                    CWnd *Owner, UINT ID);
```

Here, *dwStyle* specifies the style of the tree view control. This parameter generally includes the standard styles **WS_CHILD** and **WS_VISIBLE**. Tree views also allow additional tree-related styles to be specified when they are created, including these:

Style	Meaning
TVS_EDITLABELS	User may change (i.e., edit) the labels associated with a tree view.
TVS_HASLINES	Lines link branches in the tree.
TVS_LINESATROOT	Lines link root to the branches.
TVS_HASBUTTONS	Expand/Collapse buttons are included to the left of each branch.

Including the **TVS_HASLINES** and **TVS_LINESATROOT** styles causes lines to be drawn to each item in the tree. This gives the tree view control its "treelike" look. Including **TVS_HASBUTTONS** causes the standard expand/collapse buttons to be added. These buttons contain a plus (+) if the branch may be expanded at least one more level and a minus (–) if the branch is fully expanded. You may also click on these buttons to expand or collapse a branch. Typically, all three of these styles are included when a tree view control is created.

The **RECT** structure specified by *SizePos* specifies the size and position of the tree view. A pointer to the parent window object is passed in *Owner*. The ID associated with the tree view control is specified in *ID*. **Create( )** returns nonzero if successful and zero on failure.

When the tree view control is first created it is empty. You must add each item in the tree, as described in the next section.

Inserting Items into a Tree View

After a tree view control has been created, it is empty. To insert items into the tree view, use the **InsertItem( )** member function. There are several overloaded forms of this function. The one used by the example in this chapter is shown here:

HTREEITEM CTreeCtrl::InsertItem(TVINSERTSTRUCT *Item*);

Here, *Item* is a pointer to a **TVINSERTSTRUCT** that describes the item being inserted into the tree. The function returns a handle to the item if successful or **NULL** on failure. As you know, handles are seldom used in MFC programming. However, this is one exception.

The **TVINSERTSTRUCT** structure is shown here:

```
typedef struct tagTVINSERTSTRUCT {
  HTREEITEM hParent;
  HTREEITEM hInsertAfter;
  union {
    TVITEMEX item;
    TVITEM item;
  }
} TVINSERTSTRUCT;
```

Here, **hParent** is the handle to the parent of the item. If the item has no parent, then this field should contain **TVI_ROOT**. The value in **hInsertAfter** determines how the new item will be inserted into the tree. If it contains the handle of an item, the new item will be inserted after that item. Otherwise, **hInsertAfter** can be one of the following values:

hInsertAfter	Meaning
TVI_FIRST	Insert at beginning of list.
TVI_LAST	Insert at end of list.
TVI_SORT	Insert in alphabetical order.

The contents of **item** describe the item. This field must be either a **TVITEM** or a **TVITEMEX** structure. **TVITEMEX** is an expanded version of **TVITEM**, which provides some special-use capabilities not required by the examples in this chapter. The **TVITEM** structure is shown here:

```
typedef struct tagTVITEM {
  UINT mask;
  HTREEITEM hItem;
  UINT state;
  UINT stateMask;
  LPSTR pszText;
```

12

```
    int cchTextMax;
    int iImage;
    int iSelectedImage;
    int cChildren;
    LPARAM lParam;
} TVITEM;
```

Here, the values in **mask** determine which of the other members of
TVITEM contain valid data. The values that it may contain are shown here:

Value in mask	Meaning
TVIF_HANDLE	**hItem** contains data.
TVIF_STATE	**state** and **stateMask** contain data.
TVIF_TEXT	**pszText** and **cchTextMax** contain data.
TVIF_IMAGE	**iImage** contains data.
TVIF_SELECTEDIMAGE	**iSelectedImage** contains data.
TVIF_CHILDREN	**cChildren** contains data.
TVIF_PARAM	**lParam** contains data.

The **state** member contains the state of the tree view control. Here are some
common tree state values:

State	Meaning
TVIS_BOLD	Item is bold.
TVIS_DROPHILITED	Item is highlighted as the target of drag/drop operation.
TVIS_EXPANDED	Branch descending from item is fully expanded. (Applies to parent items only.)
TVIS_EXPANDEDONCE	Branch descending from item is expanded one (or more) levels. (Applies to parent items only.)
TVIS_SELECTED	Item is selected.

The **stateMask** determines which tab state to set or obtain. It will also be one or more of the preceding values.

When an item is being inserted into the tree, **pszText** points to the string that will be displayed in the tree. When information about an item is being obtained, **pszText** must point to an array that will receive its text. In this case, the value of **cchTextMax** specifies the size of the array pointed to by **pszText**. Otherwise, **cchTextMax** is ignored.

If there is an image list associated with the tab control, then **iImage** will contain the index of the image associated with the specified tab. If there is no image list associated with the tab control, **iImage** should be –1. **iImageSelected** contains the selected icon within the list, if such an image exists.

When information about an item is being obtained, **cChildren** will contain the number of children associated with the specified item. **lParam** contains application-defined data.

As you will see, you need to save the handle returned by **InsertItem( )** because it will be used to identify items in the tree. It is used by several other **CTreeCtrl** member functions.

Expanding and Collapsing a Tree View

After you have constructed the tree, you can display it using different views. That is, you can display various branches of the tree. To expand or collapse the tree view, use the **Expand( )** member function, shown here:

BOOL CTreeCtrl::Expand(HTREEITEM *hItem*, UINT *How*);

Here, *hItem* is the handle of the item being affected. *How* determines what action takes place. It can be one of the following values:

How	Effect
TVE_COLLAPSE	Collapses subtree.
TVE_COLLAPSERESET	Collapses tree and removes subtree.
TVE_EXPAND	Expands subtree.
TVE_TOGGLE	Reverses state of subtree.

12

It is important to understand that these actions take place on the subtree that descends from the item specified by *hItem*. For example, **TVE_COLLAPSE** only collapses the subtree below *hItem*, not the entire tree view (unless *hItem* specifies the root).

Expand( ) returns nonzero if successful and zero on failure.

Some Other Tree View Member Functions

Like the other common controls, tree views support many options. Accordingly, the **CTreeCtrl** class contains many member functions that manipulate tree view controls. Here are a few of the most common.

To determine which item in the tree is currently selected, call **GetSelectedItem( )**. Its prototype is shown here:

HTREEITEM CTreeCtrl::GetSelectedItem( );

This function returns the handle of the item in the tree that is currently highlighted. It returns **NULL** if no item is currently selected.

You can select an item in the tree by calling **Select( )**, shown here:

HTREEITEM CTreeCtrl::Select(HTREEITEM *hItem*, UINT *How*);

Here, *hItem* specifies the item being selected. The value of *How* determines precisely what occurs. If it is **TVGN_CARET**, the item is selected. If it is **TVGN_DROPHILITE**, the item is highlighted for a drag-drop operation. If it is **TVGN_FIRSTVISIBLE**, the tree view is scrolled so that the specified item is the first visible item. The function returns nonzero if successful and zero on failure.

To obtain the information associated with an item, use **GetItem( )**, shown here:

BOOL CTreeCtrl::GetItem(TVITEM **Item*);

Here, *Item* points to a **TVITEM** structure. Before the call, the **hItem** member of the **TVITEM** structure must contain the handle of the item being obtained, and the **mask** member must specify which information you desire. After the call, the structure will contain the information that you request. The function returns nonzero if successful and zero on failure.

To set the information associated with an item, use **SetItem( )**, shown here:

        BOOL CTreeCtrl::SetItem(TVITEM *Item);

Here, *Item* points to a **TVITEM** structure. Before the call, the **hItem** member of the **TVITEM** structure must contain the handle of the item being set, and the **mask** member must specify which information you want to change. The function returns nonzero if successful and zero on failure.

To remove an item from the tree, use **DeleteItem( )**. Its prototype is shown here:

        BOOL CTreeCtrl::DeleteItem(HTREE *hItem);

Here, *hItem* is the handle of the item being removed. To remove the entire tree, use **TVI_ROOT** for *hItem*. The function returns nonzero if successful and zero on failure.

Tree View Notification Messages

When a tree view control is accessed, it generates a **WM_NOTIFY** message. There are several notification messages associated with tree view controls. Commonly used ones are shown here:

Notification Message	Meaning
TVN_DELETEITEM	An item has been deleted.
TVN_ITEMEXPANDING	A branch is about to expand or collapse.
TVN_ITEMEXPANDED	A branch has expanded or collapsed.
TVN_SELCHANGING	A new item is about to be selected.
TVN_SELCHANGED	A new item has been selected.

12

These notification messages are handled by the following type of message handler:

        afx_msg void *TreeMsg*(NMHDR *hdr*, LRESULT *Result*);

For tree messages, *hdr* will point to a **NMTREEVIEW** structure. The **NMTREEVIEW** structure is shown here:

```
typedef struct tagNMTREEVIEW {
  NMHDR hdr;
  UINT action;
  TVITEM itemOld;
  TVITEM itemNew;
  POINT ptDrag;
} NMTREEVIEW;
```

Here, **hdr** is the standard **NMHDR** structure. The notification code will be contained in the **code** member of **hdr**. The handle of the tree control that generates the message is found in the **hwndFrom** member of **hdr**. The **action** member of **NMTREEVIEW** contains notification-specific information. The structures **itemOld** and **itemNew** contain information about the previously selected item (if applicable) and the newly selected item (again, if applicable). The location of the mouse at the time the message was generated is contained in **ptDrag**.

For the **TVN_SELCHANGING** and **TVN_SELCHANGED** messages, **itemOld** describes the previously selected item, and **itemNew** describes the newly selected item. For **TVN_ITEMEXPANDING** and **TVN_ITEMEX-PANDED**, **itemNew** describes the item that is the parent of the expanding branch. For **TVN_DELETEITEM**, **itemOld** describes the item that was deleted.

For **TVN_SELCHANGING** and **TVN_ITEMEXPANDING**, your message handler must set the variable pointed to by *Result* to zero to allow the change, or to nonzero to prevent it. The other messages may ignore *Result*.

NOTE: The structures associated with a tree view control have undergone a name change. Following is a list of the old and new names of the tree view structures used in this chapter. While the old names are still valid, you should use the new names for new programs or when updating old ones.

Old Name	New Name
TV_ITEM	TVITEM
TV_INSERTSTRUCT	TVINSERTSTRUCT
NM_TREEVIEW	NMTREEVIEW

A Tree View Demonstration Program

The following program demonstrates a tree view. It creates a tree view control and then inserts five items into it. The program also includes a menu that can expand one branch, expand the entire tree, or collapse a branch. Each time a new tree view item is selected, the selection is displayed in the program's window. Sample output from the program is shown in Figure 12-3.

The tree view program uses this resource file:

```
// TREE.RC

#include <afxres.h>
#include "treeids.h"

TreeMenu MENU
{
  POPUP "&Demo"
  {
    MENUITEM "&Expand One\tF2", IDM_EXPAND
    MENUITEM "Expand &All\tF3", IDM_EXPANDALL
    MENUITEM "&Collapse\tF4", IDM_COLLAPSE
    MENUITEM "E&xit\tF5", IDM_EXIT
  }
  MENUITEM "&Help", IDM_HELP
}

TreeMenu ACCELERATORS
{
  VK_F2, IDM_EXPAND, VIRTKEY
  VK_F3, IDM_EXPANDALL, VIRTKEY
  VK_F4, IDM_COLLAPSE, VIRTKEY
  VK_F5, IDM_EXIT, VIRTKEY
  VK_F1, IDM_HELP, VIRTKEY
}
```

The header file TREEIDS.H is shown here:

```
// TREEIDS.H

#define IDM_EXPAND     100
#define IDM_EXPANDALL  101
#define IDM_COLLAPSE   102
#define IDM_EXIT       103
#define IDM_HELP       104
```

12

```
#define ID_TREE        200

#define NUM              5
```

Here is the TREE.H class derivation file:

```
// TREE.H

// This is the main window class.
class CMainWin : public CFrameWnd
{
  CTreeCtrl m_Tree; // tree view control
  void InitTree();

public:
  CMainWin();

  // define menu handlers
  afx_msg void OnExpand();
  afx_msg void OnExpandAll();
  afx_msg void OnCollapse();
  afx_msg void OnExit();
  afx_msg void OnHelp();

  afx_msg void OnPaint();

  afx_msg void OnTreeChange(NMHDR *hdr,
                             LRESULT *NotUsed);

  DECLARE_MESSAGE_MAP()
};

// This is the application class.
class CApp : public CWinApp
{
public:
  BOOL InitInstance();
};
```

The tree view control program file is shown here:

```
// Demonstrate a tree view control.

#include <afxwin.h>
```

```
#include <afxcmn.h>
#include <string.h>
#include "tree.h"
#include "treeids.h"

HTREEITEM hTreeCtrl[NUM];
HTREEITEM hTreeCurrent;

CMainWin::CMainWin()
{
  Create(NULL, "Using A Tree View Control",
         WS_OVERLAPPEDWINDOW, rectDefault,
         NULL, "TreeMenu");

  // Load accelerator table
  if(!LoadAccelTable("TreeMenu"))
    MessageBox("Cannot Load Accelerators", "Error");

  INITCOMMONCONTROLSEX initCtrls;

  initCtrls.dwSize = sizeof(initCtrls);
  initCtrls.dwICC= ICC_TREEVIEW_CLASSES;
  InitCommonControlsEx(&initCtrls);

  RECT r;

  // create tree view control
  r.left = r.top  = 0;
  r.right = 120; r.bottom = 100;
  m_Tree.Create(WS_VISIBLE | WS_CHILD | WS_BORDER |
                TVS_HASLINES | TVS_HASBUTTONS |
                TVS_LINESATROOT,
                r, this, ID_TREE);

  InitTree();
}

// Initialized the tree view control.
void CMainWin::InitTree()
{
  TVINSERTSTRUCT tvs;
  TVITEM tvi;

  tvs.hInsertAfter = TVI_LAST;
  tvi.mask = TVIF_TEXT;

  tvi.pszText = "One";
```

12

```
    tvs.hParent = TVI_ROOT;
    tvs.item = tvi;
    hTreeCtrl[0] = m_Tree.InsertItem(&tvs);
    hTreeCurrent = hTreeCtrl[0]; // first item is current

    tvi.pszText = "Two";
    tvs.hParent = hTreeCtrl[0];
    tvs.item = tvi;
    hTreeCtrl[1] = m_Tree.InsertItem(&tvs);

    tvi.pszText = "Three";
    tvs.item = tvi;
    tvs.hParent = hTreeCtrl[1];
    hTreeCtrl[2] = m_Tree.InsertItem(&tvs);

    tvi.pszText = "Four";
    tvs.item = tvi;
    tvs.hParent = hTreeCtrl[2];
    hTreeCtrl[3] = m_Tree.InsertItem(&tvs);

    tvi.pszText = "Five";
    tvs.item = tvi;
    tvs.hParent = hTreeCtrl[2];
    hTreeCtrl[4] = m_Tree.InsertItem(&tvs);
}

// Initialize the application.
BOOL CApp::InitInstance()
{
  m_pMainWnd = new CMainWin;
  m_pMainWnd->ShowWindow(m_nCmdShow);
  m_pMainWnd->UpdateWindow();

  return TRUE;
}

// This is the application's message map.
BEGIN_MESSAGE_MAP(CMainWin, CFrameWnd)
  ON_COMMAND(IDM_EXPAND, OnExpand)
  ON_COMMAND(IDM_EXPANDALL, OnExpandAll)
  ON_COMMAND(IDM_COLLAPSE, OnCollapse)
  ON_NOTIFY(TVN_SELCHANGED, ID_TREE, OnTreeChange)
  ON_WM_PAINT()
  ON_COMMAND(IDM_EXIT, OnExit)
  ON_COMMAND(IDM_HELP, OnHelp)
END_MESSAGE_MAP()
```

```
// Handle WM_PAINT.
afx_msg void CMainWin::OnPaint()
{
  CPaintDC DC(this);
  TVITEM tvi;
  char str1[40];
  char str2[255];

  tvi.hItem = hTreeCurrent;
  tvi.pszText = str1;
  tvi.cchTextMax = sizeof(str1) - 1;

  tvi.mask  = TVIF_TEXT | TVIF_HANDLE;

  m_Tree.GetItem(&tvi);

  wsprintf(str2, "Current selection: %s", tvi.pszText);

  DC.TextOut(2, 150, str2, strlen(str2));
}

// Process IDM_EXPAND.
afx_msg void CMainWin::OnExpand()
{
  m_Tree.Expand(hTreeCurrent, TVE_EXPAND);
}

// Process IDM_EXPANDALL.
afx_msg void CMainWin::OnExpandAll()
{
  int i;

  for(i=0; i<NUM; i++)
    m_Tree.Expand(hTreeCtrl[i], TVE_EXPAND);
}

// Process IDM_COLLAPSE.
afx_msg void CMainWin::OnCollapse()
{
  m_Tree.Expand(hTreeCurrent, TVE_COLLAPSE);
}

// Process IDM_EXIT.
afx_msg void CMainWin::OnExit()
{
  int response;
```

12

```
     response = MessageBox("Quit the Program?",
                            "Exit", MB_YESNO);

   if(response == IDYES)
     SendMessage(WM_CLOSE); // terminate app
}

// Process IDM_HELP.
afx_msg void CMainWin::OnHelp()
{
   MessageBox("Tree View", "Help");
}

// Process tree change.
afx_msg void CMainWin::OnTreeChange(NMHDR *hdr,
                                     LRESULT *NotUsed)
{
  hTreeCurrent = m_Tree.GetSelectedItem();
  InvalidateRect(NULL);
}

CApp App; // instantiate the application
```

In the program, the function **InitTree( )** initializes the tree view control.
Notice that the handle of each item is stored in the **hTreeCtrl** array. These

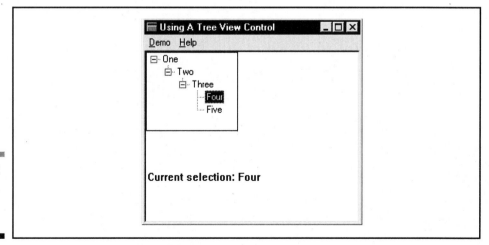

Sample output
from the tree
view program
Figure 12-3.

handles are used to make it easier to fully expand the tree. **hTreeCurrent** identifies the currently selected item. This handle is used when the user expands or collapses a branch using the menu.

Each time a new item is selected, a **WM_NOTIFY** message is received. This message is handled by **OnTreeChange( )**, which obtains the new selection by calling **GetSelectedItem( )** and then forces a window repaint. Inside **OnPaint( )**, the name of the newly selected item is obtained by calling **GetItem( )**, and displayed.

Pay special attention to the **OnExpandAll( )** handler. It expands the entire tree by calling **Expand( )** on each item in the tree. To do so, it uses the handles stored in the **hTreeCtrl** array.

While this example illustrates the most important and fundamental aspects of tree view controls, it just scratches the surface of their power. For example, using a tree view, you can drag and drop an item from one tree to another. You will want to explore this and other features on your own.

The Month Calendar Control

One very useful new common control is the month calendar. The month calendar control was added by IE 4 and is supported by Windows 98. It displays one or more months of a calendar and allows you to pick a date. By default, it displays and selects the current date. The user may change the month or year of the calendar. Various pop-up menus, up-down controls, and arrows are automatically supplied to make using the control extremely convenient. In fact, the month calendar control is so well designed that although it allows a number of interesting variations, its default mode of operation is what you will usually want. It is also visually appealing and adds professionalism to any application that needs to work with dates.

Creating a Month Calendar

To create a month calendar, you first declare an object of type **CMonthCalCtrl** and then call the **Create ( )** member function. **Create( )** has two forms. The first is shown here:

BOOL CMonthCalCtrl::Create(DWORD *dwStyle*, const RECT& *sizePos*,
                                                  CWnd* *Owner*, UINT *ID*);

12

Here, *dwStyle* specifies the style of the month calendar control. The control should include the **WS_CHILD** style. It will usually include the **WS_VISIBLE** and **WS_BORDER** styles, too. It may also include one or more of the styles shown in Table 12-2. The position and dimensions of the month calendar control are specified by the **RECT** structure specified by *sizePos*. However, when using this version of **Create( )**, the month calendar is usually created with zero dimensions because its precise size can only be determined at run time. (Its size is partially determined by the type font, for example.) As you will see, the month calendar provides an easy means of accomplishing this. A pointer to the parent window object is passed in *Owner*. The ID associated with the month calendar control is specified in *ID*. **Create ( )** returns nonzero if successful and zero on failure.

The second form of **Create( )**, shown below, automatically sizes the month calendar control to fit the dimensions of one month.

BOOL CMonthCalCtrl::Create(DWORD *dwStyle*, const POINT& *Pos*,
CWnd* *Owner*, UINT *ID*);

Here, *Pos* is a pointer to a **POINT** structure that specifies the location of the upper-left corner of the control. The other parameters are the same as the previous version. Since the first version of **Create( )** gives you more control over how a month calendar control is created, it is the form used here.

The month calendar control requires the header file AFXDTCTL.H.

Style	Effect
MCS_DAYSTATE	Calendar will request information about which days should be marked as special (such as holidays, etc.).
MCS_MULTISELECT	This allows a range of dates to be selected.
MCS_NOTODAY	The current date is not shown.
MCS_NOTODAYCIRCLE	The current date is not circled.
MCS_WEEKNUMBERS	The number of each week is displayed.

Month Calendar Style Options
Table 12-2.

Some CMonthCalCtrl Functions

CMonthCalCtrl gives you many member functions that provide detailed control over a month calendar control. Here are just a few of the more commonly used ones. To obtain the currently selected date, call **GetCurSel( )**, shown here:

BOOL CMonthCalCtrl::GetCurSel(LPSYSTEMTIME *curSelectedDate*) const;

The function returns nonzero if successful and zero on failure. *curSelectedDate* is a pointer to a **SYSTEMTIME** structure that receives the currently selected date.

To select a certain date, call **SetCurSel( )**, shown here:

BOOL CMonthCalCtrl::SetCurSel(const LPSYSTEMTIME *curSelectedDate*);

The function returns nonzero if successful and zero on failure. *curSelectedDate* is a pointer to a **SYSTEMTIME** structure that specifies the desired date.

To retrieve the current date, call **GetToday( )**, shown here:

BOOL CMonthCalCtrl::GetToday(LPSYSTEMTIME *curDate*) const;

The function returns nonzero if successful and zero on failure. *curDate* is a pointer to a **SYSTEMTIME** structure that receives the current date.

To set the current date, call **SetToday( )**, shown here:

void CMonthCalCtrl::SetToday(const LPSYSTEMTIME *curDate*);

curDate is a pointer to a **SYSTEMTIME** structure that specifies the current date.

When setting or getting a date, the date is stored in a **SYSTEMTIME** structure, which is defined like this:

```
typedef struct _SYSTEMTIME {
  WORD wYear; /* year */
  WORD wMonth; /* month (1 through 12) */
  WORD wDayOfWeek; /* day of week (0 through 6) */
  WORD wDay; /* day of month (1 through 31) */
  WORD wHour; /* hour */
```

12

```
    WORD wMinute; /* minutes */
    WORD wSecond; /* seconds */
    WORD wMilliseconds; /* milliseconds */
} SYSTEMTIME;
```

As you can see, **SYSTEMTIME** includes both date and time members. Although the calendar control does not actually deal with times, it will handle them for you. For example, when the control is created, the current time is also stored in the current date.

Sizing the Month Calendar Control

As explained, you will normally create a month calendar with zero dimensions and then resize it. To obtain the dimensions of the minimal rectangle that can hold one month, make a call to the **GetMinReqRect( )** member function, shown here:

   BOOL CMonthCalCtrl::GetMinReqRect(RECT* *minSize*) const;

On return, the minimum size for the month calendar control is contained in the **RECT** structure pointed to by *minSize*. Using the dimensions returned by this message, you can resize the month calendar using a function such as **MoveWindow( )**. Here is the sequence used by the example program to accomplish these steps:

```
RECT r;

// create month cal control
r.left = r.top  = 0;
r.right = 0; r.bottom = 0;

m_MonthCal.Create(WS_VISIBLE | WS_CHILD | WS_BORDER, r,
                  this, ID_MONTHCAL);

// now, size the calendar
m_MonthCal.GetMinReqRect(&r);
m_MonthCal.MoveWindow(0, 0, r.right, r.bottom, 1);
```

After this sequence has executed, the control will be exactly large enough to hold one month's worth of dates, plus all of the menus and controls required by the calendar. If you like, you can then alter these dimensions to give the control the precise appearance that you want. For example, you could increase the values in **r.right** and **r.bottom** slightly to add some extra space around the control.

MoveWindow( ) is the function that actually resizes the month calendar control. It is a member of **CWnd**, and its prototype is shown here:

```
void CWnd::MoveWindow(int NewX, int NewY, int NewWidth,
                      int NewHeight,
                      BOOL Repaint = TRUE);
```

The new location of the window's upper-left corner is passed in *NewX* and *NewY*. The new width and height are specified in *NewWidth* and *NewHeight*. If *Repaint* is nonzero, the window will be repainted immediately after it has been resized. Otherwise, no repainting will occur.

Demonstrating a Month Calendar Control

The following program demonstrates a month calendar. The main menu allows you to display the currently selected date. The calendar is displayed within the main window. Choosing Show Date shows the currently selected date. Sample output is shown in Figure 12-4.

The program uses the following resource file:

```
// MONTHCAL.RC

#include <afxres.h>
#include "mcalids.h"

MonthCalMenu MENU
{
  POPUP "&Demo"
  {
    MENUITEM "&Show Date\tF2", IDM_SHOWDATE
    MENUITEM "E&xit\tF5", IDM_EXIT
  }
  MENUITEM "&Help", IDM_HELP
}

MonthCalMenu ACCELERATORS
{
  VK_F2, IDM_SHOWDATE, VIRTKEY
  VK_F5, IDM_EXIT, VIRTKEY
  VK_F1, IDM_HELP, VIRTKEY
}
```

12

The header file MCALIDS.H is shown here:

```
// MCALIDS.H

#define IDM_HELP      100
#define IDM_EXIT      101
#define IDM_SHOWDATE  102

#define ID_MONTHCAL   200
```

The class derivation file MONTHCAL.H is shown here:

```
// MONTHCAL.H

// This is the main window class.
class CMainWin : public CFrameWnd
{
  CMonthCalCtrl m_MonthCal;

public:
  CMainWin();

  // define menu handlers
  afx_msg void OnShowDate();

  afx_msg void OnExit();
  afx_msg void OnHelp();

  DECLARE_MESSAGE_MAP()
};

// This is the application class.
class CApp : public CWinApp
{
public:
  BOOL InitInstance();
};
```

The program file is shown here:

```
// Demonstrate a month calendar control.

#include <afxwin.h>
#include <afxcmn.h>
#include <afxdtctl.h> //include file for date controls
#include <string.h>
#include "monthcal.h"
```

```
#include "mcalids.h"

CMainWin::CMainWin()
{
  Create(NULL, "Using A Month Calendar Control",
         WS_OVERLAPPEDWINDOW, rectDefault,
         NULL, "MonthCalMenu");

  // Load accelerator table.
  if(!LoadAccelTable("MonthCalMenu"))
     MessageBox("Cannot Load Accelerators", "Error");

  INITCOMMONCONTROLSEX initCtrls;

  initCtrls.dwSize = sizeof(initCtrls);
  initCtrls.dwICC= ICC_DATE_CLASSES;
  InitCommonControlsEx(&initCtrls);

  RECT r;

  // create month cal control
  r.left = r.top  = 0;
  r.right = 0; r.bottom = 0;

  m_MonthCal.Create(WS_VISIBLE | WS_CHILD | WS_BORDER, r,
                    this, ID_MONTHCAL);

  // now, size the calendar
  m_MonthCal.GetMinReqRect(&r);
  m_MonthCal.MoveWindow(0, 0, r.right, r.bottom, 1);
}

// Initialize the application.
BOOL CApp::InitInstance()
{
  m_pMainWnd = new CMainWin;
  m_pMainWnd->ShowWindow(m_nCmdShow);
  m_pMainWnd->UpdateWindow();

  return TRUE;
}

// This is the application's message map.
BEGIN_MESSAGE_MAP(CMainWin, CFrameWnd)
  ON_COMMAND(IDM_SHOWDATE, OnShowDate)
  ON_COMMAND(IDM_EXIT, OnExit)
  ON_COMMAND(IDM_HELP, OnHelp)
END_MESSAGE_MAP()
```

12

```
// Process IDM_SHOWDATE.
afx_msg void CMainWin::OnShowDate()
{
  SYSTEMTIME tempst;
  char str[255];

  m_MonthCal.GetCurSel(&tempst);
  sprintf(str, "%d/%d/%d", tempst.wMonth,
          tempst.wDay, tempst.wYear);
  MessageBox(str, "Date Selected", MB_OK);
}

// Process IDM_EXIT.
afx_msg void CMainWin::OnExit()
{
  int response;

  response = MessageBox("Quit the Program?",
                        "Exit", MB_YESNO);

  if(response == IDYES)
    SendMessage(WM_CLOSE); // terminate app
}

// Process IDM_HELP.
afx_msg void CMainWin::OnHelp()
{
    MessageBox("Month Calendar", "Help");
}

CApp App; // instantiate the application
```

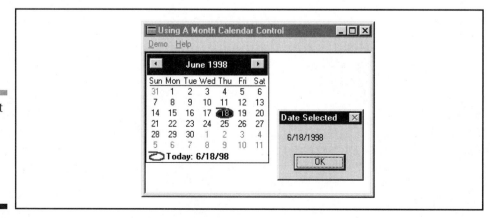

Sample output
from the
month
calendar
program
Figure 12-4.

IN DEPTH

Show More Than One Month

While most applications will display only one month at a time when using a month calendar control, you are not limited to this. To show more than one month, simply size the calendar to some multiple of the dimensions returned by **GetMinReqRect( )**. You will also need to add a little extra space for the gap between each month. For example, the following sequence creates a calendar that shows two months:

```
m_MonthCal.GetMinReqRect(&r);
m_MonthCal.MoveWindow(0, 0, (r.right*2)+10, r.bottom, 1);
```

Here is how the calendar control looks:

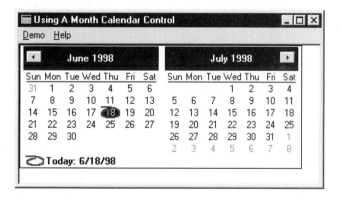

12

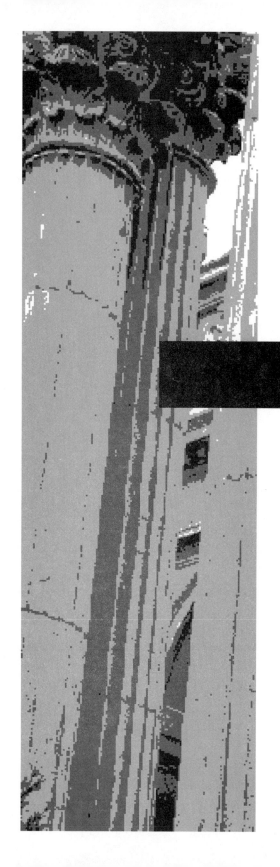

CHAPTER 13

Property Sheets
and Wizards

This chapter describes how to create one of the most exciting of the common controls: the *wizard*. As you probably know, a wizard is a sequenced set of dialog boxes that guides the user through a complex group of selections. The dialog boxes that constitute the wizard must be accessed in the order in which they are sequenced. Thus, a wizard can be used to orchestrate a "step one, step two, step three. . ." input scenario. You have probably encountered wizards several times before. For example, a wizard is activated when you install a new printer.

As you will soon see, wizards are built upon another common control: the *property sheet*. A property sheet is typically used to view and set various properties associated with some item. Although they look like the tab control described in the preceding chapter, property sheets are much more powerful.

Since the wizard is based on the property sheet, this chapter begins there.

Property Sheet Basics

Property sheets allow the user to examine or alter various properties associated with some component or subsystem of an application. For example, a property sheet is typically employed to set printer options or a modem configuration. A sample property sheet is shown in Figure 13-1. As

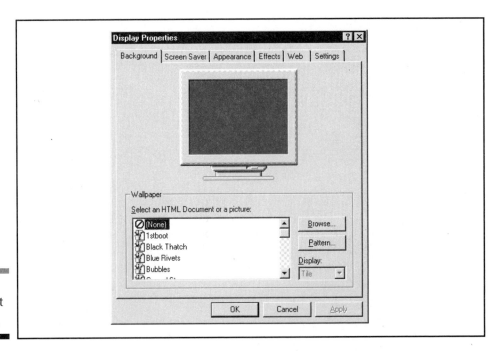

A sample
property sheet
Figure 13-1.

you can see, from the user's perspective, a property sheet consists of one or more *pages*. Each page has a tab associated with it. A page is activated by selecting its tab. This makes property sheets visually similar to tab controls, discussed in Chapter 12. However, property sheets offer far more functionality and ease of use.

From the programmer's perspective, a property sheet is a collection of one or more dialog boxes. That is, each page in a property sheet is defined by a dialog box template and interaction with the page is handled in the same way as it is with a dialog box. Most commonly, each dialog box template is specified in your application's resource file (although it can be created at run time, if necessary).

In MFC, property sheets are encapsulated by **CPropertySheet**. **CPropertySheet** is directly derived from **CWnd**. Each page of a property sheet is an object of the class **CPropertyPage**, which is derived from **CDialog**.

All property sheets contain two buttons: OK and Cancel. Often a third button, called Apply, is also included. It is important to understand that although the dialog functions associated with each page provide the mechanism by which the user sets or views the properties, only the property sheet control itself can accept or cancel the user's changes. Put differently, no page dialog box should include an OK, Cancel, or Apply button. These operations are provided by the property sheet control itself.

The page dialog boxes that constitute the property sheet are enclosed within the property sheet control. The property sheet control manages interaction with and between the individual pages. As a general rule, each page dialog box responds to its own controls in the normal fashion. That is, the individual controls that make up each page are handled in the standard way by the page's dialog class. However, each page must also respond to messages generated by the enclosing property sheet. When the property sheet needs to communicate with a page, it does so by calling various member functions of the **CPropertyPage** class. The details of this are discussed shortly.

There is one very important requirement that you must follow when creating a property sheet: The **CPropertyPage** dialog box class associated with each page must *not* close its dialog box. That is, it must not call **EndDialog( )** or **DestroyWindow( )**. Instead, the enclosing property sheet control itself will take care of this. If you do close one of the page dialog boxes, then the property sheet control will still be active but that page will be empty. This is a violation of Windows style rules, to say the least!

13

To use a property sheet, you must include the header file AFXDLGS.H in your program.

Creating a Property Sheet

In its simplest form, creating a property sheet is a two-step process: Declare an object of type **CPropertySheet**, and then add objects of type **CPropertyPage** to it. Each **CPropertyPage** object defines one page in the property sheet. However, for various reasons, including ease of use and safety, this simple approach is seldom used. Instead, a slightly more complicated implementation is required.

For most applications involving property sheets, you will not use objects of type **CPropertySheet** or **CPropertyPage** directly. Rather, you will derive your own custom versions of these classes. Typically, for each page in your property sheet, you will derive a class from **CPropertyPage** that defines the attributes associated with that page. The class that you derive from **CPropertySheet** will then include objects of each of your page classes. When a property sheet object is instantiated, the page objects will automatically be created. The advantages to this approach are:

◆ You control precisely the form and nature of your property pages.

◆ Your property pages are encapsulated within the property sheet control that uses them.

Let's look at the details of this process.

Creating Property Pages

When creating a property sheet, the first thing you must do is define its property pages. Since **CPropertyPage** is derived from **CDialog**, deriving a property page is virtually identical to deriving a dialog box. In fact, the only real difference is that the constructor for your class must execute a call to the **CPropertyPage** constructor instead of the constructor for **CDialog**. There are three forms of constructors supported by **CPropertyPage**:

CPropertyPage( );

CPropertyPage(LPCSTR *Name*, UINT *TabID* = 0);

CPropertyPage(UINT *ID*, UINT *TabID* = 0);

The first form creates a property page object, but does not initialize it. In the second form, *Name* specifies the name of the dialog box template in the resource file. In the third form, *ID* is the ID of the dialog box template. In both cases, *TabID* is the resource ID of a string that will be used as the name in the tab for the page being defined. However, if *TabID* is zero, then the name specified in the dialog box template will be used for the name of the tab.

If you use the non-parameterized form of the **CPropertyPage** constructor to declare an object, then you will need to call the **Construct( )** member function to actually create the page. Its prototypes are shown here:

> void CPropertyPage::Construct(LPCSTR *Name*, UINT *TabID* = 0);

> void CPropertyPage::Construct(UINT *ID*, UINT *TabID* = 0);

Here, *Name* specifies the name of the dialog box template in the resource file. *ID* is the ID of the dialog box template. In both cases, *TabID* is the resource ID of a string that will be used as the name in the tab for the page being defined. However, if *TabID* is zero, then the name specified in the dialog box template will be used for the name of the tab.

As mentioned, most of the time you will derive your own property page classes, using **CPropertyPage** as the base class. You will handle each of the property pages just as you handle dialog boxes derived from **CDialog**. For example, each class that you derive from **CPropertyPage** will contain its own message map and define its own message handlers.

Creating the Property Sheet Control

Once you have derived your property pages, you can derive your property sheet class from **CPropertySheet**. The constructor for your derived class must execute a call to one of **CPropertySheet**'s constructors, shown here:

> CPropertySheet( );

> CPropertySheet(UINT *TitleID*, CWnd **Owner* = NULL, UINT *Page* = 0);

> CPropertySheet(LPCSTR *lpszTitle*, CWnd **Owner* = NULL, UINT *Page* = 0);

The first form creates an uninitialized property sheet control. In the second form, *TitleID* is the string resource ID of the title of the control. In the third form, *lpszTitle* is a pointer to the title of the control. In both cases, *Owner* is a pointer to the window object that is the parent of the property sheet, and *Page* is the index of the page that will be selected when the control is created. Page indexes start at zero.

13

If you use the non-parameterized form of **CPropertySheet( )** to instantiate a property sheet, then you must initialize it using the **Construct( )** member function, shown here:

void CPropertySheet::Construct(UINT *TitleID*, CWnd **Owner* = NULL,
                   UINT *Page* = 0);

void CPropertySheet::Construct(LPCSTR *lpszTitle*, CWnd **Owner* = NULL,
                   UINT *Page* = 0);

Here, *TitleID* is the string resource ID of the title of the control. *lpszTitle* is a pointer to the title of the control. In both cases, *Owner* is a pointer to the window object that is the parent of the property sheet and *Page* is the index of the page that will be initially selected.

Adding Pages to the Property Sheet

Before you can use a property sheet, you must add to it the pages used by the control. To do this, use **AddPage( )**, which is a member function of **CPropertySheet**. Its prototype is shown here:

void CPropertySheet::AddPage(CPropertyPage **Page*);

Here, *Page* is a pointer to an object that is either of type **CPropertyPage** or an object of a class derived from **CPropertyPage**.

Pages are added to a property sheet in order from left to right. This means that the first page added is at index zero.

Activating the Property Sheet

After you have constructed a property sheet and added pages to it, you can activate the property sheet using the member function **DoModal( )**. This causes the modal version of the property sheet to be displayed. The prototype for **DoModal( )** is shown here:

virtual int CPropertySheet::DoModal( );

The return value will be either **IDOK** or **IDCANCEL**. It returns zero on failure. **DoModal( )** does not return until the property sheet has been closed. The property sheet will automatically close itself when the user selects either the OK or Cancel push buttons.

To activate a modeless property sheet, use the **Create( )** member function of **CPropertySheet**. However, most of the time, property sheets are activated as modal controls. In fact, a modeless property sheet is the exception and not the rule. Further, most of the support provided by **CPropertySheet** assumes a modal rather than modeless property sheet. (For example, modeless property sheets do not automatically have OK, Cancel, and Apply push buttons.) The examples in this chapter use modal property sheets.

Property Sheet Summary

Here is a summary of the steps that you need to take to create and activate a property sheet:

1. Define the page dialog boxes in your program's resource file.
2. Derive the necessary property page classes from **CPropertyPage**.
3. Derive a property sheet class from **CPropertySheet**. Include page objects as members of this class.
4. Create an object of the property sheet class.
5. Activate the property sheet by calling **DoModal( )**.

Soon you will see an example that implements these steps.

Property Page Message Handlers

Each page in your property sheet control is, essentially, a dialog box and is managed as such. For example, when a property page is first created, it is sent a **WM_INITDIALOG** message, which causes the built-in message handler **OnInitDialog( )** to be called. However, **CPropertyPage** includes several other built-in message handlers that relate specifically to property sheets. Following is a partial list:

Handler	Called
OnApply( )	When the user presses Apply
OnCancel( )	When the user presses Cancel
OnKillActive( )	When the page loses input focus
OnOK( )	When the user presses OK or Apply
OnReset( )	When the user presses Cancel
OnSetActive( )	When the page gains input focus

13

The prototypes for these handlers are shown here:

virtual BOOL CPropertyPage::OnApply( );

virtual void CPropertyPage::OnCancel( );

virtual BOOL CPropertyPage::OnKillActive( );

virtual void CPropertyPage::OnOK( );

virtual void CPropertyPage::OnReset( );

virtual BOOL CPropertyPage::OnSetActive( );

Your derived property page will need to override some or all of these functions, taking appropriate action. For example, when **OnOK( )** is called, any changes to the property sheet settings made by the user should be made permanent. When **OnReset( )** is called, the attributes of the property sheet should be returned to their original values. When **OnApply( )** is called, your property sheet must put the user's current selections into effect, but keep the property sheet active. For the handlers that return a Boolean result, return nonzero to indicate success, zero if a failure occurs.

Enabling the Apply Button

When a property sheet is first activated, its Apply button is disabled. To enable the button, your program must call **SetModified( )**, shown here:

void CPropertyPage::SetModified(BOOL *How* = TRUE);

Here, *How* determines whether the Apply button is enabled or disabled. If it is nonzero, then the button is enabled. It if is zero, the button is disabled.

Your program must call **SetModified( )** whenever the property sheet has been changed by the user.

Property Sheet Dialog Dimensions

The dialog box that underlies a property sheet can be of any size. However, it is recommended that your property sheets be one of the standard sizes defined by Windows. The standard sizes are shown here:

Size	Width	Height
Small	PROP_SM_CXDLG	PROP_SM_CYDLG
Medium	PROP_MED_CXDLG	PROP_MED_CYDLG
Large	PROP_LG_CXDLG	PROP_LG_CYDLG

These macros are defined by including PRSHT.H. They are specified in terms of dialog box units and should be used in the DIALOG descriptions within your application's resource file.

Older compilers may not support the property sheet dimensions macros. If this is the case with your compiler, you can use the following dimensions:

Size	Width	Height
Small	212	188
Medium	227	215
Large	252	218

A Property Sheet Demonstration Program

The following program displays a property sheet that contains three pages. Although the property sheet does not actually set any real properties, it does demonstrate the necessary procedures to create and display a property sheet. Sample output is shown in Figure 13-2.

The program uses the following resource file:

```
// Property sheet dialog boxes.
#include <afxres.h>
#include <prsht.h>
#include "ids.h"

PropertyMenu MENU
{
  POPUP "&Property Sheet"
  {
    MENUITEM "&Activate\tF2", IDM_ACTIVATE
    MENUITEM "&Exit\tF3", IDM_EXIT
  }
  MENUITEM "&Help", IDM_HELP
```

13

```
}

PropertyMenu ACCELERATORS
{
  VK_F2, IDM_ACTIVATE, VIRTKEY
  VK_F3, IDM_EXIT, VIRTKEY
  VK_F1, IDM_HELP, VIRTKEY
}

PropDialog1 DIALOG 0, 0, PROP_SM_CXDLG, PROP_SM_CYDLG
CAPTION "First Page"
STYLE WS_POPUP | WS_CAPTION | WS_SYSMENU | WS_VISIBLE
{
  DEFPUSHBUTTON "One", IDD_ONE, 11, 10, 32, 14,
           WS_CHILD | WS_VISIBLE | WS_TABSTOP
  PUSHBUTTON "Two", IDD_TWO, 11, 34, 32, 14,
           WS_CHILD | WS_VISIBLE | WS_TABSTOP
  PUSHBUTTON "Three", IDD_THREE, 11, 58, 32, 14,
           WS_CHILD | WS_VISIBLE | WS_TABSTOP
  LISTBOX IDD_LB1, 66, 25, 50, 33, LBS_NOTIFY |
           WS_VISIBLE | WS_BORDER | WS_VSCROLL | WS_TABSTOP
}

PropDialog2 DIALOG  0, 0, PROP_SM_CXDLG, PROP_SM_CYDLG
CAPTION "Second Page"
STYLE WS_POPUP | WS_CAPTION | WS_SYSMENU | WS_VISIBLE
{
  DEFPUSHBUTTON "Invert", IDD_INVERT, 11, 10, 32, 14,
           WS_CHILD | WS_VISIBLE | WS_TABSTOP
  AUTOCHECKBOX "Check Box 1", IDD_CB1, 66, 10, 70, 10
  AUTOCHECKBOX "Check Box 2", IDD_CB2, 66, 30, 70, 10
  AUTOCHECKBOX "Check Box 3", IDD_CB3, 66, 50, 70, 10
}

PropDialog3 DIALOG  0, 0, PROP_SM_CXDLG, PROP_SM_CYDLG
CAPTION "Third Page"
STYLE WS_POPUP | WS_CAPTION | WS_SYSMENU | WS_VISIBLE
{
  DEFPUSHBUTTON "Top", IDD_TOP, 11, 10, 32, 14,
           WS_CHILD | WS_VISIBLE | WS_TABSTOP
  PUSHBUTTON "Bottom", IDD_BOTTOM, 11, 34, 32, 14,
           WS_CHILD | WS_VISIBLE | WS_TABSTOP
  AUTORADIOBUTTON "Radio Button 1", IDD_RB1, 66, 10, 70, 10
  AUTORADIOBUTTON "Radio Button 2", IDD_RB2, 66, 30, 70, 10
  AUTORADIOBUTTON "Radio Button 3", IDD_RB3, 66, 50, 70, 10

}
```

The header file IDS.H is shown here:

```
#define IDM_ACTIVATE 100
#define IDM_EXIT     101
#define IDM_HELP     102

#define IDD_ONE      200
#define IDD_TWO      201
#define IDD_THREE    202
#define IDD_TOP      204
#define IDD_BOTTOM   205
#define IDD_INVERT   207

#define IDD_LB1      301

#define IDD_CB1      501
#define IDD_CB2      502
#define IDD_CB3      503

#define IDD_RB1      601
#define IDD_RB2      602
#define IDD_RB3      603

#define NUMSTRINGS     5
#define NUMPAGES       3
```

The class derivation file, PROP.H, is shown next:

```
// PROP.H

/*
   Here, the property sheet page dialog box classes
   are defined.  These pages will be used to construct
   the property sheet control.
*/

// This is the first page dialog class.
class CPropDialog1 : public CPropertyPage
{
public:
  CPropDialog1() : CPropertyPage() {};

  BOOL OnInitDialog();
  BOOL OnApply();
```

13

```
/*  You will want to override the following
    functions in real applications.

  void OnCancel(); // called when cancel button is pressed
  void OnOK(); // called when OK button is pressed
*/

  afx_msg void OnOne();
  afx_msg void OnTwo();
  afx_msg void OnThree();
  afx_msg void OnListBox();

  DECLARE_MESSAGE_MAP()
};

// This is the second page dialog class.
class CPropDialog2 : public CPropertyPage
{
public:
  CPropDialog2() : CPropertyPage() {};

  BOOL OnInitDialog();
  BOOL OnApply();

/*  You will want to override the following
    functions in real applications.

  void OnCancel(); // called when cancel button is pressed
  void OnOK(); // called when OK button is pressed
*/

  afx_msg void OnInvert();
  afx_msg void OnCB1();
  afx_msg void OnCB2();
  afx_msg void OnCB3();

  DECLARE_MESSAGE_MAP()
};

// This is the third page dialog class.
class CPropDialog3 : public CPropertyPage
{
public:
  CPropDialog3() : CPropertyPage() {};
```

```
  BOOL OnInitDialog();
  BOOL OnApply();

/*  You will want to override the following
    functions in real applications.

  void OnCancel(); // called when cancel button is pressed
  void OnOK(); // called when OK button is pressed
*/

  afx_msg void OnTop();
  afx_msg void OnBottom();

  afx_msg void OnRB1();
  afx_msg void OnRB2();
  afx_msg void OnRB3();

  DECLARE_MESSAGE_MAP()
};

// Derive a property sheet.
class CSamplePropSheet : public CPropertySheet
{
  CPropDialog1 page1; // first page
  CPropDialog2 page2; // second page
  CPropDialog3 page3; // third page
public:
  CSamplePropSheet() : CPropertySheet() {
    Construct("Sample Property Sheet", this);

    page1.Construct("PropDialog1", 0);
    page2.Construct("PropDialog2", 0);
    page3.Construct("PropDialog3", 0);
    AddPage(&page1);
    AddPage(&page2);
    AddPage(&page3);
  }
};

// This is the main window class.
class CMainWin : public CFrameWnd
{
  CSamplePropSheet m_PropSheet; // property sheet
public:
  CMainWin();
```

13

```
  afx_msg void OnActivate();
  afx_msg void OnExit();
  afx_msg void OnHelp();

  DECLARE_MESSAGE_MAP()
};

// This is the application class.
class CApp : public CWinApp
{
public:
  BOOL InitInstance();
};
```

The property sheet program file is shown here:

```
// Using a property sheet.

#include <afxwin.h>
#include <afxdlgs.h>
#include <string.h>
#include "ids.h"
#include "prop.h"

char list[][40] = {
  "Red",
  "Green",
  "Yellow",
  "Black",
  "White"
};

// Construct the main window.
CMainWin::CMainWin()
{
  Create(NULL, "Using A Property Sheet",
         WS_OVERLAPPEDWINDOW, rectDefault,
         NULL, "PropertyMenu");

  INITCOMMONCONTROLSEX initCtrls;

  initCtrls.dwSize = sizeof(initCtrls);
  initCtrls.dwICC= ICC_TAB_CLASSES;
  InitCommonControlsEx(&initCtrls);
```

```
    // Load accelerator table.
    if(!LoadAccelTable("PropertyMenu"))
       MessageBox("Cannot Load Accelerators", "Error");
}

// Initialize the application.
BOOL CApp::InitInstance()
{
  m_pMainWnd = new CMainWin;
  m_pMainWnd->ShowWindow(m_nCmdShow);
  m_pMainWnd->UpdateWindow();

  return TRUE;
}

// This is the application's message map.
BEGIN_MESSAGE_MAP(CMainWin, CFrameWnd)
  ON_COMMAND(IDM_ACTIVATE, OnActivate)
  ON_COMMAND(IDM_EXIT, OnExit)
  ON_COMMAND(IDM_HELP, OnHelp)
END_MESSAGE_MAP()

// Process IDM_ACTIVATE.
afx_msg void CMainWin::OnActivate()
{
  m_PropSheet.DoModal(); // activate modal property sheet
}

// Process IDM_EXIT.
afx_msg void CMainWin::OnExit()
{
  int response;

  response = MessageBox("Quit the Program?",
                        "Exit", MB_YESNO);

  if(response == IDYES)
    SendMessage(WM_CLOSE); // terminate app
}

// Process IDM_HELP.
afx_msg void CMainWin::OnHelp()
{
    MessageBox("Property Sheet", "Help");
```

13

```
}

// Message map for the first page dialog box.
BEGIN_MESSAGE_MAP(CPropDialog1, CPropertyPage)
  ON_COMMAND(IDD_ONE, OnOne)
  ON_COMMAND(IDD_TWO, OnTwo)
  ON_COMMAND(IDD_THREE, OnThree)
  ON_LBN_DBLCLK(IDD_LB1, OnListBox)
END_MESSAGE_MAP()

// Initialize first page dialog box.
BOOL CPropDialog1::OnInitDialog()
{
  int i;

  CPropertyPage::OnInitDialog(); // Call base class version

  CListBox *lbptr = (CListBox *) GetDlgItem(IDD_LB1);

  for(i=0; i<NUMSTRINGS; i++)
    lbptr->AddString(list[i]);

  lbptr->SetCurSel(0);

  return TRUE;
}

// A placeholder OnApply() function for CPropDialog1.
afx_msg BOOL CPropDialog1::OnApply()
{
  MessageBox("Selection Applied", "First Page");

  return TRUE;
}

// Handle IDD_ONE commands.
afx_msg void CPropDialog1::OnOne()
{
  MessageBox("One", "Button Pressed");
}

// Handle IDD_TWO commands.
afx_msg void CPropDialog1::OnTwo()
{
  MessageBox("Two", "Button Pressed");
```

```
}

// Handle IDD_THREE commands.
afx_msg void CPropDialog1::OnThree()
{
  MessageBox("Three", "Button Pressed");
}

// Handle List box notifications
afx_msg void CPropDialog1::OnListBox()
{
  int i;
  char str[255];

  CListBox *lbptr = (CListBox *) GetDlgItem(IDD_LB1);

  i = lbptr->GetCurSel();

  lbptr->GetText(i, str);

  MessageBox(str, "Selection is");
  SetModified(1);
}

// Message map for the second page dialog box.
BEGIN_MESSAGE_MAP(CPropDialog2, CPropertyPage)
  ON_COMMAND(IDD_INVERT, OnInvert)
  ON_COMMAND(IDD_CB1, OnCB1)
  ON_COMMAND(IDD_CB2, OnCB2)
  ON_COMMAND(IDD_CB3, OnCB3)
END_MESSAGE_MAP()

// Initialize second page dialog box.
BOOL CPropDialog2::OnInitDialog()
{
  CPropertyPage::OnInitDialog(); // Call base class version

  CButton *cbptr = (CButton *) GetDlgItem(IDD_CB1);

  cbptr->SetCheck(1);

  return TRUE;
}

// A placeholder OnApply() function for CPropDialog2.
```

13

```
afx_msg BOOL CPropDialog2::OnApply()
{
  MessageBox("Selection Applied", "Second Page");

  return TRUE;
}

// Handle IDD_INVERT commands.
afx_msg void CPropDialog2::OnInvert()
{
  // invert the check box selections

  CButton *lbptr1 = (CButton *) GetDlgItem(IDD_CB1);
  CButton *lbptr2 = (CButton *) GetDlgItem(IDD_CB2);
  CButton *lbptr3 = (CButton *) GetDlgItem(IDD_CB3);

  // invert the state of the check boxes
  if(lbptr1->GetCheck()) lbptr1->SetCheck(0);
  else lbptr1->SetCheck(1);

  if(lbptr2->GetCheck()) lbptr2->SetCheck(0);
  else lbptr2->SetCheck(1);

  if(lbptr3->GetCheck()) lbptr3->SetCheck(0);
  else lbptr3->SetCheck(1);

  SetModified(1);
}

// Handle IDD_CB1 commands.
afx_msg void CPropDialog2::OnCB1()
{
  SetModified(1);
}

// Handle IDD_CB2 commands.
afx_msg void CPropDialog2::OnCB2()
{
  SetModified(1);
}

// Handle IDD_CB3 commands.
afx_msg void CPropDialog2::OnCB3()
{
  SetModified(1);
```

```
}

// Message map for the third page dialog box.
BEGIN_MESSAGE_MAP(CPropDialog3, CPropertyPage)
  ON_COMMAND(IDD_TOP, OnTop)
  ON_COMMAND(IDD_BOTTOM, OnBottom)
  ON_COMMAND(IDD_RB1, OnRB1)
  ON_COMMAND(IDD_RB2, OnRB2)
  ON_COMMAND(IDD_RB3, OnRB3)
END_MESSAGE_MAP()

// Initialize third page dialog box.
BOOL CPropDialog3::OnInitDialog()
{
  CPropertyPage::OnInitDialog(); // Call base class version

  CButton *cbptr = (CButton *) GetDlgItem(IDD_RB1);

  cbptr->SetCheck(1);

  return TRUE;
}

// A placeholder OnApply() function for CPropDialog3.
afx_msg BOOL CPropDialog3::OnApply()
{
  MessageBox("Selection Applied", "Third Page");

  return TRUE;
}

// Handle IDD_TOP commands.
afx_msg void CPropDialog3::OnTop()
{
  CButton *lbptr1 = (CButton *) GetDlgItem(IDD_RB1);
  CButton *lbptr2 = (CButton *) GetDlgItem(IDD_RB2);
  CButton *lbptr3 = (CButton *) GetDlgItem(IDD_RB3);

  // turn off lower buttons
  lbptr2->SetCheck(0);
  lbptr3->SetCheck(0);

  lbptr1->SetCheck(1); // set top button

  SetModified(1);
```

13

```
}

// Handle IDD_BOTTOM commands.
afx_msg void CPropDialog3::OnBottom()
{
  CButton *lbptr1 = (CButton *) GetDlgItem(IDD_RB1);
  CButton *lbptr2 = (CButton *) GetDlgItem(IDD_RB2);
  CButton *lbptr3 = (CButton *) GetDlgItem(IDD_RB3);

  // turn off top buttons
  lbptr2->SetCheck(0);
  lbptr1->SetCheck(0);

  lbptr3->SetCheck(1); // set bottom button

  SetModified(1);
}

// Handle IDD_RB1 commands.
afx_msg void CPropDialog3::OnRB1()
{
  SetModified(1);
}

// Handle IDD_RB2 commands.
afx_msg void CPropDialog3::OnRB2()
{
  SetModified(1);
}

// Handle IDD_RB3 commands.
afx_msg void CPropDialog3::OnRB3()
{
  SetModified(1);
}

CApp App; // instantiate the application
```

The code in the program is straightforward and should present no difficulties. However, let's take a closer look at a few important aspects. PROP.H first declares the page dialog classes, called **CPropDialog1** through **CPropDialog3**. These classes are then used inside **CSamplePropSheet** to declare the page objects used by the property sheet. It is important to remember that the page objects must not go out of scope while the property sheet that relies on them is still in use. This is a crucial point and the reason why, most often, the page objects are made members of the property sheet

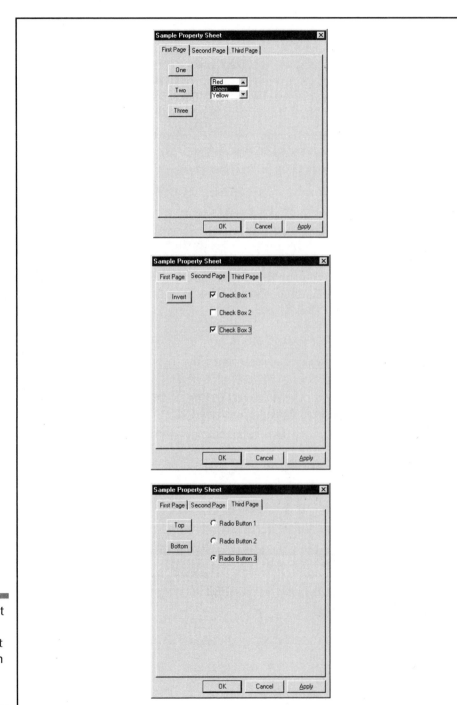

Sample output
from the
property sheet
demonstration
program

Figure 13-2.

class that you derive. They won't be destroyed before the property sheet control is terminated.

In the page classes, the **OnApply( )** function is overridden for the sake of illustration. Its implementation only displays a message box. **OnOK( )** and **OnCancel( )** are shown in PROP.H, but commented out. You will want to implement these functions in any real application that you write.

The **CMainWin** class includes a private member, called **m_PropSheet**, that is a **CSamplePropSheet** object. Thus, when the main frame window is created inside **CApp::InitInstance**, the property sheet is also created.

Creating a Wizard

Once you know how to create a property sheet, it is a simple matter to transform it into a wizard. From the programmer's point of view, a wizard is a set of sequenced property sheets. It is defined in the way just described: by declaring the property pages that comprise the wizard and then adding them to a property sheet control. To change a property sheet into a wizard requires these few extra steps:

1. Activate wizard mode.
2. Display the proper wizard buttons when each page in the wizard is activated.
3. Override **OnWizardFinish( )**, **OnWizardNext( )**, and **OnWizardBack( )** as needed.
4. If desired, add bitmaps to the pages of the wizard.

Let's see how each of these steps is accomplished.

Activating Wizard Mode

As just mentioned, a wizard is created the same way that a property sheet is created. To change your property sheet into a wizard, all that is necessary is to change the way that your property sheet is displayed. Fortunately, this is very easy to do. Simply call **SetWizardMode( )** prior to calling **DoModal( )**. **SetWizardMode( )** is a member of **CPropertySheet**. Its prototype is shown here:

```
void CPropertypSheet::SetWizardMode( );
```

After calling **SetWizardMode( )**, your property sheet will automatically be displayed as a wizard.

Enabling Wizard Buttons

Although calling **SetWizardMode( )** automatically transforms your property sheet into a wizard, there are a few more steps that you will need to take in order for your wizard to perform correctly. As you probably know, wizards use their own set of control buttons. These buttons are called Back, Next, and Finish. You will need to enable and disable these buttons manually. For example, on the first page, you will need to enable the Next button, but disable the Back button. On the last page, you will need to enable the Back button and the Finish button. On the pages between the first and last, the Next and Back buttons will have to be enabled. To accomplish this, call the **SetWizardButtons( )** function shown here:

    void CPropertySheet::SetWizardButtons(DWORD *dwWhich*);

In the *dwWhich* parameter, specify the button or buttons that you want to enable. Only those buttons that you specify will be enabled. The others will be disabled. The button macros are shown here:

PSWIZB_BACK

PSWIZB_DISABLEDFINISH

PSWIZB_FINISH

PSWIZB_NEXT

You can OR together two or more buttons. Therefore, to enable the Back and Finish buttons, you would use this statement:

```
SetWizardButtons(PSWIZB_BACK | PSWIZB_FINISH);
```

PSWIZB_DISABLEDFINISH disables the Finish button. You will disable Finish if the user has not correctly completed the sequence of dialog boxes defined by the wizard.

13

Handling the Standard Wizard Messages

There are three standard messages that relate directly to wizards. They are generated whenever the user presses one of the wizard buttons. **CPropertyPage** includes built-in message handlers for these messages, which your program may override. These message handlers are shown here:

> virtual LRESULT CPropertyPage::OnWizardBack( );
>
> virtual LRESULT CPropertyPage::OnWizardNext( );
>
> virtual BOOL CPropertyPage::OnWizardFinish( );

OnWizardBack( ) is called when the user presses the Back button. **OnWizardNext( )** is called when the user presses the Next button. For these handlers, return zero to move to the previous or next page, –1 to prevent a page change or the index of a page to move to. **OnWizardFinish( )** is called when the user presses the Finish button. Return nonzero if successful and zero on failure.

Your program will need to override these message handlers, taking appropriate action. For example, no changes should be permanent unless the user presses Finish. You may need to respond to Back or Next by resetting options or by verifying the validity of the user's choices before proceeding to the next page.

In addition to the wizard message handlers, your wizard may need to override the **OnCancel( )** message handler. This function is called when the user presses the Cancel button. It operates as described earlier.

Using a Bitmap

As you have probably noticed, most wizards specify a large bitmap on the left side of the first page. A bitmap may be specified on subsequent pages as well. This bitmap serves to identify the wizard. While not technically required, it is highly recommended that at least the first page of any wizard that you create include such a bitmap. If you wish to include a bitmap, just override the standard **OnPaint( )** handler for each page dialog box. Inside your version of **OnPaint( )**, load and display the bitmap (using the same procedure described in Chapter 7 when bitmaps were discussed).

Style Macros

Several values help you create wizards that conform to Microsoft's style rules. These values are shown here:

Value	Meaning
WIZ_CXDLG	Width of page
WIZ_CYDLG	Height of page
WIZ_CXBMP	Width of bitmap
WIZ_BODYX	X coordinate of the left side of the body of the page
WIZ_BODYCX	Width of body, excluding the bitmap area

These values are in terms of dialog box units. To have access to these values, you must include the standard header PRSHT.H in your resource file.

The style macros can be used to create wizards that are the same size and shape as those used by Windows. They also help you position each page's controls relative to the area reserved for the bitmap. Keep in mind, however, that if a page does not require a bitmap you can use the entire page area. In the example that follows, the first two pages display a bitmap and the third page does not.

A Wizard Demonstration Program

The following program demonstrates a wizard. It does so by converting the previous property sheet example into a wizard. Sample output is shown in Figure 13-3.

The wizard program uses the same IDS.H file as the preceding property sheet program. However, it requires the following resource file. This version uses the wizard style macros to create standard-sized pages.

```
// Wizard dialog boxes.
#include <afxres.h>
#include <prsht.h>
#include "ids.h"

wizbmp BITMAP bp1.bmp
```

13

```
PropertyMenu MENU
{
  POPUP "&Wizard Demo"
  {
    MENUITEM "&Activate\tF2", IDM_ACTIVATE
    MENUITEM "&Exit\tF3", IDM_EXIT
  }
  MENUITEM "&Help", IDM_HELP
}

PropertyMenu ACCELERATORS
{
  VK_F2, IDM_ACTIVATE, VIRTKEY
  VK_F3, IDM_EXIT, VIRTKEY
  VK_F1, IDM_HELP, VIRTKEY
}

PropDialog1 DIALOG 0, 0, WIZ_CXDLG, WIZ_CYDLG
CAPTION "Wizard Demo -- First Page"
STYLE WS_POPUP | WS_CAPTION | WS_SYSMENU | WS_VISIBLE
{
  DEFPUSHBUTTON "One", IDD_ONE, WIZ_BODYX, 10, 32, 14,
            WS_CHILD | WS_VISIBLE | WS_TABSTOP
  PUSHBUTTON "Two", IDD_TWO, WIZ_BODYX, 34, 32, 14,
            WS_CHILD | WS_VISIBLE | WS_TABSTOP
  PUSHBUTTON "Three", IDD_THREE, WIZ_BODYX, 58, 32, 14,
            WS_CHILD | WS_VISIBLE | WS_TABSTOP
  LISTBOX IDD_LB1, WIZ_BODYX+66, 25, 50, 33, LBS_NOTIFY |
            WS_VISIBLE | WS_BORDER | WS_VSCROLL | WS_TABSTOP
}

PropDialog2 DIALOG 0, 0, WIZ_CXDLG, WIZ_CYDLG
CAPTION "Wizard Demo -- Second Page"
STYLE WS_POPUP | WS_CAPTION | WS_SYSMENU | WS_VISIBLE
{
  DEFPUSHBUTTON "Invert", IDD_INVERT, WIZ_BODYX, 10, 32, 14,
            WS_CHILD | WS_VISIBLE | WS_TABSTOP
  AUTOCHECKBOX "Check Box 1", IDD_CB1,
            WIZ_BODYX+66, 10, 70, 10
  AUTOCHECKBOX "Check Box 2", IDD_CB2,
            WIZ_BODYX+66, 30, 70, 10
  AUTOCHECKBOX "Check Box 3", IDD_CB3,
            WIZ_BODYX+66, 50, 70, 10
}
```

```
PropDialog3 DIALOG 0, 0, WIZ_CXDLG, WIZ_CYDLG
CAPTION "Wizard Demo -- Third Page"
STYLE WS_POPUP | WS_CAPTION | WS_SYSMENU | WS_VISIBLE
{
  DEFPUSHBUTTON "Top", IDD_TOP, 11, 10, 32, 14,
            WS_CHILD | WS_VISIBLE | WS_TABSTOP
  PUSHBUTTON "Bottom", IDD_BOTTOM, 11, 34, 32, 14,
            WS_CHILD | WS_VISIBLE | WS_TABSTOP
  AUTORADIOBUTTON "Radio Button 1", IDD_RB1, 66, 10, 70, 10
  AUTORADIOBUTTON "Radio Button 2", IDD_RB2, 66, 30, 70, 10
  AUTORADIOBUTTON "Radio Button 3", IDD_RB3, 66, 50, 70, 10

}
```

The class derivation file, WIZ.H, is shown here:

```
// WIZ.H

/*
   Here, the property sheet page dialog box classes
   are defined.  These pages will be used to construct
   the wizard.
*/

// This is the first page dialog class.
class CPropDialog1 : public CPropertyPage
{
  CBitmap m_bmp;
public:
  CPropDialog1() : CPropertyPage() {};

  BOOL OnInitDialog();
  BOOL OnWizardFinish();
  BOOL OnSetActive();

/*  You will want to override the following
    functions in real applications.

  void OnCancel(); // called when cancel button is pressed
  LRESULT OnWizardBack(); // called when Back button is pressed
  LRESULT OnWizardNext(); // called when Next button is pressed
*/

  afx_msg void OnOne();
  afx_msg void OnTwo();
```

13

```cpp
  afx_msg void OnThree();
  afx_msg void OnListBox();

  afx_msg void OnPaint();

  DECLARE_MESSAGE_MAP()
};

// This is the second page dialog class.
class CPropDialog2 : public CPropertyPage
{
  CBitmap m_bmp;
public:
  CPropDialog2() : CPropertyPage() {};

  BOOL OnInitDialog();
  BOOL OnWizardFinish();
  BOOL OnSetActive();

/*  You will want to override the following
    functions in real applications.

  void OnCancel(); // called when cancel button is pressed
  LRESULT OnWizardBack(); // called when Back button is pressed
  LRESULT OnWizardNext(); // called when Next button is pressed
*/

  afx_msg void OnInvert();
  afx_msg void OnCB1();
  afx_msg void OnCB2();
  afx_msg void OnCB3();

  afx_msg void OnPaint();

  DECLARE_MESSAGE_MAP()
};

// This is the third page dialog class.
class CPropDialog3 : public CPropertyPage
{
public:
  CPropDialog3() : CPropertyPage() {};

  BOOL OnInitDialog();
  BOOL OnWizardFinish();
```

```
  BOOL OnSetActive();

/*  You will want to override the following
    functions in real applications.

  void OnCancel(); // called when cancel button is pressed
  LRESULT OnWizardBack(); // called when Back button is pressed
  LRESULT OnWizardNext(); // called when Next button is pressed
*/

  afx_msg void OnTop();
  afx_msg void OnBottom();

  afx_msg void OnRB1();
  afx_msg void OnRB2();
  afx_msg void OnRB3();

  DECLARE_MESSAGE_MAP()
};

// Derive a property sheet.
class CSamplePropSheet : public CPropertySheet
{
  CPropDialog1 page1; // first page
  CPropDialog2 page2; // second page
  CPropDialog3 page3; // third page
public:

  CSamplePropSheet() : CPropertySheet()
  {
    Construct("Sample Wizard", this);

    page1.Construct("PropDialog1", 0);
    page2.Construct("PropDialog2", 0);
    page3.Construct("PropDialog3", 0);
    AddPage(&page1);
    AddPage(&page2);
    AddPage(&page3);
  }
};

// This is the main window class.
class CMainWin : public CFrameWnd
{
  CSamplePropSheet m_PropSheet; // property sheet
```

13

```
public:
  CMainWin();

  afx_msg void OnActivate();
  afx_msg void OnExit();
  afx_msg void OnHelp();

  DECLARE_MESSAGE_MAP()
};

// This is the application class.
class CApp : public CWinApp
{
public:
  BOOL InitInstance();
};
```

Here is the wizard program file:

```
// Using a Wizard

#include <afxwin.h>
#include <afxdlgs.h>
#include <string.h>
#include "ids.h"
#include "wiz.h"

CSamplePropSheet *PropSheetPtr; // Pointer to property sheet

char list[][40] = {
  "Red",
  "Green",
  "Yellow",
  "Black",
  "White"
};

// Construct the main window.
CMainWin::CMainWin()
{
  Create(NULL, "Using A Wizard",
         WS_OVERLAPPEDWINDOW, rectDefault,
         NULL, "PropertyMenu");

  INITCOMMONCONTROLSEX initCtrls;
```

```
    initCtrls.dwSize = sizeof(initCtrls);
    initCtrls.dwICC= ICC_TAB_CLASSES;
    InitCommonControlsEx(&initCtrls);

    // Load accelerator table.
    if(!LoadAccelTable("PropertyMenu"))
        MessageBox("Cannot Load Accelerators", "Error");

    PropSheetPtr = &m_PropSheet; // save ptr to prop sheet
}

// Initialize the application.
BOOL CApp::InitInstance()
{
  m_pMainWnd = new CMainWin;
  m_pMainWnd->ShowWindow(m_nCmdShow);
  m_pMainWnd->UpdateWindow();

  return TRUE;
}

// This is the application's message map.
BEGIN_MESSAGE_MAP(CMainWin, CFrameWnd)
  ON_COMMAND(IDM_ACTIVATE, OnActivate)
  ON_COMMAND(IDM_EXIT, OnExit)
  ON_COMMAND(IDM_HELP, OnHelp)
END_MESSAGE_MAP()

// Process IDM_ACTIVATE.
afx_msg void CMainWin::OnActivate()
{
  m_PropSheet.SetWizardMode(); // activate wizard mode
  m_PropSheet.DoModal(); // activate modal property sheet
}

// Process IDM_EXIT.
afx_msg void CMainWin::OnExit()
{
  int response;

  response = MessageBox("Quit the Program?",
                        "Exit", MB_YESNO);

  if(response == IDYES)
```

13

```
      SendMessage(WM_CLOSE); // terminate app
}

// Process IDM_HELP.
afx_msg void CMainWin::OnHelp()
{
    MessageBox("Wizard", "Help");
}

// Message map for the first page dialog box.
BEGIN_MESSAGE_MAP(CPropDialog1, CPropertyPage)
  ON_WM_PAINT()
  ON_COMMAND(IDD_ONE, OnOne)
  ON_COMMAND(IDD_TWO, OnTwo)
  ON_COMMAND(IDD_THREE, OnThree)
  ON_LBN_DBLCLK(IDD_LB1, OnListBox)
END_MESSAGE_MAP()

// Initialize first page dialog box.
BOOL CPropDialog1::OnInitDialog()
{
  int i;

  CPropertyPage::OnInitDialog(); // Call base class version

  CListBox *lbptr = (CListBox *) GetDlgItem(IDD_LB1);

  for(i=0; i<NUMSTRINGS; i++)
    lbptr->AddString(list[i]);

  lbptr->SetCurSel(0);

  m_bmp.LoadBitmap("wizbmp");

  return TRUE;
}

// Display the bitmap.
afx_msg void CPropDialog1::OnPaint()
{
  CPaintDC DC(this);
  CDC memDC;

  // create a compatible DC
  memDC.CreateCompatibleDC(&DC);
```

```
   // Select bitmap into memory DC
   memDC.SelectObject(&m_bmp);

   // copy bitmap to window DC
   DC.BitBlt(0, 0, 129, 226, &memDC, 0, 0, SRCCOPY);
}

// First page is activated.
afx_msg BOOL CPropDialog1::OnSetActive()
{
   PropSheetPtr->SetWizardButtons(PSWIZB_NEXT);

   return TRUE;
}

// A placeholder OnWizardFinish() function for CPropDialog1.
afx_msg BOOL CPropDialog1::OnWizardFinish()
{
   MessageBox("Wizard Finished", "First Page");

   return TRUE;
}

// Handle IDD_ONE commands.
afx_msg void CPropDialog1::OnOne()
{
   MessageBox("One", "Button Pressed");
}

// Handle IDD_TWO commands.
afx_msg void CPropDialog1::OnTwo()
{
   MessageBox("Two", "Button Pressed");
}

// Handle IDD_THREE commands.
afx_msg void CPropDialog1::OnThree()
{
   MessageBox("Three", "Button Pressed");
}

// Handle List box notifications
afx_msg void CPropDialog1::OnListBox()
{
```

13

```
    int i;
    char str[255];

    CListBox *lbptr = (CListBox *) GetDlgItem(IDD_LB1);

    i = lbptr->GetCurSel();
    lbptr->GetText(i, str);

    MessageBox(str, "Selection is");
    SetModified(1);
}

// Message map for the second page dialog box.
BEGIN_MESSAGE_MAP(CPropDialog2, CPropertyPage)
  ON_WM_PAINT()
  ON_COMMAND(IDD_INVERT, OnInvert)
  ON_COMMAND(IDD_CB1, OnCB1)
  ON_COMMAND(IDD_CB2, OnCB2)
  ON_COMMAND(IDD_CB3, OnCB3)
END_MESSAGE_MAP()

// Initialize second page dialog box.
BOOL CPropDialog2::OnInitDialog()
{
  CPropertyPage::OnInitDialog(); // Call base class version

  CButton *cbptr = (CButton *) GetDlgItem(IDD_CB1);

  cbptr->SetCheck(1);

  m_bmp.LoadBitmap("wizbmp");

  return TRUE;
}

// Display the bitmap.
afx_msg void CPropDialog2::OnPaint()
{
  CPaintDC DC(this);
  CDC memDC;

  // create a compatible DC
  memDC.CreateCompatibleDC(&DC);

  // Select bitmap into memory DC
```

```
     memDC.SelectObject(&m_bmp);

     // copy bitmap to window DC
     DC.BitBlt(0, 0, 129, 226, &memDC, 0, 0, SRCCOPY);
   }


   // First page is activated.
   afx_msg BOOL CPropDialog2::OnSetActive()
   {
     PropSheetPtr->SetWizardButtons(PSWIZB_NEXT | PSWIZB_BACK);

     return TRUE;
   }


   // A placeholder OnWizardFinish() function for CPropDialog2.
   afx_msg BOOL CPropDialog2::OnWizardFinish()
   {
     MessageBox("Wizard Finished", "Second Page");

     return TRUE;
   }


   // Handle IDD_INVERT commands.
   afx_msg void CPropDialog2::OnInvert()
   {
     // invert the check box selections

     CButton *lbptr1 = (CButton *) GetDlgItem(IDD_CB1);
     CButton *lbptr2 = (CButton *) GetDlgItem(IDD_CB2);
     CButton *lbptr3 = (CButton *) GetDlgItem(IDD_CB3);

     // invert the state of the check boxes
     if(lbptr1->GetCheck()) lbptr1->SetCheck(0);
     else lbptr1->SetCheck(1);

     if(lbptr2->GetCheck()) lbptr2->SetCheck(0);
     else lbptr2->SetCheck(1);

     if(lbptr3->GetCheck()) lbptr3->SetCheck(0);
     else lbptr3->SetCheck(1);

     SetModified(1);
   }


   // Handle IDD_CB1 commands.
```

13

```
afx_msg void CPropDialog2::OnCB1()
{
  SetModified(1);
}

// Handle IDD_CB2 commands.
afx_msg void CPropDialog2::OnCB2()
{
  SetModified(1);
}

// Handle IDD_CB3 commands.
afx_msg void CPropDialog2::OnCB3()
{
  SetModified(1);
}

// Message map for the third page dialog box.
BEGIN_MESSAGE_MAP(CPropDialog3, CPropertyPage)
  ON_COMMAND(IDD_TOP, OnTop)
  ON_COMMAND(IDD_BOTTOM, OnBottom)
  ON_COMMAND(IDD_RB1, OnRB1)
  ON_COMMAND(IDD_RB2, OnRB2)
  ON_COMMAND(IDD_RB3, OnRB3)
END_MESSAGE_MAP()

// Initialize third page dialog box.
BOOL CPropDialog3::OnInitDialog()
{
  CPropertyPage::OnInitDialog(); // Call base class version

  CButton *cbptr = (CButton *) GetDlgItem(IDD_RB1);

  cbptr->SetCheck(1);

  return TRUE;
}

// Third page is activated.
afx_msg BOOL CPropDialog3::OnSetActive()
{
  PropSheetPtr->SetWizardButtons(PSWIZB_BACK | PSWIZB_FINISH);

  return TRUE;
}
```

```
// A placeholder OnWizardFinish() function for CPropDialog3.
afx_msg BOOL CPropDialog3::OnWizardFinish()
{
  MessageBox("Wizard Finished", "Third Page");

  return TRUE;
}

// Handle IDD_TOP commands.
afx_msg void CPropDialog3::OnTop()
{
  CButton *lbptr1 = (CButton *) GetDlgItem(IDD_RB1);
  CButton *lbptr2 = (CButton *) GetDlgItem(IDD_RB2);
  CButton *lbptr3 = (CButton *) GetDlgItem(IDD_RB3);

  // turn off lower buttons
  lbptr2->SetCheck(0);
  lbptr3->SetCheck(0);

  lbptr1->SetCheck(1); // set top button

  SetModified(1);
}

// Handle IDD_BOTTOM commands.
afx_msg void CPropDialog3::OnBottom()
{
  CButton *lbptr1 = (CButton *) GetDlgItem(IDD_RB1);
  CButton *lbptr2 = (CButton *) GetDlgItem(IDD_RB2);
  CButton *lbptr3 = (CButton *) GetDlgItem(IDD_RB3);

  // turn off top buttons
  lbptr2->SetCheck(0);
  lbptr1->SetCheck(0);

  lbptr3->SetCheck(1); // set bottom button

  SetModified(1);
}

// Handle IDD_RB1 commands.
afx_msg void CPropDialog3::OnRB1()
{
  SetModified(1);
```

13

```
}

// Handle IDD_RB2 commands.
afx_msg void CPropDialog3::OnRB2()
{
  SetModified(1);
}

// Handle IDD_RB3 commands.
afx_msg void CPropDialog3::OnRB3()
{
  SetModified(1);
}

CApp App; // instantiate the application
```

As you can see, very few changes have been required to transform the property sheet from the preceding program into a wizard. For example, **OnSetActive( )** is overridden by each property page because it is used to set the wizard buttons each time a page is activated. Also, the global variable **PropSheetPtr** has been declared in the program file. Inside **CMainWin( )**, this variable is assigned the address of the property sheet control. This pointer is used to call **SetWizardButtons( )** whenever a new page is activated. Since **OnSetActive( )** is a member of **CPropertyPage** (not **CPropertySheet**) and **SetWizardButtons( )** is a member of **CPropertySheet** (not **CPropertyPage**), **SetWizardButtons( )** cannot be called directly within the **OnSetActive( )** function. Instead, it must be called relative to the property sheet object.

One final point: Notice that the last page does not display a bitmap. In this case, the controls are not positioned relative to **WIZ_BODYX**. Instead, they are positioned relative to zero. If a page does not contain a bitmap you may use the entire page for your controls.

Using Property Sheets and Wizards

Both property sheets and wizards have become ubiquitous in modern Windows applications. Furthermore, the use of wizards as a means of guiding users through complex tasks has become the rule rather than the exception. Indeed, one of the identifying characteristics of a contemporary application is its use of property sheets and/or wizards. For these reasons, whenever you have a situation in which a large number of options must be presented or a complex series of actions must be undertaken, it is strongly recommended that you employ a property sheet or wizard. These approaches are far better than large, unwieldy dialog boxes.

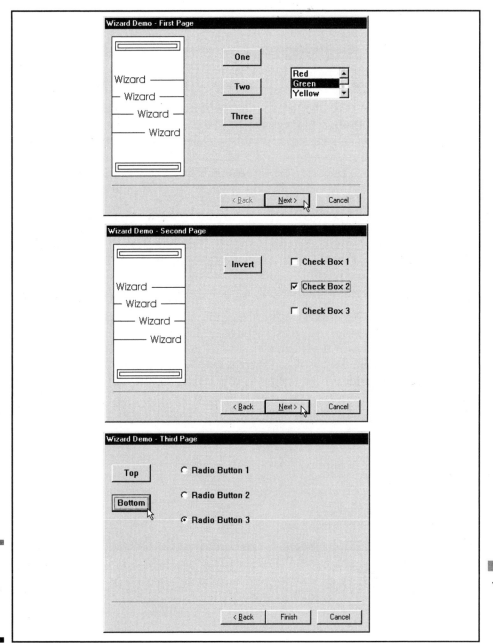

Sample output
from the
wizard sample
program
Figure 13-3.

Extended Property Sheets and Pages

In this chapter we have explored the **CPropertySheet** and **CPropertyPage** classes. However, with the advent of Windows 98 and NT 5, new functionality has been implemented for property sheets, property pages, and wizards. MFC encapsulates this functionality with two new classes: **CPropertySheetEx** and **CPropertyPageEx**.

CPropertySheetEx incorporates all the functionality of **CPropertySheet** with the addition of a new feature: a "watermark" background bitmap. This bitmap is blended into the background of the property sheet, appearing much like a traditional watermark. You can use this feature to customize the appearance of your property sheets. One possible application would be to use your company logo as a watermark for your application's property sheets.

CPropertyPageEx includes all of **CPropertyPage** and supports a new feature for property pages: a header area for titles and subtitles. This area is located at the top of your property page and runs the entire length. In this area you can display a title and a subtitle (automatically indented underneath the main title). This feature can be used to individually title your property pages.

CHAPTER 14

Thread-Based
Multitasking

Thread-based multitasking is one of the most important performance-enhancing additions made to Windows in the past several years. As you should recall from Chapter 1, modern versions of Windows support two forms of multitasking. The first type is process based. This is the type of multiprocessing that Windows has supported from its inception. A process is, essentially, a program that is executing. In process-based multitasking, two or more processes can execute concurrently. The second type of multitasking is thread based. Thread-based multitasking is supported by Win32 and is used by Windows 95, Windows 98, and Windows NT. A thread is a path (or *thread*) of execution within a process. Every Win32 process has at least one thread, but it may have two or more. Thread-based multitasking allows two or more parts of a single program to execute concurrently. This added multitasking dimension allows extremely efficient programs to be written because you, the programmer, can define the separate threads of execution and thus manage the way that your program executes. As you will soon see, MFC provides substantial support for thread-based multitasking.

The inclusion of thread-based multitasking has increased the need for a special type of multitasking feature called *synchronization*, which allows the execution of threads (and processes) to be coordinated in certain well-defined ways. Win32 has a complete subsystem devoted to synchronization. As you probably expect, MFC fully encapsulates thread synchronization.

NOTE: Windows 3.1 supports only process-based multitasking. It does not support thread-based multitasking. As such, none of the material in this chapter applies to Windows 3.1.

Thread Basics

Multithreaded multitasking adds a new dimension to your programming because it lets you, the programmer, more fully control how pieces of your program execute. This allows you to implement more efficient programs. For example, you could assign one thread of a program the job of sorting a file, another thread the job of gathering information from a remote source, and another thread the task of performing user input. Because of multithreaded multitasking, each thread could execute concurrently and no CPU time would be wasted.

It is important to understand that all processes have at least one thread of execution. For the sake of discussion, this is called the *main thread*. However, it is possible to create more than one thread of execution within the same process. In general, once a new thread is created, it also begins execution. Thus, each process starts with one thread of execution and may create one or more additional threads. Once the new threads begin running, multiple paths of execution will exist within the process. In this way, thread-based multitasking is supported.

MFC defines two types of threads: *interface* and *worker*. An interface thread is capable of receiving and processing messages. In the language of MFC, interface threads contain a *message pump*. As you can probably guess, the main thread of an MFC application (which is started when you declare an object of type **CWinApp**) is an interface thread. Worker threads do not receive or process messages. Instead, they exist to provide additional paths of execution within an interface thread. When creating multithreaded programs, you will most often add worker threads. The reason for this is that few applications need more than one message pump, but many applications benefit from additional threads of execution, which provide background processing. Since worker threads are the most common in multithreaded programs they are the only type examined here.

NOTE: It is important to understand that, at the API level, worker threads and interface threads are treated the same. The distinction exists relative to the MFC class hierarchy only.

In MFC, multithreaded multitasking is supported by the **CWinThread** class. As you might recall, **CWinThread** is a base class for **CWinApp**, which forms the main thread for your application.

To use the thread-based classes, you must include the AFXMT.H header file in your program.

Creating a Worker Thread

To create a worker thread, use the function **AfxBeginThread( )**. Its prototype is shown here:

CWinThread *AfxBeginThread(AFX_THREADPROC *ThreadFunc*, LPVOID *Param*,
        int *InitPriority* = THREAD_PRIORITY_NORMAL,
        UINT *StackSize* = 0, DWORD *dwFlags* = 0,
        LPSECURITY_ATTRIBUTES *Security* = NULL);

14

Each thread of execution begins with a call to a function, called the *thread function*, within the creating process. Execution of the thread continues until the thread function returns. The address of this function (i.e., the entry point to the thread) is specified in *ThreadFunc*. All thread functions must have this prototype:

UINT *ThreadFunc*(LPVOID *TFParam*);

The value of *Param* in **AfxBeginThread( )** is passed to the thread function in its *TFParam* parameter. This 32-bit value may be used for any purpose.

The initial priority associated with the thread is passed in *InitPriority*. If this value is zero, then the priority setting of the creating thread is used. Otherwise, it must be one of these values:

THREAD_PRIORITY_TIME_CRITICAL
THREAD_PRIORITY_HIGHEST
THREAD_PRIORITY_ABOVE_NORMAL
THREAD_PRIORITY_NORMAL
THREAD_PRIORITY_BELOW_NORMAL
THREAD_PRIORITY_LOWEST
THREAD_PRIORITY_IDLE

Each thread has its own stack. You can specify the size of the new thread's stack, in bytes, using the *StackSize* parameter. If this value is zero, then the thread will be given a stack that is the same size as the thread that creates it. In this case, the stack will be expanded if necessary. (Specifying zero is the common approach to thread stack size.)

The *dwFlags* parameter determines the execution state of the thread. If it is zero, the thread begins execution immediately. If it is **CREATE_SUSPENDED**, the thread is created in a suspended state, awaiting execution. (It may be started using a call to **CWinThread::ResumeThread( )**.)

Security is a pointer to a set of security attributes pertaining to the thread. However, if *Security* is **NULL**, the security attributes associated with the creating thread are inherited by the new thread.

AfxBeginThread( ) returns a pointer to the thread object if successful or zero if a failure occurs. You will need to save this pointer if the calling thread will need access to the new thread. For example, it will be required if the calling thread wants to set the priority or suspend the newly created thread. Otherwise, the return value can be ignored.

Terminating a Thread

As stated, a thread of execution terminates when its entry function returns. The thread may also terminate itself manually by calling **AfxEndThread( )** whose prototype is shown here:

    void AfxEndThread(UINT *Status*);

Here, *Status* is the termination status. Most of the time, it is simply easier to let the thread terminate normally when its entry function returns.

A Short Multithreaded Example

The following program demonstrates the fundamentals of multithreaded programming by creating a new worker thread each time the Execute Thread menu option is selected. The thread beeps ten times and displays the number of each beep along with its ID on the screen. Another thread can be started before the first is finished. The program uses the virtual window technology developed in Chapter 8 to repaint the window. Sample output from the program is shown in Figure 14-1.

The program uses the following resource file:

```
#include <afxres.h>
#include "ids.h"

ThreadMenu MENU
{
  POPUP "&Threads" {
    MENUITEM "Execute &Thread\tF2", IDM_THREAD
    MENUITEM "E&xit\tF3", IDM_EXIT
  }

  MENUITEM "&Help", IDM_HELP
}

ThreadMenu ACCELERATORS
{
  VK_F1, IDM_HELP, VIRTKEY
  VK_F2, IDM_THREAD, VIRTKEY
  VK_F3, IDM_EXIT, VIRTKEY
}
```

The header file IDS.H is shown next:

14

```
// IDS.H

#define IDM_THREAD 100
#define IDM_HELP   101
#define IDM_EXIT   102
```

The class derivation file, THREAD.H, is shown here:

```
// THREAD.H

// This is the main window class.
class CMainWin : public CFrameWnd
{
public:
  int m_X, m_Y; // current output location
  CDC m_memDC; // virtual window device context
  CBitmap m_bmp; // virtual window bitmap
  CBrush m_bkbrush; // brush for virtual window

  CMainWin();

  afx_msg void OnPaint();
  afx_msg void OnLButtonDown(UINT Flags, CPoint Loc);

  afx_msg void OnThread();
  afx_msg void OnExit();
  afx_msg void OnHelp();

  DECLARE_MESSAGE_MAP()
};

// This is the application class.
class CApp : public CWinApp
{
public:
  BOOL InitInstance();
};
```

Here is the thread demo program file:

```
// Demonstrate multithreaded multitasking.

#include <afxwin.h>
#include <string.h>
```

```
#include "ids.h"
#include "thread.h"

UINT MyThread(LPVOID WinObjPtr);
int ThreadID = 0;

int maxX, maxY;

// Construct the main window.
CMainWin::CMainWin()
{
  Create(NULL, "Multithreading",
         WS_OVERLAPPEDWINDOW, rectDefault,
         NULL, "ThreadMenu");

  // Load accelerator table.
  if(!LoadAccelTable("ThreadMenu"))
     MessageBox("Cannot Load Accelerators", "Error");

  m_X = m_Y = 0;

  maxX = GetSystemMetrics(SM_CXSCREEN);
  maxY = GetSystemMetrics(SM_CYSCREEN);

  CClientDC DC(this);

  // Create bitmap for virtual window.
  m_memDC.CreateCompatibleDC(&DC);
  m_bmp.CreateCompatibleBitmap(&DC, maxX, maxY);
  m_memDC.SelectObject(&m_bmp);

  // use standard background
  m_bkbrush.CreateStockObject(WHITE_BRUSH);
  m_memDC.SelectObject(&m_bkbrush);
  // paint background of virtual window
  m_memDC.PatBlt(0, 0, maxX, maxY, PATCOPY);
}

// Initialize the application.
BOOL CApp::InitInstance()
{
  m_pMainWnd = new CMainWin;
  m_pMainWnd->ShowWindow(m_nCmdShow);
  m_pMainWnd->UpdateWindow();
```

14

```
    return TRUE;
}

// This is the application's message map.
BEGIN_MESSAGE_MAP(CMainWin, CFrameWnd)
  ON_WM_PAINT()
  ON_WM_LBUTTONDOWN()
  ON_COMMAND(IDM_THREAD, OnThread)
  ON_COMMAND(IDM_EXIT, OnExit)
  ON_COMMAND(IDM_HELP, OnHelp)
END_MESSAGE_MAP()

// Update screen using contents of virtual window.
afx_msg void CMainWin::OnPaint()
{
  CPaintDC DC(this);

  DC.BitBlt(0, 0, maxX, maxY, &m_memDC, 0, 0, SRCCOPY);
}

// Reposition text when left mouse button is pressed.
afx_msg void CMainWin::OnLButtonDown(UINT Flags, CPoint Loc)
{
  m_X = Loc.x;
  m_Y = Loc.y;
}

// Process IDM_EXIT.
afx_msg void CMainWin::OnExit()
{
  int response;

  response = MessageBox("Quit the Program?",
                        "Exit", MB_YESNO);

  if(response == IDYES)
    SendMessage(WM_CLOSE); // terminate app
}

// Process IDM_HELP.
afx_msg void CMainWin::OnHelp()
{
  MessageBox("Multithreading", "Help");
}
```

```
// Process IDM_THREAD.
afx_msg void CMainWin::OnThread()
{
  AfxBeginThread(MyThread, this);
}

// A worker thread.
UINT MyThread(LPVOID WinObjPtr)
{
  int i;
  TEXTMETRIC tm;
  int Tid = ThreadID;
  char str[255];

  ThreadID++;

  CMainWin *ptr = (CMainWin *) WinObjPtr;

  // get text metrics
  ptr->m_memDC.GetTextMetrics(&tm);

  for(i=0; i<10; i++) {
    Sleep(500);
    wsprintf(str, "Thread #%d, beep #%d", Tid, i);
    ptr->m_memDC.TextOut(ptr->m_X, ptr->m_Y,
                         str, strlen(str));
    ptr->m_Y = ptr->m_Y + tm.tmHeight + tm.tmExternalLeading;
    ptr->InvalidateRect(NULL);
    MessageBeep(MB_OK);
  }
  ThreadID--;
  return 0;
}

CApp App; // instantiate the application
```

In the program, a pointer to the main window object is passed to
MyThread( ) in its parameter. This parameter is used to gain access to the
members of **CMainWin**. While useful in this example, this is not a necessary

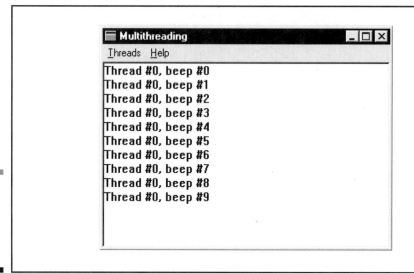

Sample output
from the
multithreaded
program

Figure 14-1.

step. The parameter to a worker thread's function may be used for any purpose you desire.

The global variable **ThreadID** keeps track of the number of concurrently executing versions of **MyThread( )**. It is incremented each time the function is entered and decremented when the function is left. This value is then displayed by the thread for the purpose of illustration. There is no other significance to this variable.

Notice that the **Sleep( )** function is called within the loop inside **MyThread( )**. This API function suspends execution of the calling thread for the specified number of milliseconds. It is used here to slow down the execution of **MyThread( )** so that you can more easily see the effects of a multithreaded program. Each time through the loop, the computer's beep is sounded using the **MessageBeep( )** API function.

Since **MyThread( )** is an independent thread of execution, while it is executing, the rest of the program is still active. For example, try the following experiment. Select Execute Thread from the main menu. Then, before the thread has finished, select Execute Thread again. As you can see, the menu bar is still active and the rest of the program is still receiving and processing messages.

Using Multiple Threads

A program can have, within reason, as many threads of execution as it wants. For example, the following version of the preceding program starts two threads each time the Execute Thread menu option is selected. Sample output from this program is shown in Figure 14-2. The program uses the resource, header, and class derivation files just shown.

```
// Demonstrate two threads of execution.

#include <afxwin.h>
#include <string.h>
#include "ids.h"
#include "thread.h"

UINT MyThread1(LPVOID WinObjPtr);
UINT MyThread2(LPVOID WinObjPtr);
int FirstThreadID = 0;
int SecondThreadID = 0;

int maxX, maxY;

// Construct the main window.
CMainWin::CMainWin()
{
  Create(NULL, "Multithreading",
         WS_OVERLAPPEDWINDOW, rectDefault,
         NULL, "ThreadMenu");

  // Load accelerator table
  if(!LoadAccelTable("ThreadMenu"))
    MessageBox("Cannot Load Accelerators", "Error");

  m_X = m_Y = 0;

  maxX = GetSystemMetrics(SM_CXSCREEN);
  maxY = GetSystemMetrics(SM_CYSCREEN);

  CClientDC DC(this);

  // Create bitmap for virtual window
  m_memDC.CreateCompatibleDC(&DC);
  m_bmp.CreateCompatibleBitmap(&DC, maxX, maxY);
  m_memDC.SelectObject(&m_bmp);
```

14

```
  // use standard background
  m_bkbrush.CreateStockObject(WHITE_BRUSH);
  m_memDC.SelectObject(&m_bkbrush);
  // paint background of virtual window
  m_memDC.PatBlt(0, 0, maxX, maxY, PATCOPY);
}

// Initialize the application.
BOOL CApp::InitInstance()
{
  m_pMainWnd = new CMainWin;
  m_pMainWnd->ShowWindow(m_nCmdShow);
  m_pMainWnd->UpdateWindow();

  return TRUE;
}

// This is the application's message map.
BEGIN_MESSAGE_MAP(CMainWin, CFrameWnd)
  ON_WM_PAINT()
  ON_WM_LBUTTONDOWN()
  ON_COMMAND(IDM_THREAD, OnThread)
  ON_COMMAND(IDM_EXIT, OnExit)
  ON_COMMAND(IDM_HELP, OnHelp)
END_MESSAGE_MAP()

// Update screen using contents of virtual window.
afx_msg void CMainWin::OnPaint()
{
  CPaintDC DC(this);

  DC.BitBlt(0, 0, maxX, maxY, &m_memDC, 0, 0, SRCCOPY);
}

// Reposition text when left mouse button is pressed.
afx_msg void CMainWin::OnLButtonDown(UINT Flags, CPoint Loc)
{
  m_X = Loc.x;
  m_Y = Loc.y;
}

// Process IDM_EXIT.
afx_msg void CMainWin::OnExit()
{
  int response;
```

```
    response = MessageBox("Quit the Program?",
                          "Exit", MB_YESNO);

  if(response == IDYES)
    SendMessage(WM_CLOSE); // terminate app
}

// Process IDM_HELP.
afx_msg void CMainWin::OnHelp()
{
   MessageBox("Multithreading", "Help");
}

// Process IDM_THREAD.
afx_msg void CMainWin::OnThread()
{
  // start two worker threads
  AfxBeginThread(MyThread1, this);
  AfxBeginThread(MyThread2, this);
}

// First worker thread.
UINT MyThread1(LPVOID WinObjPtr)
{
  int i;
  TEXTMETRIC tm;
  char str[255];
  int Tid = FirstThreadID;

  FirstThreadID++;

  CMainWin *ptr = (CMainWin *) WinObjPtr;

  // get text metrics
  ptr->m_memDC.GetTextMetrics(&tm);

  for(i=0; i<10; i++) {
    Sleep(500);
    wsprintf(str, "First Thread #%d, beep #%d",
             Tid, i);
    ptr->m_memDC.TextOut(ptr->m_X, ptr->m_Y,
                         str, strlen(str));
    ptr->m_Y = ptr->m_Y + tm.tmHeight + tm.tmExternalLeading;
    ptr->InvalidateRect(NULL);
    MessageBeep(MB_OK);
```

14

```
  }
  FirstThreadID--;
  return 0;
}

// Second worker thread.
UINT MyThread2(LPVOID WinObjPtr)
{
  int i;
  TEXTMETRIC tm;
  char str[255];
  int Tid = SecondThreadID;

  SecondThreadID++;

  CMainWin *ptr = (CMainWin *) WinObjPtr;

  // get text metrics
  ptr->m_memDC.GetTextMetrics(&tm);

  for(i=0; i<10; i++) {
    Sleep(200);
    wsprintf(str, "Second Thread #%d, beep #%d",
             Tid, i);
    ptr->m_memDC.TextOut(ptr->m_X, ptr->m_Y,
                         str, strlen(str));
    ptr->m_Y = ptr->m_Y + tm.tmHeight + tm.tmExternalLeading;
    ptr->InvalidateRect(NULL);
    MessageBeep(MB_OK);
  }
  SecondThreadID--;
  return 0;
}

CApp App; // instantiate the application
```

As this program illustrates, when using multiple threads, you must define a thread function for each thread and then start each thread separately. All the threads in the process will then execute concurrently. The concurrent execution of the threads is evidenced by the jumbled output produced by the program when they are executed.

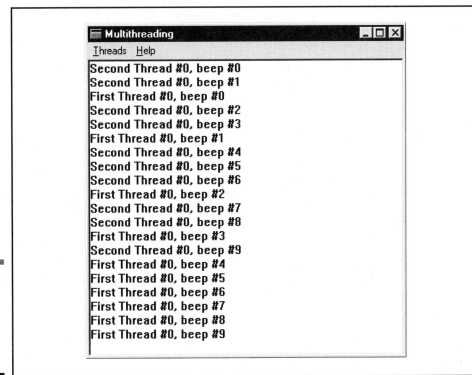

Sample output from the second multithreaded program

Figure 14-2.

Suspending and Resuming a Thread

A thread may be suspended by calling **SuspendThread( )**. When a thread is suspended it is not executed. Its execution may be resumed by calling **ResumeThread( )**. The prototypes for these functions are shown here:

DWORD CWinThread::SuspendThread( );

DWORD CWinThread::ResumeThread( );

Each thread of execution has associated with it a *suspend count*. If this count is zero, then the thread is not suspended. If it is nonzero, the thread is in a suspended state. Each call to **SuspendThread( )** increments the suspend count. Each call to **ResumeThread( )** decrements the suspend count. A suspended thread will resume only after its suspend count has reached zero.

Therefore, to resume a suspended thread implies that the number of calls to **ResumeThread( )** must be equivalent to the number of calls to **SuspendThread( )**.

Both functions return the thread's previous suspend count or –1 if an error occurs.

Managing Thread Priorities

Each thread has a priority setting associated with it. A thread's priority setting is the combination of two values: the overall priority class of the process and the priority setting of the individual thread relative to that priority class. That is, a thread's actual priority is determined by combining the process' priority class with the thread's individual priority level. A thread's priority determines how much CPU time a thread receives. Low-priority threads receive little. High-priority threads receive a lot. Of course, how much CPU time a thread receives has a profound impact on its execution characteristics and its interaction with other threads currently executing in the system.

You can obtain the current priority class by calling **GetPriorityClass( )**, and you can set the priority class by calling **SetPriorityClass( )**. Both of these are API functions. They are not members of **CWinThread**. The prototypes for these functions are shown here:

DWORD GetPriorityClass(HANDLE *hApp*);

BOOL SetPriorityClass(HANDLE *hApp*, DWORD *dwPriority*);

Here, *hApp* is the handle of the process. **GetPriorityClass( )** returns the priority class of the application. For **SetPriorityClass( )**, *dwPriority* specifies the process' new priority class. The priority class values are shown here in order of highest to lowest priority:

REALTIME_PRIORITY_CLASS
HIGH_PRIORITY_CLASS
NORMAL_PRIORITY_CLASS
IDLE_PRIORITY_CLASS

Programs are given the **NORMAL_PRIORITY_CLASS** priority by default. Usually, you won't need to alter the priority class of your program. In fact, changing a process' priority class can have negative consequences on the overall performance of the computer system. For example, if you increase a program's priority class to **REALTIME_PRIORITY_CLASS**, it will dominate the CPU. For some specialized applications, you may need to increase an application's priority class, but usually you won't. For the purposes of this chapter, the default priority setting of a process will be used.

For any given priority class, a thread's priority determines how much CPU time an individual thread receives within its process. When a thread is first created, it is given normal priority. However, you can change a thread's priority—even while it is executing.

A thread's priority is controlled by member functions of **CWinThread**. You can obtain a thread's priority setting by calling **GetThreadPriority( )**. You can increase or decrease a thread's priority using **SetThreadPriority( )**. The prototypes for these functions are shown here:

BOOL CWinThread::SetThreadPriority(int *Priority*);

int CWinThread::GetThreadPriority( );

For **SetThreadPriority( )**, *Priority* is the new priority setting. For **GetThreadPriority( )**, the current priority setting is returned. The priority settings are shown here, in order of highest to lowest:

THREAD_PRIORITY_TIME_CRITICAL
THREAD_PRIORITY_HIGHEST
THREAD_PRIORITY_ABOVE_NORMAL
THREAD_PRIORITY_NORMAL
THREAD_PRIORITY_BELOW_NORMAL
THREAD_PRIORITY_LOWEST
THREAD_PRIORITY_IDLE

Through the combination of a process' priority class and thread priority, Win32 supports 31 different priority settings.

For the most part, you can freely experiment with thread priorities without fear of negatively affecting overall system performance. In fact, you might want to try experimenting with thread priorities before moving on to the next section.

Synchronization

When using multiple threads or processes it is sometimes necessary to synchronize the activities of two or more threads. The most common reason for this is when two or more threads need access to a shared resource that may be used only by one thread at a time. For example, when one thread is writing to a file, a second thread must be prevented from doing so at the same time. The mechanism that prevents this is called *serialization*. Another

14

reason for synchronization is found when one thread is waiting for an event that is caused by another thread. In this case, there must be some means by which the first thread is held in a suspended state until the event has occurred.

There are two general states that a task may be in. First, it may be *executing* (or ready to execute as soon as it obtains its time slice). Second, a task may be *blocked*, awaiting some resource or event, in which case its execution is suspended until the needed resource is available or the event occurs.

If you are not familiar with the need for synchronization or the serialization problem and its most common solution, the semaphore, the next section discusses them. If this is familiar territory for you, skip ahead.

Understanding the Synchronization Problem

Windows must provide special services that allow access to a shared resource to be serialized because, without help from the operating system, there is no way for one process or thread to know that it has sole access to a resource. To understand this, imagine that you are writing programs for a multitasking operating system that does not provide any synchronization support. Further imagine that you have two concurrently executing processes, A and B, both of which, from time to time, require access to some resource R (such as a disk file) that must be accessed by only one task at a time. As a means of preventing one program from accessing R while the other is using it, try the following solution. First, establish a variable called **flag**, which can be accessed by both programs, and initialize it to zero. Next, before using each piece of code that accesses R, wait for the flag to be cleared, then set the flag, access R, and finally clear the flag. That is, each program executes this piece of code:

```
while(flag) ; // wait for flag to be cleared
flag = 1; // set flag

// ... access resource R ...

flag = 0; // clear the flag
```

The idea behind this code is that neither process will access R if **flag** is set. Conceptually, this approach is in the spirit of the correct solution. However, in actual fact it leaves much to be desired for one simple reason: it won't always work! Let's see why.

Using the code just given, it is possible for both processes to access R at the same time. The **while** loop is, in essence, performing repeated load and compare instructions on **flag**. In other words, it is testing the flag's value. When the flag is cleared, the next line of code sets the flag's value. The trouble is that it is possible for these two operations to be performed in two different time slices. Between the two time slices, the value of **flag** might be accessed by a different process, thus allowing R to be used by both processes at the same time. To understand this, imagine that process A enters the **while** loop and finds that **flag** is zero, which is the green light to access R. However, before it can set **flag** to 1, its time slice expires and process B resumes execution. If B executes its **while**, it too, will find that **flag** is not set and assume that it is safe to access R. However, when A resumes it will also begin accessing R. The crucial aspect of the problem is that the testing and setting of **flag** do not comprise one uninterruptable operation. Rather, as just illustrated, they can be separated by a time slice. No matter how you try, there is no way, using only application-level code, that you can absolutely guarantee that one and only one process will access R at one time.

The solution to the synchronization problem is as elegant as it is simple. The operating system (in this case, Windows) provides a routine that in one uninterrupted operation tests and, if possible, sets a flag. In the language of operating systems engineers, this is called a *test and set operation*. For historical reasons, the flags used to control serialization and provide synchronization between processes (and threads) are called *semaphores*. The Win32 API provides extensive support for semaphores and other synchronization devices. As one might expect, MFC fully encapsulates these objects.

Synchronization Objects

MFC supports four types of synchronization objects. All are based, in one way or another, on the concept of the semaphore. The first type is the classic semaphore. A semaphore can be used to allow a limited number of processes or threads access to a resource. When using a semaphore, the resource can be either completely serialized, in which case one and only one thread or process can access it at any one time, or the semaphore can be used to allow no more than a small number of processes or threads access at any one time. Semaphores are implemented using a counter that is decremented when a task is granted the semaphore and incremented when the task releases it.

The second synchronization object is the *mutex semaphore*. A mutex semaphore is used to serialize a resource so that one and only one thread or

14

process can access it at any one time. In essence, a mutex semaphore is a special case version of a standard semaphore.

The third synchronization object is the *event object*. It can be used to block access to a resource until some other thread or process signals that it may be used. That is, an event object signals that a specified event has occurred.

Finally, you can prevent a section of code from being used by more than one thread at a time by making it into a *critical section* using a critical section object. Once a critical section is entered by one thread, no other thread may use it until the first thread has left the critical section. (Critical sections apply only to threads within a process.)

With the exception of critical sections, the synchronization objects can be used to serialize threads within a process or processes themselves. In fact, semaphores are a common means of interprocess communication.

This chapter describes how to create and use a semaphore and an event object. After you understand these two synchronization objects, the other two will be easy for you to explore on your own.

The MFC Synchronization Classes

MFC encapsulates the synchronization mechanisms using the following classes:

Class	Synchronization Object Encapsulated
CCriticalSection	Critical section
CEvent	Event object
CMutex	Mutex semaphore
CSemaphore	Semaphore

These classes are derived from **CSyncObject**, which provides the basic synchronization mechanism that is common to all.

MFC defines two additional synchronization classes: **CSingleLock** and **CMultiLock**. They control access to a synchronization object. They have function members that are used to allocate and release a synchronization object. **CSingleLock** controls access to one synchronization object. **CMultiLock** can be used with multiple synchronization objects. In this chapter, only **CSingleLock** is examined. However, you will want to explore

CMultiLock on your own if you will need to control access to multiple objects.

Using CSingleLock

After you have created a synchronization object, you can control access to it by using a **CSingleLock** object. To do so, you must first construct the **CSingleLock** object, using the following constructor:

CSingleLock(CSyncObject *$SyncOb$, BOOL $InitialState$ = FALSE);

Here, $SyncOb$ is a pointer to a synchronization object, such as a semaphore. The value of $InitialState$ determines whether the constructor attempts to acquire the specified object. If $InitialState$ is nonzero, then the object is acquired. Otherwise, no attempt is made to acquire the object pointed to by $SyncOb$.

After you have created a **CSingleLock** object, you will use it to control access to the object pointed to by $SyncOb$ by using two of its member functions: **Lock( )** and **Unlock( )**. The prototypes for these functions are shown here:

BOOL CSingleLock::Lock(DWORD $dwDelay$ = INFINITE);

BOOL CSingleLock::Unlock( );

BOOL CSingleLock::Unlock(LONG $Count$, LONG *$Previous$ = NULL);

Lock( ) acquires the synchronization object. The calling thread will suspend until **Lock( )** returns. The value of $dwDelay$ specifies, in milliseconds, how long the calling routine will wait to acquire the object. Once that time has elapsed, a time-out error will be returned. To wait indefinitely, use the value **INFINITE**. The function returns nonzero when successful (that is, when access is granted). It returns zero when time out is reached. Each time **Lock( )** succeeds, the counter associated with the synchronization object is decremented.

Unlock( ) releases the synchronization object and allows another thread to use it. The first form adds 1 to the synchronization object's access count. In the second form, $Count$ determines what value will be added to the object's access counter. This value is most often used with semaphores, which can allow multiple access. $Previous$ points to a variable that will receive the previous semaphore count. If you don't need this value, pass **NULL** for this parameter. Both versions of the function return nonzero if successful and zero on failure.

14

Using **CSingleLock**, here is the general procedure that you will use to control access to a resource:

1. Create a **CSyncObject** object (such as a semaphore) that will be used to control access to a resource.
2. Create a **CSingleLock** object using the synchronization object created in step 1.
3. To gain access to the resource, call **Lock( )**.
4. Access the resource.
5. Call **Unlock( )** to release the resource.

The remainder of this chapter shows how to implement these steps using a semaphore and an event object.

NOTE: The synchronization base class **CSyncObject** also contains member functions called **Lock( )** and **Unlock( )**. These functions can be used to acquire and release a synchronization object (such as a semaphore) without using either **CSingleLock** or **CMultiLock**. However, Microsoft recommends the use of **CSingleLock** or **CMultiLock**. For this reason, that is the approach taken in this chapter.

Using a Semaphore

In this section, you will see how to use a semaphore to provide synchronization. Before you can use a semaphore, you must create one by declaring a **CSemaphore** object. The **CSemaphore** constructor is shown here:

```
CSemaphore(LONG InitialCount = 1,  LONG MaxCount = 1,
          LPSTR lpszName = NULL,
          LPSECURITY_ATTRIBUTES Security = NULL);
```

A semaphore can allow one or more threads access to an object. The number of threads allowed to simultaneously access an object is determined by the value of *MaxCount*. If this value is 1, then the semaphore acts much like a mutex semaphore, allowing one and only one thread or process access to the resource at any one time.

Semaphores use a counter to keep track of how many tasks have currently been granted access. If the count is zero, then no further access can be granted until one task releases the semaphore. The initial count of the semaphore is specified in *InitialCount*. If this value is zero, then initially all threads waiting on the semaphore will be blocked until the semaphore is released elsewhere by your program. Typically, this value is set initially to 1 or more, indicating that the semaphore can be granted to at least one task. In any event, *InitialCount* must be non-negative and less than or equal to the value specified in *MaxCount*.

lpszName points to a string that becomes the name of the semaphore object. Named semaphores are system-wide objects that may be used by other processes. As such, when two processes each open a semaphore using the same name, both are referring to the same semaphore. In this way, two processes can be synchronized. The name may also be **NULL**, in which case the semaphore is localized to one process.

Security is a pointer to the security attributes associated with the semaphore. If **NULL**, then the semaphore inherits the security attributes of the calling thread.

A Semaphore Demonstration Program

The following program demonstrates how to use a semaphore. It reworks the previous program so that the two threads will not execute concurrently. That is, it forces the threads to be serialized. Notice that the semaphore, **Sema**, is a member of **CMainWin**. Sample output is shown in Figure 14-3.

The semaphore program uses the same resource file and IDS.H file as the preceding program. Its class derivation file, SEMA.H, is shown here:

```
// SEMA.H

// This is the main window class.
class CMainWin : public CFrameWnd
{
public:
  int m_X, m_Y; // current output location
  CDC m_memDC; // virtual window device context
  CBitmap m_bmp; // virtual window bitmap
  CBrush m_bkbrush; // brush for virtual window

  CSemaphore Sema; // semaphore object

  CMainWin();
```

14

```
  afx_msg void OnPaint();
  afx_msg void OnLButtonDown(UINT Flags, CPoint Loc);

  afx_msg void OnThread();
  afx_msg void OnExit();
  afx_msg void OnHelp();

  DECLARE_MESSAGE_MAP()
};

// This is the application class.
class CApp : public CWinApp
{
public:
  BOOL InitInstance();
};
```

The semaphore program is shown next:

```
// Using a semaphore.

#include <afxwin.h>
#include <afxmt.h>
#include <string.h>
#include "ids.h"
#include "sema.h"

UINT MyThread1(LPVOID WinObjPtr);
UINT MyThread2(LPVOID WinObjPtr);
int FirstThreadID = 0;
int SecondThreadID = 0;

int maxX, maxY;

// Construct the main window.
CMainWin::CMainWin()
{
  Create(NULL, "Using a Semaphore",
         WS_OVERLAPPEDWINDOW, rectDefault,
         NULL, "ThreadMenu");

  // Load accelerator table.
  if(!LoadAccelTable("ThreadMenu"))
    MessageBox("Cannot Load Accelerators", "Error");
```

```
      m_X = m_Y = 0;

      maxX = GetSystemMetrics(SM_CXSCREEN);
      maxY = GetSystemMetrics(SM_CYSCREEN);

      CClientDC DC(this);

      // Create bitmap for virtual window.
      m_memDC.CreateCompatibleDC(&DC);
      m_bmp.CreateCompatibleBitmap(&DC, maxX, maxY);
      m_memDC.SelectObject(&m_bmp);

      // use standard background
      m_bkbrush.CreateStockObject(WHITE_BRUSH);
      m_memDC.SelectObject(&m_bkbrush);
      // paint background of virtual window
      m_memDC.PatBlt(0, 0, maxX, maxY, PATCOPY);
    }

    // Initialize the application.
    BOOL CApp::InitInstance()
    {
      m_pMainWnd = new CMainWin;
      m_pMainWnd->ShowWindow(m_nCmdShow);
      m_pMainWnd->UpdateWindow();

      return TRUE;
    }

    // This is the application's message map.
    BEGIN_MESSAGE_MAP(CMainWin, CFrameWnd)
      ON_WM_PAINT()
      ON_WM_LBUTTONDOWN()
      ON_COMMAND(IDM_THREAD, OnThread)
      ON_COMMAND(IDM_EXIT, OnExit)
      ON_COMMAND(IDM_HELP, OnHelp)
    END_MESSAGE_MAP()

    // Update screen using contents of virtual window.
    afx_msg void CMainWin::OnPaint()
    {
      CPaintDC DC(this);

      DC.BitBlt(0, 0, maxX, maxY, &m_memDC, 0, 0, SRCCOPY);
    }
```

14

```
// Reposition text when left mouse button is pressed.
afx_msg void CMainWin::OnLButtonDown(UINT Flags, CPoint Loc)
{
  m_X = Loc.x;
  m_Y = Loc.y;
}

// Process IDM_EXIT.
afx_msg void CMainWin::OnExit()
{
  int response;

  response = MessageBox("Quit the Program?",
                        "Exit", MB_YESNO);

  if(response == IDYES)
    SendMessage(WM_CLOSE); // terminate app
}

// Process IDM_HELP.
afx_msg void CMainWin::OnHelp()
{
    MessageBox("Semaphore", "Help");
}

// Process IDM_THREAD.
afx_msg void CMainWin::OnThread()
{
  AfxBeginThread(MyThread1, this);
  AfxBeginThread(MyThread2, this);
}

// First worker thread.
UINT MyThread1(LPVOID WinObjPtr)
{
  int i;
  TEXTMETRIC tm;
  char str[255];
  int Tid = FirstThreadID;

  FirstThreadID++;

  CMainWin *ptr = (CMainWin *) WinObjPtr;

  // get text metrics
```

```
  ptr->m_memDC.GetTextMetrics(&tm);

  CSingleLock SyncOb(&(ptr->Sema));
  SyncOb.Lock(); // get semaphore

  for(i=0; i<10; i++) {
    Sleep(500);
    wsprintf(str, "First Thread #%d, beep #%d",
             Tid, i);
    ptr->m_memDC.TextOut(ptr->m_X, ptr->m_Y,
                         str, strlen(str));
    ptr->m_Y = ptr->m_Y + tm.tmHeight + tm.tmExternalLeading;
    ptr->InvalidateRect(NULL);
    MessageBeep(MB_OK);
  }
  FirstThreadID--;

  SyncOb.Unlock(); // release semaphore

  return 0;
}

// Second worker thread.
UINT MyThread2(LPVOID WinObjPtr)
{
  int i;
  TEXTMETRIC tm;
  char str[255];
  int Tid = SecondThreadID;

  SecondThreadID++;

  CMainWin *ptr = (CMainWin *) WinObjPtr;

  // get text metrics
  ptr->m_memDC.GetTextMetrics(&tm);

  CSingleLock SyncOb(&(ptr->Sema));
  SyncOb.Lock(); // get semaphore

  for(i=0; i<10; i++) {
    Sleep(200);
    wsprintf(str, "Second Thread #%d, beep #%d",
             Tid, i);
    ptr->m_memDC.TextOut(ptr->m_X, ptr->m_Y,
```

14

```
                         str, strlen(str));
      ptr->m_Y = ptr->m_Y + tm.tmHeight + tm.tmExternalLeading;
      ptr->InvalidateRect(NULL);
      MessageBeep(MB_OK);
    }
    SecondThreadID--;

    SyncOb.Unlock(); // release semaphore

    return 0;
}

CApp App; // instantiate the application
```

The **CWinMain** class defines a semaphore called **Sema**. Inside both
MyThread1( ) and **MyThread2( )** this semaphore is used to serialize the
two threads. In each function, a **CSingleLock** object is created and then

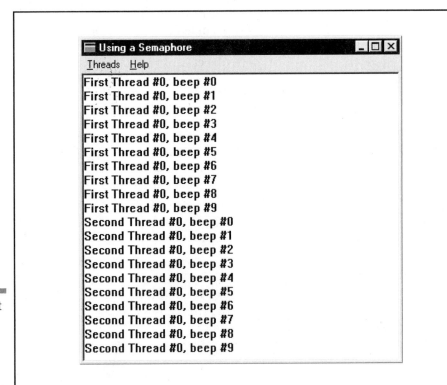

Sample output
from the
semaphore
program

Figure 14-3.

Lock( ) is called. When the first thread gains access to the semaphore, the other thread enters a suspended state until the first thread releases the semaphore by calling **Unlock( )**. Thus, the semaphore grants access to only one thread at a time. In this usage, it is similar to a mutex semaphore. On your own, experiment with granting multiple threads access to the semaphore.

Using an Event Object

As explained earlier, an event object is used to notify one thread or process when an event has occurred. To create an event object, use the **CEvent** class. Its constructor is shown here:

```
CEvent(BOOL InitialState = FALSE, BOOL Manual = FALSE,
       LPSTR lpszName = NULL,
       LPSECURITY_ATTRIBUTES Security = NULL);
```

The value of *InitialState* specifies the initial state of the object. If it is **TRUE**, the event object is set (the event is signaled). If it is **FALSE**, the event object is cleared (the event is not signaled). The value of *Manual* determines how the event object will be affected after the event has occurred. If *Manual* is **TRUE** (nonzero), then the event object is reset only by a call to the **ResetEvent( )** function. Otherwise, the event object is reset automatically after a blocked thread is granted access.

lpszName points to a string that becomes the name of the event object. Named event objects are system-wide objects that may be used by other processes. As such, when two processes each open an event object using the same name, both are referring to the same object. In this way, two processes can be synchronized. The name may also be **NULL**, in which case the object is localized to one process.

Security is a pointer to the security attributes associated with the event object. If **NULL**, then the semaphore inherits the security attributes of the calling thread.

Once an event object has been created, the thread that is waiting for the event to occur creates a **CSingleLock** object using the event object and then calls **CSingleLock::Lock( )**. This causes execution of that thread to suspend until the event occurs.

To signal that an event has occurred, use the **SetEvent( )** function, shown here:

```
BOOL CEvent::SetEvent( );
```

14

When this function is called, the first thread waiting for the event will return from **CSingleLock::Lock( )** and begin execution. The function returns nonzero if successful and zero on failure.

If you are using a manual event object, then you will need to call **ResetEvent( )** to reset the event object after it has been signaled. Here is its prototype:

```
BOOL CEvent::ResetEvent( );
```

After the call, the event object will be in the non-signaled state. The function returns nonzero if successful and zero on failure.

An Event Object Demonstration Program

To see how an event object can be used, one will be substituted for the semaphore in the preceding program. When you run this version of the program, **MyThread1( )** is blocked until **MyThread2( )** completes and signals that it is done. Thus, the conclusion of **MyThread2( )** is the event that **MyThread1( )** awaits. Sample output is shown in Figure 14-4.

The event object program uses the same resource and IDS.H files as the preceding programs. The class derivation file, EVENT.H, is shown here:

```
// EVENT.H

// This is the main window class.
class CMainWin : public CFrameWnd
{
public:
  int m_X, m_Y; // current output location
  CDC m_memDC; // virtual window device context
  CBitmap m_bmp; // virtual window bitmap
  CBrush m_bkbrush; // brush for virtual window

  CEvent Event; // event object

  CMainWin();

  afx_msg void OnPaint();
  afx_msg void OnLButtonDown(UINT Flags, CPoint Loc);

  afx_msg void OnThread();
  afx_msg void OnExit();
```

```
  afx_msg void OnHelp();

  DECLARE_MESSAGE_MAP()
};

// This is the application class.
class CApp : public CWinApp
{
public:
  BOOL InitInstance();
};
```

The event object program file is shown here:

```
// Using an event object.

#include <afxwin.h>
#include <afxmt.h>
#include <string.h>
#include "ids.h"
#include "event.h"

UINT MyThread1(LPVOID WinObjPtr);
UINT MyThread2(LPVOID WinObjPtr);
int FirstThreadID = 0;
int SecondThreadID = 0;

int maxX, maxY;

// Construct the main window.
CMainWin::CMainWin()
{
  Create(NULL, "Using an Event Object",
         WS_OVERLAPPEDWINDOW, rectDefault,
         NULL, "ThreadMenu");

  // Load accelerator table.
  if(!LoadAccelTable("ThreadMenu"))
    MessageBox("Cannot Load Accelerators", "Error");

  m_X = m_Y = 0;

  maxX = GetSystemMetrics(SM_CXSCREEN);
  maxY = GetSystemMetrics(SM_CYSCREEN);
```

14

```
  CClientDC DC(this);

  // Create bitmap for virtual window.
  m_memDC.CreateCompatibleDC(&DC);
  m_bmp.CreateCompatibleBitmap(&DC, maxX, maxY);
  m_memDC.SelectObject(&m_bmp);

  // use standard background
  m_bkbrush.CreateStockObject(WHITE_BRUSH);
  m_memDC.SelectObject(&m_bkbrush);
  // paint background of virtual window
  m_memDC.PatBlt(0, 0, maxX, maxY, PATCOPY);
}

// Initialize the application.
BOOL CApp::InitInstance()
{
  m_pMainWnd = new CMainWin;
  m_pMainWnd->ShowWindow(m_nCmdShow);
  m_pMainWnd->UpdateWindow();

  return TRUE;
}

// This is the application's message map.
BEGIN_MESSAGE_MAP(CMainWin, CFrameWnd)
  ON_WM_PAINT()
  ON_WM_LBUTTONDOWN()
  ON_COMMAND(IDM_THREAD, OnThread)
  ON_COMMAND(IDM_EXIT, OnExit)
  ON_COMMAND(IDM_HELP, OnHelp)
END_MESSAGE_MAP()

// Update screen using contents of virtual window.
afx_msg void CMainWin::OnPaint()
{
  CPaintDC DC(this);

  DC.BitBlt(0, 0, maxX, maxY, &m_memDC, 0, 0, SRCCOPY);
}

// Reposition text when left mouse button is pressed.
afx_msg void CMainWin::OnLButtonDown(UINT Flags, CPoint Loc)
{
  m_X = Loc.x;
```

```
  m_Y = Loc.y;
}

// Process IDM_EXIT.
afx_msg void CMainWin::OnExit()
{
  int response;

  response = MessageBox("Quit the Program?",
                        "Exit", MB_YESNO);

  if(response == IDYES)
    SendMessage(WM_CLOSE); // terminate app
}

// Process IDM_HELP.
afx_msg void CMainWin::OnHelp()
{
    MessageBox("Event Object", "Help");
}

// Process IDM_THREAD.
afx_msg void CMainWin::OnThread()
{
  AfxBeginThread(MyThread1, this);
  AfxBeginThread(MyThread2, this);
}

// First worker thread.
UINT MyThread1(LPVOID WinObjPtr)
{
  int i;
  TEXTMETRIC tm;
  char str[255];
  int Tid = FirstThreadID;

  FirstThreadID++;

  CMainWin *ptr = (CMainWin *) WinObjPtr;

  // get text metrics
  ptr->m_memDC.GetTextMetrics(&tm);

  CSingleLock SyncOb(&(ptr->Event));
  SyncOb.Lock(); // wait for event
```

14

```
  for(i=0; i<10; i++) {
    Sleep(500);
    wsprintf(str, "First Thread #%d, beep #%d",
             Tid, i);
    ptr->m_memDC.TextOut(ptr->m_X, ptr->m_Y,
                         str, strlen(str));
    ptr->m_Y = ptr->m_Y + tm.tmHeight + tm.tmExternalLeading;
    ptr->InvalidateRect(NULL);
    MessageBeep(MB_OK);
  }
  FirstThreadID--;

  SyncOb.Unlock(); // release semaphore

  return 0;
}

// Second worker thread.
UINT MyThread2(LPVOID WinObjPtr)
{
  int i;
  TEXTMETRIC tm;
  char str[255];
  int Tid = SecondThreadID;

  SecondThreadID++;

  CMainWin *ptr = (CMainWin *) WinObjPtr;

  // get text metrics
  ptr->m_memDC.GetTextMetrics(&tm);

  for(i=0; i<10; i++) {
    Sleep(200);
    wsprintf(str, "Second Thread #%d, beep #%d",
             Tid, i);
    ptr->m_memDC.TextOut(ptr->m_X, ptr->m_Y,
                         str, strlen(str));
    ptr->m_Y = ptr->m_Y + tm.tmHeight + tm.tmExternalLeading;
    ptr->InvalidateRect(NULL);
    MessageBeep(MB_OK);
  }
  SecondThreadID--;

  ptr->Event.SetEvent(); // signal the event
```

```
    return 0;
}

CApp App; // instantiate the application
```

This chapter really just scratches the surface of Win32's multitasking and synchronization subsystems and abilities. Some areas that you will want to explore on your own include setting and changing the scheduling priority of a thread or process. A task's priority partially determines how much CPU time it is given. Another thing to try is using a semaphore (or other synchronization objects) as a means of communicating between two processes. Finally, experiment with critical sections. In some situations, they provide the most efficient solution.

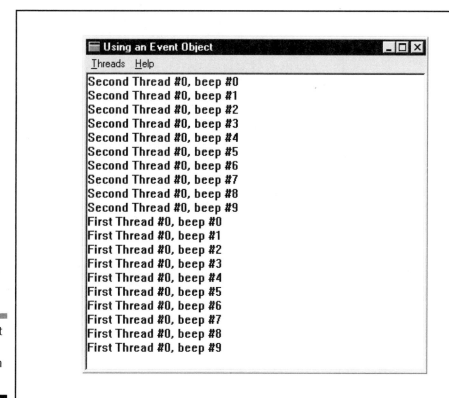

Sample output from the event program

Figure 14-4.

14

CCriticalSection and Timed Lock Requests

As explained earlier, synchronization is accomplished by creating an instance of one of the synchronization classes and then acquiring a lock by calling **CSingleLock::Lock( )**. The calling routine then waits until its lock request has been granted before continuing. This is referred to as an indefinite (or infinite) lock request and is the default behavior. However, for most synchronization objects you can change this behavior by providing a value (in milliseconds) for the *dwDelay* parameter. This forces the calling routine to abandon the request after the specified time limit has been reached. This is useful in cases where the calling routine cannot afford to wait indefinitely to be granted access.

The only synchronization class that will not accept a timed lock request is **CCriticalSection**. Unlike the other three synchronization classes, **CCriticalSection** is a thin wrapper for the underlying Win32 API functions. Because of this thin wrapper, **CCriticalSection** objects are unable to support a timed lock request because the API functions that support critical sections do not themselves directly support timed lock requests. Even if a value is supplied for the *dwDelay* parameter of **CSingleLock::Lock( )**, it is ignored and the system receives an infinite lock request. Therefore, if you need timed lock requests for your calling routines, use the **CEvent**, **CMutex**, or **CSemaphore** classes.

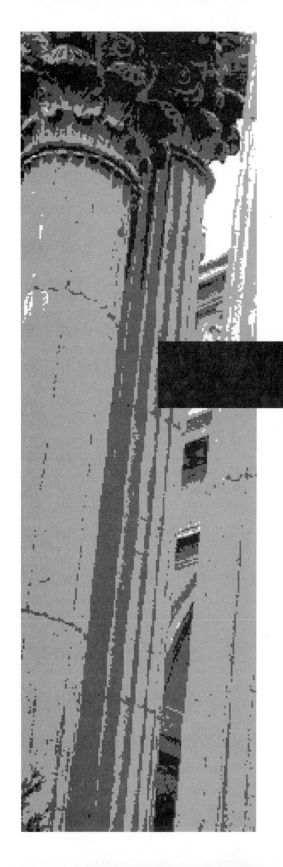

CHAPTER 15

Enhanced Menus

This chapter returns to the foundation of Windows programming: the menu. As you saw in Chapter 4, menus are straightforward, easy to handle, and on the surface, present no special programming challenges. However, when you dig a little deeper, you find that the menu subsystem is an area that contains a substantial number of sophisticated, advanced, and even exciting features. It is also a subsystem that has received added emphasis in the past few years. For example, Windows 98 makes extensive use of several menu enhancements. As you will soon see, adding enhanced menus to your application is an easy and effective way to give your programs a professional, modern look.

In this chapter we will explore two general categories of enhanced menus: dynamic and floating pop-up. Both of these give you more control over the contents of your application's menus and the way such menus can be used. However, before you can utilize Windows' advanced menus, you need to learn about another important MFC feature: *menu update handlers*. As you will see, menu update handlers are the means by which you will control the state of items in a menu. Since the menu update handlers are at the foundation of all menu activity, we will begin there.

Menu Update Handlers

Menu update handlers determine the display status of items in a menu. In an MFC program, there is a layer of processing that occurs between the time a pop-up menu is activated and the time that it is actually displayed. Between these two events, the set of menu update handlers related to that menu is called. There is one update handler for each item in the pop-up menu. The update handler for each item determines whether a menu item will be enabled or disabled. It can also set a check mark and change the text associated with an item. After all of the handlers have been called, the menu is displayed. Thus, the menu update handlers are used to determine the precise state of a pop-up menu each time it is activated. As you will soon see, it is possible for your program to define the update handlers used by the menus in your program.

Since they are so fundamental to the way that MFC manages menus, you might be wondering why menu update handlers have not been mentioned prior to this chapter. The answer is this: The built-in update handlers provided by MFC are adequate for all simple menus. Thus, we haven't had to worry about them until this point—the default handlers worked just fine. However, when your menus grow more complex, it is necessary to take control of this subsystem. Fortunately, the menu update handlers are one of MFC's easiest-to-use subsystems. But before you learn how to implement your own menu update handlers, let's start with a close look at how the menu update handler mechanism operates.

The Menu Update Mechanism

When a pop-up menu is activated, your program receives a **WM_INITMENUPOPUP** message. This message is automatically intercepted by MFC and translated into calls to menu update handlers. As mentioned, there is one update handler for each item in the pop-up menu. If your program has not defined an update handler for a menu item, then a default update handler is called.

The default menu update handlers defined by MFC implement a simple yet effective method of updating menus. They work like this: For each item in a pop-up menu, if your program has included an **ON_COMMAND** macro in its message map for the item, then its entry in the menu will be enabled. If you have not included an **ON_COMMAND** macro for the item, then it will be disabled. You can easily confirm this operation by trying the following experiment. Using one of the earlier programs in this book, remove one of the **ON_COMMAND** macros from its message map. Next, compile and run the program. As you will see, the menu item that has had its message map entry removed will be disabled and grayed.

It is important to understand that the default menu update handlers override the effects of any other operations performed on a menu. The reason for this is that they are the last agent to act upon the menu. For example, if you specify a menu item as disabled in its resource file, that specification will be nullified if an **ON_COMMAND** macro exists for the item. In this case, the default update handlers will automatically enable the item. It doesn't matter what other operations have been performed previously.

It is possible to turn off the automatic menu update mechanism. To do this, set the **m_pAutoMenuEnable** member of **CFrameWnd** to false. After this has been done, other operations on menus will have effect. This means that your program will usually need to provide its own manual control of menu items. However, you will seldom want to do this because it is easier to provide your own menu update handlers when needed.

Defining Your Own Menu Update Handlers

It is quite easy to define your own menu update handlers. To do so you need to perform only two steps: First, add an **ON_UPDATE_COMMAND_UI** macro to your program's message map for each menu item you wish to handle. Second, define the handler for that item. Let's look at each step.

The **ON_UPDATE_COMMAND_UI** macro has this general form:

ON_UPDATE_COMMAND_UI(*ID*, *Handler*)

Here, *ID* is the identifier associated with the menu item being handled. *Handler* is the name of the update handler.

Each menu update handler must have the following prototype:

afx_msg void *Handler*(CCmdUI **UIOb*);

Here, *UIOb* is a pointer to a **CCmdUI** object.

CCmdUI is a special class that exists only to support the menu update handling mechanism. It is not part of the normal MFC hierarchy—that is, it does not descend from **CObject**. It is only used as the type of the parameter in a menu update handler. It contains member functions that you will use to manage menu items. The one that we will be using in this chapter is called **Enable( )**. Its prototype is shown here:

virtual void CCmdUI::Enable(BOOL *OnOff* = TRUE);

This function sets the state of a menu item. If *OnOff* is nonzero, then the menu item will be enabled. If *OnOff* is zero, then the item will be disabled. **CCmdUI** also contains functions that set the check state of an item and the text associated with an item. You will want to explore **CCmdUI** fully, on your own.

After you have defined an update handler and entered its **ON_UPDATE-_COMMAND_UI** macro in your program's message map, then your handler will be called instead of the default handler. The example programs shown later in this chapter illustrate the use of menu update handlers.

One last point: You do not need to define your own handlers for each menu item. Those that don't have handlers will simply use the default menu update handlers provided by MFC.

NOTE: Be careful not to confuse the menu update handler with the menu item's **ON_COMMAND** handler—they are completely different. The update handler performs clerical tasks relating to how a menu is displayed. The message handler responds to a menu item's selection.

Dynamic Menus

Although most simple Windows applications statically define their menus in their resource files, more sophisticated applications frequently need to add or delete menu items dynamically, during run time, in response to changing program conditions. For example, a word processor may define different options in its File menu depending upon the type of file being edited. A compiler may include one set of debugging options for C code and another for C++ programs. Menus that change in response to conditions that occur at run time are called *dynamic menus*. The advantage of dynamic menus is that they present the user with a list of options that are appropriate to the current state of the program.

Windows includes several menu management API functions that allow you to manipulate the contents of menus during the execution of your program. These functions are encapsulated by MFC, within the **CMenu** class. Let's now take a look at a few of the functions that are most commonly used.

Adding an Item to a Menu

To add an item to a menu at run time, use **InsertMenu( )**, shown here:

BOOL CMenu::InsertMenu(UINT *Where*, UINT *Flags*, UINT *ID* = 0,
                        LPCSTR *ItemName* = NULL);

Where determines where in the menu the new item will be inserted. *ID* is the value associated with that item. Its name is specified by *ItemName*. However, the precise meanings of *Where*, *ID*, and *ItemName*, as well as other attributes, are determined by the values contained within the *Flags* parameter. These values are shown in Table 15-1. For example, assuming a menu object called **MenuOb**, to insert an item called "New Item" with a menu ID of 244 into the menu at index 2, you would use a call similar to the following:

```
MenuOb.InsertMenu(2, MF_BYPOSITION | MF_STRING, 244, "New Item");
```

InsertMenu( ) returns nonzero if successful and zero on failure.

In Table 15-1, notice the flags **MF_ENABLE** and **MF_DISABLE**. The values determine whether the inserted item will be enabled or disabled. But it is important to understand that the actions of MFC's default menu update handlers will override the **MF_ENABLE** and **MF_DISABLE** flags. Therefore, if you wish to affect the enabled/disabled state of a menu item, it is best to provide your own menu update handler and then call **CCmdUI::Enable( )**.

15

Flags Value	Meaning
MF_BYCOMMAND	*Where* must contain the menu ID of an existing item. The new item is inserted at this point.
MF_BYPOSITION	*Where* must contain the index at which point the new item is inserted. (Indexing begins at zero.) To append an item, specify *Where* as –1.
MF_CHECKED	Item is checked.
MF_DISABLED	Item is disabled.
MF_ENABLED	Item is enabled. Items are enabled by default.
MF_GRAYED	Item is disabled and grayed.
MF_HILITE	Item is highlighted.
MF_MENUBARBREAK	For menu bar, causes the item to be put on a new line. For pop-up menus, causes the item to be put in a different column. In this case, the item is separated using a bar.
MF_MENUBREAK	Same as MF_MENUBARBREAK except that no separator bar is used.
MF_OWNERDRAW	Owner-drawn item.
MF_POPUP	New item is a pop-up menu. In this case, *ID* specifies the handle of the new pop-up menu.
MF_SEPARATOR	New item is a separator. In this case, *ID* and *ItemName* are not used.
MF_STRING	New item is a normal menu entry. Its name is pointed to by *ItemName* and the ID value associated with the new item is specified by *ID*.
MF_UNCHECKED	Item is unchecked.
MF_UNHILITE	Item is unhighlighted. Items are unhighlighted by default.

Valid *Flags* Values for **InsertMenu( )** Table 15-1.

NOTE: There is an overloaded version of **InsertMenu( )** that is used to insert a bitmap into a menu. You may want to explore this on your own. Also, to append a new item to a menu, you can use **CMenu::AppendMenu( )**.

Deleting a Menu Item

To remove a menu item, use the **DeleteMenu( )** function, shown here:

    BOOL CMenu::DeleteMenu(UINT *ID*, UINT *How*);

The item to be removed is specified in *ID*. The value of *How* determines how *ID* is interpreted. If *How* is **MF_BYPOSITION**, then the value in *ID* must be the index of the item to be deleted. This index is the position of the item within the menu, with the first menu item being zero. If *How* is **MF_BYCOMMAND**, then *ID* is the ID associated with the menu item. **DeleteMenu( )** returns nonzero if successful and zero on failure.

Obtaining the Size of a Menu

Frequently, when working with menus dynamically, you will need to know how many items are in a menu. To obtain the number of menu items, use **GetMenuItemCount( )**, shown here:

    UINT CMenu::GetMenuItemCount( ) const;

The function returns the number of items in the menu, or –1 on failure.

Enabling and Disabling a Menu Item

CMenu includes a number of member functions that manage menus. One of these functions is called **EnableMenuItem( )**, and it is used to enable or disable a menu item. However, you will seldom use this function because its effects are preempted by the actions of the menu update handlers. For example, if you use **EnableMenuItem( )**, to disable a menu item, the default menu update handler will re-enable it if an **ON_COMMAND** macro is defined for that item. This of course negates the effect of your attempt to disable it! To enable or disable a menu item when using the automatic menu update feature of MFC, you must provide your own menu update handlers and then use the **Enable( )** member function of **CCmdUI**.

At this point you might be thinking that the **EnableMenuItem( )** function is pointless since its effects are nullified by the update handlers. However, this is not true. If you turn off the automatic menu update feature, its effects will be seen. However, if you will be managing menus, you are better off providing your own update handlers rather than turning off the entire menu update system.

The CMenu Constructor

Since menus are managed using **CMenu** member functions, you will need either a pointer to a **CMenu** object or a **CMenu** object itself, in order to use them. As you will see, you will often be using a pointer to the main menu of your application. However, sometimes you will need to construct a menu from scratch. To do so, you will declare a **CMenu** object using the following constructor:

CMenu( );

CMenu( ) creates an object that is initially empty. A menu must be attached to it before it can be used. (You will see two ways to do this in the course of this chapter.)

Obtaining a Pointer to the Main Menu

Most often, the main menu of a window is defined in your program's resource file. To dynamically manage the main menu (and its submenus), there must be some way to gain access to this object—and there is. To obtain a pointer to the main menu of a window, use **GetMenu( )**, shown here:

CMenu *CWnd::GetMenu( ) const;

Notice that **GetMenu( )** is a member of **CWnd**. It returns a **CMenu** pointer to the main menu of the window. It returns **NULL** on failure or if the window has no main menu. The pointer returned by **GetMenu( )** is temporary since menu objects may be moved in memory.

Given a pointer to a window's main menu, you can easily obtain the handles of the pop-up submenus contained in the main menu by using **GetSubMenu( )**. Its prototype is shown here:

CMenu *CMenu::GetSubMenu(int *Index*) const;

Here, *Index* is the position of the desired pop-up menu within the parent window. (The first position is zero.) The function returns a pointer to the specified pop-up menu or **NULL** on failure. The pointer returned by **GetSubMenu( )** is also temporary.

Dynamically Adding Menu Items

Now that the basic menu management functions have been discussed, it is time to see them in action. Let's begin with dynamically inserting and deleting an item. To do this, we will modify the graphics demonstration program shown in Chapter 9. The new version of the program contains two menus. The first is Options. The second is Graphics. The Options menu lets the user select various options relating to the program. The Graphics menu lets the user choose which graphics objects will be drawn. The following program demonstrates dynamic menu management by adding an item to or deleting an item from its Options menu. The entry added to the menu is called Reset, and it erases the current contents of the window. Sample output is shown in Figure 15-1.

The program uses the following resource file:

```
// DYNMENU.RC

#include <afxres.h>
#include "ids.h"

DynMenu MENU
{
  POPUP "&Options"
  {
    MENUITEM "&Add Item\tF2", IDM_ADDITEM
    MENUITEM "&Delete Item\tF3", IDM_DELITEM
    MENUITEM "E&xit\tF7", IDM_EXIT
  }
  POPUP "&Graphics"
  {
    MENUITEM "&Lines\tF4", IDM_LINES
    MENUITEM "&Rectangles\tF5", IDM_RECTANGLES
    MENUITEM "&Ellipses\tF6", IDM_ELLIPSES
  }
  MENUITEM "&Help", IDM_HELP
}


DynMenu ACCELERATORS
{
```

```
    VK_F1, IDM_HELP, VIRTKEY
    VK_F2, IDM_ADDITEM, VIRTKEY
    VK_F3, IDM_DELITEM, VIRTKEY
    VK_F4, IDM_LINES, VIRTKEY
    VK_F5, IDM_RECTANGLES, VIRTKEY
    VK_F6, IDM_ELLIPSES, VIRTKEY
    VK_F7, IDM_EXIT, VIRTKEY
}
```

The IDS.H header file is shown here:

```
// IDS.H

#define IDM_LINES       100
#define IDM_RECTANGLES  101
#define IDM_ELLIPSES    102
#define IDM_ADDITEM     103
#define IDM_DELITEM     104
#define IDM_HELP        105
#define IDM_EXIT        106

#define IDM_RESET       107
#define IDM_DSTINVERT   108
#define IDM_SHOWTEXT    109
```

The class derivation file, DYNMENU.H, is shown next:

```
// DYNMENU.H

// This is the main window class.
class CMainWin : public CFrameWnd
{
  CDC m_memDC; // virtual window device context
  CBitmap m_bmp; // virtual window bitmap
  CBrush m_bkbrush; // brush for virtual window

  // create pens
  CPen m_RedPen, m_YellowPen, m_GreenPen, m_BluePen;
  CPen m_OldPen;

  // flags for Add and Delete menu items
  int m_AddActive, m_DelActive;
public:
  CMainWin();
```

```
    afx_msg void OnPaint();

    // UI handlers
    afx_msg void CMainWin::OnUIAdd(CCmdUI *UI);
    afx_msg void CMainWin::OnUIDel(CCmdUI *UI);

    afx_msg void OnLines();
    afx_msg void OnRectangles();
    afx_msg void OnEllipses();
    afx_msg void OnReset();
    afx_msg void OnAdd();
    afx_msg void OnDelete();
    afx_msg void OnExit();
    afx_msg void OnHelp();

    DECLARE_MESSAGE_MAP()
};

// This is the application class.
class CApp : public CWinApp
{
public:
  BOOL InitInstance();
};
```

Here is the dynamic menu program file:

```
// Demonstrate dynamic menus.
#include <afxwin.h>
#include "dynmenu.h"
#include "ids.h"

int maxX, maxY; // screen dimensions

CMainWin::CMainWin()
{
  Create(NULL, "Demonstrate Dynamic Menus",
         WS_OVERLAPPEDWINDOW, rectDefault,
         NULL, "DynMenu");

  // Load accelerator table.
  if(!LoadAccelTable("DynMenu"))
    MessageBox("Cannot Load Accelerators", "Error");

  maxX = GetSystemMetrics(SM_CXSCREEN);
```

```
  maxY = GetSystemMetrics(SM_CYSCREEN);

  CClientDC DC(this);

  // create a virtual output window
  m_memDC.CreateCompatibleDC(&DC);
  m_bmp.CreateCompatibleBitmap(&DC, maxX, maxY);
  m_memDC.SelectObject(&m_bmp);
  // use standard background
  m_bkbrush.CreateStockObject(WHITE_BRUSH);
  m_memDC.SelectObject(&m_bkbrush);
  // paint background of virtual window
  m_memDC.PatBlt(0, 0, maxX, maxY, PATCOPY);

  // create pens
  m_RedPen.CreatePen(PS_SOLID, 1, RGB(255,0,0));
  m_GreenPen.CreatePen(PS_SOLID, 2, RGB(0,255,0));
  m_BluePen.CreatePen(PS_SOLID, 3, RGB(0,0,255));
  m_YellowPen.CreatePen(PS_SOLID, 4, RGB(255, 255, 0));

  m_OldPen.CreateStockObject(BLACK_PEN);

  m_AddActive = 1; // initialize menu flags
  m_DelActive = 0;
}

// Initialize the application.
BOOL CApp::InitInstance()
{
  m_pMainWnd = new CMainWin;
  m_pMainWnd->ShowWindow(m_nCmdShow);
  m_pMainWnd->UpdateWindow();

  return TRUE;
}

// This is the application's message map.
BEGIN_MESSAGE_MAP(CMainWin, CFrameWnd)
  ON_WM_PAINT()
  ON_UPDATE_COMMAND_UI(IDM_ADDITEM, OnUIAdd)
  ON_UPDATE_COMMAND_UI(IDM_DELITEM, OnUIDel)
  ON_COMMAND(IDM_LINES, OnLines)
  ON_COMMAND(IDM_RECTANGLES, OnRectangles)
  ON_COMMAND(IDM_ELLIPSES, OnEllipses)
  ON_COMMAND(IDM_RESET, OnReset)
```

```
        ON_COMMAND(IDM_ADDITEM, OnAdd)
        ON_COMMAND(IDM_DELITEM, OnDelete)
        ON_COMMAND(IDM_EXIT, OnExit)
        ON_COMMAND(IDM_HELP, OnHelp)
    END_MESSAGE_MAP()

    // Update screen using contents of virtual window.
    afx_msg void CMainWin::OnPaint()
    {
      CPaintDC DC(this);

      DC.BitBlt(0, 0, maxX, maxY, &m_memDC, 0, 0, SRCCOPY);
    }

    // Process IDM_EXIT.
    afx_msg void CMainWin::OnExit()
    {
      int response;

      response = MessageBox("Quit the Program?",
                            "Exit", MB_YESNO);

      if(response == IDYES)
        SendMessage(WM_CLOSE); // terminate app
    }

    // Process IDM_HELP.
    afx_msg void CMainWin::OnHelp()
    {
        MessageBox("Dynamic Menus", "Help");
    }

    // Display lines and points.
    afx_msg void CMainWin::OnLines()
    {
      // draw 4 pixels
      m_memDC.SetPixel(40, 14, RGB(255, 0, 0));
      m_memDC.SetPixel(41, 14, RGB(0, 255, 0));
      m_memDC.SetPixel(42, 14, RGB(0, 0, 255));
      m_memDC.SetPixel(43, 14, RGB(0, 0, 0));

      m_memDC.LineTo(100, 50);
      m_memDC.MoveTo(100, 50);

      // change to green pen
```

15

```
m_memDC.SelectObject(&m_GreenPen);
m_memDC.LineTo(200, 100);

// change to yellow pen
m_memDC.SelectObject(&m_YellowPen);
m_memDC.LineTo(0, 200);

// change to blue pen
m_memDC.SelectObject(&m_BluePen);
m_memDC.LineTo(200, 200);

// change to red pen
m_memDC.SelectObject(&m_RedPen);
m_memDC.LineTo(0, 0);

m_memDC.LineTo(100, 150);
m_memDC.MoveTo(0, 0);
m_memDC.LineTo(100, 250);
m_memDC.MoveTo(0, 0);
m_memDC.LineTo(100, 350);

// return to default pen
m_memDC.SelectObject(&m_OldPen);

m_memDC.Arc(0, 0, 300, 300, 0, 50, 200, 0);
// show intersecting lines that define arc
m_memDC.MoveTo(150, 150);
m_memDC.LineTo(0, 50);
m_memDC.MoveTo(150, 150);
m_memDC.LineTo(200, 0);

InvalidateRect(NULL);
}

// Display rectangles.
afx_msg void CMainWin::OnRectangles()
{
  CBrush HollowBrush;

  // display, but don't fill, rectangles
  HollowBrush.CreateStockObject(HOLLOW_BRUSH);
  m_memDC.SelectObject(&HollowBrush);

  // draw some rectangles
  m_memDC.Rectangle(50, 50, 300, 300);
```

```
   m_memDC.RoundRect(125, 125, 220, 240, 15, 13);

   // use a red pen
   m_memDC.SelectObject(&m_RedPen);
   m_memDC.Rectangle(100, 100, 200, 200);
   m_memDC.SelectObject(&m_OldPen); // return to default pen

   // restore default brush
   m_memDC.SelectObject(&m_bkbrush);

   InvalidateRect(NULL);
}

// Display ellipses.
afx_msg void CMainWin::OnEllipses()
{
   CBrush Brush;

   // make blue brush
   Brush.CreateSolidBrush(RGB(0, 0, 255));
   m_memDC.SelectObject(&Brush);

   // fill these ellipses with blue
   m_memDC.Ellipse(50, 200, 100, 280);
   m_memDC.Ellipse(75, 25, 280, 100);

   // use a red pen
   m_memDC.SelectObject(&m_RedPen);

   // create green brush
   Brush.DeleteObject(); // delete blue brush
   Brush.CreateSolidBrush(RGB(0, 255, 0));
   m_memDC.SelectObject(&Brush); // select green brush
   m_memDC.Ellipse(100, 100, 200, 200);

   // draw a pie slice
   m_memDC.Pie(200, 200, 340, 340, 225, 200, 200, 250);

   m_memDC.SelectObject(&m_OldPen); // return to default pen
   m_memDC.SelectObject(&m_bkbrush); // select default brush

   InvalidateRect(NULL);
}

// Reset screen coordinates and erase window.
```

```
afx_msg void CMainWin::OnReset()
{
  m_memDC.PatBlt(0, 0, maxX, maxY, PATCOPY);
  InvalidateRect(NULL);
}

// Add item to menu.
afx_msg void CMainWin::OnAdd()
{
  CMenu *m_MainMenu; // will point to main menu
  CMenu *SubMenu; // will point to submenu
  unsigned count;

  // get pointer to main menu
  m_MainMenu = GetMenu();

  // get pointer to first pop-up menu
  SubMenu = m_MainMenu->GetSubMenu(0);

  // get number of items in the pop-up menu
  count = SubMenu->GetMenuItemCount();

  // add a separator
  SubMenu->InsertMenu(count, MF_BYPOSITION | MF_SEPARATOR);

  // add the new menu item
  SubMenu->InsertMenu(count+1, MF_BYPOSITION | MF_STRING,
                      IDM_RESET, "&Reset");

  // update menu selections
  m_AddActive = 0;
  m_DelActive = 1;
}

// Delete item from menu.
afx_msg void CMainWin::OnDelete()
{
  CMenu *m_MainMenu; // will point to main menu
  CMenu *SubMenu; // will point to submenu
  unsigned count;

  // get pointer to main menu
  m_MainMenu = GetMenu();

  // get pointer to first pop-up menu
```

```
   SubMenu = m_MainMenu->GetSubMenu(0);

   // get number of items in the pop-up menu
   count = SubMenu->GetMenuItemCount();

   // delete the new item
   SubMenu->DeleteMenu(count-1, MF_BYPOSITION);

   // delete the separator
   SubMenu->DeleteMenu(count-2, MF_BYPOSITION);

   // update menu selections
   m_AddActive = 1;
   m_DelActive = 0;
 }

// Display Add Item.
afx_msg void CMainWin::OnUIAdd(CCmdUI *UI)
{
  UI->Enable(m_AddActive);
}

// Display Delete Item.
afx_msg void CMainWin::OnUIDel(CCmdUI *UI)
{
  UI->Enable(m_DelActive);
}

CApp App; // instantiate the application
```

A Closer Look at the First Dynamic Menu Program

When the program first begins, the Options menu initially contains only three selections: Add Item, Delete Item, and Exit. Initially, Delete Item is disabled and therefore may not be selected. To add the Reset option, select Add Item. After the Reset item has been dynamically added to the menu, the Delete Item option is activated and the Add Item option is grayed. When Delete Item is selected, Reset is removed from the menu, Add Item is reactivated, and Delete Item is once again grayed. This procedure prevents the new menu item from being added or deleted more than once.

To allow Add Item and Delete Item to be enabled and disabled, the program overrides the default menu update handlers for these two options. These handlers use the **m_AddActive** and **m_DelActive** member variables of

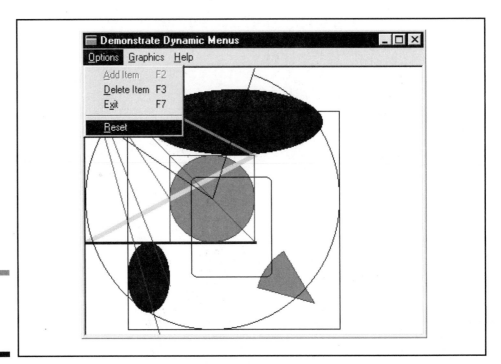

Adding menu
items
dynamically
Figure 15-1.

CMainWin to enable/disable their related items. These variables are set as needed by the program to cause the appropriate menu items to be enabled each time the Options menu is displayed.

Look closely at the code for **OnAdd( )**. Notice how a pointer to the Options pop-up menu is obtained. First, a pointer to its outer menu, which in this case is the program's main menu, is acquired using **GetMenu( )**. Next, **GetSubMenu( )** retrieves a pointer to its first pop-up menu, which is Options. Then, the program obtains a count of the number of items in the menu. This step is technically unnecessary since, in this simple example, we already know this value. Also, in this simple case, it would have been possible to just append the new items. However, these extra steps are included for the sake of illustration. Next, the program adds a separator and then the Reset menu item by using **InsertMenu( )**.

IN DEPTH

Checking Menu Items

It is possible to display a check mark next to a menu item. This is useful when an item represents an option that can be set. Check marks can be set or cleared at any time during the lifetime of your application. To set or clear a check mark, use the **CCmdUI::SetCheck( )** function, shown here:

virtual void CCmdUI::SetCheck(int *How* = 1);

The value of *How* determines the state of the check mark. If it is 1, the item is checked. If *How* is 0, the check mark is not shown.

An alternative to a standard check mark is the radio check mark. A radio check mark is a small circle. To display a radio check mark, use **CCmdUI::SetRadio( )**, shown here:

virtual void SetRadio(BOOL *How* = TRUE);

If *How* is **TRUE**, the radio check mark is shown. If it is **FALSE**, the check mark is removed. One important point: You must manually set and clear radio check marks. This is not done for you automatically.

Creating Dynamic Pop-up Menus

In addition to adding new items to an existing menu, you can dynamically create an entire pop-up menu. (That is, you can create a pop-up menu at run time.) Once you have created the menu, it can then be added to an existing menu. To dynamically create a pop-up menu, first use the function **CreatePopupMenu( )**, shown here:

BOOL CMenu::CreatePopupMenu( );

This function creates an empty pop-up menu. It returns nonzero if successful and zero on failure.

After you have created a menu, you add items to it using **InsertMenu( )**. Once the menu is fully constructed, you can add it to an existing menu, also using **InsertMenu( )**. When using **InsertMenu( )** to add a pop-up menu, you must specify the **MF_POPUP** flag and pass the handle of the new pop-up menu as the third parameter to **InsertMenu( )**. The handle of a menu is easily obtained. It is found in the **m_hMenu** member of **CMenu**.

Menus created using **CreatePopupMenu( )** must be destroyed. If the menu is attached to a window, then it will be destroyed automatically. A menu is also automatically destroyed when it is removed from a parent menu by a call to **DeleteMenu( )**. Dynamic menus can also be destroyed explicitly by calling **DestroyMenu( )**.

Demonstrating Dynamic Pop-up Menus

The following program is an enhanced version of the preceding program. It dynamically creates a pop-up menu that contains three items: Reset, Invert, and Show Text. Selecting Reset erases the window. Choosing Invert inverts the contents of the window. It does this by calling **PatBlt( )** using the **DSTINVERT** option. Choosing Show Text causes the string "Sample Text" to be displayed in the upper-left corner of the window. Pay close attention to the way that the pop-up menu is constructed and attached to the Options menu.

The program uses the same IDS.H header file as the preceding example. The resource for the program is shown here:

```
// DYNMENU2.RC

#include <afxres.h>
#include "ids.h"

DynMenu MENU
{
  POPUP "&Options"
  {
    MENUITEM "&Add Pop-up\tF2", IDM_ADDITEM
    MENUITEM "&Delete Pop-up\tF3", IDM_DELITEM
    MENUITEM "E&xit\tF7", IDM_EXIT
  }
  POPUP "&Graphics"
  {
    MENUITEM "&Lines\tF4", IDM_LINES
    MENUITEM "&Rectangles\tF5", IDM_RECTANGLES
```

```
   MENUITEM "&Ellipses\tF6", IDM_ELLIPSES
 }
 MENUITEM "&Help", IDM_HELP
}

DynMenu ACCELERATORS
{
 VK_F1, IDM_HELP, VIRTKEY
 VK_F2, IDM_ADDITEM, VIRTKEY
 VK_F3, IDM_DELITEM, VIRTKEY
 VK_F4, IDM_LINES, VIRTKEY
 VK_F5, IDM_RECTANGLES, VIRTKEY
 VK_F6, IDM_ELLIPSES, VIRTKEY
 VK_F7, IDM_EXIT, VIRTKEY
}
```

The class derivation file, DYNMENU2.H, is shown here:

```
// DYNMENU2.H

// This is the main window class.
class CMainWin : public CFrameWnd
{
  CDC m_memDC; // virtual window device context
  CBitmap m_bmp; // virtual window bitmap
  CBrush m_bkbrush; // brush for virtual window

  // create pens
  CPen m_RedPen, m_YellowPen, m_GreenPen, m_BluePen;
  CPen m_OldPen;

  CMenu *m_MainMenu; // will point to main menu

  // flags for Add and Delete menu items
  int m_AddActive, m_DelActive;

  CMenu m_Popup; // will hold dynamic pop-up menu
public:
  CMainWin();

  afx_msg void OnPaint();

  // UI handlers
  afx_msg void CMainWin::OnUIAdd(CCmdUI *UI);
  afx_msg void CMainWin::OnUIDel(CCmdUI *UI);
```

15

```
 afx_msg void OnLines();
 afx_msg void OnRectangles();
 afx_msg void OnEllipses();
 afx_msg void OnReset();
 afx_msg void OnAdd();
 afx_msg void OnDelete();
 afx_msg void OnDstInvert();
 afx_msg void OnShowText();
 afx_msg void OnExit();
 afx_msg void OnHelp();

 DECLARE_MESSAGE_MAP()
};

// This is the application class.
class CApp : public CWinApp
{
public:
 BOOL InitInstance();
};
```

The program file is shown next:

```
// Demonstrate dynamic pop-up menus.
#include <afxwin.h>
#include "dynmenu2.h"
#include "ids.h"

int maxX, maxY; // screen dimensions

CMainWin::CMainWin()
{
  Create(NULL, "Demonstrate Dynamic Pop-up Menus",
         WS_OVERLAPPEDWINDOW, rectDefault,
         NULL, "DynMenu");

  // Load accelerator table.
  if(!LoadAccelTable("DynMenu"))
    MessageBox("Cannot Load Accelerators", "Error");

  maxX = GetSystemMetrics(SM_CXSCREEN);
  maxY = GetSystemMetrics(SM_CYSCREEN);

  CClientDC DC(this);
```

```
  // create a virtual output window
  m_memDC.CreateCompatibleDC(&DC);
  m_bmp.CreateCompatibleBitmap(&DC, maxX, maxY);
  m_memDC.SelectObject(&m_bmp);
  // use standard background
  m_bkbrush.CreateStockObject(WHITE_BRUSH);
  m_memDC.SelectObject(&m_bkbrush);
  // paint background of virtual window
  m_memDC.PatBlt(0, 0, maxX, maxY, PATCOPY);

  // create pens
  m_RedPen.CreatePen(PS_SOLID, 1, RGB(255,0,0));
  m_GreenPen.CreatePen(PS_SOLID, 2, RGB(0,255,0));
  m_BluePen.CreatePen(PS_SOLID, 3, RGB(0,0,255));
  m_YellowPen.CreatePen(PS_SOLID, 4, RGB(255, 255, 0));

  m_OldPen.CreateStockObject(BLACK_PEN);

  m_AddActive = 1; // initialize menu flags
  m_DelActive = 0;
}

// Initialize the application.
BOOL CApp::InitInstance()
{
  m_pMainWnd = new CMainWin;
  m_pMainWnd->ShowWindow(m_nCmdShow);
  m_pMainWnd->UpdateWindow();

  return TRUE;
}

// This is the application's message map.
BEGIN_MESSAGE_MAP(CMainWin, CFrameWnd)
  ON_WM_PAINT()
  ON_UPDATE_COMMAND_UI(IDM_ADDITEM, OnUIAdd)
  ON_UPDATE_COMMAND_UI(IDM_DELITEM, OnUIDel)
  ON_COMMAND(IDM_LINES, OnLines)
  ON_COMMAND(IDM_RECTANGLES, OnRectangles)
  ON_COMMAND(IDM_ELLIPSES, OnEllipses)
  ON_COMMAND(IDM_RESET, OnReset)
  ON_COMMAND(IDM_ADDITEM, OnAdd)
  ON_COMMAND(IDM_DELITEM, OnDelete)
  ON_COMMAND(IDM_DSTINVERT, OnDstInvert)
  ON_COMMAND(IDM_SHOWTEXT, OnShowText)
```

```
  ON_COMMAND(IDM_EXIT, OnExit)
  ON_COMMAND(IDM_HELP, OnHelp)
END_MESSAGE_MAP()

// Update screen using contents of virtual window.
afx_msg void CMainWin::OnPaint()
{
  CPaintDC DC(this);

  DC.BitBlt(0, 0, maxX, maxY, &m_memDC, 0, 0, SRCCOPY);
}

// Process IDM_EXIT.
afx_msg void CMainWin::OnExit()
{
  int response;

  response = MessageBox("Quit the Program?",
                        "Exit", MB_YESNO);

  if(response == IDYES)
    SendMessage(WM_CLOSE); // terminate app
}

// Process IDM_HELP.
afx_msg void CMainWin::OnHelp()
{
    MessageBox("Dynamic Pop-up Menus", "Help");
}

// Display lines and points.
afx_msg void CMainWin::OnLines()
{
  // draw 4 pixels
  m_memDC.SetPixel(40, 14, RGB(255, 0, 0));
  m_memDC.SetPixel(41, 14, RGB(0, 255, 0));
  m_memDC.SetPixel(42, 14, RGB(0, 0, 255));
  m_memDC.SetPixel(43, 14, RGB(0, 0, 0));

  m_memDC.LineTo(100, 50);
  m_memDC.MoveTo(100, 50);

  // change to green pen
  m_memDC.SelectObject(&m_GreenPen);
  m_memDC.LineTo(200, 100);
```

```
         // change to yellow pen
         m_memDC.SelectObject(&m_YellowPen);
         m_memDC.LineTo(0, 200);

         // change to blue pen
         m_memDC.SelectObject(&m_BluePen);
         m_memDC.LineTo(200, 200);

         // change to red pen
         m_memDC.SelectObject(&m_RedPen);
         m_memDC.LineTo(0, 0);

         m_memDC.LineTo(100, 150);
         m_memDC.MoveTo(0, 0);
         m_memDC.LineTo(100, 250);
         m_memDC.MoveTo(0, 0);
         m_memDC.LineTo(100, 350);

         // return to default pen
         m_memDC.SelectObject(&m_OldPen);

         m_memDC.Arc(0, 0, 300, 300, 0, 50, 200, 0);
         // show intersecting lines that define arc
         m_memDC.MoveTo(150, 150);
         m_memDC.LineTo(0, 50);
         m_memDC.MoveTo(150, 150);
         m_memDC.LineTo(200, 0);

         InvalidateRect(NULL);
}

// Display rectangles.
afx_msg void CMainWin::OnRectangles()
{
   CBrush HollowBrush;

   // display, but don't fill, rectangles
   HollowBrush.CreateStockObject(HOLLOW_BRUSH);
   m_memDC.SelectObject(&HollowBrush);

   // draw some rectangles
   m_memDC.Rectangle(50, 50, 300, 300);
   m_memDC.RoundRect(125, 125, 220, 240, 15, 13);

   // use a red pen
```

```
  m_memDC.SelectObject(&m_RedPen);
  m_memDC.Rectangle(100, 100, 200, 200);
  m_memDC.SelectObject(&m_OldPen); // return to default pen

  // restore default brush
  m_memDC.SelectObject(&m_bkbrush);

  InvalidateRect(NULL);
}

// Display ellipses.
afx_msg void CMainWin::OnEllipses()
{
  CBrush Brush;

  // make blue brush
  Brush.CreateSolidBrush(RGB(0, 0, 255));
  m_memDC.SelectObject(&Brush);

  // fill these ellipses with blue
  m_memDC.Ellipse(50, 200, 100, 280);
  m_memDC.Ellipse(75, 25, 280, 100);

  // use a red pen
  m_memDC.SelectObject(&m_RedPen);

  // create green brush
  Brush.DeleteObject(); // delete blue brush
  Brush.CreateSolidBrush(RGB(0, 255, 0));
  m_memDC.SelectObject(&Brush); // select green brush
  m_memDC.Ellipse(100, 100, 200, 200);

  // draw a pie slice
  m_memDC.Pie(200, 200, 340, 340, 225, 200, 200, 250);

  m_memDC.SelectObject(&m_OldPen); // return to default pen
  m_memDC.SelectObject(&m_bkbrush); // select default brush

  InvalidateRect(NULL);
}

// Reset screen coordinates and erase window.
afx_msg void CMainWin::OnReset()
{
  m_memDC.PatBlt(0, 0, maxX, maxY, PATCOPY);
```

```
      InvalidateRect(NULL);
}

// Display some text in the window.
afx_msg void CMainWin::OnShowText()
{
  m_memDC.TextOut(1, 1, "Sample Text", 11);
  InvalidateRect(NULL);
}

// Invert the window.
afx_msg void CMainWin::OnDstInvert()
{
  m_memDC.PatBlt(0, 0, maxX, maxY, DSTINVERT);
  InvalidateRect(NULL);
}

// Add item to menu.
afx_msg void CMainWin::OnAdd()
{
  CMenu *m_MainMenu; // will point to main menu
  CMenu *SubMenu; // will point to submenu
  unsigned count;

  // get pointer to main menu
  m_MainMenu = GetMenu();

  // get pointer to first pop-up menu
  SubMenu = m_MainMenu->GetSubMenu(0);

  // get number of items in the pop-up menu
  count = SubMenu->GetMenuItemCount();

  // create a new pop-up menu
  m_Popup.CreatePopupMenu();

  // add items to new pop-up menu
  m_Popup.InsertMenu(0, MF_BYPOSITION | MF_STRING,
                        IDM_RESET, "&Reset");
  m_Popup.InsertMenu(1, MF_BYPOSITION | MF_STRING,
                        IDM_DSTINVERT, "&Invert Window");
  m_Popup.InsertMenu(2, MF_BYPOSITION | MF_STRING,
                        IDM_SHOWTEXT, "&Show Text");

  // add a separator
```

```
      SubMenu->InsertMenu(count, MF_BYPOSITION | MF_SEPARATOR);

      // Add pop-up menu to Options menu
      SubMenu->InsertMenu(count+1, MF_POPUP | MF_BYPOSITION,
                          (unsigned)m_Popup.m_hMenu, "&New Options");

      // update menu selections
      m_AddActive = 0;
      m_DelActive = 1;
    }

    // Delete item from menu.
    afx_msg void CMainWin::OnDelete()
    {
      CMenu *m_MainMenu; // will point to main menu
      CMenu *SubMenu; // will point to submenu
      unsigned count;

      // get pointer to main menu
      m_MainMenu = GetMenu();

      // get pointer to first pop-up menu
      SubMenu = m_MainMenu->GetSubMenu(0);

      // get number of items in the pop-up menu
      count = SubMenu->GetMenuItemCount();

      // delete the pop-up menu
      SubMenu->DeleteMenu(count-1, MF_BYPOSITION);

      // delete the separator
      SubMenu->DeleteMenu(count-2, MF_BYPOSITION);

      // update menu selections
      m_AddActive = 1;
      m_DelActive = 0;
    }

    // Display Add Pop-up.
    afx_msg void CMainWin::OnUIAdd(CCmdUI *UI)
    {
      UI->Enable(m_AddActive);
    }

    // Display Delete Pop-up.
```

```
afx_msg void CMainWin::OnUIDel(CCmdUI *UI)
{
  UI->Enable(m_DelActive);
}

CApp App; // instantiate the application
```

Sample output from this program is shown in Figure 15-2.

Most of the program is straightforward. However, notice one important point. After the pop-up menu has been created, it is inserted into the Options menu by calling **InsertMenu( )**. In this call, the **MF_POPUP** flag is set, and the handle of the pop-up menu is passed as the third parameter. As mentioned earlier, the handle to a menu is found in the **m_hMenu** member of a **CMenu** object. Finally, the cast to **unsigned** is necessary to prevent the compiler from reporting a type mismatch error.

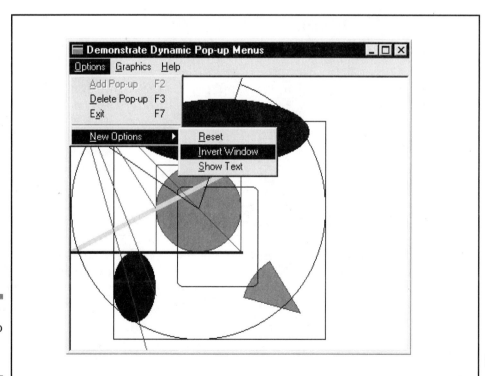

A dynamically created pop-up menu

Figure 15-2.

15

Using Floating Menus

Although stand-alone, or *floating*, menus have been available to Windows programmers for quite some time, they are increasingly important as a stylistic element. One reason for this is that floating menus are part and parcel of the modern Windows user interface. For example, when you click the right mouse button on nearly any interface item, you will activate a floating menu. Or, when you right-click on the desktop, you will see a menu that allows you to perform various functions relating to the desktop. Therefore, to conclude this chapter, a discussion of floating menus seems appropriate.

NOTE: Floating menus are also referred to as shortcut or context menus. The term *context menu* stems from the type of items that populate the menu: items that have a specific "context" within the application.

Activating a Floating Menu

A floating menu is activated using **TrackPopupMenu( )**. Its prototype is shown here:

> BOOL CMenu::TrackPopupMenu(UINT *Flags*, int *X*, int *Y*, CWnd **Owner*,
> RECT **Limits* = NULL);

Various options are specified in *Flags*. This parameter may be any valid (i.e., non-mutually exclusive) combination of the values shown in Table 15-2. You may specify zero for *Flags*. Doing so causes the default configuration to be used.

The location *on the screen* at which to display the menu is specified in *X* and *Y*. Therefore, these coordinates are in terms of screen units, not window or dialog units. To convert between screen and window units, use either the **CWnd::ClientToScreen( )** or the **CWnd::ScreenToClient( )** function. In its default configuration, **TrackPopupMenu( )** displays the menu with its upper-left corner at the location specified by *X* and *Y*. However, you can use the *Flags* parameter to alter this placement.

A pointer to the window that owns the floating menu must be passed in *Owner*.

Flags Value	Meaning
TPM_CENTERALIGN	Floating menu pops up centered relative to *X*.
TPM_LEFTALIGN	Floating menu pops up with left side at *X*. (This is the default.)
TPM_LEFTBUTTON	Left mouse button operates the menu. (This is the default.)
TPM_RIGHTALIGN	Floating menu pops up with right side at *X*.
TPM_RIGHTBUTTON	Right mouse button operates the menu.

The Values for the *Flags* Parameter of **TrackPop-upMenu( )**
Table 15-2.

Floating menus are automatically removed when the user clicks the mouse outside of a region that surrounds the menu. By default, this region is the size of the menu itself. However, you may specify the precise limits of this region. To do so, pass the extent of that region in the **RECT** structure pointed to by *Limits*. If this parameter is **NULL** (or is allowed to default), then the floating menu will be removed from the screen if the mouse is clicked on any part of the screen that is not part of the menu.

Loading a Menu

Since a floating menu is not part of the main menu of your application, it must either be constructed dynamically (using the procedures discussed in the preceding section), or it must be loaded from your program's resource file. To load a menu resource, use the **LoadMenu( )** function, shown here:

    BOOL CMenu::LoadMenu(LPCSTR *lpszMenuName*);

    BOOL CMenu::LoadMenu(UINT *MenuID*);

Here, *lpszMenuName* is a pointer to a string that specifies the name of the menu. In the second form, the menu is loaded using the ID passed in *MenuID*. The function returns nonzero if successful and zero on failure. Once loaded, the menu becomes part of the invoking **CMenu** object.

If the menu being loaded is not attached to a window, then it must be destroyed using a call to **CMenu::DestroyMenu( )** when it is no longer needed.

Demonstrating Floating Menus

The following program modifies the previous program by making the Graphics menu into a floating pop-up menu. Thus, it is no longer part of the menu bar. Instead, it is activated by pressing the right mouse button. When this occurs, the floating menu is displayed at the location of the mouse pointer when the button is pressed. Sample output is shown in Figure 15-3.

The program uses the same IDS.H header file as the preceding examples. It uses the resource file that follows. Notice that in this version, the Graphics menu is not part of the main menu bar. Instead, it is a stand-alone menu. Thus, it will not be displayed until it is invoked.

```
// DYNMENU3.RC

#include <afxres.h>
#include "ids.h"

DynMenu MENU
{
  POPUP "&Options"
  {
    MENUITEM "&Add Pop-up\tF2", IDM_ADDITEM
    MENUITEM "&Delete Pop-up\tF3", IDM_DELITEM
    MENUITEM "E&xit\tF7", IDM_EXIT
  }
  MENUITEM "&Help", IDM_HELP
}


// This menu will pop up.
GraphMenu MENU
{
  POPUP "&Graphics"
  {
    MENUITEM "&Lines\tF4", IDM_LINES
    MENUITEM "&Rectangles\tF5", IDM_RECTANGLES
    MENUITEM "&Ellipses\tF6", IDM_ELLIPSES
  }
}


DynMenu ACCELERATORS
{
  VK_F1, IDM_HELP, VIRTKEY
  VK_F2, IDM_ADDITEM, VIRTKEY
  VK_F3, IDM_DELITEM, VIRTKEY
```

```
      VK_F4, IDM_LINES, VIRTKEY
      VK_F5, IDM_RECTANGLES, VIRTKEY
      VK_F6, IDM_ELLIPSES, VIRTKEY
      VK_F7, IDM_EXIT, VIRTKEY
}
```

The class derivation file, DYNMENU3.H, is shown here:

```
// DYNMENU3.H

// This is the main window class.
class CMainWin : public CFrameWnd
{
  CDC m_memDC; // virtual window device context
  CBitmap m_bmp; // virtual window bitmap
  CBrush m_bkbrush; // brush for virtual window

  // create pens
  CPen m_RedPen, m_YellowPen, m_GreenPen, m_BluePen;
  CPen m_OldPen;

  CMenu *m_MainMenu; // will point to main menu

  // flags for Add and Delete menu items
  int m_AddActive, m_DelActive;

  CMenu m_Popup; // will hold dynamic pop-up menu
  CMenu m_FloatMenu; // will hold floating menu
public:
  CMainWin();

  afx_msg void OnPaint();
  afx_msg void OnRButtonDown(UINT Flags, CPoint Loc);

  // UI handlers
  afx_msg void CMainWin::OnUIAdd(CCmdUI *UI);
  afx_msg void CMainWin::OnUIDel(CCmdUI *UI);

  afx_msg void OnLines();
  afx_msg void OnRectangles();
  afx_msg void OnEllipses();
  afx_msg void OnReset();
  afx_msg void OnAdd();
  afx_msg void OnDelete();
  afx_msg void OnDstInvert();
```

```
afx_msg void OnShowText();
afx_msg void OnExit();
afx_msg void OnHelp();

DECLARE_MESSAGE_MAP()
};

// This is the application class.
class CApp : public CWinApp
{
public:
  BOOL InitInstance();
};
```

The program file is shown next:

```
// Demonstrate floating pop-up menus.
#include <afxwin.h>
#include "dynmenu3.h"
#include "ids.h"

int maxX, maxY; // screen dimensions

CMainWin::CMainWin()
{
  Create(NULL, "Demonstrate Floating Pop-up Menus",
         WS_OVERLAPPEDWINDOW, rectDefault,
         NULL, "DynMenu");

  // Load accelerator table.
  if(!LoadAccelTable("DynMenu"))
    MessageBox("Cannot Load Accelerators", "Error");

  maxX = GetSystemMetrics(SM_CXSCREEN);
  maxY = GetSystemMetrics(SM_CYSCREEN);

  CClientDC DC(this);

  // create a virtual output window
  m_memDC.CreateCompatibleDC(&DC);
  m_bmp.CreateCompatibleBitmap(&DC, maxX, maxY);
  m_memDC.SelectObject(&m_bmp);
  // use standard background
  m_bkbrush.CreateStockObject(WHITE_BRUSH);
  m_memDC.SelectObject(&m_bkbrush);
```

```
    // paint background of virtual window
    m_memDC.PatBlt(0, 0, maxX, maxY, PATCOPY);

    // create pens
    m_RedPen.CreatePen(PS_SOLID, 1, RGB(255,0,0));
    m_GreenPen.CreatePen(PS_SOLID, 2, RGB(0,255,0));
    m_BluePen.CreatePen(PS_SOLID, 3, RGB(0,0,255));
    m_YellowPen.CreatePen(PS_SOLID, 4, RGB(255, 255, 0));

    m_OldPen.CreateStockObject(BLACK_PEN);

    m_AddActive = 1; // initialize menu flags
    m_DelActive = 0;
}

// Initialize the application.
BOOL CApp::InitInstance()
{
    m_pMainWnd = new CMainWin;
    m_pMainWnd->ShowWindow(m_nCmdShow);
    m_pMainWnd->UpdateWindow();

    return TRUE;
}

// This is the application's message map.
BEGIN_MESSAGE_MAP(CMainWin, CFrameWnd)
    ON_WM_PAINT()
    ON_WM_RBUTTONDOWN()
    ON_UPDATE_COMMAND_UI(IDM_ADDITEM, OnUIAdd)
    ON_UPDATE_COMMAND_UI(IDM_DELITEM, OnUIDel)
    ON_COMMAND(IDM_LINES, OnLines)
    ON_COMMAND(IDM_RECTANGLES, OnRectangles)
    ON_COMMAND(IDM_ELLIPSES, OnEllipses)
    ON_COMMAND(IDM_RESET, OnReset)
    ON_COMMAND(IDM_ADDITEM, OnAdd)
    ON_COMMAND(IDM_DELITEM, OnDelete)
    ON_COMMAND(IDM_DSTINVERT, OnDstInvert)
    ON_COMMAND(IDM_SHOWTEXT, OnShowText)
    ON_COMMAND(IDM_EXIT, OnExit)
    ON_COMMAND(IDM_HELP, OnHelp)
END_MESSAGE_MAP()

// Update screen using contents of virtual window.
afx_msg void CMainWin::OnPaint()
```

15

```
{
  CPaintDC DC(this);

  DC.BitBlt(0, 0, maxX, maxY, &m_memDC, 0, 0, SRCCOPY);
}

// Process IDM_EXIT.
afx_msg void CMainWin::OnExit()
{
  int response;

  response = MessageBox("Quit the Program?",
                        "Exit", MB_YESNO);

  if(response == IDYES)
    SendMessage(WM_CLOSE); // terminate app
}

// Process IDM_HELP.
afx_msg void CMainWin::OnHelp()
{
    MessageBox("Floating Pop-up Menus", "Help");
}

// Display lines and points.
afx_msg void CMainWin::OnLines()
{
  // draw 4 pixels
  m_memDC.SetPixel(40, 14, RGB(255, 0, 0));
  m_memDC.SetPixel(41, 14, RGB(0, 255, 0));
  m_memDC.SetPixel(42, 14, RGB(0, 0, 255));
  m_memDC.SetPixel(43, 14, RGB(0, 0, 0));

  m_memDC.LineTo(100, 50);
  m_memDC.MoveTo(100, 50);

  // change to green pen
  m_memDC.SelectObject(&m_GreenPen);
  m_memDC.LineTo(200, 100);

  // change to yellow pen
  m_memDC.SelectObject(&m_YellowPen);
  m_memDC.LineTo(0, 200);

  // change to blue pen
```

```
m_memDC.SelectObject(&m_BluePen);
m_memDC.LineTo(200, 200);

// change to red pen
m_memDC.SelectObject(&m_RedPen);
m_memDC.LineTo(0, 0);

m_memDC.LineTo(100, 150);
m_memDC.MoveTo(0, 0);
m_memDC.LineTo(100, 250);
m_memDC.MoveTo(0, 0);
m_memDC.LineTo(100, 350);

// return to default pen
m_memDC.SelectObject(&m_OldPen);

m_memDC.Arc(0, 0, 300, 300, 0, 50, 200, 0);
// show intersecting lines that define arc
m_memDC.MoveTo(150, 150);
m_memDC.LineTo(0, 50);
m_memDC.MoveTo(150, 150);
m_memDC.LineTo(200, 0);

InvalidateRect(NULL);
}

// Display rectangles.
afx_msg void CMainWin::OnRectangles()
{
  CBrush HollowBrush;

  // display, but don't fill, rectangles
  HollowBrush.CreateStockObject(HOLLOW_BRUSH);
  m_memDC.SelectObject(&HollowBrush);

  // draw some rectangles
  m_memDC.Rectangle(50, 50, 300, 300);
  m_memDC.RoundRect(125, 125, 220, 240, 15, 13);

  // use a red pen
  m_memDC.SelectObject(&m_RedPen);
  m_memDC.Rectangle(100, 100, 200, 200);
  m_memDC.SelectObject(&m_OldPen); // return to default pen

  // restore default brush
```

```
  m_memDC.SelectObject(&m_bkbrush);

  InvalidateRect(NULL);
}

// Display ellipses.
afx_msg void CMainWin::OnEllipses()
{
  CBrush Brush;

  // make blue brush
  Brush.CreateSolidBrush(RGB(0, 0, 255));
  m_memDC.SelectObject(&Brush);

  // fill these ellipses with blue
  m_memDC.Ellipse(50, 200, 100, 280);
  m_memDC.Ellipse(75, 25, 280, 100);

  // use a red pen
  m_memDC.SelectObject(&m_RedPen);

  // create green brush
  Brush.DeleteObject(); // delete blue brush
  Brush.CreateSolidBrush(RGB(0, 255, 0));
  m_memDC.SelectObject(&Brush); // select green brush
  m_memDC.Ellipse(100, 100, 200, 200);

  // draw a pie slice
  m_memDC.Pie(200, 200, 340, 340, 225, 200, 200, 250);

  m_memDC.SelectObject(&m_OldPen); // return to default pen
  m_memDC.SelectObject(&m_bkbrush); // select default brush

  InvalidateRect(NULL);
}

// Reset screen coordinates and erase window.
afx_msg void CMainWin::OnReset()
{
  m_memDC.PatBlt(0, 0, maxX, maxY, PATCOPY);
  InvalidateRect(NULL);
}

// Display some text in the window.
afx_msg void CMainWin::OnShowText()
```

```
{
  m_memDC.TextOut(1, 1, "Sample Text", 11);
  InvalidateRect(NULL);
}

// Invert the window.
afx_msg void CMainWin::OnDstInvert()
{
  m_memDC.PatBlt(0, 0, maxX, maxY, DSTINVERT);
  InvalidateRect(NULL);
}

// Add item to menu.
afx_msg void CMainWin::OnAdd()
{
  CMenu *m_MainMenu; // will point to main menu
  CMenu *SubMenu; // will point to submenu
  unsigned count;

  // get pointer to main menu
  m_MainMenu = GetMenu();

  // get pointer to first pop-up menu
  SubMenu = m_MainMenu->GetSubMenu(0);

  // get number of items in the pop-up menu
  count = SubMenu->GetMenuItemCount();

  // create a new pop-up menu
  m_Popup.CreatePopupMenu();

  // add items to new pop-up menu
  m_Popup.InsertMenu(0, MF_BYPOSITION | MF_STRING,
                     IDM_RESET, "&Reset");
  m_Popup.InsertMenu(1, MF_BYPOSITION | MF_STRING,
                     IDM_DSTINVERT, "&Invert Window");
  m_Popup.InsertMenu(2, MF_BYPOSITION | MF_STRING,
                     IDM_SHOWTEXT, "&Show Text");

  // add a separator
  SubMenu->InsertMenu(count, MF_BYPOSITION | MF_SEPARATOR);

  // Add pop-up menu to Options menu
  SubMenu->InsertMenu(count+1, MF_POPUP | MF_BYPOSITION,
                     (unsigned)m_Popup.m_hMenu, "&New Options");
```

```
  // update menu selections
  m_AddActive = 0;
  m_DelActive = 1;
}

// Delete item from menu.
afx_msg void CMainWin::OnDelete()
{
  CMenu *m_MainMenu; // will point to main menu
  CMenu *SubMenu; // will point to submenu
  unsigned count;

  // get pointer to main menu
  m_MainMenu = GetMenu();

  // get pointer to first pop-up menu
  SubMenu = m_MainMenu->GetSubMenu(0);

  // get number of items in the pop-up menu
  count = SubMenu->GetMenuItemCount();

  // delete the pop-up menu
  SubMenu->DeleteMenu(count-1, MF_BYPOSITION);

  // delete the separator
  SubMenu->DeleteMenu(count-2, MF_BYPOSITION);

  // update menu selections
  m_AddActive = 1;
  m_DelActive = 0;
}

// Display Add Pop-up.
afx_msg void CMainWin::OnUIAdd(CCmdUI *UI)
{
  UI->Enable(m_AddActive);
}

// Display Delete Pop-up.
afx_msg void CMainWin::OnUIDel(CCmdUI *UI)
{
  UI->Enable(m_DelActive);
}

// Activate Floating Pop-up Menu
```

```
afx_msg void CMainWin::OnRButtonDown(UINT Flags, CPoint Loc)
{
  CMenu *SubMenu; // will point to submenu

  ClientToScreen(&Loc);

  m_FloatMenu.LoadMenu("GraphMenu");
  SubMenu = m_FloatMenu.GetSubMenu(0);

  SubMenu->TrackPopupMenu(0, Loc.x, Loc.y, this);

  m_FloatMenu.DestroyMenu();
}

CApp App; // instantiate the application
```

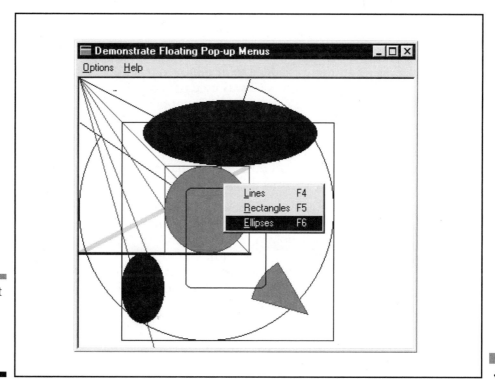

Sample output
from the
floating menu
program

Figure 15-3.

15

A Closer Look at the Floating Menu Program

Most of the program is unchanged from its previous version. However, notice the code in the **OnRButtonDown( )** message handler. It is used to activate the Graphics menu. This code pops up the menu with its upper-left corner positioned at the location of the mouse when the right button is pressed. However, since the coordinates specified in **TrackPopupMenu( )** are in terms of screen units, the program must convert the mouse's location (which is in window units) into screen units using **ClientToScreen( )**. Next, the menu must be loaded, using **LoadMenu( )**, and its first (and only) pop-up menu obtained. After these steps have been taken, the menu can be displayed.

Experimenting with Menus

The examples in this chapter show only a small portion of the things that can be done using menus. The best way to learn about the other capabilities of menus is to experiment. For instance, you might want to try using **CCmdUI::SetRadio( )** or **CCmdUI::SetCheck( )** when handling menu updates. You will also want to try the various options available to the **TrackPopupMenu( )** function.

Here is an easy experiment. In the first example program in this chapter, the Reset option was added to or removed from the Options menu manually, by the user. This approach was used only for the sake of illustration. A better way is to add or remove the Reset option automatically, under program control. For example, when the window is empty (as it is when the program begins), do not display the Reset option. As soon as the user draws something in the window, activate Reset. Once the user has erased the window, deactivate the Reset option. Automating the inclusion of the Reset option in this way reflects how dynamic menus are used in real applications.

Although menus are somewhat passé when compared to many of the new and exciting control features that are now offered by Windows, they are still the main entry point to your application. Remember that the user will generally interact with your menus more often than he or she does with any other control device in your program. Thus, their design and implementation deserve significant care and attention to detail.

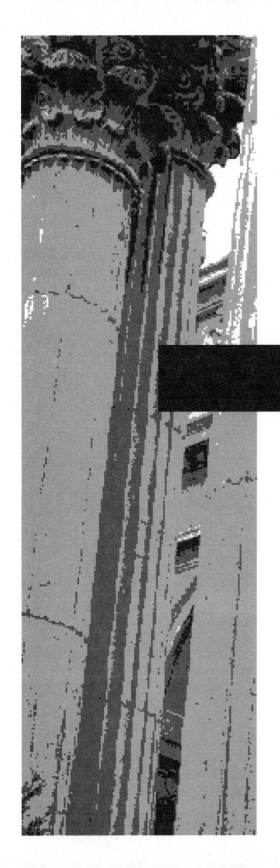

CHAPTER 16

Adding Help

O nline help is a necessary part of nearly every Windows application. A component of Windows since the beginning, online help has continually increased in its importance and scope. Years ago, it was possible to write a professional-quality application that incorporated only the most rudimentary online help. This is no longer the case. Today, no major program can be written that does not contain a full complement of help features. Indeed, online help has become an integral part of all commercial-quality applications.

Because of the importance of online Help, most programs in the preceding 15 chapters have included a placeholder menu entry for it. This placeholder was included simply to emphasize the point that help should be included in every Windows application. In this chapter you will see how to replace this placeholder with the real help system.

Two Types of Help

The Windows help system supports two general categories of help. The first is essentially online documentation and is sometimes called *reference help*. It is accessed via the standard Help window, such as the one shown in Figure 16-1. By using the standard Help window, you can display various help topics,

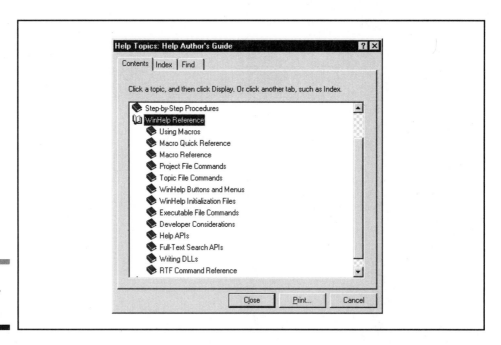

A standard
Help window
Figure 16-1.

search for other topics, or view the contents of a help file. Reference help is used to display detailed descriptions of various features supported by the application or to act as the online version of the program's user manual. The second category of help is *context-sensitive help*. Context-sensitive help displays a brief description of a specific program feature within a small window. An example is shown in Figure 16-2. Both types of help are required by a professional-quality Windows application. As you will see, although different in style, both of these categories of help are handled in much the same way.

How the User Invokes Help

To fully implement the Windows help system, your program must support the standard methods by which the user can invoke online help. Specifically, the user may obtain help by utilizing any of the following four methods:

◆ Clicking the right mouse button on an object.

◆ Clicking the **?** button and then clicking on an object.

◆ Pressing F1.

◆ Using a Help menu.

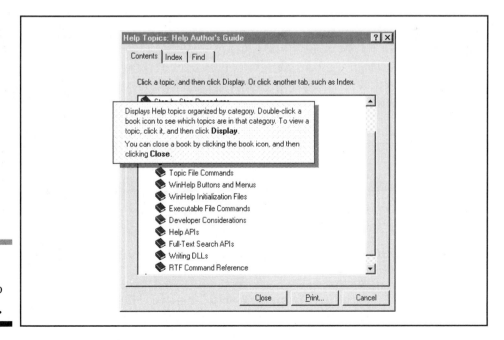

An example of context-sensitive help

Figure 16-2.

The first two methods are almost always used to invoke context-sensitive, pop-up help. In most situations, F1 is also used to invoke context-sensitive help. Occasionally, it invokes reference help. Selecting help through a menu usually invokes reference help.

It is also permissible for the application program to invoke help itself whenever it needs to do so. For example, a program might activate the help system when the user attempts an invalid operation.

As you will see, help in an MFC program is managed by **CWinApp**. Once the user has activated a help option, your application will respond to a help request by calling the **WinHelp( )** member function of **CWinApp** or, in some cases, the **WinHelp( )** API function itself. These functions automatically manage all help requests. As you will see, **WinHelp( )** is a very versatile function. However, before examining **WinHelp( )** you need to understand how to create a help file.

NOTE: To avoid confusion, when the API version of **WinHelp( )** is being referred to in text, it will be preceded with the scope resolution operator, like this: **::WinHelp( )**.

The Help File

At the core of the Windows help system is the *help file*. Both context-sensitive and reference help utilize the help file. Help files are not text files. Rather, they are specially compiled files that have the .HLP file extension. To create a help file, you must first create an .RTF (Rich Text Format) file that contains all of the help topics plus formatting, indexing, and cross-referencing information. This file will normally have the extension .RTF. This file is then compiled using a help compiler, which is usually supplied along with a Windows-compatible C++ compiler. For example, the help compiler provided by Microsoft's Visual C++ is called the Help Workshop. The output of the help compiler is a .HLP file. Thus, relative to the help compiler, the .RTF file is the source file and the .HLP file is the object file.

The Rich Text Format language contains a large number of commands. The help compiler accepts only a subset of these commands. However, the help system also recognizes several additional, help-related commands that are not part of the general purpose RTF language. All RTF commands begin with a \.

For example, **\b** is the RTF command for bold. It is far beyond the scope of this chapter to discuss all of the RTF commands. (Indeed, an entire book is needed to fully describe the RTF language.) However, this chapter describes the most important and commonly used commands relating to help files. If you will be doing extensive work with help files, you will need to acquire a full description of the RTF language.

In addition to the .RTF file, the help compiler also uses a project file. In it are various settings and values that relate to the help file. Help project files use the .HPJ extension. Since the help file is at the foundation of the Windows help system, let's begin by creating a simple one that will be used to demonstrate the help system.

Creating a Help File

As stated, the source code for a help file must be in rich text format. This means that creating the source code for a help file is not a trivial task. Fortunately, there are three ways that you can create a help file. First, you can use an automated help authoring package. Second, you can use a text editor that generates .RTF files. Third, you can use a standard text editor and manually embed RTF commands. If you will be preparing large and complex help files, the authoring package is probably the best alternative. However, for smaller applications, either of the other two choices is adequate. Since the one option that all readers will have is the third, that is the method that will be used here.

The General Form of a Help File

All help source files have certain basic elements in common. First, the entire file must be enclosed between curly braces. That is, it must begin with a **{** and end with a **}**. Immediately following the opening curly brace must be the **\rtf** command. This command identifies the file as a rich text format file and specifies which version of the rich text format specification is being used. (Help files currently use version 1.) You must then define the character set used by the file. This will generally be the ANSI character set, which is specified using the **\ansi** command. You must also define the character fonts used by the file. This is done with the **\fonttbl** command. Thus, the general form of an RTF help file will look like this:

```
{\rtf1\ansi \fonttbl ...
  Help File Contents
}
```

Within an RTF file, additional curly braces can be used to localize the effect of various RTF commands. In this capacity, the curly braces act much like they do in a C/C++ source file: they define a block.

Some RTF Commands

Before you can create even a simple help file, you need to know a few of the most important and common RTF commands. The RTF commands used in this chapter are shown in Table 16-1.

\ansi

The **\ansi** command specifies the ANSI character set. .RTF files support other character sets, such as **\mac** (Macintosh character set) or **\pc** (OEM

RTF Command	Meaning
\ansi	Specifies the ANSI character set.
\b	Turns on boldface.
\b0	Turns off boldface.
\f*n*	Selects the font specified by *n*.
\fs*n*	Sets font size to *n*.
\fonttbl	Defines a font table.
\footnote	Specifies keywords and index topics.
\i	Turns on italics.
\i0	Turns off italics.
\page	Indicates the end of a topic.
\par	Indicates the end of a paragraph.
\rtf*n*	Specifies which RTF specification is being used.
\tab	Moves to next tab position.
\uldb	Marks a "hot spot" link to another topic.
\v	Creates a topic link (used in conjunction with **\uldb**).

Selected Help-Related RTF Commands

Table 16-1.

16

character set). However, the ANSI character set is the one that is generally used for help files.

\b

The **\b** command turns on boldface. **\b0** turns it off. However, if the **\b** command is used within a block, then only the text within that block is boldfaced, and there is no need to use the **\b0** command. For example:

```
{\b this is bold} this is not
```

Here, only the text within the curly braces will be in boldface.

\fn

The **\fn** command selects a font. The font is specified by its number. The font must have been previously defined using a **\fonttbl** statement.

\fsn

The **\fsn** command sets the font size to that specified by *n*. The size is specified in half-point units. For example, **\fs24** sets the font size to 12 points.

\fonttbl

Before a font can be used, it must be included in a **\fonttbl** statement. It has the following general form:

```
{\fonttbl
 {\f1\family-name font-name;}
 {\f2\family-name font-name;}
 {\f3\family-name font-name;}
 .
 .
 .
 {\fn\family-name font-name;}
}
```

Here, *family-name* is the name of the font family (such as **froman** or **fswiss**), and *font-name* is the name of a specific font (such as Times New Roman, Arial, or Old English) within that family. The number of the font as specified in the **\f** statement will be used to select the font. A partial list of font families and names is shown here:

Family	Fonts
\froman	Times New Roman, Palatino
\fswiss	Arial
\fmodern	Courier New, Pica
\fscript	Cursive
\fdecor	Old English

For example, the following declares font 0 to be **\fswiss Arial**:

```
{\fonttbl {\f0\fswiss Arial;}}
```

\footnote

The **\footnote** statement is one of the most important RTF commands when creating a help file. The reason for this is that it is used to specify topic names, context IDs, and browse sequences. The following forms of the **\footnote** command are used in this chapter:

$\{\footnote *string*\}

K\{\footnote *string*\}

#\{\footnote *string*\}

+\{\footnote *sequence-name:sequence-order*\}

@\{\footnote *string*\}

The **$** form defines a title for a topic that is displayed in the history window of the help system. The title can include spaces. A topic title identifies the topic.

The **K** form specifies that *string* is a keyword or phrase and can include spaces. Keywords are displayed as index entries. If the first character of the string is a K, then it must be preceded by an extra space. The **K** form can only be used if a topic title has been specified.

The **#** form defines a *context ID* that is used to create links and cross-references between topics. It is also used by your application program to access portions

16

of the help file. In this form, *string* may not include spaces. As you will see, the context ID string is usually a macro that represents the ID value.

The **+** form defines a *browse sequence*. A browse sequence determines the linkage between topics when the browse arrows are pressed. (The browse arrows are the **<<** and **>>** arrow buttons on the Help window's button bar.) In this form, the content of *sequence-name* specifies the sequence and *sequence-order* determines the position of the topic in the browse sequence. Browse sequences are performed in alphabetical order or numerical order based upon the values of *sequence-order*. A help file may have one or more browse sequences. To define several sequences, both the *sequence-name* and *sequence-order* specifiers in the **\footnote** command are required. If your help file has only one browse sequence, then the *sequence-name* is not required. Examples of browse sequences are contained in the example help file shown later.

To cause browse buttons to be included in the standard help window, you must include the **BrowseButtons( )** macro in the configuration section of the project file associated with a help file that defines a browse sequence.

The **@** form of the **\footnote** command is used to embed a comment.

\i

The **\i** command turns on italics. **\i0** turns them off. However, if the **\i** command is used within a block, then only the text within that block is italicized, and there is no need to use the **\i0** command.

\page

The **\page** command signals the end of a topic.

\par

The **\par** command marks the end of a paragraph. It also causes a line to be skipped. Thus two **\par** commands in a row will skip two lines.

\rtfn

The **\rtfn** command determines which RTF specification is being used. In this chapter, version 1 is used.

\tab

The **\tab** command advances one tab stop.

\uldb

To mark a *hot spot* link, specify it using the **\uldb** command. It has the following general form:

> \uldb *text*

The *text* will be shown in the standard hot spot color and font. This command is always used in conjunction with a **\v** command.

\v

The **\v** command specifies a link to another topic. It has the following general form:

> \v *context-ID*

Here, *context-ID* must match one specified in a **#\footnote** statement. This link is executed when the hot spot associated with the **\v** command is clicked by the user.

A Sample Help File

The following help file will be used by the example program shown later in this chapter. This file contains all the common components of a help file. Call this file HELPTEST.RTF. Keep in mind that this sample help file is for demonstration purposes only. A real help file would need to contain substantially better help information!

```
{\rtf1\ansi
{\fonttbl{\f0\fswiss Arial;} {\f1\fdecor Old English;}}
\fs40
\f1
@{\footnote This is a comment.  So is the following.}
@{\footnote This is a Sample Help File.}
${\footnote Contents}
Contents of Sample Help File
\f0
\fs20
\par
\par
\tab{\uldb Main Window \v MainWindow}
\par
\tab{\uldb Push Button 1 \v PushButton1}
\par
```

16

```
\tab{\uldb Push Button 2 \v PushButton2}
\par
\tab{\uldb Push Button 3 \v PushButton3}
\par
\tab{\uldb List Box \v ListBox}
\par
\tab{\uldb Check Box \v CheckBox}
\par
\par
\f1
\fs30
Select a Topic.
\fs20
\f0
\page
#{\footnote PushButton1}
${\footnote Push Button 1}
K{\footnote Push Button 1}
+{\footnote Push:A}
{\fs24\b Push Button One}
\par
\par
This is help for the first push button.
\par
\par
See also {\uldb Push Button 2 \v PushButton2}
\page
#{\footnote IDH_PB1}
This is the popup for the first push button.
\page
#{\footnote PushButton2}
${\footnote Push Button 2}
K{\footnote Push Button 2}
+{\footnote Push:B}
{\fs24\b Push Button Two}
\par
\par
This is help for the second push button.
\par
\par
See Also {\uldb Push Button 3 \v PushButton3}
\page
#{\footnote IDH_PB2}
This is the popup for the second push button.
\page
```

```
#{\footnote PushButton3}
${\footnote Push Button 3}
K{\footnote Push Button 3}
+{\footnote Push:C}
{\fs24\b Push Button Three}
\par
\par
This is help for the third push button.
\par
\par
See Also {\uldb Push Button 1 \v PushButton1}
\page
#{\footnote IDH_PB3}
This is the popup for the third push button.
\page
#{\footnote MainWindow}
${\footnote Main Window}
K{\footnote Main Window}
{\fs24\b Main Window}
\par
\par
This is the main program window.
\page
#{\footnote IDH_MAIN}
This is the Main Window popup help message.
\page
#{\footnote IDH_DLG}
This is a dialog box.
\page
#{\footnote ListBox}
${\footnote List Box}
K{\footnote List Box}
+{\footnote BOX:A}
{\fs24\b List Box}
\par
\par
This is help for the list box.
\page
#{\footnote IDH_LB1}
This is the popup for the list box.
\page
#{\footnote CheckBox}
${\footnote Check Box}
K{\footnote Check Box}
+{\footnote BOX:B}
{\fs24\b Check Box}
```

16

```
\par
\par
This is help for the check boxes.
\page
#{\footnote IDH_CB1}
This is the popup for the check boxes.
\page
}
```

In this file, the **#\footnote** commands whose IDs begin with **IDH** are the entry points for the context-sensitive, pop-up help. The other **#\footnote** commands define links used to support reference help in the standard Help window.

After you have entered this file, you must compile it using the help compiler. This file will be used by the example program. However, before you compile the file, you must define the following MAP statements within the configuration section of the project file associated with HELPTEST.RTF:

IDH_PB1	700
IDH_PB2	701
IDH_PB3	702
IDH_LB1	703
IDH_CB1	704
IDH_MAIN	705
IDH_DLG	706

As you will soon see, these values will be used to support context-sensitive, pop-up help windows.

The easiest way to define the MAP values is to include a map file in your help project. Map files use the following format to map values to identifiers:

```
identifier1      value1
identifier2      value2
identifier3      value3
    .
    .
    .
identifierN      valueN
```

For example, here is the map file that you can use for the sample help file:

```
IDH_PB1     700
IDH_PB2     701
IDH_PB3     702
IDH_LB1     703
IDH_CB1     704
IDH_MAIN    705
IDH_DLG     706
```

You must also activate the browse buttons in the standard help window by including the **BrowseButtons( )** macro in the configuration section of your project file. Finally, if you want to give your help windows a title, you can specify one in the Options dialog box of the help compiler. If you don't specify a title, then the default title Windows Help will be used. The title used in the examples is Sample Help File.

NOTE: If you are using Visual C++, then the preceding steps can be most easily accomplished using the Help Workshop.

When you compile this help file, call the output file HELPTEST.HLP. This file will need to be in the same directory as the executable version of the example help program shown later in this chapter.

IN DEPTH

Help Macros

The **BrowseButtons( )** macro is just one of many macros supported by the Windows help system. Here are a few more:

Macro	Meaning
Annotate( )	Shows the Annotation box.
Back( )	Moves to the previous topic.
DisableButton(*ButtonID*)	Disables the standard help button specified by *ButtonID*.

16

Macro	Meaning
EnableButton(*ButtonID*)	Enables the standard help button specified by *ButtonID*.
Exit( )	Terminates the help system.
GotoMark(*mark*)	Jumps to the marker previously set by **SaveMark( )**.
History( )	Shows the history list.
Next( )	Advances to the next topic in a browse sequence. Must be executed from within a valid browse sequence.
Prev( )	Returns to the previous topic in a browse sequence. Must be executed from within a valid browse sequence.
Print( )	Prints the current topic.
SaveMark(*mark*)	Saves the current help file position in the marker specified by *mark*.

Help macros can be executed in a variety of ways. Some, such as **BrowseButtons( )**, are specified within the help project file. Others can be executed from within the help file itself. To execute a macro from within a help file, use this form of the **\footnote** RTF command:

!{\footnote *macro*( )}

Here, *macro* is the name of the macro that you wish to execute. For example, this command activates the previous topic in a browse sequence:

```
!{\footnote Prev()}
```

As you write more sophisticated help files, you will make use of several help macros because they expand your control over how the help information is presented to the user. You should spend some time exploring the help macros on your own.

A Brief Word about Help Context IDs

Before continuing, a short discussion of help context IDs is in order. As mentioned in the preceding section, a context ID is a value that is linked to a specific part of a help file. Context IDs can be defined for various Windows entities including menus, dialog boxes, and windows. You can think of a help context ID as being similar to a control or menu's command ID. It is used to identify the control relative to the help system.

MFC defines certain standard ranges for help context IDs. For example, IDs in the range 0x10000 through 0x1FFFF are reserved for menus and push buttons. The range 0x20000 through 0x2FFFF is reserved for windows and dialog boxes. The range 0 through 0xFFFF is reserved for user-defined IDs. The standard ranges should be used if your program will not be taking full control of the Help system, relying instead upon its default operation. However, from a practical point of view, you will seldom do this since users have come to expect a higher level of sophistication than can be achieved from the default operation. For these reasons, the help example in this chapter defines its own context IDs for all interface elements.

How Help Is Implemented in an MFC Program

The help system is easy to implement when using MFC. The general procedure is outlined here:

1. Add the help message handlers to your application's message map.
2. Handle **WM_CONTEXTMENU** and **WM_HELP** messages.
3. Where necessary, handle **WM_COMMANDHELP** messages.
4. Implement a Help menu item in your application's main menu bar.
5. Call **WinHelp( )** as needed.

In the following sections, you will see what each of these steps implies. Since **WinHelp( )** is at the core of the help system, let's begin there.

Using the WinHelp( ) API Function

At the time of this writing, there are some help features (especially pop-up context-sensitive help) for which it is easier to call the **WinHelp( )** API function than it is to use the **CWinApp::WinHelp( )** member function. The reason for this is that the API version gives you a little finer control over how the help system is activated. Its prototype is shown here:

BOOL WinHelp(HWND *hwnd*, LPCSTR *lpszFilename*, UINT *Command*, DWORD *dwInfo*);

Here, *hwnd* is the handle of the invoking window. This handle is easily obtained: it is found in the **m_hWnd** member of **CWnd**.

The name of the help file being activated is specified in *lpszFilename*, which may include a drive and path specifier. It is an easy matter to obtain the path to and name of the help file. When your MFC application begins, the **m_pszHelpFilePath** member of **CWinApp** will point to the path and filename of the help file associated with your application. By default, this will be the name of your application followed by the .HLP extension. However, you can set this pointer to any string you like, so your application can explicitly specify the name of the help file, if desired.

Precisely what action the **WinHelp( )** function takes is determined by *Command*. The valid values for *Command* are shown here:

Command	Purpose
HELP_COMMAND	Executes a help macro.
HELP_CONTENTS	Obsolete, use HELP_FINDER instead.
HELP_CONTEXT	Displays a specified topic.
HELP_CONTEXTMENU	Displays context-sensitive help. This includes a "What's This?" menu.
HELP_CONTEXTPOPUP	Displays context-sensitive help.
HELP_FINDER	Displays the standard Help Topics window.
HELP_FORCEFILE	Forces correct file to be displayed.
HELP_HELPONHELP	Displays help information on Help.
HELP_INDEX	Obsolete, use HELP_FINDER instead.
HELP_KEY	Displays a specific topic given its keyword.
HELP_MULTIKEY	Displays a specific topic given its alternative keyword.

Command	Purpose
HELP_PARTIALKEY	Displays a specific topic given a partial keyword.
HELP_QUIT	Closes the help window.
HELP_SETCONTENTS	Sets the contents topic.
HELP_SETINDEX	Specifies a secondary keyword index.
HELP_SETPOPUP_POS	Specifies the position of the next pop-up window displayed by the help system.
HELP_SETWINPOS	Determines the size and position of the help window and displays it, if necessary.
HELP_TCARD	This command is ORed with other commands for training card help.
HELP_WM_HELP	Displays context-sensitive help.

Some commands require additional information. When this is the case, the additional information is passed in *dwInfo*. The value of *dwInfo* for each Command is shown here:

Command	Meaning of *dwInfo*
HELP_COMMAND	Pointer to string that contains macro.
HELP_CONTENTS	Not used; set to zero.
HELP_CONTEXT	Context ID of topic.
HELP_CONTEXTMENU	See text.
HELP_CONTEXTPOPUP	Context ID of topic.
HELP_FINDER	Not used; set to zero.
HELP_FORCEFILE	Not used; set to zero.
HELP_HELPONHELP	Not used; set to zero.
HELP_INDEX	Not used; set to zero.
HELP_KEY	Pointer to string that contains the keyword.
HELP_MULTIKEY	Pointer to MULTIKEYHELP structure.
HELP_PARTIALKEY	Pointer to string containing partial keyword.

Command	Meaning of *dwInfo*
HELP_QUIT	Not used; set to zero.
HELP_SETCONTENTS	Context ID of topic.
HELP_SETINDEX	Context ID for index.
HELP_SETPOPUP_POS	Pointer to a POINTS structure.
HELP_SETWINPOS	Pointer to a HELPWININFO structure.
HELP_WM_HELP	See text.

For the **HELP_WM_HELP** and **HELP_CONTEXTMENU** commands, the meaning of *dwInfo* is a little more detailed than it is for the other commands. For these two commands, *dwInfo* is a pointer to an array of **DWORD** values. These values are organized into pairs. The first value specifies the ID of a control (such as a push button, edit box, etc.). The second value specifies the context ID of the help information linked to that control. This array must end with two zero values. These two commands are used to support context-sensitive help and to help process **WM_COMMANDHELP**, **WM_HELP**, and **WM_CONTEXTMENU** messages, which are described later.

Using CWinApp::WinHelp( )

While you are free to use the API version of **WinHelp( )** when required, most of the time you can more easily use the version defined by **CWinApp**. Its prototype is shown here:

virtual void CWinApp::WinHelp(DWORD *dwInfo*,
                                       UINT *Command* = HELP_CONTEXT);

Here, *dwInfo* and *Command* have the same meaning as their corresponding parameters in the API version of **WinHelp( )** just described.

This version of **WinHelp( )** automatically looks for the help file specified by **m_pszHelpFilePath**.

Enabling Help

To enable an MFC program to respond to help requests, you must add the following statements to your program's message map:

```
ON_COMMAND(ID_HELP, OnHelp)
ON_COMMAND(ID_HELP_FINDER, OnHelpFinder)
```

```
ON_COMMAND(ID_HELP_INDEX, OnHelpIndex)
ON_COMMAND(ID_HELP_USING, OnHelpUsing)
```

In some circumstances, you may also want to add

```
ON_COMMAND(ID_CONTEXT_HELP, OnContextHelp)
```

The functions **OnHelp( )**, **OnHelpFinder( )**, **OnHelpIndex( )**,
OnHelpUsing( ), and **OnContextHelp( )** are members of **CWinApp**.
When called, they automatically invoke **WinHelp( )**, as shown here:

Function	Action
CWinApp::OnHelp( )	Invokes **WinHelp( )** using current help context.
CWinApp::OnHelpFinder( )	Invokes **WinHelp( )** using HELP_FINDER.
CWinApp::OnHelpIndex( )	Invokes **WinHelp( )** using HELP_INDEX.
CWinApp::OnHelpUsing( )	Invokes **WinHelp( )** using HELP_HELPONHELP.
CWinApp:OnContextHelp( )	Invokes **WinHelp( )** using the current help context. The mouse cursor becomes an arrow/question mark combination. The help context is determined by the item under the cursor.

The IDs specified in the message map for these functions are defined by MFC.
Although you can use whatever IDs you like, these are the values that most
other MFC programmers will employ.

Your program will not execute calls to these functions. Placing them in your
program's message map simply enables MFC to call them as needed. Further,
versions of the handlers **OnHelpFinder( )**, **OnHelpIndex( )**, and
OnHelpUsing( ) provided by MFC are sufficient for most applications.
However, you will often need to override **OnHelp( )** and **OnContextHelp( )**
in order to provide detailed control over the help system.

Since the help functions are members of **CWinApp**, the best place to put
the help message macros is in the message map defined for your program's
main application class. This is the class derived from **CWinApp**. None of
the programs in this book have declared a message map for a program's
application class because it was not needed before now. However, it will be
used when implementing help features.

16

Handling the Help Messages

As mentioned at the beginning of this chapter, there are two broad categories of help: reference and context-sensitive. In a correctly written Windows program, the user can activate reference help (that is, activate the standard Help window) by selecting Help from a menu or, in some situations, by pressing F1. Context-sensitive help is activated by right-clicking on a control or window, by using the **?** button, or in some situations, by pressing F1. (The distinction between the two uses of F1 is discussed in the following section.)

Since your program must respond differently to different types of help requests, there must be some way to tell them apart. And there is. When F1 is pressed or when the **?** button is used, two messages are sent to the active window: **WM_COMMANDHELP** and **WM_HELP**. When the user right-clicks on a window or control, a **WM_CONTEXTMENU** message is sent to the window that contains the control. The proper processing of these three messages is crucial to the correct implementation of online help. All three messages will be examined here.

Responding to WM_COMMANDHELP

While MFC provides a minimal amount of help request handling, for some help responses you will want to write your own help handling code. To do this you will need to process the **WM_COMMANDHELP** message. This is a private message defined by MFC. To gain access to this message, you must perform the following actions. First, you must include AFXPRIV.H and AFXEXT.H. Next, include

```
ON_MESSAGE(WM_COMMANDHELP, OnCommandHelp)
```

in the message map of any window that will process the message. Finally, you must override its handler, **OnCommandHelp( )**, which is shown here:

```
afx_msg LRESULT CWnd::OnCommandHelp(WPARAM wParam,
                                    LPARAM lParam);
```

Here, *wParam* is unused. *lParam* will contain the current help context ID. This handler must return nonzero to stop further processing of the **WM_COMMANDHELP** message. That is, it must return nonzero if it handles the command. If it returns zero, the message will be passed to higher level windows.

As you will see, providing your own **OnCommandHelp( )** handler allows detailed, context-sensitive help to be easily implemented.

Responding to WM_CONTEXTMENU Messages

Each time the user presses the right mouse button, your program receives a **WM_CONTEXTMENU** command. The message handler for this message is **OnContextMenu( )**, and its prototype is shown here:

    afx_msg void CWnd::OnContextMenu(CWnd *Owner, CPoint Loc);

Here, *Owner* will point to the window in which the mouse was clicked. *Loc* contains the coordinates of the mouse when the right click occurred. To respond to a **WM_CONTEXTMENU** message, your program must invoke **::WinHelp( )** using the **m_hWnd** member of the object pointed to by *Owner* as the window handle (i.e., the first parameter to **::WinHelp( )**). It must specify **HELP_CONTEXTMENU** as the command parameter and the address of the array of IDs as the extra parameter. You will see an example of this command in the example program.

NOTE: **WM_CONTEXTMENU** is not supported by Windows 3.1.

Processing WM_HELP Messages

Each time the user presses the F1 key or uses the **?** button, your program receives a **WM_HELP** message. This message is handled by the **OnHelpInfo( )** function, shown here:

    afx_msg BOOL CWnd::OnHelpInfo(HELPINFO *HelpInfo);

HelpInfo points to a **HELPINFO** structure that contains information about the object for which the user is requesting help. Your program is free to override this handler. If it does so, it must return nonzero if it handles the message. One other point: the message map entry for **OnHelpInfo( )** is called **ON_WM_HELPINFO**.

The **HELPINFO** structure is defined like this:

16

```
typedef struct tagHELPINFO
{
  UINT cbSize;
  int iContextType;
  int iCtrlId;
  HANDLE hItemHandle;
  DWORD dwContextId;
  POINT MousePos;
} HELPINFO;
```

Here, **cbSize** contains the size of the **HELPINFO** structure.

iContextType specifies the type of object for which help is being requested. If it is for a menu item, it will contain **HELPINFO_MENUITEM**. If it is for a window or control, it will contain **HELPINFO_WINDOW**. **iCtrlId** contains the ID of the control, window, or menu item.

hItemHandle specifies the handle of the control, window, or menu. **dwContextId** contains the context ID for the window or control. **MousePos** contains the current mouse position.

If your program overrides **OnHelpInfo( )**, it will usually respond by displaying a pop-up window containing context-sensitive help. To do this, your program must invoke **::WinHelp( )** using the contents of **hItemHandle** as the window handle (i.e., the first parameter to **::WinHelp( )**). You must specify **HELP_WM_HELP** as the command parameter and the address of the array of IDs as the extra parameter. (You will see an example of this in the example program.) Invoking **::WinHelp( )** in this fashion causes it to search the array for the control ID that matches the control specified in **hItemHandle**. It then uses the corresponding context ID to obtain context-sensitive help. It displays this help in a pop-up window. It does not activate the standard help window.

Although most often your program will respond to a **WM_HELP** message by displaying context-sensitive help, this will not always be the case. As mentioned earlier, pressing F1 may be used to invoke either reference help or context-sensitive help. Here is the distinction between the two uses: When the main window has input focus (and no child window or menu is selected), then pressing F1 activates the standard Help window and displays reference help. However, pressing F1 when a control, menu, or child window is active causes context-sensitive help to be displayed. The theory behind these two uses is this: when the user presses F1 from the topmost level, the user is desiring help about the entire program, not a part of it. When responding to this situation, you will invoke the full help system. However, when a control (or other child window) is active when F1 is pressed, the user desires help about that specific item and context-sensitive help is warranted.

Since F1 may be used to activate either reference help or context-sensitive help, you might be wondering how your program will tell the two types of requests apart. That is, pressing F1 causes a **WM_HELP** to be sent no matter what type of help is being requested. The answer is quite simple: if the handle contained in **hItemHandle** is that of the main window, display reference help; otherwise, invoke context-sensitive help as described above.

Implementing the Help Menu

For most applications, you should implement a complete help menu bar option. It should allow the user to activate the help system so that it displays the following:

◆ Contents of the help file.

◆ Index of the help file.

◆ Help on Help.

You should also include an About box that describes your program. Precisely how you achieve these goals and what you name your menu entries is up to you.

Including the ? Button

As mentioned, one way to activate context-sensitive help is through the **?** button. To include the **?** button in a window you must include the extended style **WS_EX_CONTEXTHELP**. Since this is an extended style feature, you must create the window using **CWnd::CreateEx( )** rather than **CWnd::Create( )**. To display the **?** button in a dialog box, include the **DS_CONTEXTHELP** style.

A Help Demonstration Program

Now that you have learned about the various pieces and techniques involved in creating online help, it is time to put them to use. The following program demonstrates both reference help and context-sensitive help. It uses the help file shown earlier and illustrates various ways the file can be accessed using both **::WinHelp( )** and **CWinApp::WinHelp( )**. The program implements a full Help menu option on the menu bar that allows the user to activate Help On Help, the contents of the help file, or the help file index. An About box is also included. Sample output is shown in Figure 16-3.

16

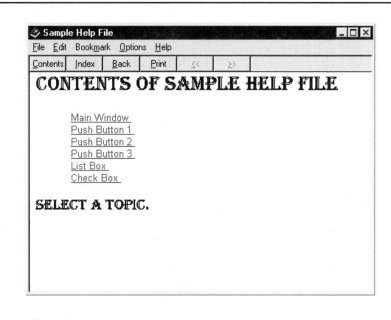

Sample output
from the help
demonstration
program

Figure 16-3.

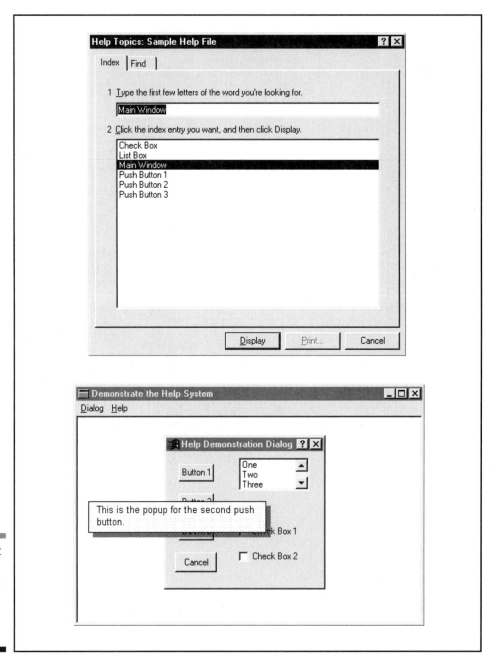

Sample output
from the help
demonstration
program
(*continued*)

Figure 16-3.

The program uses the following resource file. Notice that this file uses the extended version of the **DIALOG** statement: **DIALOGEX**. **DIALOGEX** allows a help context specifier to be included in the definition of the dialog box.

```
// HELPTEST.RC

// Demonstrate the Help system.
#include <afxres.h>
#include "ids.h"

HelpMenu MENU
{
  POPUP "&Dialog"
  {
    MENUITEM "&Dialog\tF2", IDM_DIALOG
    MENUITEM "&Exit\tF3", IDM_EXIT
  }
  POPUP "&Help"
  {
    MENUITEM "&Help Topics\tF4", ID_HELP_INDEX
    MENUITEM "&Using Help\tF5", ID_HELP_USING
    MENUITEM "Help &Finder\tF6", ID_HELP_FINDER
    MENUITEM "&About\tF7", IDM_ABOUTTHIS
  }
}


HelpTest MENU
{
  MENUITEM "&Dialog", IDM_DIALOG
  MENUITEM "&Exit", IDM_EXIT
}


HelpMenu ACCELERATORS
{
  VK_F1, ID_HELP, VIRTKEY
  VK_F2, IDM_DIALOG, VIRTKEY
  VK_F3, IDM_EXIT, VIRTKEY
  VK_F4, ID_HELP_INDEX, VIRTKEY
  VK_F5, ID_HELP_USING, VIRTKEY
  VK_F6, ID_HELP_FINDER, VIRTKEY
  VK_F7, IDM_ABOUTTHIS, VIRTKEY
}
```

```
HelpDialog DIALOGEX 10, 10, 142, 110, IDH_DLG
CAPTION "Help Demonstration Dialog"
STYLE WS_POPUP | WS_SYSMENU | WS_VISIBLE | DS_CONTEXTHELP
{
  DEFPUSHBUTTON "Button 1", IDD_PB1, 11, 10, 32, 14,
               WS_CHILD | WS_VISIBLE | WS_TABSTOP
  PUSHBUTTON "Button 2", IDD_PB2, 11, 34, 32, 14,
               WS_CHILD | WS_VISIBLE | WS_TABSTOP
  PUSHBUTTON "Button 3", IDD_PB3, 11, 58, 32, 14,
               WS_CHILD | WS_VISIBLE | WS_TABSTOP
  PUSHBUTTON "Cancel", IDCANCEL, 8, 82, 38, 16,
               WS_CHILD | WS_VISIBLE | WS_TABSTOP
  AUTOCHECKBOX "Check Box 1", IDD_CB1, 66, 50, 60, 30,
               WS_CHILD | WS_VISIBLE | WS_TABSTOP
  AUTOCHECKBOX "Check Box 2", IDD_CB2, 66, 70, 60, 30,
               WS_CHILD | WS_VISIBLE | WS_TABSTOP
  LISTBOX IDD_LB1, 66, 5, 63, 33, LBS_NOTIFY |
               WS_VISIBLE | WS_BORDER | WS_VSCROLL | WS_TABSTOP
}
```

The header file IDS.H is shown here:

```
// IDS.H

#define IDM_DIALOG    100
#define IDM_EXIT      101
#define IDM_ABOUTTHIS 102

#define IDD_PB1       200
#define IDD_PB2       201
#define IDD_PB3       202
#define IDD_LB1       203
#define IDD_CB1       205
#define IDD_CB2       206

#define IDH_PB1       700
#define IDH_PB2       701
#define IDH_PB3       702
#define IDH_LB1       703
#define IDH_CB1       704
#define IDH_MAIN      705
#define IDH_DLG       706
```

The class derivation file, called HELPTEST.H, is shown here:

```
// HELPTEST.H

// This is the main window class.
class CMainWin : public CFrameWnd
{
public:
  CMainWin();

  afx_msg LRESULT OnCommandHelp(WPARAM, LPARAM);

  // define menu handlers
  afx_msg void OnDialog();
  afx_msg void OnExit();
  afx_msg void OnAboutThis();

  DECLARE_MESSAGE_MAP()
};

// This is the application class.
class CApp : public CWinApp
{
public:
  BOOL InitInstance();

  DECLARE_MESSAGE_MAP()
};

// This is a dialog class
class CSampleDialog : public CDialog
{
public:
  CSampleDialog(char *DialogName, CWnd *Owner) :
    CDialog(DialogName, Owner) {}

  BOOL OnInitDialog();

  afx_msg BOOL OnHelpInfo(HELPINFO *p);
  afx_msg LRESULT OnCommandHelp(WPARAM, LPARAM);
  afx_msg void OnContextMenu(CWnd *Owner, CPoint Loc);

  DECLARE_MESSAGE_MAP()
};
```

The help demonstration program file is shown next. You should call this file HELPTEST.CPP so that its object file is called HELPTEST.EXE. This way, it will automatically use the help file you created earlier, which is called HELPTEST.HLP. When you run the program, make sure that HELPTEST.HLP is in the same directory as HELPTEST.EXE.

```
// Demonstrate the Help System.  Call this program HELPTEST.CPP

#include <afxwin.h>
#include <afxext.h>
#include <afxpriv.h>
#include <string.h>
#include "helptest.h"
#include "ids.h"

DWORD HelpArray[] = {
  IDD_PB1, IDH_PB1,
  IDD_PB2, IDH_PB2,
  IDD_PB3, IDH_PB3,
  IDD_LB1, IDH_LB1,
  IDD_CB1, IDH_CB1, // Here, both check boxes are
  IDD_CB2, IDH_CB1, // mapped to the same context ID.
  0, 0
};

CApp App; // instantiate the application

CMainWin::CMainWin()
{
  Create(NULL, "Demonstrate the Help System",
         WS_OVERLAPPEDWINDOW, rectDefault,
         NULL, "HelpMenu");

  // Load accelerator table.
  if(!LoadAccelTable("HelpMenu"))
    MessageBox("Cannot Load Accelerators", "Error");

}

// Initialize the application.
BOOL CApp::InitInstance()
{
  m_pMainWnd = new CMainWin;
  m_pMainWnd->ShowWindow(m_nCmdShow);
```

```
  m_pMainWnd->UpdateWindow();

  return TRUE;
}

// This is the application's message map.
BEGIN_MESSAGE_MAP(CMainWin, CFrameWnd)
  ON_MESSAGE(WM_COMMANDHELP, OnCommandHelp)
  ON_COMMAND(IDM_DIALOG, OnDialog)
  ON_COMMAND(IDM_EXIT, OnExit)
  ON_COMMAND(IDM_ABOUTTHIS, OnAboutThis)
END_MESSAGE_MAP()

// This is the CApp's message map.
BEGIN_MESSAGE_MAP(CApp, CWinApp)
  ON_COMMAND(ID_HELP, OnHelp)
  ON_COMMAND(ID_HELP_FINDER, OnHelpFinder)
  ON_COMMAND(ID_HELP_INDEX, OnHelpIndex)
  ON_COMMAND(ID_HELP_USING, OnHelpUsing)
END_MESSAGE_MAP()

// Process IDM_DIALOG.
afx_msg void CMainWin::OnDialog()
{
  CSampleDialog diagOb("HelpDialog", this);

  diagOb.DoModal(); // activate modal dialog box
}

// Process IDM_EXIT.
afx_msg void CMainWin::OnExit()
{
  int response;

  response = MessageBox("Quit the Program?",
                        "Exit", MB_YESNO);

  if(response == IDYES)
    SendMessage(WM_CLOSE); // terminate app
}

// Process IDM_ABOUTTHIS.
afx_msg void CMainWin::OnAboutThis()
{
```

```
  MessageBox("Help System Demo V1.0", "About");
}

// This is SampleDialog's message map.
BEGIN_MESSAGE_MAP(CSampleDialog, CDialog)
  ON_WM_CONTEXTMENU()
  ON_WM_HELPINFO()
END_MESSAGE_MAP()

// Initialize the dialog box.
BOOL CSampleDialog::OnInitDialog()
{
  CDialog::OnInitDialog(); // Call base class version

  CListBox *lbptr = (CListBox *) GetDlgItem(IDD_LB1);

  // initialize the list box
  lbptr->AddString("One");
  lbptr->AddString("Two");
  lbptr->AddString("Three");
  lbptr->AddString("Four");
  lbptr->AddString("Five");
  lbptr->AddString("Six");

  return TRUE;
}

// Process a right-click help request for dialog box.
afx_msg void CSampleDialog::OnContextMenu(CWnd *Owner, CPoint Loc)
{
  ::WinHelp(Owner->m_hWnd, App.m_pszHelpFilePath,
            HELP_CONTEXTMENU, (DWORD)HelpArray);
}

// Process an F1 or ? button help request for dialog box.
afx_msg BOOL CSampleDialog::OnHelpInfo(HELPINFO *ObPtr)
{
  // if user clicks on dialog box
  if((HWND) ObPtr->hItemHandle == m_hWnd)
    ::WinHelp((HWND) ObPtr->hItemHandle, App.m_pszHelpFilePath,
              HELP_CONTEXTPOPUP, IDH_DLG);
  else // if user clicks on control
    ::WinHelp((HWND) ObPtr->hItemHandle, App.m_pszHelpFilePath,
              HELP_WM_HELP, (DWORD)HelpArray);
```

16

```
    return 1;
}

// Handle F1 help request for main window.
afx_msg LRESULT CMainWin::OnCommandHelp(
                    WPARAM wParam, LPARAM lParam)
{
    App.WinHelp((DWORD) "Main Window", HELP_KEY);

    return 1;
}
```

A Closer Look at the Help Demonstration Program

Most of the help program should be clear. However, a few points warrant specific attention. First, consider the declaration of **HelpArray**. This is the array that maps control IDs to context IDs. In the IDS.H header file, the **IDH_** macros are given the same values that you defined in the HELPTEST.PRJ file when you created the help file. Notice that both check boxes map onto the same context ID. This is perfectly valid. If the same pop-up help message will be displayed for two or more controls, there is no reason to create duplicate messages.

A second point of interest is the way **OnHelpInfo( )** processes help requests. If the handle of the object is the dialog box itself, then the pop-up help window for the dialog box is displayed. Otherwise, **::WinHelp( )** is called using the **HELP_WM_HELP** option. This causes information about the requested control to be displayed.

Third, notice how **CWinApp::WinHelp( )** is invoked for the main window. It uses the keyword search mechanism to find information about the main window.

Experimenting with Help

One of the first things you will want to try is calling **WinHelp( )** using different options and observing the results. This is one of the best ways to fully understand the capabilities of the Windows Help system. Another thing to try is adding context-sensitive help to menu selections.

An exciting, newer help feature is the *training card*. Training cards are used to provide "how to" instructions to the user. For example, a word processing program might use training cards to explain, step by step, how to format a paragraph or print a document. Although training cards require some extra effort, the results are worth it.

One last point: there is no question that online, context-sensitive help will become an increasingly important part of any Windows application. It is better to build support for help into your program from the start rather than adding it later.

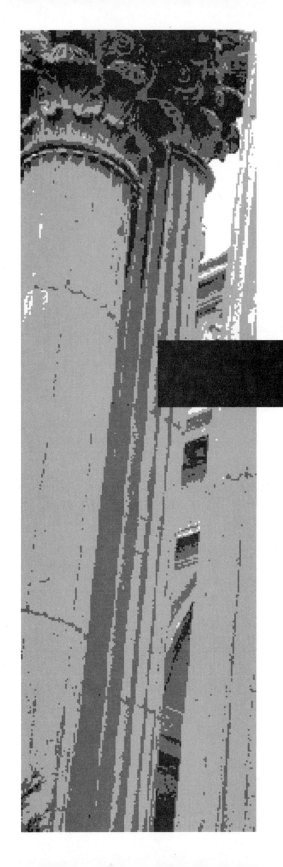

CHAPTER 17

Creating
Document/View
Applications

The preceding chapters have demonstrated the various features of MFC and Windows programming using a straightforward, easy-to-understand application skeleton. While there is certainly nothing wrong with writing programs that use that organization, there is an alternative way to organize an MFC program called the *document/view architecture* that offers many advantages. Also, if you use Visual C++'s AppWizard to generate the skeletal code for your application, then you will need to understand the document/view mechanism because it is the way the AppWizard normally structures its programs. (See Chapter 19 for an overview of the AppWizard.) Fortunately, programs that use the document/view architecture are only a bit more complex than those that do not.

In this chapter, you will learn the general theory behind the document/view model and develop a simple document/view sample application. You will also learn about another of MFC's stand-alone classes: **CArchive**. As you will see, **CArchive** provides an easy means of saving documents to disk. We will start with an overview of the document/view architecture.

The Document/View Architecture

Let's begin with some history. Prior to MFC version 2.0, all MFC programs were written using the approach found in the preceding chapters. As you know, this way of writing MFC programs creates two elemental objects: an application object and a window object. For the sake of discussion, the architecture used by this approach will be called *application/window*. A program written using the application/window approach mirrors the way that traditional, non-MFC Windows programs are written. In fact, the main difference between the two is that MFC automates and masks many of the details that a non-MFC programmer must handle explicitly. However, in terms of the general architecture, the application/window model is nearly identical to the traditional Windows program.

While the use of MFC to create application/window programs offers significant benefits to programmers (as the preceding chapters have shown), it does not take full advantage of what a class-based Windows interface can provide. For example, in an application/window–based program, the data and the rendering of that data are intertwined. Most often, data members exist within the window class—and this is the class that also determines how

17

that data is displayed. However, this is not always desirable because differing views of the same data are frequently needed. For instance, you will often need to display data in a window and print it on a printer. The point here is that in a Windows program, data is conceptually separate from the rendering of that data. However, in an application/window architecture, these two attributes are mixed together in the same window class.

In a document/view program, things work differently. The data (i.e., document) is separated from the presentation (i.e., view) of that data. This is achieved by encapsulating the data within a document class and encapsulating the mechanism that displays that data within a view class. The view class also manages user input. In a way, the separation of document and view in the document/view architecture is similar to the way data and code are separated in a program. When you create a program that uses the document/view architecture, the document is derived from **CDocument**. The view is derived from **CView** (or a derivative of **CView**).

When you create a program that uses the document/view architecture, you will still need to create a frame window class and an application class. However, the role these two classes play is diminished. For example, while **CFrameWnd** will still form the basis for your application's frame window, this window is overlayed by the view created by **CView**.

Before moving on, let's take a closer look at the precise meaning of the terms *document* and *view*.

What Is a Document?

As mentioned in the preceding section, a *document* is the data associated with your program. It is important to understand that the term "document" refers to any and all forms of data. It is not limited to, say, a text file. For example, if your program operates on bit-stream data generated by an orbiting spy satellite, this still constitutes the document associated with your program. In formal terms, a document is a unit of data operated upon by your program.

It is possible to use the document/view architecture to create both a single document interface (SDI) or a multiple document interface (MDI). However, due to the simpler structure of SDI applications, they are the only type of application examined here.

What Is a View?

As mentioned, a *view* is a rendering of a document. Put differently, a view is a physical representation of the data. The mapping of a document to view is one to many. For example, if the document associated with an application is time and your program displays this time, then there are at least four different possible views: analog 12-hour, analog 24-hour, digital 12-hour, and digital 24-hour. Keep in mind that a view is not limited to only a screen presentation. Another view is defined when a document is printed. Thus, a document is pure data and a view is a concrete representation of that data.

Document/View Manages Document Storage

The document/view classes provided by MFC automate the storage of documents to disk files. In the language of document/view, this process is called *serialization*. (The meaning of the term "serialization" as it relates to the document/view architecture is completely separate from its meaning in the context of multithreaded synchronization as described in Chapter 14.) The concept behind serialization is persistence: The current state of an object (in this case, a document) should be able to be stored and then retrieved at a later date. In practical terms, this means that a document must be able to be stored to disk and loaded later. As you will soon see, the mechanism to achieve this is built into the **CDocument** class.

Serialization is important because it is a defining characteristic of the document/view architecture. Even if your program derives a document class from **CDocument** and a view class from **CView**, if it does not support object persistence, then it is not actually a document/view application.

Understanding Dynamic Creation

In a document/view program, objects are dynamic. That is, when a document/view program is run, its frame window, document, and view objects are created dynamically at run time. This is necessary because document/view objects need to be created when one is loaded from disk or newly formed. To enable this to happen, you must use the two macros shown here:

DECLARE_DYNCREATE(*class-name*)

IMPLEMENT_DYNCREATE(*class-name*, *parent-class-name*)

Here, *class-name* is the name of the class being enabled for dynamic creation, and *parent-class-name* is the name of its MFC base class.

17

DECLARE_DYNCREATE is used inside a class declaration to allow dynamic creation of the class. **IMPLEMENT_DYNCREATE** is specified in the class' implementation file. The combination of these two macros allows a class to be used as a parameter to the **RUNTIME_CLASS** macro, shown here:

RUNTIME_CLASS(*class-name*)

Here, *class-name* is the name of the run-time class that was specified in the **DECLARE_DYNCREATE** macro. **RUNTIME_CLASS** returns a pointer to a **CRuntimeClass** structure associated with the specified class. As you will soon see, this pointer is needed when a document template is created.

Creating a Document/View Framework

To create a document/view application, you will need to follow these steps:

1. Derive your own application, frame window, document, and view classes.
2. Enable dynamic creation of your frame window, document, and view classes.
3. Create a template that links together the frame window, document, and view classes.
4. Parse and process the command line.
5. Overload various member functions, such as **CObject::Serialize( )** and **CView::OnDraw( )**.

Let's look at each step now.

Deriving the Application and Frame Window Classes

You will derive the application and frame window classes in much the same way that you have been. However, your frame window will contain less functionality and your application will contain a little more (because it is used to support serialization). As before, the application class is derived from **CWinApp**. This class does not need to be enabled for dynamic creation.

The frame window class is derived from **CFrameWnd**. It must be enabled for dynamic creation, which means that it must include the **DECLARE_DYNCREATE** macro. This class will typically be used to encapsulate any controls tied directly to the frame, such as toolbars and status windows. Here is a skeletal class derived from **CFrameWnd** that includes the **DECLARE_DYNCREATE** macro:

```
class CMainWin : public CFrameWnd
{
  DECLARE_DYNCREATE(CMainWin)

  // additional private members, here

public:
  CMainWin();

  // additional public members, here

  DECLARE_MESSAGE_MAP()
};
```

DECLARE_DYNCREATE is private in this example. However, it could be protected, or even public, if that is what is required by your application.

Deriving the Document Class

Your document class is derived from **CDocument**. This class must be enabled for dynamic creation using **DECLARE_DYNCREATE**. Typically, this class will handle any commands that affect the document and provide message map entries to this effect. From a theoretical point of view, the document class will handle manipulations on the data that comprise the document. Therefore, it will process those commands that affect the data.

The **CDocument** class contains many member functions that your program may use as is or, in some cases, override. One that you will typically override is **OnNewDocument( )**. **OnNewDocument( )** is called when the user creates a new document. Its prototype is shown here:

    virtual BOOL CDocument::OnNewDocument( );

Your overridden version of this function must first call the **CDocument** version. The function must return nonzero if successful and zero on failure.

Another function that you will typically override in your document class is **Serialize( )**, which is a member function of **CObject**. This function will be described later.

Here is a skeletal document class:

```
// This is the document class.
class CSampleDoc : public CDocument
{
  DECLARE_DYNCREATE(CSampleDoc)

  // additional private members, here
public:
  CSampleDoc();

  BOOL OnNewDocument(); // reinitialize for each new document
  void Serialize(CArchive &arch); // store or retrieve data

  // additional public members, here

  DECLARE_MESSAGE_MAP()
};
```

Deriving the View Class

The view class controls the display of the document. The view window overlays the frame window and relies on the frame window for the basic window functions, such as resizing or minimizing. The view class is derived from **CView** or from one of the view classes derived from **CView**, such as **CScrollView** (which supports scrolling). Your view class must be specified as dynamic using **DECLARE_DYNCREATE**. Your view class typically handles user interaction that affects the view.

CView contains many member functions. Of these, your derived view class must override at least one: **OnDraw( )**. This function is called whenever the view needs to be updated. This can occur when the window needs to be reconstructed because it was just uncovered or because some aspect of the view has changed. **OnDraw( )** is conceptually similar to **OnPaint( )** in an application/window style program.

The **OnDraw( )** function has the following prototype:

virtual void CView::OnDraw(CDC *DC*) = 0;

As you can see, **OnDraw( )** is a pure virtual function. This means that it must be overridden by any derived class. *DC* is a pointer to the device context of the current view. This means that your program no longer needs to obtain the device context manually, as it does when overriding **OnPaint( )**.

Here is a skeletal view class:

```
class CSampleView : public CView
{
  DECLARE_DYNCREATE(CSampleView)

  // additional private members, here

public:
  void OnDraw(CDC *DC);

  // additional public members, here

  DECLARE_MESSAGE_MAP()
};
```

Enabling Dynamic Creation

Including **DECLARE_DYNCREATE** in your derived classes is only one of two steps needed to enable dynamic creation of your document/view classes. The other step is to include **IMPLEMENT_DYNCREATE** in your implementation file. For example, here are the macros that enable the dynamic creation of the preceding classes:

```
IMPLEMENT_DYNCREATE(CMainWin, CFrameWnd)
IMPLEMENT_DYNCREATE(CSampleView, CView)
IMPLEMENT_DYNCREATE(CSampleDoc, CDocument)
```

Now these classes can be used to create a document template, as described in the next section.

Creating a Document Template

Once you have derived your document, view, and frame window classes, you can use them to create a document template. This template links together the document, view, and frame window classes and allows them to work as a unit. You can create either multi-document templates or single-document templates, which are used for MDI and SDI applications, respectively. In this chapter we will only be using a single-document template.

A single-document template is an object of the **CSingleDocTemplate** class. The only member of this class that you will use is its constructor, which is shown here:

CSingleDocTemplate::CSingleDocTemplate(UINT *ID*,
                    CRuntimeClass **Document*,
                    CRuntimeClass **FrameWindow*,
                    CRuntimeClass **View*);

Here, *ID* is the identifier for the resources used by the template. These resources include the menu and accelerator table for the frame window, its icon, and a string resource that contains various items of data related to the program. *Document* is a pointer to the document class, *FrameWindow* is a pointer to the frame window class, and *View* is a pointer to the view class. These pointers are obtained using the **RUNTIME_CLASS** macro. Thus, *Document*, *FrameWindow*, and *View* must have been specified as dynamically creatable, as described earlier.

As just stated, the *ID* parameter identifies the various resources associated with the document. It also identifies a string resource that contains the following strings, in the order shown:

◆ The title of the window.

◆ The default document name. If not specified, the default name of "Untitled" is used.

◆ The name of the document type. (This is mostly for applications that support two or more different types of documents.)

◆ The name of the file filter shown in the "Files of type" drop-down list.

◆ The file filter extension, such as .TXT.

◆ The file type identifier for use in the system registry.

◆ The name of the document file type for use in the system registry.

These items are specified, in the order shown, as substrings within one string. Each substring is separated from the next using a newline character (\n). Substrings that are not needed are represented as empty substrings. An empty substring must still contain the newline character, however. Trailing empty substrings are not required.

Resource strings are specified in your resource file using the STRINGTABLE statement. It has this general form:

```
STRINGTABLE
{
    string-ID1, "string"
    string-ID2, "string"
    string-ID3, "string"
         .
         .
         .
    string-IDn, "string"
}
```

Here, *string-ID* is a value that identifies the string. For example, here is the string resource specification for the sample program shown later in this chapter:

```
STRINGTABLE
{
  IDR_FRAMEWIN, "Test App\n\n\nDoc Type (*.pnt)\n.pnt\nDVTest\nDV Test"
}
```

In this example, **IDR_FRAMEWIN** is the macro that identifies the string resource. "Test App" is the title of the window. There is no default document name. Thus, for new documents, the default "Untitled" name is displayed. The name of the document type is also empty. The entry in the "Files of type" drop-down list is "Doc Type (*.pnt)." The file extension used by the documents is .PNT. The name of the document type identifier for use in the system registry is "DVTest." "DV Test" is the name of the file type.

IN DEPTH

Using String Resources

17

As explained, strings used by your program can be treated as resources and stored in a string table within your application's resource file. One advantage of this scheme can be seen when a program defines several standard strings that are subject to change or translation. Using string resources allows these strings to be tailored for specific uses without actually modifying the program's source code.

There are a number of ways an MFC program can load a string resource. First, it can use the API function **LoadString( )**, shown here:

    int LoadString(HINSTANCE *hInst*, UINT *ID*, LPSTR *lpStr*, int *Size*);

Here, *hInst* is the instance handle of the application (found in **CWinApp::m_hInstance**), *ID* is the identifier of the string being loaded, *lpStr* is a pointer to an array that receives the string, and *Size* specifies the length of the array pointed to by *lpStr*. The string is null-terminated. The number of characters in the string is returned. Zero is returned on error.

You may also load a string using **CString::LoadString( )**, shown here:

    BOOL CString::LoadString(UINT *ID*);

Here, *ID* is the identifier of the string resource desired. It returns nonzero on success and zero on failure. **CString** is a string class defined by MFC, but it is not part of the **CObject** hierarchy. For the most part, a **CString** object can be used anywhere that you can use a null-terminated string because a conversion from **CString** to **char *** is defined. The advantage of using **CString::LoadString( )** over **::LoadString( )** is that you need specify only the ID of the string. The rest is handled automatically.

MFC provides two useful functions that allow you to tailor a string as it is loaded. They are called **AfxFormatString1( )** and **AfxFormatString2( )**. Their prototypes are shown here:

    void AfxFormatString1(CString &*cStr*, UINT *ID*, LPCSTR *lpStr*);
    void AfxFormatString2(CString &*cStr*, UINT *ID*, LPCSTR *lpStr1*,
                          LPCSTR *lpStr2*);

For both functions, *cStr* receives the resulting formatted string and *ID* is the ID of a resource string defined in your resource file. For **AfxFormatString1( )**, the resource string must contain a placeholder marked by a "%1" that will be substituted by the string in *lpStr*. For **AfxFormatString2( )**, the resource string must contain placeholders marked by a "%1" and "%2" that will be substituted by the strings in *lpStr1* and *lpStr2*.

For example, assuming this **STRINGTABLE**:

```
#define IDS_LANG    501
STRINGTABLE PRELOAD MOVEABLE
{
   IDS_LANG, "This is the %1 version of the program."
}
```

The following code loads the string, substituting the word "English":

```
CString msgStr;
AfxFormatString1(msgStr, IDS_LANG, "English");
```

After this code has executed, the string will contain "This is the English version of the program."

Initializing the Application

As you saw early in this book, there are a certain number of steps that must be performed to initialize and start an MFC application. These steps are taken inside **CWinApp::InitInstance( )**, which is called when your application begins executing. A document/view application also uses **InitInstance( )** to initialize a program. However, it will use a different set of operations from those used by the other programs in this book. To initialize a document/view application, your program will use a function similar to that shown here:

```
// Initialize the application.
BOOL CApp::InitInstance()
{
  CSingleDocTemplate *DocPtr = new CSingleDocTemplate(
    IDR_FRAMEWIN,
    RUNTIME_CLASS (CSampleDoc),
```

```
    RUNTIME_CLASS(CMainWin),
    RUNTIME_CLASS(CSampleView)
  );

  AddDocTemplate(DocPtr);

  // register application in registry
  EnableShellOpen();
  RegisterShellFileTypes();

  CCommandLineInfo CLInfo;
  ParseCommandLine(CLInfo);

  if(!ProcessShellCommand(CLInfo)) return FALSE;

  return TRUE;
}
```

Let's examine this function closely. First, a pointer called **DocPtr** is declared and initialized to point to an allocated **CSingleDocTemplate** structure. This structure is constructed as described earlier. **DocPtr** is then used in a call to **AddDocTemplate( )**, which adds the template to the list of document templates supported by the application. It has this prototype:

   void CWinApp::AddDocTemplate(CDocTemplate **DocTemplate*);

Here, *DocTemplate* is a pointer to the new document template.

After the document template has been added, your application should call **EnableShellOpen( )** and **RegisterShellFileTypes( )**. These functions are shown here:

   void CWinApp::EnableShellOpen( );

   void CWinApp::RegisterShellFileTypes(BOOL *EnablePrinting* = FALSE);

EnableShellOpen( ) allows the user to start your application by clicking on one of its document files. **RegisterShellFileTypes( )** registers your application's document type in the system registry. If *EnablePrinting* is **TRUE**, then files created by your application can be printed by dragging them to a printer object. Remember, registry information is provided by the string resource used when a document template is created.

The next three lines of code process command-line arguments. As you know, it is possible to add command-line arguments to a Windows application when it is started using the Run option or when it is executed from the command line. In a document/view application, the command line may be used to specify a document file to open on start up. The **CCommandLineInfo** is a class that encapsulates command-line information. The **CWinApp::ParseCommandLine( )** function parses the command line. **CWinApp::ProcessShellCommand( )** processes the command line and determines its validity. If **ProcessShellCommand( )** returns zero, **InitInstance( )** must return **FALSE**. (If interpreting the command line is important to you, explore these functions further on your own.)

Storing and Retrieving Documents

One of the most impressive aspects of the document/view architecture is the ease with which you can save and load documents to and from disk. There are two reasons for this. First, **CObject** contains the **Serialize( )** member function, which is automatically called when a document will be loaded or stored. Second, MFC defines the **CArchive** class, which automates nearly all of the file handling involved. As you will see, **CArchive** overloads the << and >> I/O operators for the built-in data types and for class types defined by the MFC class hierarchy. As mentioned at the beginning of this chapter, in the terminology of document/view, storing a document is called *serialization*.

In a document/view program, **CObject::Serialize( )** is called when a document is loaded or saved. This function is declared as follows:

virtual void CObject::Serialize(CArchive &*ArchOb*);

Here, *ArchOb* is an object of type **CArchive**, which defines the archiving stream. Your document class will override **Serialize( )**. Your version will write or read your document to or from the archive stream specified by *ArchOb*.

Since **Serialize( )** is called whenever a document needs to be loaded or stored, you need some way to determine which is the case. To do this, you will use either the **IsStoring( )** or **IsLoading( )** member functions of **CArchive**. They are shown here:

BOOL CArchive::IsLoading( ) const;

BOOL CArchive::IsStoring( ) const;

IsLoading( ) returns nonzero if the document is being loaded and zero if it is being stored. On the other hand, **IsStoring( )** returns nonzero if the document is being stored and zero if it is being loaded.

Inside your overridden version of **Serialize( )**, you will use << and >> to load and store your document. The target (i.e., left-hand operator) of these operators is *ArchOb*. **CArchive** is an important—and large—class. You will want to examine it fully when writing your own applications.

NOTE: For certain serialization situations, such as those that serialize an object through a polymorphic base-class pointer, you will need to use the **DECLARE_SERIAL** and **IMPLEMENT_SERIAL** macros. These are not needed by the example in this chapter.

Two Important CDocument Member Functions

The **CDocument** class contains several member functions. While it is far beyond the scope of this book to describe them all, two of them are used by nearly all document/view programs, including the sample shown at the end of this chapter. These functions are described here.

UpdateAllViews( )

Whenever the document has changed, your application should call **UpdateAllViews( )**. This function causes all the view classes linked to the document to be notified that they must update their display representation. The prototype for **UpdateAllViews( )** is shown here:

```
void CDocument::UpdateAllViews(CView *Sender, LPARAM lParam = 0,
                               CObject *ObPtr = NULL);
```

Here, *Sender* is a pointer to the view that caused the document to change. If this parameter is **NULL**, then all views linked to the document are updated. *lParam* and *ObPtr* are parameters that you may use to optimize the updating of views. **UpdateAllViews( )** causes **CView::OnUpdate( )** to be called for all views linked to the document, except for the view specified by *Sender*. (Of course, if *Sender* is **NULL** then all views are updated.) If desired, you may override **CView::OnUpdate( )** in order to optimize updates.

SetModifiedFlag( )

Whenever a document has been changed, you must call **CDocument:: SetModifiedFlag( )**. After this function has been called, the user will be prompted to save a document before it is destroyed. The function has this prototype:

> void CDocument::SetModifiedFlag(BOOL *IsModified* = TRUE);

If *IsModified* is nonzero, then the modified flag is set. Otherwise it is cleared.

An Important CView Member Function

The **CView** class also contains numerous member functions. One that almost all document/view applications will use is called **GetDocument( )**. This function returns a pointer to the **CDocument** object that is linked to the view. As you can probably surmise, this function is frequently used when the view needs access to the document's data—especially when it must display that data. It also allows **CDocument** member functions to be called from within the view class. The prototype for **GetDocument( )** is shown here:

> CDocument *CView::GetDocument( ) const;

The function returns a pointer to the document associated with the calling view class.

The Standard IDs

Because the document/view architecture manages many of the common tasks associated with any program, such as opening and closing files, saving files, and printing, MFC has defined several standard command IDs that, when received, are automatically linked with these operations. Here are a few of the most commonly used IDs along with their corresponding functions:

ID	Calls
ID_APP_EXIT	CWinApp::OnAppExit( )
ID_FILE_CLOSE	CDocument::OnFileClose( )
ID_FILE_NEW	CWinApp::OnFileNew( )
ID_FILE_OPEN	CWinApp::OnFileOpen( )
ID_FILE_PRINT	CView::OnFilePrint( )

ID	Calls
ID_FILE_PRINT_PREVIEW	CView::OnFilePrintPreview( )
ID_FILE_PRINT_SETUP	CWinApp::OnFilePrintSetup( )
ID_FILE_SAVE	CDocument::OnFileSave( )
ID_FILE_SAVE_AS	CDocument::OnFileSaveAs( )

17

For various reasons, some of the standard IDs are automatically enabled and do not need to be included in your program's message maps. Others must be. For the IDs just shown, here is how they split:

Automatically Enabled	Must Be Included in Message Map
ID_APP_EXIT	ID_FILE_NEW
ID_FILE_CLOSE	ID_FILE_OPEN
ID_FILE_SAVE	ID_FILE_PRINT
ID_FILE_SAVE_AS	ID_FILE_PRINT_PREVIEW
	ID_FILE_PRINT_SETUP

There are many other predefined IDs that you will want to explore on your own. For example, there are standard IDs for most editing functions, such as **ID_EDIT_CUT**, **ID_EDIT_PASTE**, etc.

A Sample Document/View Application

Now that all of the theory is out of the way, this chapter concludes with a sample document/view application. Although very simple, the program demonstrates the key features and concepts that all document/view programs must contain. The document defined by the program is a record of mouse coordinates. The view of these coordinates is provided by connecting each coordinate to the next using a straight line. The user creates a document by pressing the left mouse button. Each time the button is pressed, the current location of the mouse is recorded. The program allows documents to be stored and loaded. It is also possible to remove coordinates, reset the document, or start a new document. Sample output is shown in Figure 17-1.

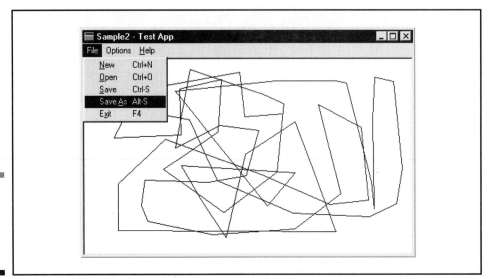

The program uses the following resource file. Notice that this file includes
AFXRES.RC. This file includes several strings used by the standard functions
called by a document/view program.

```
// DOCVIEW.RC

#include <afxres.h>
#include <afxres.rc>
#include "ids.h"

IDR_FRAMEWIN MENU
{
  POPUP "File"
  {
    MENUITEM "&New\tCtrl+N", ID_FILE_NEW
    MENUITEM "&Open\tCtrl+O", ID_FILE_OPEN
    MENUITEM "&Save\tCtrl-S", ID_FILE_SAVE
    MENUITEM "Save &As\tAlt-S", ID_FILE_SAVE_AS
    MENUITEM "E&xit\tF4", ID_APP_EXIT
  }

  POPUP "Options"
  {
    MENUITEM "&Undo\tF2", IDM_UNDO
    MENUITEM "&Reset\tF3", IDM_RESET
```

```
   }

   MENUITEM "&Help", IDM_HELP
}

IDR_FRAMEWIN ACCELERATORS
{
   VK_F2, IDM_UNDO, VIRTKEY
   VK_F3, IDM_RESET, VIRTKEY
   VK_F4, ID_APP_EXIT, VIRTKEY
   VK_F1, IDM_HELP, VIRTKEY
   "^N", ID_FILE_NEW
   "^O", ID_FILE_OPEN
   "^S", ID_FILE_SAVE
   "S", ID_FILE_SAVE_AS, ALT
}

STRINGTABLE
{
   IDR_FRAMEWIN, "Test App\n\n\nDoc Type (*.pnt)\n.pnt\nDVTest\nDV Test"
}
```

The header file, IDS.H, is shown here:

```
// IDS.H

#define IDM_UNDO      100
#define IDM_RESET     101
#define IDM_FONT      102
#define IDM_EXIT      103
#define IDM_HELP      104

#define IDR_FRAMEWIN 200

#define MAXLOC        100
```

The class derivation file, DOCVIEW.H, is shown next:

```
// DOCVIEW.H

// This is the main window class.
class CMainWin : public CFrameWnd
{
```

```
  DECLARE_DYNCREATE(CMainWin)
public:
  CMainWin();

  DECLARE_MESSAGE_MAP()
};

// This is the application class.
class CApp : public CWinApp
{
public:
  BOOL InitInstance();

  DECLARE_MESSAGE_MAP()
};

// This is the document class.
class CSampleDoc : public CDocument
{
  DECLARE_DYNCREATE(CSampleDoc)
  int m_LocIndex;
  CPoint m_Locations[MAXLOC];
public:
  CSampleDoc();

  afx_msg void OnUndo();
  afx_msg void OnReset();
  afx_msg void OnHelp();

  BOOL OnNewDocument();
  void Serialize(CArchive &arch);

  DECLARE_MESSAGE_MAP()
};

// This is the view class.
class CSampleView : public CView
{
  DECLARE_DYNCREATE(CSampleView)
public:
  void OnDraw(CDC *DC);
  afx_msg void OnLButtonDown(UINT flags, CPoint);

  DECLARE_MESSAGE_MAP()
};
```

The document/view program file is shown here:

```
// Demonstrate Document/View Architecture
#include <afxwin.h>
#include "ids.h"
#include "docview.h"

CApp App; // instantiate the application

IMPLEMENT_DYNCREATE(CMainWin, CFrameWnd)
IMPLEMENT_DYNCREATE(CSampleView, CView)
IMPLEMENT_DYNCREATE(CSampleDoc, CDocument)

// This is the application's message map.
BEGIN_MESSAGE_MAP(CApp, CWinApp)
  ON_COMMAND(ID_FILE_OPEN, CWinApp::OnFileOpen)
  ON_COMMAND(ID_FILE_NEW, CWinApp::OnFileNew)
END_MESSAGE_MAP()

// This is the view's message map.
BEGIN_MESSAGE_MAP(CSampleView, CView)
  ON_WM_LBUTTONDOWN()
END_MESSAGE_MAP()

// This is the document's message map.
BEGIN_MESSAGE_MAP(CSampleDoc, CDocument)
  ON_COMMAND(IDM_UNDO, OnUndo)
  ON_COMMAND(IDM_RESET, OnReset)
  ON_COMMAND(IDM_HELP, OnHelp)
END_MESSAGE_MAP()

// This is the frame window's message map.
BEGIN_MESSAGE_MAP(CMainWin, CFrameWnd)
  // not used by this example
END_MESSAGE_MAP()

// Initialize the main window.
CMainWin::CMainWin()
{
  // Not used by this example.
}

// Initialize the application.
BOOL CApp::InitInstance()
{
```

```
  CSingleDocTemplate *DocPtr = new CSingleDocTemplate(
    IDR_FRAMEWIN,
    RUNTIME_CLASS (CSampleDoc),
    RUNTIME_CLASS(CMainWin),
    RUNTIME_CLASS(CSampleView)
  );

  AddDocTemplate(DocPtr);

  // register application in registry
  EnableShellOpen();
  RegisterShellFileTypes();

  CCommandLineInfo CLInfo;
  ParseCommandLine(CLInfo);

  if(!ProcessShellCommand(CLInfo)) return FALSE;

  return TRUE;
}

// Initialize the document.
CSampleDoc::CSampleDoc()
{
  m_LocIndex = 0;
}

// Process IDM_HELP -- this is only placeholder help.
afx_msg void CSampleDoc::OnHelp()
{
    App.m_pMainWnd->MessageBox("Document/View Demo",
                               "Placeholder Help");
}

// Handle new document request.
BOOL CSampleDoc::OnNewDocument()
{
  if(!CDocument::OnNewDocument()) return FALSE;

  m_LocIndex = 0;

  return TRUE;
}

// Load or store document.
```

```cpp
void CSampleDoc::Serialize(CArchive &arch)
{
  int i;

  if(arch.IsLoading()) {
    arch >> m_LocIndex;
    for(i=0; i<m_LocIndex; i++)  arch >> m_Locations[i];
  }
  else {
    arch << m_LocIndex;
    for(i=0; i<m_LocIndex; i++)  arch << m_Locations[i];
  }
}


// Undo last line.
afx_msg void CSampleDoc::OnUndo()
{
  m_LocIndex--;
  if(m_LocIndex<0) m_LocIndex = 0;

  SetModifiedFlag();
  UpdateAllViews(NULL);
}

// Reset point index and erase window.
afx_msg void CSampleDoc::OnReset()
{
  m_LocIndex = 0;

  SetModifiedFlag();
  UpdateAllViews(NULL);
}

// Record position of mouse click.
afx_msg void CSampleView::OnLButtonDown(UINT flags, CPoint loc)
{
  CSampleDoc *DocPtr = (CSampleDoc *) GetDocument();

  DocPtr->m_Locations[DocPtr->m_LocIndex] = loc;
  DocPtr->m_LocIndex++;
  if(DocPtr->m_LocIndex == MAXLOC) {
    DocPtr->m_LocIndex = MAXLOC;
    App.m_pMainWnd->MessageBox("Too Many Points", "Error");
  }
  DocPtr->SetModifiedFlag();
```

```
    DocPtr->UpdateAllViews(NULL);
}

// Draw lines.
void CSampleView::OnDraw(CDC *DC)
{
    CSampleDoc *DocPtr = (CSampleDoc *) GetDocument();
    int i;

    for(i=0; i<DocPtr->m_LocIndex; i++)
        DC->LineTo(DocPtr->m_Locations[i]);
}
```

A Closer Look at the Example Document/ View Program

The program implements the document/view architecture as described in the first part of this chapter and is straightforward. The location data that constitutes the program's document is stored in the array **m_Locations**, which is a member of **CSampleDoc**. The size of this array is arbitrarily fixed at **MAXLOC** (which is defined as 100). The current index into **m_Locations** is maintained by **m_LocIndex**. Each time the user presses the left mouse button, the current location is stored in **m_Locations**, and the value of **m_LocIndex** is incremented. The user can remove a point by choosing the Undo menu option. This option simply decrements the current value of **m_LocIndex**.

Pay special attention to the way **Serialize( )** is overridden. When writing data, it first stores the value of **m_LocIndex**, and then it stores the contents of **m_Locations**. When loading a document, it first reads the value of **m_LocIndex**. It then uses this value to determine how many points to read into the **m_Locations** array. Because **CArchive** is overloaded for all of the basic data types, very little code is required to perform these operations.

When to Use the Document/View Architecture

The document/view model is currently the standard architecture used by Visual C++'s AppWizard. This fact alone assures it long-term acceptance and importance. As you have seen, the document/view approach also provides some tangible benefits. For example, it simplifies the loading and storing of your program's data. It also handles many of the mundane details associated

17

with most programs, such as activating the File Open dialog box. It is not, of course, the only way to write a great MFC application. Frankly, small applications gain little from the document/view approach. Conversely, very large, complicated applications containing many idiosyncrasies may be more easily managed using a non-document/view approach. This will be especially true for programs in which a substantial amount of "hands-on" control is needed. However, for a large class of medium-sized programs, the document/view architecture is an excellent solution.

CHAPTER 18

Exploring ActiveX Controls

ActiveX is one of the most exciting disciplines in Windows programming and it will play an increasingly important role in software development. Unfortunately, the ActiveX subsystem is both large and complex. To fully describe it requires a complete book. Frankly, if you want to create ActiveX components, expect to spend at least a few weeks studying it. Although not difficult in concept, it is an extensive subject that requires some effort to master. With this in mind, this chapter explains the basics of ActiveX and walks you through the creation of a simple ActiveX control.

Before beginning, one other point needs to be made. ActiveX controls require more sophisticated programming techniques than do the other programs discussed in this book. Because of this, many programmers will use automated development tools, such as the ActiveX Control Wizard provided by Visual C++, to produce ActiveX controls. Whether your intent is to code your own ActiveX controls or to use a tool such as the ActiveX Control Wizard, an understanding of the examples shown in this chapter will be helpful because they illustrate the fundamental characteristics of an ActiveX control.

What Is ActiveX?

In the broadest sense, ActiveX is a set of methodologies and procedures that allow you to create *software components*. A software component is a reusable, self-contained module of code that may be used by another application. A software component can be "hooked onto" another application, providing additional control or functionality. Taken to its logical conclusion, an entire application could be constructed of nothing but software components "wired" together.

Software components have been one of the long sought after goals of software engineering ever since there were computers. Although a conceptually powerful idea, component software remained a largely academic pursuit for several decades. In a world dominated by single-user, non-networked computers, component software was simply not a high priority. The reason for this is easy to understand: in a stand-alone system there is no easy way to acquire software components on demand. Thus, software for those machines was installed, intact and complete. If the user wanted to upgrade or enhance the software, he or she simply installed the latest version of the program. There was no concept of the user extending the functionality of an application by adding a component.

The key benefits of component software are best realized when a component can be acquired on demand, as needed; that is, when it can be dynamically downloaded. But this requires a means by which to acquire those components. For years, no such means existed. Of course, the advent of the Internet and the World Wide Web changed that. In the final analysis, the creation of the Internet finally moved software components to the forefront of software engineering. Using the component software model, it is possible for a user to add functionality by adding components. At the time of this writing, we are just at the beginning of the component software revolution.

As it applies to ActiveX, a software component is called an *ActiveX control*. And, indeed, by far the most common use of ActiveX is to create an ActiveX control. Although ActiveX is not limited to controls, they are the reason ActiveX exists. Controls can be downloaded dynamically over the Internet and executed within all modern browsers. They can also be used by any OLE-compliant application.

18

OLE and ActiveX

ActiveX is part of an evolutionary process that began with OLE. To understand ActiveX is to understand OLE, and vice versa. Since ActiveX begins with OLE, we will begin there too.

In its original conception, OLE was designed to allow one application to link or embed information created by another application. When this is done, a compound document is created. A compound document is also referred to as an *OLE document*. While this original purpose of OLE is still supported, it is important to understand that OLE has gone through a rather extensive evolution. OLE version 1 was devised in 1991, but it was a seldom-used system. With the advent of OLE version 2, the capabilities and applicability of OLE took a quantum leap forward. Perhaps the single most important new feature of OLE 2.0 was the definition of the component object model (COM). It is this feature that ultimately led to the ActiveX technology.

In response to the Internet, Microsoft defined ActiveX in 1996. Based on OLE, it added support for Web-based applications. However, since it supports all of OLE, the term ActiveX has nearly supplanted the term OLE.

The Component Object Model

ActiveX is based upon the component object model (COM). This model defines the way ActiveX-compliant applications interact with each other. Specifically, it defines standard interfaces that one object can use to expose its functionality to another. It is through these interfaces that one application communicates with another.

In the component object model there are two types of applications: containers and servers. In the simplest sense, a container is an application that requires data and a server is an application that supplies data. A container can be a compound document. Another term for container is *client*. The way that a container and server communicate is through the interfaces defined by COM. These are the same interfaces used by an ActiveX control. In fact, an ActiveX control is an in-process server (i.e., it runs within the process that uses it).

COM Interfaces

The nature and contents of each interface are defined by the component object model. An application that desires COM-compatibility simply implements one or more of these interfaces. A COM interface is implemented as a table of function pointers. These pointers point to the functions that comprise the interface. To expose an interface, a server returns a pointer to that interface's table. When a client seeks communication with a server, it obtains a pointer to the server's interface table. The client may then call the functions provided by the server through the pointers in the function table. The client has no knowledge of or access to the details of the implementation of the function it calls. It only knows that it is accessing a standard function through a standard interface.

Every COM interface is identified by a Globally Unique IDentifier (GUID), which distinguishes one COM interface from another. This unique identifier is made up of eleven parts: one **long**, two **WORD**s, and eight **BYTE**s. These IDs are usually generated by third-party tools. For instance, the IDs used by the sample programs in this chapter are generated using GUIDGEN.

While there are several interfaces defined by COM, most ActiveX controls will not implement them all. But the one interface they will all have is called **IUnknown**. Using the **QueryInterface( )** function defined by **IUnknown**, one application can find out what other interfaces are available in another. In the examples that follow, you won't see the **IUnknown** interface shown in the source code because this interface is implemented for you by MFC. Not having to deal with the low-level details of an ActiveX control is another advantage of using MFC.

The fundamental value in interfaces is that one COM-compliant application can take advantage of functionality provided by another COM-based program. If you think about this for a moment, the implications are enormous. It is easy to envision a computing universe populated with components that a user can simply hook together as he or she sees fit. It is also easy to imagine smart components that will seek out and use other components when they require additional functionality. These possibilities are what make ActiveX controls so exciting.

MFC and ActiveX

Starting in version 4, MFC wrapped the ActiveX technology and released it as a separate software development kit, called the OLE Controls Developer Kit (CDK). In version 4.2 of MFC, the OLE CDK was rolled into MFC as part of the library. Of course, MFC 6 continues to support ActiveX development. As with most Windows technologies, MFC implements the ActiveX control technology using a combination of classes and macros. The ActiveX control technology is implemented with three major classes (**COleControlModule**, **COleControl**, and **COlePropertyPage**). In addition to these classes, a group of macros was also designed to ease the various aspects of ActiveX control development (for example, control registration).

18

NOTE: The **COlePropertyPage** class implements a graphical interface for a control's properties. Because it is optional, and due to the scope of this chapter, this class will not be discussed. To focus the discussion, the sample projects will make use of the **COleControlModule** and **COleControl** classes only.

In addition to the MFC support, in the form of classes and macros, a variety of tools are shipped with Visual C++ to simplify the development of ActiveX controls. These tools include the GUIDGEN application (which generates GUIDs), the ActiveX Control Test Container (an application for testing all aspects of your ActiveX control), and finally the Visual C++ IDE (which generates a basic project for creating an ActiveX control). While it is true that these tools are not needed to develop an ActiveX control, they definitely make the job easier and are used throughout this chapter.

Basics of an ActiveX Project

Because of its complexity, the MFC implementation of ActiveX requires a somewhat different approach (in regard to project type and structure) compared to earlier chapters in the book. Up to this point, all the sample projects presented in this book (with a few exceptions) have shared some basic characteristics:

♦ The type of the application is a Windows executable.

♦ The project contains a **CWinApp**-derived class and a **CWnd**-derived class.

♦ The project contains resources of one or more types.

Even though ActiveX projects share some similarities with the previous sample projects, there are some key differences that need to be discussed.

Perhaps the primary difference is that an ActiveX control is implemented as a dynamic link library (DLL) instead of a Windows executable. The DLL project type fits the requirements for a software component better than the traditional Windows executable because it is modular in design and is intended for use by external clients (ActiveX control containers).

NOTE: Due to historical influences, the DLL that implements the ActiveX control has a .OCX extension. The reason being that .OCX was similar to the extension used by Visual Basic controls (which were very similar to ActiveX controls): .VBX.

This project type has a different structure and, as a result, requires a different technique for building. This technique is a little more involved than that used to build previous sample programs. For this reason, the project files needed to build each of the ActiveX control samples are made available on Osborne's Web site (**www.osborne.com**). However, the code for each example is also shown in full in this chapter.

Because the control is contained within a DLL, ActiveX projects also require a module definition (.DEF) file. This file does two things: It declares the internal name of the DLL and lists the functions that are exported. In other words, these functions are implemented in our control project but are able to be called by external applications.

Two of these functions, **DllRegisterServer( )** and **DllUnregisterServer( )**, allow the control to self-register. This means that the control (instead of another application) updates the registry with the necessary information. Later in this chapter, we will return to this topic of self-registration.

Here is the module definition file used by the sample program:

```
; TESTCTL1.DEF : Declares the module parameters.

LIBRARY "TESTCTL1.OCX"
```

```
EXPORTS
   DllCanUnloadNow      @1 PRIVATE
   DllGetClassObject    @2 PRIVATE
   DllRegisterServer    @3 PRIVATE
   DllUnregisterServer  @4 PRIVATE
```

18

Finally, the last major difference is the Object Description Language (.ODL) file. This file contains the description (hence, the title) of the various interfaces implemented by the control object. When an ActiveX project is built, one of the steps is the compilation of this file into a type library. This type library is then used as a resource in your project.

Here is the .ODL file used by the sample program:

```
// TESTCTL1.ODL : type library source for ActiveX Control project.

#include <olectl.h>
#include <idispids.h>

[ uuid(BB289DA4-0A23-11d2-ABDB-94CAF6C00000), version(1.0), control ]
library TEST1Lib
{
   importlib(STDOLE_TLB);
   importlib(STDTYPE_TLB);

   [ uuid(BB289DA2-0A23-11d2-ABDB-94CAF6C00000), hidden ]
   dispinterface _Dtest1
   {
     properties:

     methods:

   };

   [ uuid(BB289DA3-0A23-11d2-ABDB-94CAF6C00000)]
   dispinterface _DTest1Events
   {
     properties:

     methods:

   };
```

```
[ uuid(BB289DA1-0A23-11d2-ABDB-94CAF6C00000), control ]
coclass Test1
{
  [default] dispinterface _Dtest1;
  [default, source] dispinterface _DTest1Events;
};

};
```

In the preceding .ODL file, two "empty" interfaces are defined. The first
is the primary dispatch interface, **_Dtest1**. This interface will implement
the properties and methods of our ActiveX control. The second interface,
_DTest1Events, is referred to as the event interface. This interface implements
any events the control will fire. Because the sample control does not
implement any methods, properties, or events at this point, the **_Dtest1**
and **_DTest1Events** interfaces are currently empty. Later on in the chapter,
we will be adding to these interface declarations to implement methods,
properties, and events.

Notice the four GUIDs present in the .ODL file. Although they may look
like gibberish they are very important. These are the unique identifiers we
discussed earlier. They were generated using the GUIDGEN tool. The first
GUID is the ID of the **TestCtl1** type library. The second and third GUIDs are
the IDs of the primary and event dispatch interfaces respectively. The last one
is an ID for the **coclass** of the **TestCtl1** object. This **coclass** represents the
top-level object in the type library; in this case, it is the **TestCtl1** control
object. We will use these same GUIDs later when implementing various
aspects of our ActiveX control.

In addition to these three new file types, the standard header and resource
files are included. The IDS.H header file is shown here:

```
// IDS.H

#define IDS_TESTCTL1  1
#define IDB_TESTCTL1  1
```

The sample program uses the following resource file:

```
// TESTCTL1.RC

#include <afxres.h>
```

```
#include "ids.h"

IDB_TESTCTL1 BITMAP DISCARDABLE "TestCtl1.bmp"

STRINGTABLE DISCARDABLE
BEGIN
  IDS_TESTCTL1 "TestCtl1 Control"
END

1 TYPELIB "TestCtl1.tlb"
```

18

Before moving on, we would like to mention a few things about TESTCTL1.RC. First, notice the bitmap resource (**IDB_TESTCTL1**) in the preceding resource file. Before continuing, you must create a bitmap using an image editor. The size of the bitmap must be 16 × 15 pixels. This bitmap will represent the ActiveX control in a toolbar.

Also of note is the **TYPELIB** resource statement. This statement indicates that a type library is included as a resource in the project. In this example, we are including a type library, called TESTCTL1.TLB, with a resource ID of 1.

The remaining project files are the class derivation and program files. These files implement the control module class (**COleControlModule**) and the ActiveX control class (**COleControl**).

The COleControlModule Class

As mentioned previously, an ActiveX control is implemented as an in-process server (a fancy name for a DLL) rather than as a separate application. For this reason, the control is contained within a module object, implemented by a class derived from **COleControlModule**. This differs from previous sample programs, which used a class derived from **CWinApp** for the containing framework. However, you can think of these two classes as similar in purpose.

COleControlModule inherits two functions of interest, **CWinApp::InitInstance** and **CWinApp::ExitInstance**, that can be overridden in your **COleControlModule**-derived class. Override these functions to perform any custom actions during the initialization and termination of your ActiveX control module. Their prototypes are shown here:

    virtual CWinApp::BOOL InitInstance( );

    virtual int CWinApp::ExitInstance( );

As you might infer from the name, **InitInstance( )** is called when the control module is initialized. The return value indicates if the initialization was successful or not. **ExitInstance( )** is called when the control module exits. In our sample programs, we will simply call the base class implementation of these functions.

As was also the case with the **CWinApp**-derived class used in previous sample programs, you will not be working a lot with **COleControlModule**.

The COleControl Class

By far, the main focus of ActiveX control development is on the **COleControl**-derived class of the ActiveX control project. You can think of the **COleControl**-derived class as providing the same functionality as the **CWnd**-derived class used in the examples shown earlier in this book. It provides the meat of the project, implementing all the interfaces and custom functionality of your ActiveX control.

In your **COleControl**-derived class, you will commonly declare a constructor. This constructor provides a convenient place to initialize the primary dispatch and event interfaces that your control supports. In the program file, initialize your interfaces by calling the **COleControl::InitializeIIDs( )** member function. Its prototype is shown here:

> void COleControl::InitializeIIDs(const IID *DispatchInterface,
> const IID *EventInterface);

Here, *DispatchInterface* is a pointer to the primary dispatch interface ID of your control (in this case, **_Dtest1**) and *EventInterface* is a pointer to the dispatch interface ID that fires the various events of your control (in this case, **_DTest1Events**). These parameter values are provided by you and consist of two Globally Unique IDentifiers (GUIDs). As mentioned previously, these GUIDs are generated by GUIDGEN and are also present in your .ODL file. Commonly, two variables (of type **IID**) are defined in the program file and set equal to the two GUID values. The resultant definitions should resemble the following:

```
// {BB289DA2-0A23-11d2-ABDB-94CAF6C00000}
const IID BASED_CODE IID_DTestCtl1 = { 0xbb289da2, 0xa23, 0x11d2, { 0xab,
    0xdb, 0x94, 0xca, 0xf6, 0xc0, 0x0, 0x0 } };
// {BB289DA3-0A23-11d2-ABDB-94CAF6C00000}
const IID BASED_CODE IID_DTestCtl1Events = { 0xbb289da3, 0xa23, 0x11d2,
    { 0xab, 0xdb, 0x94, 0xca, 0xf6, 0xc0, 0x0, 0x0 } };
```

NOTE: A convenient feature of GUIDGEN is the supplied comment preceding each interface ID definition. You might have noticed that these values were used in the .ODL file of the control project.

If your control is visible within the control container, you need to override the **COleControl::OnDraw( )** member function. The purpose of this function is similar to the **CView::OnDraw( )** function discussed in Chapter 17: repainting the control window when needed. The **COleControl::OnDraw( )** function has the following prototype:

18

virtual void COleControl::OnDraw(CDC *DC, const CRect &*ControlRect*,
                                const CRect &*InvalidRegion*);

Here, *DC* is a pointer to the device context used by the control. *ControlRect* is the area currently used by your control to display itself (including the border of the control) and *InvalidRegion* is the area that needs to be repainted. For the sample programs, a simple ellipse and border will be drawn to represent the control's appearance.

The declaration of the constructor and override of **COleControl::OnDraw( )** are important pieces of your control's class declaration. However, the main implementation of your **COleControl**-derived class is provided by several global MFC macros. These macros, although fairly simple in use, provide the main structure of your ActiveX control.

The ActiveX Control Macros

In previous chapters, you were introduced to a few of MFC's macros, specifically **DECLARE_DYNCREATE**, **DECLARE_MESSAGE_MAP**, **IMPLEMENT_DYNCREATE**, and the **BEGIN/END_MESSAGE_MAP**. As explained, these global MFC macros are used in pairs (except for the mapping macros). The declarative macro (for example, **DECLARE_DYNCREATE**) is used in the class derivation file and the implementation macro (for example, **IMPLEMENT_DYNCREATE**) is used in the program file. Each pair of macros used in the declaration of the control class implements a specific characteristic of the ActiveX control framework. Let's examine the macro pairs required by an ActiveX control.

Dynamic Creation

As discussed in Chapter 17, the **DECLARE_DYNCREATE( )** and
IMPLEMENT_DYNCREATE( ) macros enable the target class to be created
dynamically. In the case of ActiveX controls, this allows the control to be
dynamically (instead of programatically) created upon request by the control
container.

Class Factories

To create an instance of our ActiveX control, the control container must
call a member function of our control's *class factory*. A class factory is a
separate class that is primarily responsible for creating instances of a specific
class, in this case the ActiveX control class. This class factory is required
for every COM object. Declare the control's class factory by using the
DECLARE_OLECREATE_EX( ) and **IMPLEMENT_OLECREATE_EX( )**
macros shown here:

> DECLARE_OLECREATE_EX(*ClassName*)

> IMPLEMENT_OLECREATE_EX(*ClassName*, *ExternalName*, *l*, *w1*, *w2*,
>   *b1*, *b2*, *b3*, *b4*, *b5*, *b6*, *b7*, *b8*)

Here, *ClassName* is the name of the control class that will be produced by the
class factory. *ExternalName* is the external name of the control. This is the
name used by ActiveX control containers to identify the ActiveX control to
be created. The remaining parameters of **IMPLEMENT_OLECREATE_EX( )**
are the various components of the GUID for the **coclass** object of the control.
This GUID matches the fourth GUID declared in your project's .ODL file.

Type Libraries

As mentioned previously, every ActiveX control uses a type library to describe
the interfaces exposed to ActiveX control containers. To implement the type
library for an ActiveX control, MFC provides the following two functions:

> DECLARE_OLETYPELIB(*ClassName*)

> IMPLEMENT_OLETYPELIB(*ClassName*, *TypeLibraryID*, *VerMajor*, *VerMinor*)

Here, *ClassName* is the name of the control class described by the type library.
TypeLibraryID is the GUID of the type library, matching the first GUID
declared in your project's .ODL file. The *VerMajor* and *VerMinor* parameters
describe the major and minor version of the type library. For instance, in our

sample program the version of the type library is 1.0, with 1 being the *VerMajor* value and 0 being the *VerMinor* value.

For readability, it is common to declare a constant variable, of type **GUID CDECL**, in the class derivation file. The variable is initialized with the proper GUID and then used in the call to **IMPLEMENT_OLETYPELIB( )** (in the implementation file). For instance, the following line was taken from the program file of the first sample program (shown later). It declares a variable (**_tlid**) and initializes it with the GUID of the sample control's type library.

18

```
// {BB289DA4-0A23-11d2-ABDB-94CAF6C00000}
const GUID CDECL BASED_CODE _tlid ={ 0xbb289da4, 0xa23, 0x11d2,
      { 0xab, 0xdb, 0x94, 0xca, 0xf6, 0xc0, 0x0, 0x0 } };
```

Control Type and Initial Status

The next pair of macros used in the control class declaration provides the external name of the ActiveX control, and some miscellaneous status types. The external name is a readable string, displayed in the user interface elements of an ActiveX control container containing the control. This string is defined in a string table and referenced by the ID of the string resource. In the sample program, the external string has an ID of **IDS_TESTCTL1**.

The miscellaneous status types are values that inform the container of certain requests of the control when it is first loaded. These are requests because the control container is not obligated to fulfill them. The status is created by OR'ing one or more pre-defined flags together. The common set of flags used by a standard ActiveX control (and our sample control) is as follows:

Value	Description
OLEMISC_SETCLIENTSITEFIRST	The control will access the container's ambient properties upon loading.
OLEMISC_INSIDEOUT	The control is able to be activated without additional user interface elements, such as a toolbar or a menu.
OLEMISC_CANTLINKINSIDE	The control does not support links to itself outside the container object.
OLEMISC_RECOMPOSEONRESIZE	The control will redraw itself if the display area of the control is changed by the container.

Use the following macro pair to declare the external class name and miscellaneous status:

DECLARE_OLECTLTYPE(*ClassName*)

IMPLEMENT_OLECTLTYPE(*ClassName*, *ExternalName*, *MiscStatus*)

Here, *ClassName* is the name of the control class described by the type library, *ExternalName* is the name used by ActiveX control containers, and *MiscStatus* is the OR'd result of various miscellaneous status flags.

Message Maps and Interface Maps

The remaining global macros implement the message, dispatch, and event maps of an ActiveX control. The message map is the standard map we have been using since Chapter 3. By now, you should be familiar with the **DECLARE_MESSAGE_MAP** and **BEGIN/END_MESSAGE_MAP** macros. Therefore, let's move on to the dispatch and event mapping macros.

The first pair declares and implements the primary dispatch interface of the ActiveX control. This primary dispatch interface exposes the various methods and properties supported by the ActiveX control to the ActiveX control container. In our initial sample program, this interface is empty. However, later in the chapter we will be adding some functionality to this map. The macros are as follows:

DECLARE_DISPATCH_MAP( )

BEGIN_DISPATCH_MAP(*Owner*, *Base*)

END_DISPATCH_MAP( )

Here, the name of the class that the dispatch interface map is for is specified by *Owner*. *Base* specifies the name of the base class used to derive the owner of the map. In our case, the owner class will always be **COleControl**.

The remaining map implements the event interface of the ActiveX control. The structure is similar to the dispatch interface map. The macros are as follows:

DECLARE_EVENT_MAP( )

BEGIN_EVENT_MAP(*Owner*, *Base*)

END_EVENT_MAP( )

Here, the name of the class that the event interface map is for is specified by *Owner. Base* specifies the name of the base class used to derive the owner of the map. In our case, the owner class will always be **COleControl**.

Registering the Control

As mentioned previously, before an ActiveX control can be used by ActiveX control containers, the control class and its server (the DLL) must be registered with the Windows operating system. This registration consists of several entries in the Windows registration database. These entries describe various aspects of the ActiveX control class:

◆ The type of object (control)

◆ The location of the server (the control's DLL)

◆ The initial status values

◆ The bitmap used to represent the control in a toolbar

◆ The location and ID of the type library

◆ The version of the control

Specifically, the class registration is accomplished by overriding the **COleObjectFactory::UpdateRegistry( )** member function. The server registration is accomplished by implementing two global functions, **DLLRegisterServer( )** and **DllUnregisterServer( )**, and exporting them in the .DEF file. This makes the server self-registrating.

Registering the Control Class

As mentioned previously, the primary responsibility of a control's class factory is instantiation of the control object. However, the class factory also updates the Windows registration database with important information about the control. This is accomplished by overriding the **COleObjectFactory::UpdateRegistry( )** member function of the control's class factory and performing the update within the overridden function. Its prototype follows:

virtual void COleObjectFactory::UpdateRegistry(BOOL *RegisterClass*) = 0;

As you can see, **COleObjectFactory::UpdateRegistry( )** is a pure virtual function. This means that it must be overridden by any derived class. Here, *RegisterClass* determines whether the registration database is updated or not. If *RegisterClass* is **TRUE**, the database is updated; otherwise, all trace of the control object is erased from the database.

Perform the registry update by making a call to the
AfxOleRegisterControlClass( ) function, from the override of
COleObjectFactory::UpdateRegistry( ). The prototype of
AfxOleRegisterControlClass( ) is as follows:

```
BOOL AFXAPI AfxOleRegisterControlClass(HINSTANCE hInst,
                    REFCLSID ClassID,
                    LPCSTR ProgramID, UINT ExternalNameID,
                    UINT BitmapID, int RegistryFlags,
                    DWORD MiscStatusFlags,
                    REFGUID TypeLibraryID,
                    WORD VerMajor, WORD VerMinor);
```

As you can see, all parameters require a value. This explains the abundance of
other objects and values that we have previously declared in the control class.

The first parameter, *hInst*, specifies a handle to an instance of a control object.
In this context, *hInst* contains a handle to the instance of the control module.
ClassID contains the unique class ID (or GUID) of the control object. *ProgramID*
contains the programmatic ID (or GUID) of the control. You may recall that
both GUIDs were used in the .ODL file of the project. *ExternalNameID* is the
ID of the resource string containing the external name of the control. *BitmapID*
is the resource ID of a bitmap that is used to represent your ActiveX control
in a Windows toolbar. *RegistryFlags* is a value that contains one or both of the
following flags:

Flag	Description
afxRegApartmentThreading	A registry key, describing the threading model of your control, is inserted.
afxRegInsertable	Determines if the control is available from the common Insert Object dialog box.

Our example program will use the **afxRegInsertable** flag only. *MiscStatusFlags*
contains a combination of miscellaneous status flags used by the control
container. These flags were discussed earlier in the chapter (see "Control Type
and Initial Status"). *TypeLibraryID* is the same GUID used in the .ODL file.
Finally, *VerMajor* and *VerMinor* are the major and minor values for the version
of the ActiveX control.

In addition to registering, **COleObjectFactory::UpdateRegistry( )** can
also be used to unregister a control. This action removes all registry keys

related to the control from the registry. This effectively makes the control invisible to ActiveX control containers. However, this does not mean that the control is no longer installed on your machine. It just means that Windows no longer knows about it.

Registering the Control Server

Registering the control class is only half of the registry work needed to register an ActiveX control with the Windows operating system. The other half involves registering the server for the ActiveX control.

18

You manage registration of this server by implementing the **DllRegisterServer( )** and **DllUnregisterServer( )** functions and registering or unregistering the server within. These functions are called by the control container when an instance of the control class is needed. Their prototypes are as follows:

```
STDAPI DllRegisterServer( );

STDAPI DllUnregisterServer( );
```

The implementation of **DllRegisterServer( )** simply makes calls to **AfxOle-RegistrTypeLib( )** and **COleObjectFactoryEx::UpdateRegistryAll( )**. These function calls check to see if the type library and other control information has been registered. If there are no entries, the type library and control server are registered. If entries exist for the control, no action is taken.

The implementation of **DllUnregisterServer( )** does the exact opposite of **DllRegisterServer( )**. It makes calls to **AfxOleUnregisterTypeLib( )** and **COleObjectFactoryEx::UpdateRegistryAll( )** to determine if the control has been registered. If the control is registered, all entries added by calls from within **DllRegisterServer( )** are removed.

A Simple ActiveX Control Program

Now that we have discussed all the necessary components of an ActiveX control project, let's put it all together. The following sample program demonstrates an ActiveX control framework using MFC. The resultant ActiveX control will be very basic—so basic that there are no supported methods, properties, or events! However, in later sections you will see the functionality of this control increase as we add the Caption property, the DoClick method, and finally, the Click event.

NOTE: When developing an ActiveX control, changes are usually confined to the same two or three project files (usually the program file and the .ODL file). Because of this, each sample in this chapter builds on the previous sample code, discussing only the changes made to each file. This makes modifications to the project easier to spot.

Here is the class derivation file used in our first sample program:

```
// TESTCTL1.H

class CTest1App : public COleControlModule
{
public:
  BOOL InitInstance();
  int ExitInstance();
};

class CTest1Ctrl : public COleControl
{
  DECLARE_DYNCREATE(CTest1Ctrl)

public:
  CTest1Ctrl();
  virtual void OnDraw(CDC *pdc, const CRect &rcBounds,
                      const CRect &rcInvalid);

protected:
  DECLARE_OLECREATE_EX(CTest1Ctrl)
  DECLARE_OLETYPELIB(CTest1Ctrl)
  DECLARE_OLECTLTYPE(CTest1Ctrl)
  DECLARE_MESSAGE_MAP()
  DECLARE_DISPATCH_MAP()
  DECLARE_EVENT_MAP()
};

extern const GUID CDECL _tlid;
extern const WORD _wVerMajor;
extern const WORD _wVerMinor;
```

Here is the program file:

```
// TESTCTL1.CPP
#include <afxctl.h>
#include "ids.h"
#include "TestCtl1.h"

IMPLEMENT_DYNCREATE(CTest1Ctrl, COleControl)

BEGIN_MESSAGE_MAP(CTest1Ctrl, COleControl)
END_MESSAGE_MAP()

BEGIN_DISPATCH_MAP(CTest1Ctrl, COleControl)
END_DISPATCH_MAP()

BEGIN_EVENT_MAP(CTest1Ctrl, COleControl)
END_EVENT_MAP()

// {BB289DA1-0A23-11d2-ABDB-94CAF6C00000}
IMPLEMENT_OLECREATE_EX(CTest1Ctrl, "TEST1.Test1Ctrl.1",
    0xbb289da1, 0xa23, 0x11d2, 0xab, 0xdb, 0x94, 0xca, 0xf6, 0xc0,
    0x0, 0x0);

IMPLEMENT_OLETYPELIB(CTest1Ctrl, _tlid, _wVerMajor, _wVerMinor)

// {BB289DA2-0A23-11d2-ABDB-94CAF6C00000}
const IID BASED_CODE IID_DTestCtl1 = { 0xbb289da2, 0xa23, 0x11d2, {
    0xab, 0xdb, 0x94, 0xca, 0xf6, 0xc0, 0x0, 0x0 } };
// {BB289DA3-0A23-11d2-ABDB-94CAF6C00000}
const IID BASED_CODE IID_DTestCtl1Events = { 0xbb289da3, 0xa23,
    0x11d2,
    { 0xab, 0xdb, 0x94, 0xca, 0xf6, 0xc0, 0x0, 0x0 } };

static const DWORD BASED_CODE _dwTestCtl1OleMisc =
  OLEMISC_SETCLIENTSITEFIRST |
  OLEMISC_INSIDEOUT |
  OLEMISC_CANTLINKINSIDE |
  OLEMISC_RECOMPOSEONRESIZE;
```

18

```
IMPLEMENT_OLECTLTYPE(CTest1Ctrl, IDS_TESTCTL1, _dwTestCtl1OleMisc)

BOOL CTest1Ctrl::CTest1CtrlFactory::UpdateRegistry(BOOL bRegister)
{
  if (bRegister)
    return AfxOleRegisterControlClass(
      AfxGetInstanceHandle(), m_clsid, m_lpszProgID, IDS_TESTCTL1,
      IDB_TESTCTL1, afxRegApartmentThreading, _dwTestCtl1OleMisc,
      _tlid, _wVerMajor, _wVerMinor);
  else
    return AfxOleUnregisterClass(m_clsid, m_lpszProgID);
}

CTest1Ctrl::CTest1Ctrl()
{
  InitializeIIDs(&IID_DTestCtl1, &IID_DTestCtl1Events);
}

void CTest1Ctrl::OnDraw(CDC *pdc, const CRect &rcBounds,
      const CRect &rcInvalid)
{
  pdc->FillRect(rcBounds,
    CBrush::FromHandle((HBRUSH)GetStockObject(WHITE_BRUSH)));
  pdc->Ellipse(rcBounds);
}

CTest1App theTestApp;

// {BB289DA4-0A23-11d2-ABDB-94CAF6C00000}
const GUID CDECL BASED_CODE _tlid ={ 0xbb289da4, 0xa23, 0x11d2,
      { 0xab, 0xdb, 0x94, 0xca, 0xf6, 0xc0, 0x0, 0x0 } };

const WORD _wVerMajor = 1;
const WORD _wVerMinor = 0;

BOOL CTest1App::InitInstance()
{
  return COleControlModule::InitInstance();
}

int CTest1App::ExitInstance()
{
  return COleControlModule::ExitInstance();
}
```

```
STDAPI DllRegisterServer(void)
{
  AFX_MANAGE_STATE(_afxModuleAddrThis);

  if (!AfxOleRegisterTypeLib(AfxGetInstanceHandle(), _tlid))
    return ResultFromScode(SELFREG_E_TYPELIB);

  if (!COleObjectFactoryEx::UpdateRegistryAll(TRUE))
    return ResultFromScode(SELFREG_E_CLASS);

  return NOERROR;
}

STDAPI DllUnregisterServer(void)
{
  AFX_MANAGE_STATE(_afxModuleAddrThis);

  if (!AfxOleUnregisterTypeLib(_tlid, _wVerMajor, _wVerMinor))
    return ResultFromScode(SELFREG_E_TYPELIB);

  if (!COleObjectFactoryEx::UpdateRegistryAll(FALSE))
    return ResultFromScode(SELFREG_E_CLASS);

  return NOERROR;
}
```

18

Once the control has successfully been built and registered, an instance is created by the ActiveX Control Test Container and displayed. Figure 18-1 shows the resultant control.

ActiveX Control Properties

One of the main features of ActiveX controls is their ability to expose a set of properties and methods via a primary dispatch interface. This interface is available to the control container and provides a path of communication from the control container to our control. This path of communication is a fairly unique concept compared to the previous sample programs in this book. Each previous sample program is self-contained and the only path of communication is between the user and the graphical interface of the application. However, with ActiveX controls, the dispatch interface allows the control container to access the control as a type of resource. This is the beauty and power of COM.

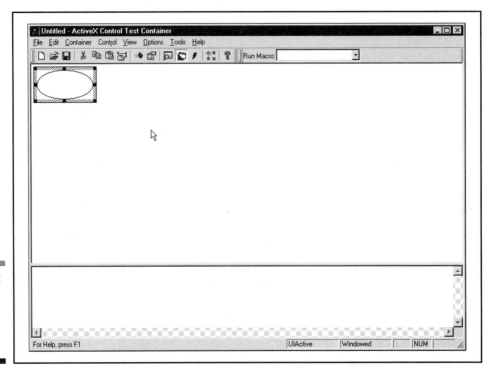

Sample output from the first demonstration program

Figure 18-1.

In the previous section of this chapter, we discussed the procedure for developing the framework of an ActiveX control. Let's narrow the discussion and look at ActiveX properties and their implementation in MFC.

ActiveX control properties expose specific attributes of the control to the control container. These properties allow a safe method of communication with the control without compromising the control's integrity. In this respect, an ActiveX control property resembles a data member of a C++ class. Common properties for a control can be as simple as a text caption or as complex as the interface between a database and the control's user. As mentioned previously, the properties of a control are implemented by the control's primary dispatch interface (in our example, **_DtestI)**. Properties come in two flavors: stock and custom.

NOTE: Custom properties, methods, and events represent a large area of ActiveX control technology and a good understanding requires extensive discussion and examples. Because the purpose of this chapter is to introduce and familiarize the reader with ActiveX control technology, we will focus only on the stock implementation of properties, methods, and events.

Stock Properties

18

Stock properties are properties whose behavior is already implemented by the **COleControl** base class. In other words, each property has a standard (or stock) behavior that cannot be altered. This property set represents the common functionality of an ActiveX control. It is not meant to encompass the entire property set of ActiveX controls (that would be impossible!). Its purpose is to provide a subset that is known by all ActiveX control containers. **COleControl** currently implements nine properties.

Stock Property	Description
Appearance	Determines if the control is flat or 3-D in appearance.
BackColor	The background color of the control.
BorderStyle	The style of border for the control. Either a standard solid border or no border.
Caption	The title of the control. Similar to the Text stock property.
Enabled	Determines if the control is enabled or disabled.
Font	The current font used by the control.
ForeColor	The foreground color of the control.
hWnd	The handle of the control's window object.
Text	The title of the control. Similar to the Caption property.

In addition to the nine properties implemented by **COleControl**, there is a set of member functions that allow the control class to get or set the current value of any stock property. If the property is exposed by the control, these functions are commonly used to implement the stock property.

For instance, if the control container makes a request to change the Caption property, the control sets the new value of the Caption property by calling **COleControl::SetText( )**. On the other hand, if the control container requests the current value of the Caption property, the control retrieves the current value by calling **COleControl::GetText( )** and then returning the result to the control container. Their prototypes are as follows:

>   void COleControl::SetText(LPCSTR *Caption*)

>   BSTR COleControl::GetText( );

Here, *Caption* is a pointer to the string containing the new value. **GetText( )** returns the current value in a variable of type **BSTR**. This data type is a 32-bit character pointer that is often used by COM objects.

In addition to the set of stock property member functions, there is another set of **COleControl** member functions that notify the control whenever a stock property (except for the **hWnd** property) is modified. Override these functions in your control class to perform additional actions when a stock property changes.

Custom Properties

Stock properties are good for general property management, but your control will have some unique properties that don't fit in the stock property category. Fortunately, MFC has a solution for this problem: custom properties. Unlike a stock property, a custom property is not implemented by the **COleControl** base class. A good example of a custom property is the owner of the ActiveX control. The ActiveX control can expose an Owner property which, when retrieved, can provide the name of the company or person who developed the control.

Because the property is custom, you provide the declaration and implementation for the custom property. However, MFC does provide a framework for declaring custom properties. There are currently four types of implementation for an ActiveX custom property:

Implementation Type	Description
Member Variable	Implemented by a member variable that is exposed to the container.

Implementation Type	Description
Member Variable with Notification	The same implementation as Member Variable except the control is notified when the property is changed.
Get/Set Methods	Implemented by a pair of exposed member functions. One gets the current property value and the other sets the current property value.
Parameterized	Implemented using the Get/Set Methods style but allows access to a group of values through a single property.

18

As mentioned, to properly present this aspect of ActiveX controls is beyond the scope of this chapter.

Implementing the Stock Caption Property

In the previous sample, we laid the groundwork for the Caption property by declaring and implementing a primary dispatch interface, **_Dtest1**. It's now time to add a property to this interface. After we are done, the stock property will be available to clients of our control.

The following sample program adds the stock Caption property. The common behavior of this property is to display the caption value in the center of the control. Because the stock Caption property is already implemented by **COleControl**, the changes to the project files are minimal. These changes are restricted to the Object Description Language file (TESTCTL1.ODL) and the program file (TESTCTL1.CPP). The remaining project files remain the same and can be copied from the previous sample.

In order for the Caption property to be exposed to a control container, it must be inserted into the primary dispatch interface of the ActiveX control. Insert the new Caption property into the primary dispatch interface by adding a new **id** statement to the **_Dtest1** interface description, declared in the .ODL file. The syntax for the **id** statement is as follows:

[**id**(*PropertyID*) [*,optional-attribute-list*]] *ReturnType ExternalName*

Here, *PropertyID* is the ID of the property, followed by a list of optional attributes. The *ReturnType* describes the type returned by the function implementing the property. *ExternalName* is the name of the function as it appears to a client of the control. The following code, taken from our sample, defines the stock Caption property, with an ID of **DISPID_CAPTION**. The external name of the property is Caption and the return is of type **BSTR**. The **bindable** and **requestedit** attributes are included in the definition.

```
[id(DISPID_CAPTION), bindable, requestedit] BSTR Caption;
```

The resultant TESTCTL1.ODL file is shown here:

```
// TESTCTL1.ODL : type library source for ActiveX Control project.

#include <olectl.h>
#include <idispids.h>

[ uuid(BB289DA4-0A23-11d2-ABDB-94CAF6C00000), version(1.0), control ]
library TEST1Lib
{
  importlib(STDOLE_TLB);
  importlib(STDTYPE_TLB);

  [ uuid(BB289DA2-0A23-11d2-ABDB-94CAF6C00000), hidden ]
  dispinterface _Dtest1
  {
    properties:
      [id(DISPID_CAPTION), bindable, requestedit] BSTR Caption;
    methods:

  };

  [ uuid(BB289DA3-0A23-11d2-ABDB-94CAF6C00000)]
  dispinterface _DTest1Events
  {
    properties:

    methods:

  };

  [ uuid(BB289DA1-0A23-11d2-ABDB-94CAF6C00000), control ]
  coclass Test1
  {
    [default] dispinterface _Dtest1;
    [default, source] dispinterface _DTest1Events;
  };

};
```

The remaining changes occur in the program file. We must add the stock Caption property to our dispatch map and implement the common behavior of displaying it in the control. First, add the **DISP_STOCKPROP_CAPTION( )** macro to the control's dispatch map. Its prototype is as follows:

```
DISP_STOCKPROP_CAPTION( )
```

The second change is to the **CTestCtl1::OnDraw( )** member function. The common behavior of this stock property is to display the caption in the center of the control. This is done by retrieving the current value of the stock Caption property with a call to **COleControl::InternalGetText(.)**. Next, we retrieve the metrics of the current font used by the control and set the alignment of the caption so that it is centered and at the top of the rectangular text field. This text alignment is done by calling **CDC::SetTextAlign( )**. Using the metrics of the current font and a simple formula, we calculate the proper coordinates that ensure the caption is always centered within the control. Finally, we draw the caption by calling **CDC::ExtTextOut( )**. Our control now implements the stock Caption property and displays the current value within the control.

18

The program file is as follows:

```
// TESTCTL1.CPP
#include <afxctl.h>
#include "ids.h"
#include "TestCtl1.h"

IMPLEMENT_DYNCREATE(CTest1Ctrl, COleControl)

BEGIN_MESSAGE_MAP(CTest1Ctrl, COleControl)
END_MESSAGE_MAP()

BEGIN_DISPATCH_MAP(CTest1Ctrl, COleControl)
  DISP_STOCKPROP_CAPTION()
END_DISPATCH_MAP()

BEGIN_EVENT_MAP(CTest1Ctrl, COleControl)
END_EVENT_MAP()

// {BB289DA1-0A23-11d2-ABDB-94CAF6C00000}
IMPLEMENT_OLECREATE_EX(CTest1Ctrl, "TEST1.Test1Ctrl.1",
    0xbb289da1, 0xa23, 0x11d2, 0xab, 0xdb, 0x94, 0xca, 0xf6, 0xc0,
    0x0, 0x0);

IMPLEMENT_OLETYPELIB(CTest1Ctrl, _tlid, _wVerMajor, _wVerMinor)
```

```
// {BB289DA2-0A23-11d2-ABDB-94CAF6C00000}
const IID BASED_CODE IID_DTestCtl1 = { 0xbb289da2, 0xa23, 0x11d2, {
    0xab,
    0xdb, 0x94, 0xca, 0xf6, 0xc0, 0x0, 0x0 } };
// {BB289DA3-0A23-11d2-ABDB-94CAF6C00000}
const IID BASED_CODE IID_DTestCtl1Events = { 0xbb289da3, 0xa23,
    0x11d2,
    { 0xab, 0xdb, 0x94, 0xca, 0xf6, 0xc0, 0x0, 0x0 } };

static const DWORD BASED_CODE _dwTestCtl1OleMisc =
  OLEMISC_SETCLIENTSITEFIRST |
  OLEMISC_INSIDEOUT |
  OLEMISC_CANTLINKINSIDE |
  OLEMISC_RECOMPOSEONRESIZE;

IMPLEMENT_OLECTLTYPE(CTest1Ctrl, IDS_TESTCTL1, _dwTestCtl1OleMisc)

BOOL CTest1Ctrl::CTest1CtrlFactory::UpdateRegistry(BOOL bRegister)
{
  if (bRegister)
    return AfxOleRegisterControlClass(
      AfxGetInstanceHandle(), m_clsid, m_lpszProgID, IDS_TESTCTL1,
      IDB_TESTCTL1, afxRegApartmentThreading, _dwTestCtl1OleMisc,
      _tlid, _wVerMajor, _wVerMinor);
  else
    return AfxOleUnregisterClass(m_clsid, m_lpszProgID);
}

CTest1Ctrl::CTest1Ctrl()
{
  InitializeIIDs(&IID_DTestCtl1, &IID_DTestCtl1Events);
}

void CTest1Ctrl::OnDraw(CDC *pdc, const CRect &rcBounds,
      const CRect &rcInvalid)
{
  pdc->FillRect(rcBounds,
    CBrush::FromHandle((HBRUSH)GetStockObject(WHITE_BRUSH)));
  pdc->Ellipse(rcBounds);

  const CString &strCaption = InternalGetText();
  TEXTMETRIC tm;

  pdc->GetTextMetrics(&tm);
```

```
  pdc->SetTextAlign(TA_CENTER | TA_TOP);
  pdc->ExtTextOut((rcBounds.left + rcBounds.right) / 2,
    (rcBounds.top + rcBounds.bottom - tm.tmHeight) / 2,
    ETO_CLIPPED, rcBounds, strCaption, strCaption.GetLength(),
    NULL);
}

CTest1App theTestApp;

// {BB289DA4-0A23-11d2-ABDB-94CAF6C00000}
const GUID CDECL BASED_CODE _tlid ={ 0xbb289da4, 0xa23, 0x11d2,
    { 0xab, 0xdb, 0x94, 0xca, 0xf6, 0xc0, 0x0, 0x0 } };

const WORD _wVerMajor = 1;
const WORD _wVerMinor = 0;

BOOL CTest1App::InitInstance()
{
  return COleControlModule::InitInstance();
}

int CTest1App::ExitInstance()
{
  return COleControlModule::ExitInstance();
}

STDAPI DllRegisterServer(void)
{
  AFX_MANAGE_STATE(_afxModuleAddrThis);

  if (!AfxOleRegisterTypeLib(AfxGetInstanceHandle(), _tlid))
    return ResultFromScode(SELFREG_E_TYPELIB);

  if (!COleObjectFactoryEx::UpdateRegistryAll(TRUE))
    return ResultFromScode(SELFREG_E_CLASS);

  return NOERROR;
}

STDAPI DllUnregisterServer(void)
{
  AFX_MANAGE_STATE(_afxModuleAddrThis);

  if (!AfxOleUnregisterTypeLib(_tlid, _wVerMajor, _wVerMinor))
    return ResultFromScode(SELFREG_E_TYPELIB);
```

```
if (!COleObjectFactoryEx::UpdateRegistryAll(FALSE))
    return ResultFromScode(SELFREG_E_CLASS);

return NOERROR;
}
```

Sample output of this stock property is shown in Figure 18-2.

ActiveX Control Methods

Continuing the work we started with ActiveX properties, let's explore the other half of the dispatch interface: methods. Unlike properties, ActiveX control methods allow the client to perform certain actions on an ActiveX control. In this respect, an ActiveX control method resembles a member function of a C++ class. For instance, a common method would be requesting the control to access a record in a database, or perhaps perform a calculation using values passed in by the container.

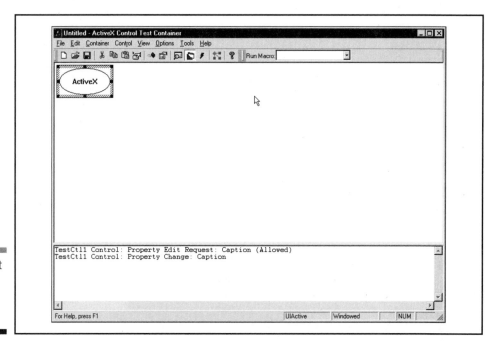

Sample output of the stock property

Figure 18-2.

Like properties, the methods of a control are implemented by the control's primary dispatch interface (in our example, **_DTest1**). Methods also come in two flavors: stock and custom.

Stock Methods

Stock methods, like stock properties, are methods whose behavior is already implemented by the **COleControl** base class. A stock method has a standard behavior that can not be altered. Currently, **COleControl** implements only two methods.

Stock Method	Description
DoClick	When the control is clicked, a stock Click event is fired.
Refresh	When this method is invoked, the control is immediately refreshed.

Unlike ActiveX stock properties, there is no set of member functions designed to work with stock methods.

Custom Methods

Like properties, custom methods are supported by the **COleControl** class. A good example of a custom method is displaying an About dialog box when requested by the user. This method, when invoked, will display an About dialog box for the ActiveX control.

MFC implements custom methods using the **DISP_FUNCTION( )** macro. Its prototype is as follows:

DISP_FUNCTION(*ClassName, ExtName, HandlerFunc, ReturnVal, Params*)

Here, *ClassName* is the name of the control class. *ExtName* is the external name of the custom method. *HandlerFunc* is the actual name of the control class' handler function and *ReturnVal* is the type of value returned from *HandlerFunc*. Finally, *Params* is a space-separated list of parameter types passed to *HandlerFunc*.

The **DISP_FUNCTION( )** macro is only part of the implementation. The handler function, referenced by the macro, must be declared in the control class and implemented in the program file of the project. The actual implementation is obviously left to the control developer. Finally, the last piece is the insertion of an **id** statement in the primary dispatch interface of the project's .ODL file.

Like custom properties, custom methods are a rich and varied area of ActiveX controls and beyond the treatment of this chapter.

Implementing the Stock DoClick Method

To demonstrate the process for adding stock methods, the following sample program adds the stock DoClick method. When invoked by the control container, this method simulates a mouse click within the control. This is done by calling the **COleControl::DoClick( )** function. Because the DoClick method is meant to simulate a mouse click within the control, a Click event is fired (if supported by the control). If the stock Click event is not supported, nothing happens.

Because the stock DoClick method is already implemented by **COleControl**, the changes to the project files are minimal. Modifications will be made to the .ODL file (TESTCTL1.ODL) and the program file (TESTCTL1.CPP). The remaining project files remain the same and are taken from the previous sample.

Like the stock property we inserted previously, the stock method is added to the **_Dtest1** dispatch interface by a new **id** statement in the .ODL file. The following code, taken from our sample, defines the stock DoClick method with no optional attributes. The ID of the method is **DISPID_DOCLICK** and the external method name is DoClick with no parameters or return value.

```
[id(DISPID_DOCLICK)] void DoClick();
```

The new TESTCTL1.ODL file is shown here:

```
// TESTCTL1.ODL : type library source for ActiveX Control project.

#include <olectl.h>
#include <idispids.h>

[ uuid(BB289DA4-0A23-11d2-ABDB-94CAF6C00000), version(1.0), control ]
library TEST1Lib
{
  importlib(STDOLE_TLB);
  importlib(STDTYPE_TLB);
```

18

```
[ uuid(BB289DA2-0A23-11d2-ABDB-94CAF6C00000), hidden ]
dispinterface _Dtest1
{
  properties:
    [id(DISPID_CAPTION), bindable, requestedit] BSTR Caption;
  methods:
    [id(DISPID_DOCLICK)] void DoClick();
};

[ uuid(BB289DA3-0A23-11d2-ABDB-94CAF6C00000)]
dispinterface _DTest1Events
{
  properties:

  methods:

};

[ uuid(BB289DA1-0A23-11d2-ABDB-94CAF6C00000), control ]
coclass Test1
{
  [default] dispinterface _Dtest1;
  [default, source] dispinterface _DTest1Events;
};

};
```

There is only one change made in the program file. The **DISP_STOCK-FUNC_DOCLICK( )** macro is added to the control's primary dispatch map. The prototype is as follows:

DISP_STOCKFUNC_DOCLICK( )

The program file is as follows:

```
// TESTCTL1.CPP
#include <afxctl.h>
#include "ids.h"
#include "TestCtl1.h"

IMPLEMENT_DYNCREATE(CTest1Ctrl, COleControl)

BEGIN_MESSAGE_MAP(CTest1Ctrl, COleControl)
END_MESSAGE_MAP()
```

```
BEGIN_DISPATCH_MAP(CTest1Ctrl, COleControl)
  DISP_STOCKPROP_CAPTION()
  DISP_STOCKFUNC_DOCLICK()
END_DISPATCH_MAP()

BEGIN_EVENT_MAP(CTest1Ctrl, COleControl)
END_EVENT_MAP()

// {BB289DA1-0A23-11d2-ABDB-94CAF6C00000}
IMPLEMENT_OLECREATE_EX(CTest1Ctrl, "TEST1.Test1Ctrl.1",
    0xbb289da1, 0xa23, 0x11d2, 0xab, 0xdb, 0x94, 0xca, 0xf6, 0xc0,
    0x0, 0x0);

IMPLEMENT_OLETYPELIB(CTest1Ctrl, _tlid, _wVerMajor, _wVerMinor)

// {BB289DA2-0A23-11d2-ABDB-94CAF6C00000}
const IID BASED_CODE IID_DTestCtl1 = { 0xbb289da2, 0xa23, 0x11d2, {
    0xab,
    0xdb, 0x94, 0xca, 0xf6, 0xc0, 0x0, 0x0 } };
// {BB289DA3-0A23-11d2-ABDB-94CAF6C00000}
const IID BASED_CODE IID_DTestCtl1Events = { 0xbb289da3, 0xa23,
    0x11d2,
    { 0xab, 0xdb, 0x94, 0xca, 0xf6, 0xc0, 0x0, 0x0 } };

static const DWORD BASED_CODE _dwTestCtl1OleMisc =
  OLEMISC_SETCLIENTSITEFIRST |
  OLEMISC_INSIDEOUT |
  OLEMISC_CANTLINKINSIDE |
  OLEMISC_RECOMPOSEONRESIZE;

IMPLEMENT_OLECTLTYPE(CTest1Ctrl, IDS_TESTCTL1, _dwTestCtl1OleMisc)

BOOL CTest1Ctrl::CTest1CtrlFactory::UpdateRegistry(BOOL bRegister)
{
  if (bRegister)
    return AfxOleRegisterControlClass(
      AfxGetInstanceHandle(), m_clsid, m_lpszProgID, IDS_TESTCTL1,
      IDB_TESTCTL1, afxRegApartmentThreading, _dwTestCtl1OleMisc,
      _tlid, _wVerMajor, _wVerMinor);
  else
    return AfxOleUnregisterClass(m_clsid, m_lpszProgID);
}

CTest1Ctrl::CTest1Ctrl()
```

```
{
  InitializeIIDs(&IID_DTestCtl1, &IID_DTestCtl1Events);
}

void CTest1Ctrl::OnDraw(CDC *pdc, const CRect &rcBounds,
      const CRect &rcInvalid)
{
  pdc->FillRect(rcBounds,
    CBrush::FromHandle((HBRUSH)GetStockObject(WHITE_BRUSH)));
  pdc->Ellipse(rcBounds);

  const CString &strCaption = InternalGetText();
  TEXTMETRIC tm;

  pdc->GetTextMetrics(&tm);
  pdc->SetTextAlign(TA_CENTER | TA_TOP);
  pdc->ExtTextOut((rcBounds.left + rcBounds.right) / 2,
    (rcBounds.top + rcBounds.bottom - tm.tmHeight) / 2,
    ETO_CLIPPED, rcBounds, strCaption, strCaption.GetLength(),
    NULL);
}

CTest1App theTestApp;

// {BB289DA4-0A23-11d2-ABDB-94CAF6C00000}
const GUID CDECL BASED_CODE _tlid ={ 0xbb289da4, 0xa23, 0x11d2,
      { 0xab, 0xdb, 0x94, 0xca, 0xf6, 0xc0, 0x0, 0x0 } };

const WORD _wVerMajor = 1;
const WORD _wVerMinor = 0;

BOOL CTest1App::InitInstance()
{
  return COleControlModule::InitInstance();
}

int CTest1App::ExitInstance()
{
  return COleControlModule::ExitInstance();
}

STDAPI DllRegisterServer(void)
{
  AFX_MANAGE_STATE(_afxModuleAddrThis);
```

```
  if (!AfxOleRegisterTypeLib(AfxGetInstanceHandle(), _tlid))
    return ResultFromScode(SELFREG_E_TYPELIB);

  if (!COleObjectFactoryEx::UpdateRegistryAll(TRUE))
    return ResultFromScode(SELFREG_E_CLASS);

  return NOERROR;
}

STDAPI DllUnregisterServer(void)
{
  AFX_MANAGE_STATE(_afxModuleAddrThis);

  if (!AfxOleUnregisterTypeLib(_tlid, _wVerMajor, _wVerMinor))
    return ResultFromScode(SELFREG_E_TYPELIB);

  if (!COleObjectFactoryEx::UpdateRegistryAll(FALSE))
    return ResultFromScode(SELFREG_E_CLASS);

  return NOERROR;
}
```

When the DoClick method is invoked, the overridable **COleControl::On-Click( )** function is called. The **COleControl::OnClick( )** function then checks the control for an implementation of the stock Click event. If one exists, the stock Click event is fired.

Because our control does not implement the stock Click event, nothing will happen except the calling of **COleControl::DoClick( )**. However, in the next section we will implement the stock Click event and tie the two together. At that point, when the DoClick method is invoked, the stock Click event will automatically fire.

ActiveX Events

Earlier, the paths of communication between an ActiveX control and its container were discussed. We have addressed how the control container communicates with the ActiveX control. It is now time to discuss the other path of communication: events. Events provide a way for the ActiveX control to notify the container that something important has happened with the control. Some typical events include mouse actions (a mouse click within the control) or key press events (the user entering data from a keyboard). Like properties and methods, MFC provides two event types: stock and custom.

The previous two sample programs have modified the primary dispatch interface (**_Dtest1**) of the control by adding a stock property and method. However, events fired by an ActiveX control are contained within a separate dispatch interface. This interface contains all the events implemented by the control, and in our sample program is identified as **_DTest1Events**. This is the interface we will be working with now.

Stock Events

18

Stock events are those that are already implemented by the **COleControl** base class. They represent the most common actions an ActiveX control might wish to support such as various mouse clicks and key presses. Note that all events require that the control be UI active before being fired. UI active simply means that the control is able to respond to user interface interaction or fire events. The stock events are shown here:

Stock Event	Description
Click	Fired when the user clicks on a control.
DblClick	Fired when the user double clicks on a control.
Error	Fired when an error has occurred within your control. The error condition is determined by you.
KeyDown	Fired when a key is pressed.
KeyPress	Fired when a key is pressed and released.
KeyUp	Fired when a key is released.
MouseDown	Fired when a mouse button is pressed within the area of the control.
MouseMove	Fired when the cursor is moved within a control.
MouseUp	Fired when a mouse button is released within the area of the control.
ReadyStateChange	Fired when the state of the control has changed. Used to indicate the different stages of loading (such as asynchronously loading data or properties).

Custom Events

Custom events are important actions or conditions that you would like to indicate have occurred and are not supported by **COleControl**. For instance, suppose your control is rendering a complex image in the background. When the image is ready, the control could fire a custom event signaling that the image has been rendered and is ready for display. The control would then update its appearance with the new image.

MFC implements custom events using the **EVENT_CUSTOM( )** macro. Its prototype is as follows:

EVENT_CUSTOM(*ExtName, FiringFunc, Params*)

Here, *ExtName* is the external name of the custom event. *FiringFunc* is the actual name of the control class' event firing function. Finally, *Params* is a space-separated list of parameter types passed to *FiringFunc*.

The **EVENT_CUSTOM( )** macro is only part of the implementation. The firing function, referenced by the macro, must be declared in the control class and implemented in the program file of the project. The actual implementation is obviously left to the control developer. Finally, the remaining piece is the insertion of an **id** statement in the dispatch interface of the project's .ODL file.

As with custom methods and properties, a deeper treatment of custom events is beyond the scope of this book.

Implementing the Stock Click Event

To demonstrate the process for adding stock events, the following sample program adds the stock Click event. The control fires this event when a mouse click has been received, or the DoClick method has been invoked. The event is fired by calling the **COleControl::FireClick( )** member function.

As with all of our modifications, implementing this stock event requires little work. Once again the work is limited to the .ODL file (TESTCTL1.ODL) and the program file (TESTCTL1.CPP). The remaining project files are the same and are carried over from the preceding example.

First, we insert a new **id** statement into the project's .ODL file. Because we are implementing an event, we will modify the **_DTest1Events** interface instead of the **_Dtest1** interface. The following code, taken from our sample, defines the stock Click event with no optional attributes. The ID of the method is **DISPID_CLICK** and the external method name is Click with no return value.

```
[id(DISPID_CLICK)] void Click( );
```

NOTE: This **id** statement is somewhat misleading as it implies that there is a function that implements the stock Click event. This is not true. The function name is supplied only because all methods on a dispatch interface must have an external name.

18

The new TESTCTL1.ODL file is shown here:

```
// TESTCTL1.ODL : type library source for ActiveX Control project.

#include <olectl.h>
#include <idispids.h>

[ uuid(BB289DA4-0A23-11d2-ABDB-94CAF6C00000), version(1.0), control ]
library TEST1Lib
{
  importlib(STDOLE_TLB);
  importlib(STDTYPE_TLB);

  [ uuid(BB289DA2-0A23-11d2-ABDB-94CAF6C00000), hidden ]
  dispinterface _Dtest1
  {
    properties:
      [id(DISPID_CAPTION), bindable, requestedit] BSTR Caption;
    methods:
      [id(DISPID_DOCLICK)] void DoClick();
  };

  [ uuid(BB289DA3-0A23-11d2-ABDB-94CAF6C00000)]
  dispinterface _DTest1Events
  {
    properties:

    methods:
      [id(DISPID_CLICK)] void Click();
  };

  [ uuid(BB289DA1-0A23-11d2-ABDB-94CAF6C00000), control ]
  coclass Test1
  {
```

```
    [default] dispinterface _Dtest1;
    [default, source] dispinterface _DTest1Events;
  };

};
```

The only change to the program file is the insertion of the
EVENT_STOCK_CLICK( ) macro to our event dispatch map. The prototype
is as follows:

    EVENT_STOCK_CLICK( )

The new program file is as follows:

```
// TESTCTL1.CPP
#include <afxctl.h>
#include "ids.h"
#include "TestCtl1.h"

IMPLEMENT_DYNCREATE(CTest1Ctrl, COleControl)

BEGIN_MESSAGE_MAP(CTest1Ctrl, COleControl)
END_MESSAGE_MAP()

BEGIN_DISPATCH_MAP(CTest1Ctrl, COleControl)
  DISP_STOCKPROP_CAPTION()
  DISP_STOCKFUNC_DOCLICK()
END_DISPATCH_MAP()

BEGIN_EVENT_MAP(CTest1Ctrl, COleControl)
  EVENT_STOCK_CLICK( )
END_EVENT_MAP()

// {BB289DA1-0A23-11d2-ABDB-94CAF6C00000}
IMPLEMENT_OLECREATE_EX(CTest1Ctrl, "TEST1.Test1Ctrl.1",
    0xbb289da1, 0xa23, 0x11d2, 0xab, 0xdb, 0x94, 0xca, 0xf6, 0xc0,
    0x0, 0x0);

IMPLEMENT_OLETYPELIB(CTest1Ctrl, _tlid, _wVerMajor, _wVerMinor)

// {BB289DA2-0A23-11d2-ABDB-94CAF6C00000}
const IID BASED_CODE IID_DTestCtl1 = { 0xbb289da2, 0xa23, 0x11d2, {
    0xab,
    0xdb, 0x94, 0xca, 0xf6, 0xc0, 0x0, 0x0 } };
```

```cpp
// {BB289DA3-0A23-11d2-ABDB-94CAF6C00000}
const IID BASED_CODE IID_DTestCtl1Events = { 0xbb289da3, 0xa23,
    0x11d2,
    { 0xab, 0xdb, 0x94, 0xca, 0xf6, 0xc0, 0x0, 0x0 } };

static const DWORD BASED_CODE _dwTestCtl1OleMisc =
  OLEMISC_SETCLIENTSITEFIRST |
  OLEMISC_INSIDEOUT |
  OLEMISC_CANTLINKINSIDE |
  OLEMISC_RECOMPOSEONRESIZE;

IMPLEMENT_OLECTLTYPE(CTest1Ctrl, IDS_TESTCTL1, _dwTestCtl1OleMisc)

BOOL CTest1Ctrl::CTest1CtrlFactory::UpdateRegistry(BOOL bRegister)
{
  if (bRegister)
    return AfxOleRegisterControlClass(
      AfxGetInstanceHandle(), m_clsid, m_lpszProgID, IDS_TESTCTL1,
      IDB_TESTCTL1, afxRegApartmentThreading, _dwTestCtl1OleMisc,
      _tlid, _wVerMajor, _wVerMinor);
  else
    return AfxOleUnregisterClass(m_clsid, m_lpszProgID);
}

CTest1Ctrl::CTest1Ctrl()
{
  InitializeIIDs(&IID_DTestCtl1, &IID_DTestCtl1Events);
}

void CTest1Ctrl::OnDraw(CDC *pdc, const CRect &rcBounds,
    const CRect &rcInvalid)
{
  pdc->FillRect(rcBounds,
    CBrush::FromHandle((HBRUSH)GetStockObject(WHITE_BRUSH)));
  pdc->Ellipse(rcBounds);

  const CString &strCaption = InternalGetText();
  TEXTMETRIC tm;

  pdc->GetTextMetrics(&tm);
  pdc->SetTextAlign(TA_CENTER | TA_TOP);
  pdc->ExtTextOut((rcBounds.left + rcBounds.right) / 2,
    (rcBounds.top + rcBounds.bottom - tm.tmHeight) / 2,
    ETO_CLIPPED, rcBounds, strCaption, strCaption.GetLength(),
    NULL);
}
```

```
CTest1App theTestApp;

// {BB289DA4-0A23-11d2-ABDB-94CAF6C00000}
const GUID CDECL BASED_CODE _tlid ={ 0xbb289da4, 0xa23, 0x11d2,
      { 0xab, 0xdb, 0x94, 0xca, 0xf6, 0xc0, 0x0, 0x0 } };

const WORD _wVerMajor = 1;
const WORD _wVerMinor = 0;

BOOL CTest1App::InitInstance()
{
  return COleControlModule::InitInstance();
}

int CTest1App::ExitInstance()
{
  return COleControlModule::ExitInstance();
}

STDAPI DllRegisterServer(void)
{
  AFX_MANAGE_STATE(_afxModuleAddrThis);

  if (!AfxOleRegisterTypeLib(AfxGetInstanceHandle(), _tlid))
    return ResultFromScode(SELFREG_E_TYPELIB);

  if (!COleObjectFactoryEx::UpdateRegistryAll(TRUE))
    return ResultFromScode(SELFREG_E_CLASS);

  return NOERROR;
}

STDAPI DllUnregisterServer(void)
{
  AFX_MANAGE_STATE(_afxModuleAddrThis);

  if (!AfxOleUnregisterTypeLib(_tlid, _wVerMajor, _wVerMinor))
    return ResultFromScode(SELFREG_E_TYPELIB);

  if (!COleObjectFactoryEx::UpdateRegistryAll(FALSE))
    return ResultFromScode(SELFREG_E_CLASS);

  return NOERROR;
}
```

18

Because we now support the stock Click event, when the user clicks on the control or invokes the DoClick method, the stock Click event will automatically fire. Sample output of this stock property is shown in Figure 18-3.

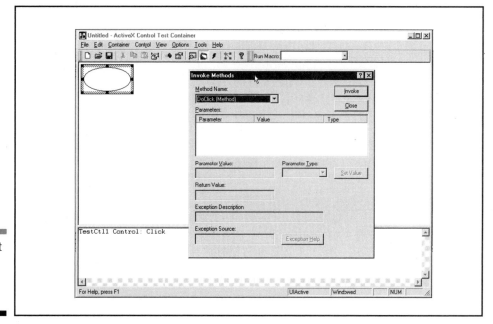

Sample output
of the stock
Click event

Figure 18-3.

IN DEPTH

ActiveX Control Containers

Throughout this chapter, we have focused on the development of ActiveX controls. Unlike normal Windows common controls, ActiveX controls implement methods and properties that are used by ActiveX clients. In turn, these controls are also able to communicate information about important occurrences (firing an event) to the ActiveX control container.

As opposed to the basic OLE container application, ActiveX control containers have built-in functionality tailored specifically for supporting ActiveX controls. This functionality includes the ability to query for specific ActiveX interfaces and invoke methods on those interfaces. In addition to manipulating the control through its dispatch interface, the control container has the ability to handle any events fired by the control, if so desired. Without these specialized control containers, ActiveX controls would not be as impressive as they are.

To ensure the ease of use and portability of these ActiveX controls, several types of ActiveX control containers exist. These applications include IE 3 (and later versions), the ActiveX Control Test Container (used to demonstrate the various incarnations of our sample control), and any OLE container built with MFC version 4 (or later). For instance, one of the application types you can build with the Microsoft AppWizard (discussed in the Chapter 19) is a dialog-based application that automatically supports ActiveX controls. It's that easy!

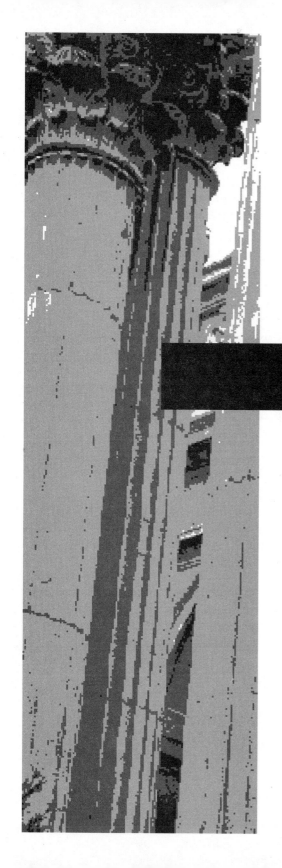

CHAPTER 19

Using the Visual C++ AppWizard and ClassWizard

The program examples in the preceding chapters were all constructed manually, in the way that you are probably accustomed to writing programs: "by hand." This approach is, of course, the best way to learn MFC. It is also the way that many real-world MFC programs are written. However, there is an important alternative method of creating MFC programs that you may want to take advantage of: the wizards supplied with the Visual C++ compiler. So, before concluding this book, we'll provide a brief overview of these important tools.

The Visual C++ wizards have been around as long as the MFC library. These tools are designed to closely support and ease the development of MFC Windows applications. The main purposes of this technology are to standardize the framework of MFC applications, exploit the innate modularity of the MFC library, and provide a framework of error-free code.

As demonstrated by the preceding chapters, MFC programming does not require you to use these wizards. In point of fact, most Windows applications these days are coded manually, in the unique style of the developer. However, there are cases where the wizards provide some real benefit and you may wish to consider them for your own program development. In this chapter, we will examine some of the benefits and abilities of the most commonly used and powerful wizards: MFC AppWizard and ClassWizard.

The MFC AppWizard

The history of the MFC AppWizard is the same as that of MFC. Both were created and released with the Visual C++ 1 product. The main purpose of AppWizard at that time (and to this day) was to quickly generate a basic project, using MFC code only, when implementing a single or multiple document (SDI or MDI) application. In the first version of AppWizard, this framework application contained MFC library code that displayed a window with a menu bar. As AppWizard was revised with each new version of MFC, greater functionality was automatically provided by the generated framework. At the current time of Visual C++ 6, AppWizard can generate an incredibly rich application framework without any additional user code.

The Basics of AppWizard

To be able to provide a functionally rich and flexible application framework, AppWizard uses a series of property pages that guide you through its myriad options. After you have removed and/or added the desired functionality (or just accepted the default options), AppWizard generates a Visual C++ project

19

that builds the resultant MFC application. Let's take a quick look at the major aspects of AppWizard, step by step.

Application Type

Each AppWizard page is composed of a bitmap representing the current properties of your AppWizard application, and a collection of controls that allow the manipulation of a group of available properties. The first page of AppWizard is shown in Figure 19-1.

The first page determines:

◆ The type of application (SDI, MDI, or dialog-based)

◆ If the application will use the document view architecture

◆ The language your application resources will use (this is for localization purposes only)

The choices made on this page affect the fundamental structure of your MFC application. The current application types offered were determined, in part, by existing trends of MFC applications. For instance, in version 1 of

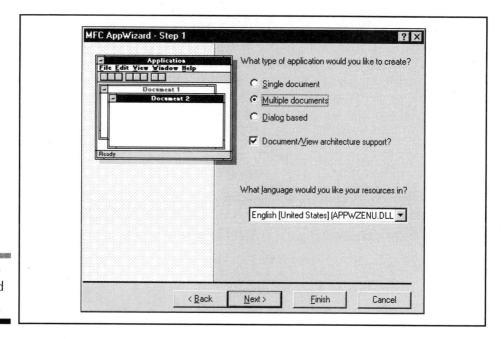

The first page
of AppWizard

Figure 19-1.

AppWizard, there was no choice for a dialog-based application; only SDI or MDI were available. However, after numerous requests from users of the product, a dialog- based option was added. With the release of Visual C++ 6, the choice to use document/view architecture (commonly referred to as doc/view support) was added to this page.

Finally, the language option allows easy localization of the standard resources provided by AppWizard. Basically, this means that the standard strings (for instance, menu items and status bar prompts) used in the application framework are already translated into their German, Spanish, French, or Italian counterparts—a very useful option for international applications.

The default options for this page are MDI, use document/view architecture, and English.

Database Options

The second page focuses on the database support provided by MFC. This page allows you to specify the type of database support, ranging from inclusion of database header files to implementation of a view object with database support. If you are including a database view object, you must provide a source for the data. This determines the type of database supported by the view object. Note that implementation of a database view object requires doc/view support (available from the first page). The default option is no database support.

Compound Document Options

The third page focuses on the compound document support provided by MFC. Previously, this was commonly referred to as "the OLE options page" but with the evolution of OLE into compound documents and COM, this page now offers additional choices beyond the standard OLE options.

The first portion lists the different "flavors" of compound document support. choices range from none, to container or mini/full server, to a combination of both Container and Server. In addition to these choices, you can also add automation and ActiveX control support. As mentioned in Chapter 18, the ActiveX controls option allows you to quickly implement an ActiveX container that accesses the full potential of ActiveX controls.

The default options include no compound document or automation support, and support for ActiveX controls.

Application Features

The fourth page focuses on a rich set of features that can be implemented by your framework application. Over time, this page has seen the majority of changes. These changes are driven by user requests and the availability of new technologies wrapped by the MFC library.

Among the features available, there are a few that are quite common and save considerable time in implementation if added by AppWizard (as opposed to manually). The implementation of basic tool and status bars can be styled in a traditional manner or with the new Internet Explorer ReBar style. AppWizard can also add the basic framework for context-sensitive help to the generated application framework. As you saw in Chapter 16, adding Help support to your application is not a trivial matter. However, with AppWizard, the process is automated and quite extensive.

19

One of the relatively unknown aspects of AppWizard can be found behind the Advanced... button on this page. This sub-page contains two tabs: one for modification of the document template string and another for window styles. The first tab allows modification of the sub-strings for the document template resource string. The purpose and structure of this resource string was introduced in Chapter 17. This string, if you recall, contains various sub-strings describing the extension of the documents created by the application, the name of the filter in the Files of Type drop-down list, and other aspects of the project. This tab allows you to modify the values of these sub-strings.

NOTE: The document template string tab is not available if you choose not to implement doc/view support in the first page.

The second tab offers the option of a split window in the view object, and optional styles for the main window and child frame window objects (if the application type is MDI). If the application type is SDI, the second section of this tab (the MDI Child Frame Styles portion) is disabled.

The default options include:

◆ A docking toolbar and initial status bar
◆ 3-D controls support

◆ Normal toolbar look and feel

◆ Four slots on the Most Recently Used (MRU) file list

Miscellaneous

The fifth page wraps up the "interview session" with some final options for the project. These options include the insertion of source file comments, options for linking with the MFC library (static or dynamic), and a new option: the style of the project.

This new option allows you to create the framework of a Windows Explorer-like project. This project type implements a window object with a split window. The left side is a tree control that you populate and the right side is a list view control. The Windows Explorer application is shown in Figure 19-2. The other choice is the standard SDI, MDI, or dialog-based project types.

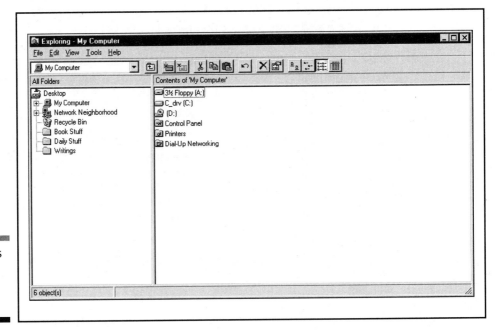

The Windows Explorer application

Figure 19-2.

Classes

The sixth, and final, page of AppWizard lists the classes that AppWizard will generate for your project, based on your current choices. This list will change depending on your earlier choices.

The purpose of this page is to allow you to modify the class names and the header and implementation filenames that implement your classes before they are generated.

NOTE: You are also able to change the class from which your view class is derived. The default is **CView** but you can change this to use a view class that supports a specific control—like **CTreeView**.

19

AppWizard Results

Now, let's take a brief look at the approach AppWizard takes to implement some of your choices by examining two areas related to the framework application. The first is the implementation of doc/view support in the generated project and the second is the context-sensitive help for the generated application.

Support for Document/View Architecture

Perhaps the most important benefit of AppWizard is the implementation of doc/view support in an MFC project. In Chapter 17 document/view was described. There, a version of the document/view architecture was implemented in a sample program. It will be instructive to compare this manual approach with that used by the AppWizard. Recall that in Chapter 17, the sample program was an SDI application that allowed the user to draw a series of connected lines. This series was stored as a collection of points in the document class and could be serialized to a permanent file (with the extension of .PNT). In the view class, these points were drawn and connected by a series of lines. In Chapter 17, the doc/view support was implemented using four classes:

- **CApp** (derived from **CWinApp**)   The main application class.

- **CMainWin** (derived from **CFrameWnd**)   The frame window class.

- **CSampleDoc** (derived from **CDocument**)   The document class, containing the data representation for the project.

- **CSampleView** (derived from **CView**)   The view class, rendering the data stored by the **CSampleDoc** class.

All four classes were declared in a single file, DOCVIEW.H.

Let's compare this class structure to a similar project generated by AppWizard, called SAMPLE. This project is created using all default options, except for the application type (SDI, instead of the default MDI). Similar to the Chapter 17 implementation, AppWizard generates four classes to implement doc/view support:

- **CSampleApp** (derived from **CWinApp**)   The main application class.

- **CMainFrame** (derived from **CFrameWnd**)   The frame window class.

- **CSampleDoc** (derived from **CDocument**)   The document class, containing the data representation for the project.

- **CSampleView** (derived from **CView**)   The view class, rendering the data stored by the **CSampleDoc** class.

As you can see, the two projects are very similar at this level. The only difference is the names of some of the classes. (Also, a separate class derivation file for each class in the SAMPLE project is generated.) However, if we look closer, additional differences become apparent. As an example, let's compare the two frame window classes.

CMainWin vs. CMainFrame

We have chosen **CMainWin** and **CMainFrame** classes for comparison because they clearly demonstrate the fundamental differences between a manual project and an AppWizard project. These differences are common for most of the classes generated by AppWizard and illustrate the benefits and deficits of a framework application generated by AppWizard.

The following is the class declaration of the manually created frame window class, **CMainWin**, from Chapter 17:

```
// This is the main window class.
class CMainWin : public CFrameWnd
{
  DECLARE_DYNCREATE(CMainWin)
public:
  CMainWin();

  DECLARE_MESSAGE_MAP()
};
```

The following is the class declaration of the SAMPLE frame window class, **CMainFrame**, created by the AppWizard:

```
class CMainFrame : public CFrameWnd
{

protected: // create from serialization only
    CMainFrame();
    DECLARE_DYNCREATE(CMainFrame)

// Attributes
public:

// Operations
public:

// Overrides
    // ClassWizard generated virtual function overrides
    //{{AFX_VIRTUAL(CMainFrame)
    virtual BOOL PreCreateWindow(CREATESTRUCT& cs);
    //}}AFX_VIRTUAL

// Implementation
public:
    virtual ~CMainFrame();
#ifdef _DEBUG
    virtual void AssertValid() const;
    virtual void Dump(CDumpContext& dc) const;
```

```
#endif

protected:  // control bar embedded members
    CStatusBar  m_wndStatusBar;
    CToolBar    m_wndToolBar;

// Generated message map functions
protected:
    //{{AFX_MSG(CMainFrame)
    afx_msg int OnCreate(LPCREATESTRUCT lpCreateStruct);
// NOTE - the ClassWizard will add and remove member functions here.
//    DO NOT EDIT what you see in these blocks of generated code!
    //}}AFX_MSG
    DECLARE_MESSAGE_MAP()
};
```

Obviously, there are quite a few differences between the two! After a general examination, one of the first things you notice are the prolific comments and access specifiers found in the declaration of **CMainFrame**. AppWizard formats each class in a similar way, with pre-defined areas delineated by the **public**, **protected**, and **private** keywords. While not necessary, they provide an easily understandable template for you to modify.

The next difference is in the number of member function declarations. AppWizard has a base set of member function declarations it will always override. This set depends on the derived class and represents the more commonly overridden member functions of the base class. These member functions are overridden by AppWizard to save you the trouble. Their function bodies are also generated and can be found in the program file for the **CMainFrame** class.

The third major difference is what is commonly referred to as the debug section of the class. AppWizard automatically defines two functions used for debugging purposes: **CObject::AssertValid( )** and **CObject::Dump( )**. Notice that these functions are defined only if the debug version of the project is being built. These functions are very useful when debugging your application. Basically, **CObject::AssertValid( )** provides a shallow check of the validity of the class. **CObject::Dump( )** dumps the contents of your class to a **CDumpContext** object. This object provides several diagnostic functions for your class. For more information, consult the Visual C++ documentation.

The toolbar and status bar provided by default are declared as two data members in the **CMainFrame** class. Their creation and initialization is provided by code found in **CMainFrame::OnCreate( )**.

Finally, notice the numerous comments at the end of the class declaration.

```
// Generated message map functions
protected:
    //{{AFX_MSG(CMainFrame)
    afx_msg int OnCreate(LPCREATESTRUCT lpCreateStruct);
// NOTE - the ClassWizard will add and remove member functions here.
//    DO NOT EDIT what you see in these blocks of generated code!
    //}}AFX_MSG
    DECLARE_MESSAGE_MAP()
```

This declares a message map for the frame window class that can be modified by another Visual C++ wizard: ClassWizard. ClassWizard, and these comments in particular, will be discussed in the second half of this chapter.

As we've seen, the main difference between the two implementations is the standard (and very structured) layout of the AppWizard class. This creates a class that is easy to read once you examine a few classes. (If you can understand one AppWizard class, you can understand them all!) In addition, AppWizard provides a generous amount of framework code. Without adding any code, this class provides declarations for the tool and status bars, debug support, and a message map whose modification is automated by using ClassWizard. You need only implement the custom functionality of your frame window class.

AppWizard Support for Application Help

Before leaving AppWizard and moving on to ClassWizard, let's look at the ease of adding a complex feature to an MFC framework application. As you may recall, Chapter 16 demonstrated the steps needed to add context-sensitive help to an existing MFC application. Briefly, they were as follows:

1. Add the help message handlers to your application's message map.
2. Handle **WM_CONTEXTMENU** and **WM_HELPINFO** messages.
3. Where necessary, handle **WM_COMMANDHELP** messages.
4. Implement a Help menu item in your application's main menu bar.

5. Call **WinHelp( )** as needed.

Each of these steps was accomplished by adding code, mainly in the form of message handler functions and implementation code, to the sample project. In addition, the source files necessary for building the help file were created and manually built as a separate step. All in all, this was quite a bit of work. As a comparison, let's see how much AppWizard does for us if we choose the Context-sensitive Help feature, located on the application features page. It will be a very close approximation of the work done in Chapter 16.

For the following example, the default AppWizard project is chosen. In addition, the Context-sensitive Help feature is also added.

Generated Context-Sensitive Help Support

After the project has been generated, a quick examination of the new project files reveals a large set of files and support for building a Help file. Let's take a closer look at these results.

The first thing of notice is the existence of a HLP sub-directory. Opening this directory reveals 30 files—the source for the project's Help file. These files are composed of:

◆ Several standard bitmap files demonstrating the standard appearance of MFC toolbar buttons and other resources. These are used in the Help file as graphical elements for Help topics.

◆ Two .RTF source files containing a framework of Help topics for the standard features of the project and placeholders for application-specific help.

◆ An entire set of Help project files needed to build the Help file of the project.

In addition to the source files, the generated project automatically rebuilds the Help file if any of the source files change. This automatic build, accomplished by a custom step, is part of the standard build process followed by Visual C++.

In addition to the source files for the actual project Help file, two help-related resources are also provided by AppWizard:

◆ A complete top-level Help menu with sub-menu items

◆ A toolbar button that invokes context-sensitive help for the application

These give the application user graphical access to related Help topics via context-sensitive help or by manually browsing through the Help topics of the Help file.

Finally, recall that in Chapter 16, a critical part of the support for context-sensitive help was in the help-specific message handlers added to the application class. It should not come as a surprise that AppWizard implements this too. The following is taken from the frame window class of the sample program:

```
BEGIN_MESSAGE_MAP(CMainFrame, CMDIFrameWnd)
    //{{AFX_MSG_MAP(CMainFrame)
// NOTE - the ClassWizard will add and remove mapping macros here.
//    DO NOT EDIT what you see in these blocks of generated code !
    ON_WM_CREATE()
    //}}AFX_MSG_MAP
    // Global help commands
    ON_COMMAND(ID_HELP_FINDER, CMDIFrameWnd::OnHelpFinder)
    ON_COMMAND(ID_HELP, CMDIFrameWnd::OnHelp)
    ON_COMMAND(ID_CONTEXT_HELP, CMDIFrameWnd::OnContextHelp)
    ON_COMMAND(ID_DEFAULT_HELP, CMDIFrameWnd::OnHelpFinder)
END_MESSAGE_MAP()
```

19

Notice the block of code in bold. This code, added by AppWizard, handles all help-related messages by routing each message to its proper handler function. Notice that the handler functions are members of the base class of our frame window object, **CMDIFrameWnd**. Therefore, all support for context-sensitive help is handled by the default implementation of MFC. Excepting the message map functions, no other code was added to our project, yet complete help coverage is included.

Some Final Comments on AppWizard

As you have seen in the previous sections, AppWizard is an extremely powerful tool for creating a *standard* framework application of tested code. Notice the stress on standard. This is a very important point and is often misunderstood by newcomers to Visual C++ and the Wizards in particular.

The main benefits in using AppWizard (i.e., standardized framework generation and default implementation of basic MFC features) are also its weaknesses. If your application is going to be a standard MFC application, then the AppWizard framework is a good place to start. In addition, if you are going to use the many MFC features without too much customization, then the framework application provides a solid foundation on which to begin implementing the various features specific to your application. However, if your application uses a unique framework or implements a unique look, then the AppWizard framework will be a difficult fit for you. In some cases, you will spend more time tearing code out than adding it. Obviously, this is not the most efficient way to develop MFC applications!

Therefore, a note of caution: AppWizard is a powerful tool, and like all tools, if you don't know what you want to do with it you will likely end up breaking it (or yourself) in the process. In other words, know the type of application you are developing and understand the basic structure of the MFC library before relying on AppWizard to generate the framework of your next MFC application.

The MFC ClassWizard

In addition to AppWizard, another MFC wizard, called ClassWizard, was also shipped with version 1 of Visual C++. From its inception, ClassWizard was designed to work closely with an AppWizard-generated project. The general structure of ClassWizard is formed by five separate pages (similar to the property pages of AppWizard) as shown in Figure 19-3. However, these pages are not meant to be used sequentially. Each page can be used independently of the others and implements a specific ability. ClassWizard has five basic abilities (one per page):

◆   Adding a message handler to an existing class

◆   Adding a member variable to an existing class

◆   Adding a method or property to an existing automation object

◆   Adding an event to an ActiveX control class

◆   Adding a new class to the project

These capabilities handle the majority of class management tasks required by most projects.

ClassWizard and Comments

One of the more commonly used abilities of ClassWizard is modifying existing message maps by adding or deleting message handlers. This is accomplished by a unique comment system known by both AppWizard and ClassWizard. As you have noticed by now, most of the files generated by

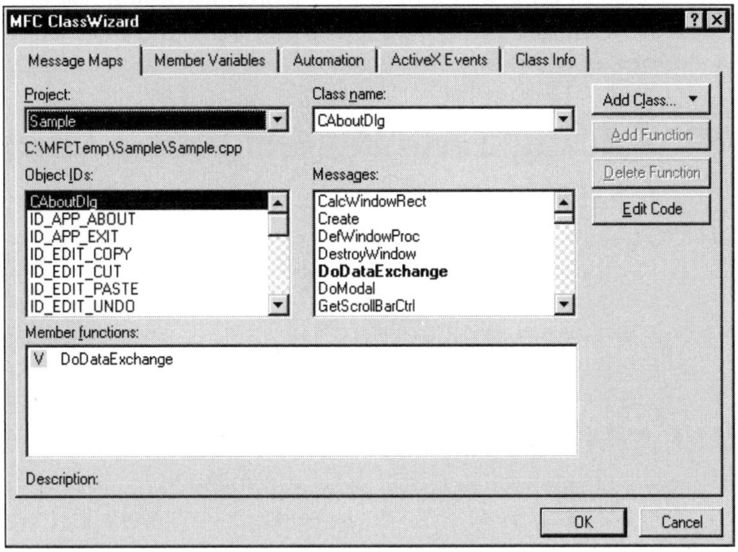

The Message
Maps page of
ClassWizard

Figure 19-3.

AppWizard contain C++-style comments. Some of these comments indicate
areas of interest in the code or are placeholders for To Do items (code
supplied by the developer). However, there is a subset that is used exclusively
by ClassWizard. The most common areas for these comments are MFC macro
maps, such as message maps. The syntax of these comments are "known" by
ClassWizard to mark areas where code can be inserted or deleted. The
following code is taken from a sample application generated by AppWizard:

```
BEGIN_MESSAGE_MAP(CMainFrame, CMDIFrameWnd)
  //{{AFX_MSG_MAP(CMainFrame)
// NOTE - the ClassWizard will add and remove mapping macros here.
//    DO NOT EDIT what you see in these blocks of generated code !
  ON_WM_CREATE()
  //}}AFX_MSG_MAP
END_MESSAGE_MAP()
```

This code sample implements a message map for a window class,
derived from **CMDIFrameWnd**. Notice the comments beginning with
//{{AFX_MSG_MAP(CMainFrame). These comments bracket the actual
message map implementation and allow ClassWizard to locate the message
map for the window and add or delete message map entries. If these comments

weren't present, ClassWizard would be unable to modify the message map. And, in fact, it would act as if the class had no message map even though one existed!

Adding a Message Handler Using ClassWizard

To demonstrate ClassWizard's ease of use, let's take the default framework application generated by AppWizard (substituting SDI for MDI) and add a message handler for **WM_CHAR** messages using ClassWizard. For the sake of comparison, we will create a program that is similar to the first example in Chapter 3.

Adding the Message Handlers

Once the project has been generated by AppWizard and loaded into the Visual C++ IDE, you are ready to add the **WM_CHAR** message handler. The easiest way to bring up ClassWizard is to press CTRL-W. This is a keyboard accelerator that invokes the ClassWizard dialog box.

Conveniently for us, ClassWizard is displaying the Message Maps page. As mentioned previously, this page allows you to add message handlers to any class in the project that implements a message map. The procedure for adding the various message handlers will be the same; only the name of the message and its associated handler function will be different.

Use the following procedure to implement the **WM_CHAR** message handler for our main view class. The sample program uses the **CSamp1View** class.

1. From the drop-down Class name combo box, choose **CView**.
2. Choose the **WM_CHAR** message, by scrolling down the Messages list box and double-clicking the **WM_CHAR** entry.
3. Click the Edit Code button.
4. Add the implementation code in the message handler function.

Just a quick comment on two things before we move on to the code. First, when you double-click on the **WM_CHAR** entry, an entry is automatically added to the Member functions list box, located at the bottom of the Message Maps page. The double click tells ClassWizard to immediately add the message map and function handler entries. Second, the Edit Code button provides a quick, convenient way to jump immediately into your code at the exact location needed to complete the implementation of the **WM_CHAR** message handler function.

19

Before we finish the implementation of the **WM_CHAR** handler, let's examine the code created by ClassWizard. In the class derivation file for **CSamp1View** (SAMP1VIEW.H), we find that ClassWizard adds the following code (in bold):

```
// Generated message map functions
protected:
  //{{AFX_MSG(CSamp1View)
afx_msg void OnChar(UINT nChar, UINT nRepCnt, UINT nFlags);
//}}AFX_MSG
```

This declares the handler function for the **WM_CHAR** function. You will recognize the standard declaration from the discussion in Chapter 3.

In the program file (SAMP1VIEW.CPP), two items were added: a message map entry for **WM_CHAR** and the handler function body. The new message map entry is as follows (in bold):

```
BEGIN_MESSAGE_MAP(CSamp1View, CView)
  //{{AFX_MSG_MAP(CSamp1View)
ON_WM_CHAR()
//}}AFX_MSG_MAP
END_MESSAGE_MAP()
```

And at the end of the file, there is the empty body of the handler function:

```
void CSamp1View::OnChar(UINT nChar, UINT nRepCnt, UINT nFlags)
{
  // TODO: Add your message handler code here and/or call default

  CView::OnChar(nChar, nRepCnt, nFlags);
}
```

The only remaining action is to add the actual code for handling this event. For simplicity, we will use the same code found in the Chapter 3 **WM_CHAR** message handler, with some modifications. The result is as follows:

```
void CSamp1View::OnChar(UINT nChar, UINT nRepCnt, UINT nFlags)
{
char str[80] = "Sample Output"; // holds output string
  CDC* pDC= GetDC();

  pDC->TextOut(1, 1, "   ", 3); // erase previous char
  wsprintf(str, "%c", nChar);
```

```
  pDC->TextOut(1, 1, str, strlen(str));
}
```

Notice that the code has changed slightly from its usage in Chapter 3. This is mainly due to the choice of using doc/view support for the project. The major difference is that the device context for the view object must first be retrieved, before being drawn to by using the **CDC::TextOut( )** function.

This completes adding the **WM_CHAR** message handler to our generated AppWizard project. As you can see, using ClassWizard largely automates the process of message handling for MFC applications. The only work required by us was the actual implementation of the function. Everything else was generated for us by ClassWizard.

Keep in mind that we have only discussed a single ability of ClassWizard—adding a message handler. There are many other procedures that ClassWizard automates, easing the tedium of Windows programming.

Should You Use the Wizards?

As the preceding tour has illustrated, the AppWizard and ClassWizard automate the creation of a framework for your MFC application. This can save you substantial time and effort, but for some projects you may find yourself fighting the framework. In general, very short projects are probably as easy to code manually as they are to create using the wizards. Very large projects often contain specialized code that may not mesh well with a wizard-generated framework. Medium-sized programs are probably the best candidates for the wizards. The wizards are also very helpful if you will be creating ActiveX controls. Of course, whether or not you use the wizards is completely up to you. However, since many MFC projects now employ wizard-generated code as a starting point, it is good to be familiar with it even if you don't plan to use the wizards for your own projects.

Final Thoughts

If you have read and worked through the examples presented in this book, you can call yourself an MFC programmer! However, make no mistake about it: this book only scratches the surface of the MFC hierarchy. Like Windows itself, MFC is a rich—and complex—programming environment. It is far too large to fully cover in any single book. However, you now have sufficient knowledge to be able to explore any of its other classes and subsystems on your own.

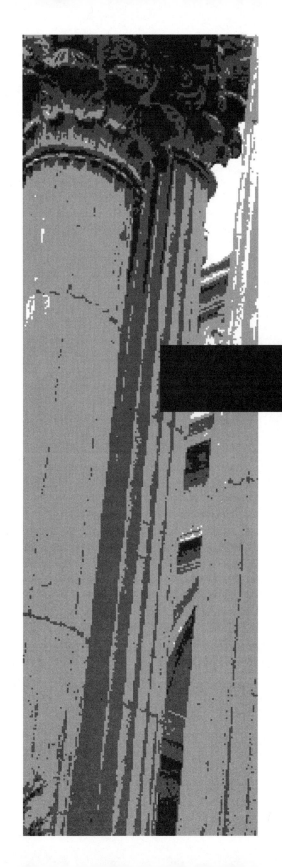

APPENDIX A

An Overview of Traditional-Style Windows Programming

As mentioned in Chapter 1, prior to MFC, Windows programs were written without the benefit of class hierarchies, member functions, or message maps. Instead, the traditional approach to Windows programming involves the direct use of the API functions and requires the programmer to handle all details. In fact, a major advantage of using MFC to program for Windows is that the class hierarchy masks many of the details associated with an API-based program. Although extensive knowledge of non-MFC Windows programming is not needed in order to create MFC-based programs, a basic understanding of its central elements is useful. For example, familiarity with traditional-style programs will be valuable if your job is to convert one to MFC! For this reason, this appendix develops a traditional-style application skeleton. In the process, it describes several of the most important parts of a Windows program, including the message loop, the window function, and **WinMain( )**. So, if you have never written a traditional-style Windows program, the material in this appendix will provide you with a general understanding.

Unlike MFC code, which is largely platform independent, a traditional-style Windows program must be targeted for a specific version of Windows. The most important differences occur between 16-bit and 32-bit versions. The skeletal code shown in this appendix is designed to run under Windows 98. However, the concepts apply to all versions of Windows, including 3.1, 95, and NT.

NOTE: This appendix is adapted from material presented in Herb Schildt's book *Windows 98 Programming from the Ground Up* (Osborne/McGraw-Hill, 1998). If you are interested in API-based Windows programming, this is a book that you will want to examine.

Some Windows Application Fundamentals

Before developing the Windows 98 application skeleton, some fundamental concepts common to all Windows programs need to be discussed. If you have already read the first few chapters of this book, then you will have learned about these elements from the perspective of MFC. Here they are presented from the traditional, API-based programming point of view.

WinMain( )

All traditional-style Windows programs begin execution with a call to **WinMain( )**. (As a general rule, Windows programs do not have a **main( )** function.) **WinMain( )** has some special properties that differentiate it from other functions in your application. It must be compiled using the **WINAPI** calling convention. (You will also see **APIENTRY** used. They both mean the same thing.) By default, functions in your C or C++ programs use the C calling convention. However, it is possible to compile a function so that it uses a different calling convention. For example, a common alternative is to use the Pascal calling convention. For various technical reasons, the calling convention used by Windows 98 to call **WinMain( )** is **WINAPI**. The return type of **WinMain( )** should be **int**.

The Window Function

All traditional-style Windows programs must contain a special function that is *not* called by your program, but is called by Windows. This function is generally called the *window function* or the *window procedure*. The window function is called by Windows when it needs to pass a message to your program. It is through this function that Windows communicates with your program. The window function receives the message in its parameters. For Windows 98, all window functions must be declared as returning type **LRESULT CALLBACK**. The type **LRESULT** is a **typedef** that (at the time of this writing) is another name for a long integer. The **CALLBACK** calling convention is used with those functions that will be called by Windows 98. In Windows terminology, any function that is called by Windows is referred to as a *callback* function.

In addition to receiving the messages sent by Windows, the window function must initiate any actions indicated by a message. Typically, a window function's body consists of a **switch** statement that links a specific response to each message that the program processes. Your program need not respond to every message that Windows will send. For messages that your program doesn't care about, you can let Windows provide default processing for them. Since there are hundreds of different messages that Windows can generate, it is common for most messages to simply be processed by Windows and not your program.

For Windows 98, all messages are 32-bit integer values. Further, all messages are linked with any additional information that the messages require.

Window Classes

When your Windows program first begins execution, it will need to define and register a *window class*. (Here, the word *class* is not being used in its C++ sense. Rather, it means *style* or *type*.) When you register a window class, you are telling Windows about the form and function of the window. However, registering the window class does not cause a window to come into existence. To actually create a window requires additional steps.

The Message Loop

As explained earlier, Windows communicates with your program by sending it messages. All Windows applications must establish a *message loop* inside the **WinMain( )** function. This loop reads any pending message from the application's message queue and then dispatches that message back to Windows, which then calls your program's window function with that message as a parameter. This may seem to be an overly complex way of passing messages, but it is, nevertheless, the way that all Windows programs must function. (Part of the reason for this is to return control to Windows so that the scheduler can allocate CPU time as it sees fit, rather than waiting for your application's time slice to end.)

Windows Data Types

If you have read the first few chapters in this book, then you already know that Windows programs do not make extensive use of standard C/C++ data types, such as **int** or **char ***. Instead, all data types used by Windows have been **typedef**ed within the WINDOWS.H file and/or its related files. This file is supplied by Microsoft (and any other company that makes a Windows C/C++ compiler) and must be included in all Windows programs. Some of the most common types are **HANDLE**, **HWND**, **BYTE**, **WORD**, **DWORD**, **UINT**, **LONG**, **BOOL**, **LPSTR**, and **LPCSTR**. For 32-bit versions of Windows (including Windows 98) **HANDLE** is a 32-bit integer that is used as a handle. There are a number of handle types, but they all are the same size as **HANDLE**. A *handle* is simply a value that identifies some resource. For example, **HWND** is a 32-bit integer that is used as a window handle. Also, all handle types begin with an H. **BYTE** is an 8-bit unsigned character. **WORD** is a 16-bit unsigned short integer. **DWORD** is an unsigned long integer.

UINT is an unsigned 32-bit integer. **LONG** is another name for **long**. **BOOL** is an integer. This type is used to indicate values that are either true or false. **LPSTR** is a pointer to a string and **LPCSTR** is a **const** pointer to a string.

In addition to the basic types described above, Windows 98 defines several structures. The two that are needed by the skeleton program are **MSG** and **WNDCLASSEX**. The **MSG** structure holds a Windows message and **WNDCLASSEX** is a structure that defines a window class. These structures will be discussed later in this appendix.

A Windows 98 Skeleton

Now that the necessary background information has been covered, we can develop a minimal Windows application. As stated, this application will be targeted for Windows 98. However, the skeleton is essentially the same for all versions of Windows. In the world of Windows programming, application skeletons are commonly used because there is a substantial "price of admission" when creating a Windows program. Unlike MFC-based programs in which a minimal program is just a few lines long, a minimal traditional-style Windows program is approximately 50 lines long. Therefore, application skeletons are commonly used when developing non-MFC Windows applications.

A

A minimal Windows program contains two functions: **WinMain( )** and the window function. The **WinMain( )** function must perform the following general steps:

1. Define a window class.
2. Register that class with Windows 98.
3. Create a window of that class.
4. Display the window.
5. Begin running the message loop.

The window function must respond to all relevant messages. Since the skeleton program does nothing but display its window, the only message that it must respond to is the one that tells the application that the user has terminated the program.

Before considering the specifics, examine the following program, which is a minimal Windows 98 skeleton. It creates a standard window that includes a title. The window also contains the system menu and, therefore, is capable of being minimized, maximized, moved, resized, and closed. It also contains the standard minimize, maximize, and close boxes. This skeleton is written in standard C/C++. It can be compiled by any C/C++ compiler capable of producing Windows 98 programs.

```c
/* A minimal Windows 98 skeleton. */

#include <windows.h>

LRESULT CALLBACK WindowFunc(HWND, UINT, WPARAM, LPARAM);

char szWinName[] = "MyWin"; /* name of window class */

int WINAPI WinMain(HINSTANCE hThisInst, HINSTANCE hPrevInst,
                   LPSTR lpszArgs, int nWinMode)
{
  HWND hwnd;
  MSG msg;
  WNDCLASSEX wcl;

  /* Define a window class. */
  wcl.hInstance = hThisInst; /* handle to this instance */
  wcl.lpszClassName = szWinName; /* window class name */
  wcl.lpfnWndProc = WindowFunc; /* window function */
  wcl.style = 0; /* default style */

  wcl.cbSize = sizeof(WNDCLASSEX); /* set size of WNDCLASSEX */

  wcl.hIcon = LoadIcon(NULL, IDI_APPLICATION); /* large icon */
  wcl.hIconSm = LoadIcon(NULL, IDI_WINLOGO); /* small icon */

  wcl.hCursor = LoadCursor(NULL, IDC_ARROW); /* cursor style */
  wcl.lpszMenuName = NULL; /* no menu */

  wcl.cbClsExtra = 0; /* no extra */
  wcl.cbWndExtra = 0; /* information needed */

  /* Make the window background white. */
  wcl.hbrBackground = (HBRUSH) GetStockObject(WHITE_BRUSH);

  /* Register the window class. */
  if(!RegisterClassEx(&wcl)) return 0;

  /* Now that a window class has been registered, a window
     can be created. */
```

```
        hwnd = CreateWindow(
          szWinName, /* name of window class */
          "Windows 98 Skeleton", /* title */
          WS_OVERLAPPEDWINDOW, /* standard window */
          CW_USEDEFAULT, /* X coordinate - let Windows decide */
          CW_USEDEFAULT, /* Y coordinate - let Windows decide */
          CW_USEDEFAULT, /* width - let Windows decide */
          CW_USEDEFAULT, /* height - let Windows decide */
          HWND_DESKTOP, /* no parent window */
          NULL, /* no menu */
          hThisInst, /* handle of this instance of the program */
          NULL /* no additional arguments */
        );

        /* Display the window. */
        ShowWindow(hwnd, nWinMode);
        UpdateWindow(hwnd);

        /* Create the message loop. */
        while(GetMessage(&msg, NULL, 0, 0))
        {
          TranslateMessage(&msg); /* allow use of keyboard */
          DispatchMessage(&msg); /* return control to Windows */
        }
        return msg.wParam;
      }


/* This function is called by Windows 98 and is passed
   messages from the message queue.
*/
LRESULT CALLBACK WindowFunc(HWND hwnd, UINT message,
                            WPARAM wParam, LPARAM lParam)
{
  switch(message) {
    case WM_DESTROY: /* terminate the program */
      PostQuitMessage(0);
      break;
    default:
      /* Let Windows 98 process any messages not specified in
         the preceding switch statement. */
      return DefWindowProc(hwnd, message, wParam, lParam);
  }
  return 0;
}
```

When you run this program, you will see a window similar to that shown in Figure A-1. Let's go through this program step by step.

All Windows programs must include the header file WINDOWS.H. As stated, this file (along with its support files) contains the API function prototypes and various types, macros, and definitions used by Windows. For example, the data types **HWND** and **WNDCLASSEX** are defined by including WINDOWS.H.

The window procedure used by the program is called **WindowFunc( )**. It is declared as a callback function because this is the function that Windows 98 calls to communicate with the program.

As stated, program execution begins with **WinMain( )**. **WinMain( )** is passed four parameters. **hThisInst** and **hPrevInst** are handles. **hThisInst** refers to the current instance of the program. Remember, Windows is a multitasking system, so it is possible that more than one instance of your program may be running at the same time. **hPrevInst** will always be **NULL**. (In Windows 3.1 programs, **hPrevInst** would be nonzero if there were other

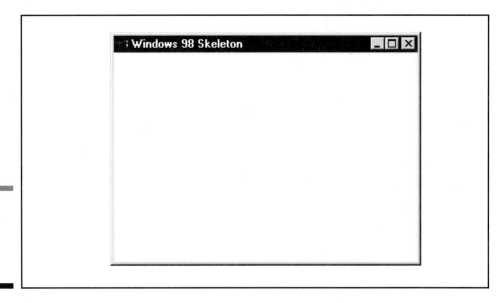

The window produced by the skeleton program

Figure A-1.

instances of the program currently executing, but this no longer applies to 32-bit versions of Windows.) The **lpszArgs** parameter is a pointer to a string that holds any command-line arguments specified when the application is begun. The **nWinMode** parameter contains a value that determines how the window will be displayed when your program begins execution.

Inside the function, three variables are created. The **hwnd** variable will hold the handle to the program's window. The **msg** structure variable will hold window messages, and the **wcl** structure variable will be used to define the window class.

Defining the Window Class

The first two actions that **WinMain( )** takes are to define a window class and then register it. A window class is defined by filling in the fields defined by the **WNDCLASSEX** structure. Its fields are shown here:

```
UINT cbSize; /* size of the WNDCLASSEX structure */
UINT style; /* type of window */
WNDPROC lpfnWndProc; /* address to window func */
int cbClsExtra; /* extra class info */
int cbWndExtra; /* extra window info */
HINSTANCE hInstance; /* handle of this instance */
HICON hIcon; /* handle of large icon */
HICON hIconSm; /* handle of small icon */
HCURSOR hCursor; /* handle of mouse cursor */
HBRUSH hbrBackground; /* background color */
LPCSTR lpszMenuName; /* name of main menu */
LPCSTR lpszClassName; /* name of window class */
```

As you can see by looking at the program, **cbSize** is assigned the size of the **WNDCLASSEX** structure. The **hInstance** field is assigned the current instance handle as specified by **hThisInst**. The name of the window class is pointed to by **lpszClassName**, which points to the string "MyWin" in this case. The address of the window function is assigned to **lpfnWndProc**.

All Windows applications need to define a default shape for the mouse cursor and for the application's icons. An application can define its own custom version of these resources or it may use one of the built-in styles, as the skeleton does. In either case, handles to these resources must be assigned to the appropriate members of the **WNDCLASSEX** structure. To see how this is done, let's begin with icons.

A Windows 98 application has two icons associated with it: one standard size and one small. The small icon is used when the application is minimized and it is also the icon that is used for the system menu. The standard icon (sometimes called the large icon) is displayed when you move or copy an application to the desktop. Typically, standard icons are 32 × 32 bitmaps and small icons are 16 × 16 bitmaps. Each icon is loaded by the API function **LoadIcon( )**, whose prototype is shown here:

HICON LoadIcon(HINSTANCE *hInst*, LPCSTR *lpszName*);

This function returns a handle to an icon. Here, *hInst* specifies the handle of the module that contains the icon and its name is specified in *lpszName*. However, to use one of the built-in icons, you must use **NULL** for the first parameter and specify one of the following macros for the second:

Icon Macro	Shape
IDI_APPLICATION	Default icon
IDI_ERROR	Error symbol
IDI_INFORMATION	Information
IDI_QUESTION	Question mark
IDI_WARNING	Exclamation point
IDI_WINLOGO	Windows logo

In the skeleton, **IDI_APPLICATION** is used for the large icon and **IDI_WINLOGO** is used for the small icon. It is also possible to define your own icons.

To load the mouse cursor, use the API **LoadCursor( )** function. This function has the following prototype:

HCURSOR LoadCursor(HINSTANCE *hInst*, LPCSTR *lpszName*);

This function returns a handle to a cursor resource. Here, *hInst* specifies the handle of the module that contains the mouse cursor and its name is specified in *lpszName*. However, to use one of the built-in cursors, you must use **NULL** for the first parameter and specify one of the built-in cursors using its macro for the second parameter. Some of the most common built-in cursors are shown here:

Cursor Macro	Shape
IDC_ARROW	Default arrow pointer
IDC_CROSS	Cross hairs
IDC_IBEAM	Vertical I-beam
IDC_WAIT	Hourglass

The background color of the window created by the skeleton is specified as white and a handle to this *brush* is obtained using the API function **GetStockObject( )**. A brush is a resource that paints the screen using a predetermined size, color, and pattern. The function **GetStockObject( )** is used to obtain a handle to a number of standard display objects, including brushes, pens (which draw lines), and character fonts. It has this prototype:

HGDIOBJ GetStockObject(int *object*);

The function returns a handle to the object specified by *object*. (The type **HGDIOBJ** is a GDI handle.) Here are some of the built-in brushes available to your program:

Brush Macro	Background Type
BLACK_BRUSH	Black
DKGRAY_BRUSH	Dark gray
HOLLOW_BRUSH	See-through window
LTGRAY_BRUSH	Light gray
WHITE_BRUSH	White

You may use these macros as parameters to **GetStockObject( )** to obtain a brush.

Once the window class has been fully specified, it is registered with Windows 98 using the API function **RegisterClassEx( )**, whose prototype is shown here:

ATOM RegisterClassEx(CONST WNDCLASSEX *lpWClass*);

The function returns a value that identifies the window class. **ATOM** is a **typedef** that means **WORD**. Each window class is given a unique value. *lpWClass* must be the address of a **WNDCLASSEX** structure.

Creating a Window

Once a window class has been defined and registered, your application can actually create a window of that class using the API function **CreateWindow( )**, whose prototype is shown here:

```
HWND CreateWindow(
  LPCSTR lpClassName,      /* name of window class */
  LPCSTR lpWinName,        /* title of window */
  DWORD dwStyle,           /* type of window */
  int X, int Y,            /* upper-left coordinates */
  int Width, int Height,   /* dimensions of window */
  HWND hParent,            /* handle of parent window */
  HMENU hMenu,             /* handle of main menu */
  HINSTANCE hThisInst,     /* handle of creator */
  LPVOID lpszAdditional    /* pointer to additional info */
);
```

As you can see by looking at the skeleton program, many of the parameters to **CreateWindow( )** may be defaulted or specified as **NULL**. In fact, most often the *X, Y, Width,* and *Height* parameters will simply use the macro **CW_USEDEFAULT**, which tells Windows 98 to select an appropriate size and location for the window. If the window has no parent, which is the case in the skeleton, then *hParent* must be specified as **HWND_DESKTOP**. (You may also use **NULL** for this parameter.) If the window does not contain a main menu, then *hMenu* must be **NULL**. Also, if no additional information is required, as is most often the case, then *lpszAdditional* is **NULL**. (The type **LPVOID** is **typedef**ed as **void ***. Historically, **LPVOID** stands for **long** pointer to **void**.)

The remaining four parameters must be explicitly set by your program. First, *lpszClassName* must point to the name of the window class. (This is the name you gave it when it was registered.) The title of the window is a string pointed to by *lpszWinName*. This can be a null string, but usually a window will be given a title. The style (or type) of window actually created is determined by the value of *dwStyle*. The **WS_OVERLAPPEDWINDOW** macro specifies a standard window that has a system menu; a border; and minimize, maximize, and close boxes. While this style of window is the most common, you can construct one to your own specifications. To accomplish this, you simply OR together the various style macros that you want. Some other common styles are shown here:

Style Macro	Window Feature
WS_OVERLAPPED	Overlapped window with border
WS_MAXIMIZEBOX	Maximize box
WS_MINIMIZEBOX	Minimize box
WS_SYSMENU	System menu
WS_HSCROLL	Horizontal scroll bar
WS_VSCROLL	Vertical scroll bar

The *hThisInst* parameter must contain the current instance handle of the application.

The **CreateWindow( )** function returns the handle of the window it creates or **NULL** if the window cannot be created.

Once the window has been created, it is still not displayed on the screen. To cause the window to be displayed, call the **ShowWindow( )** API function. This function has the following prototype:

BOOL ShowWindow(HWND *hwnd*, int *nHow*);

The handle of the window to display is specified in *hwnd*. The display mode is specified in *nHow*. The first time the window is displayed, you will want to pass **WinMain( )**'s **nWinMode** as the *nHow* parameter. Remember, the value of **nWinMode** determines how the window will be displayed when the program begins execution. Subsequent calls can display (or remove) the window as necessary. Some common values for *nHow* are shown here:

Display Macro	Effect
SW_HIDE	Removes the window.
SW_MINIMIZE	Minimizes the window into an icon.
SW_MAXIMIZE	Maximizes the window.
SW_RESTORE	Restores a window to normal size.

The **ShowWindow( )** function returns the previous display status of the window. If the window was displayed, then nonzero is returned. If the window was not displayed, zero is returned.

Although not technically necessary for the skeleton, a call to **UpdateWindow( )** is included because it is needed by virtually every Windows application that you will create. It essentially tells Windows to send a **WM_PAINT** message to your application.

The Message Loop

The final part of the skeletal **WinMain( )** is the *message loop*. The message loop is a part of all Windows applications. Its purpose is to receive and process messages sent by Windows. When an application is running, it is continually being sent messages. These messages are stored in the application's message queue until they can be read and processed. Each time your application is ready to read another message, it must call the API function **GetMessage( )**, which has this prototype:

BOOL GetMessage(LPMSG *msg*, HWND *hwnd*, UINT *min*, UINT *max*);

The message will be received by the structure pointed to by *msg*. All Window messages are of structure type **MSG**, shown here:

```
/* Message structure */
typedef struct tagMSG
{
  HWND hwnd; /* window that message is for */
  UINT message; /* message */
  WPARAM wParam; /* message-dependent info */
  LPARAM lParam; /* more message-dependent info */
  DWORD time; /* time message posted */
  POINT pt; /* X,Y location of mouse */
} MSG;
```

In **MSG**, the handle of the window for which the message is intended is contained in **hwnd**. All Windows 98 messages are 32-bit integers and the message is contained in **message**. Additional information relating to each message is passed in **wParam** and **lParam**. The type **WPARAM** is a **typedef** for **UINT**, and **LPARAM** is a **typedef** for **LONG**.

The time the message was sent (posted) is specified in milliseconds in the **time** field.

The **pt** member will contain the coordinates of the mouse when the message was sent. The coordinates are held in a **POINT** structure, which is defined as follows:

```
typedef struct tagPOINT {
  LONG x, y;
} POINT;
```

If there are no messages in the application's message queue, then a call to **GetMessage( )** will pass control back to Windows.

The *hwnd* parameter to **GetMessage( )** specifies for which window messages will be obtained. It is possible (even likely) that an application will contain several windows and you may only want to receive messages for a specific window. If you want to receive all messages directed at your application, this parameter must be **NULL**.

The remaining two parameters to **GetMessage( )** specify a range of messages that will be received. Generally, you want your application to receive all messages. To accomplish this, specify both *min* and *max* as 0, as the skeleton does.

GetMessage( ) returns zero when the user terminates the program, causing the message loop to terminate. Otherwise it returns nonzero.

Inside the message loop two functions are called. The first is the API function **TranslateMessage( )**. This function translates virtual key codes generated by Windows into character messages. Although not necessary for all applications, most programs call **TranslateMessage( )** because it is needed to allow full integration of the keyboard into your application program.

Once the message has been read and translated, it is dispatched back to Windows using the **DispatchMessage( )** API function. Windows then holds this message until it can pass it to the program's window function.

Once the message loop terminates, the **WinMain( )** function ends by returning the value of **msg.wParam** to Windows. This value contains the return code generated when your program terminates.

The Window Function

The second function in the application skeleton is its window function. In this case the function is called **WindowFunc( )**, but it could have any name you like. The window function is passed the first four members of the **MSG** structure as parameters. For the skeleton, the only parameter that is used is the message itself.

The skeleton's window function responds to only one message explicitly: **WM_DESTROY**. This message is sent when the user terminates the program. When this message is received, your program must execute a call to the API function **PostQuitMessage( )**. The argument to this function is an exit code that is returned in **msg.wParam** inside **WinMain( )**. Calling **PostQuitMessage( )** causes a **WM_QUIT** message to be sent to your application, which causes **GetMessage( )** to return false and, thus, stops your program.

Any other messages received by **WindowFunc( )** are passed along to Windows, via a call to **DefWindowProc( )**, for default processing. This step is necessary because all messages must be dealt with in one fashion or another.

Traditional-Style Programs vs. MFC

If you have read the first few chapters of this book, then you have probably noticed that several aspects of the skeleton program parallel those of an MFC program. For example, to load an icon in a traditional-style program, you use the API function **LoadIcon( )**. To load an icon in an MFC-based program, you use **CWinApp::LoadIcon( )**. However, it is obvious that the equivalent MFC-based program is far shorter—and easier to understand. As you have just seen, when you write a traditional-style Windows program, you must supply all the details. In an MFC-based program, many of these details are provided for you. Although the number of details present in the application skeleton are not so great as to overwhelm, they are still significant. But more important, the complexity of a traditional-style Windows program increases rapidly as its size grows. As you probably know from your previous programming experience, the greater the number of details that you must manage, the longer it takes to create a bug-free, functional program. This is the primary reason why many programmers are moving toward MFC for Windows development efforts.

Index

E

P

U

X